The Poverty of Progress

The Poverty of Progress

The Political Economy of American Social Problems

Written and Edited by
MILTON MANKOFF
Queens College, City University of New York

HOLT, RINEHART AND WINSTON, INC.
New York   Chicago   San Francisco   Atlanta
Dallas   Montreal   Toronto   London   Sydney

Front cover photo courtesy of VISTA.

Copyright © 1972 by Holt, Rinehart and Winston Inc.
All Rights Reserved
Library of Congress Catalog Card Number: 75-190031
ISBN: 0-03-085752-X
Printed in the United States of America
1 2 3 4 5 6 7 8 9   090   2 3 4 5

Preface

The present volume was conceived during the spring of 1970 as an antidote to the conventional wisdom found in liberal social scientific and journalistic accounts of American institutions and social problems. Liberal social analyses typically minimize the extent to which particular economic, political, cultural, and social deformations are endemic to *capitalist* society. Moreover, by urging Americans to have *faith* in the viability of existing social institutions and modes for redressing grievances, *without actually examining the historical record to determine whether such optimism has a theoretical or empirical basis,* liberalism frequently borders on demagogy.

My primary task in preparing this manuscript has been to articulate a theoretically coherent perspective that systematically relates the developing structure and dynamics of American economic and political institutions to several major social problems—imperialism, poverty and economic insecurity, racism, sexism, the misuse of knowledge, social disorganization, and personal alienation. The major thesis that emerges throughout this work is that the social problems under consideration are exacerbated in a society dominated by the capitalist mode of production and distribution, and that a satisfactory resolution of these problems may well be precluded until economic decision making is divorced from the logic of capitalist rationality and the needs and desires of a single social class.

In addition to illuminating the common economic and political roots of seemingly unrelated social problems, a second purpose of the text is to explain the reasons why Americans have generally been unwilling and/or unable to radically transform the prevailing political economy in order to improve the quality of their existence. This issue takes on greater significance in the relative tranquility of 1972 than it did two years ago when hundreds of thousands of people seemed willing to risk their future security to struggle for institutional change.

Two final and related matters—the meaning of the cultural and political revolt of the 1960s and early 1970s, and the prospects for revolutionary change in the coming generation—are considered in an epilogue which I wrote largely in early 1971, at a time when such questions seemed to have an immediate relevance. The decline in militancy and revolutionary rhetoric has rendered these issues academic for the moment; but, if my analysis in the essay is at all reasonable, the institutional contradictions that I believe to have produced upheaval from 1964 through 1970 might reproduce it on an even greater scale in the foreseeable future.

The selections by social scientists and analysts, which comprise the major portion of the work, provide an historical and comparative context within which the political economy of American social problems and the sources of societal stability and change can be grasped. Because the articles chosen were not written specifically for the purposes outlined above, it has been necessary for me to write extended introductory essays supplementing the perspectives of the various authors and placing their analyses of particular issues in a framework consistent with the general orientation of the volume.

While the thrust of the book represents a critique of capitalist society in general, and its American variant in particular, it omits what one might refer to as "constructive criticism." That is to say, except for some allusions to the possibility of transcending many of the problems discussed in the text through socialism, no concrete analysis of the forms and content of a new American institutional structure are to be found. This omission is, unfortunately, necessitated by the fact that the circumstances under which a new society comes into being severely constrict its historical options. Because it is impossible to determine whether and how socialism will come to America, it is intellectually irresponsible to paint rosy (or bleak) portraits of a socialist America.

The experience of contemporary socialist societies also serves to give one pause and helps one recognize that such societies, despite remarkable achievements, contain their own particular deformations and contradictions. Whether the social problems in socialist societies stem chiefly from the inherent features of a socialist economic structure, or from the fact that they typically had to overcome legacies of feudalism and/or capitalism, underdevelopment, the convulsions of violent revolutionary birth, and the militant hostility of the major capitalist powers, can only be assessed when these societies mature. Capitalist societies, it should be recalled, took centuries to develop, while no socialist society was established prior to 1917.

Although the historical record of socialist societies provides both positive and negative models from which Americans can and should learn, the unique characterististics of American society—notably its advanced level of technology and literacy—make it possible to approach the problem of socialist reconstruction in ways that would represent a positive advance in comparison with past efforts. Whether or not socialism is on the American agenda, and what kind of socialism it would be, depends upon the thoughts and actions of human beings as well as so-called "objective conditions." This volume will hopefully convince readers that, whatever its past accomplishments in creating the material basis for a society fit for human habitation, capitalist society inherently places extraordinary limitations on the realization of its most advanced ideals—liberty, equality, and fraternity.

Milton Mankoff

New York City
February 1972

Acknowledgments

The ideas developed in this volume largely reflect the scholarship reprinted and cited in the text. My own perspectives have been and continue to be heavily influenced by the theoretical concerns and substantive conclusions that characterize this body of intellectual work. Hence, I owe a profound debt to the scholars represented. Four years as a graduate student at the University of Wisconsin brought me into contact with numerous graduate students and members of the faculty whose critical minds provided both inspiration and guidance in my own intellectual evolution. In particular, I acknowledge the contributions of Harvey Goldberg, Richard Hamilton, Paul Mueller, Andy Rabinbach, and Evan Stark. At the University of California at Santa Barbara, where I spent three productive years and where the major portion of this work was completed, I was fortunate enough to have Bill Domhoff, Richard Flacks, Harvey Molotch, and Maurice Zeitlin as colleagues, friends, and sympathetic critics. They have read portions of this manuscript and made valuable suggestions along the way. In addition, Michael Hechter, Mary Ryan, and Kay Trimburger offered their time to provide helpful commentary.

I also wish to thank William Adams, who spent long hours preparing the manuscript; Carla Roddy and Susan Boehme, whose secretarial and editorial skills facilitated the completion of an arduous typing job; and Jan Carr and Jeanette Ninas Johnson of Holt, Rinehart and Winston, who provided needed encouragement and allowed me the necessary freedom to present my ideas in my own way. Finally, although I have received much welcome critical advice from colleagues and friends who share my intellectual and social concerns (if not always my conclusions), I must acknowledge that I bear full responsibility for the contents of this volume—the organization, choice of selections, and, of course, the introductory essays and epilogue.

Contents

PART THREE THE SOURCES OF STABILITY IN AMERICAN SOCIETY

The Poverty of Progress

Introduction

In recent years the number of academic books and articles purporting to offer the reader "radical" or "critical" social science relevant to contemporary American society has increased dramatically with the "radicalization" of significant sectors of the American population. Some social analysts, including government leaders, suggest that the growth of radical or critical academic social science in the United States has been responsible for student militancy and, to a lesser extent, urban riots. While academic intellectuals may occasionally play a significant role in reorienting the thinking of students and others through the diffusion of dissenting social thought, it would be difficult to demonstrate that extensive critical analysis of American institutions and culture by academicians preceded the contemporary breakdown of "law and order" on campuses and in ghettos. One would be on far safer ground to suggest that social movements for radical change spurred the interest in reformulating long-accepted notions about the character and stability of American economic and political institutions, racism, imperialism, and the role of social classes in societal dynamics.

In fact, some of the most creative social analysis during the past few years has originated *outside* the university and only afterward become the object of "respectable" academic inquiry.[1] Although a few radical academic intellectuals began prior to the turmoil of the sixties to utilize unorthodox approaches in comprehending the historical development of American society,[2] the scholarship of the vast majority of their colleagues simply mirrored the social theories of conventional politicians and the man in the street. Indeed, as Louis Hartz, one of the more perceptive American historians, observed about his colleagues, "the American historian at practically every stage has functioned quite inside the nation; he has tended to be an erudite reflection of the limited social perspectives of the average American himself."[3] Similar commentary has been made about the intellectual products of the sociology, political science, and economics professions.[4]

It should not be surprising that typical academic intellectuals were often well behind their students and unattached intellectuals in exploring new perspectives on American life.[5] Nevertheless, it is regrettable that many of these intellectuals are still so comfortable with traditional modes of social analysis. Even as the daily newspaper continues to bring fresh news of the contempt of the executive branch of the government for the views of the citizenry and as Congress appears as an impotent, almost vestigial, organ of state, most political scientists continue to argue that American society is

[1] The concept "institutional racism" was probably first introduced by Stokely Carmichael, the black power advocate and long-time civil rights activist, and political scientist Charles Hamilton in their *Black Power: The Politics of Liberation in America* (New York: Vintage Books, 1967). A similar development in intellectual history is the use of the concept "domestic colonialism" in analyzing American race relations. In a rare admission from an academic social scientist, Robert Blauner states that "As a good colonialist I have probably restated (read: stolen) more ideas from the writings of Kenneth Clark, Stokely Carmichael, Frantz Fanon, and especially such contributors to the Black Panther Party (Oakland) newspaper as Huey Newton, Bobby Seale, Eldridge Cleaver, and Kathleen Cleaver than I have appropriately credited or generated myself." See his "Internal Colonialism and Ghetto Revolt," *Social Problems*, vol. 16 (Spring 1969), p. 393. Also reprinted in Chapter 5 of this text.

[2] William Appleman Williams, *The Tragedy of American Diplomacy* (Cleveland: The World Publishing Company, 1959); *The Contours of American History* (Cleveland: The World Publishing Company, 1961). Paul Baran, *The Political Economy of Growth* (New York: Monthly Review Press, 1957). C. Wright Mills, *The Power Elite* (New York: Oxford University Press, 1956).

[3] Louis Hartz, *The Liberal Tradition in America: An Interpretation of American Political Thought since the Revolution* (New York: Harcourt Brace Jovanovich, Inc., 1955), p. 29.

[4] C. Wright Mills, "The Professional Ideology of Social Pathologists," *American Journal of Sociology*, vol. 59 (September 1943), pp. 165–180; *The Sociological Imagination* (New York: Oxford University Press, 1959). Alvin Gouldner, *The Coming Crisis of Western Sociology* (New York: Basic Books, Inc., 1970). James Petras, "Ideology and United States Political Scientists," *Science and Society*, vol. 29 (Spring 1965), pp. 192–216. David Mermelstein, ed., *Economics: Mainstream Readings and Radical Critiques* (New York: Random House, Inc. 1970).

[5] David Horowitz, "Billion Dollar Brains: How Wealth Puts Knowledge in Its Pocket," *Ramparts* (May 1969), pp. 36–44, analyzes the historical sources of academic adherence to paradigms that invariably support existing social structures. Also reprinted in Chapter 7 of this text.

Introduction

characterized by democratic pluralism.[6] Similarly, economists still use economic models based upon the operation of a self-regulating and competitive market when virtually every serious examination of American economic history testifies to the role of nonmarket factors such as corporate collusion and government intervention in stabilizing capitalism.[7]

Yet there has undoubtedly been an intellectual revolt which parallels the cultural and political upheaval of the sixties. The primary thrust of the political movements of the past decade has been negative, that is, they have rejected institutional ideologies and policies of the past and present without fully developing alternatives for the future. The revolt by the young intellectuals, students, and younger professors has also been largely negative. Previously accepted social theories have been mercilessly and effectively discredited, but not superseded.

We are now facing a period of transition, in which serious attempts will be made in politics, culture, and scholarship to build new edifices to replace disintegrating structures. As in all such periods there will be many false starts. The products of these experiments will often resemble some old models—discarded, if not always discredited.[8] The cultural revolution has revived the rural community of nineteenth-century America with its spartan work routine and sexual roles. Some political radicals have abandoned the participatory democracy of the early New Left for the semi-authoritarian vanguard parties reminiscent of bolshevism. Radical intellectuals, having cast off so-called bourgeois social science, have begun to experiment with what they believe to be a new social science. Unfortunately, what Marx said of revolutionaries in the political sphere also holds for those operating in the intellectual arena:

[6] For a recent example of pluralist thought about local political power see Richard Merelman, "On the Neo-elitist Critique of Community Power," *American Political Science Review,* vol. 62 (June 1968), pp. 451–460. Arnold Rose, *The Power Structure: Political Process in American Society* (New York: Oxford University Press, 1967), forcefully presents the pluralist perspective on national power. For contradictory views, see G. William Domhoff, *Who Rules America?* (Englewood Cliffs, N.J.: Prentice-Hall, Inc., 1967); *The Higher Circles: The Governing Class in America* (New York: Random House, Inc., 1970). Ralph Miliband, *The State in Capitalist Society* (New York: Basic Books, Inc., 1969). See also Milton Mankoff, "Power in Advanced Capitalist Society: A Review Essay on Recent Elitist and Marxist Criticism of Pluralist Theory," *Social Problems,* vol. 17 (Winter 1970), pp. 418–430. Also reprinted in Chapter 2 of this text.

[7] See Mermelstein, *op. cit.,* for extensive critical analysis of modern economics and the American economy. See also Karl Polanyi, *The Great Transformation: The Political and Economic Origins of Our Time* (Boston: The Beacon Press, 1957) for a brilliant analysis of the historical development of modern markets under capitalism.

[8] Frequently, social scientific models are discarded because of changing historical circumstances rather than because of any major logical or empirical weakness. Thus, sociologists emphasized "conflict" models of social development during the Great Depression and "consensus" during the tranquil 1950s largely because of the prevailing political atmosphere in each period. Today there seems to be a revival of interest in conflict in response to the social unrest of the sixties. See John Horton, "Order and Conflict Theories of Social Problems as Competing Ideologies," *American Journal of Sociology,* vol. 71 (May 1966), pp. 701–713.

Introduction   3

. . . just when they seem engaged in revolutionizing themselves and things, in creating something that has never yet existed, precisely in such periods of revolutionary crisis they anxiously conjure up the spirits of the past to their service and borrow from them names, battle cries and costumes in order to present the new scene of world history in this time-honored disguise and this borrowed language. Thus Luther donned the mask of the Apostle Paul, the Revolution of 1789 to 1814 draped itself alternately as the Roman republic and the Roman empire, and the revolution of 1848 knew nothing better to do than to parody, now 1789, now the revolutionary tradition of 1793 to 1795. In like manner a beginner who has learnt a new language always translates it back into his mother tongue, but he has assimilated the spirit of the new language and can freely express himself in it only when he finds his way in it without recalling the old and forgets his native tongue in the use of the new.[9]

Much of what the young radical intellectuals call radical social analysis is really more akin to the muckraking of the Populist and Progressive eras: documentation of injustice and inequality, conspiratorial behavior, a preoccupation with unmasking the corporate affiliations of governmental and other institutional elites, and a tendency to indict persons rather than examining the institutional context within which they operate.[10]

This skeptical consciousness is, of course, a welcome relief from the sterile apologetics of the past. Moreover, such documentation must certainly be provided in the service of a movement for social change. Unfortunately, the political as well as the intellectual payoffs resulting from muckraking per se are limited. If that were not the case the late Drew Pearson would have succeeded in establishing himself as a revolutionary intellectual and first-rate social theorist instead of remaining a minor nuisance to the ruling elites whose corruption he uncovered for a half century without understanding its social sources.

To begin the arduous task of a social analysis of social institutions one must go beyond the theoretical models of functionalism—the prevailing intellectual framework in Anglo-American academic social science—and Marxism —which has great influence throughout the non-English-speaking academic world—and incorporate the aspects from each that have provided great insight in the past.[11] From functional theory it is necessary to incorporate

[9] Karl Marx, *The Eighteenth Brumaire of Louis Bonaparte* (New York: International Publishers Co., Inc., 1968), pp. 15–16.
[10] For some of the best examples of this genre, see Domhoff, *op. cit.*, 1967; Noam Chomsky, *At War with Asia* (New York: Vintage Books, 1970); James Ridgeway, *The Closed Corporation: American Universities in Crisis* (New York: Ballantine Books, Inc., 1969).
[11] Functionalism, like Marxism, has several schools. Its distinguishing characteristic, however, is an emphasis on the dependency of whole social systems on their parts and the parts on each other. Social consensus is viewed as generating and maintaining institutions. Social conflict and the role of interest groups or classes in shaping society and benefiting from its particular organization are minimized. The best examination of functionalism can be found in Nicholas Demerath and Richard Peterson, eds., *System, Change and Conflict: A Reader on Contemporary Sociologi-*

a concern for understanding societal tendencies toward cultural consensus, that is, the crucial role that common social values and beliefs play in maintaining social stability. It is also important to consider the functional inter-relationships of institutions with each other and with the cultural sphere. At the same time—and this is where one turns more toward the Marxian perspective—one must reject the view that social institutions are somehow generated by and serve society as a whole. A sophisticated functionalism would acknowledge the disproportionate power of certain historical individuals, groups, and social classes to shape and benefit from the particular organization of institutions and culture found in a society at a given point in time, while still maintaining that all societies must offer certain *minimal* material and psychological benefits to their citizens in order to maintain stability. The functionalist beliefs that societies are in a state of dynamic equilibrium and that massive social change results from external rather than internal forces must also be questioned. While some societies such as the Eastern European nations after World War II have been transformed largely by the imposition of an outside force, others such as France in 1789 collapsed primarily because of internal contradictions.[12]

In utilizing a great deal of Marxian social theory for a new perspective with which social scientists can analyze the historical development of social structures, I am particularly impressed by the need to consider the powerful impact that the dynamics of a particular mode of economic production can have in shaping the character of other social institutions, notably the political, legal, and cultural systems, especially in periods of relative social stability. In times of extreme social upheaval, it could well be, as Marx himself recognized, that politics temporarily takes command.[13] Moreover, any mature social theory must place great importance upon the relationship of social classes to each other, that is, upon the elements of antagonism and consensus that mark their interdependency. In regard to this, I think it reasonable to assume, as did Marx, that the relationship of social classes to each other is primarily one of conflict, although ruling classes are ordinarily able to use mass persuasion (what Gramsci calls "ideological hegemony")[14] and

---

cal Theory and the Debate over Functionalism (New York: The Free Press, 1967). Gouldner, *op. cit.*, provides an important critical analysis of the work of Talcott Parsons, the preeminent functional sociologist of recent decades. For explications of Marxist theory see Irving Zeitlin, *Marxism: A Re-Examination* (Princeton, N.J.: D. Van Nostrand Company, Inc., 1967); Henri Lefebvre, *The Sociology of Marx*, translated by Norbert Guterman (New York: Vintage Books, 1969); Martin Nicolaus, "Proletariat and Middle Class in Marx: Hegelian Choreography and the Capitalist Dialectic," in James Weinstein and David Eakins, eds., *For A New America: Essays in History and Politics from Studies on the Left, 1959–1967* (New York: Vintage Books, 1970), pp. 253–283; and "The Unknown Marx," in Carl Oglesby, ed., *The New Left Reader* (New York: Grove Press, Inc., 1969), pp. 84–110.

[12] Georges Lefebvre, *The Coming of the French Revolution*, translated by R. R. Palmer (Princeton, N.J.: Princeton University Press, 1967).

[13] Marx, *op. cit.*

[14] John Cammett, *Antonio Gramsci and the Origins of Italian Communism* (Stanford, Calif.: Stanford University Press), pp. 204–206. Gwynn Williams, "Gramsci's Concept of *Egemonia*," *Journal of the History of Ideas*, vol. 21 (October–December 1960), pp. 586–599.

institutions of social control (such as the legal system) to place effective limits on any extreme manifestation of conflict. The examination of these sources of social order will take up a principal portion of any serious analysis of human societies.

While the economic mode of production and the resulting social class relationships have enormous influence on the development and maintenance of social institutions and cultural systems, one must avoid the unsophisticated Marxism that reduces all human endeavors to economic motivations and which Marx himself condemned. It is important to stress even more than Marx did that the so-called superstructural elements, the political, educational, legal, and cultural institutions, can develop a logic of their own regardless of their interpenetration by the economic system, and their semi-autonomous development can profoundly influence the economic realm. One must also criticize the element of inevitability or extreme determinism which was more characteristic of Marx's youth than his mature thought and recognize, as he came to, the ironies of historical development which could produce a socialist revolution in underdeveloped Russia and retard it in "ripe" Germany.

Essentially, the kind of analysis that I am advocating can best be called neo-Marxian. It attempts to understand the historical development of social structures by focusing upon the economic, political, and cultural relationships of social classes. It is sensitive to interdisciplinary perspectives. It asks the following basic questions: What are the dynamics and social consequences of the economic mode of production if allowed to develop freely in a society? How are these dynamics and social consequences modified, if at all, by political institutions and political culture? How are the social problems in a society related to the political economy in terms of their origin, their historically specific forms and development, and the limitations the political economy places upon their potential resolution and the mode of resolution? What are the sources of the legitimation[15] and social control that have operated and continue to operate in the service of social order? What are the social structural trends which will lead to change or stability in a society? Among contemporary social scientists a few scholars have recently begun to produce work utilizing some of these perspectives. Barrington Moore's study of revolution, Edward Thompson's history of the English working class, William Appleman Williams' analysis of American imperialism, Eugene Genovese's research on the Southern slaveholding class, and James Weinstein's work on Progressivism are perhaps the most outstanding intellectual products of this emerging school.[16]

[15] The concept of "legitimacy" in political sociology goes beyond the matter of any legal basis for the presence of a given social institution or phenomena (for example, economic inequality). It refers to a state in which the masses of people believe existing social institutions and conditions are the most appropriate ones for the society.

[16] Barrington Moore, Jr., *Social Origins of Dictatorship and Democracy: Lord and Peasant in the Making of the Modern World* (Boston: The Beacon Press, 1966). Edward P. Thompson, *The Making of the English Working Class* (New York: Vintage Books, 1963). William Appleman Williams, *op. cit.*, 1959, 1961; *The Roots of the Modern American Empire: A Study of the Growth and Shaping of Social Con-*

The present volume attempts to satisfy some of the requirements of neo-Marxist social theory outlined above. It draws principally upon the work of sociologists, historians, economists, and political scientists who have addressed themselves to the developing structure and dynamics of American political economy and the relationship between that evolving organization of economic and political life and some major American social problems: imperialism, poverty and economic insecurity, racism, sexism, the misuse of higher education, social disorganization, and personal alienation. In addition to examining the political economy and the social problems that are exacerbated by its particular character and dynamics, this volume is concerned with the historical and contemporary sources of legitimacy and social control. Finally, an extended analysis of societal trends considers the possibility of revolutionary change in the institutional structure of the country.

sciousness in a Marketplace Society (New York: Vintage Books, 1970). Eugene Genovese, The Political Economy of Slavery: Studies in the Economy and Society of the Slave South (New York: Vintage Books, 1965). James Weinstein, The Corporate Ideal in the Liberal State: 1900–1918 (Boston: The Beacon Press, 1968).

part one
The American Political Economy

chapter 1
The Structure and Dynamics of American Capitalism

When Alexis de Tocqueville visited the United States during the 1830s he was awed by what he saw as the pervasive equality that characterized the "new world."[1] Coming from Europe and being familiar with societies ridden by class antagonisms amidst great social and economic inequalities, he believed that the United States represented a great departure from the European experience. While having serious reservations about the boundless conformism and materialism of the emerging American culture, de Tocqueville nevertheless saw the possibility for a successful democratic experiment in the social equality between classes and the absence of extremes of wealth and poverty.[2] The existence of decentralized economic power—with the mass of Americans owning small farms or working as independent artisans—was in his view both a precondition for democracy and a fact of American society during the Jacksonian period.

[1] Alexis de Tocqueville, *Democracy in America*, ed. by Richard Heffner (New York: Mentor Books, 1956).

[2] Interestingly, de Tocqueville believed that both the "tyranny of the majority" and materialism were rooted in the social and economic equality that provided the promise of democracy. See Paul Eberts and Ronald Witton, "Recall from Anecdote: Alexis de Tocqueville and the Morphogenesis of America," *American Sociological Review*, vol. 35 (December 1970), pp. 1080–1097, for an explication of the

De Tocqueville's image of a democratic America, while a meaningful characterization in relation to the reality of European society, was fundamentally inaccurate. His misconception was undoubtedly due in part to the "culture shock" he experienced in visiting a society unlike his own in so many ways. America was favored by abundant natural resources, an "open class" structure (for whites), and labor scarcity which contributed to high living standards, considerable mobility, and social equality when compared to that found in Europe. Even among the nonslave population, however, a great deal of poverty and degradation existed during the period just prior to, during, and after de Tocqueville's visit.[3]

In 1827 and 1828 workingmen in Philadelphia, Boston, and New York formed political parties because they felt deprived of the opportunity for economic advancement. In particular they sought free public education for their children. Another reform which workingmen desired was the elimination of imprisonment for debt. It was estimated that 75,000 persons were sent to jail for failure to pay debts every year throughout the country; and approximately half of these cases involved debts of less than twenty dollars.[4]

In the 1830s several trade unions were formed, including the National Trades Union in 1834. These organizations were oriented primarily toward the skilled trades and sought to protect the economic position of the independent artisan in the face of a growing intercity competition brought about by the widening of markets in the wake of improved transportation. In addition to the craft unions which dominated organized labor in the 1830s, an industrial union, the New England Association of Farmers, Mechanics, and Other Workmen, was formed in 1831 to fight for the ten-hour day.

Although workers in America did have real grievances in an increasingly stratified society the ideology of early unionism was distinctly different from that of European trade unionism. American workers, unlike their European counterparts, did not have "class consciousness" in the Marxian sense. They generally did not distinguish themselves and their employers as separate classes on the basis of who owned the means of production. Rather, they were preoccupied with income differentials, job conditions, and opportunities for social and economic mobility for themselves and their children *within* the framework of a capitalist society based upon artisanship and *small* property owning. Many of the employers of the early nineteenth century were themselves ex-workers who, in Horatio Alger fashion, had prospered. Some of the early factory owners were former artisans whose mechanical inventiveness gave them an opportunity to introduce labor-saving technology into certain industries and to become employers of others' labor.

---

rather prescient "systems" analysis of American structural and cultural development undertaken by de Tocqueville.

[3] Charles Hession and Hyman Sardy, *Ascent to Affluence: A History of American Economic Development* (Boston: Allyn and Bacon, Inc., 1969) provide a useful and often detailed overview of American economic history. For a review of the historical evidence pertaining to economic distinctions among pre-Civil War Americans see Edward Pessen, "The Egalitarian Myth and the American Social Reality: Wealth, Mobility, and Equality in the 'Era of the Common Man'," *The American Historical Review,* vol. 76 (October 1971), pp. 989–1034.

[4] *Ibid.*, pp. 200–201.

The Structure and Dynamics of American Capitalism

Despite the fact that workers shared the value of private property with their employers, conflict between the two groups was often quite bitter, particularly when employers organized their own organizations to combat unionism and the business-oriented courts refused to grant legality to trade unions because they were "in restraint of trade."[5] Numerous workers were tried and convicted of "conspiracy" to restrain trade by organizing trade unions from the late 1820s until 1842, when a state court upheld labor's right to organize.

The terrible depression of the late 1830s weakened the position of labor unions even further.[6] With jobs scarce, workers were not anxious to jeopardize their employment by joining a union. The successful use of scabs in this period of job insecurity and the inability of unions to raise dues also contributed to the virtual collapse of the union movement in the 1830s. When labor attempted to use government to legislate improved working conditions employers threatened to fire anyone who voted for prolabor candidates, bought the votes of legislators, and made sure that labor laws contained enough loopholes to exempt them.

If one reads accounts of the condition of the working population after Jacksonianism a bleak picture emerges indeed. Norman Ware, in his classic volume on the working class in the two decades preceding the Civil War, attempts to describe the situation of the worker at the outset of the American industrialization process.[7] The development of advanced technology had greatly imperiled the status of independent artisans, who were forced to sell their labor to employers and work in the new factories. This status loss was accompanied by an actual decline in living standards as the factory workers had to labor longer hours for lower real wages under horrible conditions. Finally, the massive influx in the 1840s and 1850s of immigrants, an increasing proportion of whom were uneducated manual workers, also contributed to economic exploitation and polarization between social classes.[8]

Ware shows that the new working class of the pre–Civil War years was acutely aware of its exploitation. It was able to recall a more noble and independent existence and lament the loss of what appeared to be a "golden past" from the vantage point of what was felt to be "wage slavery." This term was especially apt, since many early factory owners, such as those in Lowell, Massachusetts, were firm believers in paternalism and regulated the private lives of their employees just as rigorously as their labor time.[9]

Employer paternalism was short-lived largely because of attacks against the feudal features of the institution and the costs of regulation. Another very significant factor in its demise was the demographic transformation of the factory worker. In the early period of industrialization the American labor force was ethnically homogeneous and there were many female workers. By the late 1840s large numbers of Irish immigrants had begun to replace

[5] Ibid., p. 202.
[6] Ibid., pp. 202–203.
[7] Norman Ware, The Industrial Worker: The Reaction of American Industrial Society to the Advance of the Industrial Revolution, 1840–1860 (Chicago: Quadrangle Books, 1964).
[8] Ibid., pp. 10–124. See also Hession and Sardy, op. cit., pp. 291–301.
[9] Ware, op. cit., pp. 71–105.

native American factory operatives. The widespread contempt for these foreigners made employers less concerned about and hopeful of "protecting" them from the numerous "vices" alleged to flow from factory life. The increase in male factory workers also eroded paternalism. The social costs of paternalism—lack of freedom—receded; the social costs of liberty —the "freedom" to drink, be subjected to hideous living conditions, and starve—increased.

Laborers who emigrated from Ireland to America because of the potato famine were subjected to inhuman working and living conditions because of their desperation to find any means of sustenance. Ware reports that 5 percent of the population of New York City lived in cellars. Between six and twenty persons often shared a single room among the very poor. Sanitary conditions were almost entirely absent.[10] While native workers were living somewhat better at the time, "it was with this [the conditions of immigrant labor] which they were being brought into competition, and which serves in part to explain their own tendency to lower levels of living."[11]

After the Civil War and the triumph of industrial capitalism over Southern precapitalist economic forms,[12] the United States entered a period of enormous economic expansion. In this process great amounts of capital were accumulated, unheard-of fortunes created, and considerable economic misery generated for workers, especially immigrants, whose forced savings in the form of bare subsistence wages provided an important source of capitalist development.[13]

While the emerging corporate capitalist class and its financial allies were spurring the economy on to greater heights, workers who were employed and working steadily did enjoy a rising standard of living. These workers were predominantly native Americans or Northern European immigrants. The influx of millions of persons from Southern and Eastern Europe swelled the ranks of the unskilled and unorganized in crowded urban centers.

The remarkable economic growth of the United States during the last third of the nineteenth century was not accomplished without periods of severe hardship.[14] Excess productive capacity and lack of investment outlets led to economic recessions or depressions in 1866, 1867, 1873–1879, 1883–1885, and 1891–1897. The depressions of the 1870s and 1890s were particularly severe and caused widespread unemployment. During the Civil War employment levels were high and trade union strength grew because of the accelerated demand for commodities, but with the demobilization of the armed forces demand and prices fell. As a consequence labor was placed on the defensive in the face of employer resistance to wage demands.

The instability characterizing the American economy had a profound effect upon labor history. Before the Civil War, as stated earlier, trade union-

[10] *Ibid.*, pp. 10–17.
[11] *Ibid.*, p. 16.
[12] Barrington Moore, Jr., *Social Origins of Dictatorship and Democracy: Lord and Peasant in the Making of the Modern World* (Boston: The Beacon Press, 1966), pp. 111–155.
[13] Hession and Sardy, *op. cit.*, pp. 399–403.
[14] *Ibid.*

ism was characterized neither by Marxian class consciousness nor by an effort merely to ameliorate harsh working conditions and gain higher wages. Rather, trade unionism was concerned primarily with political reforms which would put an end to the wage system and restore a society of small private property owners and artisans. This outlook led to a deemphasis on strikes which, it was argued, tended to legitimize the wage system. Moral persuasion aimed at convincing employers to enter into cooperative relations with their employees represented the principal strategy of the antebellum labor unionists. When this failed, government was looked to for redress of grievances.

The organization of the National Labor Union and its successor, the Knights of Labor, were the two most significant postwar efforts to develop reform unionism in the context of industrialization. Both unions' memberships reached the hundreds of thousands at their peak. But the leaders' unwillingness to devote themselves to vital though mundane struggles over hours and wages eventually caused both unions to decline when American workmen finally realized that a return to a "golden age" of industrial harmony was no longer feasible.[15] Paradoxically, the growth of "business unionism" indicated both an abandonment of utopianism and a heightened class militancy. Samuel Gompers, the most significant figure in American trade unionism, eschewed the visions of social transformation which had so captivated Terence V. Powderly, the architect of the Knights of Labor, and indulged in few of Powderly's illusions that the capitalist class could be reasoned with and persuaded to share its privileges with labor in a spirit of mutual respect and cooperation. Gompers realized that the threat of industrial disruption was the only way to successfully communicate with employers.

The economic and social changes of the post–Civil War decades altered the fabric of American society so dramatically that if de Tocqueville had visited America in the 1880s or 1890s, he would have doubted he had returned to the same country. If class polarization had been largely absent in 1830, it was an ever-present feature in the waning decades of the century. High unemployment (over 12 percent of the labor force in the nineties), the growing rural impoverishment (which resulted in part from increased foreign agricultural productivity), and the concentration of financial and industrial capital (unchecked by government) accentuated economic inequality in America. The rise of populism, militant trade unionism, and socialism reflected growing class conflict and added to the tensions of the capitalist takeoff.[16]

The growing agrarian and working-class unrest which characterized the last decades of the nineteenth century was met with vigorous resistance by employers, the federal government, and the courts. Private armies terrorized and even killed union organizers at the behest of respectable businessmen. Federal troops were called out to break strikes, protect scabs, and harass union leadership. In a series of major decisions, the Supreme Court

[15] Gerald Grob, *Workers and Utopia: A Study of Ideological Conflict in the American Labor Movement, 1865–1900* (Chicago: Quadrangle Books, 1969).

[16] Philip S. Foner, *A History of the American Labor Movement: From the Founding of the American Federations of Labor to the Emergence of American Imperialism* (New York: International Publishers Co., Inc., 1955).

enhanced the legal power of corporations and restricted union activity, thus consolidating corporate hegemony at a crucial moment in American history.[17]

As the twentieth century began, however, there seemed to be no end to labor militancy and the Socialist Party threatened to make major electoral gains. Corporate and governing elites began to recognize the need for limited reforms in order to stabilize capitalism.[18] The National Civic Federation (NCF) brought together representatives of giant corporations and conservative labor leaders who began to develop a corporate ideology which would permit workers a more decent life to the extent that they embraced the capitalist system and sought limited social changes within it. Ronald Radosh's article in this chapter discusses the emergence of corporate ideology among labor leaders in both the AFL and the seemingly more radical CIO. He considers the possible alternatives which were articulated by dissidents within the labor movement. Radosh probably overestimates the willingness of corporate leaders to accept even conservative "business unionism" and minimizes the fact that union militancy and protracted struggle were needed just to institutionalize labor conflict in what Galbraith calls the "New Industrial State." Moreover, state legal and military repression and the absence of an intense and widespread working-class socialist consciousness also made labor leaders willing to accept the domination of a slightly reformed capitalism and to eschew the socialist goals of European trade unionism.[19]

The "liberal" response of major corporate leaders to the abuses of the factory system and the low living standard of the American worker did not flow solely from humanitarian concerns, although some corporate leaders were truly appalled when they became aware of the living conditions of the working class. Nor can this response be understood simply as a strategy for labor co-optation in order to prevent a more radical response by labor to its situation. The reform-minded sectors of the capitalist class were able to accept limited changes in industrial relations only because their economic position was so established by the twentieth century that concessions to the working class were possible. Andrew Carnegie, who had paid labor goons to harass and occasionally shoot strikers several decades earlier, was a member of the NCF. His changing position toward labor unions must have been due at least partly to the fact that his corporate interests were no longer jeopardized by labor's demands for higher wages, shorter hours, and better working conditions. At the same time, the opposition of small business to social reform was not necessarily due to a lack of humanitarianism nor to an

[17] Arnold Paul, *Conservative Crisis and the Rule of Law: Attitudes of Bar and Bench, 1887–1895* (New York: Harper & Row, Publishers, 1969).

[18] James Weinstein, *The Decline of Socialism in America* (New York: Vintage Books, 1969); *The Corporate Ideal in the Liberal State; 1900–1918* (Boston: The Beacon Press, 1968).

[19] See Philip S. Foner's "Comment" on Radosh's article in *Studies on the Left,* vol. 6 (November–December 1966), pp. 89–96. John K. Galbraith, *The New Industrial State* (Boston: Houghton Mifflin Company, 1967), pp. 271–290. Bruce C. Johnson, "The Democratic Mirage: Notes toward a Theory of American Politics," *Berkeley Journal of Sociology,* vol. 13 (1968), pp. 104–143. Also reprinted in chapter 9 of this text.

inability to perceive the dangers of ignoring the needs of the working class. Rather, the economic situation of small business owners made it difficult for them to give in to labor. Small businessmen had to constantly cut costs because they operated in a highly competitive market with thousands of other small businesses and were unable to raise prices at will. Therefore, if costs increased, prices also had to rise, and these businessmen risked losing their share of the market. A big business, operating in competition with perhaps a few other firms, was more equipped structurally to collude with its competitors in order to maintain and increase profits even while making concessions to labor. In addition, the promotion of conservative unionism gave Big Business an opportunity to eliminate small business competition which was unable to survive increased production costs.

The basic structure of contemporary American corporate capitalism grew out of the emerging corporate ideology developed in the early decades of the twentieth century and consolidated in the New Deal period. If we examine that structure it is clear how far America has traveled from the early nineteenth-century ideal of a society of small property holders. In 1951, C. Wright Mills described transformation of property ownership in the evolution of the American economy until the beginning of World War II:

In the early nineteenth century, although there are no exact figures, probably four-fifths of the occupied population were self-employed enterprisers; by 1870 only about one-third, and in 1940, only about one-fifth, were still in this old middle class. Many of the remaining four-fifths of the people who now earn a living do so by working for the 2 or 3 per cent of the population who now own 40 or 50 per cent of the private property in the United States. Among these workers are the members of the new middle class, white-collar people on salary. For them, as for wage-workers, America has become a nation of employees for whom independent property is out of range. Labor markets, not control of property, determine their chances to receive income, exercise power, enjoy prestige, learn and use skills.[20]

The situation since the war years reinforces Mills' words. By 1969 only 9.1 percent of the population were considered self-employed.[21]

The decline in the proportion of self-employed persons in the United States, while strongly suggesting a growing centralization of economic power in the hands of a minority of property-holders, cannot be directly regarded as an indicator of such a development. It is possible, after all, that those in the employee class are paid incomes large enough to enable them to maintain a high standard of living and moreover, to become involved in capitalist forms of property ownership by purchasing stock in corporations. Thus, wage and salaried workers may still be able to maintain a certain degree of economic independence.

[20] C. Wright Mills, *White Collar: The American Middle Classes* (New York: Oxford University Press, 1951), p. 63.
[21] *Manpower Report to the President* (Washington, D.C.: Government Printing Office, 1970), p. 228.

Victor Perlo's first article in this chapter, though based on data collected in the 1950s, makes it quite obvious that the ownership of productive wealth in the form of stock is highly concentrated and the rising standard of living of American wage and salaried workers has not been translated into a significant share of "people's capitalism." Unfortunately, more recent data is unavailable, but there is no evidence to suggest the distribution of stock ownership is more equitable in 1972 than in the past. Robert Lampman's important study of wealth-holding shows that centralization in stock ownership has increased over the decades; for example, the top 1 percent of adults held 61.5 percent of corporate stock in 1922 and 76 percent in 1953.[22] Lampman also considers concentration in ownership for other forms of wealth. He notes that the top 1 percent of adults held 31.8 percent of U.S. government bonds, over 80 percent of other bonds, 12.5 percent of real estate, and more than 25 percent of cash, mortgages, and notes in 1953.[23] In general, he finds that the total personal (equity) wealth of the top 1 percent fell from 36.3 percent in 1929 to 20.8 percent in 1949, primarily because of the Depression and the resulting temporary decline in the fortunes of certain key financial and industrial elites. Yet between 1949 and 1956 the top 1 percent of wealth-holders increased their ownership of national wealth to 26 percent.[24] Once again, there is no evidence that wealth has been more equitably distributed since the fifties.

Perhaps the most recent and reliable analysis of wealth distribution in the United States was conducted by the Federal Reserve System upon data on asset holdings as of December 31, 1962.[25] This study found that the top 200,000 households, or only 0.4 percent of the total, owned 22 percent of all wealth, 32 percent of all investment assets, and 75 percent of miscellaneous assets, which are comprised primarily of trust funds. The top 1.25 percent of American households owned 65 percent of investment assets. If we compare the Federal Reserve study to Lampman's earlier work it is obvious that wealth has become much more unequally distributed in recent decades, since Lampman considers the wealth holding of *all adults,* whereas the Federal Reserve data shows concentration among *households.* Since large families are concentrated at the bottom end of the social class system, Lampman's research tends to underestimate the economic power of the top 1 percent.

While wealth-holding is highly concentrated, income distribution is somewhat more equitably distributed. According to Herman Miller, in 1959 the top 1 percent of American families received 8 percent of the national income.[26] Nevertheless, Gabriel Kolko believes, after comparing data on income distribution between 1910 and 1959, that there has been little altera-

[22] Robert Lampman, The Share of Top Wealth-Holders in National Wealth, 1922–1956 (Princeton, N.J.: Princeton University Press, 1962), p. 209.
[23] Ibid.
[24] Ibid., p. 24.
[25] Ferdinand Lundberg, The Rich and the Super-Rich: A Study in the Power of Money Today (New York: Lyle Stuart Inc., 1968), pp. 22–25, summarizes the most important findings of the Federal Reserve System study, Survey of Financial Characteristics of Consumers (Washington, D.C.: Government Printing Office, 1966).
[26] Herman Miller, Rich Man, Poor Man (New York: Signet Books, 1965), p. 24.

tion in the division of national income for almost fifty years.[27] While the trend of income distribution between 1929 and 1944 has been disputed, there is consensus that no redistribution has occurred since 1944.[28] It is also agreed that because of underreporting, the use of tax loopholes by the wealthy, and the regressive nature of state and local taxes, no fundamental transfer of income from rich to poor occurs through tax levies.[29]

The slightly more equitable distribution of income as opposed to wealth, while no doubt of comfort to the average citizen, no way suggests that the overall economic power of the top 1 percent of American families is limited. There is little doubt that wealth—that is, the ownership of such things as land, buildings, machinery, raw materials, goods in process, animals, stocks, patents, copyrights, and franchises—is a much more significant indicator of economic power than income. The wealth held by certain individuals or small groups gives them enormous power to affect others' lives. If a factory owner decides to move his plant, raise prices, cut labor costs, or invest capital abroad he may cause widespread social dislocations in a local community. When many owners make these decisions they can affect the entire fabric of society. But income, no matter how high, basically affects only the consumptive habits of the income holder. In the long run these habits may contribute to significant social changes, but the power of consumption is considerably less centralized than that of wealth. Many consumers would have to change their behavior patterns for a long time to have the effects of a small number of wealth-holders in generating societal change. Furthermore, there is good reason to believe the consumer is no longer sovereign and that corporate decision-makers play the primary role in generating demand for commodities through advertising, planned obsolescence, and influence over federal expenditures.[30]

Not only is the ownership of national wealth highly centralized but the structure of the corporate economy has been characterized by growing concentration of assets and profits. Willard Mueller, Director of the Federal Trade Commission's Bureau of Economics, in a report to the Senate Subcommittee on Anti-trust and Monopoly of the Committee of the Judiciary, presented data which vividly illustrates the domination of the American economy by a relative handful of giant corporations.[31] While there were 180,000 corporations and 240,000 partnerships in the United States as of 1962, the total

[27] Gabriel Kolko, *Wealth and Power in America: An Analysis of Social Class and Income Distribution* (New York: Frederick A. Praeger, Inc., 1962), p. 14. Since 1959 there has been no indication of major changes in income distribution. See *The American Almanac: The U.S. Book of Facts, Statistics, and Information for 1971* (New York: Grosset & Dunlap, Inc., 1971), p. 323.

[28] G. William Domhoff, *Who Rules America?* (Englewood Cliffs, N.J.: Prentice-Hall, Inc., 1967), pp. 41–42.

[29] Lundberg, *op. cit.*, pp. 321–432; Kolko, *op. cit.*, pp. 30–45; Joseph Pechman, "The Rich, the Poor, the Taxes They Pay," *The Public Interest*, No. 17 (Fall, 1969), pp. 21–43.

[30] Galbraith, *op. cit.*

[31] Willard Mueller, "Recent Changes in Industrial Concentration, and the Current Merger Movement," in Maurice Zeitlin, ed., *American Society, Inc.: Studies of the Social Structure and Political Economy of the United States* (Chicago: Markham, 1970), pp. 19–41.

The Structure and Dynamics of American Capitalism

assets of the top 20 manufacturing corporations were about equal to those of the smallest 419,000 companies. The 200 largest manufacturing corporations accounted for 56.8 percent of the total assets of all 180,000 corporations and 67.5 percent of the after-tax profits of these corporations. In 20 of 28 specific industrial groupings, the 20 top companies earned over 60 percent of industry profits. The automobile, tobacco, rubber, plastic, dairy, primary iron and steel, alcoholic beverage, petroleum refining, and industrial chemical industries are particularly dominated by a few corporations. Moreover, Mueller demonstrates that industrial concentration has increased between 1947 and 1962. This process is being spurred on by the greatest merger movement in the history of the United States. Between 1950 and 1963 about 20 percent of the largest 1000 manufacturing corporations had merged or been acquired by other firms. One third of the disappearing companies had been absorbed by corporations ranked among the top 200 corporations in 1950.[32]

Although the growing concentration of manufacturing assets and profits has been acknowledged by virtually all recent studies, the implications of economic domination by a tiny proportion of Americans has been subject to considerable debate. First, it has been maintained, even by Marxist scholars such as Paul Baran and Paul Sweezy, that corporations are now capable of financing their own expansion needs and do not have to rely upon financial institutions (for example, banks, insurance companies) as in the past.[33] This corporate self-sufficiency, if true, would tend to decentralize corporate decision-making to some degree in comparison to the earlier part of the century when a few investment banking firms like the House of Morgan exercised considerable control over a wide variety of industries. Second, the growth of enormous corporations, with huge numbers of stockholders, has led many observers to argue that the link between ownership and control of corporations has diminished. In the doctrine of the "managerial revolution" modern managers are no longer dependent upon the whims of a few stockholders as in the days of the Robber Barons. Freed from an obligatory profit-maximization orientation, the corporate executives of today are able and willing to use their inordinate power to engage in socially redeeming works.

The twin theses of corporate self-financing and managerial revolution have provided almost the only ray of hope for those scholars who, having acknowledged the growing concentration of giant corporate control over industry, seek to demonstrate that modern capitalism is less antisocial than classic entrepreneurial capitalism. Unfortunately, as Victor Perlo's second article in this chapter argues, corporate self-sufficiency is a myth in the face of the continuing dependency of giant corporations on *outside* financial

[32] For an analysis of the meaning of the merger movement see Paul Sweezy and Harry Magdoff, "The Merger Movement: A Study in Power," in David Mermelstein, ed., *Economics: Mainstream Readings and Radical Critiques* (New York: Random House, Inc., 1970), pp. 77–90.

[33] Paul Baran and Paul Sweezy, *Monopoly Capital: An Essay on the American Economic and Economic Social Order* (New York: Monthly Review Press, 1966), pp. 14–51.

capital.[34] Banks are just as significant in the financing of corporate expansion as ever. Moreover, just as in the case of manufacturing corporations, there is an increasing concentration of assets in a small number of banks, principally those operating in the New York area. When Perlo's second article is considered with Ralph Miliband's article in this chapter attacking John Kenneth Galbraith's *The New Industrial State,* which contains the most recent variation of the managerial revolution thesis, small comfort remains for those who see in the development of advanced capitalism a hidden pluralism amidst oligopoly and a trace of humanism emerging from the cost-benefit calculations of corporate decision-makers.

If neither the decentralization of corporate power nor the rise of public-spirited managers and technocrats depicts the reality of advanced American capitalism, the restoration of de Tocqueville's dream of economic democracy as the foundation of all liberty can only rest on the shoulders of labor or the state. Radosh's article in this chapter on the organized working class, together with Galbraith's analysis elsewhere of the functions of trade unionism in maintaining the stability of the modern giant corporaton,[35] leaves the reader doubtful about the past and present role of this potential agent for social change. As for the state, to rely upon its aid was, for de Tocqueville, a sad defeat for liberty.

Corporate capitalism has been discussed almost exclusively in terms of its structure. But what about the dynamics of capitalism as a system? Modern economists are generally reluctant to address themselves to questions about the natural development or "laws" of capitalism. They prefer in this age of specialization and scholarly service to industry and government to examine the operation of particular aspects of the economy (for example, monetary theory) and to try to meliorate the chronic problems such as inflation and unemployment which plague capitalism. Only a few economic theorists today seem willing to follow the footsteps of the great system builders (and destroyers) of the past, Adam Smith, Karl Marx, and John Maynard Keynes.

To some extent the paucity of grand theorists is the result of a fundamental consensus, or near-consensus, on many basic features of capitalism. Virtually all economists agree that each capitalist enterprise seeks to maxi-

[34] An important recent analysis of the role of banks in corporate affairs, emphasizing the power of these and other financial institutions over and on boards of directors and the conflicts between industrial and financial capital, is Robert Fitch and Mary Oppenheimer, "Who Rules Corporations? Parts I–III," *Socialist Revolution,* vol. 1 (July–August 1970), pp. 73–107; (September–October 1970), pp. 61–114; (November–December 1970), pp. 33–94. By 1965 the total assets of financial institutions represented 47 percent of national wealth (that is, land, structures, equipment and inventories). This proportion had increased from 14 percent in 1890 and 30 percent in 1929. See *ibid.,* (July–August 1970), p. 93. For a critique of the Fitch and Oppenheimer thesis see Paul Sweezy, "The Resurgence of Financial Control: Fact or Fancy?," *Monthly Review,* vol. 23 (November, 1971), pp. 1–33.

[35] Galbraith, *op. cit.,* pp. 271–290. It should be noted that only 22.7 percent of the labor force was unionized in 1966. This proportion has not changed significantly since 1940. Thus, even if one believes that labor unions represent a countervailing force against capitalists, it would only affect about one fifth of the labor force. See *Handbook of Labor Statistics* (Washington, D.C.: Government Printing Office, 1968), p. 300.

mize its profits and reinvest a large proportion of its earnings to expand its operations and thereby reap greater profits in the future.[36] Moreover, there is general agreement that production is geared toward profitability, and the social consequences of economic activity are largely ignored in the routine operation of the corporation. In addition, few economists would deny that capitalist competition tends to evolve into a concentration of economic power for an increasingly smaller proportion of firms in a given industry. These firms, called oligopolies or monopolies, are increasingly seen as a threat to the operation of a free market, since they can control their own prices regardless of consumer demand, regulate demand itself through their political influence (as has the automobile industry), and do not have to produce high-quality commodities. Finally, economists recognize that capitalism must constantly expand, creating new needs, products, and consumers. To stagnate is to perish, since only an increase in output permits firms to maintain and increase employment opportunities. If investment outlets dry up, labor is no longer needed and layoffs ensue, since capitalism assumes no obligation for the welfare of workers whose labor cannot be turned into profit. The business cycle with the periodic recessions endemic to capitalism reflect the uneven coordination of supply and demand, the problem of overproduction and underconsumption, which is typically rectified through lowered output and high unemployment. If these dislocations are not remedied, serious depressions may result. Under such circumstances capitalism itself, and not merely the existence of a particular company, may be in jeopardy as millions of people are forced to subsist in extreme poverty and insecurity with the knowledge that factories remain idle simply because it is no longer profitable to produce.

If there are intense conflicts among economists today they revolve chiefly around the most efficient and humane way to reconcile the logic of capitalist development with the need for human welfare. It is principally in regard to this fundamental question that the three major economic perspectives—those based upon laissez-faire principles, Keynesian notions of government regulation of demand to insure economic stability, and the Marxian critique of both laissez-faire and Keynesian economics—differ. The debate between Milton Friedman, the foremost contemporary disciple of Adam Smith in his devotion to the tenets of laissez-faire, and the many distinguished followers of Lord Keynes has revolved around the viability of unregulated competitive capitalism and its relationship to public welfare.[37] Marxists such as Paul Sweezy, Paul Baran, and Ernest Mandel accept neither the laissez-faire proponents' belief that the operation of the free market can insure economic solvency and social justice nor the Keynesians' assumption that state intervention in the economy can do what private enterprise has failed

[36] Michael Tanzer, *The Sick Society: An Economic Examination* (New York: Holt, Rinehart and Winston, Inc., 1971), pp. 7–14.
[37] Milton Friedman, *Capitalism and Freedom* (Chicago: University of Chicago Press, 1962). John Maynard Keynes, *The General Theory of Employment, Interest and Money* (New York: Harcourt Brace and World, 1936) remains the classic statement of modern liberal economics which has become the dominant perspective among contemporary economists.

to.[38] Rather, these Marxist theorists tend to view capitalism as a once-progressive economic system that created the possibility of material abundance and human liberation, but which, in its maturity, became anachronistic and regressive, being able to maintain itself only by aggressive economic expansion, militarism, and state regulation. If contemporary Marxist economists are no longer willing to predict the *inevitable* collapse of capitalism from the weight of its internal contradictions alone, they have not shared the common view that collapse is virtually impossible because of state regulation of the economy.[39]

As stated above the underlying assumptions of laissez-faire, Keynesian, and Marxian economics are not dissimilar. The laissez-faire theorists do not deny that capitalism is a basically dynamic economic system which requires constant expansion and frequently creates severe economic and social dislocations. They simply argue that *in the long run* the laws of the market will compensate for any imbalances, and government intervention will unnecessarily deprive people of freedom. Keynesians might well acknowledge that a "free market" solution works eventually, but they tend to be concerned about the short-run social and political consequences of periodic economic depressions. Because of their analysis of the anarchic nature of capitalist development Marxists share these concerns, but doubt that state regulation is sufficient to correct the inherent flaws in the capitalist mode of production. Marx in his most mature work felt that capitalism would be destroyed by its very success.[40] The creation of productive forces capable of bringing material well-being to all would conflict with the "relations of production," the necessity, under capitalism, to have people work, particularly at unnecessary alienated labor for survival.

The problem with all three economic models is their failure to place sufficient importance on the propensity of human beings not to sit idly by and permit their short- and long-run interests to be undermined by the "laws" of capitalist development. This applies at both ends of the class structure. Employers, no less than employees, will struggle to protect themselves from the ravages of the market. While workers formed unions for self-defense, capitalists forged monopolies and oligopolies; colluded to escape from ruinous competition and the fickleness of consumers; and, in a perversion of modern liberal Keynesianism, used their vast economic power to entice and coerce the representatives of the state to preserve capitalism and class privilege. Thus, laissez-faire advocates ignore social and political forces that inevitably fight against unregulated competitive capitalism in the name of the very human desire for security. Keynesians and, to a lesser extent, many

[38] Paul Sweezy, *The Theory of Capitalist Development* (New York: Monthly Review Press, 1968). Paul Baran, *The Political Economy of Growth*, 2d ed. (New York: Monthly Review Press, 1968), pp. 1–133. Ernest Mandel, *Marxist Economic Theory*, translated by Brian Pearce, 2 vols. (New York: Monthly Review Press, 1969).

[39] Tanzer, *op. cit.*, pp. 165–233.

[40] Karl Marx, *The Grundrisse*, ed. and translated by David McLellan (New York: Harper & Row, Publishers, 1971). See also Martin Nicolaus, "The Unknown Marx," in Carl Oglesby, ed., *The New Left Reader* (New York: Grove Press, Inc., 1969), pp. 84–110.

Marxists underestimate the way in which state power can be successfully employed for the benefit of private enterprise without destroying capitalism or increasing economic equality and democracy. Chapter 2 discusses this process as it evolved throughout American history.

If we must leave the realm of economic *theory* to understand why economic *history* has been so unpredictable, it is only just to recognize the significant contributions that grand economic theory has made to our general understanding of capitalism and, particularly, the profound internal contradictions which always threaten to destroy it and which contribute—as we shall see—to so many social problems.

The Structure and Dynamics of American Capitalism

Victor Perlo

PEOPLE'S CAPITALISM
AND STOCK OWNERSHIP

It has become the fashion to classify the economy of the United States as a new form, "People's Capitalism." The expression was developed by the Advertising Council, which prepared a "People's Capitalism" exhibit, shown internationally under the auspices of the United States Information Agency. The term is accepted by publicists and widely propagated in corporation reports and advertisements. It is used by some research and academic economists. Future editions of economic texts can hardly fail to discuss the theory—or slogan—of "People's Capitalism."

The central component of "People's Capitalism" is the contention that ownership of American industry has become democratic in character through the dispersion of stockholdings among the population. This is not only given the most attention, but also is the feature that involves an alleged qualitative change in structure. The present paper is devoted to this theme.

There follow typical statements by professional economists, corporations and their officers. Marcus Nadler writes:

> The economy of the United States is rapidly assuming the character of what may be termed "People's Capitalism" under which the production facilities of the nation—notably manufacturing—have come to be increasingly owned by people in the middle and lower income brackets or indirectly by mutual institutions which manage their savings.

This is the principal one of the "striking political and social transformations" which Nadler states have taken place . . . since the late 1920's. . . .

The conclusion of the analysis in this paper is that the main justification of the term "People's Capitalism"—widespread stock-ownership—is without substance.

I. Trend in Number of Stockholders

Has there actually been a sharp rise, since 1929, in the number and proportion of the population owning stocks? Table I presents available estimates. . . .

Reprinted, with deletions, from Victor Perlo, " 'People's Capitalism' and Stock-Ownership," *The American Economic Review*, vol. 48 (June 1958), pp. 333–347, by permission of the author and *The American Economic Review*. Victor Perlo is an economic consultant in New York. He is the author of several books, including *The Income "Revolution," The Empire of High Finance*, and *Militarism and Industry*.

Table I.   Proportion of Stockholders to Population in United States 1927–56

Year	Number of Stockholders	Population (millions)	Stockholders as Per Cent of Population
1927 (a)	4–6 million	119	3.5–5.0
1927 (b)	5–6 million	119	4.2–5.0
1930	9–11 million	123	7.3–8.9
1937	8–9 million	129	6.2–7.0
1952	6,490,000	157	4.1
1954	7,500,000	162	4.6
1956	8,630,000	168	5.1

Sources: Population from U.S. Bureau of Census.

1927 (a) A. A. Berle Jr. & G. C. Means, *The Modern Corporation and Private Property,* New York 1932, p. 374.

1927 (b) and 1930 N. R. Danielian and others, *The Security Markets,* New York 1935, pp. 49–50, 723 ff.

1937 Temporary National Economic Committee, Monogr. No. 29, Washington 1940, p. 168.

1952 L. H. Kimmel, *Share Ownership in the United States,* Washington 1952, p. 89.

1954 and 1956, New York Stock Exchange, shown in *Economic Report of the President, January 1957,* Washington 1957, Table D-21, p. 112.

The percentage of the population owning stock in 1956 was, if anything, lower than the corresponding percentage for 1930, but higher than that for 1927. There is a cyclical movement in the percentage of the people owning stocks. It increased sharply during the culminating years of the bull market of the 1920's; declined during the subsequent depression, and increased again during the bull market of the middle 1950's. But the statistics do not establish a secular uptrend in the proportion of the population participating directly in ownership of American industry over the past three decades.

However, the percentages in Table I understate the dispersion of stock-ownership among economic units, because one stockholder often carries the stock for the benefit of his family. Kimmel estimates that the 6,490,000 stock-owners in 1952 were distributed among 4,750,000 family units, or 9.5 per cent of the 50,000,000 such units in the country. The Michigan Survey Research Center estimated that 8 per cent of all spending units held stock in 1955. Roughly speaking, we may say that about one out of ten families own stock —a significant proportion, but hardly large enough to justify assertions of the *general* participation of the population in ownership of the means of production. . . .

Stock-ownership remains very unevenly distributed among various occupational groups and income groups. Kimmel found the per cent of different groups owning stocks ranging downward from 44.8 per cent of administrative executives and 19.4 per cent of operating supervisory officials to 1.4 per cent of semiskilled workers and 0.2 per cent of unskilled workers. Among propertied, managerial, and professional classes generally, 13.4 per cent were stock-owners, while among employee classes generally, 3.5 per cent were stock-owners. Similarly, 24.7 per cent of people in families with incomes over $10,000 owned stock, while only 1.4 per cent of those in families with incomes under $4,000 owned stock. The majority of the population was in the latter group, but it included only one-fifth of the stock-owners.

While exact comparisons are not possible, owing to changes in the purchasing power of the dollar, the proportion of lower-income individuals owning stock does not appear to be larger than estimated for 1927 by Berle and Means, or for 1937 by the TNEC. . . .

II. Concentration of Stock-Ownership

The concept of an economic democracy based on stock-ownership requires not only that there be a large number of owners, but that a large number own enough shares to have economic significance. It also requires that the situation should not be one in which a small number of stock-owners, by virtue of dominant holdings, are in a position of partial or total control.

A man owning a single share, or even 10 to 20 shares, of a typical industrial corporation, obviously has but a token stake in the ownership of the means of production. Consider the man who has invested $1,000 in corporation stocks. At recent yields, he might expect dividends of $40 per year. This is equal to about 2 days' wages for the workers in such industries as steel and automobiles. Even with allowance for possible capital appreciation, the return will not provide a significant addition to his living standard, nor represent a major degree of profit participation. After-tax profits of manufacturing corporations, in 1955, amounted to $702 per manufacturing employee, or 17½ times the dividend receipts of the $1,000 investor. The $1,000 is a similarly small fraction of the total capital invested per worker in basic industries.

This represents, in fact, the typical situation of the comparatively small number of workers owning stock. The 1955 Survey of Consumer Finances reported 3 per cent of spending units headed by skilled and semiskilled workers owning some stock. The median amount owned was between $500 and $999. None covered in the survey (or too few to be recorded in the percentage table), had as much as $5,000 in stock. The figures were identical for unskilled workers. In the case of clerical and sales workers, 9 per cent held stocks, and the median holding was a little over $1,000. All of those reported as holding over $25,000 in stock were in the managerial, propertied, and professional groups.

The Survey of Consumer Finances would indicate stock-ownership by about three-quarters of a million spending units headed by wage earners (skilled, semiskilled and unskilled workers), the figure swelled to a certain extent by the inclusion of foremen's holdings. Assuming a mean stockholding of $1,000, the total value of stocks held by all wage earners' families in the country came to something like $750 million. That was equal to 0.3 per cent of the marketable supply of stock in the United States.

The TNEC compiled, as of 1937, the main stockholdings of some wealthy families. For example the du Pont family was estimated to have $574 million in stock, the Rockefeller family $397 million, and the Mellon family $391 million.[1] Allowing only for publicly reported changes in these family holdings —and there is no evidence of their significant dispersal—by 1956 the value of holdings of the Rockefeller and Mellon families exceeded $3 billion each, and of the du Pont family $4 billion.[2]

In short, any one of these families—or more properly speaking, groups of related families—owned many times as much stock as all the wage earners in the United States. Indeed, the market value of Rockefeller holdings in a single corporation, Standard of New Jersey, was twice the market value of all the holdings of all American wage earners. . . .

The distribution of shareholdings in Standard Oil (New Jersey) is revealing. As of 1938 the 100 largest stockholders of record had 12,584,000 shares, or 46.2 per cent of the total. Most of these were various holdings of the Rockefeller, Harkness, Payne, Pratt, Whitney, and a few other families. On the other end of the scale, 103,626 stockholders, each with 100 shares or fewer, and comprising 79 per cent of all stockholders, had 2,302,000 shares, or 8.4 per cent of the total. While the number of stockholders has increased with the splitting of the stock, there is no reason to believe that there has been any material change in the distribution.

No stock is so widely dispersed as that of the American Telephone and Telegraph Co. But in 1937–39, the very small holders, with 1 to 10 shares each, numbered 358,000 and had only 9.5 per cent of the total stock; while the large holders with over 500 shares each numbered 2,478 and held 44.3 per cent of the stock. Since the share of the 20 largest holders has increased since then, there is no reason to believe there has been any material reduction in this contrast.

The over-all picture of concentration of stock-ownership is equally striking. The staff of the Senate Committee on Banking and Currency deduced from the 1952 Survey Research Center report that 8 per cent of all stock-owners, comprising: "less than one per cent of all American families owned over four-fifths of all publicly held stocks owned by individuals."

Butters, Thompson, and Bollinger made similar estimates as of 1949. They found that 50,000 spending units, or about one-tenth of one per cent of all spending units, owned over $100,000 of stock each. Their combined holdings were estimated at 65–71 per cent of the total of marketable stock outstanding. On the other extreme, 2,470,000 spending units, more than half of the total owning stock, had less than $1,000 each. Their combined holdings amounted to only 1 per cent of the total outstanding.

These authors also estimated the distribution of stockholdings by

[1] TNEC, *Investigation of Concentration of Economic Power*, Monogr. No. 29, *The Distribution of Ownership in the 200 Largest Nonfinancial Corporations*, Washington 1940, Table 6, p. 116.
[2] V. Perlo, *The Empire of High Finance*, New York 1957, Table I, p. 45. Subsequent estimates by *Fortune*, Nov. 1957, LVI, 177, for individual members of these families are consistent with the cited figures.

family-income level. Naturally, the degree of concentration shown in this way was somewhat less, because not all of the largest stockholders are in the highest income group. Their minimum estimates of the concentration at the top were: 1 per cent of the spending units (with incomes over $15,000) held 65 per cent of the stock; one-half of one per cent of the spending units (incomes over $25,000) held slightly over 50 per cent of all stock; and one-tenth of one per cent of the spending units (incomes over $50,000) held 35 per cent of all stock.

Prewar studies showed a similar concentration. Kuznets showed that there has been a decline in the percentage of concentration of dividend receipts among the top 1 per cent of the population, from 71 per cent of total dividends in 1929 to 53 per cent in 1948. However, this estimate is not adjusted for the effects of changes in the tax laws on the methods of individual income reporting. Butters and associates, taking this into account, made the estimate for 1949, already cited, of 65 per cent, not far below Kuznets' 71 per cent for 1929. Qualifications cited by Butters and associates, and the reasonable range of statistical error, could account for the entire difference. At any rate, it is evident that the concentration of stock-ownership among a comparatively few individuals and families remains exceedingly great. The important stock-owners are numbered in the hundreds of thousands, rather than the millions. And the decisive stock-owners are numbered in the tens of thousands.

This conclusion is further supported by the specialized data available concerning current concentration in stockholdings within individual corporations. Information is limited to public utility and railroad corporations required to submit to government agencies figures as to the holdings of the largest stockholders of record. The data show, for most railroad and communication companies, an increase in the proportion of stock owned by the 20 largest holders of record since 1937. The 10 largest holders of stock in electric power companies in 1954 generally held a smaller share than in 1937, owing to the forced distribution of holding company shares under the Public Utility Holding Company Act. Examples, for the largest companies, are shown in Table II.

Study of comparable data for smaller railroad and power companies shows that the results of Table II are representative. Unfortunately, similar data are not available for industrial corporations for the postwar period. However, the special legal conditions which caused a decline in power-company stockholding concentration were not duplicated among industrial corporations. The slight increase in concentration in American Telephone and Telegraph shares is noteworthy, since this is the most popular stock of all.

The evidence, limited as it is, certainly gives no support for the hypothesis that stock-ownership has become less concentrated than prior to the second world war. The largest holders of record for companies supplying such data are almost all financial institutions, and the domination of institutions among the largest holders is more marked than in 1937. This is consistent with the known fact that institutional holdings of stock have increased relatively as well as absolutely.

Table II. Percentage of Common Stock Owned by 20 Largest Holders of Record Specified Corporations,[a] 1937 and 1954

	1937	1954
Communications		
American Tel. & Tel.	3.8	4.2
Western Union	12.9	24.1
Railroads		
Pennsylvania	6.1	19.2
New York Central	23.7	42.6
Southern Pacific	15.0	15.3
Power companies (largest 10 holders)		
Pacific Gas & Electric[b]	25.1	10.0
Consolidated Edison	12.9	8.9
Commonwealth Edison	18.2	7.7

[a] The railroads and power companies shown are the three largest. 1954 statistics for General Telephone, 2nd largest communications company, are not available.
[b] Holders of common and preferred combined.
Sources: 1937 from TNEC Monogr. No. 29. 1954 from reports to the Federal Communications Commission, Interstate Commerce Commission, and Federal Power Commission.

III. Institutional Stockholdings

Goldsmith estimated that the share of financial intermediaries in total domestic stock outstanding increased from 7.9 per cent in 1900 to 14.2 per cent in 1929 and 23.6 per cent in 1949.[3] I. Friend estimated a further rise in the proportion of institutional holdings subsequently. My estimate for 1954, on a basis not strictly comparable with Goldsmith's, is 33 per cent. Nadler and others interpret the growth of institutional holdings as a further evidence of the widespread distribution of ownership of the means of production.

Nadler gives particular stress to stock-ownership by mutual institutions, apparently regarding it as a more important means by which the mass of the population participates in ownership of equity capital than by direct ownership. Examples he cites include life insurance companies, mutual savings banks, and mutual investment funds. It is my contention, however, that the great bulk of financial-institution stockholdings are of a character that cannot by any stretch of the imagination be regarded as representing ownership by masses of the population; that institutional holdings, in fact, reinforce the extreme concentration of stock-ownership in the hands of a small minority in the upper-income brackets.

Table III shows the New York Stock Exchange estimate of distribution of institutional holdings of corporation stocks, as of the end of 1954. These figures are close to estimates prepared by the Securities and Exchange Commission. They compare with estimates of the total potential market supply

[3] R. W. Goldsmith, *The Share of Financial Intermediaries in National Wealth and National Assets, 1900–1949*, New York 1954, Table 16, p. 69.

of stocks of $250 billion and $268 billion. Thus institutions accounted at the end of 1954 for about one-fourth of all stockholdings, strictly financial institutions accounting for 21-22 per cent.

Two facts stand out in Table III. The stock owned by institutions of a "mutual" character, in which large numbers of the general public have any degree of proprietary interest, is a small part of the total. Holdings of life insurance companies, most of which are mutual, mutual savings banks, mutual-fund investment companies, and pension funds total $12,960 million. Close to half of this, or $5,840 million, consists of the mutual-fund holdings. Since the stockholders in these are included in the estimated totals of direct stock-owners, they represent no addition to the numbers participating in ownership of the means of production. That leaves $7,120 million as the combined stockholdings of mutual institutions through which many millions of people, not otherwise involved in equity ownership, have an indirect beneficial interest, however attenuated. This sum represents a little over one-tenth of all institutional stockholdings, and roughly 3 per cent of all outstanding stock.

The other notable feature is the domination of institutional stockholdings by one type, the bank-administered personal trust funds. This situation has prevailed throughout the 20th century, although the extent of domination has fluctuated. The share of personal trust departments in total stockholdings has grown markedly: according to Goldsmith's figures, from 5.1 per cent in 1900 to 8.4 per cent in 1929 and 15.2 per cent in 1949.

It is, however, doubtful whether the New York Stock Exchange estimate of 1954 holdings by trust departments, cited in Table III, is adequate. The

Table III. Estimated Institutional Holdings of Equity Securities, 1954
(million dollars)

Type of Institution	Market Value
Financial institutions:	
Bank-administered personal trust funds	$37,800
Fire and casualty insurance companies	6,460
Open-end investment companies (mutual funds)	5,840
Life insurance companies	3,400
Closed-end investment companies	1,450
Mutual savings banks	620
Subtotal	$55,570
Other institutions:	
Pension funds (noninsured)	3,100
College-university endowment funds	2,500
Foundations, religious, and other charitable organizations	5,100
Grand Total	$66,270

Source: U.S. Senate, Committee on Banking and Currency, Staff Report, Factors Affecting the Stock Market, Washington 1955, Table 6, p. 96.

periodical *Trusts and Estates,* which specializes in the study of trust departments of banks, estimated that stockholdings of the latter amounted at the end of 1954 to $62.6 billion. Using the *Trusts and Estates* figures, the personal trust departments of banks hold close to one-fourth of all corporation stocks, and by either estimate, they hold more than all other types of institutional investors put together.

Are these massive holdings an evidence of "People's Capitalism," or of a still greater concentration of stockholdings in the hands of the very wealthy than measured by their nonfiduciary holdings alone? In 1954 trust departments of national banks administered 289,000 personal trust accounts with $43.4 billion of assets. The main concentration of personal trust business is in New York, and it is primarily handled by state banks, hence for the most part not included in the report of the Comptroller of the Currency. The Federal Reserve Bank of New York reported that in 1954, 83 banks in the 2nd Federal Reserve District handled 115,000 personal trust accounts with $48 billion of assets.

From these figures it is clear that the enormous holdings of stocks and other properties by trust departments represent but a few hundred thousand accounts, quite large in average size. Since a single individual is often the beneficiary of several trusts, and since there are often a number of individuals in the same family for whom separate trusts are established, the number of families beneficiaries of these trusts may be but a fraction of the number of accounts.

Moreover, these largely coincide with the largest direct stockholders. Butters, Thompson, and Bollinger found that among a sample of active investors, the proportion who were beneficial owners of trusts increased from 3 per cent among those with less than $25,000 of wealth to 48 per cent for those with over a million dollars of wealth. Millionaires with trusts had 47 per cent of their wealth in that form.

Thus the effect of the main form of institutional stockholding is to *increase* the concentration of stock-ownership. Butters and associates recognized this, commenting in relation to their estimates of concentration in stock-ownership cited above: "These figures would all be several percentage points higher if stock managed by corporate trustees for individual beneficiaries were included in the total."

The "several" percentage points may be quite substantial indeed. The authors' estimates of personal trust stockholdings preceded the publication of data by the New York Federal Reserve Bank revealing that the New York banks alone held as much in personal trust accounts as had previously been estimated for the entire country, and before the recent *Trusts and Estates* estimates of a higher value of personal trust stockholdings than others current.

IV.   Influence in Corporate Affairs

Effective participation in the business life of the country requires not only the beneficial ownership of a corporation's stock, but also at least a minimum of influence in the affairs of the corporation. It is scarcely necessary to belabor the point that the millions of small stockholders, and even the hundreds of thousands of medium-sized stockholders, have not an iota of influence in corporate affairs. The great majority of small stockholders either ignore corporate business, or limit their participation to signing proxies sent to them by a committee of the Board of Directors. Even in those corporations with highly publicized annual meetings, only a tiny proportion of stockholders attend. In the case of General Electric, where the proportion is unusually high, it slightly exceeds one per cent.

Moreover, even if all of the small stockholders could combine their forces to influence corporate affairs—an unlikely event—their votes would be insufficient. The 94 per cent of all stockholders having $25,000 of stock or less have only 15–18 per cent of the total stock, and hence of the total votes. As for the 55 per cent owning under $1,000 of stock, and with combined holdings of 1 per cent of the total, they are utterly powerless.

On the other hand, the 50,000 spending units with $100,000 or more of stock, and two-thirds of the total stock, or part of these 50,000, are the group in a position to have genuine influence in corporate affairs. Of course, comparatively few of these 50,000 are stock-owners in any given corporation. But it is from among these few that the dominant forces arise.

In 1937–39, the 20 largest stockholders of record in each of the 200 largest nonfinancial corporations owned altogether 31.6 per cent of the common stock and 30.47 per cent of the preferred stock. In practical terms, these 20 very large holders, voting typically about one-third of the stock, exercise full effective voting control of the corporation. Thus Samuelson writes of large corporations: "The largest single minority ownership groups typically hold only about a fifth of all voting stock. Such a small fraction has been deemed more than enough to maintain 'working control.' " Reports of proxy contests during recent years make it clear that invariably both groups are led by those among the very largest holders. In short, contests are not between the small group of very large stockholders and the mass of small stockholders, but between rival groups of giant stockholders.

Concentration of control is furthered by the role of institutional stockholders, particularly the large trustee banks. Just nine New York City banks handled four-fifths of the city's personal trust business in 1954, and hence perhaps two-fifths of the national total. These New York banks appear again and again among the 20 largest stockholders of record in the country's largest corporations in the prewar TNEC tabulations. The National City Bank appears in 8 of the 10 largest nonfinancial corporations. The Hanover bank, which published Sadler's pamphlet, appeared among the leading stockholders in 6 of the 10 largest nonfinancial corporations. The resulting influence is expressed, among other ways, by particularly frequent representations on boards of directors. In 1955 five New York banks, among the leaders in trust business, each had interlocking directorates with scores of corporations having combined assets ranging from $45 billion to $70 billion.

One can search far and not find a real representative of small stockholders among the directors of large corporations, whether a representative is defined as one having an occupation similar to that of the typical small stockholder (small business man, salaried employee, wage-earner), or being an official of an organization of any of these groups. Nor has there been any real change since the 1930's. Individuals have died off or retired, but the interests represented on the boards of such corporations as American Telephone and Telegraph, General Electric, and most others are virtually the same as they were 20 years ago, except for certain changes in the distribution of influence as between particular financial houses (as in the case of A.T. & T.) . . .

V. Conclusion

The basic claim of "People's Capitalism," that the rank and file of the population are becoming owners of the means of production in American industry, is without foundation in fact. The widespread diffusion of this theory signifies only the effectiveness of organized propaganda.

Victor Perlo

WALL STREET STILL RULES

Rising Industrial Concentration

A whole series of government reports establish the fact of continually rising concentration in industry. . . . In 1920, the 200 largest non-financial corporations obtained 33.4% of total non-financial corporate profits, in 1929, 43.2%, and in 1955, 57.4%.

The share of the 200 largest manufacturing corporations in total manufacturing sales rose from 37.7% in 1935 to 40.5% in 1950 and 45.5% in 1955. During the first 15-year interval, including most of the New Deal period, the increase in concentration was comparatively slow. The anti-monopoly legislation of the Roosevelt Administration had not turned back the trend towards monopoly, but merely slowed its growth. By the 1950's the limited practical effect of these laws was cancelled out by a government hostile to its purposes. Concentration increased almost twice as much in five years as it had during the previous fifteen years.

Today defenders of the system generally concede its monopoly character. Berle, for example, speaks of the state of American industry as representing "a concentration of economic ownership greater perhaps than any recorded in history . . . a system, industry by industry, in which a few large corporations dominate the trade. Two or three, or at most, five, corporations will have more than half the business, the remainder being divided among a greater or less number of smaller concerns who must necessarily live within the conditions made for them by the 'Big Two' or 'Big Three' or 'Big Five' as the case may be."

True, Berle defines these giants as "concentrates," and various academic economists call them "oligopolies," to distinguish the situation described above from one in which a single company makes *all* of a given product. However, we here are not concerned with these academic niceties. The power and functioning of the "Big Twos" and "Big Fives" is of the same kind as that of the "Big Ones" (which do exist for a number of important products). The popular term monopoly is the correct one to describe the real situation. . . .

In New York City, according to a Congressional report, the share of the four largest banks in deposits increased from 21% in 1900 to 60% in 1955. Most of the increase in concentration occurred after 1929. Nor was the process limited to New York: "in 10 of the nation's 16 leading financial centers, 4 banks own more than 50 per cent of all commercial bank assets. In 9 of these financial centers, 2 banks own more than 60 per cent."

Reprinted, with deletions, from Victor Perlo, *The Empire of High Finance* (New York: International Publishers, 1957), pp. 18–35. Reprinted by permission of INTERNATIONAL PUBLISHERS CO., INC. Copyright © 1957.

The Mellon Bank in Pittsburgh, the Bank of America in San Francisco, and the First National Bank in Boston each control more than half the assets in their respective cities.

With all the multiplication of financial activity, the total number of banks in the country fell from 30,419 in 1921 to 25,113 in 1929 and 14,243, in 1955. And the 10 largest banks increased their share of the national business from 10% in 1923 to 21% in 1955.

Monopoly is more complete in finance than in industry, it grows more rapidly, and the all-important links between financial and industrial monopolies have been strengthened.

One must examine the financial world to find the control center of American monopoly. But it is exactly at this point that the academicians and publicists have failed most dismally. With scarcely any exceptions, they have either ignored the whole question since World War II, or presented a Pollyanna view of American finance having no relation to reality.

Apologetics of the Vanishing Banker

During the . . . New Deal period, the masters of capital, while not relaxing their grip in any respect, dropped a heavier curtain of secrecy around their operations, adopting a pose of innocent servant of industry and of government.

Experts bending to the reactionary political winds came forward to give the blessings of "science" to the supposed demise of "Wall Street," and the apologetics became bolder even as the financiers returned increasingly to the center of the stage after World War II. . . .

What are the arguments advanced by most of these writers? They are:

1. The banker's voice in industrial affairs has become insignificant.
2. Industrial corporations have become so powerful in their own right that they no longer depend on banks for funds, and are run by a new group of "industrial managers."
3. Government regulation and "hostility" prevents financial domination.

The basic facts about the growth in the scope of financial institutions undercut all of these arguments. Raymond Goldsmith, a conservative economist, provides a convenient summary in a recent monograph. He estimates the national wealth in 1949 at $898 billion, of which the banks, insurance companies, and other financial institutions held $432 billion, or almost half. These financial assets were multiplied 23 times in a half century. More significant was the increase in their share of the national wealth. In 1900 they owned 21%, in 1929, 35%, and in 1949, 48%. The bankers increased their power not only during the period of open manipulations, mergers, and pyramiding of fortunes that culminated in the stock market crash of 1929. They increased it even more rapidly thereafter, when a "hostile government" and the "managerial revolution" were supposedly sapping their strength!

When we differentiate among various kinds of wealth, the rising share of the financial oligarchy is even more impressive. Securities, in modern capitalism, are the decisive claims to ownership and control of industry. In 1900 the financial institutions held 23% of all securities; in 1929 this had increased only to 26%. But by 1949 it had risen to 58%. The huge wartime rise in the federal debt, mainly held by the banks, contributed to this, but the post-1929 rise in the bankers' share of corporate securities was almost as dramatic.

As is typical of those National Bureau publications which contain significant information, the author is constrained to avoid explaining the meaning of his findings except in the most innocuous and generalized fashion. Thus Goldsmith says: "From the economists' point of view, the development of financial intermediaries and the trend of their share in national assets and wealth deserve attention as an indication of the extent and character of financial interrelations, which in turn help to determine how capital expenditures are financed and how existing assets are shifted among owners."

But the lesson which Goldsmith did not draw is clear enough: The "extent and character of financial interrelations" has intensified greatly. The control of capital expenditures is more firmly than ever in the hands of the financial oligarchy, and "existing assets are shifted" more and more into their hands.

Here is more evidence, concerning the identity of the very largest, most powerful corporations. In 1935, out of 62 corporations with assets of over $500 million, 28 were banks and insurance companies, and they had 42% of the assets of the 62 giants. Seventeen years later, in 1952, out of 66 corporations with assets of over a billion dollars, 38 were banks and insurance companies, and these had 64% of all the assets of the 66 giants.

The share of profits siphoned off by the financial institutions has also increased. The after-tax profits of financial corporations (including real estate) increased from $0.9 billion in 1925 to $4.7 billion in 1952, and from 14% of the profits of all corporations to 24% of the total. Under capitalism, profits are the ultimate arbiter of power and position. The ability of the financial corporations to extract a rising share of profits is the surest sign that the dependence of industry, and of capitalist society generally, on financial power has increased, and not diminished.

These growing shares of national wealth and income accrue to a smaller number of financial institutions, for, as we have seen, concentration of capital proceeds with especial rapidity in banking.

Now let us turn to the connecting links between finance and industry, and see whether the financiers have really been pushed out. Paul Sweezy, who did important work in the analysis of the structure of finance capital during the New Deal period, wrote in 1942 that bankers' power had become divorced from economic function, and "is bound to weaken and eventually disappear. . . . Bank capital, having had its day of glory, falls back again to a position subsidiary to industrial capital, thus re-establishing the relation which existed prior to the combination movement . . . today the entire banking system could be 'seized' in the United States, for example, without creating more than a temporary ripple in the ranks of big capital."

The Federal Trade Commission in 1951 analyzed the interlocking directorates of the largest thousand industrial companies. In almost every basic industry, the financial corporations had more representatives than any other group. Among 727 interlocks of 112 machinery companies, 224, or 31%, were with banks, investment bankers, investment trusts, and insurance companies —an average of two financier-directors per machinery company. This government report commented:

> The high frequency of machinery company interlocks with financial institutions reflects the fact that the industry requires, particularly in its larger operations, huge aggregates of capital for plant and heavy equipment. Sources of finance capital have played significant roles in the formation, expansion, reorganization, consolidation, operation, and policy-making of many of the largest machinery corporations. These financial institutions also served as the prime connecting link among the leading machinery producers, as well as between machinery companies and their potential competitors or their potential suppliers or customers in other industries.

There is really only one significant piece of evidence offered to prove the supposed weakening of financial-industrial links. That is the increase in corporate self-financing. The theory of the financially self-contained corporation grew during the stagnant 1930's, when there was little expansion of capacity, and internal funds largely sufficed for the replacement of equipment that took place. However, in the boom after World War II, corporations turned increasingly to outside financing to keep ahead in the race for automation of production and expansion of capacity.

Owing to higher tax rates, large stockholders often prefer to collect smaller dividends, and reinvest profits without removing them from the corporate network. But the extent of dependence on outside funds remains larger than implied by Berle and others, and quite decisive in industrial expansion. Government tabulations show that in the 11 years 1946–1956, some 64% of gross capital spending was from retained profits and depreciation reserves, while 36% was from outside sources.

To interpret these figures, it is necessary to analyze how the funds are used. Since World War II about half of corporate capital spending has been for replacement of obsolete and worn-out capital, and about half for expansion. The former is financed out of depreciation reserves, and to the extent necessary, out of retained profits. Comparatively little internal funds are left for expansion. Roughly and approximately, we have the following: as against the 50% of total spending for expansion, there is left 14% of internal funds and the 36% of outside funds which must be raised for the purpose. Thus the outside funds account for as much as 72% of the expansion capital.

This is the decisive part of the investment. It determines which corporation will get ahead, which must fall behind and either be absorbed through merger or wrecked through bankruptcy. The giant American Telephone and Telegraph Corporation borrows almost $2 billion yearly through financial institutions. There is hardly a major industrial company which has not gone to the capital markets since 1950. The debt of all corporations increased $111.5 billion or 131% in the decade after World War II, as compared with $35.6 billion, or 67% in the decade after World War I.

Clearly, if there has been a statistical decline since the 1920's in the

The Structure and Dynamics of American Capitalism

proportion of capital funds obtained through financial institutions, it has been insufficient to cause any qualitative change in the dependent relation of industry on these institutions. And this is only part of the story.

What many overlook is that the *merging* of financial and industrial capital means just that. This is expressed most directly in the ownership by the same groups of controlling shares in banks and industries, and the ownership by financial institutions of industrial shares . . .

The Auto Industry and the Banks

Very well, some say, the bankers are still powerful, but the really big industrial giants do not need them any more. General Motors, the corporation with the largest profits in the world, is an oft-cited example. It has over a billion dollars in net current assets, and until recently it was debt-free. Its erstwhile President, Charles E. Wilson, is hailed as the man who rose to the top as a manager of a great industry, and thence to the Cabinet of the United States.

But actually General Motors and the auto industry as a whole provide an outstanding example of the interlocking of industrial and financial power, of the domination of great corporations by a financial oligarchy, and of the decisive weight of the banking element in crucial periods.

The auto industry is in the midst of a bitter power struggle. General Motors and Ford achieved outstanding gains during the years 1954–56; Chrysler absorbed serious losses. Meanwhile the "independents" dropped from 15% of the market in 1949 to 4.5% in 1955, after having been reduced to two in number, the rest having been absorbed by mergers or forced out of production.

The battle rages in the field of capital expenditures, in distribution, in securing reliable sources of materials and parts, and in the striving for mergers and acquisitions. And in all of these areas of combat the financiers have the last word.

Consider the huge capital spending to reduce costs and locate factories more favorably, so that more horsepower and gadgets can be loaded into the "package" designed to win the customer's favor. General Motors and Ford threatened to squeeze out Chrysler partly because they were able to outstrip the latter in capital spending.

Until 1953, the major companies kept up the race from accumulated profits and reserves. But now this is not enough; the bankers must play a key role. General Motors borrowed $300 million. The largest industrial loan ever publicly floated up to that time, it was sold through a syndicate headed by Morgan, Stanley & Co. In a desperate attempt to catch up, Chrysler borrowed $250 million for 100 years from the Prudential Insurance Co. (which has directors in common with the principal Morgan banks as well as with Chrysler) and with its aid *did* regain some lost ground in 1957. Again in 1955, General Motors sold shares to existing stockholders for $329 million, with Morgan, Stanley underwriting the issue. Finally, at the beginning of 1956, The Ford Motor Company, which had always boasted independence of the bankers, authorized the Ford Foundation to sell 10,200,000 shares for $663 million dollars, through a large Wall Street syndicate headed by Blyth & Co. (connected with the First National City Bank). This sale of Ford shares did not directly make funds available to Ford Motors for expansion, but paved the way for future sales of shares for that purpose.

The role of banking is even more important in financing distribution of cars than in financing production. The corporation which can loan its dealers funds for cut-throat competition, and which can provide the easiest install-ment credit to car buyers, will survive and rise to the top.

General Motors, through the General Motors Acceptance Corp. and its Motors Holding Plan, has advanced $2 billion to car buyers and dealers. The dealers, backed financially by the corporation, can hold the stock of cars with which GM saddles them, can afford to slice their profit margins, and to engage in all sorts of sharp practices. Chrysler, until recently, had no scheme for financing its dealers, and the largest Chrysler dealer, Bishop, McCormick and Bishop, had to go out of business early in 1954, a serious blow to the Chrysler Corp.

But the extent of GM's financial backing of dealers and buyers is not a measure of its "independent" financial strength, but rather of the strength of the financial circles with which it is connected. At the end of 1955 General Motors carried an investment of $231 million in General Motors Acceptance Corp. But the banks and insurance companies had over $3 billion invested in GMAC. The banking investment in GMAC increased more than 15 times between 1947 and 1955.

Combining the producing company and its sales subsidiary, new securi-ties issues in the three years 1953–55 alone totalled $2,340 million. *No indus-trial company has ever before gone so deeply into debt to the leading financial interests as General Motors has since World War II.*

Now let us turn to the internal structure of General Motors and the role of financiers within it. To begin with, General Motors today is itself more a financial holding company than an industrial corporation. Even with-out *any* outside banking funds, the ruling group in General Motors would be in truth a financial oligarchy. This is quite apart from the widespread lending activities of General Motors, such as loans to steel suppliers, dealers, and customers. It is seen more basically in the much-advertised operating independence of the various manufacturing divisions.

What is the mechanism by which the top circles of General Motors coordinate the activities of its various divisions? Donaldson Brown, then vice-president and still a director of General Motors, wrote 34 years ago in a paper presented to the American Management Association:

In the case of General Motors, the Board of Directors has two subcommit-tees, a finance committee responsible for general financial policies, and an executive committee responsible for operating policies. The finance com-mittee includes men of large affairs identified with banking and with big business, apart from General Motors, while the executive committee is composed of men giving all of their time to the affairs of General Motors. In a limited sense, the executive committee is subject to the finance com-mittee in that operations are dependent upon financial policies. At the

The Structure and Dynamics of American Capitalism

same time, financial policies must be maintained so that operations will not be deprived of any legitimate development . . .

The structure is virtually the same today, except that the Executive Committee is now called the Operations Policy Committee. Thus GM is organized as a center for controlling the operations of a series of manufacturing companies; and the principal organ of control is the Financial Policy Committee.

Who are the men of "large affairs" that run the decisive Financial Policy Committee? The controlling stock of General Motors, 23% of it, is owned by the du Pont Company, which has (as of the beginning of 1956) five representatives on the GM Board of Directors, three of them on its Financial Policy Committee. The du Ponts themselves are a section of the financial oligarchy, controlling important banks in addition to their industrial empire. But the financial resources controlled by the du Ponts are far from sufficient to insure the preeminence of GM. The billions which have flowed into GM in recent years reflect the interest of a group of financiers with still greater resources.

This is the famous House of Morgan, banker for both the du Pont Corp. itself and for GM. The chairman of the board and the president of J. P. Morgan & Co. are directors of GM, while the chairman of GM is a director of J. P. Morgan & Co. as well as of du Pont. These two Morgan men are both on the Financial Policy Committee, together with the three du Pont men and the Morgan–du Pont chairman of GM. Presumably, the du Pont voice is more powerful than that of the Morgans in GM affairs, if only because in the event of conflict the du Ponts, with the controlling block of shares, could switch GM financing to the equally wealthy institutions centering around the Rockefeller interests. But the balance between the du Pont and Morgan financial interests in GM is not the point at issue. Clearly, their representatives, and not Charles E. Wilson nor his successor as chief executive, Harlowe H. Curtice, dominate the affairs of GM.

For all its power, General Motors Corp. cannot be regarded as an *independent* center of finance capital, but as a major part of the still larger Morgan and du Pont empires.

Lastly, consider the role of the financial oligarchy in one of the recent big mergers. The Studebaker-Packard merger was worked out by three Wall Street houses, Lehman Bros. (Studebaker's "traditional banker"), Glore Forgan & Co. (also on the Studebaker Board), and Kuhn Loeb & Co. Here is how the bankers worked: "If present plans develop, a merger program . . . will be submitted to Studebaker-Packard management within 20 days. . . . Several suggested methods of bringing Studebaker-Packard under one roof have been scrapped without ever reaching the attention of the principals . . . only one house will submit the final suggestion for bringing the companies together."

Thus the fate of these two companies was worked out *wholly* by the banking houses, with the industrial managers not even being informed as to what was going on, and the final result was brought to them as a *fait accompli* by the bankers' spokesmen. . . .

Wall Street

The center of the money market is in downtown New York City, clustered irregularly around Wall Street. . . . This area bounds the location of the head offices of the ten or fifteen banks which . . . provide the major part of the facilities needed to effect the transfers of money, advices in confirmation of agreements, and the securities themselves, which flow largely on the basis of word-of-mouth agreements over the telephone between men who are known to each other and whose integrity cannot be questioned.

So writes a Federal Reserve Bank official, Robert V. Roosa, in the most authoritative description of the present-day money market.

The economic life of the country is largely controlled from this area no larger than a baseball field. Wall Street is the apex of monopoly power, and a symbol of the extreme concentration of that power under modern conditions.

Supplementing the arguments of the supposed "disappearance" of the power of the financiers is the argument that Wall Street no longer predominates in finance; that the remaining financial power is diffused throughout the country.

Again, a most valuable argument for big business. Convince the people that the traditional target of their anti-monopoly campaigns has been dissipated, its power diffused, and anti-monopoly actions will become correspondingly more diffused and confused.

Sweezy, who is not trying to help big business, claims that New York no longer dominates financially, but is merely first among equals. As one argument he states that financial centers outside of New York formerly "looked up to and sought guidance from and actually followed" New York, but no longer do so to a decisive extent.

This substitutes a subjective criterion—whether the out-of-town centers "seek guidance" from New York—for objective relationships. The desire for an independent role, for getting away from the "guidance" of Wall Street, was always there. During the 1920's the Chicago bankers set up their "own" public utility empire, the ill-fated Insull combine. Giannini, rising to the top in West Coast finance, struck out to establish a nation-wide and ultimately world-wide banking chain. Both of these attempts were beaten back by objective factors, principally the financial domination of Wall Street, which came into full play during the economic crisis of the 1930's. Wall Street emerged more powerful, more dominant than ever.

Again, during the postwar boom, the struggle of out-of-town groups for a "place in the sun" has become significant. The California financiers once more are spreading out within the country and overseas. The Chicago interests have gained control of important corporations formerly run by Wall Street. The Cleveland capitalists and some of the Texas oil millionaires have moved into the fray. Their most dramatic accomplishment was the successful attempt, headed by Robert R. Young, to wrest control of the New York Central from the Morgan-Vanderbilt interests. Correspondingly, these groups seek a greater voice in political affairs at the expense of the New York Behemoths.

But the existence of different financial centers, and struggles among them, does not assure a decisive change in the balance of power. Alongside the much publicized specific gains of out-of-town groups, New York circles have quietly extended their positions in the original areas of operation of their rivals. Even without a detailed analysis of these struggles . . . it is possible to examine the overall evidence to determine whether Wall Street has actually been undermined.

The facts show that New York remains far ahead in all financial statistics. Its lead has diminished in some, but increased in others of greater significance. Its premier position is most marked in the new and rising forms of financial power. Altogether, the financial domination of The Street is unshaken, while with the continuation of centralization of economic power as a whole, its overall weight in the life of the country is enhanced.

The most summary measure of financial activity is the volume of bank clearings. These totalled $531 billion in New York City in 1955. This was nine times the clearings of the second most active city, Philadelphia, and exceeded the combined clearings of the next twenty cities. One might say, considering all *secondary* centers, that Philadelphia is "first among equals." But this is not the case with New York. Handling each year more dollars than the total national income of the United States, it is in a class by itself.

The standard statistical evidence cited to "prove" the demise of Wall Street domination is the decline in New York's city's share of commercial bank deposits from over 30% in 1940 to 18% in 1954. However, this comparison uses an unrepresentative starting point and does not include all banks. Deposits of all banks in New York State during the early 1950's were 25% of the national total, as against 28% during most of the period 1914–1929. This is a drop, but not of major proportions.

Even this smaller decline does not signify a diffusion of financial power. It reflects the growth of "retail" or consumer banking . . . which is spread out geographically more or less according to population. "Wholesale" or big business banking is the decisive instrument of financial power. It is the traditional means of banking penetration into industry, of the merging of financial and industrial capital.

In this crucial field, the role of the New York City banks has not diminished at all as compared with immediate prewar years, and has increased markedly as compared with the 1920's. The share of all banks in New York State in the business loans of the country was 32.5% in 1939, rising to 34.1% in 1953.

Over a longer period, referring to member banks in the Federal Reserve System, the share of those in New York City rose from 19% in 1928 to 29% in 1953. Just eight New York City banks account for close to half the national total of loans to giant corporations with assets of $100 million.

The share of New York banks in financial loans, connected most intimately with stock market manipulations and the control of corporations, increased just as markedly, and by 1953–54 amounted to almost 60% of the national total. . . .

Centralization of World-Wide Profits

A favorite explanation of the supposed decline in Wall Street's importance has been the movement of population to the West, and the "shift by industry to new centers."

The physical fact of this dispersal is irrelevant. Gulf Oil and Standard of New Jersey have shifted much of their industrial operations out of the United States, and get most of their crude oil abroad. But this merely signifies a great *increase* in the power of the United States oil companies. Within the United States there has been a significant movement of industry away from the higher-wage, older northeastern centers. But William Zeckendorf, large-scale New York real estate developer, pointed out that industries leaving New York have been replaced with executive units "ten times more valuable than industrial space." Since 1947, he said, 20 million square feet of office space has been newly constructed or planned in New York City, more than the entire office space in the city of Chicago. The office space is "ten times more valuable" because it is used as a center of control to draw the profits from developing industry all over the country and abroad.

Commercial banking throughout the country is dominated from the main centers by the correspondent relationship with out-of-town banks and industries. The smaller correspondent banks maintain funds on deposit in a metropolitan bank, to be used for purchase of securities, loan participations, etc. The headquarters bank supervises, to a considerable extent, the lending activities of the smaller bank, channeling selected securities into its portfolio and suggesting loan participations. It also often holds stock in correspondent banks.

The First National City Bank, with over a billion in inter-bank deposits, writes: "Of the hundred largest non-financial corporations in the country, 95 have accounts with our bank. Our correspondent banking relationships are similarly wide. All of the hundred largest banks in the country outside New York City maintain accounts with us. We work jointly with our correspondent banks in cases where business in their areas is of a size and importance to warrant including a New York bank as depositary and lender."

Large midwestern banks have important correspondent relationships also. But, considering those connections carrying influence as distinct from purely nominal deposits, the banks in other cities generally exert only regional influence while the New York banks alone exert truly national influence.

Foreign banking is a field of crucial importance; it affects international relations; it involves close connections with the most profitable foreign dealings of U.S. corporations. Because of the increased world role of the dollar, this foreign business has become more important and in some respects has multiplied in volume. For example, deposits of foreigners in United States banks increased eight times between 1931 and 1954.

A recent Federal Reserve study showed that 15 banks wholly dominate foreign transactions. Of these, ten New York City banks held 76% of the total claims on foreigners, and 84% of the total deposits of foreigners.

There are just nine U.S. banks with foreign branches or subsidiaries.

Two Wall Street banks account for the majority of branches and over half the deposits in foreign offices. These are the First National City Bank, traditional bank of the raw materials merchants, and Chase Manhattan, bank of the international oil companies. Four other New York banks with foreign offices bring the city's share of deposits abroad up to two-thirds.

If one passes from the field of ordinary commercial banking to other fields of finance, the predominance of Wall Street is shown to be even greater.

In investment banking, during the period 1950–54, 16 large New York City firms headed the underwriting of 66.5% of all securities issued.

In stock exchange transactions, 92% of the 1953 national total were on the New York exchanges.

In life insurance, New York and Newark companies held 61.4% of all life insurance company corporate loans at the end of 1952. Nine-tenths of all such loans are held by life insurance companies operating from 5 northeastern centers. Trust departments of banks in New York City handle almost half of this vital business.

The activities of these various forms of financial institutions are coordinated by the interlocking oligarchy of Wall Street. . . .

Sweezy thinks that "economic and political changes in the last thirty years (especially changes in the structure and functions of the banking system and the expansion of the economic role of the state) have reduced the relative importance of New York to a marked degree."

The development of life insurance companies, trust departments, and international financial connections are among the more important changes in financial structure and forms during the past thirty years. But as can be seen, these all serve to enhance the domination of Wall Street, rather than the opposite. . . .

Ralph Miliband

PROFESSOR GALBRAITH AND AMERICAN CAPITALISM: THE MANAGERIAL REVOLUTION REVISITED

The intellectual defence of capitalism has long ceased to be confined to the simple celebration of its virtues; or even to the argument that, whatever might be said against it, it was still a much better system, on economic, social and political grounds, than any conceivable alternative to it. Such arguments are of course still extensively used. But they belong to an older school of apologetics; and for some considerable time now, many people, who see themselves as part of the "democratic left," as liberal and even radical critics of the existing social order, and as anything but its apologists, have argued that the question of alternatives to capitalism had been rendered obsolete by the internal developments of the system itself; capitalism, the argument goes, has been so thoroughly transformed in the last few decades that the need to abolish it has conveniently disappeared. The job, for all practical purposes, has been done by the "logic of industrialization," which is well on the way to erasing all meaningful differences between "industrial systems," whatever misleading labels they may choose to pin upon themselves. Dinosaur socialists will, no doubt, continue to peddle their unwanted ideological wares; for their part, serious men with a bent for reform will address themselves to the *real* problems of what Mr. Crosland long ago called "post-capitalist" societies.

The New Industrial State[1] is a further version of this by now familiar thesis. Professor Galbraith, however, does not conceal his belief that he is here unrolling a map of American capitalism (or of "what is commonly called capitalism") which is entirely new, and immeasurably more accurate than any previous one. The former claim is rather exaggerated, but it is perfectly true that there is much in his essay which is indeed new. The question, however, is whether what is new is also true, and whether the combination of old and new really does provide an accurate, reliable map of American economic life. The answer, as I propose to argue in this review, is that it does not; and that much more interesting than the revelation which it purports to bring about the true nature of American capitalism is what it reveals of the confusion and bafflement of the latter-day liberalism which Professor Galbraith

Reprinted from Ralph Miliband, "Professor Galbraith and American Capitalism," *The Socialist Register* (London: Merlin Press Ltd., 1968), pp. 215–229, by permission of the author and publisher. Ralph Miliband is a Senior Lecturer in Political Science at the London School of Economics. He is the author of *Parliamentary Socialism* and *The State in Capitalist Society* as well as numerous articles.
    [1] J. K. Galbraith, *The New Industrial State* (Boston: Houghton Mifflin Company, 1967), p. 430.

represents, in regard to an "industrial system" which it approaches with a mixture of admiration and distaste, and whose basic irrationality, some aspects which it perceives, it is either unable or unwilling to locate and transcend. It is not surprising that Professor Galbraith should sometimes be seen as a critic of the system and sometimes as its defender. For he is both, at one moment belabouring conservative economists, yet echoing, in more elegant language, their own vulgar apologetics, at another trembling on the brink of radical criticism, yet unable to jump. The famous style of exposition itself, the laboured humour, the straining after ironic effect, the attempt at cool wit, all testify to the ideological tension. Professor Galbraith perceives that an advanced industrial system *requires* the transcendance of private appropriation and much of his book is in fact a documented though seemingly unconscious comment on Marx's prediction that, with the development of capitalism, "centralization of the means of production and socialization of labour at last reach a point where they become incompatible with their capitalist integument." But the central point of the book, which is also its central weakness, is that the "industrial system" has actually *solved* the problem, and that whatever adjustments it further requires can be achieved within its present framework, and without, perish the thought, the invocation of the old socialist gods. The tone is critical and so is the intent, but the result is all the same profoundly apologetic.

In *American Capitalism: The Concept of Countervailing Power,* first published in 1952, Professor Galbraith advanced the notion that, while the growing concentration of economic enterprise might appear to entail a dangerous increase in the power of business, traditional liberal, not to speak of socialist, fears on this score were really misconceived: for the power of business was, he argued, effectively balanced and checked by a variety of forces and agencies, such as organized labour, other economic interests, the state, the consumer, and so forth. This notion of "countervailing power," coming as it did in the early days of an ideological, political and military struggle which counterposed power-diffused democracy to monolithic communism was an exceptionally useful ideological weapon; and it served as one of the foundations of a theory of political pluralism which has since greatly prospered, to the point of becoming the dominant orthodoxy of Western political and social theories of power in capitalist societies: in these societies, a plurality of "interests" (classes being rather *vieux jeu*) compete under the watchful eye of a democratic state, and achieve, as a result of that competition, a rough equilibrium in which everybody has some power and no one has, or can have, too much.

In *The New Industrial State,* Professor Galbraith has now come to discard the notion of "countervailing power." Unions, he now believes, are a declining force, consumers are the manipulated prisoners of induced demand, the state serves the goals of the "industrial system," and there is no "interest" remotely comparable in importance to the five or six hundred large corporations which are "the heartland of the modern economy."

Nothing [Professor Galbraith writes] so characterizes the industrial system as the scale of the modern corporate enterprise. In 1962 the five largest industrial corporations in the United States, with combined assets in excess of $36 billion, possessed over 12 per cent of all assets used in manufacturing. The fifty largest corporations had over a third of all manufacturing assets. The 500 largest had well over two-thirds. Corporations with assets in excess of $10,000,000, some 2,000 in all, accounted for about 80 per cent of all the resources used in manufacturing in the United States. In the mid nineteen-fifties, 28 corporations provided approximately 10 per cent of all employment in manufacturing, mining and retail and wholesale trade. Twenty-three corporations provided 15 per cent of all employment in manufacturing. In the first half of the decade (June 1950–June 1956) a hundred firms received two-thirds by value of all defence contracts; ten firms received one-third. In 1960 four corporations accounted for an estimated 22 per cent of all industrial research and development expenditure. Three hundred and eighty-four corporations employing 5,000 or more workers accounted for 55 per cent of these expenditures; 260,000 firms employing fewer than 1,000 accounted for only 7 per cent. (pp. 74–75).

This, is, indeed, impressive and Professor Galbraith is certainly right to place this formidable complex at the centre of the picture, since those who control it might also reasonably be thought to concentrate in their hands a vast amount of power, not only economic but political and cultural as well.

Not so at all, Professor Galbraith hastens to reassure us. For while *resources* are concentrated, *power* is not. Power, in the "industrial system" is not in the hands of the old-style owner-capitalist, who has, he suggests, all but disappeared; nor of course is it held by essentially passive shareholders; nor even by that managerial élite which had long been claimed to have inherited the power of both. The people to whom corporate power *has* passed, Professor Galbraith insists again and again, is an entirely different element, so far overlooked by all other toilers in this field, namely "the technostructure." On this, it is necessary to quote Professor Galbraith at some length, firstly because much of his thesis rests on this discovery, and secondly because it will be argued here that the "technostructure" as the new repository of corporate power is unmitigated nonsense.

The "technostructure" comprises a "very large" group of people who "contribute information to group decisions" and who "extend from the most senior officials of the corporation to where it meets, at the outer perimeter, the white and blue collar workers whose function is to conform more or less mechanically to instructions or routine. It embraces all who bring specialized knowledge, talent or experience to group decision-making" (p. 71). "It will be evident that nearly all powers—initiative, character of development, rejection or acceptance—are exercised deep in the company. It is not the managers who decide. Effective power of decision is lodged deeply in the technical, planning and other specialized staff" (p. 69). Indeed, Professor Galbraith, later in the book, goes even further. For, he tells us, "distinctions between those who make decisions and those who carry them out, and between employer and employee, are obscured[2] by the technicians, scientists, market

---

[2] The fact that power is "obscured" (if it is a fact) would not, one would have thought, mean that it does not exist, but simply that it is more difficult to perceive, which is something very different.

The Structure and Dynamics of American Capitalism

analysts, computer programmers, industrial stylists and other specialists who do, or are both. A continuum thus exists between the centre of the techno-structure and the more routine white-collar workers on the fringe" (p. 268).

On this view, the demon Power has once again been exorcized, without the help of "countervailing power": for the "technostructure" is very large, and the power which accrues to it is therefore diffuse, shared—indeed, why not say it? democratic.

In examining this remarkable argument, it may, to begin with, be noted that much of it rests on the by now well-intrenched notion of the separation of ownership from control, which Professor Galbraith pushes to its furthest limits: for him, those who control the corporations are now virtually owner-less, and ownership is in any event wholly irrelevant to corporate policy.

A considerable amount of evidence and argument, which Professor Galbraith does not discuss, has been produced over the years to rebut or at least to qualify this thesis; and some interesting further evidence against it has recently appeared in *Fortune* magazine.

In an article entitled "Proprietors in the World of Big Business," and concerned with ownership and control in the 500 largest corporations in the United States, Mr. Robert Sheehan writes that "in approximately 150 com-panies on the current *Fortune* list (i.e. of the 500 largest industrial corpora-tions) controlling ownership rests in the hands of an individual or of the members of a single family"; and, he adds, "the evidence that 30 per cent of the 500 largest industrials are clearly controlled by identifiable individuals, or by family groups . . . suggests that the demise of the traditional American proprietor has been slightly exaggerated and that the much-advertised triumph of the organization is far from total."[3] Mr. Sheehan, it should be explained, also notes that he has used a very conservative criterion of con-trol, i.e. that his list only includes companies in which the largest individual stockholder owns 10 per cent or more of the voting stock or in which the largest block of shares—representing 10 per cent or more of the total votes—is held by members of a single family. This, he points out, leaves out "coali-tions" which may assure working control for small groups of associates in many companies; and also businessmen known to wield great influence with holdings of less than 10 per cent.[4] Even so, "at least 10 family-controlled companies rank among the top 100, and several of these are actively owner-managed";[5] and "approximately seventy family-named companies among the 500 are still controlled by the founding family."[6]

Even if these pretty severe qualifications to the thesis of the disappear-ance of the owner-controller are ignored (and Professor Galbraith was in no position to consider them, since they appeared after he had written his book) the question remains as to the managerial élite's relation to ownership. Pro-fessor Galbraith, as noted, wholeheartedly endorses the thesis of managerial

[3] R. Sheehan, "Proprietors in the World of Big Business" in *Fortune*, June 15, 1967, p. 178.
[4] *Ibid.*, p. 179.
[5] *Ibid.*, p. 180.
[6] *Ibid.*, p. 182.

ownerlessness. Thus: "stock holdings by management are small and often non-existent"; "even the small stock interest of the top officers is no longer the rule"; and so on.

This, too, however, is rather extreme. For, as one writer among many has noted, "the managerial class is the largest single group in the stockholding population, and a greater proportion of this class owns stock than any other."[7] Another writer notes that "a recent study by the National Industrial Conference Board shows that 73 per cent of 215 top executives during the period 1950–1960 gained at least 50,000 dollars through the use of stock options, that 32 per cent gained 250,000 dollars, and that 8 per cent gained at least 1,000,000 dollars";[8] and by 1957, it may also be noted, option plans for the purchase of stock had been instituted by 77 per cent of the manufacturing corporations listed in the New York or American Stock Exchange.[9] Managers, the evidence shows, are by no means as ownerless as Professor Galbraith, following many others, maintains.

On the other hand, how often ownership determines control is a rather more complex question. That it does not has of course been an article of faith with managerial revolutionists ever since Berle and Means claimed in 1932 that "ownership is so widely distributed that no individual or small group has even a minority interest large enough to dominate the affairs of the company."[10] This too has long been held to be far too categorical. There is dispersal of ownership (though even this should not be exaggerated) but, as Mr. Clive Beed, of the University of Melbourne has recently argued, the method used by Berle and Means "is unable to separate ownership from control because it does not establish empirically the proportion of votes needed for control in the real as distant from the legal company situation . . . since ownership is very widely dispersed (among different names) in management controlled companies, either it could mean, with Berle and Means, that no one individual or small group could gain sufficient votes for control, or, contradicting Berle and Means, that only a few per cent of votes was required for control."[11]

Various such percentages have at one time or another been advanced. As Mr. Sheehan suggests, 10 per cent is a very conservative estimate. Mr. Villarejo took 5 per cent as the amount of stock required to control a corpora-

[7] G. Kolko, *Wealth and Power in America* (1962), p. 13. See also C. W. Mills, *The Power Elite* (1956) and D. Villarejo "Stock Ownership and the Control of Corporations" in *New University Thought* II (Autumn 1961 and Winter 1962). For Britain, a survey of share owning, published in 1955, showed that directors of companies held shares to an average value of £28,000 and that this was the largest average holding of all the groups about which information was available (*Bulletin of the Oxford Institute of Statistics*, November 1965 in P. Anderson and R. Blackburn, eds., *Towards Socialism* (1965), pp. 116–117).

[8] R. C. Heilbronner, "The View from the Top. Reflections on a Changing Business Ideology," in E. F. Cheit, ed., *The Business Establishment* (1960), p. 25.

[9] E. F. Cheit, "The New Place of Business. Why Managers Cultivate Social Responsibilities," *ibid.*, p. 178.

[10] A. A. Berle and C. C. Means, *The Modern Corporation and Private Property* (1932), p. 84.

[11] Clive S. Beed, "The Separation of Ownership from Control," *Journal of Economic Studies* (University of Aberdeen), vol. I, no. 2, p. 31. Italics in text.

tion whose stock is widely dispersed, and found that in at least 76 of the 232 largest United States corporations, ownership on boards of directors was sufficient to ensure working control;[12] and Mr. Bede also notes that Professor Gordon's 1945 study, *Business Leadership in the Large Corporations,* on which Professor Galbraith greatly relies, held that 3 per cent ultimate ownership might exercise control.[13] In fact, as Mr. Bede suggests, "the possibility of *'any percentage'* control does exist."[14] And where it does, that control-through-ownership is most likely to be in the hands of top managers. Moreover, one place where it is *not* likely to be lodged is in Professor Galbraith's "technostructure." For it is scarcely to be thought that "the technical, planning and other specialized staff" in which, according to him, "the effective power of decision is lodged" ("deeply") are to be counted among the "large owners" of corporate stock.

This, however, is by no means the main reason for thinking that the claim is invalid. For even if it is assumed—which is obviously often the case —that top managers do not exercise control through ownership, the notion that they do not exercise control *at all*, and that the men at the top of the corporate structure are, as Professor Galbraith claims, virtually powerless and ceremonial figures, whose function within the corporation is "to give the equivalent of the royal assent to agreements, contracts and indentures" (p. 93)—this notion too must invite complete disbelief, the more so since Professor Galbraith provides no concrete evidence whatever to buttress his claim.

That claim, in fact, would appear to rest on an extreme "technocratic" view of the degree of influence which hierarchically subordinate technical experts of one sort or another (and the corporation is of course a highly hierarchical, and hierarchy-conscious organization) may wield with men upon whom the power of managerial decision rests. There may be "mature corporations" where the top men are *rois fainéants* or constitutional monarchs. But hard evidence to that effect is lacking. Professor Galbraith claims that the expert influence in the corporation is decisive. There is every reason to think that, here as in government, it is nothing of the kind. The expert does not decide policy: he works out how best to carry it out. In that role, he may well affect policy, but this is hardly synonymous with the dramatic reversal of roles—the experts on top, the managers on tap—which Professor Galbraith claims to be the present reality of the "industrial system."

Having lodged the "effective power of decision" in the "technostructure," Professor Galbraith proceeds to discuss the latter's "motivations." Since there is no good evidence to suggest that the "technostructure" does have such power, it might seem superfluous to follow him in this exercise. But since much that he has to say about the motivations of the "technostructure" also concerns wider issues of corporate policy, it is worth while preserving.

[12] Villarejo, *op. cit.,* vol. II, no. 2, p. 52.
[13] Bede, *op. cit.,* footnote 22.
[14] *Ibid.,* p. 32. Italics in text.

Theories of motivation have been closely linked with the thesis of ownerless management. That thesis was not, it may be surmised, so passionately embraced by so many writers because of its irresistible conceptual beauty. Ideology came into it as well. For from the view that the new class of managers neither owned the resources it controlled, nor was subject to the control of owners, it was but the shortest step, which was eagerly taken, to the claim that managers were, in their running of the corporation, moved by impulses altogether different from those of old-style capitalist owner-entrepreneurs, or from those of passive shareholders, and that these impulses were not only different, but *better,* less "selfish," more "socially responsible." It was this notion which Professor Carl Kaysen once epitomized in the phrase "the soulful corporation." "No longer the agent of proprietorship seeking to maximize return on investment," he claimed, "management sees itself as responsible to stockholders, employees, customers, the general public, and perhaps most important, the firm itself as an institution . . . there is no display of greed and graspingness;[15] there is no attempt to push off onto the workers or the community at large part of the social costs of the enterprise. The modern corporation is a soulful corporation."[16] This, incidentally, was also the view of Mr. C. A. R. Crosland, who wrote in *The Conservative Enemy* that "now perhaps most typical amongst very large firms, is the company which pursues rapid growth and high profits—but subject to its sense of social responsibility and its desire for good labour and public relations. . . . Its goals are a 'fair' rather than a maximum profit, reasonably rapid growth and the warm glow which comes from a sense of public duty."[17] Much the same view, it may be recalled, also found expression in a major Labour Party policy document, which proclaimed that "under increasingly professional management, large firms are as a whole serving the nation well."[18]

This notion of soulful managerialism has often been challenged on two different grounds. Firstly, on the ground that top managers do, as "large owners," often have a direct financial interest in "profit maximization." Thus, Mr. Sheehan, in the article quoted earlier, notes that "Chairman Frederic C. Donner, for example, owns only 0.017 per cent of G.M.'s outstanding stock, but it was worth about $3,917,000 recently. Chairman Lynn A. Townsend owns 0.117 per cent of Chrysler, worth about $2,380,000. Their interest in the earnings of those investments is hardly an impersonal one."[19] And Professor Kolko also notes that "in early 1957, 25 General Motors officers owned an average of 11,500 shares each. Collectively their holdings

[15] The argument that there is no *display* of greed and graspingness would seem a poor basis for the claim that it does not exist. It could, after all, be that "greed and graspingness" are now simply less ostentatious, better concealed, not least by a vast public relations industry of which many academic economists appear to be honorary members.

[16] C. Kaysen, "The Social Significance of the Modern Corporation" in *American Economic Review*, May 1957, pp. 313–314.

[17] C. A. R. Crosland, *The Conservative Enemy* (1962), pp. 88–89.

[18] *Industry and Society* (1957), p. 48.

[19] Sheehan, *op. cit.*, p. 242. See also my earlier references to gains through stock options and Villarejo, *op. cit.*, Part III.

would have been inconsequential if they had chosen to try and obtain control of G.M. through their stocks. Yet each of these men had a personal share of roughly half a million dollars in the company. . . ."[20] The largest part of managerial income may not be derived from ownership, or depend upon such ownership, but managers are hardly likely, all the same, to ignore their shareholdings in their view of what their firms ought to be about. As indeed why should they?

The second and more important reason why managers *are* concerned with "profit maximization" has been well put by Baran and Sweezy: "The primary objectives of corporate policy," they write, "—which are at the same time and inevitably the personal objectives of the corporate managers—are thus strength, rate of growth and size. There is no general formula for quantifying or combining these objectives—nor is there any need for one. For they are reducible to the single common denominator of profitability. Profits provide the internal funds for expansion. Profits are the sinews and muscle of strength, which in turn gives access to outside funds if and when they are needed. . . . Thus profits, even though not the ultimate goal, are the necessary means to all ultimate goals. As such, they become the immediate, unique, unifying, quantitative aim of corporate policies, the touchstone of corporate rationality, the measure of corporate success."[21]

As it happens, the inventor of the "soulful corporation" himself concedes a good deal to this view. "It may be argued," Professor Kaysen writes "that all this (i.e. the managers' multiple responsibilities) amounts to no more than long-run profit maximization, and thus that management in the modern corporation does no more than business management has always tried to do, allowing for changed circumstances"; furthermore "only the ability to continue to earn a substantial surplus over costs makes possible a variety of expenditures who benefits are broad, uncertain and distant."[22] This is also Mr. Sheehan's conclusion: "Very few executives argue that the managers of a widely held company run their business any differently from the proprietors of a closely held company"; "it is unrealistic to assume that because a manager holds only a small fraction of his company's stock he lacks the incentive to drive up the profits."[23] Indeed, Professor James Earley has even gone further and suggested, very plausibly, that the modern manager may be better placed to pursue profit than the old-style entrepreneur, because with "the rapidly growing use of economists, market analysis, other types of specialists and management consultants by our larger businesses . . . profit-oriented rationality is likely to be more and more representative of business behaviour."[24]

For his part, Professor Galbraith will have none of this. Profit maximization, he holds, excludes other goals. But this can only be true if "profit-

[20] Kolko, *op. cit.*, p. 65.

[21] P. Baran and P. Sweezy, *Monopoly Capital* (1966), pp. 39–40.

[22] C. Kaysen, "The Social Significance of the Modern Corporation," *op. cit.*, pp. 313, 315.

[23] Sheehan, *op. cit.*, pp. 183, 242.

[24] J. S. Earley, "Contribution to the discussion on the impact of some new developments in economic theory: exposition and evaluation" in *American Economic Review*, May 1957, pp. 333–334.

maximization" is taken to mean, as Professor Galbraith appears to mean, a reckless and wholly irrational pursuit of immediately realizable profit, regardless of any longer term consideration. And this is a purely arbitrary definition, which is applicable neither to corporate management, nor, for that matter, to owner-entrepreneurs.

In any case it is not the motivation of managers, but of the "technostructure" which, in Professor Galbraith's view, is what matters. The professional and salaried staff who mainly compose it are, he insists, even less concerned with "profit-maximation" than top managers. This may well be the case, but would only be significant if one were to accept the view that the corporation "as an instrument of power" is used "to serve the deeper interests and goals of the technostructure." And there are no good grounds, as I have suggested, for accepting this view.

Even so, it may be worth examining what, according to Professor Galbraith, these "goals" of the "technostructure" are, since his discussion illustrates so well the extreme difficulty of finding a rationale for corporate enterprise clearly distinct from financial reward.

Despite solemn announcements of motivational revelations, the motives and goals which Professor Galbraith ascribes to the "technostructure" (purely on the basis of supposition and inference) turn out, upon examination, to be no different from the goals which have often been ascribed to top management—the survival of the firm, its growth, its independence from outside control. But these are precisely the kinds of issues which the technical and professional staffs within the corporation are least likely to be called upon to decide.

Nor is Professor Galbraith at all successful in locating the larger "social" goals which, he claims, move the "technostructure." "The individual," he tells us, "will identify himself with the goals of the corporation only if the corporation is identified with, *as the individual sees it,* some significant social goal" (p. 162, my italics). On the other hand, "the individual," he also tells us, "serves organization because of the possibility of accommodating its goals more closely to his own" (p. 163). But *then,* we also find that "he will normally think that the goals he seeks have social purpose," "for individuals have a well-marked capacity to attach high social purpose to whatever— more scientific research, better zoning laws, manufacture of the lethal weapons just mentioned—*serves their personal interest*" (p. 163, my italics). Moreover, it does not appear to matter in the least *what* the corporation produces, whether "life saving drugs" or "an exotic missile fuel, or a better trigger for a nuclear warhead" (p. 163).

What this amounts to is that whatever "goals" members of the "technostructure" may have will be seen, *by them,* as having a "social purpose"; and whatever the corporation produces will be deemed, *by them,* to have an equally "social purpose." As Professor Galbraith puts it, "what counts here is what is believed" (p. 163). But this surely renders the discussion of "goals" quite meaningless. For why should we accept the "goals" of the "technostructure" as having a "social purpose" simply because its members happen to *believe* this to be the case?

In any case, Professor Galbraith himself is compelled to attribute more importance to "pecuniary compensation" than many of his formulations would tend to suggest. For it appears that other "goals" only operate *after* a certain level of income has been achieved; it is only "above a certain level" that other motivations "may operate independently of income" (p. 138); "the participants are well compensated" and "few regard their compensation with disinterest" (p. 141). On one page, "pecuniary compensation, as an explanation of effort, has now a much diminished role" (p. 141); twenty pages later, "pecuniary compensation is an extremely important stimulus to individual members of the technostructure up to a point. If they are not paid this acceptable and expected salary, they will not work" (p. 161). As a "general theory of motivation," these extraordinary contortions may be thought to leave something to be desired.

One of Professor Galbraith's most insistent themes is that modern economic life requires planning. But this requirement, it would appear, is already largely met in the American "industrial system"; for the United States, *mirabile dictu*, is "a largely planned economy" (p. 356). This remarkable assertion rests on the notion that the "mature corporation" is able to plan because it is no longer subject to the vagaries of a market which it controls, or to the cold winds of competition; and its planning is the more secure in that the state controls aggregate demand: "the firm is the basic planning unit in the western economies. In the Soviet system it is still the state" (p. 105). This is surely pushing "convergence" beyond the bounds of sense. For whatever may be thought of Soviet planning, it is hardly to be assimilated to the "planning" of which Professor Galbraith speaks. Even if one leaves aside his dubious elimination of the market and of competition from the "industrial system," and his no less dubious assurance that the state has perfected its mechanism of control of aggregate demand (i.e. that depression is now not only unlikely but impossible), the planning in which individual corporations engage bears no relation to, and is in fact the opposite of, any meaningful concept of national planning. Professor Galbraith may *wish* to overcome the anarchy of production characteristic of his "industrial system"; but the wish ought not to be taken for a fact.

As for "state intervention," Professor Galbraith clearly sees that what he calls "the public sector," i.e. government expenditure, is the "fulcrum" for the regulation of demand. And he also notes that "plainly military expenditures are the pivot on which the fulcrum rests" (p. 229). This he finds regrettable. But all he has to offer, concretely, as an alternative to military expenditure is expenditure on space competition. "In relation to the needs of the industrial system, the space competition is nearly ideal" (p. 341). He is then moved to ask: "Are there not better uses for the resources so employed?" And he answers, in a remarkable and revealing phrase: "There is no rational answer to these questions as there is none to a query as to why negotiated disarmament is inherently more dangerous than a continuance of the weapons competition. *Truth in both instances is subordinate to need and the needed belief.* But this does not affect the value of the space competition in meeting the needs of the industrial system in a comparatively harmless instead of an extremely dangerous competition" (p. 341, my italics).

This would do very well as a satire on the "industrial system," of the kind presented, deliberately or unwittingly, by *Report from Iron Mountain*. But Professor Galbraith is not here, to all appearances, in the least satirical. And his prescription therefore betokens, in the fact of genuine human need, an illuminating willingness to sacrifice reason so as to meet the "need and the needed belief" of the "industrial system."

But what, in any case, if armaments expenditure is not simply produced by a deluded view, as Professor Galbraith suggests, of the "Soviet threat"? What if it is the inevitable expression of the determination to maintain the largest possible area of the globe open to the "industrial system," and to a consequent determination to counter by every means, including military means, all attempts to resist that penetration? What, in other words, if military expenditure is the necessary concomitant of the expansionist needs of the "industrial system" itself? Professor Galbraith has not a word to say about *this* aspect of the "industrial system," of its relation to the world, of its imperialist urges; and it is only by ignoring it, and by ignoring the supreme irrationality of his prescription, that he is able to urge "space competition" as an alternative to armaments.

In a sense, his default is all the greater in that he does see that the system "generally ignores or holds as unimportant those services of the state which are not closely related to the system's needs (p. 345); and that a state attuned to capitalist purposes therefore neglects those services.

Yet even here, there is a typical disregard of the *scale* of the human needs which are left unfulfilled. Professor Galbraith is of course concerned with poverty. But in *The New Industrial State* as in *The Affluent Society,* he treats it as an all but marginal, "special" problem. The latter book rendered an immense service to the "industrial system" by helping to popularize the notion that capitalism had all but eliminated poverty, or that it had at least reduced it to marginal, "minority" proportions. In *The Affluent Society,* he described poverty as mainly confined to "special" sections of the population: either "some quality peculiar to the individual or family involved—mental deficiency, bad health, inability to adapt to the discipline of modern economic life, excessive procreation, alcohol, insufficient education, or perhaps a combination of several of these handicaps—has kept these individuals from participating in the *general* well-being"[25] (the notion that these are qualities "peculiar to the individual" is distinctly odd, but let it pass); or, alternatively poverty was an "insular" phenomenon, which had "something to do with the desire of a comparatively large number of people to spend their lives at or near the place of their birth."[26] In either case, his readers, presumably mentally alert, healthy, disciplined, sexually sophisticated, non-alcoholic, educated and mobile, were given to understand, for this was the theme of the whole book, that here *was* a special problem, which might be thought to involve, since Professor Galbraith did not venture figures, a quite easily manageable minority. Poverty might be a "disgrace" to an "affluent society"; but the very idea of the affluent society exiled the poor to its outer fringes, and greatly helped to obscure them from view.

[25] J. K. Galbraith, *The Affluent Society* (1958), p. 254. My italics.
[26] *Ibid.,* p. 254.

It was not long after the publication of *The Affluent Society* that poverty was rediscovered in the United States (and in Britain), not as a marginal and special phenomenon, on the way to eradication in "post-capitalist" societies, but as a literally massive phenomenon, of quite gruesome proportions. Harry Magdoff has summarized thus, to take but one example, the findings of an impeccably official Conference on Economic Progress which reported in April 1962: "The simple summary of the Conference Report on the 1960 income situation in the U.S. is as follows: 34 million people in families and 4 million unattached individuals (that is, unattached economically to a family unit) lived in poverty; 37 million people in families and 2 million unattached individuals lived in deprivation. The total of 77 million comprised two-fifths of the U.S. population in 1960."[27] This is not, as Professor Galbraith had it, "private affluence and public squalor," but public squalor *and* private poverty.

There is nothing in *The New Industrial State* to suggest that Professor Galbraith has taken note of such findings, nothing to qualify his view of poverty as a special, marginal and easily soluble "problem." Certain "tasks" —"the care of the ill, aged and physically or mentally infirm, the provision of health services in general, the provision of parks and many other services"— "are badly performed to the general public's discomfort or worse. Were it recognized that they require planning, and in the context of a largely planned economy [*sic*] have been left unplanned, there would be no hesitation or apology in the use of all the necessary instruments for planning. Performance would be much better" (p. 356). In fact, nothing is more certain than that it would require much more than "recognition" for performance to be much better. Here is not simply optimism but blindness to the reality which Professor Galbraith so insistently claims, throughout his book, to portray; and it is a blindness induced by the wish to see all "problems" of the "industrial system" as readily soluble within its framework, and without the need to look beyond it.

The final question raised by Professor Galbraith's modest discontents with the "industrial system" concerns the likely agencies of its reform. Not labour, certainly; for in that system, "everything is more benign. Compulsion will have receded. In consequence, there is little or no alienation; the way is open for the worker to accept the goals of the organization" (p. 137); "interests that were once radically opposed are now much more nearly in harmony" (p. 263). Demand for change cannot, clearly, be expected from the happy industrial family which Professor Galbraith has conjured up; where, but fifteen short years ago, there were large reserves of countervailing power, there is now unalienated integration. But all hope is not lost, for there remains, in growing numbers and strength, the "educational and scientific estate." "It is possible," Professor Galbraith suggests, "that the educational and scientific estate requires only a strongly creative political hand to

[27] H. Magdoff, "Problems of United States Capitalism" in *The Socialist Register, 1965*, p. 73. "Deprivation" was held by the Conference to include people living above the stark poverty level but below what a Labour Department investigation found to be a "modest but adequate" worker's family budget (*ibid.*, p. 73). See also e.g. Baran and Sweezy, *op. cit.*, Chapter 10, and M. Harrington, *The Other America* (1962).

become a decisive instrument of political power" (p. 294). "A decisive instrument of political power" is pitching it rather high, and the notion of people as "an instrument" of political power, decisive or otherwise, is ambiguous and unattractive. Still, there is everything to be said for the stress on the responsibility and possible power of intellectuals. But the question then arises —political power for what? Professor Galbraith has no serious answer to that question. In fact, his whole soothingly complacent view of the "industrial system" and of American society precludes him from providing such an answer. For all the verbal iconoclasm, and the seeming dismissal of "conventional wisdom" and orthodox economics, there is too much here of apologetics and obfuscation, too little genuine probing, too ready an acceptance of the "logic" of the system, too cramped a view of its contradictions, too much underlying intellectual and political timidity, notwithstanding the self-conscious *enfant terrible* posturings, for Professor Galbraith to speak seriously to the American condition, or to those who seriously seek to change it. For such people, *The New Industrial State* has little to offer, either by way of diagnosis, or of prescription. What it does offer is a further demonstration of the limitations, both in diagnosis and in prescription, of a type of liberalism which constitutes not an alternative but a variant of that conservatism which Professor Galbraith claims to condemn.

Ronald Radosh

THE CORPORATE IDEOLOGY
OF AMERICAN LABOR LEADERS
FROM GOMPERS TO HILLMAN

Historians of American labor usually describe two strains in trade unionism: the "pure and simple" business unionism of Samuel Gompers, and the social unionism of Sidney Hillman or Walter Reuther. But beneath these avowed differences there is a fundamental consensus shared by both kinds of labor leaders—that a corporate society offers the best means of achieving industrial stability, order and social harmony.

Corporate thinkers view society as composed of various functional economic groups caused by the division of labor. Workers are defined as producers rather than as a social class. Therefore they hold an equal stake with management in developing efficient industrial production. The goal of such thinkers is peaceful industrial relations in which each sector of the economy has political representation and is coordinated by an impartial administration. Ideally, an economic congress should be created in which each functional group would be represented. Such a congress of economic groups would work more equitably than the system in which the different groups blindly scramble for power.

C. Wright Mills was perhaps the first social scientist to emphasize that labor leaders framed unions as instruments for integration into the existing political economy, not levers for changing it. It was the labor leader's desire to "join with owners and managers in running the corporate enterprise system and influencing decisively the political economy as a whole." The result, in Mills' words, was a "kind of 'procapitalist syndicalism from the top.'"

In this paper I hope to present some tentative but provocative suggestions as to the way in which Samuel Gompers in the 1920's, and Sidney Hillman in the 1930's, sought to find a place for labor within a corporate capitalist economic structure.

After defeats suffered by labor in the Homestead, Pullman and Coeur d'Alene strikes of the 1890's, Samuel Gompers concluded that unions could not beat the growing "trusts" in head-on collisions. Accepting the growth of the large corporations as natural and inevitable, Gompers sought to organize the worker within the system as an alternative to socialism. The problem was to find means whereby the employer and worker could function together harmoniously.

Reprinted, with footnotes deleted, from Ronald Radosh, "The Corporate Ideology of American Labor Leaders from Gompers to Hillman," *Studies on the Left*, vol. 6 (November–December 1966), pp. 66–88, by permission of *Studies on the Left*. Ronald Radosh teaches history at Queensborough Community College, City University of New York. He is the author of *American Labor and United States Foreign Policy* and co-editor of *Teach-ins U.S.A., Reports, Opinions, Documents* as well as a contributor to *The Nation* and other periodicals.

This problem was met by espousing labor participation in the National Civic Federation. Organized in 1900 by Ralph Easley, Mark Hanna and Samuel Gompers, the Federation sought to resolve class conflict and institute cooperative relations between capital and labor. The employer who led the Civic Federation hoped to establish a community of interest between previously warring groups and create one unified corporate body. Gompers' association with men like Hanna led him to believe that industrial peace would reign, since the "men who control wealth in this country are at bottom human and adaptable to the changed order of relations." Hanna signed a collective bargaining agreement with the AFL union in his steel plant, and worked to convince capitalists to concede "the rightful demands of labor."

From the birth of the Civic Federation to 1914, Gompers' ideas about labor were molded by his association with those sophisticated employers who saw the AFL as a conservative and disciplined junior partner in a stable corporate order. It was Gompers' wartime experience, however, that led to maturation of his thought. The wartime need for an uninterrupted flow of goods and services, the participation of union leaders in the Administration and the growth of union membership impressed upon labor leaders the desirability of taking a new position. Before the war the AFL was indifferent to production and efficiency, scorned productivity theories and was hostile to the scientific management movement. The war years taught the AFL leaders the value of preaching cooperation and efficiency to increase production. It was then that Gompers began a close association with scientific engineers from the Taylor school.

During the war the Wilson Administration tried to institutionalize cooperative relations between labor, industry and government. The War Industries Board, Bernard Baruch reported, established price fixing, allocation and priorities policies under which the "manufacturing facilities of the Nation were almost as effectively transformed into governmental agencies as though the Government had absorbed them." Baruch's board worked with Gompers and sought to adjust disputes over wages, hours of labor and working conditions. Gompers was never "a class champion obstructionist," Board secretary Grosvenor B. Clarkson reported, and he proved a "strong believer in the scheme of close cooperation with industry and was one of the first to endorse the program of industrial group committees to facilitate government dealings with private business."

As the government developed a large cartelizing program that kept up prices and stabilized industry under administration tutelage, Gompers came into contact with leading corporate figures involved in this reorganization. Daniel Willard, President of the Baltimore and Ohio Railroad and the first head of the War Industries Board, was close to Gompers. As members of the Advisory Commission to the Council of National Defense in 1916, Willard noted that he and Gompers found themselves "in very full accord concerning most questions of fundamental importance."

After the war Gompers' contact with such sophisticated industrialists continued. The 1920's saw a revival of the National Civic Federation. Industrialists such as Edward A. Filene, of Filene and Sons, and former Secretary of Commerce William C. Redfield were among the luminaries active in trying to forge a new community of interest. Charles A. Coffin, chairman of the Board of General Electric, expressed the Civic Federation's position when he observed that the task of industry was to find methods by which the "best among labor and the best among the employers" could cooperate. Coffin branded employers who supported the open-shop movement as "oppressive." "Sympathetic, broad-minded employers," he said, should be ready to "discipline and denounce the radicals among the employers, and to meet on that ground men like Mr. Gompers and his associates who are combatting the radical movement in labor." The NCF position was also supported by former Assistant Secretary of the Navy Franklin D. Roosevelt, who sat on the Civic Federation Executive Committee. During the seven and one half years that he supervised a ship building industry of 100,000, Roosevelt did not have "a single strike in a single trade in a single Navy yard." FDR attributed this stability to the agreement that if a dispute occurred, management and labor would "sit around the table and talk it over," a plan which always worked. Roosevelt criticized both the old-fashioned employer who refused to accept modern conditions and the radical worker who dreamt of far-off ideals. He urged labor-capital cooperation to meet domestic problems, and called for elimination of misleading socialist schemes such as those emanating from the Rand School in New York.

The man whose thought most affected Gompers was the prolabor Secretary of Commerce Herbert Clark Hoover. Hoover analyzed the American industrial system as composed of three basic units—capital, labor and government. His objective was to have these groups function together harmoniously. He therefore demanded a voice in labor policy in President Harding's Cabinet. Defining labor and management as producers, not as social classes, Hoover saw large areas of mutual interest that had to be cultivated. Once in office Hoover began the pattern of prolabor intervention by government that culminated in the New Deal. As coordinator of Woodrow Wilson's Second Industrial Conference, Hoover had favored collective bargaining, had criticized company unions and urged an end to child labor. E. D. Howard, the labor negotiator for the firm of Hart, Schaffner and Marx, was among those who in 1920 urged that "it would be a great step forward if Mr. Hoover were appointed Secretary of Labor." While there was evidence that many "reactionary employers" wanted to eliminate unions, there were "also a great number of more thoughtful and more liberal-minded employers who would like to carry on the work started by the President's conference," and "block the efforts of the reactionaries and also of the radical people on the other side" and "do something constructive."

In May of 1924 Hoover gave a speech before the United States Chamber of Commerce in which he presented his concept of self-determination in industry. Hoover pleaded that new regulations favoring human rights had to be developed out of the voluntary forces in the nation. Legislation entered the business world only when abuses existed, and remedies had to come "out of the conscience and organization of business itself; these restraints which will cure abuse . . . eliminate waste . . . that will march with larger social understanding." The United States, Hoover stated, was "in the midst of a great revolution," a transformation from a period of "extremely individualistic action into a period of associational activities." Through autonomous associational bodies, America was moving "towards some sort of industrial democracy."

After reading his speech Samuel Gompers wrote Hoover that he found "genuine inspiration" in the address; it was "the most valuable contribution to the understanding of industrial organizations" and would "without doubt further constructive progress for which I share your concern." Gompers proceeded to use the speech as a vehicle for a major statement. Writing that Hoover's views met and "match perfectly the policy and philosophy of the American Federation of Labor," Gompers agreed that those who sought "retention of our basic institutions" had to cure "the abuses which naturally" develop. Gompers endorsed the concept of self-government in industry, claiming that the legislative world lacked the informed intelligence necessary to deal with industrial problems. American labor "goes all the way with Mr. Hoover," Gompers wrote, "or Mr. Hoover goes all the way with Labor." Hoover had a "keen understanding of our industrial order, including Labor's part in the operation thereof—and that is all Labor asks of any man." Gompers departed from Hoover in only one respect; he emphasized the need to grant unions "greater participation in the impending changes."

Gompers' evolving corporatist outlook became clear in his evaluation of the wartime experience. 1924 saw Bernard Baruch argue for a new scheme to institute price fixing of all commodities and to reinstitute wartime type controls, when "wages had to be the same as were then prevailing in the industry." While labor was satisfied with that, Baruch wrote Gompers, he was concerned that Gompers was "opposed to . . . my plan for mobilizing industry." Baruch could not understand this because he knew that "neither you nor any of the men associated with me . . . during the war, could be opposed . . . because it is only what we were endeavoring to put into execution at that time."

Gompers assured Baruch that he was aware that many did not have "your sympathetic attitude towards labor." Moreover, labor had given its wholehearted support during the war because the War Industries Board recognized unions, and had arranged that "representation be provided for all elements concerned in producing including labor." Industrial policy of the future would have to be the result of decisions reached by "a thoroughly representative group" which would have the "confidence of industry."

Gompers believed that society moved not through the exercise of political power, but through the recognition that decision making power was concentrated directly in autonomous functional economic units. He emphasized that the WIB worked through "the organized agencies of industry and enforced decisions by economic means." The methods, machinery of operation and decisions were far different than any which could be secured through political means. In fact, Gompers recalled, "the complete collapse of political machinery during the war emergency has remained in my mind as a most significant feature. During the months of our intense activity we were scarcely aware of the existence of Congress."

Baruch was pleased to find that Gompers shared his conception. "It gave me great pleasure to receive your letter," he wrote, and to find that "your thoughts are exactly in accord with me on this whole subject." Baruch expressed his debt to Samuel Gompers. "My recommendations," he informed him, "were based on our mutual experiences. None of my contacts in Washington were of more benefit or of greater pleasure to me than the one I had with you."

The attempt to organize, balance and coordinate functional economic groups took final shape in the demand that a new economic parliament be created. As AFL Vice-President Matthew Woll expressed it, the Federation hoped that there would "come into existence an economic and industrial chamber, in which all factors in industry will be fairly represented, and which will determine the rules and regulations that industries will impose upon themselves." The most explicit statement was to be made at the 1923 Convention in the Executive Board's statement "Industry's Manifest Duty." Here the AFL leadership revealed that it sought the "conscious organization of one of the most vital functional elements for enlightened participation in a democracy of industry." State regulation was undesirable because decisions that affected people's daily lives were made by men in autonomous economic groups. Functional elements in our national life had to work out their own problems without regulation. The mission of industrial groups was "to legislate in peace," and to develop an "industrial franchise comparable to our political franchise." It was Gompers' corporate conception that led him to respond positively to Benito Mussolini's attempt to build a corporate state in Italy. Despite differences in method, Gompers saw a set of common assumptions shared by Italian fascists and liberal American trade unionists.

Gompers' corporate overview, with its stress on functional democracy, efficiency and production, is often viewed as a pragmatic response to paternalism of open-shop employers. When confronted with benevolent employers, some argue, labor sought to prove that "it was industry's most able helpmeet." Others view the AFL's emphasis on efficiency as an admission that they were in a period of decline. By striving to improve output, the declining AFL hoped to gain the employer's acceptance. As one labor historian has written, the emphasis on production was "a kind of 'if you can't lick 'em, join 'em philosophy,' " to which most employers "did not want to be 'joined.' "

Writers taking this view contrast the AFL approach with that developed by CIO leaders in the 30's. The latter are praised for organizing unskilled workers, for their use of militant tactics and for purportedly developing a new labor ideology. But the corporate ideology of American labor leaders actually matures in the New Deal era. CIO leaders stressed efficiency and productivity, and favored a formal corporate state. The difference was that in the 30's they hoped that the CIO industrial unions would be the labor bodies given representation in the new industrial parliament.

In the 1930's labor leaders became involved with a new group of far-sighted industrialists who wanted to establish a place for unionism in the corporate capitalist economy. Gerard P. Swope, architect of his own plan for a corporate state—the Swope Plan—was one industrialist who wanted to integrate labor into the system. As early as 1926 Swope had sought to convince William Green to form a nation-wide union of electrical workers organized on an industrial basis. Swope felt that having an industrial union might mean "the difference between an organization with which we could work on a business like basis and one that would be a source of endless difficulties."

William Green, maintaining his commitment to the craft union bloc in the AFL, rejected Swope's pleas. Swope preferred industrial organization for one simple reason; he saw his industry "intolerably handicapped if the bulk of our employees were organized into different and often competing craft unions." They could deal easily with one bargaining agent, but not with more than one dozen. When the CIO was organized and the left-led United Electrical Workers began to organize G.E., Swope rejoiced. He informed one of his vice-presidents that "if you can't get along with these fellows and settle matters, there's something wrong with you." The UE was praised by Swope as "well led, the discipline good." Julius Emspak, a top official of the union, recalled that Swope was an "enlightened" employer who told him that the time had come when "industry would have to recognize that" a union representative should sit on the company's board of directors.

Not only did Swope favor industrial organization, but he supported the Black Bill for a 30-hour week and the minimum wage amendment introduced by Francis Perkins. While William Green opposed the amendment urging that it would reduce the hourly earning of skilled labor, Swope supported it because he claimed that the AFL did not cover all unskilled labor. It was a necessity since out of the "millions of men employed in industry, a very small proportion is in the American Federation of Labor." The legislation was on behalf of the unskilled worker "who needs protection . . . those who have no organization working for them." Congress, Swope said, had to act on behalf of the "millions of men who are not members" of the AFL and "for whom no one is talking."

The early New Deal was to be characterized by the introduction of planning techniques that had antecedents in the trade associations of the 1920's. The War Industries Board cartelization reached fruition in the National Recovery Administration. One of NRA's key architects was Donald Richberg, who had been chosen for his position because of his labor background. As a young Chicago lawyer, Richberg had written both the Railway Labor Act of 1926 and the Norris–La Guardia Act of 1932. In 1933 Richberg argued that industrial unions would have to be the prerequisite for an American corporation. "If industrial workers were adequately organized," he wrote, "it would be entirely practical to create industrial councils composed of representatives of managers, investors and workers and then to create a national council composed of similar representatives of all essential industries." In the council "all producing and consuming interests would be so represented that one group could hardly obtain sanction for a policy clearly contrary to the general welfare." Richberg was critical of craft union leaders. "He wished that they had "seized" labor's "great opportunity to organize the unemployed," and had ignored "the hampering tradition of craft unionism," simply organizing men and women "denied their inherent right to work." Labor should have demanded that "their government should no longer be controlled by rulers of commerce and finance who" had failed to "meet their obligations." If such a movement had been built, if labor had created one "mighty arm and voice" of the "unemployed millions," Congress would have listened to the dispossessed.

Richberg also forecast the conservative role which industrial unions would play. "Let me warn those who desire to preserve the existing order," he cautioned, "but intend to do nothing to reform it, that if this depression continues much longer the unemployed will be organized and action of a revolutionary character will be demanded." To avoid this people had to be put back to work. The answer was to mobilize the nation "through the immediate creation of a national planning council, composed of representatives of major economic interests who recognize the necessity of a planned economy," or, in other words, the American corporate state—or the NRA.

NRA, as Eugene Golub has observed, revealed that "the basic idea of corporatism had been accepted as part of the American scene." Businessmen in each industry were given exemption from antitrust prosecution, and were granted permission to draw up codes of fair competition which the government would enforce as law. The codes also established minimum wages in each industry, and price and production quotas. Labor was to receive the protection offered in Section 7-a, which guaranteed its right to organize. Despite the obvious corporate origins and function of NRA, liberals and radicals ignored its conservative heritage because of what Arthur K. Ekirch called their "widespread confidence in the broad nature and humanitarian goals of the New Deal's planning." FDR's use of big business methods and wartime regimentation was forgotten because the goal was more jobs and better working conditions. The commitment to support reform if liberals would bypass criticism of the conservative nature of NRA was understood by Richberg himself. NRA would win the allegiance of liberals by providing Title II which offered a program of public works. In a draft prepared for the NRA planning committee Richberg suggested that "it would be at least a tactical error not to begin the bill with a public works program," with the provision for trade agreements following as further stimulation to stabilization of industry. "If this is not done," he explained, "the reaction of the host of people expecting, advocating and convinced of the value of public works will be antagonistic to the general program." If "industrial control leads off, with public works as a secondary, incidental part of the program, it will be difficult to avoid violent opposition from those now clamoring for public works who might swallow a somewhat 'fascist' proposal to get their 'democratic' measure of relief." In facetiously using the terms he expected critics to cite in the future, Richberg showed awareness that reformers would acquiesce in the corporate state if reform was part of its program.

The most significant success that the Roosevelt Administration had was the integration of organized labor into the corporate system. The old line craft unions were insufficiently structured to aid unskilled labor. Therefore unions that had a sudden revival under NRA were industrial outfits such as the United Mine Workers and the Amalgamated Clothing Workers. NRA turned unionism into a semipublic institution whose organization was part of the new government program. NRA officials understood that the AFL unions were not capable of fulfilling the NRA program for a rise in labor's condition. As Benjamin Stolberg wrote in 1933, "in short, the socialist unions, whose militancy has been kept alive these last few years by an inner left wing opposition, fitted very easily into the drift toward state capitalism, which characterizes the New Deal."

It is not surprising to find that Sidney Hillman, the Jewish immigrant who built the Amalgamated Clothing Workers, would emerge as a major exponent of a corporate state in which labor would be guaranteed a formal position. Hillman's contribution to corporate ideology is usually ignored. Hillman was originally a socialist and led a union whose rank and file was Marxist inclined. Moreover, he favored industrial unionism and his own Amalgamated was created in an internal rebellion against the AFL garment union in Chicago.

The truth about Hillman's attitude was carefully explained by William H. Johnston, the President of the AFL Machinists. Trying to reassure Baltimore and Ohio President Daniel Willard about the effect of radical workers on the B and O, Johnston urged that Willard disregard rhetoric and look at reality. "I believe it is a mistake to be too much disturbed by every unfortunate phrase or differing angle" some labor groups use, he wrote. What Willard had to realize is that "in labor circles discussion is free and often acrimonious, that labor people have their own traditions" and use their own terminology. It was essential "not to confuse phrases with the reality." Johnston's example was relations between the hat firm of Hart, Schaffner and Marx and Hillman's Amalgamated Clothing Workers, "no strikes having taken place in the plant and cooperative experiments having been developed to a high degree." Yet, Johnston commented, "the union itself is full of 'revolutionary' propaganda, and even its officers are far more outspoken in their radical political and industrial doctrines than the officers of any railroad unions." If the "well disposed employers had taken this sort of thing too seriously or had allowed themselves to be upset by everything that was said in the union, then friendly relations with their employees might have been broken off a hundred times." But these employers "were realistic and concentrated on the job in hand. They did not confuse realities with phrases."

The record indicates that the employers acted wisely in disregarding the Amalgamated's radical rhetoric. Hillman's role was that of champion of cooperative schemes in the garment industry. Like Gompers, Hillman received the aid of government during the First World War. In August of 1917 Secretary of War Newton D. Baker had composed a directive assuring that sound industrial conditions would be in force in firms manufacturing army uniforms. A control board was established to see that standard wages, the eight hour day and union conditions were met. With this agreement the Amalgamated grew rapidly and organized most of the clothing industry. By 1919 Hillman was advocating stabilization of the industry by creation of one national organization of clothing manufacturers, a move opposed at the time by other union officers. As Hillman's biographer observed, his "intellectual approach . . . was sympathetic to 'statism,' an attitude formed during World War I, when a constructive policy toward organized labor had been adopted by the Federal Government."

When rank and file unionists opposed administration policy, such as American participation in the World War, the union moved to curb antiwar agitation. Amalgamated officer Frank Rosenblum wrote that the union's newspaper had "overdone itself in its criticism of the government." While

Rosenblum agreed that the war was unjust, he felt that attacks on it should not be given "the space and prominence it has until now," and that the union should "not do anything which will antagonize any one." To Rosenblum it was "a question of expediency." To criticize the war meant an opening for those who wanted to harm the union, since there were "enough forces in and out of the labor movement seeking to destroy the Amalgamated without getting the U.S. Government on the job to assist them." If it kept up an anti-war stance, the union would "lose friends which it might need in the future."

The union did not lose its friends. By the 1920's Hillman was the leading advocate of "the new unionism," whose supporters put their stress on efficiency. They argued that an industry which was not productive could not be prosperous, and that industry would yield benefits to all groups if it was efficiently administered. Hillman introduced what were called standards of production into the clothing trade, in which a specified shop production was agreed to by representatives of both sides, and was guaranteed by the union.

For this attitude Hillman won praise from important figures. Ray Stannard Baker saw the Amalgamated representing "in the labor question what the League of Nations represents in international relations," substituting in place of militancy "a system for the prevention of war and conflicts between employers and employees." The result of Hillman's program would be that workers would not be "compelled in despair to turn to radical movements in the hope of securing what they consider their right—a joint voice with the employer in the determination of conditions of labor." Since the Amalgamated was supposedly a radical union, this was a substantial achievement.

Most satisfied with the work of the Amalgamated were employers. Joseph Schaffner had signed the first binding agreement with the union. The result, he stated in 1915, was that "in our own business, employing thousands of persons . . . many of them in opposition to the wage system and hostile to employers as a class, we have observed astonishing changes in their attitude during the four years under the influence of our labor arrangement." Workers knew that "justice will be done them" once the company gave the union a voice. Another employer explained that before the union entered his New York firm the workers often simply refused to produce. After he signed with the union the Amalgamated gave its permission to dismiss hostile workers, "and with their sanction we discharged every man in the shop, and are now building up a new force." Years ago, the employer explained, such discharges would have meant a "general strike," but now his firm "had the disciplinary power of the union behind us." The union's worth was also demonstrated by E. Strouse, a leading Baltimore clothing manufacturer. Writing to Hillman in October of 1919, Strouse complained that the local leader in Baltimore was so loaded down with work that he was unable to be reached "when we need him most." Asking that the union representative meet with him once a day, Strouse noted that, "I have been trying to get more production for weeks and have been unable to do so." Could you "not do something that we might have him oftener," Strouse asked, "because I feel that with his finesse he is able to get for us what we want, better than we can ourselves and it is urgent from many angles that we get our production."

By 1919 Hillman had called for "the organization of every industry, beginning from the raw materials, completing with the agencies for distribution, and providing representation from all the factors in industry, and placing upon all of them the responsibility of running the industry." The result, Robert W. Bruere wrote, was that continuity of production was guaranteed, and strikes and lockouts did not occur. Hillman had proved the "ability of rightminded employers and trade union leaders to sublimate class conflict into integral class concert." Labor's concern shifted from the haggles of getting more to the joint concern for achieving "efficient production." Like Samuel Gompers, Hillman's approach led him into the camp of Herbert Hoover. After Hoover was elected to the Presidency Hillman termed his efforts the "first definite national move to carry out the plans favored by the Amalgamated for the last fifteen years."

By 1931 Hillman actively called for creation of a formal corporate state structure. Speaking at a conference held in March with leading progressive Senators, Hillman demanded that government step in to alleviate bread lines and the plight of the poor, which he attributed to the lack of "planning in industry." Hillman called for creation of an "economic council for industry" similar to the one Bernard Baruch operated during the First World War. The council should have "representatives of all the parts that make up industry management, capital, labor and government representing the public," and should be empowered to make recommendations to both industrial leaders and Congress.

From 1931 on Hillman became the main labor advocate of a corporate society. Gerard Swope and other industrialists favored mobilization of industries into trade associations that would regulate and stabilize prices and production. Hillman's model differed only in that it demanded labor representation as an equal factor in industry. "Planless production for uncoordinated distribution" was attacked by Hillman as the "core of our individualistic social system." Instead of laissez-faire one had to substitute "purposive intervention in social processes," and begin to think "in terms of economic planning" by creating a national economic council. Hillman made it clear that he did not favor socialist planning in which capitalists would play no role. Rather, he envisioned a corporate state in which authority would rest in a "national house of industrial representatives" on which both management and labor leaders sat.

Hillman had come to sound like Hoover in the 1920's, since he emphasized a joint employer-worker attack on instability by "increasing individual productivity, reducing cost, eliminating waste . . . and taking advantage of the new technical advances in industry." Unions would assume greatly increased responsibility for the quantity and quality of output, which meant "a revolutionary change in the attitude of the worker toward his job." But for this to work nationally, a government "instrumentality" was needed to "guide a national economic plan." The national program that would gain Hillman's favor was the NRA, and Hillman became its most ardent champion. NRA, he wrote, provided "for a measure of national economic planning, in business enterprise and productive activity." It could be used by labor to throw open union doors, and hence "unorganized industries and areas must be invaded by union organizers. Existing and functioning organizations," Hillman warned, "must abandon the narrow craft outlook. Labor must think of itself in terms of the whole working class."

Speaking to the 1934 Amalgamated convention, Hillman told delegates that NRA was " a new constitution for both labor and industry." By eliminating the sweatshop employer it provided "a basis of equality for labor." Hillman predicted that NRA would "remain a permanent part of our industrial life," because it recognized the "need for planning" and because the codes of fair competition made "further development possible." NRA gave labor "representation in the governing of industry and it assigns to the government the place of an umpire." Roosevelt had seen the need to create an organization representing "all elements in industry." NRA, Hillman asserted, proved that a social organization could be changed within its own shell. It aimed at a coordinated balance of production, and saw the "fundamental necessity for government regulation and supervision of industrial processes and of economic forces." It was "the beginning of national economic planning," and those who wanted "to ride into the land of promise" had to first "lay the road." Moreover, employers through NRA were "becoming accustomed to consider the demands of labor an integral part of the industrial situation."

In March of 1935 Hillman cited NRA as proof that "we have come to maturity as a nation in our understanding and in our handling of the problems arising out of a complex economic system." Workers knew that they had "an economic interest with employers in the successful operation of the establishment." That is why they favored increased productivity, and denied the autocratic employer who held that business was their own exclusive affair. It was to NRA's credit that it recognized the social "nature of industry." It truly forecast "a new birth in industrial relations," and the "responsible labor leaders" had learned "the lessons of cooperative relations under the New Deal." They knew that "the source of our prosperity is increased production," and Hillman guaranteed that labor thought in these terms whenever it strived to gain a just share of the product. As he put it, "organized labor, with the full feeling that 'it belongs' and that everyone recognizes it is an essential part in industry, will cooperate to make it more efficient, more productive, more humane."

Hillman's support of NRA was unique in that he backed its extension long after the majority of organized labor had concluded that NRA was resulting in the spread of company unions. Attacking those Congressional liberals who blamed NRA for monopolistic price-fixing, Hillman compared them with those who favored ending unions because they were not perfect. Asking radicals "not to hurry things beyond their natural course," Hillman asked that labor support NRA and demand increased authority to "impose a code on every industry."

Hillman then worked in Washington to effect a rapprochement between dissident labor leaders and the administration. The labor leaders agreed to stop attacking NRA, Philip Murray was appointed to the National Industrial Recovery Board and the administration began to show a sympathetic attitude to the pending Wagner labor disputes bill. More important, Hillman's close associate Robert Soule revealed that Hillman began "discussions which may lead to the evolution of a labor organization which can cooperate with the government in place of the American Federation of Labor." Labor, adopting this path, would "have ready access to the White House."

Hillman had begun to take steps that would lead to representation for industrial unions in the corporate state. The industrial unions, he assured all, would function responsibly. In a 1937 interview Hillman stressed that the CIO emphasized "that industry is based on three factors of equal importance," and that the "labor factor" was entitled to a fair share. The CIO was "not a movement to change the competitive system," but was, rather, trying "to make the system workable." It asked only a "proportionate share of the progress of industry" in which labor was one of the three "vital and participating elements." Commenting accurately that Hillman subscribed to the "principle enunciated by the late Samuel Gompers," the interviewer quoted Hillman as advising that after a contract was signed, "every employee should lend himself to complete cooperation with the employer in the interest of efficient management of industry." Responsible labor shared a set of common economic goals with the employer. Hillman stressed that the CIO objected in principle to sit-down strikes. He "chuckled" as he told the press that "Wall Street is beginning to recognize the CIO."

Hillman always stressed that if studied, industry would see that the CIO recognized the need for a prosperous industry. In fact, the CIO had contributed to this end "in choosing the form of industrial organization." It had rejected craft unionism precisely because "it permits of no responsibility in the relationship between labor and management." Sounding like Gerard Swope, Hillman pointed out that no employer could enter into seventeen agreements with seventeen unions, and be sure of avoiding jurisdictional strikes "which made it impossible to have responsible leadership." By 1933 Hillman was explaining that "efficiency in the men's clothing industry" had reached its highest point. The union had "helped many manufacturers to introduce efficiency methods because" at the same time they helped their members by enabling the employers to stay in business. Hillman added, *"Industry-wide union organization is, of course, essential if cooperation and efficiency are to be brought to this degree."*

While Sidney Hillman was leading the industrial workers into absorption in the corporate capitalist system and towards political commitment to the Roosevelt Administration, some criticism was beginning to emerge from labor's ranks. It came, however, from the remaining descendants of the Gompers machine in the AFL. Men trained by Gompers, such as Matthew Woll, president of the Photo-Engravers and an AFL Vice-President, and the old prowar socialist William English Walling, were two who quickly became disenchanted with NRA and became outspoken critics of the New Deal. Originally both had hoped that NRA would lead to a new partnership between equal factors in industry. As it turned out, workers were not given equal protection, and no guarantee existed that labor was to be organized as efficiently as the employers were in trade associations. Woll and Walling dissented from Hugh Johnson's belief that strikes were economic sabotage against the government. They defended the right to strike as the sole assurance workers had as a preventative to compulsory labor. As for the plea of Johnson that labor be subject to government control, Woll and Walling viewed that demand as one pointing "in the direction of Fascism" and as the "opposite of self-government in industry."

In 1935 Woll emerged as a full-scale critic of the New Deal. While he favored an economic congress that would represent functional groups, Woll wanted it to be voluntary and labor to be afforded equal representation. NRA gave only a "semblance of recognition" to all factors. It worked not to create unity, but to accentuate differences and to "undermine every vestige of concord in the functional groups in industry." Industry was functioning under a form of "capitalistic syndicalism" in which labor had no direct voice. Under NRA codes monopoly had grown, cartelization of the economy had been encouraged and "corporate control had been permitted to strengthen its grip upon the economic life of the nation." Woll felt that while NRA held out the promise of a corporate society, the goal had been subverted by its actual practice. Labor "might well assert," he wrote, "that the seed of Fascism had been transplanted" and that political government reigned supreme. The NRA's system of "compulsory trade association, of code membership, and of code observance borders closely upon the corporate or syndicalist form of organization characterized by Fascism in Italy." Labor might "well be concerned regarding its future hope and policy to deal effectually with such a strongly entrenched and cartelized system of industry."

Rather than urge compliance with code authorities, Woll suggested that labor should remove its support from the concept of NRA itself. "Not anywhere this side of Fascism, or complete control by the Government," Woll wrote, "could code provisions be adequately enforced." Woll worried that the unions might become the equivalent of Fascist labor groups, in which industries were organized "along lines somewhat akin to what has taken place in each of our major industries operating under a code." In Italy labor was subordinate to the state in the guise of governmentally controlled unions. Woll explained that "the cartelization of American industry which has gone on under codes is a familiar story in the early history of Fascist Italy." "Are we," Woll queried, "heading toward a business Fascism?"

Another aspect of New Deal policy questioned by Woll was American foreign policy. Woll argued that an economic surplus was being invested abroad instead of being put to use at home. While the internationalist view was "put before the world as a form of idealism," it was sustained "mainly by private international banking and trading interests." Implying that internationalism actually meant interventionism, Woll saw no relation between "the internationalist idea of free trade and peace." On the contrary, "economic activities of private interests outside of national boundaries were likely to "carry us toward war than toward peace." Many plans for economic ties were meant to "cover growing economic conflicts" due to foreign investments.

Commenting that many saw the "chief cure for the present depression and for unemployment . . . in the development of the export market," Woll dissented from Cordell Hull's path of gaining security through increase of reciprocal trade treaties. "The arguments of those who made possible" that legislation, Woll wrote, "are precisely the same as have been used by all those who see the solution of our present economic problem not in the increase of American purchasing power, but in plunging our nation into the mad and illusory race for foreign markets." While Woll's vision of creating a viable home market for existing surpluses was marred by the faulty argument that the export trade was unimportant for the economy, he did not hesitate to demand creation of an order that did no have to seek its prosperity through foreign expansion. "To attempt any radical extension of our foreign trade through 'reciprocal tariffs,' " he stressed, "is not only likely to get us into economic conflict with the nations excluded . . . but involves us in difficulties due to 'most favored nation' provisions." The only solution was at home. Woll hoped that capitalism would prove itself by developing full employment through a highly developed home market. Rising surpluses had to be absorbed by the home market "through increasing the income of wage-earners."

The 1930's revealed the apparently strange picture of conservative craft union leaders developing a fairly rigorous critique of the direction taken by the leaders of corporate capitalism. They urged that problems be solved at home, and opposed the expansionist course of the New Deal abroad and its corporatism at home. During these years industrial unions were flourishing under a New Deal aegis. Their leaders renounced a critical approach, and urged the absorption of labor into the very mechanism of the corporate state. Although the AFL leaders began to criticize, their reliance on craft organization made their critique irrelevant and allowed it to go virtually unnoticed. Most misread their views as the desperate pleading of old-line conservatives. Liberals and radical forgot that the militant tactics of the CIO soon ended, and as William A. Williams has explained, the "labor movement rather rapidly settled down into the syndicalist pattern that was by then clearly emerging from the excitement and flux of the New Deal."

The labor movement and its leadership chose to align itself with American business and its path of foreign expansion. In exchange labor received government protection as it entered a stage of rapid growth. The labor leaders developed an ideological view of reality in which they asserted that the old capitalist system with its manifold problems had basically changed. In failing to point out the fallacies of this view, and by failing to explain that labor's victories were byproducts of continued expansion abroad, American radicals quietly forfeited their responsibility of providing a radical alternative.

While radicals worked hard to organize workers into industrial unions and at times won the leadership of CIO branches, they unwittingly became the allies of those whose concern was to fit labor into the corporate structure. John L. Lewis explained in December of 1935 that the "dangerous state of affairs" might very well have led to " 'class consciousness' " and "revolution as well." Lewis hoped that it could "be avoided," and he pledged that his own industrial union was "doing everything in their power to make the system work and thereby avoid it." The CIO leaders gained the aid of the left in the attempt to make the system work. Once it was on its feet the services of the left were no longer appreciated, and radicals were purged from the labor movement with only a ripple of protest emanating from the rank and file. Labor's postwar position of acquiescence in the policies of different conservative administrations had been assured, and the corporate ideology of American labor leaders remained dominant and unchallenged.

chapter 2

The American State:
The Private Use of Public Power

In Chapter 1 the structure and dynamics of the American economy were considered in some detail. The evidence clearly suggested that corporate capitalism represents a "private" government. The decisions made in the corporate sector have as great an impact upon our lives as those made in the "public" sector, perhaps more. Corporate decisions can bring affluence or poverty to any region of the United States or the world; they can eliminate occupations (and the livelihoods of thousands of dependent families); they can foster or retard technological innovation. Yet almost all this power ultimately resides in financial institutions, large corporate stockholders and boards of directors, and high-level management. Under ordinary circumstances, there are no possibilities for petition, referendum, and recall by those who are the "subjects" in this basically feudal structure. When the old "government" is replaced by retirement or death, its offspring, the inheritors of great wealth, assume the mantle of corporate responsibility.[1]

---

[1] While great fortunes have been made since World Wars I and II, the bulk of American corporate wealth is based upon the accumulation of assets by family dynasties which began their economic ascent in the late nineteenth century or earlier. Ferdinand Lundberg, *The Rich and the Super-Rich: A Study in the Power of Money Today* (New York: Lyle Stuart, Inc., 1968), pp. 38–98, 132–203.

Many of the heirs have already been socialized by formal and informal education in elite private schools, private clubs, and summer and winter resorts.[2] They have presumably developed a "class consciousness" which permits them to understand the larger needs of the system that sustains the privileges of private government.

In the face of the power of private government, social analysts who adhere to democratic principles have sought desperately to discover a countervailing force or set of forces which could check, if not override, the influence of the capitalist class. In this connection, the articles by Ralph Miliband and Ronald Radosh in Chapter 1 seem to eliminate organized labor and the emergence of a "soulful corporation" run by autonomous and "soulful" managers or technocrats as effective countervailing forces.

Given the impotence or irrelevance of potential agencies of change within the economic structure, the only institutionalized power that could realistically be used to serve the interests of the masses of Americans and to validate the characterization of the United States as a democratic society resides in the state.[3] The accumulation of wealth and the growing inequality of economic power between social classes have brought about a paradoxical situation where state power, so feared in the classical liberal tradition, has become the only potential source of freedom and security. Accordingly, this chapter will consider whether the formal structure of the American state, the informal modes of influencing public policy, and the functions of the government and other state institutions have and can provide opportunities to effectively oppose corporate power and shape American institutions to promote "the general welfare."[4]

One of the major debates in political science and sociology has raged over the question of state power. On the one hand, the dominant "pluralist" tradition, while rejecting the notion that the American state is primarily subject to the influence of mass participation in decision-making, accepts the view that state power is wielded in behalf of many different competing and co-existing organized interest groups. Among these interest groups, according to the pluralists, are business, labor, ethnic, and religious groups. These groups may have "spheres of influence," but no single one has decisive influence in all spheres of state activity.

The pluralist position as articulated by David Truman, Robert Dahl,

[2] G. William Domhoff, *The Higher Circles: The Governing Class in America* (New York: Random House, Inc., 1970), pp. 9–32, 57–99. See E. Digby Baltzell, *Philadelphia Gentleman: The Making of a National Upper Class* (New York: The Free Press, 1958), for an historical analysis of the development and maintenance of a "business aristocracy" during the nineteenth and twentieth centuries.

[3] The "state" consists of the executive, legislative, and judicial branches of the federal, state, and municipal governments as well as the governmental administrative bureaucracies and the armed forces.

[4] The primary emphasis will be on the power of the federal government, particularly the executive and legislative branches. Power in local communities, although the focus of enormous research efforts, has taken on secondary importance with the growth of a *national* political economy and culture. See Arthur Vidich and Joseph Bensman, *Small Town in Mass Society* (New York: Doubleday & Company, Inc., 1960). Don Martindale and R. Galen Hanson, *Small Town and the Nation: The Conflict of Local and Translocal Forces* (Westport, Conn.: Greenwood, 1969). The political role of the military and the judiciary will be considered in somewhat greater depth in Chapters 3 and 9, respectively.

Nelson Polsby, and Arnold Rose does not deny the existence of elites.[5] It merely argues that no *single* elite group or social class, generally conceived as the business class, has the power to consistently use the state for its own ends and prevent other groups from using the state to threaten its vital interests. Pluralist theory maintains that certain state decisions which seem to benefit the business class are not necessarily taken because of business pressure, but because they are perceived as being beneficial to society on the whole. Those who deny that America operates in a pluralist manner must present evidence to show that the elite's preferences systematically override the preferences and interests of the nonelites.

The modern pluralist perspective on national state power developed primarily in response to several important studies of life in small American communities. In the 1920s and 1930s Robert and Helen Lynd published two books on power in a small midwestern town. They argued that many aspects of life in "Middletown" (Muncie, Indiana) were strongly influenced by the economic elite of the town, and, in particular, one extremely wealthy family.[6] In the early 1950s Floyd Hunter, following the lead of the Lynds, wrote a book which attempted to document the inordinate amount of power exercised by economic elites in the political affairs of "Regional City" (Atlanta, Georgia).[7] Hunter used a "reputational" methodology; that is, he relied primarily upon the subjective evaluations of Regional City "influentials" in determining who held power. Then he interviewed those perceived to be powerful to understand the workings of the power structure. Although neither the Lynds' nor Hunter's work denies that the power of elites are limited in some ways, vocal critics have accused these writers of suggesting that elites had nearly total control of the cities studied.[8] In this way the critics were able to set up straw men who could be easily toppled with evidence that denied monolithic and total elite power, although it indicated that a great deal of power was held by economic elites in local communities. In such a manner pluralism became the hegemonous doctrine in social science.

While the pluralist-elitist argument was originally based on empirical studies of local power, the conclusions of each camp were applied *by analogy* to the issue of national state power. Almost no significant empirical research on this topic was undertaken until the mid-1950s. C. Wright Mills' *The Power Elite,* published in 1956, was a major empirical work on national state power which directly challenged the dominant pluralist perspective.[9] Mills distinguished himself from Marxists and pluralists by denying that

---

[5] David Truman, *The Governmental Process: Political Interests and Public Opinion* (New York: Alfred A. Knopf, 1951). Robert Dahl, *Who Governs?* (New Haven, Conn.: Yale University Press, 1961). Nelson Polsby, *Community Power and Political Theory* (New Haven, Conn.: Yale University Press, 1963). Arnold Rose, *The Power Structure: Political Processes in American Society* (New York: Oxford University Press, 1967).

[6] Robert and Helen Lynd, *Middletown* (New York: Harcourt Brace Jovanovich, Inc., 1929); *Middletown in Transition: A Study in Cultural Conflicts* (New York: Harcourt Brace Jovanovich, Inc., 1937).

[7] Floyd Hunter, *Community Power Structure* (Chapel Hill, N.C.: University of North Carolina Press, 1952).

[8] Allan Rosenbaum, "Community Power and Political Theory: A Case of Misperception," *Berkeley Journal of Sociology,* vol. 12 (1967), pp. 91–116.

[9] C. Wright Mills, *The Power Elite* (New York: Oxford University Press, 1956).

economic elites, the masses, or a multitude of *conflicting* interest groups dominated society. Rather, he saw a triumvirate formed by economic elites joined with autonomous political and military elites. While he recognized that the elites in each of the three institutional orders—economic, political, and military—frequently differed on small issues, Mills believed they reached consensus on major ones such as foreign policy. He felt that common class backgrounds, interests, and personal associations created preconditions for cooperation among the three institutional elites.

Although Mills rejected pluralism as a theory of national power, he felt it might accurately describe the local political scene and the struggle of interest groups in the congress, the "middle levels of power." Decisions at these levels had significant consequences for many people, but not the overwhelming import of decisions made at the highest levels. Finally, Mills stated, below the middle levels of power were the masses, almost totally powerless on national and local issues because of their elite-manipulated ignorance and lack of organization.

Mills' book was met with great hostility by traditional academics, established journalists, and social commentators.[10] His professional career was hampered because of his inability to get research support. Nevertheless, Mills was probably the most influential American sociologist of the past generation in stimulating serious thought about national power.

Since Mills' death in 1962 at the age of forty-six his work has been carried on by a growing number of scholars in different disciplines. My article on elitist and Marxist critiques of pluralist theory attempts to summarize the arguments presented by several social scientists whose recent work bears upon the questions Mills so forcefully raised. This article documents the predominant power of the business class throughout the twentieth century, while questioning the neutrality of the state structure. The article does not cover the military role in any depth, but in the introductory essay to Chapter 3, I argue that Mills was mistaken in his emphasis upon the military's power. The article also tries to address the methodological objections that pluralists such as Robert Dahl have made to the "positional" approach of Mills and other elitists, who draw conclusions about power primarily from analysis of the social backgrounds of decision-makers. In essence the article supports what I call a neo-Marxist perspective in criticizing both pluralism and elitism. The discussion of the role of the capitalist state under social democratic control is particularly crucial in considering the limitations even anticapitalist governments face because of the pressure of economic elites to maintain the capitalist system and their privileged position within it.

While my article discusses the processes by which a small but powerful sector of the economic elite has exercised influence and decisive power over state action, it does not address itself to some questions typically raised by scholars and laymen who are largely unfamiliar with the solid literature in political science on the electoral process, the role of Congress, and so on. My concerns presuppose an understanding of the structure and process of

---

[10] G. William Domhoff and Hoyt Ballard, ed., *C. Wright Mills and the Power Elite* (Boston: The Beacon Press, 1968).

government in the United States and dwell instead upon the often neglected forces that *have* acted and *can* act upon *any* government in capitalist society. For the purposes of this text, however, it may be worthwhile to summarize briefly the development of America's republican form of government and the role of that structure in minimizing challenges to economic elites.

The Founding Fathers are often seen as having a great commitment to democracy in contrast to the leaders of the authoritarian regimes so prevalent around the world at the time of the American Revolution and the writing of the Constitution. It is true that the preeminent revolutionary and post-revolutionary leaders believed far more than their foreign contemporaries in a certain amount of popular influence upon government. Nevertheless, whatever matters these men disagreed on in forming a postrevolutionary polity, they were united in their hostility to direct rule by the masses and majoritarian principles.

Virtually all the creators of the Constitution were men of extraordinary wealth and status. They were public security holders, slaveholders, real estate and land speculators, manufacturers, shippers, planters, investors, and lenders. They were highly educated for their times and eschewed provincialism in favor of a nationalist consciousness rooted in the strengthening of capitalism and republicanism.[11]

The American Revolution, though relatively mild in comparison to the French Revolution, still stirred up great mass feelings against privilege. The abolition of feudal rights, seizure of Tory estates, abolition of debts owed to British merchants, and the acts of violence against authority in general frightened American political and economic elites.[12] Shay's Rebellion in 1786—in which debtors, largely farmers, artisans, and laborers, attempted a military uprising against local elites—was the most spectacular example of insurrectionary sentiment and stimulated the development of the Constitution to create a national society and contain popular discontent.

If one examines the debates of the Constitutional Convention of 1787, it is clear that the Founding Fathers wished to develop a political structure that would ensure the rights of property, including the ownership of slaves, above all. Their concern for liberty was something of an afterthought, and, in fact, the Bill of Rights was *amended* to the Constitution after mounting concern by the citizenry, including some elite figures, jeopardized the Constitution's chances for ratification.

The final draft of the Constitution was a masterpiece in terms of the political and economic needs of a highly class-conscious propertied elite. The Constitution provided for federal assessment and collection of taxes which were needed to create an infrastructure for capitalist development as well as to repay the war debts of the revolutionary government. The creditors

[11] Thomas Dye and L. H. Zeigler, *The Irony of Democracy: An Uncommon Introduction to American Politics* (Belmont, Calif.: Wadsworth Publishing Company, Inc., 1970), pp. 23–55, provides an excellent portrait of the Founding Fathers, their social backgrounds, ideology, and political behavior.

[12] Jesse Lemisch, "The American Revolution Seen from the Bottom Up," in Barton Bernstein, ed., *Towards a New Past: Dissenting Essays in American History* (New York: Vintage Books, 1969), pp. 3–45.

were, of course, the nation's financial magnates such as Robert Morris, who feared that local governments if left to their own devices would repudiate these debts. A provision in Article VI linked taxation with debt collection by stating that "All the debts contracted and engagements entered into before the adoption of this Constitution shall be valid against the United States under this Constitution as under the Confederation." While they endorsed taxation, the Founding Fathers opposed income and property taxes and favored placing the burden on consumers in the form of excise taxes and custom duties. The provision that taxes could be levied only on the basis of population, and not on wealth, inhibited the development of any form of progressive taxation until the twentieth century.

An important constitutional feature was federal power over interstate commerce; this prevented states from erecting trade barriers which would affect commerce between the states of the Union. The federal government also was given the sole right to coin, print, and regulate the value of money; to pass copyright and patent laws to protect authors and inventors; as well as other rights that helped the business class to obtain an integrated national market.

The political needs of economic elites were satisfied in specific substantive provisions of the Constitution as well as in the creation of mechanisms for political change. The federal power to raise armies and subordinate state and local militias to federal authority was designed to insure adequate social control in case of domestic insurrection as well as to create a powerful military force to protect the nation from foreign enemies. A substantial naval presence was considered vital for the protection of American overseas trade, which from the outset was perceived as essential in maintaining domestic prosperity and social stability.

The "supremacy clause" of Article VI was perhaps the most significant portion of the Constitution because it made federal law and the Constitution the ultimate sources of authority, overriding state and local autonomy except in matters not specifically enumerated in the Constitution or federal law. This clause permitted the national government to dominate the financial, commercial, military, and political affairs of the nation.

Because the Founding Fathers were interested in creating a document that would maintain and augment their class privileges, they were farsighted enough to include procedural provisions in the Constitution which would make it extremely difficult for popular majorities to bring about rapid and extreme social change.

Almost all major national political institutions were not under direct popular control. Voters could directly elect Representatives to Congress, but Senators were chosen by state legislators. The President was selected by electors, who were chosen in any way state legislators wished. Federal judges, and most significantly, justices of the Supreme Court, were appointed by the President for life terms. The Founding Fathers felt that such a selection procedure would remove government from the "tyranny of the majority" and place responsibility in the hands of men of wealth and prestige. The separation of powers between the executive, legislative, and judicial branches of government was also conceived largely as a bulwark against mass political influence, since power was not concentrated in any one branch. Even if the electorate managed to send radical legislators to Congress, for example, the President could veto threatening bills, and, if necessary, the Court could declare them unconstitutional.

The fact that the President served for four years, Senators for six (one third of the Senate being replaced every two years), and Representatives for two insured that any popular desire for radical social change could not be realized rapidly. The *lifetime* tenure of federal and Supreme Court justices meant, of course, that the judiciary would be the last stronghold of elite power if the legislative and executive branches of government were controlled by the masses. After *Marbury* v. *Madison* (1803) the Supreme Court granted itself judicial review with the power to interpret the Constitution and invalidate not only the state laws and constitutions but congressional laws which violated the Constitution. This sweeping set of powers was used throughout the nineteenth century to invalidate legislative limits on property rights and to outlaw trade union activity.[13]

The ideology of federalism, as manifested in the Constitution and the *Federalist Papers,* was translated into institutional reality because of the enormous economic, political, and organizational power of the Founding Fathers and their elite supporters. A major handicap of anti-Federalists was the fact that a large proportion of the population was legally barred from engaging in political activity.[14] Most states had property qualifications for voting and holding office. It is estimated that of the entire male population at the time of constitutional ratification, 40 percent—of whom half were slaves and half were poor white tenant farmers and indentured servants—were totally disenfranchised. Only the financial, commercial, and professional elites were actually involved in political affairs. The small middle class had some voting power, while "freeholders"—the great bulk of Americans who owned small farms and could vote—were too preoccupied with physical survival and isolated to even bother voting. It is believed that only 5 percent of the population and one sixth of the adult males actually participated in the ratification of the Constitution, with about 60,000 of the 160,000 votes cast against its adoption.

The Federalist domination of the national government was not seriously challenged until the Jacksonian era. Jefferson's election brought to the presidency a man of somewhat more democratic tastes, but one who was nevertheless committed to government by men of property, particularly landed property. "Jacksonian Democracy," as it has been called, did involve a considerable reformation of the political structure by incorporating Western elites into the governing class and widening the franchise and office-holding rights to include virtually all white adult males. Jackson was opposed to the Eastern elite and sought not the leveling of social classes, but a "natural aristocracy" based upon achievement rather than family background. His supporters were wealthy Western businessmen and landowners as well as the beleaguered "common man," those who were both rising and declining economically.[15] In addition to extending political rights to almost all adult

---

[13] Arnold Paul, *Conservative Crisis and the Rule of Law: Attitudes of Bar and Bench, 1887–1895* (New York: Harper & Row, Publishers, 1969).
[14] Zeigler and Dye, *op. cit.*, pp. 25, 50–51. Lemisch, *op. cit.*, pp. 6–10.
[15] Michael Lebowitz, "The Jacksonians: Paradox Lost?" in Bernstein, *op. cit.*, pp. 65–89. Zeigler and Dye, *op. cit.*, pp. 64–67.

white males, Jackson introduced the popular election of presidential electors and discarded the older system of selection, which had left the method of choosing to the discretion of state legislators. This change in the structure of choosing government leaders was the last major political reform until the franchise was extended to blacks and women and United States Senators were chosen by popular vote (the last two reforms did not occur until the early twentieth century). While these structural changes in the process of electing public officials appeared to make the political system more open to nonelite influence, a combination of economic and social developments intertwined with the formal structure of government and the electoral process to insure continuing political domination by economic elites.

The pattern of economic growth after the Civil War consolidated the development of a rigidified class system characterized at the extremes by enormous wealth and abject poverty.[16] This rigidity permitted economic elites to amass the resources to finance political campaigns and influence legislation on an unprecedented scale. Moreover, the need for a large pool of cheap labor encouraged massive immigration, which accomplished as a side effect the destruction of any homogeneous working-class culture. Ethnic and racial groups, rather than uniting to combat increasingly miserable conditions in the factories and slums constantly competed with each other for scarce jobs and territory in the inner cities. The more resourceful and organized capitalist class was able to play sections of the under class off against each other and to maintain political rule. To some extent this was accomplished by what Bruce Johnson calls "internal stratification," the creation of "privileged" subgroups, often based upon race or ethnicity, in the working class.[17] The fragmentation of the working class has hindered militant trade unionism and political action to this day.

The formal characteristics of the government and electoral structure also played and still play an important role in preventing the diverse needs of class, regional, racial, and ethnic groupings from finding expression in viable new political parties. The absence of the European system of proportional representation in municipal, state, and national legislatures has contributed to the stabilization of a sterile two-party system characterized by preelectoral rather than postelectoral coalitions. The fact that the "winner takes all" in elections has meant that "extremist" demands have had to be moderated or eliminated in an attempt to appeal to the largest number of voters in any given election campaign.[18] Complex voting registration procedures[19] and the lack of financial resources have diminished working-class

[16] Stephan Thernstrom, *Poverty and Progress: Social Mobility in a Nineteenth Century City* (Cambridge, Mass.: Harvard University Press, 1964); "Urbanization, Migration and Social Mobility in Late Nineteenth Century America," in Bernstein, *op. cit.*, pp. 158–175.

[17] Bruce C. Johnson, "The Democratic Mirage: Notes toward a Theory of Politics," *Berkeley Journal of Sociology*, vol. 13 (1968), pp. 119–124. Also reprinted in this Chapter 9 of this text.

[18] While it is often assumed that interparty competition necessarily leads to the promotion of the will of the majority, it is more feasible to argue that mass preferences, already largely shaped by an elite-manipulated political socialization (see Chapter 9) are realized only to the extent that they do not go beyond the limits set

electoral participation. Finally, the seniority system in Congress, the numerous possibilities for legislative obstruction by Congressional minorities, and the powerful system of checks and balances by governmental branches have prevented nonelite power from being exercised, given the *conservative* context which it faced in the electoral arena.

The few alterations made in American government in the twentieth century have resulted largely from the pressures of America's world role and the increasing difficulty in maintaining a complex capitalist economic and social structure. A major modern trend is the decline of the power of Congress, which now more than ever acts at the command of the executive branch as a rubber stamp. The growth of the executive branch and, in particular, the increasing influence of appointed officials and "experts" have removed the government even further from the control of nonelites. Drawing upon the work of Weinstein, Domhoff, and Kolko, my article suggests how such developments have given economic elites major new opportunities for formal and informal governmental influence.

This chapter concludes with James O'Connor's detailed examination of the state budget, which shows the consequences of business domination of government. As stated in Chapter 1, capitalism is inherently unstable and constantly requires expansion to function properly. O'Connor documents how the power of taxation, so valued by the Founding Fathers, is employed today to strengthen corporate capitalism. The benefits nonelites appear to have derived from the actions of government in a given period are primarily a by-product of the dominant sector of the economic elite's pursuing its own long-run interests. Political struggle throughout American history has rarely pitted nonelites against elites. Rather it has involved interelite conflict— Northern businessmen versus Southern and Western landowners and businessmen; big businessmen versus small businessmen. In these historic confrontations nonelites have been largely powerless spectators whose inability to use government for their own needs has meant that America, more than any other capitalist society, has been a business civilization.

---

by the ideology of political candidates' financial backers; general corporate pressure; and the political, economic, and status needs of party officials and administrative bureaucrats. Richard Hamilton, "Notes on the Study of Mass Political Behavior," unpublished ms. (Department of Sociology, University of Wisconsin, 1968), pp. 2–11. See also Richard Dawson and James Robinson, "Inter-Party Competition, Economic Variables, and Welfare Policies in the American States," *Journal of Politics*, vol. 2 (1963), pp. 265–289. Thomas Dye, *Politics, Economics, and the Public: Policy Outcomes in the American States* (Skokie, Ill.: Rand McNally & Company, 1966). Ralph Miliband, *The State in Capitalist Society: An Analysis of the Western System of Power* (New York: Basic Books, Inc., 1969).

[19] Walter Burnham, "The Changing Shape of the American Political Universe," *American Political Science Review*, vol. 59 (March, 1965), pp. 7–28.

[20] Paul Baran, *The Political Economy of Growth* (New York: Monthly Review Press, 1957), pp. 87–133, complements O'Connor's analysis by indicating why government in capitalist society is limited to the amount and kind of expenditures which do not interfere with the interests of private enterprise. His work suggests that the "welfare" state must primarily serve the capitalist class.

Milton Mankoff

POWER IN ADVANCED CAPITALIST SOCIETY: A REVIEW ESSAY ON RECENT ELITIST AND MARXIST CRITICISM OF PLURALIST THEORY

Men make their own history, but they do not make it just as they please; they do not make it under circumstances chosen by themselves, but under circumstances directly encountered, given, and transmitted from the past. The tradition of all dead generations weighs like a nightmare on the brain of the living.—Karl Marx, "The Eighteenth Brumaire of Louis Bonaparte"

It has been said that in war truth is the first casualty. Yet the escalation of the war in Vietnam and the conflagration of the cities may well have served to reveal a great deal about the structure of power in American society that might otherwise have remained obscured during an era of tranquility. The liberal consensus of the late 1950's and early 1960's made it possible to "refute" Mills' *The Power Elite* (1956) merely by referring to Dahl's (1961) study of political power in a small American city. The crisis of the middle and late 1960's has inevitably focused the attention of social scientists toward national and even international power.

While American political science long ago replaced classical democratic theory with the theory of "democratic elitism" (Bachrach, 1967), in which government "by the people" is replaced by the competition of various organized interest groups for governmental favor, the dominant pluralist tradition denies that any one interest can marshal the power regularly to impose its will upon the larger society through decisive control over governmental decision-making. Thus, the business class is seen as only one of a series of powerful interests attempting to influence the polity and the shape of the social order. Today, pluralist theory is being challenged by a resurgence of the elitist perspective and, even more, by the development of a sophisticated empirically based Marxist approach to power in American society.

The present essay will attempt to present the basic thrust of contemporary "revisionism" as manifested in the recent work of elitist and Marxist critics of pluralism. In order to gain greater understanding of the decisive power of the capitalist class in America . . . it will be necessary to transcend the limitations of American history to some extent. Thus, I shall examine

Reprinted, with deletions and slight revision, from Milton Mankoff, "Power in Advanced Capitalist Society: A Review Essay on Recent Elitist and Marxist Criticism of Pluralist Theory," *Social Problems*, vol. 17 (Winter 1970), pp. 418–430, by permission of Milton Mankoff, *Social Problems*, and THE SOCIETY FOR THE STUDY OF SOCIAL PROBLEMS. Milton Mankoff teaches sociology at Queens College, City University of New York. He has written articles on the American student movement and social deviance.

the important comparative study of national power in the advanced capitalist societies of the west by Miliband (1969). . . . Comparative studies of this kind illustrate the parochialism of research based solely on the American experience which precludes the opportunity to study the *performance* of avowedly anti-capitalist governments operating within the context of advanced capitalist societies. By such study it is possible to make a more thorough test of pluralist theory.[1]

Pluralism vs. Elitism: The Hollow Debate

One of the major criticisms leveled by pluralists against Mills and other elitists has been that they employed a faulty methodology in assessing the structure of power. According to Dahl (1958), the ruling elite hypothesis can only be tested if:

1. The hypothetical ruling elite is a well defined group.
2. There is a fair sample of cases involving key political decisions in which the preferences of the hypothetical ruling elite run counter to those of any other likely group that might be suggested.
3. In such cases, the preferences of the elite regularly prevail.

Given the fact that Mills, for example, never adequately described the goals of the "power elite" it was difficult for him to demonstrate that their political decisions ran counter to the preferences of most members of society. While claiming that the power elite was not "responsible" to the masses, Mills never discussed what responsibility would entail. The lack of a decisional methodology followed from this inability to articulate the goals of the elite.

In response to the demand that power structure studies employ a decisional methodology rather than reputational or positional methods, Bachrach and Baratz (1962; 1963), among others, claimed that:

1. Social issues threatening elite interests have never become the focus of political decision-making because elites have co-opted non-elites through ideological hegemony so that a "false consciousness" is created among the non-elites.
2. Even when ideological dissensus existed, the non-elites, fearing that they could not prevail in political competition, would not attempt to raise issues publicly.
3. Even if issues were raised publicly, various forms of ideological, bureaucratic, or coercive methods could be brought to bear by elites to crush opposition in order to avoid making certain political decisions which would threaten their interests.

---

[1] The pluralist perspective on national power has been articulated in *The Power Structure* (1967) by Arnold Rose. Rose's work has received considerable praise (Domhoff, 1969: 36) and will serve as the best example of this genre.

In this theoretical breakthrough the "neo-elitists," as they have been called, seemed to argue for a historically based research program which would examine in great detail the origins and development of the institutional context within which contemporary men "make their own history." Pluralist theory is incredibly ahistorical, as if power struggles were conducted on Robinson Crusoe's island or in the world of William Golding's novel, *Lord of the Flies*. All current participants in competition over scarce resources (political, economic, military) appear to be stripped of any built-in advantages afforded by their strategic location in an ongoing society with a particular economic and cultural history. When the "tradition of all dead generations" is mentioned on occasion (Rose, 1967: 18–20, 38, 492) it is only to indicate the "lack of alternatives." The human economic and political decisions which created "tradition" are viewed as irrelevant. The tradition is now seemingly fixed for all time. Thus, for example, when political competition is limited, even by coercion, to parties willing to offer only different programs for governing the *same* economic system, pluralist theory has no difficulty denying the existing economic elite has any decisive advantages in the competitive struggle.

Unfortunately, the neo-elitist insight about the importance of non-decisions in studying power was obscured by the fact that, once again, there was no serious attempt to define the goals of elites or the historical context within which they operated. Thus, a potentially fruitful methodology, albeit one which would require extensive historical analysis, was never fully employed. Instead, neo-elitists spoke of power in the same formalistic way pluralists did, considering the possibilities for power without rule by economic elites, but never spelling out the historical basis for such possibilities.

Recently the weakness of purely formalistic neo-elitist theorizing such as that of Bachrach and Baratz has been exposed by an equally formalistic critique (Merelman, 1968). It is impossible to dwell at great length here on the numerous logical flaws Merelman attributes to neo-elitist theory. Nevertheless, his own critique ultimately fails because it suffers from the same devotion to logical possibilities instead of historical analysis. For example, at one point Merelman finds fault with Bachrach and Baratz's contention that economic dominants often abstain from certain political issues because they are trivial.

> . . . Bachrach and Baratz have no difficulty believing that economic dominants who take no role in a decision do so from their own disinterest in the issues at stake. However, it may instead be true that, anticipating a defeat, they downgrade the importance of the issues. Rationalization is a ubiquitous and powerful defense mechanism.

In analyzing Merelman's remarks it is indeed *logically* possible that economic elites might rationalize away anticipated political defeat by playing down the significance of threatening public issues. Because Merelman does not give a meaningful historical example to illustrate this possibility, his point is of little value. If the political issue at stake involved nationalizing the elite's property, as it has in many historical cases, though not in America during recent times, Merelman would be unlikely to encounter the disinterest of economic elites. Thus, when economic elites appear to be disinterested in a political decision it is more than likely that it *is* because the issue is not threatening to their interest.

Capitalism and Class Consciousness

It is in the light of the prevailing poverty of pluralist and elitist theory that James Weinstein's *Corporate Ideal in the Liberal State: 1900–1918* (1969), G. William Domhoff's *Who Rules America?* (1967) and his more recent work (Domhoff, 1969), and Gabriel Kolko's *The Roots of American Foreign Policy: An Analysis of Power and Purpose* (1969) represent an important step forward in the study of national power in American society and its consequences for domestic and international government policy. These books make explicit the fact that America is a capitalist society, that is, it has an economic system where the major portion of economic activity is conducted on the basis of the private ownership and control of the means of production and financial institutions and the private appropriation of economic surplus. Preserving capitalism has been the primary goal of *the most articulate and politically powerful sector of the economic elite* during the 20th century because it is inextricably tied to the maintenance of class privilege (i.e., a disproportionate share of world and national wealth and its translation into power, status, and increased life chances for the members of the economic elite and their progeny). In the political arena they have successfully prevailed over the potentially threatening opposition of less powerful and enlightened economic elites, labor, and radical dissenters, at home and abroad.[2]

The theoretical and methodological importance of discussing the capitalist nature of American society and the role and purpose of the leading sectors of the capitalist class in the society cannot be over-emphasized. To begin with, it becomes possible for scholars to develop adequate criteria for what constitutes "key political decisions," and it raises the more fundamental question: How important are *political* decisions made by governments and the administrative and judicial sectors of the state in distributing and redistributing wealth, life chances, status, etc. compared to the *economic* decisions of financiers and corporate owners and managers? When banks raise interest rates, when corporations cut production, invest in foreign markets, transfer capital from one geographic region to another, or raise prices, the social fabric is probably affected considerably more than it is when governments carry out welfare reforms. For example, if we consider the relative share of national income appropriated by employees (in wages

[2] It is not necessary for non-elites to express socialist ideology to make them an objective threat to the hegemony of the capitalist class. The survival of pre-industrial values can be just as disruptive of industrial capitalism as Marxist ones. If the question of redistribution *per se* was not articulated by non-elites very often an examination of the gap between office-seekers' campaign promises and their fulfillment over the decades might be a better indicator of mass preferences (and a fruitful area of study for non-decisional theory).

and salaries) from 1929–1953 (Kerr, 1957) it is clear that redistribution has not been characteristic of the American system. In fact, Kerr believes that the share of income going to employees has not shifted noticeably since 1870. The more recent work of Kolko (1962), Domhoff (1967: 38–62), and Lundberg (1968: 15–25) corroborate Kerr's research findings and extend them to include wealth-holding (e.g., stock ownership).

By taking what Kolko (1969) calls a "functional view of American reform," in terms of its redistributive effects on wealth and life chances, it is possible to make fairly precise statements about the long run power of various interest groups in American society to influence government and society at large.

One of the questions that has always been raised when the question of capitalists' class interests come up is whether it is possible to demonstrate any genuine unity of purpose among the economic elite. Pluralists have admitted that there is an enormous concentration of wealth in the hands of a relatively tiny proportion of the population. Yet, the internal conflicts within the business community (e.g., the historic rivalry between small and big business) and the fact that many studies have shown businessmen relatively unmotivated and incompetent in dealing with the larger interests of their class as opposed to the specific needs of their own businesses have led pluralists to contend that business is often incapable of articulating, much less pursuing its class interests (Rose, 1967: 89–92).

If one examines the works of Domhoff, Weinstein, and Kolko, however, it becomes clear that despite the general disunity of the business class and the parochial concerns of most businessmen, there have been highly articulate members of this class who have been able to shape government policy through their enormous wealth and strategic location in the largest corporations, financial institutions, corporation-oriented law firms, and the state itself.

Weinstein's book deals with the period of American social reform known as The Progressive Era. Rather than characterizing these crucial years as ones in which the power of the business community was restrained by other elements in the society Weinstein suggests that:

> ... The ideal of a liberal corporate social order was formulated and developed under the aegis and supervision of those who then, as now, enjoyed ideological and political hegemony in the United States: the more sophisticated leaders of America's largest corporations and financial institutions.

While not proposing a conspiracy theory of history Weinstein does posit:

> ... a conscious and successful effort to guide and control the economic policies of federal, state, and municipal governments by various business groupings in their own long-range interest as they perceived it. Businessmen were not always, or even normally, the first to advocate reforms or regulations in the common interest. The original impetus for many reforms came from those at or near the bottom of the American social structure, from those who benefited least from the rapid increase in the productivity of the industrial plant of the United States and from expansion at home

and abroad. But in the current century, particularly on the federal level, few reforms were enacted without the tacit approval, if not the guidance, of the large corporate interests. And much more important, businessmen were able to harness to their own ends the desires of intellectuals and middle-class reformers to bring together "thoughtful men of all classes" in "a vanguard for the building of the good community." These ends were the stabilization, rationalization, and continued expansion of the existing political economy, and, subsumed under that, the circumscription of the Socialist movement with its ill-formed, but nevertheless dangerous ideas for an alternative form of social organization.

The major evidence that Weinstein presents to demonstrate his thesis is a detailed analysis of the history of the National Civic Federation, founded in 1900, an organization which was led and dominated by big businessmen such as Marcus A. Hanna, Samuel Insull, and Andrew Carnegie, among others. By 1903, the NCF had representatives from almost one-third of the 367 corporations with assets of more than ten million dollars and 16 of the 67 largest railroads in the country. In addition to representatives from the corporate elite, the NCF included public figures such as Grover Cleveland and William Howard Taft and top labor leaders such as Samuel Gompers and John Mitchell of the United Mine Workers.

The NCF was devoted to solving the conflicts between management and labor which had become exacerbated in the wake of periodic economic crises throughout the last part of the 19th century and the first decade of the 20th. The leading figures of the NCF were as concerned about the "anarchism" of the manufacturing class who adhered to the ideology of *laissez-faire* (and were represented by the National Association of Manufacturers) as by the Socialists who were making strong electoral gains during the period 1904–1918. The NCF was interested in making businessmen recognize the necessity for accepting social welfare reforms and even conservative trade unions to avert state socialism. In this task it promoted various welfare measures and directed intensive propaganda campaigns for business responsibility. At the same time it:

asked of the conservative trade unionists . . . that they become mediating agents between the workers and the corporations, rather than act simply as the representatives of the workers in confrontation with their employers.

In the pursuits, the NCF was bitterly opposed by the NAM, significant sectors of labor, and the Socialists, but was able to prevail. Weinstein argues that the First World War, with the mobilization and regulation of economic activity by the War Industries Board, the recognition of conservative trade unionism, in exchange for war support, and the suppression of Socialist and militant labor dissent, firmly established the political and economic framework for the New Deal, Fair Deal, New Frontier, and Great Society.

Weinstein's book has great significance in the debate on national power. He is able to demonstrate that there was a genuine conflict between capital and labor at the turn of the century and that labor was attracted to a considerable extent to anti-capitalist perspectives. At the same time, he documents the presence of class conscious businessmen, with important government contacts, not opposed to governmental intervention in the economy or social reform, who were instrumental in stabilizing capitalism and preserving class privileges. It is this kind of historical data which undercuts much of the pluralist view that business has been traditionally opposed to social reform. Pluralists tend to confuse the smaller business interests, as represented in the NAM and Chambers of Commerce, with business in general (Rose, 1967: 30). Weinstein clearly indicates that these conservative economic elites were unable to prevail over the more liberal and powerful industrial and financial interests.

The research of Domhoff (1967: 63–77, 1969: 39–48) can be used to supplement Weinstein's analysis for the post-World War Two period. Domhoff discusses the role of foundations, and organizations such as the National Planning Association, Committee on Economic Development, Council on Foreign Relations, Foreign Policy Association, and the Brookings Institution in the formulation of government policy. These organizations, financed by the economic elite, train future government leaders and permit corporate leaders to communicate with each other and academic experts as well. Economic elites also serve on presidentially-appointed commissions and task forces and special committees of the executive branch departments to furnish expertise to the federal government on specific industries as well as being frequently appointed to the executive branch of government as cabinet or sub-cabinet officials. Domhoff feels that it is possible to compare important domestic and international policy recommendations drawn up by the various economic elite organizations and the actual governmental policies which emerged (e.g., Employment Act of 1946, Taft-Hartley Act of 1947, Alliance for Progress). Once again, pluralists tend to ignore these avenues of economic elite influence on the government or underestimate their importance in policy making.

Gabriel Kolko's monograph on the sources of American foreign policy extends the analyses of Weinstein and Domhoff into the sphere of international relations. By an analysis of the class origins of top governmental decision-makers he shows that American foreign policy has been conducted, from 1944–1960, primarily by a relatively small number of representatives from the largest corporations, banks, investment houses, and Wall Street law firms which serve the corporate world. He also supports the pluralist attack on Mills' view that the military shares power with economic and political elites. Foreign policy making, he argues, is totally in the hands of civilians.

In addition to a class origins analysis, and more importantly, Kolko establishes the vital importance of access to raw materials and captive investment and sales markets for the preservation of American economic prosperity. Without American economic control over vast territories, he argues, world economic power would soon shift to Western Europe and Japan, and social unrest would grow at home because of a profit squeeze and the necessity to attack labor's share of national income. Such a situation, he feels, would exacerbate social conflict and mean the end to liberal capitalist democracy or possibly lead to the radicalization of the non-elites. Together with Magdoff's (1969) recent work on the economics of American foreign policy, Kolko's research is extremely convincing, on the whole, in establishing a genuine basis for a *class* interest in economic imperialism.[3]

Finally, Kolko analyzes the development of American world economic, political, and military policy buttressed by the arguments of various decision-makers, which leave little illusion as to the "false consciousness" of economic elites serving as government officials or informal advisors to these officials. His section on Vietnam policy is particularly incisive.

It should be pointed out, in passing, that it is not possible to demonstrate that American foreign policy has been formulated by elites over the opposition of non-elites *within* the United States. Nevertheless, there are few students of foreign policy formation who believe that public opinion is a significant factor in the process (Rose, 1967: 92–93, 488). While Americans largely support all foreign policy initiatives of the President, it should be noted that those persons most affected by these initiatives, foreign elites and non-elites, have been bitterly opposed to little avail. An examination of the share of world wealth appropriated by the United States and the protests by Europeans and peoples of the so-called Third World make it clear that American foreign policy is not conducted with the approval of significant sectors of the world population.

The Limits of Government

The research of Weinstein, Domhoff, and Kolko represents an important step forward in the development of a functional and motivational analysis of American social reform at home and imperialism abroad. Class interests are outlined and class consciousness is demonstrated. Given the serious challenge to the pluralists who have rather consistently viewed businessmen as almost uniformly hostile to reform and incapable of class consciousness the question arises whether other sectors of society (notably labor) can possibly use the federal government to wrest political (and ultimately economic) power away from the capitalist class.

Most of the conventional elitist literature has focused on the monopolization of political office (elected and appointed) by members of the upper and upper middle class. Domhoff (1967) is particularly thorough in documenting the lack of working class participation in the executive and legislative branches of the American government. Pluralists such as Rose (1967: 27–28) have retorted by claiming that wealthy men can serve the interests of the working classes (a claim somewhat vitiated by the apparent failure of reform legislation to redistribute wealth). Explicit in the elitist perspective (and also suggested to some extent by the Marxist analyses of Kolko and Weinstein) is the notion that the capitalist class or their representatives must govern in order for class privileges to be maintained.

[3] Imperialism is not ordinarily considered to be in the "national" interest because while the costs of Empire (material and human) are socialized, profit is disproportionately appropriated by one class.

Because America has never had a powerful Labor or Socialist Party in control of the federal government and the Congress it is possible to consider that if only such a party was able to achieve political power through parliamentary methods, the privileges of the capitalist class could be successfully curbed if not altogether eliminated. This strategy has indeed been adopted by the European Social Democratic parties in advanced capitalist societies.

Ralph Miliband (1969), in his exhaustive study of *The State in Capitalist Society,* attempts, in part, to understand why the *occasional* ascension of avowedly anti-capitalist parties to governmental power (e.g., Germany, 1918; France, 1936; England, 1945, 1964), and the *stable* Social Democratic rule in Sweden over several decades has not significantly redistributed wealth and life chances in those countries, much less ushered in socialism. Miliband's comparative analysis of the state systems in western advanced capitalist societies shows the limited utility of studying power by examining the class origins of political office-holders. While Miliband often shares the same predilection of Mills, Domhoff, and other elitist theorists to link government officials' decision-making to their social class backgrounds, his more sophisticated passages argue that it is not necessarily "who governs" but the strategic structural advantages the capitalist class enjoys in existing capitalist societies that ultimately determines the limits of governmental policy.

To begin with, Miliband clearly delineates the composition of the state. He argues that it includes not only the executive and legislative branches of national government, but the civil service, sub-central government (e.g., state governors, mayors), judiciary, military, security, and police forces. Miliband considers the "state system" to be the interaction of the above institutions. He argues against the view that the executive branch of national government is synonymous with the state itself. The government speaks for the state but historically there have been times when the executive branch has been weak and, while formally invested with state power, may not actually control that power. The case of France during the Fourth Republic illustrates this possibility. Miliband's point is well taken because the threat of "sabotage" by other elements in the state system is often ignored by analysts who believe that the formal aspects of parliamentary democracy assure the potential for carrying out major redistributive reforms (or even nonviolent social revolution) once a party of change is elected to office.

Miliband is sensitive to the fact that a new anti-capitalist government must work with other members of the state system who are more or less permanent fixtures selected and socialized by class background and political pressures under the old regime. Thus, civil servants, military elites, and judges are not likely to come from working class backgrounds and, hence, are unlikely to be ideologically predisposed to carry out truly radical social change. Their "neutrality" or conception of serving "the national interest" may be sincerely felt, but "neutrality" has always meant serving pro-capitalist governments in the past which differed on many issues *save* those of *radical* social change. Security clearances have generally been used precisely to weed out radical civil servants.

Moreover, non-governmental members of the state system are likely to have extensive contact with the business community or their representatives in the course of their careers, which make it useful for them to maintain cordial relations. It is well known, for example, that high civil servants serving on regulatory agencies and top military officers often end their careers by working for large corporations. This career pattern is not calculated to make such state elites hostile to corporate interests. Labor organizations, Miliband notes, are unlikely to be able to offer comparable rewards for "cooperation."

Finally, a new government committed to massive social change would undoubtedly wish to make profound administrative, judicial, and military changes which would threaten the power and even the livelihood of the existing members of the state system. It could hardly be doubted that such a possibility would be resisted. Miliband's work serves as a corrective to many analysts who speak of a neutral or apolitical technocracy, judiciary, or military. Kolko (1969: 13) is not strictly accurate when he states that "bureaucracy serves constituted power, not itself." The "neutrality" of the state elite has never seriously been tested in the United States or Western Europe because of the non-threatening records of reform and even Socialist governments.

One must also consider the possibility that a Socialist government might be able to remain in power for a long enough period to gradually overhaul the social composition and functions of the various non-governmental sectors of the state system. In Sweden, for example, Social Democrats have ruled for several decades with economic activity remaining primarily under private management and control and with the existence of class privilege (Anderson, 1961, 1961a). Under these circumstances how does the capitalist class continue to wield decisive power over governmental decisions?

To begin with, the capitalist class through its ownership and control over industry, commerce, and finance is able potentially to disrupt the social fabric if its interests are threatened. In Italy in 1920, for example, even when workers seized factories and actually attempted to continue production, the industrialists made sure that the workers were unable to procure raw materials, dispose of finished products, or obtain credit (Cammett, 1967: 111–122). The power to halt production and distribution of commodities, or transfer capital abroad, on the part of a business community hostile to government would imperil the viability of that government. Miliband discusses the reluctance of local SPD officials in Germany to tax corporations too heavily for fear they will relocate. On a national level, there are, of course, various ways to pass on the burden of increased taxation to consumers.

Another important advantage that capitalist interests have in preventing radical government action is that such governments would inevitably be faced with enormous pressure from "foreign capitalist interests and forces, foreign firms, central banks, private international finance, official international credit organizations like the International Monetary Fund and the World Bank . . ." (Miliband, 1969: 153). While American government officials and capitalists are somewhat more likely to initiate such retaliatory action against anti-capitalist governments than be the *recipients* of such action, the recent gold crisis illustrated the potential fear even the wealthiest country in the world has of losing the confidence of the international capitalist "community."

While it is true that capitalists do have, and have occasionally employed, the above resources is it not also true that labor has enormous potential power which can serve as a countervailing force? Miliband, as a Marxist, does believe that labor has this potential, but he discusses several reasons why the actual use of such power is limited in practice. Labor is often divided ideologically, by skill, race, and ethnicity. National and international labor organizations are not nearly as representative of labor or as powerful as groups such as the Business Advisory Council or the World Bank are representative of national and international capital. Labor is almost always on the defensive when it goes on strike . . . its ultimate weapon. This is not only because of lack of endurance dictated by insufficient strike funds, but because labor is trying to upset the status quo and can be made to appear as a "special" interest opposed to the "national" interest.

> The demands of business, in contrast, are always claimed to be in the 'national interest' . . . business demands which are designed to strengthen the position of individual firms or of particular industries, or of capitalist enterprise at large, can always be presented, with a high degree of plausibility, given the capitalist context in which they are made, as congruent with the 'national interest.'

Because the basic role of government, to serve the national interest, is inextricably tied to the health and expansion of the existing economy, governmental leaders in capitalist societies, even if they are ideologically anticapitalist, tend to support measures which, while strengthening the economy, function to strengthen capitalism and class privilege. This is no less true of reform and even Social Democratic governments, and perhaps more so, than for conservative governments. . . .

REFERENCES

Anderson, Perry (1961) "Sweden: Mr. Crosland's Dreamland." *New Left Review* 7 (January–February): 4–12.
———— (1961a) "Sweden II. Study in Social Democracy." *New Left Review* 9 (May–June): 34–45.
Bachrach, Peter (1967) *The Theory of Democratic Elitism: A Critique.* Boston: Little Brown and Company.
———— (1962) "Two faces of power." *American Political Science Review* 56 (December): 947–952.
———— (1963) "Decisions and non-decisions: An analytical framework." *American Political Science Review* 57 (September): 632–642.
Cammett, John (1967) *Antonio Gramsci and the Origins of Italian Communism.* Stanford, California: Stanford University Press.
Dahl, Robert (1958) "A critique of the ruling elite model." *American Political Science Review* 52 (June): 463–469.
———— (1961) *Who Governs?* New Haven: Yale University Press.
Domhoff, G. William (1967) *Who Rules America?* Englewood Cliffs, New Jersey: Prentice-Hall.
———— (1969) "Where a pluralist goes wrong?" *Berkeley Journal of Sociology* 14: 35–57.

Kerr, Clark (1957) "Labor's income share and the labor movement." In George Taylor and Frank Pierson (eds.), *New Concepts in Wage Determination*. New York: McGraw-Hill: 260–298.

Kolko, Gabriel (1962) *Wealth and Power in America: An Analysis of Social Class and Income Distribution*. New York: Praeger.

——— (1969) *The Roots of American Foreign Policy: An Analysis of Power and Purpose*. Boston: Beacon Press.

Lundberg, Ferdinand (1968) *The Rich and the Super-Rich: A Study in the Power of Money Today*. New York: Lyle Stuart.

Magdoff, Harry (1969) *The Age of Imperialism: The Economics of U.S. Foreign Policy*. New York: Monthly Review Press.

Merelman, Richard (1968) "On the neo-elitist critique of community power." *American Political Science Review* 62 (June): 451–460.

Miliband, Ralph (1969) *The State in Capitalist Society: An Analysis of the Western System of Power*. New York: Basic Books.

Mills, C. Wright (1956) *The Power Elite*. New York: Oxford University Press.

Rose, Arnold (1967) *The Power Structure: Political Process in American Society*. New York: Oxford University Press.

Weinstein, James (1969) *The Corporate Ideal in the Liberal State: 1900–1918*. Boston: Beacon Press.

James O'Connor

THE PRIVATE WELFARE STATE

The Functions of the State Budget

The [state] budget reflects the particular and general economic needs of corporate capital, on the one hand, and the general political needs of the ruling class as a whole, on the other. Preliminary to an investigation of these needs, and their budgetary reflections, it should be stressed that there are no specific budgetary items which mirror *exclusively* any particular or general need. There are no hard and fast theoretical categories applicable to the analysis of the budget because there are no precise, real, historical budgetary categories. Individual expenditure items do not reflect with absolute precision any particular interest; quite the contrary, a particular item may express imperfectly a multitude of interests. To cite one outstanding example, state financed railroad construction in the nineteenth century was determined by a combination of related economic and political factors. . . . The primary motives for the first United States transcontinental railroad were the opening of new markets, new sources of raw material supply, and the settlement of new lands. Railroads were built in the great majority of export economies very simply to get raw materials out of the country. Yet in India, "really large-scale [railroad] construction began . . . only after the popular uprising of 1857-59, when the colonialists fully grasped the significance of communication lines to maintain their domination." Railroad construction in Russia bore a similar thrust, beginning in earnest in the 1860's after the Crimean War had revealed the military importance of good land transportation. Yet the decision to build the Trans-Siberian Railway was made only in 1891 when it became apparent that Britain was seeking to penetrate the markets of South Manchuria.

Today, there are few state expenditures which fail to serve a number of different, although related ends. Johnson's War on Poverty aimed simultaneously to insure social peace, upgrade labor skills, subsidize labor training for the corporations, and help finance local governments. Highway expenditures complement private investments in manufacturing and distribution facilities, encourage new private investments, link up the major metropolitan centers in accordance with the needs of the Department of Defense, facilitate the mobility of labor, and provide a kind of social consumption—or goods and

Reprinted, with deletions and added headings, from James O'Connor, "The Fiscal Crisis of the State: Parts I–II," *Socialist Revolution*, vol. 1 (January–February 1970), pp. 12–54; (March–April 1970), pp. 34–94, by permission of *Socialist Revolution*. James O'Connor teaches economics at San Jose State College and is the author of *The Origins of Socialism in Cuba*.

services consumed in common. Outlays on other forms of transport, communications, water supplies, utilities, and the like also simultaneously provide inputs to private capital and services to the working class. Nevertheless, it is useful to categorize specific expenditures into four major groups, not for purposes of exposition, but rather because there is always a preponderant set of social forces determining the amount, type, and location of the particular facility.

STATE AID TO SPECIFIC INDUSTRIES

The first major category of expenditures consists of facilities which are valuable to a specific industry, or group of related industries. These are projects which are useful to specific interests and whose financial needs are so large that they exceed the resources of the interests affected. They also consist of projects in which the financial outcome is subject to so much uncertainty that they exceed the risk-taking propensities of the interests involved. Finally, these are projects which realize external economies and economies of large-scale production for the particular industries.

These projects fall into two sub-categories: first, *complementary* investments; second, *discretionary* investments. Both types of investments, like private investments, increase the stock of tangible or intangible capital. But the first consists of facilities without which private projects would be unprofitable. Complementary investments are determined completely by the rhythm of private capital accumulation, or by the spheres that private capital has chosen to expand and by the technical relations or coefficients between private investment and complementary activities. Complementary investments are thus a special form of private investment: their determination rests squarely on the determination of private commodity production and accumulation. And since private accumulation is increasingly social—since the economy is increasingly interdependent—there is no economic or technical limit on state expenditures for facilities which complement private facilities. The most dramatic example of complementary investments are infrastructure projects in backward capitalist economies which specialize in the production of one or two primary commodities for export. The relationship between state and private capital is here seen in its pure form. Private investments in agriculture and mining completely determine the location, scale, function, and degree of flexibility of infrastructure projects. Railroads, ports, roads, communication and power facilities are oriented to serve one or two industries making up the export sector.

The purpose of the second type of state investment is to provide incentives for private accumulation. In practice, there is no hard line drawn between complementary and discretionary investments; highway extensions, for example, facilitate the movement of goods and also encourage new investments. While complementary investments are part of the normal rhythm of capital accumulation, discretionary investments are ordinarily made during times of crisis—when profitable opportunities for capital as a whole are lacking, or in the event that declining industries depress certain regions. Both kinds of investments are oriented by profit, although the latter may or may not raise the rate of profit.

Because discretionary investments are not oriented by immediate profitability criteria, they run the risk of being condemned as "inefficient" and "wasteful." Efficiency in a capitalist society is defined by reference to the pattern of resource use prevailing under conditions of competition. Investments which do not have to meet the "test of the market" are by definition inefficient. How wasteful discretionary investments can be is suggested by the existence in France until 1902 of large-scale subsidies to sailing ships, precisely at the time of the ascendency of steamships. The result was that France developed the most technically backward fleet of all the advanced capitalist countries. A dramatic contemporary example is provided by the first U.S. government subsidized nuclear-powered merchant ship, which originally cost $54 million and whose operating costs of $3 million yearly far exceeded revenues. Because discretionary investments are not likely to pass the "test of the market" they ordinarily have little quantitative importance in the budget.

Yet in the context of the Federal system and the fiscal crisis, which compels local governments to compete with one another for new tax-producing industrial and commercial properties by providing low cost or free facilities to specific investors, and in the context of an industrial structure dependent on the state for contracts and subsidized to develop new technical "solutions" for "crime control," institutional administration, transportation systems, and so on, more and more discretionary investments are being financed by the state.

The most important state investments serving the interests of specific industries are highway expenditures.[1] Domestic economic growth since World War II has been led by automobile production and suburban residential construction, which requires an enormous network of complementary highways, roads, and ancillary facilities. Rejecting public transportation, on the one hand, and toll highways, on the other the state has "socialized intercity highway systems paid for by the taxpayer—not without great encouragement for the rubber, petroleum, and auto industries." From 1944, when Congress passed the Federal Aid to Highways Act, to 1961, the Federal government expended its entire transportation budget on roads and highways. Today, approximately twenty per cent of non-military government spending at all levels is destined for highways; inland waterway and airport expenditures total less than one billion yearly; and railroads and local rapid transit receive little or nothing. And in area redevelopment schemes, highways receive the lion's share of the subsidies; more than eighty per cent of the funds allocated by the Federal government to Appalachia for economic development, for example, have been destined for road construction. The reason was that the Federal planners needed the cooperation of the local governors, who together with electric power, steel and other companies combined to block other "solutions." The power of the "auto complex" has

---

[1] Weapon expenditures fall partly into this category, but since their ultimate determinant lies elsewhere discussion of military spending is postponed until later.

been documented many times; two more examples must suffice. In 1962, the combined forces of the truckers, port groups, and barge companies blocked legislation which sought to give the railroads more freedom to cut rates; in 1965, an attempt by Johnson to compel truckers to pay higher user charges failed completely.

Initiated and supported by the auto complex, sometimes along and sometimes allied with other industries, road transport nevertheless receives powerful support from the large part of private capital as a whole, as well as from the suburbs. From the standpoint of private capital the availability of truck transport is the key factor in location decisions. For the car-owning commuter, the transportation budget constitutes a giant subsidy. First, because although the determinant of highway construction is found in the auto complex, highways have technical characteristics—mainly free access and unused capacity—which afford easy use by car owners.[2] Second, because "the auto owner enjoys a low marginal price per mile by auto once he commits himself to ownership," in turn, because he must meet fixed car payments, for this reason, his use of public transportation is minimal.

The social cost of auto transport is extraordinarily high, hence the enormous fiscal burden on the state. In the United States, about twenty per cent of total product is spent on transportation (in the Soviet Union, roughly seven per cent), chiefly because of the high capital requirements of moving people from one destination to another, together with the existence of vast unused physical capacity—partial underutilization of highways during non-peak hours, and autos in transit, and full underutilization of autos during working hours.

Costs, and the fiscal burden, are also rising; it has become a standard complaint that the construction of freeways does not end, but rather intensifies congestion. The basic reason is that auto use is subsidized; hence expanding the freeway system leads to the expansion of the demand for its use. Furthermore, the state cannot free itself fiscally by constructing more freeways, because the freeway system has spawned more and more suburban developments—where road expenditures per capita are much greater than in the cities—at greater distances from the urban centers.

Further, road transport intensifies the fiscal crisis of the cities, owing to the removal of land from the tax rolls for freeways, access roads, and ancillary facilities. Simultaneously, the cities' commuting population places an extra burden on city expenditures in the form of traffic control, parking facilities, and the like.

For all of these reasons, not only does the social cost of transportation steadily rise, but also transport costs borne by capital itself increase. Local capital and the state itself are responding to the monster created in Detroit, Akron, and other centers of the auto complex with programs for public

[2] A provocative thesis is that the argument that roads "benefit" everything in a capitalist society is the same as the argument that slave quarters "benefit" everyone in a slave society. Both roads and slave quarters, because of their physical features, can be used for recreation. The political consensus that developed in the 1950's—grand era of road building and suburbanization—thus is attributable partly to the technical features of roads, and so on, not to any consciously designed plan for promoting the general well-being.

The Private Welfare State

transport, two of which have been implemented in San Francisco and Washington. The Pittsburgh ruling class, worried about the relative decline of sheet steel orders from Detroit, immediately responded with a plan for "transit-expressways"—elevated trains mounted on steel structures. The project is sponsored by the Port Authority of Allegheny County, and dominated by the Mellon interests, big steel, and Westinghouse Electric Corp. Backed financially by the State of Pennsylvania, the project also receives help from the Housing and Home Finance Agency in the United States Department of Commerce. But far from solving the transportation problem, this and similar efforts are bound to add to the total irrationality of transportation patterns, and to the fiscal crisis. At present, there are more than thirty agencies at the Federal level regulating or promoting particular modes of transport. Many of these agencies are in competition with one another, paralleling the competition for state funds among different branches of industry. To date, the Federal government has been unable to rationalize and streamline transportation, because it has not been able to acquire sufficient independence from the conflicting and contradictory interests of particular industries to deprive the state agencies which represent these specific interests of their independence. Another reason to expect the transportation budget to rise in the future is that the development of rapid transport will push the suburbs out even further from the urban centers, and put even more distance between places of work, residence, and recreation. Far from contributing to an environment which will free suburbanites from congestion and pollution, rapid transport will simply displace the traffic jams to the present perimeters of the suburbs, thereby requiring still more freeway construction. The only general solution is planned urban development as a whole, and neither corporate capital nor local capital is willing or able to take this step.

Integrally related to transport outlays are urban renewal expenditures, which figure more and more in local, State and Federal budgets, and which are the main response to the decline in profits of downtown business interests. The decline in profitability in turn is attributable to the profoundly exploitative relationship which has developed between the suburb and the city.

The suburb and the city have evolved a relationship very similar to the one which developed between the imperial powers and their colonies specializing in the production and export of primary commodities. Just as the export economy offers a natural resource, a gift of nature, the city provides at no cost its central location and hence enormous advantages to economic activities in the sphere of trade and exchange. If trade and exchange are the very reason-for-being of the city, *centrality* is its most valuable resource. Thus central city services—banks and other financial houses, law offices, research, advertising and public relations services, and central office administration for the giant corporations—which are essential to corporate capital undergo a rapid expansion. Meanwhile, manufacturing, storage, transportation and other facilities move to the periphery, taking the better-paid industrial working class jobs with them. What is left is small-scale manufacturing, retail trade and food and other services, where productivity and wages are relatively low. One difference between the export economy and the city is that the exploitation of a natural resource sooner or later must come to an end, while the value of a central location not only fails to contract but increases with more intensive use. This simple fact goes a long way toward explaining the simultaneous dynamism and decay of the central city.

The export sector in the colonies was partly or wholly owned by foreign capital, and sometimes even the working force was of foreign extraction. The key downtown economic activities are partly owned by suburbanites. The wage share generated by these sectors is small and the share going to salaries (and therefore suburbanites) is correspondingly large. "The central cities are becoming more and more specialized in functions which require chiefly professional, technical and clerical workers," one economist has written. "But the skilled and literate groups are precisely those segments of the population which are increasingly choosing to live outside the urban center." When the export economy expanded the large part of the rise in income was channeled abroad in the form of repatriated profits and workers remittances. When the economy of the city expands, there occur similar spending "leakages" as increments to income in the form of profits and salaries are repatriated to the suburb. To be sure, suburbanites patronize central city stores, thus contributing to revenues from sales taxes and bear some of the burden of property taxes on suburbanite-owned real assets. Moreover, income taxes siphon off some of the flow and grants-in-aid from State and Federal Governments return it to the city. Nevertheless, the only study available indicates that the income-employment multiplier is low in the central city compared with the outlying districts; incomes earned in the central city tend to be "exported" to the suburbs. Thus from the standpoint of both the imperial power and the suburb, the system is partly self-financing: resources are transferred from the colony and the city and paid for with the increased income (repatriated earnings and profits) generated by the expansion of demand for central city services. This one-way transfer of resources tends to pauperize the colony and city alike.

Extending the analogy further, commodities and services which were not available locally to the colonists were imported. For the "new colonists," suburban living itself takes the place of luxury and other goods not available locally. Foreigners in the colonies utilized the local social and community services at little or no cost. Suburbanites appropriate the transport, hospital, police, fire, and other services for little or nothing. Thus the suburbanite appropriates two sets of social services. Meanwhile, as we have seen, the central city must widen its highways to accommodate peak rush-hour traffic, invest in more parking and police services and traffic control systems, and bear the burden of generally increased costs of congestion, including air pollution. The flight of industry erodes the value of the existing tax base, and, at the same time, the removal of land from the tax rolls reduces the tax base itself. The argument that the central city population will refuse to vote expenditures to meet the needs of the suburbanites (and thus that city expenditures may be less than "optimum") ignores the fact that the city bureaucracy has little choice in the matter, and that the voters have little or nothing to say in connection with either the volume or composition of city expenditures. As Julius Margolis has shown in a study of fifty-five city governments in the San Francisco-Oakland area, the property tax rate and level of per capita expenditures in the central city were higher than in the dormitory, industrial or balanced suburbs. The dormitory suburb enjoyed the lowest tax rate and per capita expenditures were only fifty-eight per cent of those in the central city. Like the Margolis study, an analysis by Harvey E. Brazer is also suggestive of suburban parasitism. Brazer showed that the expanding population in the suburbs was correlated with all categories of city expenditure except outlays for recreation facilities, while the population of the central city itself did not appear to influence the level of per capita expenditures.

The exploitation by the "new working class," middle class, and ruling class suburbanites of the predominantly working class city has probably intensified since World War II. There has been a historic shift in the terms of trade between the suburb and the city to the advantage of the former. This is expressed in the tendency for salaries to advance more rapidly than wage payments, and finds its reflection in the increasing number of residential, as compared with industrial, suburbs. What is more, although the typical metropolitan area has become more economically self-sufficient, more autarkic, the central city increasingly specializes in the "export" services.

It is in this context that urban renewal should be interpreted. The market still determines the contours of urban and regional development. More important, the supra-municipal authorities and quasi-public regional development agencies which control urban renewal *reinforce* the "decisions" of the market. The state budget has thus contributed to the dynamism of the downtown sections and the decay of the remainder of the city. Urban renewal expenditures are thus bound to expand in the future because they do not correct the irrationalities of capitalist development, but rather intensify them.[3]

[3] For example, Detroit is the top candidate for HUD's "demonstration city" program. Detroit's plan calls for $2.5 billion in Federal funds over a ten year period. Nearly all of the proposed expenditure items will have the effect of *reinforcing* the existing social structure and pattern of resource use. Public transportation receives no attention in the plan; instead, $300 million is requested for freeways and city streets. Nor does new working class housing rate attention; instead, Detroit wants $50 million for slum clearance in order to make room for five industrial development areas, and $73 million for middle class recreational and cultural facilities in order to reverse the middle class migration to the suburbs. While the largest request is $1.7 billion for schools, the key to the entire plan is the neighborhood family centers. These appear to be giant settlement houses, which will provide employment services, "delinquency control teams," clinics, staff homemakers, hobby, education, and other activities. Clearly, Detroit's plan, considered by HUD to be the best proposal put forth by any city, confirms and *formalizes* the existence of the ghetto, inequality, and the class system (*Wall Street Journal*, January 1, 1966).

A similar conclusion can be drawn about rural redevelopment expenditures. In 1965, Congress voted over three billion dollars to "depressed areas." According to the Administration bill, "the bulk of the money would be earmarked for Federal grants to public works projects such as water works, waste treatment plants, industrial streets and roads, airport and other facilities useful in attracting private industry (*New York Times*, June 2, 1965). In the absence of planned directly productive investments this kind of program will only make the depressed areas more depressed.

Specifically, spending on urban reconstruction takes the form of multi-project investments which harmonize the specific expenditure items in the interests of local capital as a whole. The main aspects of urban renewal include: reconstruction of downtown areas in the interests of retailers suffering from sharp suburban competition; stadium and other recreational investments which seek to give restaurants, clubs, and so on a new lease on life; multiplication of parking and other facilities for suburbanites working in downtown office buildings; deacceleration of the deterioration of middle class neighborhoods, and acceleration of the decline of working class neighborhoods;[4] in general, the recreation and intensification of profitability conditions for builders, banks, utilities, retailers, brokers, and land speculators. To the degree that urban renewal reconstructs cities which complement suburban development, the development of the suburbs and the underdevelopment of the cities are intensified; to the degree that urban renewal reconstructs cities which compete with the suburbs, the underdevelopment of the cities is deaccelerated, at the expense of the duplication and multiplication of facilities of all kinds. . . .

SUBSIDIZING THE GENERAL ECONOMIC NEEDS OF CAPITALISM

The second major determinant of state expenditures stems from the immediate economic interests of corporate capital as a whole. The budgetary expression of these interests takes many forms—economic infrastructure investments, expenditures on education, general business subsidies, credit guarantees and insurance, social consumption, and so on. In the United States, most of these forms appeared or developed fully only in the twentieth century, although in Europe state capitalism emerged in an earlier period—in France, during the First Empire, generalized state promotion buoyed the private economy; in Germany, state economic policy received great impetus from political unification and war; in Italy, laissez-faire principles did not prevent the state from actively financing and promoting accumulation in the major spheres of heavy industry; and everywhere liberal notions of small,

---

[4] The practical experience and literature on this subject is vast, and the general conclusions widely accepted. Urban renewal means people removal, especially black removal, owing to the transfer of families from the downtown periphery to deteriorating districts elsewhere in the city, the blighting of neighborhoods by freeway construction, and the chaining of public housing to slum clearance and, thus, the impossibility of using open spaces. As Charles Abrams has written (*The City is the Frontier*, N.Y., 1966), "since the welfare of the building industry had won equal place with the people's welfare in the 1949 Housing Act, it seemed inevitable that sooner or later the interests of lower-income families would be forgotten. When the entrepreneurial and the general welfare are bracketed in the same legislation, it should not be surprising that the social purpose will be subordinated. It was."

Martin Anderson's *The Federal Bulldozer* (Cambridge, 1964) analyzes the coalition of banks, newspapers, department stores, downtown real estate owners, academic intellectuals, city planners, and city politicians who have made urban renewal what it is. Originally introduced at the expense of both the urban working class and small business, urban renewal began to protect the latter in 1964 when Congress passed a housing bill which provides concessions and compensation to small business.

balanced budgets and indirect taxation came face to face with the fiscal realities of wartime economies.

In the United States, the budget remained small throughout the nineteenth century; transportation investments were chiefly private, and natural resource, conservation, public health, education and related outlays were insignificant. The state served the economic needs of capital as a whole mainly in non-fiscal ways—land tenure, monetary, immigration, tariff, and patent policies all "represented and strengthened the particular legal framework within which private business was organized."[5] State subsidies to capital as a whole were confined to the State government and local levels and were largely the product of mercantile, rather than industrial capital, impulses.[6]

In the twentieth century, however, corporate capital has combined with state capital to create a new organic whole. Corporate capital is not subordinated to state capital, or vice versa, but rather they are synthesized into a qualitatively new phenomenon, rooted in the development of the productive forces and the concentration and centralization of capital. More specifically, the rapid advance of technology has increased the pace of general economic change, the risk of capital investments, and the amount of uncontrollable overhead costs. Further, capital equipment is subject to more rapid obsolescence, and there exists a longer lead time before the typical investment is in full operation and thus is able to pay for itself. The development of the production relations has also compelled corporate capital to employ state power in its economic interests as a whole, and socialize production costs. The struggles of the labor movement have reinforced the general tendency for the rate of profit to decline and have thus compelled corporate capital to use the state to mobilize capital funds from the liquid savings of the general population. And, finally, the onset of general realization crises have forced large-scale business to use the budget to subsidize the demand for commodities.

The most expensive economic needs of corporate capital as a whole are the costs of research, development of new products, new production processes, and so on, and, above all, the costs of training and retraining the labor force, in particular, technical, administrative, and non-manual workers. Preliminary to an investigation of the process of the *socialization* of these costs,[7] a brief review of the relationships between technology, on the one hand, and the production relations, on the other, is required.

[5] Henry W. Broude, "The Role of the State in American Economic Development, 1820–1890," in Harry N. Scheiber, editor, *United States Economic History: Selected Readings*, New York, 1964.

[6] Louis Hartz, *Economic Policy and Democratic Thought: Pennsylvania, 1776–1860*, Cambridge (Mass.), 1948, pp. 290–291.

[7] All or even a majority of education expenditures are not determined by corporate capital's drive to socialize these costs. A large part of the education budget consists of social consumption for middle class children; that is, education is required to complement private consumption, and as a way to create and maintain prestige and status for middle class and ruling class families. Further, the main purpose of elementary education is to structure personalities, behavior patterns, and thoughts in accordance with the need for maintaining the social order as a

The forces of production include available land, constant capital, labor skills, methods of work organization, and, last but not least, technology, which is a part of, but not totally identified with, the social productive forces. The advance of technology, the uses of technology, and its distribution between the various branches of the economy are all determined in the last analysis by the relations of production. The transformation from a labor-using to a labor-saving technology in mid-nineteenth century Europe was ultimately caused by the disappearance of opportunities for industrial capitalists to recruit labor "extensively" from the artisan and peasant classes at the given wage rate. During the last half of the nineteenth century, the established industrial proletariat faced less competition, their organizations were strengthened, and they were better able to win wage advances. Thus, it was the class struggle that compelled capital to introduce labor-saving innovations.[8]

Despite the rapid advance of technology during the first half of the twentieth century, until World War II the industrial corporations trained the largest part of their labor force, excluding basic skills such as literacy. In the context of the further technological possibilities latent in the scientific discoveries of the nineteenth and twentieth centuries, this was a profoundly irrational mode of social organization.

The reason is that knowledge, unlike other forms of capital, cannot be monopolized by one or a few industrial-finance interests. Capital-as-knowledge resides in the skills and abilities of the working class itself. In the context of a free labor market—that is, in the absence of a feudal-like industrial state which prohibits labor mobility, a flat impossibility in the capitalist mode of production—no one industrial-finance interest can afford to train its own labor force or channel profits into the requisite amount of research and development. The reason is that, apart from the patent system, there is absolutely no guarantee that their "investments" will not seek employment in other corporations or industries. The cost of losing trained

---

whole. And, lastly, to the degree that education teaches consumer and related skills, there is obviously a large element of economic waste in the education budget. All of these functions of education, however, excepting the last one, are traditional. In our discussion of the education budget we concentrate on what is new and unique—namely, the socialization of production costs. To put it another way, the practical element in education has become of crucial importance. Veblen was one of the first to take note of this: business "feels the need of a free supply of trained subordinates at reasonable wages," parents "are anxious to see their sons equipped for material success," and youth "are eager to seek gainful careers" (*The Higher Learning in America*, N.Y., 1957, p. 144). According to studies now in progress by Herb Gintis, the *practical* element in education today is precisely "personality structuring" in accordance with the need to produce "human capital."

[8] The change in technology then "works back upon" or modifies the relations of production, but not mechanically nor owing to any "imperative." The immediate decision to accelerate labor-saving technology belonged to capitalists; the ultimate decision lay in the production relations. The acceleration of labor-saving techniques had the long term effect of stratifying the working class into many unskilled, semi-skilled, and skilled layers. Broad-based working class organizations, the development of class consciousness, and class unity were subsequently more difficult to achieve.

manpower is especially high in those industries which employ technical workers with skills which are specific to a particular industrial process.

World War II provided the opportunity to rationalize the entire organization of technology in the United States. As Dobb writes, "a modern war is of such a kind as to require all-out mobilization of economic resources, rapidly executed decisions about transfer of labor and productive equipment, and the growth of war industry, which ordinary market-mechanisms would be powerless to achieve. Consequently, it occasions a considerable growth of state capitalism . . ." The intervention of the state through government grants to finance research programs, develop new technical processes, and construct new facilities and the forced mobilization of resources converted production to a more social process. The division of labor and specialization of work functions intensified, industrial plants were diversified, the technical requirements of employment became more complex, and, in some cases, more advanced. The end result was a startling acceleration of technology.

At the end of the war, corporate capital was once again faced with the necessity of financing its own research and training its own technical work force. The continued rationalization of the work process required new forms of social integration which would enable social production to advance still further. The first step was the introduction of the GI Bill, which socialized the costs of training (including the living expenses of labor trainees) and eventually helped to create a labor force which could exploit the stockpile of technology created during the war. The second step was the creation of a vast system of lower and higher technical education at the local and State level, the transformation of private universities into Federal universities through research grants, and the creation of a system to exploit technology in a systematic, organized way which included not only the education system, but also the foundations, private research organizations, the Pentagon, and countless other Federal government agencies. . . . In turn, this reorganization of the labor process, and, in particular, the free availability of masses of technical-scientific workers, made possible the rapid acceleration of technology.[9] With the new, rationalized social organization of technology and

[9] This is an overstatement. The Federal System prevents the full rationalization of the labor process from the standpoint of profitability. Ordinarily, local business dominates the Boards of local and State institutions of higher learning; further, junior colleges are normally financed at least in part from local taxes. Owing to the mobility of labor and the existence of market-determined wages, there is a tendency for local capital to under-invest in education, and rely instead on high wages and salaries to attract technical labor trained in other localities and States. This is probably why technical and trade schools located in working class districts tend to be underfinanced, and frequently oriented towards training people for skills which are no longer needed by private capital.

Thus, higher organs of the state, which are able to act in the name of larger strata of capital, are beginning to rationalize the education process still further. A number of States, including New York, are imitating California's Master Plan. North Carolina, a growing industrial state with few traditional industrial interests to fight against "modernization," has established a State-wide system of 20 industrial education centers which today enroll more than 40,000 students. Again, Federal aid to education can only result in more Federal control, and thus over-all rationalization, of local education systems.

the labor process completed, technical knowledge became the main form of labor power and capital. There occurred a decline in the relative importance of living labor, and an increase in the importance of dead labor in the production process. Thus, statistical studies, beginning in the mid-1950's and multiplying rapidly since then, indicate that the growth of aggregate production is caused increasingly less by an expansion in labor "inputs" and the stock of physical assets, and more by upgrading labor skills, improvements in the quality of physical assets, and better organization of work. One famous study demonstrated that increased education accounted for over three-fifths of the growth of output per man-hour in the United States from 1929–1957.

The continued substitution of "mind" work for manual work is bound to place a growing burden on state budgets at local, State and Federal levels. Equally important, the increased demand for higher education will add to the fiscal crisis. Education remains "private property" in the sense that the material benefits from training accrue not to society at large but to the technical worker himself. Higher individual incomes are only partly "paid for" by the individual's family during his school years. Of course, full tuition requirements, or a tax on future earnings attributable to education, would reduce the number of applications for admissions to colleges and universities; on the other hand, new tuitions or fresh taxes would tend to dry up the supply of technical labor. And this is not a likely possibility: in 1966 the United States government estimated that current annual expenditures of institutions of higher learning would rise from $5.3 billion in that year to $7.2 billion in 1970; comparable estimates for the elementary and secondary schools were $18.6 billion and $22.3 billion, respectively. . . .

Another rising expense facing corporate capital as a whole consists of investments in economic infra-structure—plant and equipment for education and research; water, power, and similar projects; and harbor, air, and other transportation facilities. Specific industries or groups of related industries normally do not provide the political impetus for these expenditures, but rather regional or corporate capital as a whole does. These kinds of economic infra-structure ordinarily serve a wide variety of industries, either precede or coincide with private capital accumulation, and generate many-sided, long-term, economic effects. They are also capital-intensive projects that are characterized by large "indivisibilities"; they require large original capital outlays and normally are constructed in large, discrete units. To cite one example, the Boeing 747 jetliner will make most existing air terminal facilities obsolete, and will require the construction of entirely new airports, rather than a gradual modernization of existing facilities.

These projects place a growing burden on the state budget for three reasons: first, their absolute size is increasingly large, owing to their capital-intensive and "indivisible" character; second, corporate capital needs more economic infra-structure, due to the increased complexity and interdependence of production; and, third, state and local governments seeking to attract branch-plants of large corporations by subsidizing infra-structure projects tend to produce an over-supply of projects. For all these reasons, federal outlays and grants-in-aid and state and local bond issues for "capital improvements" will continue to expand.

Still another fiscal burden heaped on the state by corporate capital are the *expenses of selling*. The need for state programs to expand individual commodity demand springs from the rapid development of the productive forces that have reached the stage at which most individual economic needs —needs formed by goods production itself—can be easily satisfied. As a result the corporate bourgeoisie is compelled to lay out larger and larger portions of profits on selling expenses—for packaging, advertising, model and style changes, product differentiation, and forced commodity obsolescence—in order to discourage savings and maintain and expand the volume of consumption.

The corporate ruling class has learned to use the state budget to subsidize commodity demand by reinforcing and accelerating the production of waste. Government "full employment" policies lead to a large volume of waste production. Safety laws, truth-in-lending, truth-in-packaging, food and drug laws, and other forms of "consumer protection" are designed to buoy up the market by officially sanctioning particular commodity lines. Highway expenditures increase the demand for automobiles and contribute to urban and suburban sprawl. They indirectly expand the demand not only for consumer durable goods needed in private dwellings, but also for social consumption expenditures in the suburbs. Owing to the extreme individualistic character of the suburbanization process—single-unit dwellings, and the increased separation of places of work, residence, and recreation—the burden on local budgets arising from the need for more education, recreational, and similar facilities continues to mount.

The corporate ruling class has also learned to use the state and federal colleges and universities as proving grounds for new marketing ideas, new products, and new brands of full employment economics. The activities of these "marketing departments" of the corporate ruling class range from market research courses, home economics departments and seminars in Keynesian economics to the art and industrial design schools that train, mobilize, and apply creative talent to the latest problems of product design and packaging.

The state also underwrites consumer credit—the process of borrowing purchasing power from the future to realize surplus value in the present—in many fields; in particular, housing. The state guarantees and subsidizes private, single-unit-housing in order to expand the demand for residential construction, automobiles, appliances, and other consumer durable goods. Partly for this reason, mortgage debt on non-farm residential properties has risen from about $25 billion during World War II to roughly $250 billion in 1968, when there was an outstanding $50 billion in FHA-insured mortgage loans, and another $34 billion in VA-guaranteed mortgages.

From a theoretical standpoint, the need for state spending destined to underwrite private commodity demand is limitless. Capital "accumulates or dies" and in the absence of regular increases in private commodity demand, which in the current era require fresh state subsidies, accumulation comes to a halt. Moreover, a few particular commodities receive the greatest share of state subsidies. Highways and education receive the most direct subsidies and private suburban housing and development receive the greatest indirect subsidies. Politically, it is difficult for the state to shift resources from highway construction to other modes of transportation, from suburban residential development to urban housing, and from social consumption in the suburbs to social consumption in the cities. . . .

The uncontrolled expansion of production by corporate capital as a whole creates still another fiscal burden on the state in the form of outlays required to meet the *social costs of private production* (as contrasted with the socialization of private costs of production, which we have discussed above). Motor transportation is an important source of social costs in the consumption of oxygen, the production of crop- and animal-destroying smog, the pollution of rivers and oceans by lead additives to gasoline, the construction of freeways that foul the land, and the generation of urban sprawl. These costs do not enter into the accounts of the automobile industry, which is compelled to minimize its own costs and maximize production and sales. Corporate capital is unwilling to treat toxic chemical waste or to develop substitute sources of energy for fossil-fuels that pollute the air. (There are exceptions to this general rule. In Pittsburgh, for example, the Mellon interests reduced air pollution produced by its steel mills in order to preserve the values of its downtown real estate.) And corporate farming—the production of agricultural commodities for exchange alone—generates still more social costs by minimizing crop losses (and thus costs) through the unlimited use of DDT and other chemicals that are harmful to crops, animals, water purity and human life itself.

By and large, private capital refuses to bear the costs of reducing or eliminating air and water pollution, lowering highway and air accidents, easing traffic jams, preserving forests, wilderness areas, and wildlife sanctuaries, and conserving the soils. In the past these costs were largely ignored. Today, owing to the increasingly social character of production, these costs are damaging not only the ecological structure, but also profitable accumulation itself, particularly in real estate, recreation, agriculture, and other branches of the economy in which land, water, and air are valuable resources to capital. The portion of the state budget devoted to reducing social costs has therefore begun to mount.[10] In the future, the automobile industry can be expected to receive large-scale subsidies to help finance the transition to the electric or fuel-cell car. Capital as a whole will receive more subsidies in the form of new public transportation systems. Subsidies to public utilities to finance the transition to solar, nuclear, or sea energy will expand. Corporate farmers will insist on being "compensated" for crop losses arising from bans on the use of DDT and other harmful chemicals. And more Federal funds will

[10] These and other costs of maintaining the social order have been estimated at roughly $109 billion (Alexander L. Crosby, "The Price of Utopia," *Monthly Review*, May 1968). Private capital attempts to profit from the environmental conditions it has produced itself. For example, one corporation advertises private solutions to the social problem of pollution in the form of eye drops.

be poured into the states to help regulate outdoor advertising, alleviate conditions in recreational areas, finance the costs of land purchase or condemnation, and landscaping and roadside development, and otherwise meet the costs of "aesthetic pollution."

Some local and national leaders are seeking to reduce pressures on the budget arising from these social costs by attempting to shift the burden to private capital. For example, the State of Illinois is attempting to force the airlines using Chicago's airports to install air-pollution control devices on their aircraft. Former Secretary of the Interior Udall has stated that "waste treatment is a proper business cost." And the Water Quality Act of 1965—introduced into Congress by the Federal executive—requires State governments to establish and enforce water purity levels for interstate waterways within their boundaries.

Law suits, legislation and moral suasion cannot be expected to provide a *total* solution to the problem of social costs. Total environmental planning is needed to socialize the costs of protecting the natural environment while simultaneously avoiding sharp financial pressures on the specific corporation or industry interests involved. No one corporate farmer can afford the costs of conserving soils, water and plant, animal, and human life. No single manufacturer can bear the expense of manufacturing automobiles that do not pollute the air. No airline alone can meet the expenses of "sound pollution" or by itself modernize air traffic facilities and control. These facts are understood by the Congress, which represents the interests of specific capitals and local business interests, and which continues to vote more state subsidies to specific industries and local and state governments.

POLITICAL STABILIZATION OF WORLD CAPITALISM

The third major category of state expenditures consists of the expenses of stabilizing the world capitalist social order: the costs of creating a safe political environmental for profitable investment and trade. These expenditures include the costs of politically containing the proletariat at home and abroad, the costs of keeping small-scale, local, and regional capital at home, safely within the ruling corporate liberal consensus, and the costs of maintaining the comprador ruling classes abroad.

These political expenses take the form of income transfers and direct or indirect subsidies, and are attributable fundamentally to the unplanned and anarchic character of capitalist development. Unrestrained capital accumulation and technological change creates three broad, related economic and social imbalances. First, capitalist development forces great stresses and strains on local and regional economies; second, capitalist growth generates imbalances between various industries and sectors of the economy; third, accumulation and technical change reproduce inequalities in the distribution of wealth and income and generate poverty. The imbalance—described by Eric Hobsbawm as "the rhythm of social disruption"—not only are integral to capitalist development, but also are considered by the ruling class to be a sign of "healthy growth and change." What is more, the forces of the marketplace, far from ameliorating the imbalances, in fact magnify them by the multiplier effects of changes in demand on production. The decline of coal mining in Appalachia, for example, compelled other businesses and able-bodied workers to abandon the region, reinforcing tendencies toward economic stagnation and social impoverishment.

These imbalances are present in both the competitive and monopoly phases of capitalism. Both systems are unplanned and anarchic as a whole. But monopoly capitalism is different from competitive capitalism in two fundamental respects that explain why political subsidies are budgetary phenomena mainly associated with monopoly capitalism.

First, an economy dominated by giant corporations operating in oligopolistic industries tends to be more unstable and to generate more inequalities than a competitive economy. The source of both instability and inequality is oligopolistic price-fixing, since the interplay of supply and demand that clears specific commodity markets is no longer present. Shortages and surpluses of individual commodities now manifest themselves in the form of social imbalances. In addition, the national (and, increasingly, the international) character of markets means that economic and social instability and imbalances are no longer confined to a particular region, industry, or occupation, but rather tend to spread through the economy as a whole. Finally, Federal government policies for economic stability and growth soften the effects of economic recessions, lead to the survival of inefficient businesses, and, hence, in the long-run to the need for more subsidies.

The second difference between competitive and monopoly capitalism concerns the way in which economic and social imbalances are perceived by capital and wage-labor. In a regime of competitive capitalism, businessmen exercise relatively little control over prices, production and distribution. Unemployment, regional underdevelopment, and industrial bankruptcy appear to be "natural" concomitants of "free markets." Moreover, the level and structure of wages are determined competitively, individual capitals are not able to develop and implement a wage policy, and, thus, the impact of wage changes on the volume and composition of production, the deployment of technology, and unemployment, appear to be the consequence of impersonal forces beyond human control. Because imbalances of all kinds are accepted by capital as natural and even desirable, and because the ideology of capital is the ruling ideology, the inevitability and permanence of imbalances and transitory crises tend to be accepted by society as a whole.

With the evolution of monopoly capitalism and the growth of the proletariat as a whole, this fatalistic attitude undergoes profound changes. Business enterprise gradually develops economic and political techniques of production and market control. Gradually, oligopolistic corporations adopt what Baran and Sweezy have termed a "live-and-let-live attitude" toward each other. In this setting, the imbalances generated by capitalist development begin to be attributed to the conscious policies of large corporations and big unions, rather than to the impersonal forces of the market. Corporate capital, small-scale capital, and the working class alike begin to fix responsibility for the specific policies on particular human agents. Only in this context can the proletariat, local and regional capital, and the comprador classes be contained and accommodated by corporate capital.

The political containment of the proletariat requires the expense of maintaining corporate liberal ideological hegemony, and, where that fails, the cost of physically repressing populations in revolt. In the first category are the expenses of medicare, unemployment, old age, and other social insurance, a portion of education expenditures, the welfare budget, the anti-poverty programs, non-miltary "foreign aid," and the administrative costs of maintaining corporate liberalism at home and the imperialist system abroad—the expenses incurred by the National Labor Relations Board, Office of Economic Opportunity, Agency for International Development and similar organizations. The rising flow of these expenditures has two major tributaries.

In point of time, the first is the development of the corporate liberal political consensus between large-scale capital and organized labor.[11] Through the 19th century, private charity remained the chief form of economic relief for unemployed, retired, and physically disabled workers, even though some state and local governments occasionally allocated funds for unemployed workers in times of severe crisis. It was not until the eve of the 20th century that state and local governments introduced regular relief and pension programs. Until the Great Depression, however, welfare programs organized by the corporations themselves were more significant than government programs. Economic prosperity and the extension of "welfare capitalism" throughout the 1920s made it unnecessary for the federal government to make funds available (in the form of loans to the state) for economic relief until 1932.

The onset of the Great Depression, the labor struggles that ensued, and the need to consolidate the corporate liberal consensus in order to contain these struggles, all led finally to state guarantees of high levels of employment, wage advances in line with productivity increases, and a standard of health, education, and welfare commensurate with the need to maintain labor's reproductive powers and the hegemony of the corporate liberal labor unions over the masses of industrial workers.

The need for this consensus, always threatened by the expansion and increasing alienation of the proletariat, is rooted in the antagonistic production relations. But the imperatives of the consensus are constantly changing under the impact of the developing forces of production. Today, the advance of modern technology reduces the relative number of workers in goods-producing industries, and the absolute number of workers in mining and certain key manufacturing industries. In turn, "technological unemployment" potentially threatens labor bureaucracy control over rank-and-file unionists. The big unions are under constant pressure from their membership to fight for programs that will protect unemployed workers, members forced into early retirement, and others whose normal work life is subject to profound convulsions arising from capital accumulation, the introduction of new technology, and rapid changes in the composition of demand. Unable to win adequate retirement benefits, guaranteed annual wages, and funds for other compensatory programs from the corporations themselves, the unions turn

[11] The five hundred largest mining and manufacturing corporations employ roughly 65 percent of total mining and manufacturing workers.

to the state, constituting themselves as the chief lobbies for expanded social insurance. The human costs of capital accumulation—unemployment, retirement, sickness, and so on—are shifted to the state budget, that is, to the taxpaying working class as a whole.[12] In this way, the corporations successfully defend their profits, the unions conserve their hegemony, and redundant union labor receives material relief. And social insurance outlays continue to rise, limited only by the limits on the industrial application of modern technology.

The second tributary runs parallel with, but runs faster and stronger than, the first, and flows from the same source—the development of modern technology. Corporate capital at home and abroad increasingly employs a capital-intensive technology, despite a surplus of unskilled labor, partly because of relative capital abundance in the advanced economies, and partly because of the ready supply of technical-administrative labor power. From the standpoint of large-scale capital, it is more rational to combine in production technical labor power with capital-intensive technology than to combine unskilled or semi-skilled labor power with labor-intensive technology. As we have seen, the fundamental reason is that many of the costs of training technical labor power are met by taxation falling on the working class as a whole.

Advanced capitalism thus creates a large and growing stratum of untrained, unskilled white, black and other Third-World workers that strictly speaking is not part of the industrial proletariat. The relative size of this stratum does not regulate the level of wages, because unskilled labor power does not compete with technical labor power in the context of capital-intensive technology. This stratum is not produced by economic recession and depression, but by prosperity; it does not constitute a reserve army of the unemployed for the economy as a whole. Unemployed, under-employed, and employed in menial jobs in declining sectors of the private economy (e.g., household servants), these workers increasingly depend on the state. "Make-work" state employment, health, welfare, and housing programs, and new agencies charged with the task of exercising social control (to substitute for the social discipline afforded by the wages system itself) proliferate. The expansion of the welfare rolls accompanies the expansion of employment. For the first time in history, the ruling class is beginning to recognize that welfare expenditures cannot be temporary expedients but rather must be permanent features of the political economy: that poverty is integral to the capitalist system. Thus, the ruling class is beginning to experiment with "negative income taxes" and similar schemes that represent permanent concessions to the poor. Complementing these concessions with programs that tie welfare payments to work (e.g., the current Nixon proposal), the ruling class may be able in the future to expand welfare spending without dangerously undermining the social discipline of the wage system.

Further, there is every reason to expect an expansion of other programs —particularly in the areas of education and health—designed to soften the

[12] Social insurance represents a "forced savings"—to cite Oscar Ewing, FSA administrator under Truman—imposed on the working class as a whole.

impact of poverty. And the system of higher education, in this respect inseparable from the state bureaucracy, will expand its budget, because it is becoming more and more preoccupied with questions of "social stability," "law and order," and "social reform."

Abroad, in all of the urban centers of the underdeveloped economic colonies and semi-colonies of the United States, there is a vast growing impoverished population, unable to find employment in the capital-intensive branch plants and subsidiaries of the international corporations. This increasingly restless, potentially revolutionary population is a growing source of concern for the corporate and government leaders charged with administering the empire—a concern that is translated into requests for more "foreign aid," loans, grants, and technical assistance. The general aim of "foreign aid" programs is to maintain the world capitalist social order intact, and to create the conditions for its further expansion. The need for welfare programs, "wars on poverty," "foreign aid," and other ameliorative programs knows no limit, or, more accurately, is limited only by the boundaries on the application of modern technology and the spread of capitalism itself.

The second major cost of politically containing the proletariat at home and abroad (including the proletariat in the socialist world) consists of police and military expenditures required to suppress sections of the world proletariat in revolt. These expenditures place the single greatest drain on the state budget. A full analysis of these expenditures would require detailed development of the theory of imperialism, which cannot be undertaken here. However, we can identify those factors in the arms race, the structure of the "military-industrial space complex," the wars against national liberation struggles abroad, and the physical suppression of revolutionary movements at home that are likely to force the ruling class to expand the military budget in the forseeable future.

First, the continuous expansion of social production, the extension of capitalism into the Third World, and the proletarianization of the world population enlarges the arena both for capital accumulation and for class conflict. The increasing instability of the world capitalist social order, the transformation of nationalist movements led by compromise-minded national bourgeoisies into national liberation struggles led by revolutionary armies, and the birth of new socialist societies, have all required greater levels of military expenditure in the "mother country." Today, overseas expansion meets more resistance and the defense of the empire is more costly. Responding to the needs of the giant international corporations that seek to penetrate and dominate Third World economies in a politically hostile environment, the United States government has been compelled to develop a series of military blocs, a far-flung network of military bases, and an enormous military establishment at home. Further, the cold war requires the constant upgrading of military technology in order to maintain parity in the balance of terror; and the absence of popular support at home for the imperialist war in Vietnam requires the development of technological substitutes for the fire power traditionally supplied by foot soldiers.

Second, a large and growing military establishment is needed to initiate technological advance in *civilian* production. In the past, the military often has been the medium for the modernization of civilian production. The reason is that the military sphere has always been the most acceptable sphere politically for the development of technology beyond the financial capabilities of private capital. In present-day advanced capitalist economies, which normally generate more economic surplus than the private sector is able to absorb profitably, economic growth depends on the *systematic* introduction of innovations in production, and hence the role of the military in supplying technology for non-military uses is greatly expanded. Most of the major growth industries in the United States (for example, electronics, aerospace, and scientific instruments), directly or indirectly owe their expansion to war and militarism.

In turn, the civilian development of military technology under the auspices of private corporations and the universities augments military requirements still further and activates even more military production. Originally developed to power the first battleships, the dynamo later found a market in urban lighting, underwent improvement at the hands of civilian engineers, and finally was reintroduced into military production at a higher level of efficiency. The story of the development of aircraft, atomic power, and electronics is similar.

Third, not only is the economy as a whole more dependent on rising military expenditures, but also the major "private" military contractors have established permanent beachheads in the state budget, and thus have a permanent stake in the arms race itself. The largest 50 defense contractors received 58 per cent of all military orders during World War II, 56 per cent during the Korean War, and 66 per cent in 1963–1964. In military production, "the initiative, risk-bearing and similar manifestations of enterprise appear to have become characteristics of the buyer rather than the seller," and thus the big military contractors cooperate readily with government defense programs independent of the rationality of these programs for overall ruling class interests.

The proof that a handful of large corporations has a permanent hold on the budget lies in the fact that the companies that were the major defense contractors a decade or so ago continue to receive the greater share of military expenditures today *despite* the rapidly changing *composition* of defense spending. The resources of most of these corporations are so specialized, the emphasis on quality and high technology rather than high volume and low price is so great, and the absence of mass distribution is so pronounced that they are unable to shift a significant amount of resources to non-military production and hence must be subsidized indefinitely by the taxpaying public. Attempts to help these corporations to divert military production to civilian production by and large have failed. In the words of one expert, "In view of the consistently poor results that these diversification efforts have yielded in the past and the extreme reluctance of the company managements to invest substantial amounts of their own funds in these ventures [government subsidies to do commercial work] would seem to offer little encouragement."

For these reasons, the ruling class has little discretion in the determination of either the volume or type of military expenditures. Department of

Defense research and development spending—which rose from less than $1 billion in 1950 to about $7 billion in 1965 (and to over $13 billion, including space and atomic energy research)—will continue to mount. Military payrolls will continue to increase, not only (or even mainly) due to a growth in the armed forces, but also because of the need to expand pay scales to attract and keep technically competent military personnel. Present and future wars of national liberation will compel the United States to augment "conventional" military forces and the new "counter-insurgency" forces. And, last but not least, the "China threat" and the inability to achieve a detente with the Soviet Union (and thus a reduction in hostilities in the Middle East and elsewhere) will lead to an expansion in the production of existing and new nuclear weapons and delivery systems.[13]

The final expense of stabilizing the world capitalist social order consists of the funds needed to keep local and regional capital securely within the corporate liberal political consensus at home and the costs of maintaining the comprador ruling classes abroad. The latter take the form of foreign aid: in particular, balance-of-payments assistance through the International Monetary Fund; infrastructure loans by the World Bank and AID that economically strengthen export industries in the Third World and politically harden the rule of local bourgeoisies whose economic interests are based on export production, processing, and trade; and outright military and non-military grants-in-aid.

At home, corporate capital must make alliances with traditional agricultural interests (especially those of the Southern oligarchy) and small-scale capital. In the Congress, the votes of Southern and Midwest farm legislators and other representatives bound to local and regional economic interests, for example, shipping, soft coal mining, and the fishing industry, are indispensable for the legislative victories of corporate liberal policies. Support for Federal programs in the areas of urban renewal, education, health, housing, and transportation by state legislators, municipal governments, and local newspapers, TV stations, and other "opinion-makers" is equally important.

The political support of small businessmen, farmers, and other local and regional interests is extremely costly. Billions of dollars of direct and indirect subsidies are required by the farmers, especially the large growers who dominate the farm associations and many local and state governments. The first New Deal farm plan—the so-called domestic allotment plan—was introduced to quell a farm revolt organized in the Midwest. Since the 1930s, price support, acreage restriction, credit, soil conservation, and rural redevelopment and rehabilitation programs—all designed with the aim of politically conservatizing the farmers—have proliferated. "It was soon discovered that these programs were, on the whole, more helpful to the 'top third' of the farmers than they were to the 'lower two-thirds' . . . The small landowners, tenants, sharecroppers, wage hands, and migrant workers who composed

---

[13] According to Charles Schultz, taking into account weapons systems already approved and the expected costs of improving them, a $100 billion Vietnam "dividend" (added to the anticipated increases in taxes due to economic growth) will be reduced to $30 billion by 1974 (*The Progressive*, 37, 6, June 1969, pp. 41–42).

the majority of the farm population received only indirect benefits and, in some cases, were actually harmed by these programs." Today, the large, commercial farmers make up less than 15 per cent of the farm population, but receive an estimated 63 per cent of farm subsidies.

Subsidies in various forms—in particular, allowances to finance the relocation of small business—are also required to placate small-scale capital adversely affected by corporate-oriented urban renewal programs. The Small Business Administration has an extensive financial-aid program, including a policy of underwriting small banks. The fishing industry receives capital grants for new boat construction. In shipping, the Federal government pays the difference between the cost of constructing ships in the United States and the estimated costs in foreign shipyards, which amounts to roughly 50 per cent of total construction costs. Further, the state expends about $125 million annually to help pay for merchant shipping operating costs. Finally, stockpiling of "strategic materials," favorable buying prices offered the textile industry, and the licensing of various occupations also fall wholly or partly into the category of political subsidies.[14]

CONCLUSION

In the preceding sections, we have attempted to analyze state expenditures in terms of the development of the forces and relations of production. We have seen that the increasingly social character of production requires the organization and distribution of production by the state. In effect, neo-capitalism fuses the "base" and "superstructure"—the economic and political systems—and thus places an enormous fiscal burden on the state budget. . . .

[14] Ideologically, these expenditures cannot be justified in terms of either economic efficiency or economic growth. In part or in whole political subsidies must be concealed or disguised (examples are the provision of state services at less than cost and tax exemptions) or rationalized in terms of "national defense" (stockpiling of raw materials, for example).

part two

The Political Economy of American Social Problems

chapter 3

American Imperialism and Militarism

Until the late 1950s and early 1960s American foreign economic, political, and military relations were not generally considered problematic, except insofar as interventionism in behalf of "freedom" represented a drain on national human and material resources. The mythology of the Cold War, accepted by virtually all academicians, laymen, and perhaps even economic and political elites, cast the United States in the role of selfless defender of the so-called Free World. Opposed to American beneficence was the Soviet Union, a wartime ally who opportunistically attempted to sabotage world peace in order to dominate other peoples in the name of communism. The other Communist countries, of Eastern Europe and even China, were perceived as satellites totally under the domination of Soviet power. In addition to facing Communist threats, America was seen as bedeviled by fair-weather Western European allies who were anxious to receive the protection of American military might and economic aid but unwilling to make sacrifices for their freedom. Finally, a large number of neutral underdeveloped countries tried to benefit from the Cold War by securing foreign aid from both democratic and totalitarian camps, without committing themselves to either.

To some extent this general interpretation of the postwar period is still the most acceptable to the masses of American citizens because of a lack of knowledge and to many economic and political elites for its ideological utility. However, the events of 1953–1963 caused a growing number of academicians to challenge the previously accepted perspective with which they viewed international relations. Stalin's death, the Hungarian revolution, the thaw in the Cold War resulting from the need to make certain accommodations to the reality of the Soviet Union's nuclear capabilities, the promulgation of the doctrine of "peaceful coexistence," and the later Sino-Soviet split all contributed to a reconsideration of Soviet-American relations.

The early "revisionist" historians began to develop the view that although Russian expansionist ideology was the ultimate source of the Cold War, a good deal of the heat generated in that conflict was not simply the result of Soviet duplicity, but stemmed from the giant powers' mutual suspicion about each other's *immediate* intentions. Numerous instances of misunderstanding were documented in order to show that both sides were at fault in generating world tensions. Moreover, communism was no longer viewed as having one guiding force, the Soviet Union, but appeared to be polycentric. Nevertheless, this more balanced analysis still examined the Cold War from an American perspective. American goals were not questioned; only the judgment of our policy-makers in regard to Russia's *immediate* postwar aims was challenged.[1]

Even as the revisionists argued for a more detached perspective on the Cold War—one that saw blame on both sides, while still remaining loyal to the American camp—a few scholars remained unsatisfied. William Appleman Williams, D. F. Fleming, Gar Alperovitz, and David Horowitz, in particular, maintained that the United States had provoked the Cold War and sought to maintain it despite Soviet passivity.[2]

This heresy was quickly dismissed by a host of academic specialists, but the experience of the Bay of Pigs, the invasion of the Dominican Republic, and, above all, the seemingly endless escalation of the war in Vietnam served to heighten the dilemmas of the "neutralists." Moreover, the relatively mild antagonism between the Soviet Union and the United States by the mid-sixties served to draw attention away from the origins of the Cold War and toward American relations with the Third World. The publication of Carl Oglesby's monograph on postwar foreign policy was a major breakthrough in the direc-

[1] John Lukacs, *A History of the Cold War* (New York: Doubleday & Company, Inc., 1961).

[2] William Appleman Williams, *The Tragedy of American Diplomacy* (Cleveland: The World Publishing Company, 1959); *The Contours of American History* (Cleveland: The World Publishing Company, 1961). Williams actually went far beyond the Left critics of Cold War historiography and early revisionism by maintaining that America had always pursued an empire, albeit a largely noncolonial one. His analysis, however, was based more on examination of the ideology of statesmen than actual documentation of American imperial activity.

D. F. Fleming, *The Cold War and Its Origins, 1917–1960* (New York: Doubleday & Company, Inc., 1961). Gar Alperovitz, *Atomic Diplomacy: Hiroshima and Potsdam* (New York: Vintage Books, 1965); *Cold War Essays* (New York: Doubleday & Company, Inc., 1970). David Horowitz, *The Free World Colossus: A Critique of American Foreign Policy in the Cold War* (New York: Hill & Wang, Inc., 1965).

American Imperialism and Militarism

tion of analyzing the sources of what had, by that time, been acknowledged by many academicians as a long history of American opposition to revolutionary movements in underdeveloped areas.[3]

Oglesby saw the problem of American counterinsurgency in Greece, Vietnam, and Latin America as one that could best be understood in terms of the logic of imperialism. He documented the advantages American businessmen realized from trade with and investment in underdeveloped countries having pro-Western governments. He suggested that American support for military dictatorships or authoritarian civilian regimes was related to the hospitality of these generally unpopular governments to American business activity in their countries. Genuine nationalist and social revolutionary movements, on the other hand, sought the elimination of economic dependence upon the West. Claiming that "neocolonialism"—economic control over a country's natural and human resources and markets by another nation despite an absence of formal colonial domination—represented an obstacle to economic development, these nationalist movements directly or indirectly jeopardized American business interests.[4]

Oglesby's work set the stage for a revival of study on the general topic of imperialism and the specific role of American economic interests in generating foreign policy. William Appleman Williams' controversial thesis that America had followed an expansionist policy throughout its history received renewed attention, and the scholarship of some of his former students added credence to his position.[5] Williams has recently written a highly acclaimed volume which attempts to locate the source of modern American economic expansionism in the agricultural crises of the last third of the nineteenth century.[6] Gareth Stedman Jones' article in this chapter uses the work of Williams, his students, and others to provide an illuminating overview of the political economy of American imperialism from 1776 to the period of the Russian Revolution.

The work of Williams and his students on the historical origins of American neocolonial imperialism has been matched in the past few years by some equally compelling analyses of American imperialist ambitions and practice after World War II. These new analyses totally recast the relationship

[3] Carl Oglesby, "Vietnamese Crucible: An Essay on the Meaning of the Cold War," in Carl Oglesby and Richard Schaull, *Containment and Change: Two Dissenting Views of American Society and Foreign Policy in the New Revolutionary Age* (New York: Crowell-Collier and Macmillan, Inc., 1967), pp. 3–176.

[4] Celso Furtado, *Development and Underdevelopment*, translated by Ricardo W. de Aguiar and Eric Charles Drysdale (Berkeley, Calif.: University of California Press, 1967), presents the views of the non-Marxist opposition to neocolonialism. The revolutionary Marxist perspective is exemplified by Bahman Nirumand, *Iran: The New Imperialism in Action* (New York: Monthly Review Press, 1969).

[5] Williams, *op. cit.*, 1959; 1961. Walter LaFeber, *The New Empire: An Interpretation of American Expansion, 1860–1898* (Ithaca, N.Y.: Cornell University Press, 1963). Lloyd Gardner, *Economic Aspects of New Deal Diplomacy* (Madison, Wis.: University of Wisconsin Press, 1964); *Architects of Illusion: Men and Ideas in American Foreign Policy, 1941–1949* (Chicago: Quadrangle Books, 1970).

[6] William Appleman Williams, *The Roots of the Modern American Empire: A Study of the Growth and Shaping of Social Consciousness in a Marketplace Society* (New York: Vintage Books, 1969).

among the United States and the Soviet Union, America's wartime allies in Western Europe, and the revolutionary movements which erupted during the struggle against fascism.

In one of the most thoroughly documented volumes on diplomatic history, Gabriel Kolko views world history since 1917 as an ongoing international civil war.[7] On one side of this conflict has been the United States and its Western European capitalist allies, on the other side the Soviet Union and the peoples of the underdeveloped world. The role of Germany and Japan has shifted during the century from dangerous imperialist rivals of the United States, England, and France to allies against the world revolutionary currents which have threatened global capitalist economic, political, and military dominance.

Kolko's research begins with World War II. He argues that military victory over German and Japanese fascism was the predominant goal of the Allies prior to 1943. After that date, when ultimate victory seemed assured, American political leaders began to concern themselves with the shaping of the postwar environment. In order to be in a position to dominate the postwar world economy, American policy-makers sought not only to contain and weaken the Soviet Union and Communist-led popular resistance movements but also to undermine British and French colonialism.

Government leaders strongly believed that the Great Depression and war were brought about by economic nationalism and sought a world of free and extensive international trade. While such a policy superficially appeared to benefit all trading partners, the postwar economic balance of power made such a proposal a cover for American world economic hegemony. After the war America's human and material resources and physical productive capacity were largely intact while those of her allies and old and new enemies, including the Soviet Union, were in a greatly weakened state. Thus, America was able to impose economic and political conditions upon countries in need of aid, conditions which effectively permitted American business to penetrate all parts of the world.

The Soviet Union is presented by Kolko as a passive, if not counter-revolutionary, force during and immediately after World War II. With half her industrial capacity destroyed and 20 million dead after she had borne the brunt of Nazi military power, the Soviet Union was in no condition—as America and her other allies well knew—to foment revolution in Western Europe. Stalin basically wished to secure Western Allied compensation for Russia's wartime sacrifices, which exceeded those of all her allies, or to obtain massive reparations from Germany and the other Axis powers. In an attempt to obtain such aid Stalin actively discouraged Communist parties and even the Communist-led popular resistance movements forged to combat

[7] Gabriel Kolko, *The Politics of War: The World and United States Foreign Policy, 1943–1945* (New York: Vintage Books, 1970). See David Horowitz, *Empire and Revolution: A Radical Interpretation of Contemporary History* (New York: Vintage Books, 1970) for a similar analysis which takes the international significance of the Bolshevik Revolution as its focal point. See also Arno J. Mayer, *Politics and Diplomacy of Peacemaking: Containment and Counterrevolution at Versailles, 1918–1919* (New York: Alfred A. Knopf, 1967).

Nazism in Greece, Italy, and France from making revolution. He urged coalition with liberal and even reactionary regimes. Most notably, he tried to convince Mao-Tse-Tung to support Chiang-Kai-Shek, who had lost the support of the Chinese people and was close to defeat in Civil War.

Soviet efforts at appeasement proved fruitless. Contrary to the popular belief that Stalin started the Cold War by establishing total control in Eastern Europe, he was only responding to American and British behavior in Western Europe. In Italy, for example, America and Britain maintained *exclusive* governance of occupied territory, disarmed resistance personnel, and attempted despite great popular opposition to restore monarchism and right-wing army leadership. In Greece, the British, relying upon American support, fought the anti-Nazi resistance, which was led by Communists, and restored the power of Nazi collaborators who would align themselves with the Free World.

Kolko's selection in this chapter is a natural sequel to his massive work on wartime diplomacy and its aftermath. It leaves little doubt as to the considerable success of American imperial planning by extensively documenting both the stake that American capitalism has in world economic domination and the fruits of imperial policies. With the important recent volume by Harry Magdoff and more specialized studies such as Michael Tanzer's extensive analysis of the role of international oil companies, primarily American owned, in perpetuating underdevelopment,[8] Kolko's research has succeeded in shifting the terms of scholarly, if not political, debate on the question of American imperialism. Thus, a serious student of the political economy of American foreign policy is no longer able to deny that American capitalism derives great advantages from overseas economic activity and the particular pattern of governmental alliances and militarism. Moreover, it is becoming rather apparent from the now-voluminous literature on neocolonialism that American foreign policy contributes heavily to the increasing immiseration of much of the world's population.[9]

While it is fairly simple to appreciate the capitalist class's imperialist orientation given capitalism's chronic need for raw materials and sales and investment outlets, students of American foreign affairs have traditionally denied any suggestion that *governmental* foreign policy could be erected on such foundations.

One of the arguments that conventional scholars make to counter any suggestion that economic goals ultimately dominate governmental decisions in the foreign policy arena is that those in the business class are often unaware of their class interests and hopelessly divided among themselves on many issues.

[8] Harry Magdoff, *The Age of Imperialism: The Economics of U.S. Foreign Policy* (New York: Monthly Review Press, 1969). Michael Tanzer, *The Political Economy of International Oil and the Underdeveloped Countries* (Boston: The Beacon Press, 1969).

[9] Paul Baran, *The Political Economy of Growth* (New York: Monthly Review Press, 1957). Andre Gunder Frank, *Capitalism and Underdevelopment in Latin America: Historical Studies of Chile and Brazil* (New York: Monthly Review Press, 1967). Tanzer, *op. cit.* Nirumand, *op. cit.*

My article in Chapter 2 attempted to document the fact that in the twentieth century a powerful sector of the business class was able to unite and develop long- and short-run policies to serve its own interest. Private organizations such as the Council on Foreign Relations, the Committee for Economic Development, and the Foreign Policy Association provide opportunities for corporate elites to mingle with academic experts and each other in order to determine the most appropriate ways to deal with pressing world problems.[10] These organizations are funded primarily by the giant foundations (such as Rockefeller, Ford, Carnegie) created by corporate elites as mechanisms for tax evasion and as means to support research and development which is necessary for the continued functioning of the *existing* political economy. Members of these organizations and their academic advisers are appointed to governmental bodies and special committees to study foreign policy problems. Governmental advisory boards such as the National Security Council and study commissions such as the Gaither and Clay committees on military preparedness and foreign aid policy, respectively, are dominated by members of the American business aristocracy, their legal representaives, foundation executives, and academics affiliated with establishment foundations or corporations.

Kolko, in a study of foreign policy decision-makers, examines the social backgrounds of high-ranking American foreign policy officers in several branches of the federal government (the departments of State, Defense, Treasury, and Commerce) and in comparable positions of the army, air force, navy, and other foreign policy-related organizations such as the White House staff.[11] He considers data covering the period from 1944 to 1960. Kolko finds that "men who came from big business, investment, and law held 59.6 percent of the posts. . . . The very top foreign policy decision-makers were therefore intimately connected with dominant business circles and their law firms."[12]

Although the documentation of business overrepresentation on official foreign policy decision-making bodies and the discovery of its informal influence through private organizations such as the Council on Foreign Relations has been noted fairly recently, few social scientists ever maintained that Congress or public opinion played a significant role in foreign affairs.[13] It is almost universally acknowledged that since World War II, at least, the executive branch has dominated foreign policy making. This executive power has been justified largely by the claim that world crises in the nuclear age demand a rapid response that only the President can make. In regard to the role of public opinion in formulating foreign policy, even pluralists feel public opinion is generally manipulated by the media rather than based upon independent analysis by the citizenry. Arnold Rose acknowledges this when he observes:

[10] G. William Domhoff, *The Higher Circles: The Governing Class in America* (New York: Random House, Inc., 1970), pp. 111–155.

[11] Gabriel Kolko, *The Roots of American Foreign Policy: An Analysis of Power and Purpose* (Boston: The Beacon Press, 1969), pp. 3–26.

[12] *Ibid.*, p. 19.

[13] Domhoff, *op. cit.*, pp. 139–153.

American Imperialism and Militarism

One reason, I think, for the public's "unenlightened" views on questions of foreign policy is its lack of a "reference frame" independent of the mass media. A union-hating paper will not be very persuasive on the subject of unions to a man in a good union, but the average man's only contact with foreign policy issues is through the mass media.[14]

If there is a consensus that only a few people make foreign policy, there is less agreement about the motivations of the decision-makers. While a few social analysts believe class interests are paramount in foreign policy formation, most agree with Rose, who argues that policy-makers act in "their conception of the national interest."[15] These two views are not necessarily in conflict if one recognizes that policy-makers, who frequently come from business backgrounds or work with and for businessmen, are apt to consider any policy that seriously hampers the existing economy harmful to the national interest. To this extent helping the national interest means aiding capitalism. This is particularly true when the national interest has been increasingly identified with economic growth rather than with an internal redistribution of resources. In any case, given the antagonistic interests of various social strata and classes, it is difficult to imagine how political elites—short of a concern for the physical survival of the citizenry—could formulate a policy in the national interest which would not give advantages to certain social groups at the expense of others.

Since the "pursuit of the national interest" thesis raises more questions than it answers, some scholars have sought more understanding of the roots of American foreign policy by focusing on the "anti-Communist crusade" which has been the primary governmental rationale for diplomatic and military maneuvers in recent decades.[16] Yet what does the Communist threat entail? If communism must be opposed because it is antidemocratic—as American statesmen proclaim—how can we justify active support for rightwing dictatorships in South Vietnam, Spain, Greece, South Korea, and Brazil? What is the essence of "unfreedom" that makes Cuba an enemy and Greece an ally and a member of the Free World?

If communism is a greater threat to freedom than rightwing dictatorship because it is perceived to be expansionist and a threat to the self-determination of small states, why did the United States tolerate the fascist expansionism of Italy, Germany, and Japan until provoked by acts or declarations of war? Why did the American government intervene militarily in Russia in 1918 before it could possibly be aware of any Soviet expansionist impulse?

[14] Arnold Rose, *The Power Structure: Political Process in American Society* (New York: Oxford University Press, 1967), p. 93, fn. 11. See James Aronson, *The Press and the Cold War* (Indianapolis: The Bobbs-Merrill Company, Inc., 1970).

[15] Rose, *op. cit.*, p. 93.

[16] Edmund Stillman and William Pfaff, *Power and Impotence: The Failure of American Foreign Policy* (New York: Random House, Inc., 1966). It is not necessary to deny the operation of ideology in the making of foreign policy. No doubt it has its role and certain government elites such as John Foster Dulles seem to have been obsessed with "anti-Communism." Nevertheless, as the recent abrupt thaw in the relations between China and the United States suggests, ideology can be quickly cast aside if more practical considerations intrude.

Why did the United States fail to fight British and French colonialism with the tenacity that characterizes her anti-Communist crusade?

When all the contradictions of American foreign policy are brought to light, the most reasonable explanation of the double standard applied to Communist countries appears to be not their denial of political liberty to their own citizens or to the citizens of other lands, but their hostility to the freedom the capitalist class holds most dear—that is, the freedom to penetrate all possible markets.[17]

The quest for an Open Door as the guiding principle of American foreign policy can help explain why communism represents the greatest threat to the national interest as defined by governing elites. To the extent that communism appeals to the peoples of the world, capitalist investment and trade opportunities largely disappear. While they have always suspected the intentions of other major capitalist powers such as England, France, Germany, and Japan, American elites could tolerate these nations' actions as long as they did not seriously impede the expansion of American economic power. That both world wars resulted from imperialist rivalries should not obscure the fact that the leaders of the billigerent camps were fighting over the distribution of the world market. The international civil war that has been fought since the Bolshevik Revolution involves a more profound challenge: the continued *existence* of the world market, if not capitalism itself. This accounts for imperial rivals' desires to weaken but not totally destroy each other and thus endanger the survival of world capitalism.

The final major framework employed by scholars to explain American foreign policy has been a favorite of liberal critics of militarism and counter-revolution. This view stresses the role of a "military-industrial complex" dominated by generals, admirals, and defense contractors, who exert decisive influence over foreign policy decision-makers through propaganda and lobbying. In this perspective, the military's thirst for power and status is seen as dovetailing with the arms manufacturers' desire for large profits from federal defense expenditures.[18]

In assessing the position of the military in the complex, Domhoff and

---

[17] Critics of the view that American foreign policy has imperial underpinnings often cite the excessive cost of the Vietnam War and business opposition to the war as proof that noneconomic factors lie behind foreign policy. Yet, the cost of the war has been excessive because it has been impossible to win (unlike previous American interventions). Few government leaders expected Vietnamese resistance to be so tenacious. As for possible imperial gains compensating for war costs, it should be noted that after-tax corporate profits rose steadily from 1961 to 1966 and only dropped significantly during 1970. Since business was not bearing the cost of the war, Asian investment opportunities, if forthcoming, could only be icing on the cake. The increasing opposition to the war from the business community is primarily of recent vintage, coinciding with a dollar crisis, economic recession, domestic turmoil, and the growing conviction that the war is unwinnable. Even so, *Fortune*, vol. 83 (May 1971), pp. 168–169, reports that three quarters of the chief executives of the largest corporations still support President Nixon's war policy.

[18] C. Wright Mills, *The Power Elite* (New York: Oxford University Press, 1956). Fred Cook, *The Warfare State* (New York: Crowell-Collier and Macmillan, Inc., 1962). Seymour Melman, *Our Depleted Society* (New York: Holt, Rinehart and Winston, Inc., 1965).

American Imperialism and Militarism

Kolko, pluralists such as Rose, and "insider" academicians such as Samuel Huntington and Morris Janowitz all agree that military men and institutions play a very minor role in developing foreign policy.[19] The increasing civilian domination of the Department of Defense; the powerful interservice rivalries over budgetary matters and strategic policy; the civilian orientation of military elites; and the growing complexity of military strategy—with its reliance upon physical and social scientists rather than "heroic" field commanders—have weakened whatever meager power the American military had in determining foreign policy. If the United States has embarked upon a path of militarism it is because the civilians who make foreign policy have accepted a "military definition of reality" and believe that the foreign aspirations of the United States can best be implemented with an armed presence.

Since the military does not appear to have much independent weight, it seems that the industrial sector of the complex must have the decisive power to distort national priorities.

The principal evidence proponents of the military-industrial theory offer is the enormous size of the military and defense budget; the great waste, in the form of overkill, built into this budget; and the inability of opponents of military spending to reduce the war economy.[20] While agreeing with all the data scholars present to support the thesis of a military-industrial complex, I believe it is necessary to reinterpret this data in the light of what we know about the political economy of American capitalism.

The existence of a huge and wasteful defense budget may be irrational in terms of cost-benefit analysis if the criterion for benefit is the allocation of American natural and human resources that will bring the greatest good to the greatest number of citizens. Since it is obvious from our earlier discussion of the political economy that this criterion is not employed by economic or political elites, the defense budget is no more irrational than the federal transportation budget, which is devoted almost totally to maintaining the automobile as the chief mode of transportation despite its human and material costs and untoward ecological effects.

Military spending, however irrational from the point of social benefit, is

[19] G. William Domhoff, *Who Rules America?* (Englewood Cliffs, N.J.: Prentice-Hall, Inc., 1967), pp. 115–126. Kolko, *op. cit.*, 1969, pp. 27–47. Rose, *op. cit.*, pp. 134–152. Samuel Huntington, *The Common Defense: Strategic Programs in National Politics* (New York: Columbia University Press). Morris Janowitz, *The Professional Soldier* (New York: The Free Press, 1960).

[20] Richard Barnet, *Intervention and Revolution: The United States in the Third World* (Cleveland: The World Publishing Company, 1968) and Seymour Melman, *Pentagon Capitalism: The Political Economy of War* (New York: McGraw-Hill, Inc., 1970) posit an autonomous aggressive "national security" management, or "Pentagon capitalist" class, which promotes war and massive defense outlays to serve its bureaucratic need for growth and power. Their thesis is a variant of the military-industrial complex formula because it conceives militarism as stemming from the goals of parochial interest groups unresponsive to the genuine security needs of the nation. Barnet and Melman ignore or minimize the fact that top civilian foreign policy and defense policy-makers are generally men whose primary career ties are to the world of corporate capital and who do not expect to have long-term tenure in government. Their abbreviated public "service" and their sensitivity to the needs of capitalism make it difficult to characterize them as autonomous elites oriented towards perpetual growth in the defense sector.

extremely useful to the capitalist class. First, military spending is not for the production of ordinary commodities, but for *weapons.* These weapons are needed to carry out imperialist objectives. The threat of military intervention and its occasional use have helped keep large parts of the world "free" for American economic penetration. Second, weapon sales are also helpful in enabling our Free World client governments to defend themselves against revolutionary movements so that we do not have to intervene directly in these matters. Third, arms exports are very important in maintaining a balance of payments threatened by foreign investment and militarism.[21] Fourth, another vital function of military spending is the maintenance of a relatively high level of employment. Harry Magdoff estimates that unemployment might be in the neighborhood of 24.3 percent in the absence of the military budget because 8.3 million people are employed in defense-related work, and it is estimated that every $1 of defense spending stimulates another $1 to $1.40 of national product, creating more jobs.[22] Magdoff admits that unemployment insurance and a decline in interest rates and taxes would take up the slack along with a related rise in welfare outlays, construction, and municipal and state investment. Nevertheless, he argues that the inflationary effects of military spending and stock market speculation in the past generation have brought general economic prosperity which would be threatened by a trend toward disarmament. Finally, military spending has stimulated research and development whose fruits have been turned over to private industry.

As the case has been presented so far, military spending can be seen as rational because of *America's* economic interests. Only when the actual human and material costs exacted by militarism are enumerated can military spending be judged detrimental to the interests of the vast majority of the American people.[23] Military spending, as Paul Baran suggests, is indeed one way to solve or try to solve problems of chronic underinvestment in the private sector of a monopolistic capitalist economy.[24] It is the chosen method because it creates long-term investment opportunities for giant corporations which need a military umbrella for their highly valued foreign economic activity and also provides profitable, endless, and low risk investment in defense-related production, research, and development. Victor Perlo has shown that the top five hundred corporations, which are the heaviest foreign investors, are also the major beneficiaries of defense contracts.[25] Using these corporations' annual reports, which frequently break down the source of profits, he estimates that profits from foreign investments make up 25.2 per-

[21] Melman, *op. cit.*, 1965, pp. 131–155.
[22] Harry Magdoff, "Militarism and Imperialism," *Monthly Review*, vol. 21 (February, 1970), pp. 10–12.
[23] Melman, *op. cit.*, 1970, pp. 184–205.
[24] Baran, *op. cit.*, 1957, pp. 44–133. That it is not the *only* way open to capitalist societies is exemplified by Japan and Sweden. Yet both countries are heavily dependent on foreign trade and America's military presence provides protection for all world capitalists to peacefully pursue trade and investment at home and abroad.
[25] Victor Perlo, *Militarism and Industry: Arms Profiteering in the Missile Age* (New York: International Publishers Co., Inc., 1963).

cent of the total after-tax profits of these firms, while military-based profits account for an additional 16.8 percent.[26] Thus, by Perlo's method of calculation, 42 percent of the profits after taxes of the dominant American industries are attributable to imperialism and militarism.

Perlo admits that even some of these corporations might benefit, principally through tax reductions, from lower military budgets. He feels that profit ratios of 37 percent from foreign and military spending would be needed to offset the corporate taxes which support military expenditures—assuming that 50 percent of the profits from foreign investments would be retained without a military umbrella. According to Perlo's estimates, thirteen of the top twenty-five corporations, would be in a position to profit from military spending, while twelve would not.[27] Of course, as Perlo acknowledges, it is wrong to try to reduce corporate support for military spending simply to immediate economic interest. Many business elites might believe that a small tax loss relative to profits might be well advised to protect Americans from communism's social and political aims.

In addition, the capitalists as a class may feel—as Williams, Kolko, and Perlo suggest[28]—that the alternative to militarism and imperialism is the renewed struggle between business and the working class over the distribution of a smaller pie at home. The Cold War has witnessed the economic subordination of the labor movement to the needs of Big Business, the cutback of domestic welfare legislation, and the diminution of labor's political role. A demilitarized, postimperial America would require vast social changes, provide opportunities for labor militancy, and reduce the economic and political privileges now enjoyed by the business class.

For all these reasons the military-industrial complex thesis must be rejected in its simplest form. It too often sees the sources of militarism and war profits as the basis of the elite's support for a war economy without appreciating the important functions of military spending for the maintenance of *class* privilege. Moreover, the defense industries are often seen as a marginal sector rather than as a major part of the corporate capitalist system. In addition, the thesis frequently assumes that all the citizenry can and will reject what is irrational for the society as a whole. Too often, the critics of the military-industrial complex forget that what is irrational for the society is functional for many of the leading elements of the capitalist class, who will resist social reform. Given the power of this portion of the ruling class, it is doubtful that the war economy and imperialism can easily be eliminated. On the one hand, it is clear that capitalist countries can survive the "end of Empire." Britain's imperial role is now highly restricted. The capitalist world has not been destroyed by the loss of Communist Chinese and Russian markets and natural resources. Yet, as Harry Magdoff points out, these setbacks to the world capitalist class required painful adjustments—wars, depressions, increasing power for labor, the reduction of capitalist political and economic

[26] *Ibid.*, pp. 71–83.
[27] *Ibid.*, pp. 119–126.
[28] Williams, *op. cit.*, 1959; 1961; 1970. Kolko, *op. cit.*, 1969, pp. 87, 138. Perlo, *op. cit.*, pp. 115–116.

hegemony in the affected nations.[29] Despite these defeats, capitalists have not reconciled themselves to a restricted world role. They rely more on government support and still seek expansion, a goal they will not renounce without a struggle. It is perhaps wisest to say that capitalist classes engage in imperialist practices whenever possible, but probably can at a considerable cost adjust to a diminishing world and national economic and political role.[30] To say this is to say that capitalism and imperialism are linked, all other things being equal. The sole countervailing force operating against this unholy alliance is the ability and determination of the victims of this process to alter the situation.

[29] Harry Magdoff, "The Logic of Imperialism," *Social Policy*, vol. 1 (September–October, 1970), pp. 20–29. This article is a reply to a critique of Magdoff, *op. cit.*, 1969, by S. M. Miller, Roy Bennet, and Cyril Alapatt, "Does the U.S. Economy Require Imperialism," *Social Policy*, vol. 1 (September–October, 1970), pp. 12–19. This debate, which also includes a rejoinder by Roy Bennet and S. M. Miller under the same title as their original piece, *Social Policy*, vol. 1 (November–December, 1970), pp. 54–61, is one of the most stimulating discussions of the subject in print. While I tend to side with Magdoff's analysis of the tendencies of the system and feel that his critics fail to make a distinction between the needs and desires of a ruling class and economic rationality for a whole society, I concur to some extent with the critics' claim that the American empire is becoming progressively weaker. Whether capitalism survives in the United States may depend upon how the ruling class responds to this crisis. For a penetrating analysis of Britain's postimperial crisis and its threat to British capitalism see Andrew Glyn and Bob Sutcliffe, "The Critical Condition of British Capital," *New Left Review*, no. 66 (March–April, 1971), pp. 3–33.

[30] The role of the Soviet Union in Eastern Europe during the past generation inevitably raises the question of the relationship between socialism and imperialism. Although a socialist economy does not depend upon the continual expansion of sales and investment markets the Soviet case suggests that political and economic decision-makers in socialist societies can embark upon an imperialist path if they value *national* economic growth more than social and cultural revolution. The Chinese seem to be opting for a nonimperialist future which emphasizes economic and political equality. Thus, imperialism appears to be primarily a matter of choice for socialist countries, whereas in advanced capitalist societies, at least, imperialism is the preferred solution to *inherent* problems generated by the natural workings of the economy.

Gareth Stedman Jones

THE SPECIFICITY
OF U.S. IMPERIALISM

Since the Russian Revolution, the rulers of America have been increasingly concerned to justify their imperial system against revolutionary attack. They have employed two constant methods to maintain their domination. The first has been physical—the proliferation of US bases, the mobility of the American fleet, the alertness of the marine, the manoeuverings of the CIA, the bribery of friendly politicians. All this is well known. The second method has been ideological: the construction of a mythological, non-communist, non-socialist and even non-nationalist road to political independence for the countries of the Third World. To woo the aspiring politicians of these new states, the US has offered them the model of the "American Revolution" of 1776. It was on this basis that Franklin Roosevelt considered that the US was uniquely equipped to advise India on the road to independence, and it was again on the basis of this claim that Eisenhower felt entitled to ditch his Anglo-French imperialist allies at the time of the Suez crisis in 1956. America, in the estimation of her ruling politicians, was the first ex-colony, and so was uniquely equipped to steer a benevolent course through the stormy waters of post-war decolonization.

Of course, one embarrassing feature of this otherwise roseate vista was America's own imperial record—as a colonial power. For it was impossible to deny that the Spanish-American war of 1898 had resulted in the acquisition of Puerto Rico and the Philippines, or that Hawaii had been annexed to the metropolitan power. To circumvent these difficulties, a large school of official historians has attempted to provide satisfactory legalistic or at least non-economic explanations for America's unexpected lapse into the colonialism associated with the Old World. With as much ingenuity as their self-imposed myopia would permit, the historians came up with a satisfactory solution. The notorious Monroe doctrine was a defensive reaction against the colonial ambitions of European powers. Its purpose was simply to provide the necessary defensive bulwarks behind which the new nation could be consolidated. According to one official historian, 19th-century American leaders "were at most only incidentally concerned with real or imagined interests abroad." The events of the 1890's had no precedent. They were "an aberration." America lurched into an empire in a fit of absent-mindedness—"it had greatness thrust upon it." A Schumpeterian explanation was advanced

Reprinted, with deletions, from Gareth Stedman Jones, "The Specificity of U.S. Imperialism," *New Left Review,* no. 60 (March–April 1970), pp. 59–86, by permission of *New Left Review.* The original article included footnotes which have generally been deleted. Gareth Stedman Jones is a Research Fellow at Nuffield College, Oxford University, England. He is the author of *The Social Crisis of Victorian London* and is currently writing a biography of Engels. He is on the editorial board of *New Left Review.*

for the Spanish-American War. Incursions into the Caribbean and the Philippines were not in any sense determined by real economic interests, but were the result of the machinations of the cheap yellow press. The war was necessary to satisfy the frenzied and hysterical emotions of the people. The United States was forced to intervene to prevent new colonial incursions into the American hemisphere. America had not engaged in a determined war of economic expansion but had reluctantly assumed the Anglo-Saxon burden of helping backward peoples forward to liberty and democracy.

This official interpretation of the background to 20th-century American power has been skilfully elaborated in hundreds of volumes replete with an apparent apparatus of scholarship. For the most part, these legends have taken the form of a knowing or unknowing confusion between imperialism and colonialism. The *invisibility* of American imperialism when compared with the territorial colonialism of European countries, has been internalized by its historians to such an extent, that with a clear conscience they have denied its very existence. . . .

Until recently alternative interpretations put forward by radical or socialist critics have scarcely been more satisfactory. While official historians have celebrated the American ascent to world power either in terms of a beneficent and inexorable manifest destiny or else in terms of an unavoidable geopolitical logic of power, radical critics have tended to see American history as a progressive betrayal of the ideals and possibilities of a lost golden age: Beard's triumph of *personalty* (mobile capital) over *realty* (agrarianism).[1] In the heroic epoch of simple agrarians and small entrepreneurs, according to C. Wright Mills, "a free man, not a man exploited, and an independent man, not a man bound by tradition, here confronted a continent and, grappling with it, turned it into a million commodities." America was a country unburdened by a feudal or militaristic past and unmarred by the social and religious strife of Europe; but the foundation of an independent America contained a promise that its subsequent history failed to fulfil. David Horowitz could write in 1965: "When America set out on her post-war path to contain revolution throughout the world, and threw her immense power and influence into the balance against the rising movement for social justice among the poverty-stricken two-thirds of the world's population, the first victim of her deeds were the very ideals for a better world—liberty, equality and self-determination—which she herself, in her infancy, had done so much to foster."

In recent years the work of William Appleman Williams has also tried to break away from conventional patriotic fantasies.[2] Williams has rejected the myth of a golden age and laid bare the deep national historical roots of American imperialism. Nevertheless, for all its virtues, Williams's work has remained imprisoned in a similar idealistic-moralistic problematic. Williams's argument is best understood as a response to the Turner thesis which associated American democracy with the existence of an expanding frontier to

[1] Beard's interpretation of the American Revolution is to be found in *An Economic Interpretation of the Constitution of the United States*, 1913, and *Economic Origins of Jeffersonian Democracy*, 1915.

[2] William Appleman Williams, *The Contours of American History*, 1961; and see also, *The Tragedy of American Diplomacy*, 1957.

the West. According to Turner, "whenever social conditions tended to crystallize in the East, whenever capital tended to press upon labour or political restraints to impede the freedom of the mass, there was this gate of escape to the free conditions of the frontier. These free lands promoted individualism, economic equality, freedom to rise, democracy." Williams turns this thesis on its head. According to Williams, American history can be seen as the compound of two conflicting themes. The first of these themes has been the conception of a corporate Christian Commonwealth based upon the ideal of social responsibility; the second has been the untrammelled individualism based upon the ideals of private property. In Williams's eyes, the expanding westward frontier which in the 20th century became metamorphosed into a global American imperialism has always been the dominant means by which Americans have evaded the possibility of building a genuine democracy, of constructing the true Christian Socialist Commonwealth which has always remained immanent in American history. Thus American history is not basically seen as the product of the struggle and interaction of classes within a particular social formation, but of the clash between "weltanschauungs". The development of American Imperialism is seen not so much as the result of the inner logic of capitalist development, but rather as the product of a conscious evasion. Like Hobson before him, Williams seems to envisage the possibility of a modified American capitalism shorn of its unnecessary imperialist outworks, and asks whether the ruling class of corporation capitalism has "the nerve to abandon the frontier as Utopia" and "to turn its back on expansion as the open door of escape."

Despite these shortcomings, however, Williams's work possesses one major virtue: it shows expansionism to have been a consistent theme running throughout American history from its very beginning. On the basis of his work and that of his followers, it is possible to raise more adequately the problem of the specificity of American imperialism. Discussion among Marxist and Socialist writers has tended to concentrate perhaps too insistently upon the analysis of imperialism as a global stage of capitalist development. Such discussion has generally neglected the subsidiary but nevertheless crucial problem of the relationship between the historical determinants of a particular social formation and the specific mode of imperialist domination engendered by it.

Twentieth century American Imperialism may be said to have been characterized by two distinctive features which have clearly differentiated it from other imperialist systems. These are:

1. Its *non-territorial* character. Unlike the mode of imperialism employed by the British, French, German, Italian or Japanese, American imperialism has generally been characterized by its non-possession of a formal colonial empire. In this sense, official historians are partially correct when they speak of the Spanish-American war as "an aberration." The acquisition of Puerto Rico and the Philippines was a deviation, not as official historians have thought from an otherwise peaceful and non-expansionist American history, but rather from the typical economic, political and ideological forms of domination already characteristic of American imperialism.

The 20th century American empire, in intention at least, has been *an invisible empire*. American imperialism has been characterized by the concealment of American imperial interests behind a shield of supra-national or inter-governmental organizations—the League of Nations, the UN, the World Bank, the Marshall Plan, the OAS, the Alliance for Progress. Secondly, it is noticeable that the United States has attempted to evade formal political control even when client governments have nakedly relied upon American military and political power—South Vietnam, South Korea, Taiwan, and certain Latin American states (the classical example is Cuba after the Platt Amendment).

2. Its possession of a *formally anti-imperialist* ideology. The twin bases upon which this ideology rests are firstly the self-image of the United States as the first ex-colony, and secondly the creation and constant reproduction of a theory of "Communist aggression" which has justified "defensive" interventions of the part of the United States in the interests of 'freedom' and the territorial integrity of independent states. Thus the Cold War, the creation of NATO, the proliferation of US bases throughout the world, the Bay of Pigs and the US intervention in Vietnam are generally seen by official US ideologues as part of an anti-imperialist crusade, as a struggle to contain Communist aggrandisement.

Until recently American Imperialism and the Cold War have been treated even by the Left as two separate subjects. This conceptual apartheid has resulted in economic reductionism in the one case and psychologistic interpretations in the other. The intention of this essay is to examine the development of American imperialism from the moment of the formation of the United States as an independent political entity to the epoch of the First World War and the Russian Revolution. It is hoped that this tentative sketch will provide some of the elements necessary to resolve the question: *how far the characteristic modern form of American imperialism is a product of the Cold War, and how far it is an independent product resulting from the particularity of American historical development.*

1. The American "Revolution": Struggle for a National Imperialism

The claim that American Independence was the result of an anti-colonial revolution will bear little examination. Modern industrial imperialism is a mode of economic and social domination characteristic of capitalism at a mature stage of development. The question of political sovereignty has ultimately been contingent to the practice of this type of imperialism. Modern anti-colonial revolutions have been revolts against social systems based upon foreign exploitation, in which the national question could only be resolved by a social revolution.

A comparison between this specific system of oppression and the colonial status of North America under the mercantile system would reveal only the most meaningless and abstract resemblances. The truly colonized and exploited peoples were not the White American settlers, but the Indians and the Black slaves. The American "Revolution," far from procuring their liberation, tightened their chains of dependence, and in the case of the

Indians, accelerated the speed of their extermination.[3] While the mercantile system may have inhibited certain forms of industrial production in the thirteen colonies and was to become the source of some administrative and fiscal inconvenience, this was marginal beside the impetus given to indigenous capital accumulation through the development of the triangular trade, and the advantages conferred by a ready supply of slaves for the plantation economies and the provision of military protection against the Indians. The essential fact is that white settlers in North America were partners in English mercantile imperialism, and not its victims. They were no more part of some pre-industrial *damnés de la terre* than are white Rhodesian planters or Hong Kong merchants today. The white settlers accepted the English mercantile system until they were strong enough to do without it. The purpose of American independence, as John Adams put it in 1774, was the formation of "an independent empire."

If it is difficult to categorize the American War of Independence as anti-imperialist, it is equally difficult to describe the American "Revolution" as a bourgeois revolution, or indeed as a social revolution of any kind. While most historians have agreed that the internal struggle between different social groups was quite secondary to the national war of independence, some have nevertheless attempted to draw analogies with the French Revolution. Advocates of this position point to the immediately fiscal origins of both struggles, draw attention to the separation of church and state in both cases and go on to compare the confiscation of French emigré lands with the confiscation of Tory estates, the destruction of feudalism in France with the abolition of quit rents and entails in America, the Declaration of Independence with the Oath of the Tennis Court. While of course it would be absurd to deny the important detonating effects of the American Revolution abroad, such analogies only highlight the immense difference between the two movements. Unlike the French Revolution, the American Revolution produced no clearcut contest between social classes, but tended to divide allegiances across class lines. Secondly, the American Revolution was virtually untouched by any social challenge from below. A radical alliance between the subordinate classes failed to emerge. Small subsistence farmers in the interior—the nearest thing to an American peasantry—failed to make significant contact with artisans in the towns. The spectre of slave revolt exercised a major subterranean influence upon the course of the American Revolution. The promise of freedom in exchange for loyalism provoked large scale waves of slave desertions near the British lines. But slaves did not participate in the struggle as a coherent political force and found few allies in the classes above them. The leadership of the movement for national independence and the construction of a new Constitution ended, as it had begun, in the hands of a coalition of slave-owning agrarian capitalists in the South and mercantile capitalists in the North-East. Thirdly, it may be argued that a bourgeois

[3] Thomas Jefferson, one of the founding fathers, expressed the dominant attitude to the Indians—or at least of those who did not wish to exterminate them outright. He was glad "to see the good and influential individuals among the Indians in debt; because we observe that when these debts get beyond what the individuals can pay, they become willing to lop them off by a cession of land."

revolution, by definition, must entail a radical change in anterior forms of property relationship. It would be difficult to argue that the American Revolution produced any such transformation. Feudal vestiges such as entails and quit rents had long been rendered meaningless by American conditions, and their abolition was most ardently supported by the supposedly "feudal class"—indebted Southern planters in need of a more fluid market in land. The real seeds of future conflict lay in the uneasy coexistence between a form of capitalism based upon free labour and a form of capitalism based upon slavery, within a single polity still in the process of expansion. But in the Revolutionary period, this fundamental tension was overridden by the sectional conflict between the large scale capitalist property-owning class as a whole (including commercial farmers, Northern Merchants *and* Southern slave owners) and indebted subsistence farmers in the interior: a struggle which reached its climax in 1787–88 with Shay's Rebellion and the making of the Constitution. As Staughton Lynd writes, "the United States Constitution represented, not a triumph of capitalism over a landed aristocracy . . . but a compromise or coalition between men of wealth in the cities and men of wealth on the land."

The United States was then already structurally an imperialist state at the moment of its foundation. The foundation of the United States was in no sense an anti-imperialist or even an anti-colonial revolution. If anything the American Revolution accelerated the development of American Imperialism by freeing westward expansion from the controls imposed by the British. Westward expansion and settlement at the expense of the Indians was eventually to secure the United States the crucial advantage of possessing the largest single domestic market in the world. But already at the time of the Revolution, its political advantages were realised. The famous Turner thesis was understood from the beginning by the more sophisticated American politicians. Madison, for instance, in his Federalist Papers, clearly understood the purpose of the frontier—for by the almost indefinite provision of cheap land further and further to the West, the dangers of class warfare resulting from unequal distribution of property, could be postponed. Just as an expanding internal frontier in Sweden had resulted in relatively weak instruments of feudal domination, so it was hoped that the Western frontier would act as the self-perpetuating safeguard of property and democracy in America.

2. Two Forms of Expansion—Prelude to the Civil War

Even at the beginning of the 19th century, Americans were looking beyond the West, in their fantasies of a new world Empire. A Kentuckian boasted in 1810, for example, "that his countrymen were full of enterprise" and "although not poor, are greedy after plunder as ever the old Roman were. Mexico glitters in our eyes—the word is all we wait for." The war of 1812 with England possessed many elements of a war of inter-imperialist competition. It was certainly hoped that Canada would be conquered, and some Congressmen pressed for an invasion of Florida and Cuba, while others suggested that the war offered a legitimate excuse for finishing off the

Indians. The famous Monroe Doctrine was also a much more expansionist statement than conventional American historians will admit—by keeping Europeans away from territorial footholds in the Americas, the field would be left open for American economic predominance. As Henry Clay, Monroe's contemporary, predicted, in half a century North Americans in relation to South America "would occupy the same position as the people of New England do to the rest of United States."

But there were basic limits to the rate of expansion in the first half of the 19th century. The most obvious of these was the as yet inadequate development of the forces of production. America, at least before the 1840's,[4] could not be described as an industrialized country. A second reason was the necessary time spent in Western expansion. American historians who speak complacently of the absence of the settler-type colonialism characteristic of European powers merely conceal the fact that the whole *internal* history of US Imperialism was one vast process of territorial seizure and occupation. The absence of territorialism "abroad" was founded on an unprecedented territorialism "at home." A third reason was the growing conflict between North and South. Here also the basic issue was Western expansion. The effect of the English industrial revolution was to give an enormous boost to the slave-based cotton crop economy of the South.[5] Slavery was certainly not in danger of dying a natural death as an economic anachronism. In the case of cotton, slavery was an efficient method of production, and as a dynamic sector of the economy slave-based cotton production was moving west in the South just as small independent farmers producing cereals were moving west in the North. The most productive cotton crop areas moved from the Eastern seaboard into Alabama and Mississippi— and after 1840 into Texas. This had politically explosive implications because it threatened to upset the balance that had been established between the relative number of slave and free states.

The problem had existed in embryo since the 1790's when the 1790 census had threatened the South with numerical minority and consequent loss of influence over the direction of the federal government. But it had been hoped at that time that the South could make up its losses by gains in the West. By the 1820's open conflict was only narrowly averted by a compromise which established Missouri as a slave state in exchange for Maine as a free state. In the 1830's the South was more ominously threatened by the "transportation revolution" which progressively undermined the economic basis of the traditional alliance of South and West (via the Mississippi and New Orleans) by connecting the West with the North-East. By the 1840's the problem had become menacing. President Polk came into power in 1845 determined upon a course of aggressive expansion. His aim was to take Oregon, Texas and California. In a strident war against Mexico he captured Texas and California, but decided to deal with the British and compromise over Oregon. The result was recrimination from the North and the West over

[4] The turning point comes in the late 1830's. See Douglas C. North, *The Economic Growth of the United States 1790–1860*, 1961.
[5] In the 1830's cotton represented two thirds of the total value of American exports and remained well over half until the Civil War.

the supposed betrayal of Northern interests. After much conflict a compromise was made in 1850, establishing California as a free state and leaving Texas unallocated for competition. It was the determination of the North and West to break down this compromise that led to Civil War.

The competition between two different forms of production in some respects slowed down the rate of US expansion—for it was liable to lead to the same forms of conflict as those raised by Western expansion itself. This problem had already been posed in the 1820's. When Adams became President in 1826, he suggested a conference of the newly established Spanish American Republics. "As navigators and manufacturers," he wrote, "we are already so far advanced upon a career which they are yet to enter, that we may for many years after the conclusion of the war maintain with them a commercial intercourse, highly beneficial to both parties." Southerners strongly objected, for this implied a blow at their conception of empire. Many of them wanted Cuba as a new slave territory. Southern expansion, in other words, would have necessitated *territorial* expansion. Similarly Southerners resented the importation of ideas of laissez-faire liberal democracy into American foreign policy, whose purpose was to benefit Northern manufacturers, and which implied a threat to slave-owning society. As industrial capitalism took more and more hold in the North, articulate Southerners emphasized more and more their "preindustrial" traits—courtesy, grace, cultivation, the broad outlook versus money grubbing. Their ambitions for Cuba remained. They had assumed with John Quincy Adams that the laws of political gravitation would push Cuba inevitably into the arms of the United States. But this did not happen. By the 1850's the South was becoming increasingly impatient with "the apple that refused to fall from the tree." Southerners attempted to persuade Spain to sell the island and when this did not work, they issued the Ostend Manifesto proclaiming their right to take it. The Manifesto was quickly disclaimed by Northerners in Washington. It was not that expansion was unpopular, but rather that Northerners were not prepared to sanction the expansion of the slave economy.

The Civil War was also a necessary precondition of a fully developed American Imperialism in a second sense. For the War can justly be described in the words of Barrington Moore, "as the last revolutionary offensive on the part of urban or bourgeois capitalist democracy." Industrialization itself had of course, started well before the War. In fact its pace had been rapidly increasing since 1837. What the War accomplished was the removal of the political and institutional fetters upon industrial capitalism. Legislation passed by the Northern-dominated War Congresses included measures for stronger central banking, high tariffs to protect new industries, a contract labour law to provide a steady flow of cheap immigrant labour, the Homestead Act to gain the support of the West and Federal assistance for internal improvements (the granting of generous loans and free land to build rail links between the industries of the East and the farms of the West, thus unifying the domestic market). It is instructive to compare this legislation, as Moore has done, with the planters' programme of 1860: federal enforcement of slavery, no high protective tariffs, no subsidies nor expensive tax-creating internal improvements, no national banking and currency system. The extent to which the Plantation Economy had imposed fetters upon the emancipation of capital and the scale of the Northern capitalist victory after the Civil War are both evident.

3. The Triumph of Bourgeois Imperialism

From the 1840's, Eastern Capitalists had begun to show increasing interest in overseas economic expansion, especially in the supposedly vast China market, and in such areas as California and Hawaii, which were seen as stepping stones to it. But they had lacked the legislative power to enforce their policies. In the period after 1870 these empire builders succeeded because the Civil War had given them the political power to implement their plans. The territorial colonialism of Southerners, primarily interested in the extension of the plantation system, was finally superseded by the bourgeois empire of Northerners primarily interested in overseas economic control as an outlet for profitable investment and surplus commodities. The control of policy-making by industrialists and financiers was a pre-condition to the creation of a new commercial empire in its two chief spheres—South America and the Far East.

Indeed it might be argued that the rapidly increasing rate of industrialization, triggered by victory in the Civil War, made such an empire not only possible but also necessary. As efficient machines produced more and more industrial and agricultural goods, consumption could not maintain the pace. The resulting deflation "needed only the impetus derived from the failures of large banks or Wall Street firms to push the whole economy into full scale depression."[6] Of the 25 years after 1873, half were years of depression: 1873–78, 1882–85 and 1893–97. If the general price index is figured as 100 in 1873, then it fell to 77 in a few years, in the 1880's it again fell from 87 to 76 and again from 78 in 1890 to 71 in 1894. The break in the 1880's was particularly sharp, since agricultural prices fell when good European crops combined with still greater American wheat production. Industrial prices followed suit. Between 1880 and 1884 business failures tripled to almost 12,000 annually.

The result of these cataclysmic depressions was to accelerate cartelization and concentration of ownership. Speaking of the 1873 panic Andrew Carnegie recollected, "so many of my friends needed money, that they begged me to repay them. I did so and bought out five or six of them. That was to give me my leading interest in the steel business." The depression of 1883 similarly allowed him to purchase the Homestead steel plant. Out of this expanded plant came vast amounts of steel, much of which sought foreign markets in the 1890's because of insufficient demand at home. Simultaneous to this process, the rate of foreign investment continued to expand until it reached 3 billion 300 million dollars in 1899. This capital accumulated from

[6] Walter LaFeber, *The Empire—An Interpretation of American Expansion 1860–98*, 1963, p. 8. This is the best detailed examination of American expansion in the second half of the 19th century, and the factual material in this section is largely taken from it.

the profits of the American industrial revolution was reinvested in new machinery and plants, but an increasing volume also flowed into Latin America, Canada and Asia.

The problem of foreign outlets was even more intense for the agricultural sector. With the opening of vast new lands in 1855 and the progress of farm mechanization, production soared way beyond home needs—and sometimes world needs. The result was a sharp decline in prices—and an increase in farm bankruptcies. At the beginning of the Reconstruction period it was thought that the lands of the West would provide limitless opportunities for another 100 years. Even the semi-desert areas, it was claimed, would soon be made profitable by ploughing, settlement and the planting of trees. Taking such promises literally, farmers, cattlemen and speculators settled more land in 30 years than they had in the previous 300. In the 1880's this dream turned into a nightmare—the fall of prices and the exhaustion of bad soil made the land barely sufficient for subsistence. Between 1888 and 1892 half the population of Western Kansas left their farms in search of new opportunities. But the end of the frontier had already been reached. This had another important consequence—for by 1886 the American railroad system had been more or less completed: 200,000 men had been employed on railroad construction, who were now forced to find other jobs. Similarly iron makers were now forced to find other markets, having increased their output enormously between the 1860's and the 1880's.

The three major depression periods coincided with outbreaks of industrial violence perhaps unmatched in other capitalist countries of the period— the railway strike of 1877, the Chicago Haymarket riot of 1886, and the Pullman Strike and Coxey's march of the unemployed upon Washington in the 1890's. Madison's prediction that class war would follow the closing of the frontier seemed to be coming true.

The aftermath of the Civil War thus produced an economic substructure that impelled a fully fledged modern imperialism. The victory over the Southern planters ensured that the nature of imperial expansion would not generally follow the European pattern of formal political domination over vast colonial areas—except within the borders of the United States itself. There was no prominent military-agrarian class vying for proconsular employment. The new American empire was to be a strictly bourgeois product. It would both solve the problem of surplus disposal and reduce discontent at home. The open class conflict unleashed by the industrial depressions from the 1870's to the 1890's swung the vast majority of the anxious middle class behind a policy of informal but careful planned economic domination in Asia and Latin America.

The lines of this new policy were prophesied with remarkable accuracy by William Seward, Republican Secretary of State at the end of the 1860's. Seward understood that the primary objective of expansion would no longer be territorial, once the economy had been more industrialized. He considered that commercial expansion would now be the key to making America "the master of the world." The new commercial empire would no longer need territory for colonization, which in Seward's view raised the danger of a standing army; it only needed certain land bases to protect the flow of trade and investment. The key to this new world empire was to be Asia. As early as 1853, he had warned of the growing competition there. France, England and Russia, he wrote, are the great rivals. "Watch them with jealousy, and baffle their designs against you . . . you are already the great continental power of America. But does that content you? I trust it does not. You want the commerce of the world. This must be looked for on the Pacific. The nation that draws most from the earth and fabricates most, and sells the most to foreign nations, must be and will be the great power of the earth."

In 1867 Seward purchased Alaska. This was far from a white elephant. It was designed to sandwich British Columbia between American territory and thereby, Seward hoped, increase the pressure upon Canada to join the USA. More important, however, it established what he called a "drawbridge between America and Asia." Seward regarded Alaska as the Northern protected-flank in his aim to dominate the Pacific. The Southern flank would be ensured by an American controlled Panama Canal. In the centre would be California and Hawaii. In pursuit of this policy Seward promoted the American representative in Hawaii to Minister Resident in 1863, and four years later tried to prepare the islands for the hug of annexation by pulling the country into a reciprocity treaty. This was vetoed by the Senate, but he was successful in annexing the Midway Islands 1,200 miles west of Hawaii in 1867. The importance of these islands was not their intrinsic economic value, but their crucial position as safe coaling stations for American ships.

In the late 1860's and early 1870's there was little widespread interest in Seward's policy, but with the onset of depression in the 1870's, and the only fitful prosperity of the 1880's and 1890's, the necessity of empire became more apparent. In the depression of the 1870's, the new Secretary of State negotiated a treaty with Hawaii, and moved more actively towards control of Latin America. The United States intervened in Cuba and Venezuela, and encouraged investment in the South of Mexico—a move to secure more surely the projected line of the Panama canal. The 1878 revolution in Cuba destroyed many Spanish and Cuban planters by forcing them to sell their remaining holdings to pay debts. American capital entered the island in large quantities when the expansion of European beet sugar production drove down prices and bankrupted inefficient growers, who sold out cheaply. As the *North American Review* boasted in 1888, this species of ownership gave Americans the financial fruits without political responsibilities. A few years later there was systematic penetration of American capital into Mexico. With the ending of railroad construction in the US a group of capitalists moved across the border and obtained Mexican government subsidies of 2 million dollars and concessions for the construction of five major railways. The victory of Northern capitalism in the Civil War had meant the triumph of a policy of high tariffs. One factor which differentiated British and American imperialism in the last half of the century was the American exploitation of tariffs as an instrument of informal empire. This mode of domination in South America increasingly took the form of the reciprocity treaty. Using the high all-around protective tariff as a bargaining counter, Frelinghuysen, then US Secretary of State, negotiated this form of treaty with Mexico, Cuba, Puerto Rico, Santo Domingo, Salvador and Colombia. In return for a virtually free entrance for American manufactures, he reduced the tariff on certain imported raw materials—thus increasing the subordination of Latin American states to the US economy. As he himself explained, reciprocity in the case of the Caribbean islands, "brings the islands into close commercial connection with United States and confers upon us and them all the benefits that would result from annexation were that possible."

The expansion of the frontier by trade into South America and the Pacific in the 1880's and early 1890's was increasingly associated with ideas of an ever expanding commercial frontier which would alleviate discontent at home. Frederick Turner in the 1890's produced his famous frontier thesis of American Democracy. His ideas heavily influenced both Theodore Roosevelt and Woodrow Wilson (who considered himself to be carrying Turner's ideas into practice). Turner regarded commercial expansion as the magic escape route from his otherwise depressing conclusions. The march to the Pacific would not stop at the shore line. Turner saw the necessity of continued expansion, and for strong government support of enterprising capitalists. "Once fully afloat on the sea of world wide economic interests," he wrote, "we shall develop political interests. Our fisheries dispute furnishes one example; our Samoan interests another; our Congo relations a third. But perhaps most important are our present and future relations with South America, coupled with our Monroe doctrine. It is a settled maxim of international law that the government of a foreign state whose subjects have lent money to another state may interfere to protect the right of bond-holders, if they are endangered by the borrowing state."

Turner was not alone in his idea of the necessity of developing the new frontier. Similar ideas were put forward with much force in the best selling works of Josiah Strong, the Protestant Missionary. Strong stressed the political significance of the disappearance of public lands. Many expect revolution, warned Strong, and the Christian church was all that stood in the way. Strong's writings cast an interesting light on the frequent assertion by academic historians, that missionary activity bore no relation to economic interest. According to him, the Anglo-Saxon with his two virtues of civil liberty and spiritual Christianity would move down on Mexico and Central America, out upon the islands of the sea, over Africa and beyond, and "can anyone doubt that the result of this competition of races will be the survival of the fittest?" The expansion of Anglo-Saxon Christianity would also solve the fundamental problems of overproduction. Noting that "steam and electricity have mightily compressed the earth," so that "our markets are to be greatly extended," he commented, "commerce follows the missionary . . . a Christian civilization performs the miracle of loaves and fishes, and feeds its thousands in a desert." Missionary activity encouraged native peoples to adopt Western habits and Western dress, thus missionary and trader were in perpetual alliance.

By the 1890's, there was a growing consensus among business men and politicians that further expansion was necessary to avert economic depression. This policy had been implicit in the 1880's, when Congress sanctioned a large increase in naval spending. There was opposition to territorial expansion in non-contiguous areas. It was argued that colonialism of this kind would lead to the dangers that had brought down the Roman Empire—through the necessity of large standing armies and an increasingly strong military caste. But there was no disagreement about the wisdom of informal methods of domination. This much is illustrated by the role of President Cleveland who is popularly recorded in American history books as a fervent anti-colonialist. The Brazilian Revolution of 1894–5 threatened the growing American trade with that country. Vigorous pressures for intervention were made by Standard Oil and W. S. Crossman and Brothers. As a result, Cleveland ordered the navy to intervene to check the rebels, and it was kept on duty off Rio for a further year to check any further danger to American property. Cleveland's attitude to British interference in Venezuela was similarly vigorous. England was forced to back down, since, as Secretary of State Olney claimed, "Today the United States is practically sovereign on this continent, and its fiat is law upon the subjects to which it confines its interposition." Henry Cabot Lodge remarked, in a significant reformulation of the Monroe doctrine: "The doctrine has no bearing on the extension of United States, but simply holds that no European power shall establish itself in the Americas or interfere with American governments."

4. The Advent of the Spanish-American War

It was the fierce depression of the 1890's that set America on the final path towards war with Spain. When the depression burst in 1893, there was a considerable body of business opinion that attributed the slump in trade to incorrect monetary policy. But the attempt of the Cleveland Administration to provide a monetary cure for the crisis made little difference. The result was a growing agreement that the crisis was one of overproduction and the lack of markets. This consensus was expressed by McKinley in 1895: "No worthier cause than the expansion of trade can engage our energies. . . . We want our markets for our manufactures, and agricultural products. . . . We want a foreign market for our surplus products. . . . We want a reciprocity which will give us foreign markets for our surplus products, and in turn that will open our markets to foreigners for those products which they produce and we do not." The National Association of Manufacturers took up this cause enthusiastically, and were particularly keen on entry into the fabled Asian market. In Japan and Korea it met with some success. Japan doubled her imports of cotton in 1895, and Americans gained substantial contracts in shipbuilding. In Korea, Horace Allen, a missionary who was also the economic secretary of the American legation, was able to gain the concession of the Un San mines, the richest gold mines in the Far East. Allen then reorganized the Korean Cabinet so that pro-Japanese elements were unable to oppose the grant and persuaded the Korean government to institute the death penalty for Japanese traders copying American goods in the area. Accompanying this thrust of finance and manufacture in the Far East was an intensified missionary effort in the area. One missionary stated his role bluntly in the *Congregationist Magazine*: "If I were asked to state what would be the best form of advertising (in China) for the great American Steel Trust or Standard

Oil or Baldwin Locomotives . . . or Singer Sewing machine . . . I should say, take up the support of one or two dozen mission stations." Despite such sterling efforts, however, US imperialism found stiff competition from Japan, Russia, England and France in China. Because of the collusion of other powers, American capitalists lost the chance to finance China's war indemnity to Japan, and thus the railroad concession that went with it. Anxiety about the Chinese market played a considerable part in determining the annexation of the Philippines in the Spanish-American war.

In 1895 there was a further Cuban revolution directed against Spain. The causes of discontent in the island were in fact a direct result of the Reciprocity Treaty negotiated with the US. A new American tariff in 1895 had eliminated the privileged position of Cuba in the American sugar market, and plantations were consequently forced to discharge hands. In the Revolution that followed considerable damage was done to Cuban-American property. Powerful US corporations launched a campaign for intervention in the island. Initial support for the revolution changed into a demand for intervention to support moderate and conservative elements in Cuba. At the same time business men who did not have assets to defend and who had hitherto opposed the war, considered that the situation was creating an atmosphere of business uncertainty, and that intervention was necessary to stabilize the situation so that domestic recovery and Asian expansion could proceed uninterrupted. The causes of the War were quite blatantly stated in a note from the American Government to Spain. It read: "The extraordinary, because direct and not merely theoretical or sentimental, interest of the US in the Cuban situation cannot be ignored. . . . Not only are our citizens largely concerned in the ownership of property and in the industrial and commercial ventures . . . but the chronic condition of trouble causes disturbance in the social and political conditions of our own peoples. . . . A continuous irritation within our borders injuriously affects the normal functions of business, and tends to delay the condition of prosperity to which this country is entitled."

The war proceeded very much along the lines prophesied by Seward 40 years before. Hawaii and the Philippines were annexed as necessary stepping stones to the penetration of China. The annexation of the Philippines aroused opposition because it seemed to be the first step towards a European type of colonialism, which entailed a growing military sector and increased taxes. But such was not McKinley's original intention. All that was initally needed was an adequate naval base. It was the Filipino rebellion against US occupation, that made annexation an unfortunate necessity. In Cuba itself, this necessity was averted by a resolution from Senator Platt of Connecticut, to the effect that the government and control of the island would be left in the hands of its peoples, subject only to a restriction of its relations with foreign powers, a limit on the national debt, support for American actions, and the provision of bases. This was a decidedly better solution than the Puerto Rican annexation, since it maintained effective control without the threat of immigration to racist sentiment.

The War itself was only a prelude to an attempt to make a full scale economic penetration of Asia, and particularly China. The Secretary of State in 1899 issued a demand for equal access and fair treatment for US economic power in China. A further note asserted America's direct interest in maintaining the territorial and administrative integrity of that country. These Open Door notes were America's characteristic contribution to the practice of Imperialism. It was not akin to British imperial policy in the period. London's version of the policy acknowledged spheres of interest whereas the US demanded absolute equality of treatment. Convinced of the necessity to expand and yet wanting to avoid the pitfalls of a formal colonial empire (with the consequent necessity of war against rivals), the USA employed the strategy of the Open Door to exploit its growing economic power.

The depression of the 1890's had a further important consequence for the changing practice of American imperialism: the growing domination of finance capital over industrial capital. Significantly, Rockefeller became a financier, while older giant capitalists like Carnegie sold out and retired. In the depression the great majority of industrial capitalists became temporarily dependent on finance capital, like that represented by the house of Morgan. Banks, like Morgan and Rockefeller were able to control the vast capital assets tied up in life insurance companies in addition to the security and profits derived from industrial plants such as Standard Oil and US Steel. The conflict between finance and industrial capital had certain repercussions on the character of the American Empire. Since poor countries had to have money to buy American exports of goods and services, they had to accumulate it, either by increasing their export of raw materials or else by borrowing it from abroad. The result was what Taft referred to as "dollar diplomacy." Backward countries needed capital, but financiers needed government help at home in order to attract capital from the great number of individual savers who were unfamiliar and doubtful about the security of such overseas investment. This made financiers particularly keen to win firm guarantees of repayment from debtor nations.

5.   The Maturation of the US Imperial System

With the Open Door policy, the implementation of dollar diplomacy and the seizure of the Panama Canal zone from Colombia, the main infra-structure of the early US Imperialist system was completed. Theodore Roosevelt produced the final metamorphosis of the Monroe doctrine when he declared, "I regard the Monroe doctrine as being equivalent to the open door in South America." He went on to assure each Latin American nation that it could count on the friendship of United States, if it "acted with reasonable efficiency and decency in social and political matters" and "if it keeps its orders and pays its obligations." If nations behaved they would enjoy prosperity, if not they would be punished by American intervention.

This system was to be exemplified in the American treatment of Cuba. A revolt in 1917 immediately evoked protests from the resident US business community, and as a matter of course the Marines were sent in. State Department historians claim that this intervention was necessitated by the danger of German activity in the island—but not surprisingly have produced no evidence to support this assertion. The purpose of intervention was to restore political stability and thus create conditions for profitable business activity. As part of this stabilization policy, General Enoch Crowder was appointed to supervise a new electoral code, and oversee the elections of 1920. Crowder proceeded to draw up six necessary qualifications for a Cuban president and member of the Cuban cabinet. The first condition was stated to be "a thorough acquaintance with the desires of the US government," and the sixth condition was "amenability to suggestions which might be made to him by the American Legation." At the instance of the house of Morgan, Crowder was appointed ambassador to Cuba, although it had hitherto been illegal for a soldier to hold a diplomatic post. A bank loan to the Cuban government by Morgan was endorsed by the American government, and timid attempts by the Cuban government to raise revenue by a 4 per cent profits tax were satisfactorily replaced by a 1 per cent sales tax. Although particularly blatant, this episode was a typical product of the heavy involvement of American finance capital in South America.

Conventionally, historians tend to contrast the swashbuckling crudity of dollar diplomacy by Roosevelt and Taft with the high-minded idealism, "the legalistic-moralistic approach to international problems" associated with Wilson, and the arbitration movement. The contrast between Roosevelt and Wilson is presented as one between the "realist" and the "moralist." While Roosevelt is seen as the wielder of the "big stick" and creator of the Great White Fleet, Wilson is seen as the fierce critic of dollar diplomacy, the hammer of the trusts and the naive champion of world peace. In this context, much is made of Wilson's repudiation of the Taft-backed International Banking Consortium as evidence of Wilsonian moralism. This is a misunderstanding, however. Wilson did not oppose loans to China as such, he merely opposed loans in which the American banking group could not have the controlling interest. As he explained to the bankers, he intended the United States to "participate and participate very generously in the opening to the Chinese and to the use of the world of the almost untouched and perhaps unrivalled resources of China." He kept his word by exempting expanding corporations from anti-trust legislation, and providing the legislative encouragement that the financiers desired.

In fact Woodrow Wilson provided 20th century American Imperialism with its most coherent and self-righteous defender. As an early adherent of the Turner frontier thesis, Wilson defined the nation's natural politico-economic development and its prosperity as a function of Westward expansion. With the end of the continental frontier, expansion into world markets with the nation's surplus economic goods and capital was, in his view, indispensable to the stability and prosperity of the economy. It was also no more than a natural development in the life of any industrial nation, and in no way morally invidious; for in his view, the nation's economic expansion was a civilizing force that carried with its principles of democracy and Christianity, bonds of international understanding and peace. Given superior US industrial efficiency, the United States would assume supremacy in the world's markets, provided artificial barriers to her economic expansion were eliminated. Accordingly, Wilson admired and championed Hay's Open Door policy and advocated vigorous government diplomacy to attain these ends. In a speech in 1921, he stated, "If we are not going to stifle economically, we have got to find our way out into the great international exchanges of the world. . . . The nation's irresistible energy has got to be released for the commercial conquest of the world." As a policy for achieving this he advocated a strong mercantile marine, a downward revision of the tariff and laws encouraging American overseas banking. Wilson's beliefs about universal peace were inextricably linked with his commercial philosophy.

Wilson hoped to stay out of the First World War and then dominate the peace settlement as the undisputed economic master of the world. He nevertheless feared the commercial threat of Germany and hated its military-dominated government. In addition prominent finance houses like Dupont and Morgan provided economic support to the Allied war effort. Wilson's war aims were genuinely expressed in his rules for the League of Nations. For there was no fundamental incompatibility between the ambitions of American Imperialism and the sermonizing tones of the Covenant. There, like the Ten Commandments, were the principles of American economic expansion—the open door, the freedom of the seas, the prohibition of territorial changes except in accordance with the wishes of the inhabitants, compromises between advanced powers and underdeveloped territories that ensured the economic expansion of the former, and a political system of control which would be dominated by US, Britain, France and Japan.

This grandiose bourgeois evangelism was upset by the very cupidity of the capitalist system, which Wilson had so idealized. In October 1917, his scheme was threatened by the accomplishment of the Bolshevik Revolution.[7] Wilson's position on socialism had been unambiguous. The President's thought, records his official biographer, "disclosed itself as antipathetic to unsettled political conduct and to revolution as a method of government." Such a philosophy had formed the justification for his extensive interventions in Haiti, Nicaragua, the Dominican Republic and in the Mexican Revolution. Wilson, in his own words, had set about "to teach the South American Republics to elect good men" and to establish a government in Mexico "under which all contracts and business and concessions will be safer than they have been."

Despite his announcement that he "stood resolutely and absolutely for the right of every people to determine its own destiny and its own affairs," Wilson wasted little time on deciding that the Bolsheviks constituted an exception to his principle of self-determination. By defining the Bolsheviks as German agents, the task of self-justification was made relatively simple. It was not moral scruple that prevented Wilson from making a swift and effective intervention in Russia, nor even the dictates of the War with Germany, for Wilson made the decision to intervene with American troops before the Germans were stopped short in the second battle of the Marne. What prevented proper intervention by the Pacific Imperialist powers was their expansionist greed and mutual suspicions. America could not afford to leave the

[7] For an account of the politics of American counter-revolutionary intervention in Russia, see Appleman Williams's essay in Horowitz (ed.), *Containment and Revolution*, 1967.

Manchurian railway in the control of the Japanese, and was more concerned to prevent covert Japanese expansion in China and Siberia at the expense of American economic interests, than to make an all-out attack on Bolshevism. Here Wilson made a massive but characteristic mistake. The eventual result of this local imperialist squabble was, of course, Pearl Harbour and the Pacific War.

6. Conclusions

Several critical factors differentiated America from European imperialist powers in the 19th century. America lacked a powerful militarily-oriented aristocracy, was free from the land hunger which sustained European colonial settlement and was exceptionally well-endowed in necessary raw materials. The Northern victory in the Civil War ensured the emergence of a bourgeois non-territorial imperial system whose primary rationale was initially not the supply of raw materials but the provision of markets for American goods and outlets for American capital. By the beginning of the 20th century, the basic structure of the American imperial system had been completed. The growth of this system had neither been anomic nor indiscriminate. American power from the beginning had been concentrated upon Latin America and the Far East. These areas were guaranteed by the two classic statements of American Imperialism—the Monroe doctrine and the Open Door Note.

At the end of the 19th century it seemed that American ambitions in these two areas were soon to be completely fulfilled. In the previous half century, the main obstacle to American economic expansion had been the entrenched positions already occupied by the British. By the turn of the century, however, the balance of economic power had shifted. British economic hegemony in South America had begun to give way before the encroachments of American capital. For Americans this shift was symbolized by the settlement of the Venezuelan dispute in 1895. Traditional hostility or suspicion towards Britain was increasingly replaced by the idea of an Anglo-American partnership which would smooth the transition between the Pax Britannica and the Pax Americana. This would allow the United States all the fruits of imperial control without its concomitant fiscal and military burdens. America had no need of a formal colonial empire but could increase her imperial power simply by relying upon her superior economy.[8] Just as early

[8] United States was probably the most self-sufficient country in the world in this period. Nevertheless in 1910 America was the world's third largest trader. US exports only constituted 4–5 per cent of GNP in the years before 1914. Her main imports were capital and labour. In 1914 foreign investment in the US constituted 7.2 billion dollars, while US investment abroad constituted 3.5 billion dollars. This balance was almost exactly reversed during the First World War. The semi-autarchic nature of the US economy in the 19th century might at first sight contradict an economic interpretation of the rise of US imperialism. In the period 1870–1900 the population increased by 97 per cent, and home consumers consumed 90 per cent of US total production. By 1898, however, this 10 per cent amounted to 1 billion dollars worth and was heavily concentrated in iron, steel, textiles and agricultural machinery—precisely the industries which pushed hardest for overseas expansion.

British imperialism had honeycombed the Portuguese empire while protecting its formal structure, so a similar special relationship might be established between the United States and the British Empire. The USA could afford to move from the crude territorial expansionism of Polk to a peaceful and ordered world governed by due respect for property and the Open Door. Just as British industrial supremacy had produced the pacifism of John Bright, so American industrial supremacy was to produce the sanctimonious moralism of Woodrow Wilson and the League of Nations.

It was increasingly evident, however, in the years before 1914, that America's economic power would not go unchallenged. America's reservation in the Far East was increasingly threatened by Japan in the years after the Russo-Japanese war, while the rise of German "militaristic" imperialism might pose a threat to American penetration of Eastern Europe and the Middle East. Moreover, in the second decade of the century, a yet more ominous phenomenon appeared in the shape of indigenous movements against imperialism under the banner of nationalism or socialism. The Chinese Revolution of 1911, the Mexican Revolution and then the Russian Revolution posed a drastic threat to the ideology of Wilsonism.

Wilson's League of Nations was therefore conceived both as a means of securing American imperial supremacy without recourse either to formal colonial empire or to inter-imperialist warfare, and secondly as a means of building a Holy Alliance of industrial powers to hold down the rebellious forces of the underdeveloped world. It envisaged the consolidation of an informal American empire in which each dependent country would be tied to the United States on the model of the Platt amendment. As is well known, Wilson's proposal of the League was rejected by the American electorate after the war. What had been devised as an inexpensive means of securing the permanence of the Open Door international order had begun to appear like an open-ended commitment to police the globe in the defence of non-essential interests. It would be a mistake, however, to interpret the rejection of the League as a retreat to a naive isolationism. The American ambition to establish an Open Door world remained unchanged. But in the 1920's it was considered possible to achieve this end without the dangerous organizational commitments implied by the League. The Washington Conference of 1921 was designed to lay down Open Door rules for the Far East and to ensure that Japan remained a subordinate imperialist partner in an Anglo-American domain. The Kellog-Briand Pact and the Lausanne Conference, together with the Dawes plan, similarly employed American economic power to ensure the extension of the Open Door principle into Europe, the Middle East and Africa. The contradiction between the industrial supremacy of United States after the First World War and its limited interventions in world politics was more apparent than real.

The Great Depression and the coming of the Second World War, however, brought to an end this prospect of informal economic domination. The collapse of the world market brought with it an intensified struggle between the established imperialist powers (USA, Britain, France) and aspirant contenders (Germany and Japan). The massive unemployment and growing social discontent in America expressed itself once more, as in the 1890's, in an intensified search for new export markets and the protection of existing preserves. The American objective of penetrating the British Empire through the Open Door was made difficult by the establishment of Imperial Preference in the Ottawa agreement. But the worse sufferers were Germany and Japan. Japanese goods were systematically excluded from the USA and from US dependencies. Given the structure of her imperial system, the US thus had little option later but to participate both in the European and in the Pacific Wars. For the rise of Japanese militarism posed a threat to the Open Door in Asia, while the possibility of the German domination threatened to close down markets in Europe and to encroach upon US preserves in Latin America. When France collapsed and Britain seemed on the verge of defeat in 1940–1, however, America was in a strong position to prop up the tottering British empire on her own terms. In return for American aid, the British were forced to accept completely the rules of the Open Door and to modify the Ottawa agreements to allow American economic penetration. With the undermining of British imperialism, the collapse of Germany and the imposition of an American diktat on Japan, the USA assumed its long-anticipated place as the undisputed leader of world capitalism.

It should thus be clear that there has been considerable continuity both in ideology and in political form between the American imperialism that developed in the second half of the 19th century and the American imperialism that has manifested itself since 1945. The ideology and political expression of American Imperialism in the century before 1914 was shaped by the exigencies of inter-imperialist struggle. Americans before the first World War had no reason to disguise their plans and methods of economic domination. This was because they did not consider their form of imperialism to constitute imperialism. It did not occur to "liberals" like Wilson or the dollar diplomatists who preceded him, that investment in and ownership of other nations' raw materials, transport, industry and financial apparatus constituted an imperialist form of exploitation. Imperialism to them meant British and European style territorial expansion and monopolistic spheres of interest held down by large and threatening military castes. Exploitation meant exorbitantly profitable concessions gained by undue influence over government officials—in short the supposed "unfair practices" which in the liberal mythology of domestic progressivism, distinguished the unhealthiness of the trust from the healthiness of the corporation.

Open Door expansion, on the other hand, appeared to them unproblematically as a natural division of labour between industrialized and agrarian nations; it meant mutually beneficial business relationships and trade; it meant the assumption by the United States of its natural place in the world economy through the elimination of "artificial" impediments to the operation of the laws of competitive commerce. In the words of President Truman, "the Open Door policy is not imperialism, it is free trade."

The October Revolution of 1917 traumatized American imperialism, because it proved that it was possible to carry through a successful socialist and anti-imperialist revolution. After its initial attempt to put down the Revolution by force, the United States ostracized the Soviet Union in the clear expectation that a régime at such variance to domestic and international liberal practice

American Imperialism and Militarism

was doomed to collapse. But it did not collapse and managed to survive in defiance of all the social-Darwinist laws which Wilson believed to govern international relations. The subsequent survival of the Chinese, Korean, Vietnamese and Cuban revolutions has only confirmed this frightened sense of bewilderment. Yet functionally Communism is also "the sustaining menace." For not only does it provide the rationale for massive defence expenditure (ABM's), but it also breathes new life into the official anti-imperialist mythology.

US Imperialism has also tried to preserve its original non-territorial character. The mythology of American "advisers," even when they number tens of thousands, and the cover operations of the CIA testify to this. But efforts to preserve the informal empire during the past quarter of the century have been progressively undermined by the very success of American capitalism in encroaching upon rival imperial systems. In the Second World War the USA flattened the imperial pretensions of Japan, contributed to the collapse of Germany and seriously undermined the economic viability of British imperialism. Faced by the threat of anti-imperialist movements in these moribund colonial systems, the USA has been to an increasing extent forced to fill the vacuum and bear the military and financial costs. The result has been a strange reversal of roles. While the Americans police the world and bear a high proportion of the infa-structural costs of the defense of the international capitalist system, Germany and Japan—only lightly burdened by defence costs —have expanded dramatically under the American military umbrella and now compete in American markets. The "invisible empire" of the USA has disappeared, and in its place stands a conspicuous military machine raining destruction upon Vietnam. The old American fear of the professional soldier has been largely realized by the consequent growth of the military-industrial complex. History has turned full circle. The territorialism so despised by the bourgeois empire builders of the North is now being practised on a massive scale throughout the world by a Southern-dominated standing army.

Gabriel Kolko

THE UNITED STATES
AND WORLD ECONOMIC POWER

There is no comprehensive theory of the contemporary world crisis. That both conventional academic or Left scholars have failed or been unable to assess the causes and meaning of the most significant events of our time in large part reflects their unwillingness to confront directly the nature of American interests and power. Theories of imperialism are now the dry-as-dust topics of academic tomes, and all too few have made a serious effort to scratch beneath the ideology of American expansion to define its larger needs, imperatives, and functions as a system.

Earlier studies of imperialism left no doubt as to what one had to examine in order to comprehend the role of a state in the world. Whether it was imperialist rivalries for economic and strategic power, the atavism of feudal ideologies, reaction and counterrevolution, or the desire to integrate and stabilize a world economy, the study of foreign policy was specific, real, and discounted the notion of error, myth, and exuberance as the sources of conduct as explanations sufficient only for national patriots. American scholars have not translated their ability to perceive correctly the roots of diplomacy in the past into a description of contemporary American policy, even though the same categories and analogies may be equally relevant today.

To understand the unique economic interests and aspirations of the United States in the world, and the degree to which it benefits or loses within the existing distribution and structure of power and the world economy, is to define a crucial basis for comprehending as well as predicting its role overseas. The nature of the international crisis, and the limited American responses to it, tell us why the United States is in Vietnam and why in fact American intervention inevitably colors the direction of the vast changes in the world political and social system which are the hallmarks of modern history. In brief, the manner in which the United States has expanded its problems and objectives overseas, transforming the American crisis into a global one, also explains its consistent interventionism.

It is critical, as part of a comprehensive theory of the world crisis, to study the control and organization of the international economy, who gains and who loses in it, and how we have arrived at the present impasse. We should neither dismiss nor make too much of the issue of ideology or the less systematic belief, as former Secretary of Defense James Forrestal once put it, that ". . . our security is not merely the capacity or ability to repel invasion,

Reprinted, with deletions, from the Roots of *American Foreign Policy* (Boston: The Beacon Press, 1969), pp. 48–87. Reprinted by permission of The Beacon Press, copyright © 1969 by Gabriel Kolko. Gabriel Kolko is Professor of History at York University in Toronto, Canada. He has written several books, including *The Triumph of Conservatism, Wealth and Power in America,* and *The Politics of War.*

it is our ability to contribute to the reconstruction of the world. . . ." For American ideology is a vague synthesis that embodies, once its surface is scratched, economic and strategic objectives and priorities that a thin rhetoric rationalizes into doctrines more interesting for what they imply than for what they state. For purposes of this chapter I shall deal only with the structure and the material components of the world economy that set the context for the repeated local interventions and crises that are the major characteristics of the modern world scene.

The United States and Raw Materials

The role of raw materials is qualitative rather than merely quantitative, and neither volume nor price can measure their ultimate significance and consequences. The economies and technologies of the advanced industrial nations, the United States in particular, are so intricate that the removal of even a small part, as in a watch, can stop the mechanism. The steel industry must add approximately thirteen pounds of manganese to each ton of steel, and though the weight and value of the increase is a tiny fraction of the total, a modern diversified steel industry *must* have manganese. The same analogy is true of the entire relationship between the industrial and so-called developing nations: The nations of the Third World may be poor, but in the last analysis the industrial world needs their resources more than these nations need the West, for poverty is nothing new to peasantry cut off from export sectors, and trading with industrial states has not ended their subsistence living standards. In case of a total rupture between the industrial and supplier nations, it is the population of the industrial world that proportionately will suffer the most.

Since the Second World War the leaders of the United States have been acutely aware of their vital reliance on raw materials, and the fact, to quote Paul G. Hoffman, former Marshall Plan administrator, that ". . . our own dynamic economy has made us dependent on the outside world for many critical raw materials." Successive Administrations have been incessantly concerned over the ability and necessity of the United States to develop these resources everywhere, given the paucity of local capital and technology, and their interest extends far beyond short-term profits of investment. In areas such as Africa this obsession has defined American policy on every major issue.

At the beginning of this century the United States was a net earner in the export of minerals and commodities, but by 1926–30 it had a vast annual deficit of crude materials, and in 1930 imported 5 percent of its iron ore, 64 percent of its bauxite (aluminum), 65 percent of its copper, 9 percent of its lead and 4 percent of its zinc. Imports of these five critical metals by 1960 had increased to 32 percent for iron ore, 98 percent for bauxite, 35 percent for lead, and 60 percent for zinc, and only in the case of copper declined to 46 percent. As a percentage of the new supply, the United States in 1956 imported at least 80 percent of thirty-nine necessary commodities, 50 to 79 percent of fifteen commodities, 10 to 49 percent of twenty commodities, and less than 10 percent of another twenty-three—all with a total import value of $6.6 billion. There was no doubt, as one Senate report concluded in 1954, that Washington knew that should the mineral-rich nations cut off these resources, "To a very dangerous extent, the vital security of this Nation is in serious jeopardy."[1]

By 1956–60 the United States was importing over half of all its required metals and almost 60 percent of its wool. It imported all tropical foodstuffs, such as cocoa, coffee, and bananas, as well as over half the sugar supply. When, in 1963, Resources for the Future completed its monumental survey of raw materials and projected American needs for the next forty years, it predicted a vast multiplication of American demands that made imperative, in its estimate, ". . . that in the future even larger amounts of certain items will have to be drawn from foreign sources if demand is to be satisfied without marked increases in cost." Its medium projections suggested immensely increased needs for nearly all metals, ranging as high as nine times for molybdenum to about two and one-half times for lead. Within three years, however, all of the critical output, consumption, and population assumptions upon which the Resources for the Future experts based their speculations proved to be far too conservative, the omnivorous demands of the economy were far greater than they had expected.

A critical shift in the location of the world's most vital mineral output and reserves has accompanied the imperative need for raw materials in the United States. In 1913 the developing nations accounted for 3 percent of the world's total iron ore output and 15 percent of its petroleum, as opposed to 37 percent and 65 percent, respectively, in 1965. Its share of bauxite output increased from 21 percent in 1928 to 69 percent in 1965. The United States share of world oil output fell from 61 percent in 1938 to 29 percent in 1964, as the known world reserves shifted toward the Middle East.

Despite the introduction of synthetics between 1938 and 1954, which reduced by about one-fifth the quantity of natural raw materials needed for the average constant quantity of goods produced in the industrial nations, the vast increase in world industrial output has more than compensated for the shift and greatly increased pressures on raw materials supplies from the industrial nations. In effect, the United States has become more dependent on imported raw materials as its share of the consumption of the world's total has declined sharply in the face of European and Japanese competition for supplies. The United States, which consumed slightly less than half of

[1] U.S. Senate, Committee on Interior and Insular Affairs, *Report, Accessibility of Strategic and Critical Materials to the United States in Time of War and for Our Expanding Economy,* 83:2, July 9, 1954 (Washington, 1954), 1. See also statements of Paul H. Nitze in *Department of State Bulletin,* February 26, 1947, 300, and November 21, 1948, 626–27; Department of State, *The United States and Africa* (Washington, 1964), *passim; New York Times,* August 18, 1963; Percy W. Bidwell, *Raw Materials: A Study of American Policy* (New York, 1958), 2, 6; Hans H. Landsberg, Leonard L. Fischman, and Joseph L. Fisher, *Resources in America's Future: Patterns of Requirements and Availabilities, 1960–2000* (Baltimore, 1963), 427. Certain of these themes for the period 1943–45 are explored in detail in my *The Politics of War* (New York, 1968), and for 1946–55 in a forthcoming history of the period my wife and I are presently writing.

American Imperialism and Militarism

the world's total output of copper, lead, zinc, aluminum, and steel in 1948–50, consumed slightly over one-quarter in 1960, save for aluminum, where the percentage decline was still great. This essentially European demand, which has grown far more rapidly than in the United States, has challenged the American predominance in the world raw materials trade in a manner which makes the maintenance and expansion of existing sources in the ex-colonial regions doubly imperative to it.[2]

American and European industry can find most of these future sources of supply, so vital to their economic growth, only in the continents in upheaval and revolution. Over half of United States iron ore imports in 1960 came from Venezuela and three equally precarious Latin American countries. Over half the known world reserves of manganese are in Russia and China, and most of the remainder is in Brazil, India, Gabon, and South Africa. South Africa and Rhodesia account for nearly all the world's chromium reserves, Cuba and New Caledonia for half the nickel, China for over two-thirds the tungsten, and Chile, Northern Rhodesia, Congo, and Peru for well over two-thirds of the foreign copper reserves. Guyana has about six times the American reserves of bauxite, and China has three times, while Malaya, Indonesia, and Thailand alone have two-thirds the world tin reserves, with Bolivia and the Congo possessing most of the balance. Only zinc and lead, among the major metals, are in politically stable regions, from the American viewpoint.[3]

It is extraordinarily difficult to estimate the potential role and value of these scarce minerals to the United States, but certain approximate definitions are quite sufficient to make the point that the future of American economic power is too deeply involved for this nation to permit the rest of the world to take its own political and revolutionary course in a manner that imperils the American freedom to use them. Suffice it to say, the ultimate significance of the importation of certain critical raw materials is not their cost to American business but rather the end value of the industries that *must* employ these materials, even in small quantities, or pass out of existence. And in the larger sense, confident access to raw materials is a necessary precondition for industrial expansion into new or existing fields of technology, without the fear of limiting shortages which the United States' sole reliance on its national resources would entail. Intangibly, it is really the political and psychological assurance of total freedom of development of national economic power that is vital to American economic growth. Beyond this, United States profits abroad are made on overseas investments in local export industries, giving the Americans the profits of the suppliers as well

[2] *Ibid.*, 428; *New York Times*, April 17, 1966; *The Economist*, June 5, 1965, 1155; General Agreement on Tariffs and Trade [GATT], *Trends in International Trade: A Report by a Panel of Experts* (Geneva, 1958), 43; Paul Bairoch, *Diagnostic de l'Évolution Économique du Tiers-Monde, 1900–1966* (Paris, 1967), 76; U.S. President's Materials Policy Commission, *Resources for Freedom*, June 1952 (Washington, 1952), I, 9. Bairoch's book is the best available study on the relationship of the Third World to the world economy.
[3] Landsberg et al., *Resources in America's Future*, 430, 437, 440, 443, 448, 456, 459, 464, 466, 468.

as the consumer. An isolated America would lose all this, and much more.

It is not enough, therefore, to state that nonfood raw materials imports doubled in value between 1953 and 1966, and that $16.6 billion in imports for the food and industrial users in 1966 was vitally necessary to American prosperity. More relevant is the fact that in 1963 the Census valued the iron and steel industry's shipments at $22.3 billion, the aluminum's at $3.9 billion, metal cans at $2.1 billion, copper at $3.1 billion, asbestos at a half billion, zinc at a half billion, coffee at $1.9 billion, sugar and chocolate at $1.7 billion —and that all of these industries and many others, to some critical extent, depended on their access to the world's supply of raw materials. Without the availability of such goods for decades, at prices favorable to the United States, the American economy would have been far different—and much poorer.

To suggest that the United States could solve its natural shortages by attempting to live within its raw materials limits would also require a drastic reduction in its exports of finished goods, and this the leaders of the American system would never voluntarily permit, for it would bring profound economic repercussions for a capitalist economy in the form of vast unemployment and lower profits. While only four or five percent of American steel mill products went to exports in 1955–60, this proportion reached nearly one-quarter in the aluminum and one-fifth in the copper industries. In this context the United States has become a processor of the world's raw materials in a number of fields not simply to satisfy domestic needs but also its global export trade and military ambitions. At home, a policy of self-sufficiency would, in the case of aluminum, seriously affect the building construction industry, consumer and producer durables, and transport industries. The same is true for copper, which is critical for producer durables, building construction, communications, and electric power. Minor metals, of which the United States is largely deficient, are essential to any technologically advanced nation, especially to the chemical, electrical, and electronics industries.

America's ability to procure at will such materials as it needs, and at a price it can afford, is one of the keystones of its economic power in this century. The stakes are vast, and its capacity to keep intact something like the existing integrated but unequal relations between the poor, weak nations and the United States is vital to the future of its mastery of the international economy.

The United States and World Exports

The dominant interest of the United States is in world economic stability, and anything that undermines that condition presents a danger to its present hegemony. Countering, neutralizing and containing the disturbing political and social trends thus becomes the most imperative objective of its foreign policy.

For the developing nations, the postwar experience has been one of relative decline in world commerce, a pattern that has vastly benefited the

American Imperialism and Militarism

industrial nations of Europe and the United States, who have done almost nothing to alter a situation that has greatly favored their own economies. No matter what the source, all agree that since 1948 the overall share of the developing nations in the world export trade has decreased consistently, the specific aspects and causes of this reduction deserving more detail later in this chapter. Taking the United Nations data, from 1950 to 1966 the share of the developing nations in world exports fell from 31.2 percent to 19.1 percent. Latin America suffered worst in this regard. Though the absolute value of the exports of developing nations had steadily increased, it has been at a much slower growth rate than among industrial nations, where, in turn, the Common Market nations and Japan, long after their wartime recovery, have not only consistently and greatly outstripped the developing nations, but Great Britain and the United States as well. Moreover, just as the industrialized nations have shared more of their export trade among themselves, the Common Market nations have set the pace by trading among themselves to an unprecedented degree. They have collectively displaced the United States as the major importer from the Third World and since 1953 have almost equaled the United States in exports to these nations.

In 1954–56 the United States accounted for 30.5 percent of the world export trade for principal manufacturers, by 1961 had slipped to 25.3 percent, and in 1966 to 22.7 percent. Given the faster growth rate in exports of goods such as machinery and transport equipment, processed food, beverages, and highly finished articles, the exceptional success of the Common Market nations in intra-Market trade, Africa, and especially Latin America has meant the gradual weakening of United States power in the world manufacturing export market and the re-emergence of Europe as a major, viable competitor with the United States in classic, traditional capitalist terms. West Europe is succeeding, as well, in carving out an even larger share of the trade of the Third World, where the United States proportion of exports has significantly declined, reducing the magnitude of American access to vital raw materials.

At the same time that the United States has been losing in competition against the other major capitalist industrialized nations as an exporter of manufactures, its relationship to the Third World for control of the world trade in agricultural commodities indicates a long-term pattern of American success at the expense of the poorer countries. For the United States is not only a highly industrialized nation, consuming raw materials, but its immense agricultural output requires it to sell ever-growing quantities of food abroad, closing possible markets and earnings to developing nations. America's agricultural exports grew from $2.9 billion in 1950 to $6.9 billion in 1966, its agricultural imports increasing only by one-eighth during that period.

While it is difficult to estimate the extent to which the vast increase of United States shares in world exports of certain foods, such as wheat, was due to temporary relief, it is certain that for two decades the active, aggressive export expansion of the agricultural sector has been a fundamental American policy having little to do with humanitarian concerns. It has often contributed to world gluts within the market economy and lower Third World earnings, bringing the poor nations, ultimately, more misery. Table I illustrates the increase of the United States share of the world agricultural

Table I. United States Share in World Exports and Production of
Selected Agricultural Products 1934–35, 1955–57, and 1965

	Percentage Share in World Exports			Percentage Share in World Production		
	1934–35	*1955–57*	*1965*	*1934–35*	*1955–57*	*1965*
Wheat	6.4	46.1	38.0	21.0	20.2	14.5
Oats	5.9	29.3	19.4	31.0	37.1	29.7
Corn	9.0	63.9	60.6	59.3	59.2	45.7
Rice	.8	14.8	21.7	1.0	1.8	1.4
Cotton	43.0	43.6	27.0*	51.9	35.5	20.2*
Tobacco	41.0	37.6	45.0	30.2	32.3	20.5
Soybeans	2.3	82.0	89.1	9.5	51.3	63.0

* 1966

Calculated from data in U.S. Senate, Committee on Foreign Relations, *United States-Latin American Relations.* ["Compilation of Studies"] 86:2. August 31, 1960 (Washington, 1960), 452; United Nations, Statistical Office, *Statistical Yearbook, 1966* (New York, 1967); U.S. Department of Agriculture, *Handbook of Agricultural Charts, 1967* (Washington, 1967), and monthly issues of *World Agricultural Production and Trade*; Food and Agricultural Organization of the United Nations, *Trade Yearbook, 1966* (Rome, 1967).

export market, generally far in excess of the American share of world production. Briefly, it reveals that the highly commercial American policy in agriculture, which resulted in the export of 42 percent of its rice, and one third is wheat and cotton output in 1954–58, led to a crucial and unprecedented American domination of the world agricultural food and cotton trade. Even more important, if we calculate the United States share of the total world agricultural export trade, from 1953 to 1966 it increased from 12 to 19 percent, significantly offsetting America's loss to Europe in the manufacturing trade market.

It is within this larger setting—American losses to Europe in the industrial export sector, dependence on the raw materials of the developing world, and mastery over the developing nations in many world agricultural exports —that Washington pursues its foreign policy. The details of these economic relationships and their causes reveal more fully the purposes and objectives of America in the world today.

World Trade and World Misery

If the postwar experience is any indication, the nonsocialist developing nations have precious little reason to hope that they can terminate the vast misery of their masses. For in reality the industrialized nations have increased their advantages over them in the world economy by almost any standard one might care to use.

The terms of trade—the unit value or cost of goods a region imports compared to its exports—have consistently disfavored the developing nations since 1958, ignoring altogether the fact that the world prices of raw materials prior to that time were never a measure of equity. Using 1958 as a base year, by 1966 the value of the exports of developing areas had fallen to 97, those of the industrial nations had risen to 104. Using the most extreme example of this shift, from 1954 to 1962 the terms of trade deteriorated 38 percent against the developing nations, for an income loss in 1962 of about $11 billion, or 30 percent more than the financial aid the Third World received that year. Even during 1961–66, when the terms of trade remained almost constant, their loss in potential income was $13.4 billion, wiping away 38 percent of the income from official foreign aid plans of every sort.

Since about one-half the exports of the developing countries are mining products, and about two-fifths agricultural, fishery, and forestry products, the comparative patterns in the prices and output of these goods reveal somewhat more.

The developing nations' food export prices have fallen, particularly coffee and sugar, for an overall decline of 7 percent between 1950–54 and 1961–65. Nonfood agricultural prices fell 9 percent during that time, but the price of minerals and fuels rose only 3 percent—together, the decline has spelled greater misery for the Third World.

The developing nations have compensated for this price decrease by exporting 60 percent more in 1966 than 1958, as opposed to an 87 percent increase for the industrialized nations. The result was a serious reduction in their share of world trade. But minerals and petroleum accounted for much of the increase in quantity, with an absolute quantity decline on types of nonfood agriculture. In effect, relatively inflexible demand for certain foods, the introduction of synthetic textiles, rubber, and the like, and the rising prices of industrial goods contributed to the already groaning problems of the developing world. All of this has revealed once more that rather than the existence of a harmony between the rich and poor nations, the drift of affairs and, as we shall see, Western policies have led to a further aggravation of the condition of the majority of the world's peoples.[4]

In fact, whether intended or otherwise, low prices and economic stagnation in the Third World directly benefit the industrialized nations. Should the developing nations ever industrialize to the extent that they begin consuming a significant portion of their own oil and mineral output, they would reduce the available supply to the United States and prices would rise. And there has never been any question that conservative American studies of the subject have treated the inability of the Third World to industrialize seriously as a cause for optimism in raw materials planning. Their optimism is fully warranted, since nations dependent on the world market for the capital to industrialize are unlikely to succeed, for when prices of raw materials are high they tend to concentrate on selling more raw materials, and when prices

[4] Bairoch, *Diagnostic*, 160–65; United Nations, Department of Economic and Social Affairs, *Yearbook of International Trade Statistics, 1965* (New York, 1967), 33–34; UNCTAD, "Commodity Problems and Policies," November 10, 1967 (mimeo, 1967), 4, 9; GATT, *International Trade, 1966: GATT-Report 1967* (Geneva, 1967), 2–3, 9, 43, 47, 50; UNCTAD, "Review of International Trade and Development," 35–36.

are low their earnings are insufficient to raise capital for diversification. The United States especially gears its investments, private and public, to increasing the output of exportable minerals and agricultural commodities, instead of balanced economic development. With relatively high capital-labor intensive investment and feeding transport facilities to port areas rather than to the population, such investments hardly scratch the living standards of the great majority of the local peasantry or make possible the large increases in agricultural output that are a precondition of a sustained industrial expansion. Indeed, the total flow of private and public foreign capital to the developing areas, amounting to $10.1 billion in 1965, has only increased the output of resources needed in the Western world, and the flight of local capital toward safe Western banks has partially offset even this form of capital influx.

Taking the value of world manufacturing produced in the developing areas, after a period of decline, the share of this region in 1961 finally attained its 1938 portion of 9.3 percent of the world's manufacturing output, excluding Russia and East Europe. If we add mining, a function of service mainly to the industrial states, then between 1938 and 1961 the proportion increased from 9.9 percent to 11.3 percent. In terms of the world's gross domestic product, the developing nations' share declined from 17.6 percent to 17.4 percent over this period, which their percentage of the population grew from 67.3 to 70.3. Stagnation, therefore, has been the primary characteristic of the Third World.

A closer look at the data, however, reveals that the developing countries have remained essentially agricultural even where annual manufacturing growth is substantial, in part because foreign investments have been capital intensive and employ fewer workers, and also because light manufacturing still predominates in these instances. In terms of world export trade, the developing nations tend to trade with each other for such manufactures as they may produce, and if we remove Hong Kong and Israel from the calculations as two most untypical examples, the share of Third World manufactured products in international trade drops dramatically. What is much more significant is that despite modest increases in absolute output, per capita food production in the Third World between 1934–38 and 1961–65 declined in Africa and Latin America and remained static in the Far and Near East. Between 1958–59 and 1963–64 the per capita food consumption in Latin America fell a drastic 7 percent. Another measure of this trend, the average income per inhabitant in the noncommunist developing nations and the noncommunist industrial sector, reveals a ratio of inequality of about one to six in 1900 and one to twelve in 1965.

Dual Standard Policy

Although the United States for over two decades has advocated that all nations sharply lower their tariffs and rely on a world economy of essentially free trade, it has never been willing to implement this policy when it was not to the interest of powerful American industries. This American refusal to open fully its own economy to the world, which would undoubtedly gain thereby, is the vital difference between a desire to dominate the world economy—a new imperialism—and a theory of free trade or the "Open Door." The net effect of this dual standard has been to enlarge United States economic power in the Third World and partially to stem the decisive advantages that West Europe increasingly holds in the industrial sector. For since 1949, when the United States refused to ratify an International Trade Organization it had initiated, everyone understood that the United States would advocate one economic doctrine for the rest of the world merely as a pretense for mastering the world economy to the maximum extent possible—but at the same time practice another code itself.

The United States maintains import quotas and tariff barriers on agricultural products and minerals in order to sustain high prices for its own producers, while simultaneously depriving Third World nations of an export market they could probably command in at least several critical fields.

In 1960 the United States had quotas and tariffs on nine Third World products, including petroleum, sugar, and cotton, and while it removed restrictions from zinc and lead at the end of 1965, the possibility of reimposing them remains. An effective "sanitary" embargo on live cattle and dressed beef and veal also existed, while Congress placed tariffs on many other agricultural and primary products. There is no way a nation can export a sack of sugar to the United States if Congress has not already allocated a quota to it under the Sugar Act, which reserves a majority of the quota for United States producers and the Philippines, where American owners dominate the industry. "The agricultural export sales policies and the import quotas on minerals," one leading United States trader warned President Eisenhower in 1958, "put the United States in the role of perhaps the world's greatest violator of the principles that it advocates in international competition and tries to sell to others through GATT."

Changes in domesic programs for sugar, cotton, and oil within the United States, and to a lesser degree Europe, profoundly influence the sales and prices of Third World exports. United States price supports for cotton, for example, have helped determine plantings in Latin American nations, and extensive United States self-sufficiency in both oil and sugar has been a major loss of income to developing states. Latin American and Japanese exporters have for many years publicly complained, and the Latins have threatened retaliation, but for a variety of compelling economic reasons connected with the United States loan and investment program have been unable to implement their menacing words. In brief, the United States has attempted to maintain the most convenient aspects of both protectionism and free trade. For to have opened its doors to foreign agricultural surpluses and oil on a free market basis merely to be ideologically consistent would have resulted in enormous damage to America's coveted supremacy in the world economy.

The United States has been able to obtain its share of world agricultural exports, thwart retaliation, open needed raw materials supplies, and prevent an even more rapid decline in the share of manufacturing exports through adroitly using its foreign aid and loans to the world. Even before the Marshall

Plan in 1947 the United States was ready to make foreign aid useful to itself by introducing ever greater emphasis on its value in developing raw materials sources and stockpiles the United States might someday need. The Foreign Assistance Act of 1948 (the Marshall Plan) required that aid recipients make at least 5 percent of the local "counterpart" currencies available to the United States to purchase raw materials, as well as open the European nations and their colonies to American investors on an equal basis. And between 1945 and 1951 the percentage of Export-Import Bank loans devoted to developing new foreign supplies of raw materials increased from 6 to 30 percent. By mid-1953 United States counterpart funds purchased $115 million in raw materials for American use, plus a larger amount in United States dollar purchases for direct stockpiling after the Korean War.

These policies were not exceptional, for raw materials guided every aspect of American policy toward the Third World, and the keystone of the Point Four program from 1950 onward was the accelerated expansion of world raw materials supplies and sources. In the case of India, which after the 1948 Russian embargo on manganese exports became the major available source of supply, Congress quickly made loans for grain and other needs contingent on repayment in manganese and other minerals, and although the final loan terms moderated the bluntness of some congressional enthusiasts, manganese as a factor in Indian-American economic relations became the basis of a vital *quid pro quo*. Congressmen frankly stated the reasons for this policy: "Manganese today is far more important to us . . . because it is used in the production of steel. We have to have it," as one North Carolina member phrased it. More bluntly, a Pittsburgh congressman made it plain that "We use tremendous quantities of manganese in the steel industry . . . and if we do not get this strategic material, our mills and our economy will shut down."

The Americans got their Indian manganese, and using Point Four and the Export-Import Bank they later opened up Brazilian supplies during the 1950's as well. The various Administrations and Congresses consistently geared the bulk of American foreign aid funds to this function throughout the world, making the Third World more dependent on the needs and inconsistencies of the industrial nations, the United States in particular. "Not for one minute," John Foster Dulles told Congress in 1958 concerning one foreign aid proposal, "do I think the purpose . . . is to make friends. The purpose . . . is to look out for the interests of the United States."

Another example of this assumption, and the manner in which it has operated to the detriment of Third World nations, was the raw materials stockpiling program which began in 1946 and accelerated after the Korean War. By the end of 1961 the United States Government had spent $8.9 billion and eventually found it had, in effect, also undertaken a partial subsidy program for domestic producers. When the Kennedy Administration sought to begin discarding vast holdings that far exceeded amounts required for national emergencies, it soon found it was having a depressing effect on world prices, especially on tin. As the United States Government quickly learned, it had also developed a means of hedging against higher raw materials prices, a fact that only helped keep the value of Third World exports at a lower level.

The long standing opposition of the United States to commodity agreements which would stabilize at a high level the rapidly and continuously fluctuating prices of many of the world's key raw materials has been no less significant. This opposition, which dates back to the 1920's, reflects America's practice of maximizing its wealth by buying as cheaply as possible while it dumps agricultural goods on the world market and restricts imports damaging to its own producers. To the developing nations, price stability is the most attractive, fastest, and simplest means to increase their foreign exchange. In Latin America, for example, during 1960–63 nine minerals and agricultural commodities provided 70 percent of the foreign exchange earnings, the prices of most of them vacillating wildly as a matter of course. These fluctuations have vast significance, for a one-cent-a-pound increase in coffee could mean $65 million a year additional income to the exporting countries, or $100 million for rice producers—and increased costs to the American consumers. Since foreign aid and investment of every variety provide slightly more than one-tenth of the foreign exchange receipts of developing nations, their ability to raise and sustain the prices of such exportable assets as they have is the heart of any effective development program. Quite as significant, of course, is the internal redistribution of income via land reform and the elimination of United States investments in those export sectors that would obtain higher earnings.

Under these circumstances, effective commodity agreement programs would have a far-reaching impact on the distribution of the world's income and living standards. Experts conservatively estimated that a moderate world commodity program for coffee, tea, cocoa, sugar, and bananas in 1961 alone could have added $700 million to the incomes of the producer nations. Quite apart from the fact that such agreements would partially benefit American overseas investors in those fields as well, for whatever its motives the United States Government has always managed to oppose such comprehensive regulation of the vital minerals and agricultural goods it needs. This fact has contributed greatly to the high American standard of living.

Because the United States opposed the commodity agreements provisions that the developing nations offered at the International Trade Organization conference in 1948, the Charter was watered down to impotence, but Congress still refused to ratify it. Later that year the United States delegation entered a reservation on the subject at the Bogotá Conference, voted against a similar resolution at the Caracas Conference in 1954, abstained at another that year, issued another reservation at the Buenos Aires Conference of 1957, opposed a strong O.A.S. position, and in general has as tactfully as possible thwarted the desire of Latin American and other nations to earn more of their exports.

The United States has seen the dependence of the developing world on income from such raw materials as an opportunity to open the doors of those nations to increased investment and force greater output. "While we do not believe that commodity agreements, in general, serve the objective of obtaining more efficient production and distribution," the United States delegate to the February 1959 hemispheric conference declared, ". . . we recognize that they may serve temporarily . . . on a commodity-by-commodity basis." Such temporary expediencies have served more to thwart the dangerous potential of the agreements and protect the American consumer than to advance the welfare of the developing states. ". . . our first duty," the State Department made clear in November 1962, "is to protect the American consumer."

A detailed survey of the specific agreements in which the United States has participated, such as coffee and sugar, confirms that Washington enters such arrangements to fulfill its explicit public goal of serving its own interests. In the case of the 1964 coffee discussions, at which time the Latin American producers hoped for a twenty-cent-a-pound increase that experts estimated would cost American consumers about a billion dollars a year or more, the United States arranged a voting structure which gave it, in effect, a veto. It also left itself the right of withdrawal within ninety days, which would have led to the destruction of the agreement. Coffee prices by 1967 fell to one-quarter less than the average for 1953–62. The United States has consistently nullified the price-increasing effects of commodity agreements, or has opposed them altogether. That it has gained immeasurably thereby is reflected in the sorry economic state of the nations exporting to keep United States industry running and its people, relative to the rest of the world, affluent.

American Tools for Success

The United States vast expansion in its agricultural exports, and the billions of dollars of lost income to the Third World, reveals the success of the brilliant American synthesis of aid, pressure, and exclusion that is the main characteristic of its foreign economic diplomacy.

The United States is the world's leading state trader, even though it has consistently attacked this principle when other industrial nations used it to advance their own neocolonial export positions. Official American agricultural export subsidy programs involved $3 billion annually in 1957 and 1967, with sums approaching that amount in the interim years. Most of these subsidized exports went to developing nations, often, as in the case of India, in return for vital concessions that aided America's industry, just as agricultural exports aided its big commercial farmers.

Given United States exclusion of many cheaper, freely exportable goods and commodities, and its opposition to higher prices for Third World exports, one can only regard the foreign aid program as a subsidy to American farmers and industry rather than as a gesture of concern for the world's poor. Between 1948 and 1958 ships sailing under the American flag carried 57 percent of the foreign aid despatched from the United States, and Americans owned many of the other vessels flying foreign flags. The United States required aid recipients to spend 68 percent of the aid program expenditures during that period in the United States; American-controlled Middle Eastern oil absorbing part of the remainder. By 1965 over one-third of United States exports to developing countries, which now absorbed nearly one-third of American exports, were directly financed on a tied basis. There were few humanitarian reasons for exporting vast amounts of cotton abroad under these programs, and in fact cheaper cotton was usually available to developing nations from other Third World countries. In reality, the American program cut into intra-Third World trade on behalf of a standing United States policy to maintain a "fair historical share" of the world cotton market for the United States, a figure somewhere around five million bales a year and in no sense a standard of equity.

The aid programs have generated vast quantities of counterpart funds in local currencies, amounting to nearly $2 billion by June 1965, as a result of the obligation of recipient nations to deposit the proceeds of the sales of American aid in jointly controlled accounts. Though not convertible to dollars, these funds have deprived recipient nations of dollar incomes that would have otherwsie been available in cases of outright American grants of aid.

American expenses in counterpart countries, ranging from embassy overhead to C.I.A. activities, are limited by convention, but this is optional and the United States can use nearly half of the counterpart resources. In India, which has accounted for half the counterpart funds, United States-controlled rupees were equivalent to more than one-half the money in circulation, and America's ability to dislocate India's economy is now openly acknowledged and discussed. Possible economic warfare aside, counterpart funds not only reflect the United States search for agricultural markets but the desire, as Draper Committee experts recommended in 1959, ". . . to encourage through a form of subsidy without actual cost to the US taxpayer, desirable US industrial investment in selected areas and fields. . . ."

Public Law 480 in 1954 already partially embodied such sophistication. It authorized the United States to use counterpart funds to stockpile raw materials, and the Government acquired $295 million worth of such commodities by September 1956. By 1964 it had used some $1.7 billion in counterpart funds to build military bases and housing, as loans to American businesses, to find new agricultural markets, and similar functions. Despite the rhetorical conservative business complaints about "give-aways," foreign aid essentially has been a means of subsidizing American interests while extending American power in the world economy. "I wish," President Kennedy reminded them in September 1963, "American businessmen who keep talking against the program would realize how significant it has been in assisting them to get into markets where they would have no entry and no experience and which has traditionally been European. . . . Last year 11 percent of our exports were financed under our aid program. And the importance of this aid to our exports is increasing as our developing assistance is increasing, now almost entirely tied to American purchases."

The Loan Syndrome

The Marshall Plan consisted essentially of outright grants to industrialized and potentially rich European nations because it was a program to save

Western capitalism, an objective so fundamental in importance to the United States that $13 billion appeared a small price to pay for the survival of world capitalism. The impoverished Third World receives tied American loans, not grants, because this is a major means to extend capitalism and economic control into that sphere. In brief, loans have become a species of imperialism —in many nations more complex and subtle but no less thorough.

By March 1957, when the President's Fairless Committee on foreign aid reported, most American foreign economic planners were inclined to shift more emphatically to a policy of harder loans, repayable in dollars. At the same time, the United States had to solve its growing and persistent balance of payments problem, and in late 1959 it even more firmly tied loans to the required export of American goods as a precondition. In principle, during these years and thereafter, the United States opposed European tied loans, ostensibly because Europe was not faced with a balance of payments problem. If the Latin American nations complained that as a result of such strings associated with the Alliance for Progress loans the United States agencies only forced them to purchase goods far above the cost of European or Japanese equivalents, they were told, as Lincoln Gordon phrased it in March 1966, that the "struggle for freedom in Vietnam" required the practice.

Until the Kennedy Administration, most United States International Cooperation Administration or Development Loan Fund loans were repayable in local funds rather than dollars, and assistance was geared more to contingent grants than loans. After 1961, when Washington created the Agency for International Development, it made development loans repayable in dollars, and by 1965 70 percent of United States development aid was in the form of loans. During this period Congress raised minimum loan rates from three-quarters of 1 percent to 2 and one-half percent, while the Export-Import Bank and World Bank were averaging 5 and one-half percent. As a result, whereas in 1955 debt servicing in the form of interest and repayments offset 8 percent of external assistance to developing countries, by 1964 it had reached 30 percent. In terms of debt servicing as a percentage of income of the recipient nations from foreign exports, the increase was from 3.7 percent in 1956 to 9.1 percent in 1963, with the possibility of more than doubling by 1975. For Latin America the problem is even more grave, as its debt servicing increased from 7.7 percent of its export income in 1957 to 17 percent in 1967. By 1967 servicing external public debt absorbed three-quarters of the gross capital inflow into Latin America, causing a near impasse in regional development via foreign aid. In short, servicing aid was beginning to wipe out the advantages of loans to the developing nations, so that in 1964, for example, the Export-Import Bank received $100 million more from Latin America than it lent to it. Indeed, Export-Import loans result in a net outflow of resources from all its borrowers after about eight years. Since it is the plan of A.I.D. to harden its loan terms, despite the fact that there has already been a rescheduling of the payments of a number of hard-pressed nations, the end result will aggravate the economic position of the developing states.

Then why does the United States loan funds to poor nations that in the long run will lose thereby? First, most of the loans go to build an internal infrastructure which is a vital prerequisite to the development of resources and direct United States private investments. Then there is the fact that to repay loans in dollars requires the borrowing nations to export goods capable of earning them, which is to say, raw materials of every sort. Development in this form increases the Third World's dependence on Western capitalist nations, so that loans become integrating and binding liens. And lastly, as A.I.D. itself explains it,

Our foreign economic assistance program as a whole has had by-products of substantial benefit to the U.S. economy. For example, Food for Peace has helped us manage our agricultural surpluses while making its important contribution to development. A.I.D. development loan dollars, now spent in large preponderance in the U.S., contribute substantially to employment in our export industries, and have created important footholds for future U.S. export markets after U.S. assistance is phased out. (Indeed, in considering projects for development financing, A.I.D. now also takes into account any special potential for future trading relationships between the U.S. and recipient countries.)

United States Investment and Trade

The true extent of American investments and control in the world economy is too complex a topic for precise description, for the quality of the data is such that only rough estimates reveal the broad configurations of the vital problem. The known values of United States investments abroad hardly expose the true worth and profitability of American-controlled industries. Using foreign corporate intermediaries, and acquiring local firms via outright purchase (833 in 1965–66 alone), makes the gathering of accurate data all the more difficult. The extensive use of tax havens and false reports on overseas profits and holdings pose yet other problems. Less than one-quarter of the total funds available for all United States investments abroad in 1957 were based on exported dollars; reinvested profits, local borrowing, and depreciation provided the larger bulk. Therefore the investment of American corporate funds abroad carries with it a vast power of internal expansion and multiplication that exceeds known appraisals. The Department of Commerce readily admits that it bases official data on book values rather than true market worth and replacement costs, which Emilio G. Collado of Standard Oil of New Jersey has suggested are at least double the book assessments. By any criterion, what we call United States investment abroad is much more foreign resources mobilized in American hands, generating its own capital in a manner that pyramids the American penetration of the world economy. Whatever else they may be, profits on such investments are not primarily the reward for the the transfer of American capital abroad.

With these statistical limitations in mind, direct United States private investments abroad had a book value of $7.5 billion in 1929, and in 1950 were still only $11.8 billion. By 1966 those investments were about five times greater, or $54.6 billion, with an additional $32 billion in other forms of private holdings. Manufacturing investments accounted for $22 billion of this sum, and were preponderately located in Canada and West Europe. Canada and Latin America absorbed the large bulk of the $4.1 billion in mining and smelting, while substantial portions of the $16.3 billion in petroleum were found everywhere, most of all, of course, in the Middle East.[5]

Translated into different terms, indicating economic power and not depending on artificially deflated investment data, United States firms controlled the better part of the world's oil industry. In Germany in 1964, foreign corporations, among whom American companies predominated, owned 90 percent of the petroleum industry, 40 percent of the food, drink, and tobacco industries, and 23 percent each in the automobile and electronics industries. In France, where United States firms accounted for over one-half of the foreign investments, by 1962 eighteen of the one hundred largest French corporations were foreign owned, giving them a powerful position in the leading sector of the economy. And by 1967 American firms in Italy represented at least six percent of all corporate investments there, with especially strong positions in the oil and electronics industries. In 1957 such American-owned firms everywhere in the world supplied 27 percent of the United States imports, with the concentration being much higher in petroleum, minerals, and agricultural commodities. They accounted for one-third of Latin American exports to the world during 1967. Their function, therefore, was not merely to produce vast profits but to supply essential American needs. Their relative economic power in the countries in which they operated was, at the very least, great.

Despite Washington's more recent desire to balance its payments via lower dollar exports, it has directed this restrictive program mainly to West Europe rather than the developing world, for investments in the latter are critical to sustain and expand the output of raw materials the United States requires. In fact, the recent leveling off in European economic growth, devaluation and further threats of it, have all contributed to a slight reduction in American investments in Europe since 1966 in any case. But these are transitory fluctuations which in no way diminish the powerful position of American industry and finance abroad, and its profound involvement in the fate of the world economy and everything that affects it.

American foreign investments are unusually parasitic, not merely in the manner in which they use a minimum amount of dollars to mobilize maximum foreign resources, but also because of the United States crucial position in the world raw-materials price structure both as consumer and exporter. This is especially true in the developing regions, where extractive industries and cheap labor result in the smallest permanent foreign contributions to national wealth. In Latin America in 1957, for example, 36 percent of United States manufacturing investments, as opposed to 56 percent in Europe and 78 percent in Canada, went for plant and equipment. And wages as a per-

[5] U.S. Department of Commerce, *U.S. Business Investments in Foreign Countries* (Washington 1960), 60–64, 90, 92, 139; Emilio G. Collado and Jack F. Bennett, "Private Investment and Economic Development," *Foreign Affairs*, XXXV (July 1957), 633–34; *Survey of Current Business*, September 1967, 40, 45, 49; Committee on Foreign Relations, *United States-Latin American Relations*, 511; *New York Times*, November 17, 1963.

centage of operating costs in United States manufacturing investments are far lower in Third World nations than Europe or Canada.

Actual annual profits on United States investments abroad are difficult to calculate, not only for the same complexities mentioned in estimating the true worth of investments, but for larger structural reasons as well. For example, the United States industry's predominance in Middle Eastern oil sources also makes possible its control over Western European oil refining and sales, and opens new means of earning profits on Third World investments. Suffice it to say, the official figures are quite minimal, as the Commerce Department readily admits. Even so, between 1950 and 1966 the annual yields in all United States direct private investments abroad were at least a low of 11.5 percent in 1966 to at least a high of 19 percent in 1951. However, this lumps Europe and the Third World, manufacturing and oil, together in a totally meaningless fashion, for American profits in the Third World are generally greater. United States petroleum earnings on investment in Latin America between 1951–55, *after* local taxes, were an annual average of 25.6 percent, and 20.5 percent in 1956–58. Petroleum quite consistently has returned the largest annual returns on any form of investment, and this has meant resources depletion and a vast loss to the Third World, if not in the past under feudal and reactionary regimes then most assuredly in the future.

Several other indices are perhaps more to the point in suggesting the relative significance of world trade and the developing nations to United States prosperity. The sales of the foreign affiliates of American manufacturing firms in the first half of this decade grew much faster than those of their domestic components, and one can haphazardly measure this comparatively high profit and sales in a manner that reveals the dimensions of American interests. International oil firms, of course, are well known for their dependence on world sources. But in 1961 the foreign subsidiaries of the Aluminum Corporation of America generated 65 percent of its net income, 80 percent of Yale & Towne's net earnings, 78 percent of Colgate-Palmolive's profits, 35 percent of Corn Products' sales, and 48 percent of Pfizer's total volume. Forty-four of the one hundred top United States industrial corporations in the same year were no less dependent on their overseas branches for sales and profits, and during the mid-1960's only 70 United States firms accounted for nearly one-half of the American investments in developing countries.

Another approach is to estimate the ability of direct United States investments to originate profits. For example, between 1950–60 the $30.5 billion in earnings in all areas was almost equal to the accumulated book value of all American direct investments in the world, though in Latin America profits were higher than the total investments there. During 1961–66 earnings in the entire world added another $28.8 billion, making the return on investment in only seventeen years considerably larger than its total book value since the post-1890 period. This profit was again more pronounced from Latin America and the Middle East. Even assuming that the book value represents the net capital outflow from the United States, which is certainly not the case, profits on foreign investments have been extremely large during the postwar period of Third World revolution and hunger.

Seen in this light, United States foreign aid has been a tool for penetrating and making lucrative the Third World in particular and the entire non-socialist world in general. The small price for saving European capitalism made possible later vast dividends, the expansion of American capitalism, and ever greater power and profits. It is this broader capability eventually to expand and realize the ultimate potential of a region that we must recall when short-term cost accounting and a narrow view make costly American commitments to a nation or region inexplicable. Quite apart from profits on investments, during 1950–60 the United States allocated $27.3 billion in nonmilitary grants, including the agricultural disposal program. During that same period it exported $166 billion in goods on a commercial basis, and imported materials essential to the very operation of the American economy. It is these vast flows of goods, profits, and wealth that set the fundamental context for the implementation and direction of United States foreign policy in the world.

The United States and the Price of Stability

Under conditions in which the United States has been the major beneficiary of a world economy geared to serve it, the continued, invariable American opposition to basic innovations and reforms in world economic relations is entirely predictable. Not merely resistance to stabilizing commodity and price agreements, or non-tied grants and loans, but to every imperatively needed structural change has characterized United States policy toward the Third World. In short, the United States is today the bastion of the *ancien regime*, of stagnation and continued poverty for the Third World.

There was never any secret in the decade and a half after the war that the basic foreign economic policy of the United States posited that "The U.S. is convinced that private ownership and operation of industrial and extractive enterprises contribute more effectively than public ownership and operation to the general improvement of the economy of a country. . . . It is therefore a basic policy of the I.C.A. to employ U.S. assistance to aid-receiving countries in such a way as will encourage the development of the private sectors of their economies." Both personally and publicly, American leaders felt, as Douglas Dillon "most emphatically" phrased it, ". . . aid to a foreign country is no substitute for the adoption of sound economic policies on the part of that country."

Invariably, this meant opening the doors of developing nations to American investments and the support for pliable *comprador* elements wherever they could be found, in the belief, to cite Secretary of Treasury George M. Humphrey, that "There are hundreds of energetic people in the world who are better equipped than governments ever can be to risk huge sums in search, exploration, and development wherever the laws of the country will give them half a chance."

The implications of such a policy were great, requiring intervention to save American investors and friendly conservative governments, and above all the maximization of raw materials production for export to the fluctuating world market. "Our purpose," Percy W. Bidwell wrote in his studies for the

Council on Foreign Relations, "should be to encourage the expansion of low-cost production and to make sure that neither nationalistic policies nor Communist influences deny American industries access on reasonable terms to the basic materials necessary to the continued growth of the American economy." Hence nationalism and modest but genuine reform were quite as great an enemy as bolshevism. This meant that via diplomatic pressures and contingent loans and aid the United States engaged in what Eugene Black has called "development diplomacy" throughout the world, a strategy that attempts to show that "The desire for autarky will not be tempered until there is more awareness of how, by underemphasizing exports, the leaders of these nations are prolonging the poverty of their people." That fluctuating raw materials prices and immense foreign profits were crucial handicaps to the problems of development was of no consequence, since the primary objective of the United States was to serve its own interests.

The advancement of American capitalism and an open field for development in the Third World were the guiding principles of American diplomacy, both on the part of government and business leaders. This has required, in turn, specific opposition to every measure likely to alleviate Third World misery at the expense of the industrial nations. Land reform, especially in Latin American nations, is now regarded essentially as a problem of increasing productivity rather than broadening tenure or redistributing land. The United States has opposed measures to stop the so-called "brain drain" which now brings 30,000 professionals and technically trained migrants to the United States each year (not counting nonreturning foreign students who are educated here), about one-third of them from Third World countries. In fact this also represents the annual transfer of hundreds of millions of dollars of educational investment to the United States.

Global efforts to revise the terms of trade go beyond commodity agreements, but the United States opposed such reforms at the United Nations Conference on Trade and Development at Geneva in March 1964, where the American delegation found itself in the uncomfortable position of disputing nearly all Third World proposals. At the Delhi session in March 1968 the United States position was seemingly more liberal, but geared to the unattainable precondition that France and England give up their preferential agreements with former colonies, even though the United States has its own with the Philippines and Puerto Rico. Significantly, the United States has also consistently opposed the creation of a meaningful Latin American "free trade" area. In principle, if such blocs lower costs of production, conserve scarce exchange, or improve the terms of trade, they can develop into effective means for development. In fact, both the Common Market and European special agreements in Africa and Asia have filled the United States with profound reservations concerning all new exclusionary trade blocs, for in practice they have tended to close off United States trade. Indeed, a Latin American trade zone would not make sense if it qualified as a true free-trade bloc into which the United States could export and invest without planned economic development, and since only restrictionism in one form or another will improve Latin economic conditions the United States has ranged itself against meaningful Latin American economic integration.

The numerous American interventions to protect its investors throughout the world, and the United States ability to use foreign aid and loans as a lever to extract required conformity and concessions, have been more significant as a measure of its practice. The instances of this are too plentiful to detail here, but the remarkable relationship between American complaints on this score and the demise of objectionable local political leaders deserves more than passing reference.

When, in May 1963, the Indonesian Government insisted on taking over its oil industry, the American threat to discontinue foreign aid forced Sukarno to accept an agreement that left the American firms with effective control of the industry. Later that year similar scenarios were repeated in Peru and Argentina, also involving oil, as the United States linked the future of aid and the Alliance for Progress directly to its private investments. At the end of the year President Goulart of Brazil attacked the Alliance as a means of United States hemispheric domination and a poor substitute for a Latin trade bloc intended to obtain higher earnings for exports. Some months later, in April 1964, President Johnson sent his "warmest wishes" to the leaders of the coup who had overthrown Goulart, and at the end of 1964 Hanna Mining and Bethlehem Steel obtained vast iron ore concessions in Brazil.

The relationship between the objectives of foreign economic policy and direct political and military intervention therefore has been a continuous and intimate one—indeed, very often identical. If historians have glossed over this dimension, in part because of lack of access to data but also due to a fashionable theory of economic nondeterminism, it is sufficient to point out that the critical premises and world view of America's leaders make this element in American foreign policy since the Second World War the one that needs far greater appreciation and inquiry. During the early stage of the Suez Crisis, in August 1956, John Foster Dulles, in a meeting with the presidents of American oil firms, made explicit the premise that, as a Socony Vacuum executive recorded his words, ". . . the United States would not acquiesce in the rights of nationalization that would affect any other facilities in our own economic interests. . . . He commented that international law recognizes the right to nationalize if adequate compensation is paid, but he admits that actually adequate compensation is never really paid and nationalization, in effect, thereby becomes confiscation. . . . the United States felt it was O.K. to nationalize only if assets were not impressed with international interest. What he meant by international interest was where a foreign government had made promises of fixed duration in the form of concessions or contracts, upon which other nations would rely on fixing their courses of action and their own economies. . . . Therefore . . . nationalization of this kind of an asset impressed with international interest goes far beyond composition of shareholders alone, and should call for international intervention."

This formula, as vague as it is concerning the unknown value of minerals in the ground or the ideological basis of necessary economic planning, was broad enough to lead to United States belligerence toward the Cuban revolution from its very first days and to a whole host of other crises involving American property abroad. Succinctly, it aligned the United States against any radical changes in the internal affairs of national economies in which it had some interest, and required interventionism as a consistent response. Where United States troops and threats of violence did not accompany the intervention, various economic pressures, embargoes, and the like accomplished the task. Hoping to stem the tide of Third World economic conflicts with American objectives, by October 1964 the United States had signed investment guaranty treaties against convertibility changes with sixty-six countries and against expropriation with sixty-four. Congress, with enthusiasm that often exceeded even that of the Executive branch, has repeatedly declared its support for private investment as the best means for economic development in the Third World, and in summer 1964 surpassed itself in unsuccessfully attempting to transfer to American courts the right to judge the legality of foreign expropriations. The effort was superfluous, for in the preceding decades and later years the United States Government made it abundantly clear that its function in the world was to protect and advance American economic power in the control of the world economy.

That function, in the final analysis, required a monumental inconsistency between America's practice and what it advocated as acceptable conduct for the rest of the world. Such a role demanded, as well, that the United States take a stand against every political and economic movement in the world designed not even to revolutionize national societies but merely to shift the distribution of the world's wealth away from American borders. In effect, this conservative policy compelled the United States to confront the competitive European nations as well as Left nationalist and revolutionary governments, and its choice of responses depends on the stakes and countervailing power involved.

A Theory of United States Global Role

In their brilliant essay on the political economy of nineteenth century British imperialism, John Gallagher and Ronald Robinson have described a process that parallels the nature of United States expansion after 1945:

> Imperialism, perhaps, may be defined as a sufficient political function of this process of integrating new regions into the expanding economy; its character is largely decided by the various and changing relationships between the political and economic elements of expansion in any particular region and time. Two qualifications must be made. First, imperialism may be only indirectly connected with economic integration in that it sometimes extends beyond areas of economic development, but acts for their strategic protection. Secondly, although imperialism is a function of economic expansion, it is not a necessary function. Whether imperialist phenomena show themselves or not, is determined not only by the factors of economic expansion, but equally by the political and social organization of the regions brought into the orbit of the expansive society, and also by the world situation in general.
>
> It is only when the politics of these new regions fail to provide satisfactory conditions for commercial or strategic integration and when their relative weakness allows, that power is used imperialistically to adjust those conditions. Economic expansion, it is true, will tend to flow into the

,regions of maximum opportunity, but maximum opportunity depends as much upon political considerations of security as upon questions of profit. Consequently, in any particular region, if economic opportunity seems large but political security small, then full absorption into the extending economy tends to be frustrated until power is exerted upon the state in question. Conversely, in proportion as satisfactory political frameworks are brought into being in this way, the frequency of imperialist intervention lessens and imperialist control is correspondingly relaxed . . .

In today's context, we should regard United States political and strategic intervention as a rational overhead charge for its present and future freedom to act and expand. One must also point out that however high that cost may appear today, in the history of United States diplomacy specific American economic interests in a country or region have often defined the national interest on the assumption that the nation can identify its welfare with the profits of some of its citizens—whether in oil, cotton, or bananas. The costs to the state as a whole are less consequential than the desires and profits of specific class strata and their need to operate everywhere in a manner that, collectively, brings vast prosperity to the United States and its rulers.

Today it is a fact that capitalism in one country is a long-term physical and economic impossibility without a drastic shift in the distribution of the world's income. Isolated, the United States would face those domestic backlogged economic and social problems and weaknesses it has deferred confronting for over two decades, and its disappearing strength in a global context would soon open the door to the internal dynamics which might jeopardize the very existence of liberal corporate capitalism at home. It is logical to regard Vietnam, therefore, as the inevitable cost of maintaining United States imperial power, a step toward saving the future in something akin to its present form by revealing to others in the Third World what they too may encounter should they also seek to control their own development. That Vietnam itself has relatively little of value to the United States is all the more significant as an example of America's determination to hold the line as a matter of principle against revolutionary movements. What is at stake, according to the "domino" theory with which Washington accurately perceives the world, is the control of Vietnam's neighbors, Southeast Asia and, ultimately, Latin America. . . .

The existing global political and economic structure, with all its stagnation and misery, has not only brought the United States billions but has made possible, above all, a vast power that requires total world economic integration not on the basis of equality but of domination. And to preserve this form of world is vital to the men who run the American economy and politics at the highest levels. If some of them now reluctantly believe that Vietnam was not the place to make the final defense against tides of unpredictable revolutionary change, they all concede that they must do it somewhere, and the logic of their larger view makes their shift on Vietnam a matter of expediency or tactics rather than of principle. All the various American leaders believe in global stability which they are committed to defend against revolution that may threaten the existing distribution of economic power in the world.

chapter 4

Poverty, Economic Insecurity, and the Welfare State

From the 1950s until the beginning of the 1960s it was widely believed by academicians as well as laymen that America had eliminated poverty. The social reforms of the New Deal and the prosperity of the late 1940s and 1950s seemed to have accomplished an "income revolution" unprecedented in the history of mankind.[1] Looking back upon this recent age of innocence, one wonders how the often deteriorating living conditions of the rural and urban poor and the special plights of racial and ethnic minorities and the aged could have been ignored. Perhaps the existence of poverty was easy to deny when it was no longer characteristic of a large proportion of the population as it had been during the terrible years of the Great Depression. Moreover, the Cold War paranoia that gripped the land during the early 1950s made it almost treasonous to suggest that American capitalism had

---

[1] Some sociologists who practiced their craft during this period argued that the very concept of "social stratification" no longer had meaning in America. John Pease, William Form, Joan Huber Rytina, "Ideological Currents in American Stratification Literature," *American Sociologist*, vol. 5 (May 1970), p. 132.

not succeeded in eliminating the conditions which communists and socialists believed to be inherent in the nature of an economy based upon private enterprise and a limited regulation of market forces.

The almost total neglect of poverty in the fifties was transformed in the next decade into a nearly compulsive concern for those "other Americans" who were left out of the "affluent society."[2] Unfortunately, the recent proliferation of social scientific research on poverty has tended to obscure crucial aspects of this phenomenon.

This chapter attempts to describe the economic and social well-being of Americans, to account for the failure of the wealthiest nation in the world to eliminate hard-core poverty and material insecurity, and to examine the role of the so-called welfare state as a solution to these problems.

In the past decade much energy has been expended investigating the living standards and life chances of Americans. From the dry statistics of the annual economic reports to the President to the dramatic presentations of Harry Caudill and Michael Harrington.[3] Americans have been inundated with accounts of extreme misery in the United States. Using the government's own income definition of poverty status, we see that the proportion of American families living in great poverty has declined substantially in recent years. Nevertheless, as of 1968 25.4 million persons, or 12.8 percent of the population, were considered to be living below the poverty level.[4]

What are the consequences of extreme economic deprivation on life style? If we consider housing, health, education, legal services, and transportation, low incomes are translated into physical and social poverty. In 1960, according to the Census Bureau, 16 percent of all housing units were classified as deteriorating or dilapidated, with 39 percent of those with incomes under $2000 and 20 percent of those with incomes from $3000 to $3999 living in such units. In addition to a significant possibility of living in substandard housing, persons with very low incomes are disadvantaged in several other ways in the housing market. For example, it is generally difficult for them to obtain insurance against property damage or theft, because they reside in high-risk areas. It is also difficult for them to maintain or enhance the conditions of their homes because of the prohibitive preconditions for obtaining loans. Moreover, people with low incomes are often ineligible for federally subsidized housing because they cannot *afford* to live there.[5]

[2] Michael Harrington's The Other America: Poverty in the United States (New York, Crowell-Collier and Macmillan, Inc., 1962), played a major role in dramatizing the "new" poverty.

[3] Harry Caudill, Night Comes to the Cumberlands: The Biography of a Depressed Area (Boston: Little, Brown & Company, 1963). Harrington, op. cit.

[4] The American Almanac: The U.S. Book of Facts, Statistics, and Information for 1971 (New York: Grosset & Dunlap, Inc., 1971), p. 328. Recently, the absolute number and proportion of poor in the United States has increased slightly reversing a trend of many years. This has been the consequence of severe economic recession, which has dramatically increased unemployment levels.

[5] S. M. Miller, Martin Rein, Pamela Roby, Bertam W. Gross, "Poverty, Inequality, and Conflict," Annals of the American Academy of Political and Social Science, vol. 373 (September 1967), pp. 26–28.

In terms of health and educational services the economically deprived American family is likely to suffer perhaps even more than in terms of housing. Many studies indicate that the quantity and quality of medical care and education increase with family income.[6] Yet persons with low incomes, who cannot afford these services, are considerably more likely to be in poor health and to lack adequate educations. In 1963, for example, 50 percent of the young men examined by the Selective Service System for induction into the armed forces were rejected because of physical and/or educational deficiencies.[7] This contrasted with a figure of 30 percent during World War II using similar standards. Even allowing for stricter enforcement of the standards during wartime and minor distortions because of deceptive practices on the part of inductees seeking to avoid military service, these figures suggest that an incredible proportion of young Americans are suffering from ill health and are functionally illiterate. Another survey, conducted by the Department of Health, Education and Welfare in 1964, found that 22.3 percent of the white and 63 percent of the nonwhite children aged five to fourteen in the United States had never been to a dentist.[8] When broken down by family income, the data indicated that 39.6 percent of the children whose parents earned between $2000 and $3999 per year had never visited a dentist.

In addition to fairly widespread deficiencies in housing, health care, and education, low-income Americans and a considerable number with allegedly adequate incomes are disadvantaged when they need legal services, transportation, and "neighborhood amenities," namely, sanitation control, police and fire protection, recreation facilities, libraries, parks, adequate streets and roads.[9]

Although the so-called objective indicators of poverty status are worthy of continual emphasis, it is the "culture of poverty" observed by Oscar Lewis in his cross-cultural ethnographic research that is perhaps most tragic in its social and psychological consequences for the extremely poor in any society. Lewis' conception of the importance of cultural characteristics is often confused with the school that attributes the sources of poverty status to the institutions, values, beliefs, and practices of poor people. While his scholarship does contribute to this school of thought, which shall be discussed shortly, his sadly neglected observations in the introduction to *La Vida* should be considered:

[6] *Ibid.*, pp. 32–35, Patricia Cayo Sexton, *Education and Income: Inequalities in Our Public Schools* (New York: The Viking Press, Inc., 1964).

[7] Seymour Melman, *Our Depleted Society* (New York: Holt, Rinehart and Winston, Inc., 1965), pp. 114–116. Although Melman does not report the rejection rate by social class it is well known that the poor are more likely to be eligible for induction because they generally are unable to qualify for student or occupational deferments and are rejected on the basis of deficiencies. Thus, the population of potential inductees was probably disproportionately overrepresented by the poor as were the rejectees.

[8] *Ibid.*, p. 119.

[9] Miller et al., *op. cit.*, pp. 35–37.

. . . On the basis of my limited experience in one socialist country—Cuba— and on the basis of my reading, I am inclined to believe that the culture of poverty does not exist in the socialist countries. I first went to Cuba in 1947 as a visiting professor for the State Department. At that time I began a study of a sugar plantation in Melena del Sur and of a slum in Havana. After the Castro revolution I made my second trip to Cuba as a correspondent for a major magazine, and I visited the same slum and some of the same families. The physical aspects of the slum had changed very little, except for a beautiful new nursery school. It was clear that the people were still desperately poor, but I found much less of the despair, apathy and hopelessness which are so diagnostic of urban slums in the culture of poverty. They expressed great confidence in their leaders and hope for a better life. The slum itself was now highly organized, with block committees, educational committees, party committees. The people had a new sense of power and importance. They were armed and were given a doctrine which glorified the lower class as the hope of humanity. . . . In socialist, fascist and in highly developed capitalist societies with a welfare state, the culture of poverty tends to decline. I suspect that the culture of poverty flourishes in, and is generic to, the early free enterprise stage of capitalism and that it is also endemic in colonialism.[10]

An examination of scholarly work on the rural white poor and black ghetto dwellers[11] suggests that the experience of unmitigated despair, apathy, and helplessness—components of Lewis' "culture of poverty"—is not foreign to the United States. If Lewis' hypothesis about the kinds of societies that nurture such a poverty syndrome is accurate, one would have to contend that many Americans today are living under conditions of early industrial capitalism or colonialism. In fact, the large pool of cheap labor and undercapitalization of the rural South and the urban ghettos do seem comparable to the conditions of these earlier settings and times.

The Harlems and Appalachias of today may even be considered more fertile soil for the development of social despair than were the old colonies or the nineteenth-century European capitalist societies. The forced migration of blacks from Africa and the violation of their culture made social and psychological resistance to oppression much more difficult than in the case of colonial peoples who maintained contact with their physical environment and culture.[12]

Like the African and Asian peoples whose societies were colonized, the European working classes developed distinctive cultural orientations and social institutions which helped them in resisting some of the terrible material, social, and cultural dislocations of industrialization.[13] In contrast,

[10] Oscar Lewis, La Vida: A Puerto Rican Family in the Culture of Poverty—San Juan and New York (New York: Random House, Inc., 1965), pp. xlix–1.
[11] Caudil, op. cit., discusses poor whites; Elliot Liebow, Tally's Corner: A Study of Negro Streetcorner Men (Boston: Little, Brown & Company, 1967), considers the black ghetto.
[12] Robert Blauner, "Internal Colonialism and Ghetto Revolt," Social Problems, vol. 16 (Spring 1969), pp. 393–408. Also reprinted in Chapter 5 of this text.
[13] Edward Thompson, The Making of the English Working Class (New York: Vintage Books, 1963).

blacks, poor rural whites, and the aged—among the groups most mired in the culture of hopelessness in contemporary America—have virtually no autonomous cultural tradition which would permit them to maintain their dignity in chronic poverty. Self-denigration has probably also been more characteristic of the American poor than the deprived of any other industrial nation because of the absence of an organized anticapitalist ideological force, such as can be found in the European trade unions and Social Democratic parties. In addition, the enormous economic growth of the United States and the upgrading of the occupational structure have permitted enough job mobility for some poor people to accept at least part of the Horatio Alger mythology.[14]

While maintaining that millions of Americans do live under conditions of material, social, and psychological degradation, the preceding discussion has not adequately depicted the more general economic insecurity that most Americans experience. Donald Light's article in this chapter suggests that about 45 to 60 percent of American families have incomes that do not permit a living standard which is "moderate but adequate," according to the criteria of the Bureau of Labor Statistics.

Light's careful empirical research comparing the bureau's periodic estimates for a "moderate but adequate city worker's family budget" with the actual distribution of family incomes during selected years lends weight to the argument that the well-being of Americans has not improved—and may actually have declined slightly—in the past two decades. Other evidence such as that on liquid savings also suggests that the average American family is only one major illness or job layoff away from disaster.[15] Finally, a definitive study of the financial characteristics of consumers conducted by the Federal Reserve Board showed that 45 percent of American consumer units had a net worth (assets less debt) of less than $5000 in 1962, with 28 percent having a net worth under $1000.[16]

It is necessary, at this point, to counter the argument made by critics of Light's position that the average American family today obviously has a much higher standard of living than ever before because of the vast increase in educational opportunities and goods and services available in this

[14] In 1967, the Gallup poll asked a random sample of Americans, "In your opinion, which is more to blame if a person is poor—lack of an effort on his own part or circumstances beyond his control?" Forty-two percent of the entire sample and 30 percent of those earning less than $3000 per year chose "lack of an effort." Only 19 percent of the total sample and 30 percent of those with incomes less than $3000 chose "circumstances." *Gallup Opinion Index*, no. 25 (July 1967), p. 17. Yet Blau and Duncan's study indicates that only about 10 percent of the male offspring of working-class (craftsmen, operatives, laborers) fathers become professionals compared to almost 40 percent of the male sons of professionals. Peter Blau and Otis Dudley Duncan, *The American Occupational Structure* (New York: John Wiley & Sons, Inc., 1967), p. 28.
[15] As of 1969, 45 percent of American families had liquid assets (checking and savings accounts and nonmarketable U.S. savings bonds) of less than $500. See *The American Almanac, op. cit.*, p. 321.
[16] Ferdinand Lundberg, *The Rich and the Super-Rich: A Study in the Power of Money Today* (New York: Lyle Stuart, Inc.) pp. 22–25. Net worth refers not simply to liquid assets but also includes all other forms of property (for example, clothing, furniture, phonograph records).

era of constant technological innovation. This argument claims that family budgets are felt to be inadequate only because our expectations are so much higher than previous generations.

Whenever one discusses "economic well-being" it is important to realize that the term has meaning primarily in an historical context. American citizens have higher living standards than their ancestors in many respects, but historical comparisons make little sense in view of the greater requirements for "adequate" well-being today. While total illiteracy did not represent a major social problem in 1850 when most laborers worked the land, so-called functional illiteracy in the 1970s takes on enormous significance, given the nature of contemporary work. Similarly, the fact that most Americans own automobiles is often offered as proof that material comfort in the United States is widespread. Yet the American farmer or worker of the past century had little need for sophisticated modes of transportation unlike the urban dweller of today who must often commute over an hour to find suitable work. When public transportation systems are nonexistent or inadequate, the contemporary laborer must purchase an automobile not as a luxury item, but as a means of survival. Much of what is considered progress upon inspection turns out to be the introduction of new means to satisfy basic human needs in ways not clearly superior to those of the past. The automobile, for example, that permits such freedom to travel long distances also permits the establishment of essential services far away from the home. Travel to and from work should be added to the workday rather than to "leisure time." Thus, Sebastian de Grazia estimates that the conditions of modern work allow less leisure time than did those of medieval agrarianism.[17]

It has been suggested that a fairly large number of Americans are extremely poor and perhaps a majority are economically insecure. But what are the sources of these phenomena? The major debate between social scientists over the past decade has pitted those who believe that the personal characteristics of the poor are the cause of their plight against those who trace economic deprivation and insecurity to the normal workings of a capitalist economy.

While governmental elites—very willing to believe that America offers success to all who have talent and motivation—have widely accepted theories of poverty emphasizing the cultural, social, and psychological characteristics of the poor, such theories have had little support in the academic world of late. Alleged characteristics of the poor such as an absence of social and organizational contacts; an inability and/or unwillingness to defer gratification and think in terms of the future; feelings of helplessness, fatalism, dependency, are at best applicable only to sectors of the poor population.[18] In other words, even within a capitalist context the culture of poverty does not

[17] Sebastion de Grazia, *Of Time, Work and Leisure* (New York: Doubleday & Company, Inc., 1964), pp. 57–83.

[18] David Elesh and Seymour Spilerman, "Poverty Theories and Income Maintenance: Substantive Validity and Policy Relevance," unpublished ms. (Department of Sociology, University of Wisconsin, 1970), provide a critical review of the literature relevant to this controversy. See also Charles Valentine, *Culture and Poverty: Critique and Counter-Proposals* (Chicago: University of Chicago Press, 1968).

Poverty, Economic Insecurity, and the Welfare State

apply to all who are extremely deprived economically and in terms of social services. Certainly, it applies to even fewer of those who have incomes slightly below what is "moderate but adequate." It is perhaps best to view the phenomena described by Lewis and others as relevant to sections of the poor and the insecure who face chronic economic deprivation, often because they work in nonunionized, low-wage industries and have failed to maintain or develop a viable cultural tradition which permits explanations for poverty and insecurity that do not involve the self-denigration fostered by capitalist culture.

A variant of the culture of poverty thesis is the view that the poor and insecure experience deprivation because they lack sufficient education to qualify for the increasingly complex jobs spawned by advanced technology. Although there is an obvious correlation between educational attainment and income, considerable evidence contradicts the theory of educational deprivation. First, among certain groups noneconomic discrimination reduces the utility of education in obtaining high-paying jobs. Thus, black college graduates earn only slightly more than white high school dropouts because of racial discrimination.[19] Similarly, women, who are the breadwinners in many American families, also suffer from economic discrimination, regardless of their educational achievements.[20] Second, many educational qualifications necessary to obtain certain jobs have little or no relationship to the skills actually necessary to do adequate work. Many if not most workers are overeducated for the jobs they hold.[21] Does a person really need a college degree to be a social worker? The current plight of unemployed engineers, many with postgraduate degrees, who have been laid off because of cuts in defense spending testifies to the limited relationship between education and economic well-being.

Except in a few cases, educational criteria for employment reflects a lack of jobs relative to job applicants. If very few persons wanted to be mailmen or social workers or if communities decided they needed many more persons in these occupations, the educational qualifications might be lowered. If high school dropouts returned to school in large numbers, their job prospects might not be improved, unless many new jobs were created for them. Otherwise, their high school diplomas would be of little advantage in commanding a higher income. The same could well be true for college graduates in the near future.

Having questioned the importance of personal characteristics of the poor in the maintenance of extreme poverty and general economic insecurity, we may discuss the economic features which make it difficult for all capitalist societies to totally eliminate material concerns from the mind of the average citizen. One basic characteristic of economic decision-making under capitalism is that it is accomplished by a small number of owners, directors,

[19] Paul Siegal, "On the Cost of Being Negro," *Sociological Inquiry*, vol. 35 (Winter 1965), p. 53.
[20] Marlene Dixon, "Why Women's Liberation?" *Ramparts*, December 1969, pp. 61–62.
[21] Ivar Berg, *Education and Jobs: The Great Training Robbery* (New York: Frederick A. Praeger, Inc., 1970).

and managers of businesses oriented towards maximizing profitable investment and economic growth. This essential feature of capitalism, whether in
its early or advanced phases, means that investment, pricing, employment,
marketing, and other economic decisions will not be made in accordance
with *community* needs. If the institutionalization of private greed leads to
public good so much the better, but this is at best an accidental by-product
of corporate activity.

One of the goals all capitalists must accept in operating their enterprises
is that the costs of production must be kept to a minimum. Historically, this
has meant that wages and salaries will be set as low as an employer can get
away with and labor-saving machinery will be introduced, if possible, when
workers' wage and salary demands make human labor too costly. The drive
to cut costs should not be seen as a reflection of the personal inhumanity or
greed of capitalists. Rather, in a competitive environment (and even monopolies and oligopolies compete internationally if not nationally) failure to maintain a competitive price brings disaster to a firm. Paying high wages is not
merely a matter of accepting lower profits for many small businesses. High
labor costs necessitating high prices may actually drive marginal enterprises
out of business if they cannot control their markets. The average life span
for a business in the United States is approximately six years, although giant,
monopolistic corporations are virtually impregnable unless commodity sub-
stitutions or new technologies eliminate the need for their products or services.

The need for the lowest possible production costs reflects itself in the
extent and distribution of poverty in the United States. Many industries suffering from extreme competition and seeking to employ only a small number
of persons from a large pool of available laborers are in an excellent position
to contribute to poverty by paying extremely low wages.

Besides being caused by low-wage industries, poverty is very much
related to general levels of employment, since material well-being in a
capitalist society is inextricably tied to work. Once again, unemployment and
its consequences are not uniform features of all societies. In Western Europe,
trade union militancy and a socialist or labor political presence has kept
unemployment levels much lower than in the United States for many years.[22]
In socialist countries unemployment is virtually absent.[23] Unemployment
occurs in capitalist countries when there is a reduced demand for goods and
services or when employers decide to replace human labor with machinery.
In the first case, employers may respond to reduced demand by laying off
workers and thus cutting unnecessary production costs. In the second case,
the employers' desire to increase productivity relative to labor costs so as to
maintain or enhance the competitive position of the firm or simply to extend

[22] Melman, *op. cit.*, pp. 127–129.

[23] Economic "liberalization" in socialist countries such as Yugoslavia has, in
recent years, increased levels of unemployment and income inequality by utilizing
market criteria for the allocation of resources and emphasizing material incentives
to boost productivity. See Frank Parkin, *Class Inequality and Political Order: Social
Stratification in Capitalist and Communist Societies* (New York: Frederick A.
Praeger, Inc., 1971).

Poverty, Economic Insecurity, and the Welfare State

its market without cost reduction is the general source of automation. In neither case are the needs of workers considered a sufficient condition for maintaining employment levels. In an economy not primarily organized around profit and capital accumulation (for example, feudalism, socialism) involuntary unemployment can be eliminated.

Other features of capitalist economic behavior also contribute to poverty. Not only can businessmen decide how much to pay employees and whether to hire or fire them but they can also determine prices, what products to produce and how durable to make them, and where to invest their capital. Each of these decisions made by individuals with no need to obtain community sanction contributes to economic conditions that affect millions of other persons. Thus, when workers strike and win wage increases, businessmen can and do raise their prices at the expense of the same and other workers as consumers. When businessmen decide to build automobiles guaranteed to deteriorate in five years despite the technical possibility of producing longer-lasting vehicles, consumers must expend a larger portion of their incomes on transportation than is necessary. Finally, if businessmen find investment more profitable for themselves in Canada than in Harlem or West Virginia, the citizens of the latter areas have no right to demand their share of capital investment.

This discussion of the major economic sources of poverty should clearly indicate that poverty theories emphasizing personal characteristics of the deprived are significant primarily in determining the poor's relative disadvantage within the context of widespread insecurity caused by the operation of the capitalist economic organization. The economic sources of extreme poverty are only more acute instances of the general effects which make the majority of Americans insecure about the size and stability of their incomes and their inability to improve their standards of living despite increased consumption.

The above analysis has focused on the tendencies of an unchecked capitalist economy to generate chronic economic deprivation and insecurity. While readily admitting these socially undesirable features of capitalism, contemporary liberals, at least until recently, have contended that the development of social reform legislation and the birth of the welfare state had succeeded in curbing the worst abuses of the unregulated market economy and in reducing considerably the economic and social inequalities of capitalism. Unfortunately, as Dorothy Wedderburn shows in her article in this chapter, the social welfare systems in advanced Western capitalist societies have not fulfilled the hopes of social reformers. Moreover, Wedderburn's comparative analysis indicates that the United States has the least-developed social welfare system and should not be considered as having even a diluted welfare state.[24]

Wedderburn's evidence on the inability of welfare systems under

[24] An analysis of the motivations behind and functions of American welfare legislation can be found in Frances Fox Piven and Richard Cloward, *Regulating the Poor: The Functions of Public Welfare* (New York: Pantheon Books, Inc., 1971). See also Richard Elman, *The Poorhouse State: The American Way of Life on Public Assistance* (New York: Dell Publishing Co., Inc., 1966).

capitalism to redistribute property wealth and income is drawn primarily from the British case. Thus, it should be noted again (as in Chapter 1) that studies of American wealth and income distribution by Lampman, Kolko, and the Federal Reserve System corroborate the British findings.[25] Similarly, research on the effects of taxation in transferring income from rich to poor in America indicates that despite the seemingly progressive nature of tax laws, approximately the same proportion of income from all social classes is appropriated.[26]

While Wedderburn's emphasis on Britain means that all her data is not strictly relevant to the United States, the findings do suggest that even if a genuine revolution in welfare legislation occurred in this country, the problems of poverty, inequality, and insecurity would at best be mitigated. The absence of powerful Labor or Social Democratic parties and the weaknesses of a trade union movement that had organized only 22.7 percent of the labor force by 1966[27] probably make even a British-style welfare state a utopian prospect.

Why a genuine welfare state never developed in the United States has been partially discussed in Chapter 2 and will be considered from a different perspective in Chapter 9. The present chapter demonstrates that American affluence has been insignificant as a cause of this failure.

[25] Robert Lampman, *The Share of Top Wealth-holders in National Wealth, 1922–1956* (Princeton, N.J.: Princeton University Press, 1962). Gabriel Kolko, *Wealth and Power in America: An Analysis of Social Class and Income Distribution* (New York: Frederick A. Praeger, Inc., 1962), pp. 9–29, 46–54. Lundberg, *op. cit.*

[26] Kolko, *op. cit.*, pp. 30–45. See also Joseph Pechman, "The Rich, the Poor, the Taxes They Pay," *The Public Interest*, No. 17 (Fall, 1969), pp. 21–43.

[27] *Handbook of Labor Statistics* (Washington, D.C.: Government Printing Office, 1968), p. 300.

Donald Light

INCOME DISTRIBUTION: THE FIRST STAGE IN THE CONSIDERATION OF POVERTY

What is undoubtedly one of the most neglected fields in contemporary western economics is the area of income distribution. After the status quo is rationalized by the statement that everyone's income is equal to what the market bids for the factors of production which he owns, and making some vague references to the wishes of society to redistribute income by transfer payments in order to maximize some concept of social welfare, economists have been anxious to move onto more quantitative and "scientific" fields. Within the past ten years certain painfully obvious social conditions, namely the plight of urban populations and of the Negro urban population in particular, have forced economists to go back and make further explorations and pronouncements about income distribution in the United States. . . .

. . . For the last twenty-five years, the B.L.S. [Bureau of Labor Statistics] has periodically published a "moderate but adequate" city workers' family budget. In 1948 it stated that the income designated by this budget enables families to purchase the kinds and amounts of goods and services which "men commonly expect to enjoy, feel that they have lost status and are experiencing privation if they cannot enjoy, and what they insist on having." The same theme was elaborated in the 1969 version which stated that the budget "provides for maintenance of physical health and social well-being, the nurture of children, and participation in community activities."

In order to determine the budget, the B.L.S. . . . assembled a complete budget for an urban family of a thirty-eight-year-old man, his wife, a boy thirteen, and a girl eight. This budget specified the amounts and kinds of all the goods and services which the family would consume over a year, and it priced these goods and services according to field surveys conducted in twenty or thirty major American cities (the number varying from year to year). For food, B.L.S. used the standards provided by the Department of Agriculture in its low and moderate cost diets and by the Food and Nutrition Board of the National Research Council. For shelter, the B.L.S. used the minimum housing standards of the American Public Health Association and the Federal Public Housing Administration. This is a pre-tax budget, so the proper amount of federal, state, and local taxes were computed for each city.

Other goods and services which the family would purchase are clothing,

Reprinted, with deletions, from Donald Light, "Income Distribution: The First Stage in the Consideration of Poverty," *Occasional Papers of the Union for Radical Political Economics*, vol. 1 (December 1969), pp. 1–8, by permission of the *Union for Radical Politics Economics*. Donald Light is a graduate of Princeton University. He is employed by the Department of Health of the City of New York.

house furnishing, transportation, medical care, household operation, reading, recreation, tobacco, education, gifts and contributions, and miscellaneous expenses. B.L.S. determined amounts in each category by examining budget studies that are made every ten years of consumer expenditures to find the amount of each good which is purchased by a family when quantity-income elasticity is at a maximum. The rationale is that for normal goods, a family will consume larger and larger amounts as its income increases. If its income is initially very low, a family will purchase progressively greater amounts of a good as its income rises. At some point the proportion of its budget which it spends on this good reaches a maximum (of quantity-income elasticity), and it will start buying other or better goods rather than more and more of the good being considered. Of course this method of finding the proper amount of goods and services in a "moderate but adequate" budget is open to criticisms, but it does have the virtue of giving an empirically based estimate of what American families feel are minimally necessary requirements for their daily life.

An examination of the amounts used in the "moderate but adequate" budget shows that they are less than extravagant. Clothes are replaced over a period of two to four years and furniture over a longer period. Transportation is by used-car unless the city has a well-developed public transportation system. There is no hired help for the wife in her housekeeping chores. The recreation allowance permits only a movie every two or three weeks. The education category covers only day-to-day school expenses such as book fees and materials—it does not provide for money to be put away for college or any kind of post-high school training. The entire budget in fact makes no provision for savings of any kind to meet future major expenses. It may be said to be quite un-American in that it does not recognize social mobility as a necessary "good" to be consumed. This budget also makes no provision for legal assistance—people who live under this budget are basically powerless to contest official actions concerning them. By the standards of what many American families presently receive, the medical category is quite generous —fifteen visits to the doctor for the entire family and one hospital stay per year.

As would be expected with the post-war prosperity the entire basket of goods has been upgraded from 1948 to 1969. Originally no provision was made for either a phone or a television in every home, but now there is. The "usedness" of the used car has gradually decreased from eight to two years. The proportion of families assumed to own their dwelling has increased from far under half to 75 percent. And the families in 1969 are assumed to be covered by group insurance plans which was not true for the earlier years.

Four "moderate but adequate" budgets are considered here for the years 1966–1967, 1959, 1951, and 1946–1947 (see Table 1). Only for the most recent year did the B.L.S. give a composite figure for the entire country. For all other years, a median figure was selected—half the cities' budgets were above it and half were below it. This procedure probably tends to understate a true national average because included in the cities which are above the median are the largest population centers such as New York, Chicago, and Los Angeles. Various editions of the *Statistical Abstract of the United*

Table 1.   Income Distribution and the Moderate but Adequate Budget[a]

Year	Moderate but Adequate Budget (dollars)	Percent of Families below MBA Budget	Number of Families below MBA Budget (millions)	Equity Gap (billions of dollars)
1966–1967	9,100	59.4	28.5	119
1959	6,200	29.9	13.8	29.7
1951	4,200	52.5	14.1	22.6
1946–1947	3,000	46.7	Not Available	Not Available

[a] All figures are in current dollars.

States were used to find figures on income distribution for families. For 1966–1967 and 1959, figures for all families, urban and non-urban, had to be used. But for the 1951 and 1946–1947 figures, a breakdown by urban and non-urban population was utilized. Given that by the '60's only about 10 percent of the population remained on the farm, using total family figures does not result in a serious distortion.

A more important question is just how accurately the figures in Table 1 reflect the total number of individuals in the country living on a less than "moderate but adequate" budget. No attempt has been made to account for individuals who are not living in a family unit (where family is defined by the presence of two or more people who are related to one another). Therefore, the loners are not counted at all, and it is known that this group (especially lone women) have many individuals who are living in poverty by any standards. Also, it presumably costs less than the "moderate but adequate" budget to live decently if there are fewer than four members of a family and more if there are more than four. In 1966 there were 48,278,000 families in the United States and their average size was 3.72 members. This size has been quite constant through the '60's, although it was a bit smaller in the '50's when a slightly different definition of family was used. Since a reduction in size of a family of 24 percent (from four to three persons) does not reduce costs 25 percent, it may be seen that the methodology used in compiling Table 1 only overstates the number of families with a less than adequate income by perhaps 5–10 percent. And given that in 1966 there were 12,471,000 unattached individuals in the United States, the total true percentage of people living on less than adequate budgets is probably reasonably close to the figures cited.

Given these problems of data which make the statistics in Table 1 only a first approximation to a crucial area of economic enquiry, a study of the table still reveals several startling facts. First, the notion that America is an affluent society is simply a myth for anywhere from 45 percent to 60 percent of all American families—the people in these living units do not have sufficient income at their disposal to purchase the goods and services which "men commonly expect to enjoy, feel that they have lost status and are experiencing privation if they cannot enjoy, and that they insist on having." Second, the amount of wealth which is necessary to truly eliminate poverty in this country—what is sometimes called the poverty gap, and what in

Table 1 is called an equity gap—is far in excess of the usually named figures entailing an expenditure on the order of $120 billion. This figure was calculated by multiplying the number of families in each income group below the one necessary or a "moderate but adequate" budget times the difference between the median income of that group and the size of the "moderate but adequate" budget. Naturally the same criticisms apply to this $120 billion figure as apply to the number of families below the "moderate but adequate" budget; however, the order of magnitude is not open to dispute. And some of the political implications of this figure begin falling into perspective when it is viewed with respect to the level of government expenditures on all levels in 1966 which was $154 billion or the gross corporate profits of 1966 of $82 billion.

The one set of figures standing in contradistinction to the trend depicted above is the one for 1959. The proportion of families in that year living on less than a "moderate but adequate" budget and the size of the equity gap while still formidable are less mind-boggling and more capable of being handled in the context of conventional analysis and institutions. However, a good case can be made that the 1959 figures are simply the result of a statistical anomaly which, if there were some way of correcting it, would yield results much more similar to those obtained for the other years. The crux of the problem is that the "moderate but adequate" basket of goods is in a continual process of evolution as the overall productivity of the society steadily increases. As more and more of all goods are produced for the average worker to consume, he becomes more likely to consider as obtainable things which he and his family really need but which in former years they have had a life-style which enabled them to live without. It is the function of the maximum quantity-income elasticity criterion to determine what goods at a given point in time are now in fact within grasp of most American families. It turns out that the quantities and kinds of goods produced by this criterion for the 1959 budget were provided by consumer studies which were conducted in 1950. In other words, the methodology was to use post-war consumption patterns and expectations to determine what constitutes a normative standard of living when purchased at the end of the decade of the '50's. The same sort of understating methodology is also true of the 1946–1947 figures, since they were based on depression budget studies. Use of more contemporary and relevant data sources would provide a picture more consistent with those of other years.

There are a number of hypotheses which gain support from the analysis presented above. What was referred to at the beginning of the paper as the traditional economic rationalization of the status quo, namely, the marginal productivity theory of income, has been shown to be adequate only as a very first approximation as to what should be the ultimate power to command the goods and services which are produced by the national economy. Granting the premise of an equitable society with respect to certain essentials, it is clear that the present system of letting productivity and certain limited redistribution which takes place in goods and services through governmental expenditures and in income through transfer payments are grossly inadequate to the task. Furthermore, there would seem to be a real limit as to how

Poverty, Economic Insecurity, and the Welfare State

far currently proposed remedies could actually go towards a real solution. Any proposal of a guaranteed annual income for everyone in the society (with family responsibilities) of $9,000 at present probably would result in a very severe disruption of present work systems. With a guaranteed annual income of $9,000 embodied in some sort of negative income tax plan so as to preserve as much incentive for additional work as possible, two outcomes would occur: that families with incomes between $10,000 and $20,000 would be receiving subsidies, and that effective taxation of everyone else (persons, corporations, and previously untaxed entities) would have to be much, much greater than it presently is. How, why, and whether these sorts of changes could take place within the framework of the present society, i.e., within the present system of Constitutional government and capitalist economic organization, are questions which must be painstakingly and honestly addressed by any economists who would claim that they are interested in bringing about a society without want and a society where all men have an equal claim to dignity as human beings.

Dorothy Wedderburn

FACTS AND THEORIES
OF THE WELFARE STATE

. . . In the immediate post-war years the "welfare state" was generally regarded as an almost exclusively British phenomenon. It was identified as the "achievement" of the 1945 Labour government and it acquired in those years a "socialist flavour." Only critics of the far or idiosyncratic Left were to be found asking: What was "socialist" about it? In what ways had the capitalist system been fundamentally modified by it? Or, if not, by what other tests did it rank as a socialist achievement?

Now twenty years later the intellectual fashion has changed. Sociologists of various political persuasions observe that the "welfare state" is a common phenomenon of all capitalist societies. In its most extreme form this view maintains that the "welfare state" is but one aspect of "industrial society" as such, be it capitalist, communist or any other. It is part of the "logic" of industrialisation which "everywhere has its managers, its managed and a pattern of interaction." This particular theory is discussed more fully below. But in the course of the debate in which this change of emphasis has occurred certain insights into developments in society and the nature of the forces producing these developments have emerged. This article reviews some of the major contributions to the discussion, and indicates certain of the areas which particularly require further attention and analysis by socialists. As a starting point, however, we must examine the facts of the "welfare state" in capitalist society.

Meaning of the Welfare State

First, what do we take as the "welfare state" for the purpose of this essay? The various meanings given to the phrase would be worth an essay in themselves and some of the argument about whether the welfare state has or has not meant a fundamental change in capitalist society is no more than a semantic disagreement about definitions. There is often confusion, too, between objectives themselves and the means of attaining those objectives. There is, though, a central core of agreement that the welfare state implies a state commitment of some degree which modifies the play of market forces in order to ensure a minimum real income for all. By implication, if not explicitly, this is done to protect individuals against the hazards of incapacity

Reprinted, with deletions, from Dorothy Wedderburn, "Facts and Theories of the Welfare State," in Ralph Miliband and John Saville, eds., *The Socialist Register* (London: Merlin Press Ltd., 1965), pp. 127–146, by permission of the author and publisher. Dorothy Wedderburn is Reader in Industrial Sociology, Industrial Sociology Unit, Imperial College, University of London.

for work arising through sickness, old age, and unemployment. There is also general agreement that the objectives of the welfare state will include a guarantee of treatment and benefit for sickness and injury, and the provision of education. There is less agreement about whether the essential goal will also include the maintenance of full employment, economic growth or even ensuring "that all citizens without distinction of status or class are offered the best standards available in relation to a certain agreed range of social services."

Few people will use the term as widely as Professor Meade when he says: "I mean the taxation of incomes of the rich to subsidise directly or indirectly the incomes of the poor." Others may imply that such redistribution is a necessary *consequence* of legislation, say, to guarantee a minimum income. But just as the trend has been towards an acceptance of the view that the welfare state is an "essential" feature of capitalist society, so also there has been a trend towards a narrowing of the content of the concept itself.

Education requires volumes to itself; and the present discussion is confined to an examination of the facts of the welfare state in so far as it is concerned to guarantee minimum health and income for members of the society; and also in so far as the measures necessary to achieve those ends do or do not contribute to the reduction of economic inequality in the society.

The Welfare State in Western Europe

Most Western European capitalist societies today accept the need for state intervention to provide minimum incomes and to protect against social contingencies through legislation related to achieving these ends. It came as something of a surprise to the insular British to discover at the time of the major debate over entry into the Common Market, that many Western European countries had social security provisions which could provide better benefits than did their British counterparts. In all of these countries there are state programmes to provide old age pensions, sickness and maternity benefits, industrial injury provisions, unemployment benefits and family allowances.[1] In many of them such provisions have a continuous history from the beginning of the century. Major changes have occurred since 1945 and in two cases, Britain and France, there was a great period of legislative activity at the end of the war. Development has been towards a more and more complete coverage of the whole population and away from restricted groups of manual workers. It had also been towards more generous levels of benefit.

Important differences remain, however, which could be of considerable importance in contributing to an understanding of the "welfare state." The method of ensuring a minimum income is in most countries two-tier. The first

---

[1] For a summary of basic provisions see U.S. Department of Health, Education and Welfare, *Social Security Programmes Throughout the World*. (Washington, 1962.)

is the state itself using, or enforcing via other bodies the use of, the market principle of contributions to guarantee benefits. This is the system of social insurance. "Need" is recognized, but only providing the necessary price in the form of contributions has been paid. The rôle of the State varies considerably. In Britain and the Scandinavian countries the general exchequer plays a much greater part in the financing of this insurance than in France, West Germany or Belgium. In some of the continental countries and for some of the schemes coverage is only of "employed persons." Since some of these countries have large peasant sectors this can mean major exceptions from coverage. In Britain, since the war, everyone has been included. Again in most of the continental countries the main contribution and benefits are wage-related. The judgment of the market on the individual's ability to pay contributions and, more important, on his standard of need is accepted. In Britain there is still, despite small changes in 1959, basically a flat-rate contribution and a flat-rate benefit which is supposed to represent a "subsistence income." In Britain the major elements of social insurance are unified under one National Insurance scheme. In other countries they are frequently administered separately.

The second tier of the system in all countries is some form of public assistance—that is the provision of support not on terms of the market, i.e. the contribution, but on satisfaction of some test of need (usually defined in monetary terms). The stringency and the punitive nature of the tests again varies. In Britain there remains (despite major improvement in 1948) a strong flavour of the Victorian poor law. Family allowances in Britain are paid out of general taxation but remain at a very low level. But elsewhere, in France and Italy for instance, they are financed by contributions from employers and the level of benefit can represent a considerable addition to wages. A further example is in the health service. In Britain this is universal and free (subject to prescription charges which the Labour Government is pledged to remove). In France and Italy part, at least, of the cost of medical care may be recovered by certain groups. This is also the case in Sweden for doctors and medicines, where there is a scheme of compulsory insurance which reimburses patients. If we had to summarize these differences which have been touched on here only superficially it would be to say that they lie in the extent to which various provisions are close to, or further away from the simulation of a market situation. But what all the countries have in common is the recognition of a similar range of needs and states of dependency.

The Welfare State in the United States

But what of the U.S.A.? Insufficient attention has been given to the extent to which America is outside the mainstream of capitalist societies in so far as welfare state provisions are concerned.

There is overt commitment by the Federal Government to the goal of a minimum income for all, but it is not backed by the necessary legislation. The only Federal scheme in operation to guarantee a minimum income is that which provides old age pensions and survivors benefits. Other provisions are

Poverty, Economic Insecurity, and the Welfare State

left to individual states with varying degrees of direct encouragement and financial support from the federal government. One authority on American welfare policies has written that "the gaps in coverage are serious in both workmen's compensation and in unemployment insurance."[2] More than a fifth of all wage and salary workers are excluded from the federal-state unemployment insurance, and many states do not provide supplements for dependants of the unemployed worker. It has been estimated that only 60 per cent of workers are covered by schemes to provide cash benefits when sick, and in all but four states these schemes are in private hands; and there are no family allowances of any kind.

The position of the unemployed worker is particularly worthy of note. Most European insurance schemes limit the right to benefit when unemployed. In Britain, for instance, if full contributions have been paid benefit may still only be drawn in the first place for 180 days and then up to a maximum of 492 days. After entitlement is exhausted, however, the worker can have recourse to national assistance, which will certainly provide him and his family with a bare minimum income. But in the United States, as Margaret Gordon points out:

> The American unemployed worker who exhausts his benefit right is at a disadvantage compared with his counterpart in most other industrial countries . . . since in many parts of the U.S. public assistance has been unavailable to an unemployed worker or is available only on the most meagre, restrictive and humiliatory terms.

The nineteenth-century view of the virtue of work and the sin of idleness dies hard everywhere, but nowhere harder than in America.

Another area in which the United States noticeably lags behind European capitalism is in the provision of some form of state financed medical care. In America the heavy burden imposed upon individuals by the system of paid medical care is well known. Progressives have followed with interest the battle of first Kennedy and then Johnson to get even a limited system for meeting the medical care costs of the aged agreed upon. Finally, public assistance is administered entirely on a state or county basis and there are wide divergences of approach. In many states the means test is so severe that people have to be practically destitute before they become eligible for relief.

In the light of these deficiencies it is questionable how far the phenomenon of the welfare state can be said to exist in the U.S.A. To argue that many welfare provisions supplied in other countries by government are supplied in the U.S.A. by industry is to miss an essential quality of welfare state provision in Europe. Even where, as in Germany, emphasis is laid upon social insurance being an arrangement between employers and workers, it is, of course, between the collectivity of employers and workers. It is not an individual trade union negotiating the best terms it can for its members and irrespective of those who are not its members. In any case the coverage of

[2] Margaret S. Gordon. "U.S. Welfare Policies in Perspective," *Industrial Relations*, vol. 2. (February 1963.)

such market negotiated provisions within the U.S.A. is extremely limited. The main feature of the European systems of social security is that by one organizational means or another the provision of at least minimum security shall be supplied outside of the market to large sections of the population.

Doubts about whether, in the most restricted sense, a welfare state exists in America are reinforced if account is taken of the accumulating evidence about the nature and extent of poverty in America today. The only European country for which even roughly comparable data is available is Britain. Most American estimates suggest that 20 percent of the population have incomes below the poverty line; the British estimates show 8 to 10 percent. Both these estimates are based on a poverty line appropriate to the standard of living in the particular country concerned. In real terms the American poverty line is much higher up the scale than the British one, although judged in relation to average earnings in each country the two poverty lines are about equal. Even if some allowance is made for the American standard being higher absolutely than the British, the interesting fact emerges that in Britain those below the poverty line are only a little way below it. This is achieved because of extensive reliance upon public assistance nationally administered, but generally available to all who satisfy the financial conditions. In this way the British welfare state has a floor built into it. In America, on the other hand, millions are a long way below the poverty line as defined, and live in what, by British standards, might be called destitution. Low wages and earnings for the largely unorganized service and farm workers; low wages, too, for those sections of the population against whom discrimination is practised, like Negroes and Puerto Ricans. But illness, unemployment and old age are also major problems in America. In Britain these particular matters are cared for by social security legislation and public assistance at least to the point of keeping the majority of people so afflicted at, or only very little below, the poverty line.

Data on the extent of poverty in other European countries, in a form from which comparisons can be made, is badly needed before the achievements of the welfare state can be judged against the goal of a minimum income for all. Some of the countries like Italy and France, with large agricultural sectors and rapid structural change are much less homogeneous than Britain. They may well present a more diverse picture of economic levels at the lower end of the income scale however comprehensive and effective the social security legislation may be. There are difficulties in comparisons on the basis of general observation because the standard of living generally in these countries is lower than in Britain. But the social security legislation does at least exist. In this respect the welfare state can be said to be a fact of Western European capitalist society but not of American society. What is, perhaps, most significant of all to the outside observer is that any extension of welfare legislation seems scarcely on the agenda for public discussion in the United States. In the 1964 programme to combat poverty there are the "job corps," "work-training programmes" and "employment and investment incentives." There is no suggestion that the provision of a minimum income for the old, the sick, the unemployed or the widowed mother through social security and public assistance legislation is administratively very simple. Politically, of course, it is another matter.

The Welfare State and Redistribution

Although we pointed out that redistribution is not generally accepted as a goal for the welfare state of capitalist society it may be useful to conclude this necessarily brief review of the "facts" with reference to the nature and extent of redistribution. An important part of the mythology surrounding the "welfare state" of the fifties which became incorporated in theories of radical transformation of capitalist society was that first, there had been a major reduction in the inequality of pre-tax income distribution; and second (although perhaps less widely held) that welfare state measures had made a major contribution to the further reduction in inequality observable in post-tax income distribution. Of recent years both these views have been subjected to sustained and devastating criticism on two main grounds. First, the basic data on income has been properly criticized for its unreliability and incompleteness. The growth of devices like expense allowances, methods of redistributing family income to reduce tax liability, and the problems of distinguishing capital from income all make the income tax returns of very limited value as a basis for evaluating reductions in inequality. Second, criticism arose because of the impossibility of making comparisons over time in terms of tax units when there have been major demographic and social changes such as reductions in the size of the family and the increased incidence of married women working. For Britain the most sustained critique along these lines has come from Professor Titmuss.[3] But his approach was already foreshadowed in many ways in a study of income redistribution in the main European countries carried out by the Economic Survey for Europe in 1956,[4] and this revealed remarkably similar trends in most Western European countries.

In so far as the taxation authorities' figures could be said to show an improvement in income equality, some economists have argued that this was the result of a permanent trend in modern capitalism. The data for the last few years do not bear this out for Britain, and in the U.S.A., where the figures also showed an apparent shift towards greater income equality in the immediate post-war years, it is argued that this was the result of wartime changes and the once and for all achievement of a higher level of employment in the post-war period. A leading American economist has summed up the position:

> There is some evidence that the movement towards equalization was a consequence of the wartime recovery from depression and of the more or less sustained prosperity of the post-war period. And, equally significant, it is a sea change which roughly parallels the developments in the advanced industrial countries of Western Europe during the same period.[5]

The contribution, if any, of welfare state legislation to any post-tax reduction in inequality must be seen in the total context of state taxation and

[3] R. Titmuss. *Income Distribution and Social Change*. (George Allen and Unwin, London, 1962.)
[4] *Economic Survey of Europe in 1956*. (United Nations, Geneva, 1957.)
[5] R. Solow. "Income Inequality Since the War" in *Post-war Economic Trends in the U.S.*, ed. R. Freeman. (Harper, New York, 1960.)

state provision of benefits. There have been one or two studies of the post-war British position which again suggested that the amount of post-tax redistribution in total was not as great as some people believed. It was suggested, for instance, that "horizontal redistribution" was more important than "vertical redistribution," i.e. there was redistribution from smokers to non-smokers, or people without children to people with children, rather than from rich to poor in the sense, simply, of income level. Recently there has been published an interesting study by J. L. Nicholson, more complete than any previously attempted. Again it is restricted to Britain, and it is possible that a different situation would be revealed elsewhere. But since it has widely been held that Britain is the country where redistribution has gone further than elsewhere as a result of deliberate government policy, that may be thought unlikely.

Nicholson is concerned, first of all, with what has happened in the post-war period, and he is constrained by his data to begin with 1953. His analysis suggests that pre-distribution income showed much the same degree of inequality in 1953 and 1959; and although the total effect of government taxes and benefits was a reduction of inequality, again it was of the same order of magnitude in the two years. Nicholson estimates that in those two years the total effect of government redistributive activity was to reduce the measure of inequality by one-fifth of what it was originally. In the process of doing this he makes some interesting estimates of the power of various types of tax or benefit in contributing to a reduction of inequality. In an appendix he also makes a comparison between his measures of post-war inequality and those made in 1937 by Barna. He stresses the fact that because of the differences of method this can only be a very rough comparison, but he arrives at the interesting conclusion that "There appears to have been little increase in the amount of vertical redistribution between 1937 and 1959."

Nicholson's approach is to make his calculations first for families of different size and composition in different income ranges, and then to derive global estimates by reweighting according to the estimated true proportions of these family size and income types in the total population. We are then able to see that the extent of vertical redistribution varies very considerably for families of different composition. This brings home the complexity of the notion of inequality. Up to the present most attempts at measuring inequality of income distribution have been concerned with global measures. But these can be misleading in that an overall reduction of inequality may mark a growth in inequality as between certain groups (perhaps of considerable importance in political terms, or in terms of social injustice) because reduction in inequality elsewhere is sufficient to outweigh it in the overall measure. A sociologist, J. H. Goldthorpe, has commented upon this when he says:

> For example there may be a tendency towards greater equality in that the number of middle-range incomes is growing; but at the same time the position of the lower income groups relative to the upper and middle groups alike may be worsening.

Finally we must note that the available statistics still point also to considerable inequalities in the ownership of wealth. In so far as international comparison can be made, the position of inequalities of wealth in the capitalist countries seems to have paralleled that of pre-tax income. There has been some reduction of inequality comparing the pre- and the post-war period, but it is not a dramatic reduction and there is little evidence to support any view that there is a long-term trend towards equality. Professor Meade has recently written that: "The problem is already a very real one in the highly industrialized developed countries in many of which there is a really fantastic inequality in the ownership of property"; and he then quotes estimates from a recent new survey in Britain which shows the following position.

Percentage of Population	Percentages of Total Wealth		
	1911–13	1936–38	1960
1	69	56	42
5	87	79	75
10	92	88	83

No socialist can fail to be shocked that the top 5 per cent of the population in Britain in 1960 still owned 75 per cent of the wealth. As Professor Meade further points out, inequality in the ownership of wealth is significant apart from any income inequality which it implies:

A man with much property has great bargaining strength and a great sense of security, independence and freedom; and he enjoys these things not only vis-à-vis his propertyless fellow citizens but also vis-à-vis the public authorities. . . . An unequal distribution of property means an unequal distribution of power and status even if it is prevented from causing too unequal a distribution of income.

A summary of this necessarily rather sketchy review runs the risk of over simplification. But it might be reasonable to say that if the welfare state is defined in a fairly narrow way to mean state intervention to achieve the goal of guaranteeing a minimum income against the natural calamities of life —sickness, unemployment, old age, and some protection against ill health, it exists in most Western European capitalist countries, but it is extremely doubtful whether it exists in America. There is, however, no evidence to support the view that the welfare state, so defined, is a significant factor contributing to a growth of equality in capitalist society. There is limited evidence that in capitalist society there has been some reduction in the past forty or fifty years both in inequality in the ownership of wealth and in the distribution of pre-tax income; though it is hardly of major proportions and there has been much technical criticism of the income statistics in recent years. There is meagre evidence to support the view that this represents a continuing trend. As for the total results of Government activity as taxer and as provider of benefits, this does result in some reduction in inequality, but the suggestion is that the reduction is about the same order of magnitude now as before the war.

Theories of the Welfare State
(i) THE ANTI-COLLECTIVISTS

We turn now to a consideration of the attempts to explain the emergence and development of the welfare state. Of course many of these theories will represent attempts to explain things which our survey of facts have shown not to exist or not to be true. It is necessary also to recognize the degree of "pure ideology" contained in most of the attempts at analysis and explanation. Both from the left and right, historians and sociologists of the welfare state have injected into their work strong overtones of what, in their view, should be, as well as of what is or has been. This can be seen perhaps most clearly in the anti-collectivist school from Dicey through to Hayek where analysis is at a minimum and polemic against the growth of state intervention in the field of social policy the main concern. Goldthorpe has shown that in so far as Dicey offered any "explanation" of the departure from *laissez-faire* it was almost solely in terms of the success of the ideas of individuals who held collectivist views in capturing public opinion. Public opinion, then, in its turn succeeded in carrying legislation. Later writers of this school have substituted "pressure groups" like trade unions or monopolists for the "ideas" of the great men as the agency responsible for bringing about a continual increase in the power of the state.

In a moderated form this *laissez-faire* approach has provided the foundation for the work of a group of contemporary liberal economists in Britain like Seldon and Professors Peacock and Forgarty. They see the welfare state as a phase to be passed through at a particular stage of industrialization, but which can be increasingly dispensed with as output increases. Economic growth, so they argue, provides a vision "of increasingly independent individuals who make use of a variety of means—state, occupational, personal—for providing against the common contingencies of life."[6]

Features of this school of thought worth noting are, first of all, its devotion to the superiority of the market mechanism for the allocation of resources wherever possible. Secondly, and a corollary of the first, it is believed that the structure of the welfare state can be progressively dismantled as output grows. Recently, for instance, this group of writers has argued for larger sections of health and education services to be returned to the market and to the operation of the pricing mechanism. In both regards there is a complete failure to examine the conditions which create "the common contingencies of life" and to ask whether these may change in character rather than disappear as economic growth proceeds. There is singularly little attempt by these writers to examine the situation in the United States, where as Myrdal's recent analysis shows, there is nothing automatic in the way in which increasing real output can solve the real and pressing problems of poverty.[7] Lastly and interesting, because less recognized, there is implied in all the arguments of the anti-collectivists a particular viewpoint about

[6] M. Forgarty, "Social Welfare" in *Agenda for a Free Society*, ed. A. Seldon. (Hutchinson, London, 1961.)
[7] G. Myrdal. *Challenge to Affluence*. (Gollancz, London, 1963.)

human behaviour. As Professor Peacock has written: "The true object of the Welfare State . . . is to teach people how to do without it."

These writers tend to assume, for example, that monetary incentives are essential to make men work; and that state provision of income runs the risk of undermining an individual's independence and desire to work. Their judgments are heavily loaded with the value systems associated with the Victorian bourgeoisie, with the emphasis upon the desirability of thrift, self-help and independence. Existing welfare state legislation in Britain already carries some overtones of such values. Two of what could be described as the essential features of the welfare state reflect the Victorian norms. The contributory principle for the financing of social security which is found in most countries is, above all others, an example of the triumph of the "virtue of thrift." The beneficiaries must in some way be made to pay for their benefits. The notion of "minimum" income itself also implies that the income provided by the state must be kept at such a low level as not to remove incentives for the individual to make efforts to better himself in other directions.

These positions might be regarded as unfortunate legacies of the past. Certainly their uncritical adoption today is difficult to justify because there is an accumulating body of data which casts doubt upon their validity. Most studies of unemployment show that apart from a small group who are usually found to have physical and psychological difficulties, men's main concern is to have a job. Work implies other satisfactions—of interest, status, social contacts—as well as just monetary reward.

The adoption, by the anti-collectivists, of the model of economic man sufficiently well informed, and economically powerful enough, to exercise "choice" and "rational" choice (in some sense) when confronted with the "contingencies of life," is a major barrier towards a real understanding of the problems of the welfare state. It ignores the role of social institutions and forces both in shaping the needs and the preferences of the individuals concerned. Evidence from psychological studies of behaviour might enable serious students, rather than propagandists, to make some headway in understanding this relationship.[8]

(ii) THE FUNCTIONALIST APPROACH

Apart from the Marxist opposition to the anti-collectivists, the main body of Left writing on the nature and origin of the welfare state first concentrated upon what a modern sociologist would call a functionalist approach. This sees the welfare state as "necessary" to the survival of capitalist society. Such a view can be found in the work of E. H. Carr, Polanyi, Beales and others, and "necessity" as Goldthorpe shows may be postulated in two ways; to avoid the waste and inefficiency of *laissez-faire* capitalism or to prevent the class struggle breaking out into open rebellion and so

[8] For a trenchant criticism of some of the anti-collectivist views of human behaviour, see B. Wootton, *Social Science and Social Pathology*. (George Allen and Unwin, London, 1959.)

rupturing the fabric of society. There are affinities between this approach to an explanation of the growth of the welfare state and that Marxist position which sees social reform simply as a palliative; that is, concessions made by the ruling class in order to prevent more serious attacks being made upon their position. The welfare state is here seen as a convenience to capitalism, a "shock absorber," as John Saville has called it.[9] Both approaches, the functionalists and the Marxist, begin from observable conditions, like poverty and ill health, which cause hardship and social unrest. Social legislation is then a response to those objective conditions. The difference lies in the process connecting the condition and the response. In the "necessity" school it might be simply a recognition of the problem by the more enlightened legislators, in the Marxist school the essential channel is the pressure applied by the organizations of the working class. From a non-Marxist standpoint Goldthorpe argues the limitation of an over-simple "necessity" approach convincingly. He is concerned with its failure to provide a satisfactory account of the connection between condition and response without which, he argues, we cannot understand the different pace and forms of development in different countries.

> In other words when it is said by historians that a particular social problem "had to be dealt with" or that a particular piece of legislation was "imperative" or "inevitable," what apparently is meant is that the alternative to action of the kind taken was such as to be clearly incompatible with the ends of those, at least, who were in a position to make the effective decision.

One of the most thoughtful and stimulating commentators on the welfare state is Professor Titmuss. In one sense he might be described as a functionalist because he sees the welfare state as the collective recognition of certain socially determined needs:

> All collectively provided resources are deliberately designed to meet certain socially recognized "needs"; they are manifestations, first, of society's will to survive as an organic whole, and secondly, of the expressed wish of all the people to assist the survival of some people.[10]

The great value of this particular approach is that it is dynamic. There is no once and for all set of "needs" which having been provided for can then set a limit to the development of social policy. The process of the creation of needs is a continuing one. Technical change, measures taken to meet needs in one sphere (i.e. raising of the compulsory school-leaving age) all can create new dependencies and needs elsewhere (i.e. for assistance to the family in supporting the child during the extended period of dependence). His analysis provides moreover greater insight into why certain "needs" receive recognition first in terms of social legislation. In this way Titmuss has supplied a

[9] John Saville, "The Welfare State, An Historical Approach," *New Reasoner* (No. 3, 1957–58).

[10] R. Titmuss, *Essays on the Welfare State.* (George Allen and Unwin, London, 1958.)

devastating critique of the view that the British welfare state is an act of collective charity. Moreover he has drawn attention to the continuous growth of new and subtle forms of privilege.

A welcome feature of Professor Titmuss's analysis is the emphasis placed upon the rôle of capitalist institutions, and the distribution of economic power in creating social needs, or in blocking the measures necessary to meet those needs. In attacking the view that the fundamental problems of the industrial revolution have been solved and that the welfare state has contributed to their solution, he writes:

> Implicit in the thesis is the assumption that the industrial revolution was a once-and-for-all affair. Thus, it ignores the evidence concerning the trend towards monopolistic concentration of economic power, the rôle of the corporation as private government with taxing powers, the problems of social disorganization and cultural deprivation, and the growing impact of automation and new techniques of production and distribution in economically advanced societies. If the first phase of the so-called revolution was to force all men to work, the phase we are now entering may be to force many men not to work.[11]

In his study of the development of individual services in the welfare state (for instance the health service) Professor Titmuss has produced a revealing model of the way in which the conflict of different interest groups can shape and mould the final form of legislation which emerges. What is missing, however, is any notion of class conflict as crucial in creating the overall balance of political forces which determines whether or not social legislation is enacted, or as an influence upon the final form of that legislation. At times it is as though classes, shaped by the overall distribution of economic power and authority in industrial society, did not exist. It is significant that in one of his most recent essays on the development of the welfare state Professor Titmuss places his main emphasis not upon the trade unions but upon nineteenth-century friendly societies, which he describes as "microscopic welfare states,"

> aptly and significantly named, during a century of unbridled competition they were the humanistic institution of the artisan and his family far outdistancing in active membership all trade unions, political parties and religious bodies.

(iii) THE CITIZENSHIP VIEW

Much of the writing on the left has been concerned to trace the origins of the welfare state in order to show that it was not "socialist." One of the sociologists who perceived this earliest and who contributes much to an understanding of the welfare state as part of the process of the development of capitalism is Professor T. H. Marshall.[12] In 1949 he was already arguing that

[11] R. Titmuss, "Merits of the Welfare State" in *New Left Review* (No. 27, 1964).
[12] T. H. Marshall. "Citizenship and Social Class" in *Sociology at the Crossroads*. (Heinemann, London, 1963.)

the development of the social services did not represent a move towards economic equality as such (indeed financed in certain ways and with certain forms of benefit, he noted, they might positively increase economic inequality). But they were to be seen as an essential ingredient in what he called the achievement of equality of status required for the functioning of the market mechanism. There are three elements in Marshall's notion of citizenship, civil (equality before the law), political (equality in voting) and social (equal right to a minimum income and other social services). Together these make up the "status of citizenship, which provided the foundation of equality on which the structure of inequality could be built." Marshall was well aware that while formal equality might be achieved in these three areas, in reality inequalities would and did persist. But at that time (1949) he was optimistic about the possibility of moving towards more equality in the content of the status of citizenship and through it towards less economic inequality:

> the preservation of economic inequalities has been made more difficult by the enrichment of the status of citizenship.

These predictions were set very clearly in the context of Britain, and in later writing Professor Marshall suggests that there was a special feature of the British Welfare State which distinguished it, for a period at least, from the parallel developments in other European countries. This was the ideological position of a society committed, as he put it, to "fair shares for all," expressing itself first in the principle of universality in the provision of social security, but, more important, in the provision of certain welfare services, notably the health service, free to all. As we have noted, social insurance, even when universal, still retains the notion of contribution in order to qualify for benefit. The health service requires only the establishment of "need" before benefit can be enjoyed. But even the development of social insurance in post-war Britain was imbued with an emphasis upon need which might be contrasted with the following kind of statement of the philosophy behind the German welfare system:

> Social policy is not a policy administered by the rich on behalf of the poor; it aims to harmonize the social relationships of the whole people and to guarantee to each the status he has achieved by his own efforts within the general order.

On that basis the welfare state reinforces and legitimizes the activities of the market, whereas "fair shares for all," as Marshall puts it, implies

> a distribution of real income which could be rationally justified and was not the unpredictable result of the supposedly blind forces of a competitive market.

Marshall sees the emergence of this special element in the British Welfare State system as a consequence of the consensus of the war years, and the post-war period of austerity. In 1961 he was writing:

That phase has ended, as it was bound to do ... it was also the product of an explosion of forces which chance and history had brought together in Britain's unique experience in the war and in the transition to a state of peace. As this situation dissolved the society changed and the thing to which we had first given the name of "Welfare State" passed away. Its institutions, practices, procedures and expertise are still with us, but they are operating in a different setting and without the original consensus which welded them into a social system with a distinctive spirit of its own.

This attention to the "superstructure," to the role of ideas in interaction with the objective interests of different groups in the sociey is important. It is echoed in a short but interesting contribution to the debate from Dorothy Thomson.[13] She criticized the essay by John Saville already referred to above on the grounds that he had adopted an over-simple "palliative" view of reform. She agreed that the welfare state of Britain was not "a new form of society qualitatively different from Socialism or Capitalism," continuing:

What is important in the British situation is that a range of benefits are provided purely on the basis of *need* and not of cash payment, or even on any abstract conception of social value. This conception is a profoundly anti-capitalist one ...

and following T. H. Marshall she went on:

The Welfare Services, like the civil rights which are enjoyed in England, and which have also been fought for over the years, are enjoyed by all sections of the community. But their greatest significance is for those without property or power.

(iv) THE INTEGRATIONIST SCHOOL

A final important trend in the analysis of the welfare state, which has already been hinted at in our account of the functionalist approach, and also in Professor Marshall's analysis, is what may be called the "integrationist school." Dahrendorf, for instance, starts from a position akin to that of Marshall by maintaining first that the social rights of citizenship (including old-age pensions, public health insurance and a minimum standard of living) ensure that "conflicts and differences of class are at the very least no longer based on inequalities of status in a strict sense of this term."[14] He then suggests that enforced recognition of such civil rights becomes part of the process of the institutionalization of class conflict:

organization presupposes the legitimacy of conflict groups, and it thereby removes the permanent and incalculable threat of guerrilla warfare. At the same time it makes systematic regulation of conflicts possible.

This particular passage was written primarily in the context of the development of collective bargaining institutions, but clearly the welfare state,

[13] Dorothy Thomson, "The Welfare State," *The New Reasoner* (No. 4 1958).
[14] R. Dahrendorf, *Class and Class Conflict in an Industrial Society.* (Routledge and Kegan Paul, London, 1959.)

which guarantees at least a minimum income to all, can be viewed as part of the "rules of the game" of capitalist society.

One might say this was close to John Strachey's position although the terminology is different. Strachey maintains that if the democratic countervailing pressures can become strong enough to make the distribution of the national income significantly more favourable to the mass of the population, then wage earners acquire a stake in society. Old-age pensions, the health service are all part of the stake.

Once such rights as these have been acquired democracy becomes much more strongly entrenched than before. For then the struggle to maintain and extend democracy can be undertaken as a struggle to preserve known and tangible rights not merely as a struggle to achieve theoretically desirable ideals.

Dahrendorf did not see the process of institutionalization of conflict as necessarily implying the end of conflict—indeed he specifically refers to conflict emerging in new forms. But by the time we get to the attempt by Clark Kerr and other American sociologists to formulate the grand theory of industrial society this point is almost lost. In *Industrialism and Industrial Man* the authors are concerned with a much wider canvas than that of the welfare state alone. Indeed they seek to develop a theory of the development of society which lays its emphasis upon the similarity of demands made upon social organization in all countries by technology itself. In this sense all industrial societies are becoming increasingly similar; capitalist and communist societies are converging. One example of this claim is that:

In the logic of industrialization the responsibility for guaranteeing the minimum welfare and security of industrial man rests in large measure upon his manager and his government.

This guaranteeing of minimum welfare is common to capitalist and communist countries alike and moreover is part of the essential process in industrial society by which inequalities of all kinds, of status, of income and wealth, and of political power are reduced.

Our earlier examination of the available evidence on the reduction in economic inequality is enough to raise serious doubts about the validity of this theory, and for the U.S.A. it is at least arguable that no agency, or group of agencies, exist for guaranteeing minimum welfare. In a general critique of the whole thesis Goldthorpe suggests that apart from doubts about much of the evidence upon which these authors draw, there is a crucial difference between any existing inequalities or systems of stratification in capitalist and those in communist societies.

In the industrial societies of the West, one could say, the action of the state sets limits to the extent of social inequalities which derive basically from the operation of a market economy: in Soviet society the pattern of inequality also results in part from 'market' forces, but in this case these

are subordinated to political control up to the limits set by the requirements of the industrial system.[15]

Thus the welfare state in capitalist society is to be seen as a part of the
mechanism for setting limits to the extent of social inequalities; and, following Myrdal, Goldthorpe argues that the limits set differ in different capitalist
societies because of differences in the balance of political forces:

> If then Myrdal's analysis has any general validity—and it has yet, I think,
> to be seriously disputed—it follows that we should look somewhat doubt-
> fully on arguments about a new equality which 'has nothing to do with
> ideology' but which is the direct outcome of technological and economic
> advance. Such new equality there may be for some. But for those at the
> base of stratification hierarchies at least, how equal they are likely to
> become seems to have a good deal to do with ideology, or at any rate
> with purposive social action, or lack of this, stemming from specific social
> values and political creeds as well as from interests.

Conclusions

This survey of some of the main strands in recent thinking about the
welfare state immediately raises a central theoretical problem for all socialists: what have been the crucial changes in the nature of capitalism in recent
years? The "welfare state" is but one aspect of those changes which has to
be fitted into the wider analytical framework. In so far as some theorists
have claimed that the welfare state is an "essential" and universal feature of
capitalist or industrial society they have directed attention at the undoubted
fact that the process of economic growth itself appears to make possible a
more rational handling of the problems set by the "natural contingencies of
life."

But to explain some of the important differences which exist between
different capitalist countries we have to examine political forces. We have
to focus attention upon the demands of the working class for social justice
and upon an analysis of the political strength of the working class; and its
success in winning allies from particular pressure and interest groups then
becomes an essential part of the story. On another level, although we may
not go all the way with Professor Marshall in believing that the British Welfare State from 1945 to the 1950s constituted a specific social system, it is
none the less important to note that the post-war consensus appears to have
been greater in Britain than in the U.S.A. or even in most other European
countries (even where, as in France, major programmes of social reform were
enacted). Hence the predominance during the years of the post-war Labour
government, of devotion to the norms of equality and fair shares, which did
lend a special flavour to, and in some areas affected the specific form of
British legislation. An important question is what led to the dissipation of the
consensus? Some suggest that it may be "affluence" itself; but part of the
explanation must surely be the willingness of the Labour government and
its spokesmen to be blinded by, and indeed to propagate actively, the myth

[15] J. H. Goldthorpe, "Social Stratification in Industrial Society" in *Development
of Industrial Societies*, Sociological Review Monograph No. 8. (Keele, 1964.)

that "equality" had been achieved. Another feature which from a study of the U.S.A. we might judge to be important in the British situation (and one could add the Scandinavian as well) is the hitherto homogeneous structure of British society. There are few extremes of agricultural and industrial sectors or of different racial or religious groupings. This, too, must have contributed to the high degree of consensus in the past, although it is legitimate to ask for how long it will remain in the light of recent developments (the growth, for example, of the immigrant population and the emergence for the first time in the 1964 election of colour as a major political issue).

This survey of fact and theory also reveals the limitations of viewing the "welfare state" as a static achievement, "conceded by the capitalist," "inevitable in an industrial society" or any of the once and for all explanations which fail to see the continuing process of change and struggle. This has profound implications for the programme of socialist parties and groups. But so, too, has the fact that there is nothing about any of the particular bits of social welfare legislation which is specifically or "essentially" socialist. At all points, the actual effect of welfare legislation (i.e. whether it contributes to a reduction of inequality), the values embodied in welfare legislation (i.e. whether it is fair shares for all, or help to those who have paid), represent a compromise between the market and *laissez-faire* on the one hand, and planned egalitarianism on the other. How near to either extreme a particular piece of legislation falls depends both upon the balance of political forces and upon the awareness of the reformers of the difficulties and dangers of doing what Professor Marshall said the Labour Party were attempting with their national superannuation proposals, which "narrows the arrangements of private enterprise and sets out to beat it at its own game." The dangers are especially great, because a social reform won at a particular point of time can become adapted, modified, less effective as a result of market forces acting upon it. . . .

There are certain needs where it may well be relatively easy to get general agreement to abandon the market; and to recognize, for instance, that all needs are equal in respect of care in ill health, or for education of children. But in social insurance we are touching on the market at its most vulnerable point, the distribution of incomes. The "need" for income is in part determined by the market itself in that men become accustomed to standards of living and ways of life. Should we not then abandon what must be an artificial notion of equality, for instance in pensions, particularly when it may mean equality in poverty for many, but equality in comfort for those with private wealth or occupational pensions? But in abandoning this false equality are we not then to accept the judgment of, and the inequalities in, the market——for this is what we do if we accept wage-relation as a basis for fixing social security benefits. . . . A socialist cannot be simply concerned to perpetuate and to emphasize in state legislation the values of the market; he must be involved with the ideological struggle against these very values.

Welfare state legislation in capitalist society is a battleground not only for the short-term solution of immediate social problems but also for the longer-term battle of ideas. The former has received much attention from the Left; the latter all too little.

chapter 5

Racism: Domestic Colonialism and Neocolonialism

This chapter will deal almost exclusively with the experience of black people in the United States. While Indians, Mexican-Americans, and other minority groups have suffered from intense prejudice and discrimination throughout American history, black people have been the largest oppressed minority and their fate has been the most crucial in shaping American society. Their slave labor was essential to the growth of the American economy—the cotton trade being considered by modern economic historians as the major source of the economic surplus which generated industrial growth in the nineteenth century. Moreover, the dispute over the institution of slavery profoundly influenced the constitutional debates after the Revolutionary War and contributed to the economic and political conflict that culminated in the Civil War. In the contemporary period the urbanization of blacks and their growing militancy has placed them in a strategic position in the political economy. Thus, they are a source of great potential power and a continuing threat to the stability of parliamentary capitalism.

Although their suffering may be of as great a magnitude as that of the blacks, other oppressed minorities such as the Indians have lost or do not yet have the potential to fatally disrupt the national political economy. To a great extent the current plight and prospects of these other minorities are similar to those of black people, and their fate may well be dependent upon the resolution of the general economic, political, and cultural problems that victimize blacks.

Readers interested in the historical experience of American Indians, Mexican-Americans, Chinese- and Japanese-Americans and Hawaiians should consult the bibliography at the end of this text, and, in particular, Paul Jacobs and Saul Landau, eds., To Serve the Devil: A Documentary Analysis of America's Racial History and Why It Has Been Kept Hidden.

If imperialism is the major world problem America has *exported,* racism has surely been its most tragic *import.* Winthrop Jordon, in what is perhaps the most exhaustive study of the origins of American racism, traces the roots of colonial racial stereotypes to the experiences of English voyagers to Africa.[1] The dark color of the Africans and the unfortunate discovery of the great apes on the continent led many Englishmen to believe that the African, unlike the Caucasian, was closely linked to the animal world. In addition, the heathen religion of Africans was shocking to Christian Europeans and further enabled them to consider Africans a subhuman species. Jordon argues in great detail that racial feelings long preceded any desire to enslave the black. At the same time, he suggests that enslavement accentuated many of the stereotypes about the black's inferiority and his inherent threat to the white man, which was often perceived in violent and sexual terms.

There is little doubt that the reason for the introduction and maintenance of slavery in the United States was economic. Slavery provided a cheap and controlled supply of labor which was desirable in a land devoid of sophisticated technology and underpopulated. Moreover, the isolation of the wilderness relaxed many normal civil and ecclesiastical controls upon the colonists' behavior. Finally, indentured servants were prevalent at the time, and this practice permitted the settlers to legitimize bound labor. However, the reason why *blacks* were enslaved cannot be answered without reference to the way white settlers perceived them. As Jordon observes:

> . . . it seems likely that the colonists' initial sense of difference from the Negro was founded not on a single characteristic but on a congeries of qualities which, taken as a whole, seemed to set the Negro apart. Virtually every quality in the Negro invited pejorative feelings. What may have been his two most striking characteristics, his heathenism and his appearance, were probably prerequisite to his complete debasement. His heathenism alone could never have led to permanent enslavement since conversion easily wiped out that failing. If his appearance, his racial characteristics, meant nothing to the English settlers, it is difficult to see how slavery based on race ever emerged, how the concept of complexion as the mark of slavery ever entered the colonists' minds. Even if the colonists were most unfavorably struck by the Negro's color, though blackness itself did not

[1] Winthrop Jordon, *White over Black: American Attitudes toward The Negro, 1550–1812* (Baltimore: Penguin Books, Inc., 1969).

urge the complete debasement of slavery, other qualities—the utter strangeness of his language, gestures, eating habits, and so on—certainly must have contributed to the colonists' sense that he was very different, perhaps disturbingly so. In Africa these qualities had for Englishmen added up to *savagery;* they were major components in that sense of *difference* which provided the mental margin absolutely requisite for placing the European on the deck of the slave ship and the Negro in the hold.[2]

Although other settlers, such as the Irish, were looked down upon and discriminated against, they were not enslaved primarily because they could not be perceived as distinct forms of beings as were blacks. The one group that resembled Africans was the American Indian. And brief attempts were made to enslave Indians but these efforts failed. The settlers were not able to adapt Indians to settled agriculture. They were a fairly unified people who were willing and able to conduct military reprisals against whites when their own interests were threatened. Thus, whites were more often forced to commit genocide against Indians than to use them as slaves. At other times good relations with friendly Indian tribes were used to wage war against other less cooperative ones. Sometimes one tribe could be played off against another. This required a certain amount of diplomacy and reciprocity between settlers and the Indians and prevented the total cultural alienation that characterized white relations with the imported African slaves.

Whatever its complicated origins, slavery became institutionalized in a rather shaky manner and the slave trade was carried on until the early nineteenth century. During the period just prior to and after the Revolutionary War some white Americans began to question the morality of the institution, particularly since it conflicted so strongly with the sentiments of the Declaration of Independence. The use of the Declaration as an inspiration to revolutionaries abroad, including the French and Santo Domingans, as well as American slaves, made other white Americans repudiate such libertarian notions. The retreat from revolutionary idealism led to a strengthening of the restrictions on the rights of free blacks, so that they became more isolated from white society, physically and socially. This development was, of course, most pronounced in the South, where a full-blown ideology based upon the virtue of a slaveholding society came to the fore.[3]

Throughout the past century historians have had many disputes about the sources of the Civil War. In recent years the belief that it was fought chiefly because of a clash of idealisms and abolitionist fervor has been largely discarded. Among the most provocative theses are those of Barrington Moore and Eugene Genovese.[4] Moore argues that the Civil War represented the "last capitalist revolution" and was fought because the differing needs of feudal

[2] *Ibid.*, p. 97.

[3] Eugene Genovese, *The World the Slaveholders Made: Two Essays in Interpretation* (New York: Pantheon Books, Inc., 1969).

[4] Barrington Moore, Jr., *Social Origins of Dictatorship and Democracy: Lord and Peasant in the Making of the Modern World* (Boston: The Beacon Press, 1966), pp. 111–155. Eugene Genovese, *The Political Economy of Slavery: Studies in the Economy and Society of the Slave South* (New York: Vintage Books, 1965).

and capitalist economic institutions made it increasingly difficult for them to coexist under a single government. Genovese places great stock in the tenaciousness with which Southern slaveholders clung to an agrarian aristocratic ideal.

Several volumes have been published in the past few years which describe race relations outside the South before and after the Civil War. The conclusion drawn from this body of scholarship is that racism was pervasive in the "free" states and, moreover, was a major factor in abolitionist thought.[5] The chief argument in behalf of emancipation was that if slavery continued a large population of blacks would eventually migrate into nonslave areas. Many Midwestern states passed laws excluding free blacks or restricting their rights. Famous abolitionists denounced the notion of racial equality. The areas which were strongholds of abolition were also opposed to extending many elementary rights to blacks. The Lincoln government, which went to war with the intention of permitting slavery to continue in the South, eventually fought for abolitionism; but at no time did the administration commit itself to racial equality or a policy of northern migration. Lincoln himself favored the deportation and colonization of the former slaves in the Caribbean, but this experiment failed.

Given its economic irrationality, the slave system might eventually have died more or less peacefully, if it had not been for the tenacity of the southern slaveholders in attempting to preserve their class privileges. J. H. Plumb suggests that the eighteenth century witnessed a nearly worldwide disappearance of slave labor not for humanistic reasons, but because of the economic advantages of free labor.[6] Before this time attitudes and behavior toward the poor were not terribly different from those toward slaves. Intermarriage between wealthy and poor was cause for social ostracism. The poor, like slaves, were the object of sexual exploitation and stereotyping. It could even be argued that slaves were somewhat better off than free laborers because their masters considered slaves valuable property and had to provide minimal care for them. With the Industrial Revolution employers recognized that it would be far more costly to pay for the upkeep of slaves, especially during the frequent business depressions, than to hire cheap labor as needed. Moreover, an incentive system could favorably increase the productivity of "wage-slaves" rather than them, who had little reason to work hard. In Plumb's view, then, it is impossible to consider the development and abolition of slavery apart from a general history of labor exploitation.

Reconstruction did little to give former slaves land and actually helped channel them as free labor to white landowners and businessmen in the South. While some committed abolitionists also desired racial equality and integration, the political and economic situation as well as the deep-seated racial fears of whites prevented a radical social reconstruction of the South.

[5] C. Vann Woodward, "White Racism and Black 'Emancipation,'" *The New York Review of Books*, vol. 12 (February 27, 1969), pp. 5–11, provides a fine summary of the relevant literature in this area. See also George Fredrickson, *The Black Image in the White Mind: The Debate on Afro-American Character and Destiny, 1817–1914* (New York: Harper & Row, Publishers, 1971).

[6] J. H. Plumb, "Slavery, Race and the Poor," *The New York Review of Books*, vol. 12 (March 13, 1969), pp. 3–5.

Racism: Domestic Colonialism and Neocolonialism

When Northern and Southern elites made peace in the election of 1876 and federal troops were finally removed from the defeated South, a repressive social order was gradually re-created.[7]

In the context of the above discussion it is useful to examine the relationship of the slave experience to the current situation of blacks in the United States. Genovese, in one of the most controversial articles on the effects of slavery on black social and political development, suggests that the peculiar features of American slavery prevented the blacks from liberating themselves through violent means (as occurred, for example, in Latin America) and thus placed them in a fruitless dependency upon white men for the achievement of their civil rights and economic progress.[8]

Notwithstanding a few well-publicized but short-lived revolts, American slaves were relatively docile because of several factors. First, they came largely from parts of Africa which had a population already adjusted to servitude in contrast, for example, to Brazilian slaves, whose strong military, religious, and cultural traditions made them hard to subjugate. Another reason was that the North American slave trade ended quite early and there were fewer immigrants as years wore on. It was generally the newly imported slaves who proved to be most rebellious. Slave revolts in the Caribbean and Brazil were also facilitated because the whites themselves were divided and the state was weak. This permitted slaves to revolt or run away without great difficulty, whereas in the United States the slaveholders and other whites were united against such occurrences. The relative stability of the American slave system was also due to the fact that the white population was larger than that of the slaves, unlike in Brazil and the Caribbean where sugar cultivation led to plantations with as many as two hundred slaves and only a small white population. This relative paucity of slaves also contributed to the destruction of African religion and culture in the face of white hegemony—particularly since American slaveholders resided on their plantations and were not absentee owners, as in Latin America. Finally, the tradition of paternalism, the carrot and the stick, also helped undermine slave solidarity because individuals could win special favors through obedience.

The consequence of these aspects of American slavery was that slave revolt often took passive forms such as low work productivity, minor sabotage or destruction of tools, and, more infrequently, violent but unorganized insurrection. Slaves were ultimately "liberated" by the Union Army not themselves. The reliance upon Republican reconstructionists, the Union Army, and the Freedmen's Bureau proved disastrous, because of the weak

[7] John Hope Franklin, *Reconstruction: After the Civil War* (Chicago: University of Chicago Press, 1961). William McFeely, *Yankee Stepfather: General O. O. Howard and the Freedmen* (New Haven, Conn.: Yale University Press, 1968). C. Vann Woodward, *The Strange Career of Jim Crow* (New York: Oxford University Press, 1966), pp. 3–109.

[8] Eugene Genovese, "The Legacy of Slavery and the Roots of Black Nationalism," *Studies on the Left*, vol. 6 (November–December 1966), pp. 3–26. See also critical comments by Herbert Aptheker, C. Vann Woodward, and Frank Kofsky on Genovese's article and his rejoinder in *Studies on the Left*, vol. 6 (November–December, 1966), pp. 27–65. Recently Genovese has revised some of his earlier thoughts on the nature of the slave experience; see his "American Slaves and Their History," *The New York Review of Books*, vol. 15 (December 3, 1970), pp. 34–43.

commitment of these groups to genuine racial equality. At no time did blacks organize politically, economically, and militarily to retain and extend their paper freedoms.

The reinstitution of white supremacy in the South after 1876 went virtually unchallenged until 1954, when the Supreme Court ruled segregation in public facilities unconstitutional in *Brown v. Board of Education of Topeka*. Until that time blacks existed without hope in economic, political, legal, and social subordination. Migration offered the only possibility for betterment.[9] Between 1910 and 1960 the total black population of the United States nearly doubled from 9.8 million to 18.5 million, but the number of rural Southern blacks declined from 6.9 to 4.7 million. Northern and Western urban blacks increased from 1 to 7.2 million, and urban Southern blacks grew from 1.9 to 6.6 million. The migration boom was due primarily to labor shortages during the world wars and the mechanization of southern agriculture. Between 1950 and 1960 alone, approximately 1.5 million blacks moved north, as many as had migrated during the thirty years between 1910 and 1940.

Unfortunately, migration proved to be a limited solution in terms of increasing blacks' opportunities for a decent standard of living. This situation has not changed very dramatically, despite other recent attempts by the courts and the federal government to solve some of these problems. Why has the granting of formal legal and political rights, even when enforced, failed to eliminate racism in the United States? To some extent the answer lies in the continuing presence of racial prejudice and discrimination. Yet recent evidence suggests that Americans are less likely to accept racial stereotypes and express prejudicial sentiments than ever before. While their expressed belief in biological equality may simply reflect a sensitivity toward the opinion expected of Americans on racial matters, it is probable that increasing levels of education have reduced the level of overt personal prejudice and even racial discrimination among Americans in the past few decades. The reduction in hostile racial attitudes, however, has minimal effects on the problems facing most black people.[10]

The major obstacle to ending racism in America today is not white racially motivated attitudes and behavior toward blacks. *Institutional racism* now keeps submerged groups down. This term implies that the normal impersonal functioning of economic, political, and legal institutions results in the maintenance of black subordination, even when personal racial prejudice and discrimination are not present. Thus, if a man is poor he is less likely to be able to afford to give his children a decent education even if there are no formal obstacles to college attendance. Similarly, a businessman who wants to make a bank loan to expand his ghetto business will have

---

[9] Daniel Fusfeld, "The Basic Economics of the Urban and Racial Crisis," *Conference Papers of the Union for Radical Political Economics* (Ann Arbor, Mich.: December 1968), pp. 55–84, summarizes the interaction between black migration and changes in the American economy during the twentieth century and analyzes the resulting impact upon the condition of the black population.

[10] Howard Schuman, "Sociological Racism," *Trans action*, vol. 7 (December 1969), pp. 44–48, shows how the reduction of racial prejudice can serve to increase resistance to black demands for economic and social justice.

more difficulty in obtaining it because ghetto businesses are poor financial risks.

Because prejudice and discrimination in the past have deprived black people of the educational and organizational skills necessary for obtaining economic and political power, seemingly neutral institutions presently function in a way that prevents substantial progress within the black community. Poverty and degradation in one generation incapacitates the next. Because the past weighs heavily on the present and future, the simple removal of legal barriers to equality has had little effect on the position of blacks. Lieberson and Fuguitt show that it would take several generations to eliminate black-white occupational differences, even if all discrimination ended.[11] When the *actual* rate of occupational mobility between 1940 and 1960 was projected into the future, it was estimated that *centuries* would pass before blacks had equal representation in business and the professions.[12]

In the present, progress is largely the hope of middle-class blacks who have by their good fortune, exceptional skill, or favored birth the opportunity to rise according to the impersonal standards of the job market. A. James Gregor has shown how the operation of institutional racism has split the black community into two distinct groups with entirely different positions vis-à-vis white society and, thus, opposing strategies for liberation.[13]

Middle-class blacks have sought integration because they have been more able to obtain equality of condition, given equal opportunity to compete with whites. The masses of blacks, on the other hand, are ill equipped for economic competition, given the dynamics of capitalist enterprise. They seek collective advancement, reverse discrimination, and other compensatory programs to attain equality of condition. The absence of initiative by business or government to suspend the rules of the game by providing incentives to compensate blacks for centuries of oppression has meant that black nationalism has periodically arisen as the popular solution to black subordination. While nationalism once took the form of a "back to Africa" movement, it has more recently attempted to develop strategies for gaining black control of ghetto economic, political, cultural, and social institutions.

Robert Blauner's article in this chapter suggests that the spontaneous ghetto riots of the 1960s, which were supported by a significant proportion of ghetto residents, were the first stage in the process of asserting territorial rights in black communities. These mass actions gave the ghetto dwellers a sense of power and solidarity and served a necessary function in mobilizing the population to develop programs for local control. Blauner argues that in many ways the current black nationalist upsurge is reminiscent of anticolonial struggles. While blacks are a minority within the confines of white America, they have had several experiences characteristic of colonized peoples. Blacks, like colonial subjects, were *forced* into a relationship with an

[11] Stanley Lieberson and Glen Fuguitt, "Negro-White Occupational Differences in the Absence of Discrimination," *American Journal of Sociology*, vol. 73 (September 1967), pp. 188–200.

[12] Leonard Broom and Norval Glenn, *The Transformation of the Negro American* (New York: Harper & Row, Publishers, 1965), pp. 109–115.

[13] A. James Gregor, "Black Nationalism: A Preliminary Analysis of Negro Radicalism," *Science and Society*, vol. 27 (Fall 1963), pp. 415–432.

oppressive dominant society. Their culture and social organization were destroyed—perhaps more thoroughly than in a traditional colonial relationship. In addition, they were subordinated to administrative control by the dominant society. White businessmen, politicians, educators, judges, juries, and police comprised the agents of ghetto control. Although the presence of a few token blacks has created the illusion of local control (for example, black store managers, politicians, teachers and principals, police), these individuals actually serve the interests of white society—which continues to control the ghetto.

In addition to bearing the characteristics of colonization ghetto dwellers may be exploited in ways that the subjects of traditional colonial powers were.[14] For example, black consumers spend their money in white-owned stores. The money leaves the ghetto and is not invested in local development projects. This is true even of black-owned banks. Concerned as they must be with profit rather than ghetto development, these institutions channel deposits into outside business loans and investment. Blacks also represent a large pool of cheap labor sought by labor-intensive industries. In addition, the enormous demand for even substandard slums in a segregated housing market enables landlords to charge large rents, which they use not to keep their buildings in good repair, but to restore their own capital investment. Thus, capital expenditures are accompanied by the deterioration rather than the improvement of the physical environment. The public facilities in the ghetto also deteriorate because whites are not willing to tax themselves to support blacks. Finally, blacks in the armed forces serve interests irrelevant to their needs.

In the face of the extreme exploitation of blacks and the potentially explosive situation in the increasingly overcrowded ghettos, reforms have been almost nonexistent. A reliance upon educational upgrading has failed to provide blacks with jobs because many companies, particularly in high-wage industries, are located outside the central cities adjacent to de facto segregated residential areas. Moreover, educational facilities and policies are totally inadequate, and the economy has not been able to generate enough jobs to insure genuine full employment even if it were desirable in a capitalist economy. Black unemployment is approximately twice as high as white unemployment, and black incomes are about 60 percent of white income.[15] These problems are exacerbated by the high black birth rate—almost 50 percent greater than the white rate in the decade between 1950 and 1960. The children of this "baby boom" are now entering the labor market.

The failure of traditional strategies to improve chances for individual upward mobility and the white business resistance to compensatory pro-

[14] Fusfeld, op. cit., pp. 66–75.

[15] The recent rise in the proportion of black income to white income can be traced primarily to continued northern migration, the decrease in personal prejudice and discrimination which has affected the life chances of educated blacks, and the employment opportunities which have invariably accompanied wartime. The current economic recession is now threatening to erode the temporary gains caused by the Vietnam war. See Thomas Cook, "Benign Neglect: Minimum Feasible Understanding," Social Problems, vol. 18 (Fall, 1970), pp. 145–152.

grams that would suspend prevailing standards for hiring and investing, have contributed to the growth of black nationalism and militancy. These movements have been aided also by a growing solidarity with anticolonial movements in Africa, Asia, and Latin America, which have given black people confidence that oppression can be successfully fought; as well as by the influence of mass communications (especially television), which have heightened the sense of deprivation in the black community.

Ghetto revolt and the rise of militant black nationalist groups such as the Black Panthers have increased the tensions between the black and white communities. Because of the substantial economic interests of white realtors, financial institutions, and corporations in the maintenance of inhabitable urban areas and the genuine threat of protracted and costly violence, liberal far-sighted business leaders and their governmental allies have attempted to develop a last-ditch set of strategies to meliorate ghetto conditions *without* restructuring the balance of economic and political power. David Wellman and Jan Dizard's article in this chapter discusses this corporate liberal strategy for ghetto pacification and the formidable obstacles it will encounter. Given the failure of traditional remedies, legal and legislative reform, and welfare measures, it would seem that the racial problem in the United States may ultimately be resolved by genocide against the black population, as a regrettable outcome of protracted revolt.[16] Without economic independence, the increasing black political power in cities has led and will lead to growing frustration for poor blacks, not to integration into the mainstream of American society.[17] Yet it is doubtful that black liberation through violence can succeed without considerable active white support and the aid of other dispossessed minority groups.[18] The only other solution, if blacks were unwilling to indefinitely acquiesce in the role of a colonized people, would be for economic and political elites to accept a greatly reduced influence over the urban political economy, and, by suspending the normal rules of institutional operation, risk a general transformation of the political, economic, and cultural foundations of American capitalism.

[16] Sidney Willhelm, "Red Man, Black Man and White America," *Catalyst*, vol. 4 (Spring 1969), pp. 1–62, draws a tragic comparison between the historical experience of the American Indian and that of black people.

[17] Edward Greer, "The 'Liberation' of Gary, Indiana," *Trans action*, vol. 8 (January 1971), pp. 30–39, 63.

[18] Martin Oppenheimer, *The Urban Guerrilla* (Chicago: Quadrangle Books, 1969).

Robert Blauner

INTERNAL COLONIALISM
AND GHETTO REVOLT

It is becoming almost fashionable to analyze American racial conflict today in terms of the colonial analogy. I shall argue in this paper that the utility of this perspective depends upon a distinction between colonization as a process and colonialism as a social, economic, and political system. It is the experience of colonization that Afro-Americans share with many of the non-white people of the world. But this subjugation has taken place in a societal context that differs in important respects from the situation of "classical colonialism." In the body of this essay I shall look at some major developments in Black protest—the urban riots, cultural nationalism, and the movement for ghetto control—as collective responses to colonized status. Viewing our domestic situation as a special form of colonization outside a context of a colonial system will help explain some of the dilemmas and ambiguities within these movements.

The present crisis in American life has brought about changes in social perspectives and the questioning of long accepted frameworks. Intellectuals and social scientists have been forced by the pressure of events to look at old definitions of the character of our society, the role of racism, and the workings of basic institutions. The depth and volatility of contemporary racial conflict challenge sociologists in particular to question the adequacy of theoretical models by which we have explained American race relations in the past.

For a long time the distinctiveness of the Negro situations among the ethnic minorities was placed in terms of color, and the systematic discrimination that follows from our deep-seated racial prejudices. This was sometimes called the caste theory, and while provocative, it missed essential and dynamic features of American race relations. In the past ten years there has been a tendency to view Afro-Americans as another ethnic group not basically different in experience from previous ethnics and whose "immigration" condition in the North would in time follow their upward course. The inadequacy of this model is now clear—even the Kerner Report devotes a chapter to criticizing this analogy. A more recent (though hardly new) approach views the essence of racial subordination in economic class terms: Black people as an underclass are to a degree specially exploited and to a degree economically dispensable in an automating society. Important as are economic factors, the power of race and racism in America cannot be sufficiently

Reprinted, with deletions, from Robert Blauner, "Internal Colonialism and Ghetto Revolt," *Social Problems*, vol. 16 (Spring, 1969), pp. 393–408, by permission of Robert Blauner, *Social Problems*, and The Society for the Study of Social Problems. Robert Blauner teaches sociology at the University of California at Berkeley. He is the author of *Alienation and Freedom*.

explained through class analysis. Into this theory vacuum steps the model of internal colonialism. Problematic and imprecise as it is, it gives hope of becoming a framework that can integrate the insights of caste and racism, ethnicity, culture, and economic exploitation into an overall conceptual scheme. At the same time, the danger of the colonial model is the imposition of an artificial analogy which might keep us from facing up to the fact (to quote Harold Cruse) that "the American black and white social phenomenon is a uniquely new world thing."

During the late 1950's, identification with African nations and other colonial or formerly colonized peoples grew in importance among Black militants. As a result the U.S. was increasingly seen as a colonial power and the concept of domestic colonialism was introduced into the political analysis and rhetoric of militant nationalists. During the same period Black social theorists began developing this frame of reference for explaining American realities. As early as 1962, Cruse characterized race relations in this country as "domestic colonialism." Three years later in *Dark Ghetto*, Kenneth Clark demonstrated how the political, economic, and social structure of Harlem was essentially that of a colony. Finally in 1967, a full-blown elaboration of "internal colonialism" provided the theoretical framework for Carmichael and Hamilton's widely read *Black Power*. The following year the colonial analogy gained currency and new "respectability" when Senator McCarthy habitually referred to Black Americans as a colonized people during his campaign. While the rhetoric of internal colonialism was catching on, other social scientists began to raise questions about its appropriateness as a scheme of analysis.

The colonial analysis has been rejected as obscurantist and misleading by scholars who point to the significant differences in history and social-political conditions between our domestic patterns and what took place in Africa and India. Colonialism traditionally refers to the establishment of domination over a geographically external political unit, most often inhabited by people of a different race and culture, where this domination is political and economic, and the colony exists subordinated to and dependent upon the mother country. Typically the colonizers exploit the land, the raw materials, the labor, and other resources of the colonized nation; in addition a formal recognition is given to the difference in power, autonomy, and political status, and various agencies are set up to maintain this subordination. Seemingly the analogy must be stretched beyond usefulness if the American version is to be forced into this model. For here we are talking about group relations within a society; the mother country—colony separation in geography is absent. Though whites certainly colonized the territory of the original Americans, internal colonization of Afro-Americans did not involve the settlement of whites in any land that was unequivocably Black. And unlike the colonial situation, there has been no formal recognition of differing power since slavery was abolished outside the South. Classic colonialism involved the control and exploitation of the majority of a nation by a minority of outsiders. Whereas in America the people who are oppressed were themselves originally outsiders and are a numerical minority.

This conventional critique of "internal colonialism" is useful in pointing to the differences between our domestic patterns and the overseas situation. But in its bold attack it tends to lose sight of common experiences that have been historically shared by the most subjugated racial minorities in America and non-white peoples in some other parts of the world. For understanding the most dramatic recent developments on the race scene, this common core element—which I shall call colonization—may be more important than the undeniable divergences between the two contexts.

The common features ultimately relate to the fact that the classical colonialism of the imperialist era and American racism developed out of the same historical situation and reflected a common world economic and power stratificaiton. The slave trade for the most part preceded the imperialist partition and economic exploitation of Africa, and in fact may have been a necessary prerequisite for colonial conquest—since it helped deplete and pacify Africa, undermining the resistance to direct occupation. Slavery contributed one of the basic raw materials for the textile industry which provided much of the capital for the West's industrial development and need for economic expansionism. The essential condition for both American slavery and European colonialism was the power domination and the technological superiority of the Western world in its relation to peoples of non-Western and non-white origins. This objective supremacy in technology and military power buttressed the West's sense of cultural superiority, laying the basis for racist ideologies that were elaborated to justify control and exploitation of non-white people. Thus because classical colonialism and America's internal version developed out of a similar balance of technological, cultural, and power relations, a common *process* of social oppression characterized the racial patterns in the two contexts—despite the variation in political and social structure.

There appear to be four basic components of the colonization complex. The first refers to how the racial group enters into the dominant society (whether colonial power or not). Colonization begins with a forced, involuntary entry. Second, there is an impact on the culture and social organization of the colonized people which is more than just a result of such "natural" processes as contact and acculturation. The colonizing power carries out a policy which constrains, transforms, or destroys indigenous values, orientations, and ways of life. Third, colonization involves a relationship by which members of the colonized group tend to be administered by representatives of the dominant power. There is an experience of being managed and manipulated by outsiders in terms of ethnic status.

A final fundament of colonization is racism. Racism is a principle of social domination by which a group seen as inferior or different in terms of alleged biological characteristics is exploited, controlled, and oppressed socially and physically by a superordinate group. Except for the marginal case of Japanese imperialism, the major examples of colonialism have involved the subjugation of non-white Asian, African, and Latin American peoples by white European powers. Thus racism has generally accompanied colonialism. Race prejudice can exist without colonization—the experience of Asian-American minorities is a case in point—but racism as a system of domination is part of the complex of colonization.

The concept of colonization stresses the enormous fatefulness of the historical factor, namely the manner in which a minority group becomes a part of the dominant society. The crucial difference between the colonized Americans and the ethnic immigrant minorities is that the latter have always been able to operate fairly competitively within that relatively open section of the social and economic order because these groups came voluntarily in search of a better life, because their movements in society were not administratively controlled, and because they transformed their culture at their own pace—giving up ethnic values and institutions when it was seen as a desirable exchange for improvements in social position.

In present-day America, a major device of Black colonization is the powerless ghetto. As Kenneth Clark describes the situation:

> Ghettoes are the consequence of the imposition of external power and the institutionalization of powerlessness. In this respect, they are in fact social, political, educational, and above all—economic colonies. Those confined within the ghetto walls are subject peoples. They are victims of the greed, cruelty, insensitivity, guilt and fear of their masters. . . .
>
> The community can best be described in terms of the analogy of a powerless colony. Its political leadership is divided, and all but one or two of its political leaders are shortsighted and dependent upon the larger political power structure. Its social agencies are financially precarious and dependent upon sources of support outside the community. Its churches are isolated or dependent. Its economy is dominated by small businesses which are largely owned by absentee owners, and its tenements and other real property are also owned by absentee landlords.
>
> Under a system of centralization, Harlem's schools are controlled by forces outside of the community. Programs and policies are supervised and determined by individuals who do not live in the community. . . .

Of course many ethnic groups in America have lived in ghettoes. What make the Black ghettoes an expression of colonized status are three special features. First, the ethnic ghettoes arose more from voluntary choice, both in the sense of the choice to immigrate to America and the decision to live among one's fellow ethnics. Second, the immigrant ghettoes tended to be a one- and two-generation phenomenon; they were actually way-stations in the process of acculturation and assimilation. When they continue to persist as in the case of San Francisco's Chinatown, it is because they are big business for the ethnics themselves and there is a new stream of immigrants. The Black ghetto on the other hand has been a more permanent phenomenon, although some individuals do escape it. But most relevant is the third point. European ethnic groups like the Poles, Italians, and Jews generally only experienced a brief period, often less than a generation, during which their residential buildings, commercial stores, and other enterprises were owned by outsiders. The Chinese and Japanese faced handicaps of color prejudice that were almost as strong as the Blacks faced, but very soon gained control of their internal communities, because their traditional ethnic culture and social organization had not been destroyed by slavery and internal colonization. But Afro-Americans are distinct in the extent to which their segregated communities have remained controlled economically, politically, and administratively from the outside. One indicator of this difference is the estimate that the "income of Chinese-Americans from Chinese-owned businesses is in proportion to their numbers 45 times as great as the income of Negroes from Negro-owned businesses." But what is true of business is also true for the other social institutions that operate within the ghetto. The educators, policemen, social workers, politicians, and others who administer the affairs of ghetto residents are typically whites who live outside the Black community. Thus the ghetto plays a strategic role as the focus for the administration by outsiders which is also essential to the structure of overseas colonialism.[1]

The colonial status of the Negro community goes beyond the issue of ownership and decision-making within Black neighborhoods. The Afro-American population in most cities has very little influence on the power structure and institutions of the larger metropolis, despite the fact that in numerical terms, Blacks tend to be the most sizeable of the various interest groups. A recent analysis of policy-making in Chicago estimates that "Negroes really hold less than 1 per cent of the effective power in the Chicago metropolitan area. [Negroes are 20 per cent of Cook County's population.] Realistically the power structure of Chicago is hardly less white than that of Mississippi."

Colonization outside of a traditional colonial structure has its own special conditions. The group culture and social structure of the colonized in America is less developed; it is also less autonomous. In addition, the colonized are a numerical minority, and furthermore they are ghettoized more totally and are more dispersed than people under classic colonialism. Though these realities affect the magnitude and direction of response, it is my basic thesis that the most important expressions of protest in the Black community during the recent years reflect the colonized status of Afro-America. Riots, programs of separation, politics of community control, the Black revolutionary movements, and cultural nationalism each represents a different strategy of attack on domestic colonialism in America. Let us now examine some of these movements.

[1] "When we speak of Negro social disabilities under capitalism . . . we refer to the fact that he does not own anything—even what is ownable in his own community. Thus to fight for black liberation is to fight for his right to own. The Negro is politically compromised today because he owns nothing. He has little voice in the affairs of state because he owns nothing. The fundamental reason why the Negro bourgeois-democratic revolution has been aborted is because American capitalism has prevented the development of a black class of capitalist owners of institutions and economic tools. To take one crucial example, Negro radicals today are severely hampered in their tasks of educating the black masses on political issues because Negroes do not own any of the necessary means of propaganda and communication. The Negro owns no printing presses, he has no stake in the networks of the means of communication. Inside his own communities he does not own the house he lives in, the property he lives on, nor the wholesale and retail sources from which he buys his commodities. He does not own the edifices in which he enjoys culture and entertainment or in which he socializes. In capitalist society, an individual or group that does not own anything is powerless." H. Cruse, "Behind the Black Power Slogan," in Cruse, Rebellion or Revolution, op. cit., pp. 238–39.

Racism: Domestic Colonialism and Neocolonialism

Riot or Revolt?

The so-called riots are being increasingly recognized as a preliminary if primitive form of mass rebellion against a colonial status. There is still a tendency to absorb their meaning within the conventional scope of assimilation-integration politics: some commentators stress the material motives involved in looting as a sign that the rioters want to join America's middle-class affluence just like everyone else. That motives are mixed and often unconscious, that Black people want good furniture and television sets like whites, is beside the point. The guiding impulse in most major outbreaks has not been integration with American society, but an attempt to stake out a sphere of control by moving against that society and destroying the symbols of its oppression.

In my critique of the McCone report I observed that the rioters were asserting a claim to territoriality, an unorganized and rather inchoate attempt to gain control over their community or "turf." In succeeding disorders also the thrust of the action has been the attempt to clear out an alien presence, white men and officials, rather than a drive to kill whites as in a conventional race riot. The main attacks have been directed at the property of white business men and at the police who operate in the Black community "like an army of occupation" protecting the interests of outside exploiters and maintaining the domination over the ghetto by the central metropolitan power structure. The Kerner report misleads when it attempts to explain riots in terms of integration: "What the riots appear to be seeking was fuller participation in the social order and the material benefits enjoyed by the majority of American citizens. Rather than rejecting the American system, they were anxious to obtain a place for themselves in it." More accurately, the revolts pointed to alienation from this system on the part of many poor and also not-so-poor Blacks. The sacredness of private property, that unconsciously accepted bulwark of our social arrangements, was rejected; people who looted apparently without guilt generally remarked that they were taking things that "really belonged" to them anyway. Obviously the society's bases of legitimacy and authority have been attacked. Law and order has long been viewed as the white man's law and order by Afro-Americans; but now this perspective characteristic of a colonized people is out in the open. And the Kerner Report's own data question how well ghetto rebels are buying the system: In Newark only 33 per cent of self-reported rioters said they thought this country was worth fighting for in the event of a major war; in the Detroit sample the figure was 55 per cent.

One of the most significant consequences of the process of colonization is a weakening of the colonized's individual and collective will to resist his oppression. It has been easier to contain and control Black ghettoes because communal bonds and group solidarity have been weakened through divisions among leadership, failures of organization, and a general dispiritment that accompanies social oppression. The riots are a signal that the will to resist has broken the mold of accommodation. In some cities, as in Watts, they also represented nascent movements toward community identity. In several riot-torn ghettoes the outbursts have stimulated new organizations and movements. If it is true that the riot phenomenon of 1964–68 has passed its peak, its historical import may be more for the "internal" organizing momentum generated than for any profound "external" response of the larger society facing up to underlying causes.

Despite the appeal of Frantz Fanon to young Black revolutionaries, America is not Algeria. It is difficult to foresee how riots in our cities can play a role equivalent to rioting in the colonial situation as an integral phase in a movement for national liberation. In 1968 some militant groups (for example, the Black Panther Party in Oakland) had concluded that ghetto riots were self-defeating of the lives and interests of Black people in the present balance of organization and gunpower, though they had served a role to stimulate both Black consciousness and white awareness of the depths of racial crisis. Such militants have been influential in "cooling" their communities during periods of high riot potential. Theoretically oriented Black radicals see riots as spontaneous mass behavior which must be replaced by a revolutionary organization and consciousness. But despite the differences in objective conditions, the violence of the 1960's seems to serve the same psychic function, assertions of dignity and manhood for young Blacks in urban ghettoes, as it did for the colonized of North Africa described by Fanon and Memmi.

Cultural Nationalism

Cultural conflict is generic to the colonial relation because colonization involves the domination of Western technological values over the more communal cultures of non-Western peoples. Colonialism played havoc with the national integrity of the peoples it brought under its sway. Of course, all traditional cultures are threatened by industrialism, the city, and modernization in communication, transportation, health, and education. What is special are the political and administrative decisions of colonizers in managing and controlling colonized peoples. The boundaries of African colonies, for example, were drawn to suit the political conveniences of the European nations without regard to the social organization and cultures of African tribes and kingdoms. Thus Nigeria as blocked out by the British included the Yorubas and the Ibos, whose civil war today is a residuum of the colonialist's disrespect for the integrity of indigenous cultures.

The most total destruction of culture in the colonization process took place not in traditional colonialism but in America. As Frazier stressed, the integral cultures of the diverse African peoples who furnished the slave trade were destroyed because slaves from different tribes, kingdoms, and linguistic groups were purposely separated to maximize domination and control. Thus language, religion, and national loyalties were lost in North America much more completely than in the Caribbean and Brazil where slavery developed somewhat differently. Thus on this key point America's internal colonization has been more total and extreme than situations of classic colonialism. For the British in India and the European powers in Africa were not able—as outnumbered minorities—to destroy the national and tribal cultures of the

colonized. Recall that American slavery lasted 250 years and its racist aftermath another 100. Colonial dependency in the case of British Kenya and
French Algeria lasted only 77 and 125 years respectively. In the wake of this
more drastic uprooting and destruction of culture and social organization,
much more powerful agencies of social, political, and psychological domination developed in the American case.

Colonial control of many peoples inhabiting the colonies was more a goal
than a fact, and at Independence there were undoubtedly fairly large
numbers of Africans who had never seen a colonial administrator. The
gradual process of extension of control from the administrative center on
the African coast contrasts sharply with the total uprooting involved in
the slave trade and the totalitarian aspects of slavery in the United States.
Whether or not Elkins is correct in treating slavery as a total institution,
it undoubtedly had a far more radical and pervasive impact on American
slaves than did colonialism on the vast majority of Africans.

Yet a similar cultural process unfolds in both contexts of colonialism.
To the extent that they are involved in the larger society and economy, the
colonized are caught up in a conflict between two cultures. Fanon has
described how the assimilation-oriented schools of Martinique taught him to
reject his own culture and Blackness in favor of Westernized, French, and
white values. Both the colonized elites under traditional colonialism and
perhaps the majority of Afro-Americans today experience a parallel split in
identity, cultural loyalty, and political orientation.

The colonizers use their culture to socialize the colonized elites (intellectuals, politicians, and middle class) into an identification with the colonial
system. Because Western culture has the prestige, the power, and the key to
open the limited opportunity that a minority of the colonized may achieve,
the first reaction seems to be an acceptance of the dominant values. Call it
brainwashing as the Black Muslims put it; call it identifying with the aggres-
sor if you prefer Freudian terminology; call it a natural response to the hope
and belief that integration and democratization can really take place if you
favor a more commonsense explanation, this initial acceptance in time
crumbles on the realities of racism and colonialism. The colonized, seeing
that his success within colonialism is at the expense of his group and his
own inner identity, moves radically toward a rejection of the Western culture
and develops a nationalist outlook that celebrates his people and their traditions. As Memmi describes it:

Assimilation being abandoned, the colonized's liberation must be carried
out through a recovery of self and of autonomous dignity. Attempts at
imitating the colonizer required self-denial; the colonizer's rejection is the
indispensible prelude to self-discovery. That accusing and annihilating
image must be shaken off; oppression must be attacked boldly since it is
impossible to go around it. After having been rejected for so long by the
colonizer, the day has come when it is the colonized who must refuse the
colonizer.

Memmi's book, *The Colonizer and the Colonized*, is based on his experience as a Tunisian Jew in a marginal position between the French and the colonized Arab majority. The uncanny parallels between the North African situation he describes and the course of Black-white relations in our society is the best impressionist argument I know for the thesis that we have a colonized group and a colonizing system in America. His discussion of why even the most radical French anti-colonialist cannot participate in the struggle of the colonized is directly applicable to the situation of the white liberal and radical vis-à-vis the Black movement. His portrait of the colonized is as good an analysis of the psychology behind Black Power and Black nationalism as anything that has been written in the U.S. Consider for example:

> Considered en bloc as *them*, *they*, or *those*, different from every point of view, homogeneous in a radical heterogeneity, the colonized reacts by rejecting all the colonizers en bloc. The distinction between deed and intent has no great significance in the colonial situation. In the eyes of the colonized, all Europeans in the colonies are de facto colonizers, and whether they want to be or not, they are colonizers in some ways. By their privileged economic position, by belonging to the political system of oppression, or by participating in an effectively negative complex toward the colonized, they are colonizers. . . . They are supporters or at least unconscious accomplices of that great collective aggression of Europe.

> The same passion which made him admire and absorb Europe shall make him assert his differences; since those differences, after all, are within him and correctly constitute his true self.

> The important thing now is to rebuild his people, whatever be their authentic nature; to reforge their unity, communicate with it, and to feel that they belong.

Cultural revitalization movements play a key role in anti-colonial movements. They follow an inner necessity and logic of their own that comes from the consequences of colonialism on groups and personal identities; they are also essential to provide the solidarity which the political or military phase of the anti-colonial revolution requires. In the U.S. an Afro-American culture has been developing since slavery out of the ingredients of African worldviews, the experience of bondage, Southern values and customs, migration and the Northern lower-class ghettoes, and most importantly, the political history of the Black population in its struggle against racism. That Afro-Americans are moving toward cultural nationalism in a period when ethnic loyalties tend to be weak (and perhaps on the decline) in this country is another confirmation of the unique colonized position of the Black group. (A similar nationalism seems to be growing among American Indians and Mexican-Americans.)

The Movement for Ghetto Control

The call for Black Power unites a number of varied movements and tendencies. Though no clear-cut program has yet emerged, the most important emphasis seems to be the movement for control of the ghetto. Black leaders and organizations are increasingly concerned with owning and controlling those institutions that exist within or impinge upon their community. The colonial model provides a key to the understanding of this movement, and indeed ghetto control advocates have increasingly invoked the language of colonialism in pressing for local home rule. The framework of anti-colonialism explains why the struggle for poor people's or community control of poverty programs has been more central in many cities than the content of these programs and why it has been crucial to exclude whites from leadership positions in Black organizations.

The key institutions that anti-colonialists want to take over or control are business, social services, schools, and the police. Though many spokesmen have advocated the exclusion of white landlords and small businessmen from the ghetto, this program has evidently not struck fire with the Black population and little concrete movement toward economic expropriation has yet developed. Welfare recipients have organized in many cities to protect their rights and gain a greater voice in the decisions that affect them, but whole communities have not yet been able to mount direct action against welfare colonialism. Thus schools and the police seem now to be the burning issues of ghetto control politics.

During the past few years there has been a dramatic shift from educational integration as the primary goal to that of community control of the schools. Afro-Americans are demanding their own school boards, with the power to hire and fire principals and teachers and to construct a curriculum which would be relevant to the special needs and culture style of ghetto youth. Especially active in high schools and colleges have been Black students, whose protests have centered on the incorporation of Black Power and Black culture into the educational system. Consider how similar is the spirit behind these developments to the attitude of the colonized North African toward European education:

He will prefer a long period of educational mistakes to the continuance of the colonizer's school organization. He will choose institutional disorder in order to destroy the institutions built by the colonizer as soon as possible. There we will see, indeed a reactive drive of profound protest. He will no longer owe anything to the colonizer and will have definitely broken with him.

Protest and institutional disorder over the issue of school control came to a head in 1968 in New York City. The procrastination in the Albany State legislature, the several crippling strikes called by the teachers union, and the almost frenzied response of Jewish organizations make it clear that decolonization of education faces the resistance of powerful vested interests. The situation is too dynamic at present to assess probable future results. However, it can be safely predicted that some form of school decentralization will be institutionalized in New York, and the movement for community control of education will spread to more cities.

This movement reflects some of the problems and ambiguities that stem from the situation of colonization outside an immediate colonial context. The Afro-American community is not parallel in structure to the communities of colonized nations under traditional colonialism. The significant difference here is the lack of fully developed indigenous institutions besides the church. Outside of some areas of the South there is really no Black economy, and most Afro-Americans are inevitably caught up in the larger society's structure of occupations, education, and mass communication. Thus the ethnic nationalist orientation which reflects the reality of colonization exists alongside an integrationist orientation which corresponds to the reality that the institutions of the larger society are much more developed than those of the incipient nation. As would be expected the movement for school control reflects both tendencies. The militant leaders who spearhead such local movements may be primarily motivated by the desire to gain control over the community's institutions—they are anti-colonialists first and foremost. Many parents who support them may share this goal also, but the majority are probably more concerned about creating a new education that will enable their children to "make it" in the society and the economy as a whole—they know that the present school system fails ghetto children and does not prepare them for participation in American life.

There is a growing recognition that the police are the most crucial institution maintaining the colonized status of Black Americans. And of all establishment institutions, police departments probably include the highest proportion of individual racists. This is no accident since central to the workings of racism (an essential component of colonization) are attacks on the humanity and dignity of the subject group. Through their normal routines the police constrict Afro-Americans to Black neighborhoods by harassing and questioning them when found outside the ghetto; they break up groups of youth congregating on corners or in cars without any provocation; and they continue to use offensive and racist language no matter how many intergroup understanding seminars have been built into the police academy. They also shoot to kill ghetto residents for alleged crimes such as car thefts and running from police officers.

Police are key agents in the power equation as well as the drama of dehumanization. In the final analysis they do the dirty work for the larger system by restricting the striking back of Black rebels to skirmishes inside the ghetto, thus deflecting energies and attacks from the communities and institutions of the larger power structure. In a historical review, Gary Marx notes that since the French revolution, police and other authorities have killed large numbers of demonstrators and rioters; the rebellious "rabble" rarely destroys human life. The same pattern has been repeated in America's recent revolts.[2] Journalistic accounts appearing in the press recently suggest

[2] "In the Gordon Riots of 1780 demonstrators destroyed property and freed prisoners, but did not seem to kill anyone, while authorities killed several hundred rioters and hung an additional 25. In the Rebellion Riots of the French Revolution, though several hundred rioters were killed, they killed no one. Up to the end of the Summer of 1967, this pattern had clearly been repeated, as police, not rioters, were responsible for most of the more than 100 deaths that have occurred. Similarly, in a related context, the more than 100 civil rights murders of recent years have been matched by almost no murders of racist whites." G. Marx, "Civil Disorders and the Agents of Social Control," *Journal of Social Issues*, vol. 26 (Winter 1970), pp. 19–57.

that police see themselves as defending the interests of white people against a tide of Black insurgence; furthermore the majority of whites appear to view "blue power" in this light. There is probably no other opinion on which the races are as far apart today as they are on the question of attitudes toward the police.

In many cases set off by a confrontation between a policeman and a Black citizen, the ghetto uprisings have dramatized the role of law enforcement and the issue of police brutality. In their aftermath, movements have arisen to contain police activity. One of the first was the Community Alert Patrol in Los Angeles, a method of policing the police in order to keep them honest and constrain their violations of personal dignity. This was the first tactic of the Black Panther Party which originated in Oakland, perhaps the most significant group to challenge the police role in maintaining the ghetto as a colony. The Panthers' later policy of openly carrying guns (a legally protected right) and their intention of defending themselves against police aggression has brought on a series of confrontations with the Oakland police department. All indications are that the authorities intend to destroy the Panthers by shooting, framing up, or legally harassing their leadership— diverting the group's energies away from its primary purpose of self-defense and organization of the Black community to that of legal defense and gaining support in the white community.

There are three major approaches to "police colonialism" that correspond to reformist and revolutionary readings of the situation. The most elementary and also superficial sees colonialism in the fact that ghettoes are overwhelmingly patrolled by white rather than by Black officers. The proposal—supported today by many police departments—to increase the number of Blacks on local forces to something like their distribution in the city would then make it possible to reduce the use of white cops in the ghetto. This reform should be supported, for a variety of obvious reasons, but it does not get to the heart of the police role as agents of colonization.

The Kerner Report documents the fact that in some cases Black policemen can be as brutal as their white counterparts. The report does not tell us who polices the ghetto, but they have compiled the proportion of Negroes on the forces of the major cities. In some cities the disparity is so striking that white police inevitably dominate ghetto patrols. (In Oakland 31 per cent of the population and only 4 per cent of the police are Black; in Detroit the figures are 39 per cent and 5 per cent; and in New Orleans 41 and 4.) In other cities, however, the proportion of Black cops is approaching the distribution in the city: Philadelphia 29 per cent and 20 per cent; Chicago 27 per cent and 17 per cent. These figures also suggest that both the extent and the pattern of colonization may vary from one city to another. It would be useful to study how Black communities differ in degree of control over internal institutions as well as in economic and political power in the metropolitan area.

A second demand which gets more to the issue is that police should live in the communities they patrol. The idea here is that Black cops who lived in the ghetto would have to be accountable to the community; if they came on like white cops then "the brothers would take care of business" and make their lives miserable. The third or maximalist position is based on the premise that the police play no positive role in the ghettoes. It calls for the withdrawal of metropolitan officers from Black communities and the substitution of an autonomous indigenous force that would maintain order without oppressing the population. The precise relationship between such an independent police, the city and county law enforcement agencies, a ghetto governing body that would supervise and finance it, and especially the law itself is yet unclear. It is unlikely that we will soon face these problems directly as they have arisen in the case of New York's schools. Of all the programs of decolonization, police autonomy will be most resisted. It gets to the heart of how the state functions to control and contain the Black community through delegating the legitimate use of violence to police authority.

The various "Black Power" programs that are aimed at gaining control of individual ghettoes—buying up property and businesses, running the schools through community boards, taking over anti-poverty programs and other social agencies, diminishing the arbitrary power of the police—can serve to revitalize the institutions of the ghetto and build up an economic, professional, and political power base. These programs seem limited; we do not know at present if they are enough in themselves to end colonized status. But they are certainly a necessary first step.

The Role of Whites

What makes the Kerner Report a less-than-radical document is its superficial treatment of racism and its reluctance to confront the colonized relationship between Black people and the larger society. The report emphasizes the attitudes and feelings that make up white racism, rather than the system of privilege and control which is the heart of the matter. With all its discussion of the ghetto and its problems, it never faces the question of the stake that white Americans have in racism and ghettoization.

This is not a simple question, but this paper should not end with the impression that police are the major villains. All white Americans gain some privileges and advantage from the colonization of Black communities. The majority of whites also lose something from this oppression and division in society. Serious research should be directed to the ways in which white individuals and institutions are tied into the ghetto. In closing let me suggest some possible parameters.

1. It is my guess that only a small minority of whites make a direct economic profit from ghetto colonization. This is hopeful in that the ouster of white businessmen may become politically feasible. Much more significant, however, are the private and corporate interests in the land and residential property of the Black community; their holdings and influence on urban decision-making must be exposed and combated.

2. A much larger minority have occupational and professional interests in the present arrangements. The Kerner Commission reports that 1.3 million non-white men would have to be up-graded occupationally in order to make the Black job distribution roughly similar to the white. They advocate this

without mentioning that 1.3 million specially privileged white workers would lose in the bargain. In addition there are those professionals who carry out what Lee Rainwater has called the "dirty work" of administering the lives of the ghetto poor: the social workers, the school teachers, the urban development people, and of course the police. The social problems of the Black community will ultimately be solved only by people and organizations from that community; thus the emphasis within these professions must shift toward training such a cadre of minority personnel. Social scientists who teach and study problems of race and poverty likewise have an obligation to replace themselves by bringing into the graduate schools and college faculties men of color who will become the future experts in these areas. For cultural and intellectual imperialism is as real as welfare colonialism, though it is currently screened behind such unassailable shibboleths as universalism and the objectivity of scientific inquiry.

3. Without downgrading the vested interests of profit and profession, the real nitty-gritty elements of the white stake are political power and bureaucratic security. Whereas few whites have much understanding of the realities of race relations and ghetto life, I think most give tacit or at least subconscious support for the containment and control of the Black population. Whereas most whites have extremely distorted images of Black Power, many—if not most—would still be frightened by actual Black political power. Racial groups and identities are real in American life; white Americans sense they are on top, and they fear possible reprisals or disruptions were power to be more equalized. There seems to be a paranoid fear in the white psyche of Black dominance; the belief that black autonomy would mean unbridled license is so ingrained that such reasonable outcomes as Black political majorities and independent Black police forces will be bitterly resisted.

On this level the major mass bulwark of colonization is the administrative need for bureaucratic security so that the middle classes can go about their life and business in peace and quiet. The Black militant movement is a threat to the orderly procedures by which bureaucracies and suburbs manage their existence, and I think today there are more people who feel a stake in conventional procedures than there are those who gain directly from racism. For in their fight for institutional control, the colonized will not play by the white rules of the game. These administrative rules have kept them down and out of the system; therefore they have no necessary intention of running institutions in the image of the white middle class.

The liberal, humanist value that violence is the worst sin cannot be defended today if one is committed squarely against racism and for self-determination. For some violence is almost inevitable in the decolonization process; unfortunately racism in America has been so effective that the greatest power Afro-Americans (and perhaps also Mexican-Americans) wield today is the power to disrupt. If we are going to swing with these revolutionary times and at least respond positively to the anti-colonial movement, we will have to learn to live with conflict, confrontation, constant change, and what may be real or apparent chaos and disorder.

A positive response from the white majority needs to be in two major directions at the same time. First, community liberation movements should be supported in every way by pulling out white instruments of direct control and exploitation and substituting technical assistance to the community when this is asked for. But it is not enough to relate affirmatively to the nationalist movement for ghetto control without at the same time radically opening doors for full participation in the institutions of the mainstream. Otherwise the liberal and radical position is little different than the traditional segregationist. Freedom in the special conditions of American colonization means that the colonized must have the choice between participation in the larger society and in their own independent structures.

David Wellman and Jan Dizard

CORPORATE LIBERALISM, RACISM, AND EMERGING STRATEGIES FOR GHETTO CONTROL

With the publication of the President's Commission on Civil Disorders (the Kerner Report), the beginnings of a blueprint for ghetto control emerged. The report identifies the problem as "white racism," and urges businessmen to take a direct hand in counteracting this racism, loosely and conveniently defined as an attitude of their employees, not of businessmen themselves. The report encourages white businessmen to increase job opportunities— compensatory hiring, not just equal opportunity hiring—and develop the investment climate in the black ghetto, either for themselves or, if the current mood of the black community prevails, for black entrepreneurs. The Kerner Report did not advance anything that had not been talked about for some time: more jobs through "positive recruitment," revision of entrance requirements for jobs, advanced training, college entrance, etc., and investment in urban areas. The Report did, however, provide the early formulation of an ideological synthesis that charts the course to be taken. To understand the significance of the new strategy, it is important to understand the black challenge to corporate America.

The Black Challenge

So long as there have been black people in America they have posed a challenge to the institutions and the ideology that have made America a distinctive country. America's response to the challenge of whether to accommodate black people (and if so, how?) has hardly been consistent. America has enslaved, "set free," employed, cast aside, preached at and viciously beaten down and repressed black people. Through all these vagaries, the litany of the past forty years has insisted that blacks were already, or would soon be, on the same road of assimilation as the one traveled by European ethnic groups. Black people, it was argued (and hoped), would be distributed more or less proportionately throughout the occupational structure and especially among white collar and stable working-class strata. And life chances, access to goods and services, would somehow be distributed with reasonable equity. This optimistic faith in the capacity of American society to absorb has been shattered for all save the most celebrationist.

Reprinted, with a footnote deleted, from David Wellman and Jan Dizard, " 'I Love Ralph Bunche but I Can't Eat Him for Lunch': Corporate Liberalism, Racism, and Emerging Strategies for Ghetto Control," Leviathan, vol. 1 (July–August 1969), pp. 46–52, by permission of the authors and Leviathan. David Wellman teaches sociology at the University of Oregon. He has written for Trans action and several political journals. Jan Dizard teaches sociology at Amherst College.

Much of the mobility of blacks that has encouraged optimism among certain people turns out, on closer inspection, to be simply the result of the move from the rural south to the urban north and west: from the bottom of an archaic social order to the bottom of a modern industrial social order. Thus, while constituting roughly 12 percent of the American population, black people account for only 2.5 percent of professional and technical workers and only 4.2 percent of all foremen and craftsmen. By contrast, blacks make up 44.7 percent of all private household workers and 25 percent of all unskilled laborers. ("Unskilled" is a characteristic of the job held, not necessarily of the person holding the job.) And it is precisely these unskilled jobs which provide blacks with the lowest prospects for mobility and, hence, the bleakest future.

A consideration of the much-vaunted growth of the black middle class demonstrates that blacks are not following the path traveled by other ethnic groups. Although the black middle class has been expanding rapidly since 1950, it still embraces no more than one-fifth of the black population. (This should be compared to the forty to fifty per cent of the white population which is considered middle class by the same considerations of occupation and income.) But, significantly, as Department of Labor statistics indicate, this development is *not* part of a general upward movement among blacks. Quite the contrary, the income gap between the black middle class and the rest of the black population is widening, with nearly forty percent of the black population suffering a *deterioration* in economic status during this same period. Moreover, even the rapid growth of the black middle class has, generally, failed to keep pace with the advancements being made by whites. Thus, in spite of the growth of the black middle class, class differences between the races are becoming sharper, not declining.

The degree of unemployment among blacks indicates their concentration at the bottom of the industrial order. Black unemployment routinely runs double that of whites, on the order of 7 to 9 percent as compared to 3.5 to 4.5 percent throughout most of the post-World War II years. The above statistics, based on a monthly average unemployment rates, translate into the fact that between thirty and forty percent of adult black men (and indeterminably more women) fail to work a complete year. Race and class, blackness and poorness, remain superimposed.

In the face of poverty and humiliation, blacks have repeatedly struggled to overcome white economic, political, and cultural hegemony. While the development of this struggle is by no means unilinear, it is clear that the present level of mobilization of the black population has drawn mightily on historical experiences. In the process, a group consciousness has begun to re-emerge that once more threatens to lay bare and repudiate one of the principal ideological assumptions that has continually propped up the American system of class privilege and inequality: the assumption that problems of poverty and subordination are individual problems solvable through individual efforts and achievement. As long as blacks remained largely fragmented, unwilling or afraid to see themselves as a group, the "carrot" of individual success held people's fascinated attention. Token gains, miraculous success stories, or minimal legalistic gains were substituted for genuine collective advances. No matter that the successful individual often returned to the ghetto only to reinforce the hegemony of whites. "Success" implied that one ceased to be black, ceased having obligations to the black community. As Thomas Dent points out: "Our middle-class heroes in America have too often been tied to what whites think. In the thirties and forties each success who became a Negro 'first'—a Joe Louis, a Roland Hayes, a Marian Anderson, a Ralph Bunche—became precious *because* they were acclaimed by whites (who called them credits to your race)." Needless to say, these "credits to the black race" were also credits to the fairness and generosity of the white race. As long as blacks accepted the tokens, they were forced to accept this implication.

The development of black power and black pride has seriously challenged this dominant mode of "race relations" by insisting that spectacular individual gains and legislative programs like the civil rights acts are not a substitute for group gains. It is no quirk of fate that some of the most disturbing militant actions of late have come largely from blacks who have begun to "make it." It is precisely on these people that the pressures are greatest: there is the pressure from whites to "set an example," and there is the pressure from less fortunate blacks to be relevant to the entire community. Moreover, as the general level of militancy increases, the white community reacts with decreasing discretion, rounding up and brutalizing the "good" and the "bad," forcing those who would perhaps wish otherwise to acknowledge the common fate they share with the entire black community.

The implications of this growing solidarity among black people are important. The more blacks act as a group, the less token concessions can satisfy them. Those who benefit from token gains no longer simply view themselves as individual successes. They increasingly weigh their own "good fortune" against the misery of the collectivity. More important, the demand for collective solutions tends to undermine the influence of the black middle class, when it is largely dependent upon whites for authority and unable to respond to the aspirations of the black community.

All this is not to suggest that anything approaching unanimity exists within the black population on the matter of collective versus individual strategies. The NAACP and other like-minded groups still have substantial influence in the black community and command respect for their efforts to make this society open to the individual achievements of black people. And the movement that is groping toward a sense of collective identity and the articulation of a program for collective advancement and transformation of America is, itself, less a movement than an uneasy alliance between quite disparate tendencies. This movement contains groupings that advocate a separate black state in the South, black capitalism, and an as yet ill-defined socialism. These tendencies have arisen and gained support less from the internal logic of the black community than from white hostility to opening up avenues of individual mobility needed to transform the present half-hearted thrust toward integration to a more genuine equality. The continued hope that white America will deliver on its rhetoric of equal opportunity, and the new hope that whites may aid in the formation of black capitalism have been sufficiently credible to guarantee division in the black community, even though this division now appears to be diminishing.

From this perspective, the future of the black middle class is problematic. Middle class blacks can move in a number of political directions. They can opt for a kind of traditional accommodation with and acceptance of the social-political dictates of white society. Recent developments toward group consciousness and militancy within the overall black community, however, make this choice more difficult than before. Middle class blacks who align themselves with white society today reduce their political credibility within the community. In some cities middle class blacks who are identified as representatives of white society cannot safely walk ghetto streets. More often, the community has ignored these elements. To the extent that the black middle class is ignored or opposed by the community, their position becomes untenable and whites can no longer look to them for ghetto control.

Another option for middle class blacks is political quiescence or neutrality concerning events in the black community, a perpetuation of the phenomenon described by E. Franklin Frazier in his *Black Bourgeoisie*. Given the increasing racial polarization in America, this response also seems untenable. As polarization deepens, the public world intrudes pervasively into the private world of those who prefer noninvolvement. The only other major alternative open to middle class blacks who wish to be politically relevant is to identify themselves with developments in the black community from a base within the community. This response is increasingly characteristic of the black middle class. It includes hustling poverty programs, attempting to use federal money for small businesses, the alignment of black school administrators with their community against centralized school boards, or working with revolutionary organizations. This political diversity among the black middle class reflects the heterogeneity of the black community and indicates that any response to emerging strategies will not be homogeneous. It should be clear, however, that attempts on the part of the black middle class to relate to the black community will effectively be shaped by the white response to increasing black militancy. Political diversity among middle class blacks is in large part a function of the flexible and differentiated response of white corporate America toward black demands. As long as the political hegemony of the black middle class is shaped by what white society says and does, its influence will at best be unstable.

Strategies for Maintaining Rule

As the crisis deepens in the black community, it is forcing the discontent of other groups to the surface. Implicit in the demands raised by blacks is the demand for a redistribution of wealth and power. At the same time, the collapse of liberalism in the face of growing black demands has also fed an increasingly powerful reactionary force that has begun to seriously challenge the rule of corporate liberalism from the right, demanding an end to tampering and "pampering" and calling for strong measures of repression and control. While the right has typically been strongest in local and state politics, there can be little doubt that the Nixon administration, especially in the Department of "Justice," is responding to this growing force. This situation is forcing the liberal rulers of America to attempt to maintain order without redistributing wealth and power but also without generalized repression.

The demands for repression and redistribution have been raised from the outset of American independence. Business and government elites have consistently responded to the agitation of agrarians and workers in the following manner: First, they sought to stimulate economic growth to provide the illusion of redistribution; and, second, they systematically invoked repression on a limited scale directed at specific targets.

The response of the corporate elite and of the political interests dependent upon it proceeds on the basis of two widely accepted postulates. First, redistribution of wealth, and to a lesser extent, redistribution of income, is intolerable. Redistribution has been invoked on a small scale during short periods of desperate crisis (for example, the failure of recovery after 1934–36), but the secular trend in American society favors the maintenance and enhancement of economic privilege. Thus, while there has been a slight redistribution of incomes over the course of the past forty years, the concentration of wealth has, at best, remained constant; and there are, moreover, strong indications that the distribution of wealth has become more regressive.

Second, the corporate elite has not particularly wanted the thorough-going repression that has repeatedly been demanded by reactionary elements within American society. Thorough repression would require abandoning the liberal ideology of equality and freedom that has served to enlist the masses of Americans in a system which the corporate elite can manage and lead. But repression has been an integral part of the corporate liberal strategy. Repression, like redistribution, has been used as a tactical weapon, a means for getting out of a specific difficulty and, as such, has typically been selective and focused, much to the dismay of the right.

While corporate liberals have regularly rejected generalized repression as an instrument of policy, the repression they start on a more or less selective basis often becomes generalized, despite their ideological and pragmatic concerns. For example, it was the anti-communism of the corporate elite and their ideologists that ultimately legitimated the rampant and diffuse anti-communism of the fifties. But, importantly, McCarthy was defeated not by popular outrage, but rather by the liberal wing of the corporate elite itself. Repressive periods such as McCarthyism are not aberrations in American political life as some liberal critics have argued. The tool of repression is integral to the maintenance of the corporate structure. What is aberrant is the generalization of repression. Ordinarily, the right is forced to remain content with exercising their repressive program through local district attorneys' offices and state legislatures.

Were it not for the corporate elite's continued ability to rely on the alternative of economic growth, the right's demand for repression would be nearly irresistible. Under conditions of economic growth, class cleavages tend to be obscured as a result of expanded mobility opportunities and increased levels of consumption. As a result, while contradictions endemic to capitalism are not averted, these contradictions tend to remain beyond the pale of politics. Failures of the system are often perceived as individual failings and personal shortcomings or as problems which can be solved by minor adjustments. Economic growth is likely to diminish the pressure from below for more goods and services, without requiring a change in the economic structure that produces inequality. Under conditions of economic stagnation, by contrast, the corporate elite sees the demand from below as a demand for a more equitable distribution. Without mass discontent, it becomes easier to isolate radicals and separate them from any constituency, while at the same time confining the reactionaries to local politics.

All things considered, the strategy of economic growth has worked well in preventing disaffection and, especially, the political expression of disaffection. Black people are a major exception to this because racist exclusion has vitiated the defusing effects of economic growth and mobility. The realization that economic expansion was having little, if any, effect on changing the relative positions of blacks and whites has led to a peculiar set of intellectual responses by those who have assigned themselves the task of making sense of the nonsense. Since liberal apologists cannot see the "Negro problem" as the result of an improperly functioning economy, they reason that blacks are falling behind because "they don't have skills," or because "they've developed a welfare dependency." Indeed, from this perspective the economy has been functioning within such narrow limits that to apply the necessary measures to alleviate the inordinate unemployment among black workers, that is, to apply standard full employment measures, would be to seriously overheat the economy. Maintaining high and increasing levels of aggregate demand does not produce jobs for ghetto dwellers. As this realization dawned a frantic search for ways of modifying the traditional aggregate growth policy began. That policy had, in general, served quite well for incorporating whites. It is usual at this point in the chronicle to herald the coming of the "War on Poverty" as an example of the "coping behavior" of the corporate liberals. Actually, it was hardly anything of the sort. Insufficient funding aside, the War on Poverty represented a hodgepodge of quite unremarkable programs, most predicated on the assumption that the problem was, again, Negroes—so we tried to give them "new skills" (which were, more often than not, old, useless skills), new attitudes toward work, head starts, and so forth.

The three major components of the emerging program for dealing with the "urban crisis," while maintaining if not enhancing the strength of the corporate structures, are but variations on the theme of responses to past dilemmas: First, to moderate the caste-like effects of racism so that blacks can move more freely through the social and class structure; second, to continue the long-range aggregate growth policy, but to create policies that focus a disproportionate share of current growth specifically on the ghetto and its population; and, third, to rationalize law enforcement agencies to make them more useful in the task of selective repression. Let us consider

Racism: Domestic Colonialism and Neocolonialism

each in somewhat greater detail before we move on to an evaluation of the limitations of the emergent program.

The commitment to reduce centuries-old impediments to mobility was, in principle, made years ago with the passage of the first modern civil rights legislation, the Fair Employment Practices Act of 1947. New to the scene is the realization that legislation no longer has the soporific effects it once had, coupled with the recognition that the system predicated on tokenism has ceased being useful. Compensatory programs are now envisioned in which employers are joined with various governmental agencies in organizations like the Urban Coalition and the National Alliance of Businessmen, theoretically to coordinate job placement for the unemployed, accelerate training on the job (with the help of governmental subsidies, of course), and other similar attempts to create a vacuum into which blacks can flow.

In addition, many colleges and universities are making room for expanded numbers of black students by modifying or waiving outright the very admissions standards so successful in the past in preserving this major avenue of social mobility for the middle class white and the especially promising working class white. By the same token, bureaucracies, principally governmental, are opening their embrace to increasing numbers of black applicants, creating thereby a whole new spectrum of low and middle level white collar jos. In all of these respects, the third and fourth order privileges that have accrued to whites by virtue of racism (as distinct from the major privileges that have accrued to the corporate elite and its minions, privileges which such documents as the Kerner Report obscure from view) are contemplated as targets for reform.

Yet increasing the potential for blacks to become mobile within the society is not, in and of itself, enough. Accomplishing this presupposes continued and even accelerated economic growth while maintaining sufficient deflationary pressure to keep in balance the other commitments and interests that combine to make the social system. As we have pointed out, relying solely on aggregate policies has failed, and, at least partly in response to that failure, new ways are being found to funnel a portion of new investment directly into the ghetto—i.e., not to wait for general investments to trickle down to this level.

Numerous programs are either in initial stages of operation or on the drawing boards. They range from granting fast tax write-offs to corporate investments in ghetto housing and business, to low interest loans through the Small Business Administration to black entrepreneurs. While the former type of program is likely to account, in the long run, for the bulk of the effort at focused economic development of the black community, it is the latter that has attracted most attention under the catch-phrase of "black capitalism." Many enterprises are envisioned under this program. Some are standard small retailing outlets. Others are more substantial. For example, various large corporations have set about establishing subsidiaries that are scheduled to be turned over to black executives. These subsidiaries, presumably, will employ mostly residents of the black communities in which they locate. In San Francisco, for example, Safeway has released one of its top store managers to an infant black cooperative market to serve as a trainer-consultant-temporary manager until the enterprise gets on its feet—at which point, perhaps, it will stock Safeway products.

The mobility and focused growth aspects of the emergent policy are interdependent. The growth of industry and the enlargement of black business create mobility opportunities that will be more or less reserved for blacks— in much the same way that other ethnic groups have reserved niches for group members. In addition, increasing mobility external to the black community also creates increased consumer demand, at least some of which can be counted on by the aspiring black merchants—particularly if the black pride and identity energies can be fashioned into a "buy black" ethos. In this sense, what is clearly hoped for is a Rostow-like "take-off into self-sustained growth." It must be kept in mind, though, that this "self-sustained growth" is not to be equated with independence or autonomy. Rather what is clearly envisioned is growth that is responsive to and dependent upon major centers of corporate wealth, in the same fashion that Rostow's notion of economic development for third world countries leaves these countries dominated by Western capital.

Closely linked to these plans to incorporate blacks into the political economy is a systematic program of repression of those elements in the black community—and within the white radical movements as well—who are attempting to create bases from which to resist this incorporation. Repression is nearly always, as we have suggested, double-edged: aid and encourage those groups that has mastered an effective—in this context, militant— rhetoric but which also have a reformist program; at the same time, smash the more "recalcitrant" groups. Thus, the Ford Foundation shows extensive noblesse oblige to CORE and its attempts to promote black capitalism in Cleveland while the Justice Department prepares, according to recent reports, Smith Act indictments against the Black Panthers.

To make this carrot and stick policy workable, however, police departments need to be "modernized"—that is, made to recognize that not all black militants are "bad." Thus, the Kerner Commission and, more recently, the Eisenhower (Violence) Commission have made police practices the subject of intense scrutiny. The results have been uniform: the police must be more highly trained, made more efficient in "crowd control," and be sensitized to problems of "human relations" (distinguishing between "good" and "bad niggers"). The fact that police victimization of the black community has played a large role in the growing black hostility to white society has not been lost on the corporate and political elite. But "modernization," at a time when repression is a necessity, produces "professional" police organizations that wage political campaigns which often run counter to liberal reforms. So, for example, in New York City the Policemen's Benevolent Association successfully defeated Lindsay's civilian review board; and in Detroit police associations are attempting to impeach a liberal black judge.

It should be clear even from our schematic portrayal of current plans and operations that the strategy for maintaining order is intricate and diverse. It is not our contention that some small—or even large—group of corporate liberals has somewhere a Pentagon-like control center from which the various strands of policy are coordinated. While it is obvious that the elite has no problem generating individuals and organizations who do engage in long-term planning and coordination functions, it should also be abundantly clear that what we have collected together here and called a "strategy" consists primarily of programs that numerous, on the whole like-minded, people have developed in response to a commonly perceived set of dilemmas. Kennedy with his set of advisors pushes one particular approach while Rockefeller, with a different set of advisors, pursues another tactic. Competition even arises between proponents of different approaches. But this should in no way obscure the fundamental coherence of what is emerging.

It is not a foregone conclusion that the strategy we have just outlined can, in fact, be put into practice. Nor is it clear that even if programs are implemented, they will work as expected. All the programs face limitations that are clearly rooted in the structure of American society, limits which cannot be seen as ad hoc temporary phenomena.

Limitations on Liberal Reform

One of the reasons traditional aggregate growth policies have failed to ease the oppression of black people is the pervasive racism which has prevented social mobility for black people. While a considerable portion of this restriction is accounted for by unintentional—i.e., institutional—racism, nevertheless large numbers of people have a substantial stake in maintaining institutional patterns, not to mention the stake of those who like real estate interests directly benefit from explicit restriction. Thus while the corporate elite in and out of the executive branch of the federal government may be able, and even anxious, to rid themselves of a commitment to the more perverse aspects of the status quo, it is by no means clear that they can convince to do likewise others whose view of things is considerably less empyrean. Two considerations make this task problematic.

First, the benefits of racist restriction are not evenly distributed throughout the society. As a general rule, it seems that as one goes from the transnational to the local business interests, the direct stake in racism increases. This can be seen even within the large corporation. The central headquarters, housing the most cosmopolitan, internationally involved staffs, has in many instances sent down orders for hiring more blacks to its far-flung local branches. In the process of implementation at the local level, these orders rarely get the attention the front office thinks they deserve. The local branch managers have to worry about production, maintaining peace with the local union, paying deference to local customs and job market connections, and so on, all of which present cross-pressures that contradict the intent of the original directive. This is clearly one of the reasons why top executives can announce plans to hire 100,000 "hard core unemployed" and wind up with some number significantly below that mark.

This same scene was acted out in more conventional political terms within the "war on poverty." Although the reasons for failure are many, an important one was that local power structures simply could not tolerate the challenges to their rule implicit in many of the programs, especially in the Community Action Programs. Supporting local agitation for jobs, better welfare services, more responsive government, firmer controls over police, and the like in no way threatened the security of elites resting on a national base. In fact, success in these local areas would serve to make their rule more secure by eliminating some of the harshest abuses endemic in this society. But this is not the case for those rooted in the local scene.

Local resistance to reforms from above is always troublesome, no matter what the area. If it were simply a matter of enforcing tighter discipline on subordinates as it is in the organizational context, rational elites would only be faced with an irritant and an impediment to speedy action. But power relations between national and local elites are not such that one can apply the organization analogy. Local businessmen and politicians are not simply lackeys to those in positions of greater power. Moreover, national elites—the heads of major corporations, foundation executives, members of the executive branch, and some members of Congress—have historically divested themselves of direct involvement in the politics of local rule; they have had much bigger fish to fry. This has meant that local elites are not always controllable on terms the corporate liberals prefer. It is recognition of this fact that no doubt has provided one of the major spurs to regional government (cf. *Leviathan,* April 1969).

It is clear that the implementation of the reforms we have been speaking of is no simple matter when one considers the substantial commitments to racist restriction on the part of local elites and their ability to formulate independent positions at least in the short run. Real political struggle has to be waged, the more so as new programs reach deeper into the strongholds of local power. The general resistance to new programs that smack of welfare "give-aways" or "rewarding violence and sloth" that have come to typify state and local governmental "deliberations" are cases in point. If we were dealing with a formal organization, we would be talking about the insubordination of middle and lower level management. The accelerated closing of police ranks and their increasing independence in city after city; the response of the UFT in New York to the brainstorm of McGeorge Bundy of the Ford Foundation; the difficulties encountered by the National Alliance of Businessmen in enlisting the cooperation of local businesses—all point to the fact that implementation is by no means assured.

In other words, substantial entrenched interests with considerable political power currently stand in opposition to major aspects of the corporate liberal strategy of reform. Those aspects of the overall strategy that call for opening up mobility channels to blacks are especially vulnerable to these forces. Local politicians have taken advantage of the growing fears among whites who are faced with increased taxes and whose sources of security and gratification are increasingly being ridiculed by their children and jeopardized, in their view by the demands of black people. And local political brokers are using these fears as a political base from which to resist the incursions of the national elite.

Rear-guard political resistance is not the only barrier to implementation of corporate strategies. There are also fiscal problems. One of the central problems is inflation. In general, inflation occurs in response to two forces: increasing demand that tends to push prices up and increasing wages that, in turn, cause price increases as business attempts to offset wage increases and maintain or increase profit margins. Inflation is dangerous to the economy insofar as 1) rising prices reduce the competitive position of American products on the international market and also make the domestic market vulnerable to penetrations from foreign firms offering lower prices; and 2) it necessitates tax increases in order that government services at all levels can at least be maintained. Standard means of combatting inflation usually include discouraging new investments in the domestic economy with consequent reduced levels of employment and reduced consumer spending. Tighter restrictions on federal spending and monetary policies that put brakes on lending are the chief deflationary weapons. Given the fact that we are currently in a period of rapid inflation—the cost of living index is showing yearly increases of over five per cent and the prime interest rate is currently at its highest point since the beginning of this century—the fiscal problems now confronting the nation make the high levels of investment required to bring off attempts at focused economic development problematic at best.

Compounding the problem is an old story—investors will not go into uncharted areas without guarantees. This has meant that corporations are generally reluctant—to put it mildly—to invest in the black community without significant concessions from government in the form of accelerated tax write-offs, guaranteed profits ("cost plus" contracts, typically specifying a minimum of ten per cent return), or some other "incentive" that will make such investment at least as attractive as other conceivable investments. While the federal government has always been willing to underwrite private gain, inflation and the costs of maintaining an empire are currently restricting the extent to which the federal government can use funds in this way. The recent cutbacks in poverty program funds, the recent decision by the Nixon administration to scratch several Job Corps training centers (many of which have been operated by corporations on a lucrative "cost plus" arrangement), demonstrate this.

Will It Work?

Let us assume for the moment that the strategy is implemented. The question yet remains: Will it work? Radicals have traditionally underestimated America's ability to contain unrest under the guise of social reform, but the emerging strategy to contain black people is hardly sure of success. There are a number of significant factors working against it.

Even if the economy were able to avoid recession and thus facilitate the elimination of unemployment, the success of job aid programs in opening avenues for social mobility is likely to remain minimal. A study prepared for the Urban Coalition reports that fewer than ten thousand new jobholders received special training last year. The findings are based on a survey of 224 companies with 8.7 million employees in fifteen major urban areas. The study also labels as a "phony numbers game" the NAB claim of more than 100,000 "hard core" unemployed hired last year. This figure includes hiring that would have been done in any case and companies with high turnover rates are credited as having more recruits. In addition, many of the jobs into which the unemployed are placed are jobs facing imminent elimination through technological change.

Reducing unemployment is only one aim of these programs. Another is reducing militancy in the black community. If unemployment is reduced— so the formula seems to read—militancy will be reduced. If this is a criterion for success, then job training programs are more of a failure than statistics showing a decrease in unemployment might suggest. According to the Coalition report, militancy among blacks *increases* as employees become more secure in their work situation. People demand a greater voice in union affairs, more upgrading opportunities and alterations in seniority provisions which perpetuate racism. This fact is corroborated by the organizing successes among black workers by radical groups like the League of Revolutionary Black Workers in Detroit. The ghetto rebellions of 1967 also reflect the relation of employment to militancy: Young black workers—according to the Kerner Commission—played a very important part in the uprisings. Thus, it is not at all clear that programs aimed at increasing job mobility will be effective in the short run in reducing either unemployment or militancy.

The frailty of the corporate liberal program is dramatically illustrated in a recent article in *Business Week* on the rebellion of black workers. In addition to the now widely publicized militant black workers' groups, the article cites rising incidents of machines sabotaged, union officials rejected, and, perhaps most importantly, black supervisors derided for "doing the man's job." In the latter vein, the article reports one incident in which a production employee of Chrysler stabbed a black official of the company when the official informed the worker of a disciplinary lay-off. Thus it appears that the black administrative corps being created by new recruitment measures is not sufficient to the task expected of it—assuring the cooperation of black underlings.

Colleges and universities are another area in which social mobility for blacks is opening up. Educational rationalizers expect that through intense recruitment of people with high learning potential and changes in outmoded entrance requirements, blacks will be able to enter colleges and begin to advance themselves throughout the "opportunity" structure. The success of these programs has been limited. The number of blacks entering major colleges and universities is still quite low. The programs have not reduced militancy, but have created the base for a radical black student movement. More and more young blacks entering college are insistent upon relating their college careers to the ghettoes. This can be seen most graphically in the ongoing struggles for the removal of all entrance requirements at many schools. In other words, they are rejecting the university as simply an avenue for individual mobility: they are insisting that their advantage be generalized.

Government employment as a vehicle for social mobility is a last resort effort, even in the eyes of the corporate liberal strategy. Most government jobs for minority people are dead ends. Realizing this, the corporate leadership is attempting to channel minority people elsewhere. The government as an employer cannot, short of becoming a total corporate state, hire all the people private enterprise rejects or casts to the side. In fact, if government ends up having to do most of the hiring of black people, it will mark the *failure* of the strategy we have outlined.

The attempt to develop small businesses within America's black ghettoes is a crucial aspect of the corporate strategy. American society, however, is obviously not a small business society. Small business has been declining in importance since at least the turn of this century. The decline is highlighted by the high failure rate of small businesses. As C. Wright Mills noted in *White Collar,* while sixteen million firms began operation during the four decades preceding World War II, fourteen million went out of business. When an increasing number of small businesses compete for a small share of the market, a high rate of failure is to be expected.

Assuming the limitation cited above, the corporate liberal strategy does address one traditional problem plaguing the development of small business: capital. Government and business programs will ostensibly provide money with which to start small businesses. The business to which this capital will give birth, however, will not gain much leverage in the American economy. Black-owned businesses will be central to neither the growth areas of the national nor ghetto economies. They will either distribute the products of national corporations or be subcontractors to them. Thus, the "profits" derived from black-owned business will be of little immediate benefit to the general black community. For years to come, money that might flow into the ghetto—profits which need not be plowed back for expansion purposes—will be drained off in interest and debt payments to the corporations which initially put up the capital. Some black entrepreneurs will undoubtedly benefit but it is difficult to see how this will affect greatly the economic and political dependency of the black community, which is currently among the principal sources of dissatisfaction.

The emerging strategy does not confront crucial aspects of the relationship of black people to white society. The ghetto does not provide a substantial base for economic development. Land cost, taxation, transportation, deteriorated facilities, crime and social instability restrict the possibilities for development to consumer services for the existing black population and to some small or marginal industrial facilities. It is unlikely, moreover, that small businesses could successfully compete as independent enterprises against such giant firms as Safeway, A. & P., or IBM. Moreover, the economic growth areas outside the ghetto—e.g., personal services, land development, and complex technology—offer little possibility of black business penetration from a ghetto base. The development programs—even if we accept the dubious proposition that they might be implemented—do not deal with economic power beyond the ghetto. As such, the programs do not confront a basic reality of America: Blacks have been and apparently will continue to be an underclass of surplus labor which is segregated within ghetto boundaries and which is of marginal productive utility to the surrounding economy.

Another aspect of the economic growth strategy is encouraging industry to relocate plants in the ghetto. This, it is assumed, will lend itself to alleviating unemployment and create new consumer markets. While hardly constituting "black capitalism," as it will involve new capital which is not even nominally controlled by blacks, the strategy faces serious obstacles once implemented. For one, most white middle level management, as well as skilled workers, live outside the central city and will not be easily persuaded to commute each day. In fact, the opposite is true. Plants are moving outside central cities and one of the long list of disadvantages of being an unskilled worker is that *he* must do the commuting. When they can, plants leave cities for three basic reasons. Property taxes in cities are extremely high and suburbs use low tax rates to attract desirable industries. Insurance rates in central cities are prohibitive. And, finally, the employees to whom they are most responsive, managers and skilled workers, are moving to the suburbs to avoid blacks. Plants move outside the city for real economic reasons. A recent poll conducted by the *Wall Street Journal* asked major corporations if they were willing to relocate back to the city. Very few said they would. Expecting them to return without changing the conditions which caused them to leave originally is liberal daydreaming.

A third feature of the growth strategy is investment in central city housing. This is another way of attracting industry by halting the white exodus out of the cities, hopefully lowering the crime rate, and developing a taxable base in the cities. Most projects of this nature have been remarkably unsuccessful. For many reasons, none of which are difficult to pinpoint, middle-class Americans are not willing to return to the cities. Many of the new central city high-rises have continually had to contend with low levels of occupancy. Central city housing developments have also involved removing black people by means of such euphemisms as "urban renewal." The negative political and social consequences of "urban renewal" often render negligible the positive aspects (from the corporate perspective) of relocation.

Even if these problems were overcome, there is yet another to face. A good portion of the capital to back these ventures will have to come from either government subsidies or guarantees like cost-plus fixed fees. Congress, however, has not seen any decline in black militancy in the limited time that corporate liberal strategies have had to prove their effectiveness. Moreover, at each juncture in which blacks are pushed up into the occupational or educational hierarchy there has been an attendant clash with whites who see black uplift as a threat to their interests. All indications are that Congress, the bastion of localism, will use the so-called backlash as an excuse to cut back on funds to be used for the liberal strategy.

Perhaps the largest potential obstacle to the success of ghetto strategies is the surrounding white community. The corporate liberals are having one hell of a time selling this strategy to the white public. Any program that includes the notion of "preferential treatment" raises the ideological hackles of most white Americans. In their minds it challenges the universalistic principles of equality upon which America is supposedly based. ("We made it the hard way. We started at the bottom with no help from the government. They should too. I'm not prejudiced. We're all equal. We should be treated as equals with no help from the government.") In fact, of course, the universalistic assumptions of liberalism have become the justification for a new ideological twist to racism.

As most organizers know, and as corporate liberals are finding out, white people will not easily relinquish the privileges of white skin in American society. Whites are a political as well as ideological obstacle to emerging strategies. Preferential hiring programs are going to evoke serious problems for labor and industry when and if skilled white workers are not hired. In anticipation of this problem unions in the clothing industry have already obtained prohibitions in manpower legislation against the use of government funds for training in job skills in their industry. Thus, those who would push the new ghetto strategies are politically vulnerable. If the programs they push infringe upon the privileges of whites, they are likely to be replaced. But if programs *don't* infringe on white privileges they are almost worthless for black people. Political vulnerability in a period of increasing hostility toward any kind of social change could well result in the retreat of corporate liberal strategies.

Although we are obviously not optimistic about the chances for the corporate strategy working, sufficient energies, capital, and political power may in fact be mobilized to create enough of a sense of reform to significantly moderate current levels of conflict. While successful in this restricted, though obviously important sense, the broader bases upon which the ability of American corporate capitalism rests will make this incorporation of blacks less attractive than might otherwise be the case. Specifically, the experience of the past thirty years has demonstrated clearly the very close dependence of continued domestic prosperity—economic growth—on the twin engines of militarism and the increased penetration of foreign markets and national economies.

The record to date has been anything but promising. Plans and promises are many, results few and largely overinflated. All the while, of course, repression is increasingly being applied. But in the absence of the carrot the stick works in peculiar ways. For example, the heightened attacks on the Black Panthers, rather than isolating them, seem to be gaining them support. The black community is less and less disposed to credit hollow promises wanting of delivery. The political and economic disfigurations of contemporary American society, increasingly apparent as the result of unrelenting anti-communism and imperial militarism, may be producing a situation in which corporate liberalism finds itself unrelentingly propelled toward a heavily repressive, tightly managed "garrison state."

chapter 6

Sexism and Society

There is little doubt that sex roles have probably been, along with religion, the most stable institutional features of civilization throughout history. Possibly because of its durability or the threat to other social institutions that its dissolution might entail, the scholarly examination of this area of human experience has been extraordinarily unimaginative when it has been undertaken at all. The role that *women's* exploitation has played in the development of societies has been particularly neglected. As Aileen Kraditor observes:

> Until toward the end of the nineteenth century, most history was written in terms of kings' reigns and presidents' administrations, of wars and revolutions; in these, women took little or no part. And, since women wrote as little history as they made, it is not surprising that historiography faithfully reflected their exclusion from those events historians considered important enough to record.[1]

[1] Aileen Kraditor, *Up from the Pedestal: Selected Documents from the History of American Feminism* (Chicago, Quadrangle Books, 1968), p. 3.

246

The recent resurgence of feminism in the United States has forced social analysts to grapple with the phenomena of sex roles and sexism, just as the black liberation movement compelled a reexamination of American racism. The growing literature on the role of women in contemporary American society reveals quite clearly that fifty years of suffrage has done little to emancipate women from economic, political, social, and sexual oppression.[2]

Marlene Dixon's article in this chapter not only gives a vivid description of the oppression of American women in the home and on the labor market but provides a functional analysis of sexism; that is, it links the exploitation of women to the needs of advanced capitalism. Women, and particularly wives, in their role as consumers provide the impetus for male participation in the work force; women undercut the production costs of capitalism by serving as a reserve army of low paid part-time laborers and by providing free labor in the form of housework. By their work inside or outside the home, women supplement their husbands' salaries and unwittingly enable employers to exploit them by not paying an adequate wage to either. In addition, women play a nurturant, supportive role, giving emotional and sexual rewards to men for playing an "instrumental" breadwinner role, rewards which are essential if men are to be capable of suppressing their "expressive" tendencies in the world of alienated labor.[3]

Dixon's work is also valuable because she is sensitive to the differential impact of sexism on white middle-class women and black and white working-class women as well as the resultant contradictions within the women's movement.

While covering a wide range of topics, Dixon's analysis should be supplemented by mention of the role women play in family socialization and "tension management." In general, wives are expected to transmit the values of hard work, discipline, and self-blame in order to gear the whole family to the task of survival. As Kathy McAfee and Myrna Wood put it, "the role of wife is one of social mediator and pacifier. She shields her family from the direct impact of class oppression. She is the true opiate of the masses."[4] Moreover, the subordinate status of women in the family permits men to displace hostility toward their employers and other authority figures onto their wives. This too helps stabilize the existing social order.

Although Dixon discusses the historical relationship between capitalist development and sexism in passing, it should perhaps be considered more fully. If we briefly examine American history, the particular form of sex role relationships appears to have changed dramatically in response to the evolution of the capitalist mode of production. Prior to the onset of industrial

[2] Robin Morgan, ed., *Sisterhood Is Powerful* (New York: Vintage Books, 1970), has compiled the best anthology of writings on the status and experiences of contemporary women to date.

[3] Morris Zelditch, Jr., "Role Differentiation in the Nuclear Family: A Comparative Study" in Talcott Parsons and Robert F. Bales, *Family, Socialization and Interaction Process* (New York: The Free Press, 1955), pp. 307–351.

[4] Kathy McAfee and Myrna Wood, "Bread and Roses," *Leviathan,* vol. 1 (June 1969), p. 9.

capitalism the family was totally involved *as a unit* in economic production. While men and women performed different tasks along with their offspring and sexual repression was the norm, there was a certain egalitarianism in sex roles simply because both sexes, working where they lived, performed manual tasks necessary for family survival.[5] The work pace was more relaxed than in later years and family members lived together in what at least could have been a more harmonious manner.

With the advent of the Industrial Revolution, the family as a unit of production broke down. At various times, children, men, and women were sent to the factory to work long hours for pitiful wages.[6] In the early stages of industrialization there was considerable hostility towards the new system of "wage slavery." Consequently, the need for a docile labor force played a crucial part in taking women out of the factory and returning them to the home where they could socialize (that is, pacify) future generations of workers.

Between 1830 and 1860 an increasing volume of popular literature was devoted to the idealization of the "household" and the particular "feminine" virtues that permitted women to assume the role of the conscience of society.[7] In this period female sexuality was most repressed, possibly serving the function of reducing the birthrate and facilitating social mobility as well as reinforcing social conservatism.

These changes in sex roles mainly affected middle-class women. Industrial development under capitalism did not permit the lower classes to reestablish a stable home life to the extent that those who were somewhat more materially secure were able. Women and children continued to swell the ranks of factory workers, and socialization could not proceed as thoroughly as in the middle classes. Nevertheless, the "feminine mystique" probably seeped down to the lower orders and coexisted with a sex role structure based upon more practical considerations.[8]

As capitalism developed and became more secure in the twentieth century, the social foundations of the feminine mystique were gradually undermined. Women were no longer needed to pacify a restive male labor force to the extent they had been in the pre–Civil War era. But until the past few decades women's labor was only useful on a part-time basis, since employers were anxious to have a stable and increasingly skilled work force.

[5] John Demos, *A Little Commonwealth: Family Life in Plymouth Colony* (New York, Oxford University Press, 1970).

[6] Norman Ware, *The Industrial Worker: The Reaction of American Industrial Society to the Advance of the Industrial Revolution, 1840–1860* (Chicago: Quadrangle Books, 1964), pp. 10–124.

[7] Mary P. Ryan, an historian at Pitzer College and a student of domesticity in the pre–Civil War era, has provided great insight into the transformation of the female role during the early stages of industrialization. See her "American Society and the Cult of Domesticity, 1830–1860," unpublished PhD. dissertation (Department of History, University of California at Santa Barbara, 1971).

[8] Hyman Rodman, "The Lower-class Value Stretch," *Social Forces*, vol. 42 (December 1963), pp. 205–215, suggests a model for this mode of adaptation to conflicting normative and social pressures. The normative ideals are not forsaken; rather they are stretched to accommodate the realities of a social situation that offers few rewards and even punishment for normative fidelity.

Because they could become pregnant (and leave their jobs) and because they lacked training, women failed to qualify.

The increasing demand for educated labor, the small gains registered by feminist agitation during the transition from early to late industrialization, and the valuable labor services performed by women during the Great Depression and both world wars made it more difficult to maintain the ideological basis of sexism after World War II. As young people's entrance into the job market was postponed because of the need for highly skilled "brain" workers, women were encouraged to enter or reenter the world of paid labor to replace young men who were continuing their formal education after high school. Given the need for a burgeoning female labor force and the increased educational achievement of women in the postwar period, the traditional roles of wife and mother became more anachronistic than ever. The possibility of transcending the "career" of housework and the gradual encroachment by educational institutions and the mass media on the maternal obligation to socialize the young provided the structural sources for a redefinition of sex roles.[9] Unfortunately, as Dixon shows, the dissaffection with the traditional female role has not led to the emancipation of women, but only to their increasing frustration with a cultural and social function that seems to have no rational foundation. Despite the great increase in the proportion of women who have graduated from college since World War II, sex differences in economic status have not diminished. In fact, there is evidence that things have gotten worse since the early 1960s.[10] Nor has the role of wife and mother been redefined.

The tenacity of sexism in the United States is enigmatic. It would be simplistic to say that the capitalist system alone accounts for the oppression of women when their liberation in socialist societies, though more profound than under capitalism, is still incomplete.[11] Although capitalism certainly exaggerates the economic and cultural functions of sexism because it thrives on an inexhaustible supply of cheap labor, consumer ideology, passivity, and the displacement of aggression within the confines of the family, there is little doubt that sexism is a force to be reckoned with in any society as it has been throughout history.

Juliet Mitchell's article in this chapter attempts to go beyond an analysis of sexism as simply a by-product of *capitalist* development, while also rejecting the view that biopsychic factors account for the historical subjugation of women. Moreover, Mitchell attempts to come to grips with the structural preconditions for women's liberation. Her work makes it clear that

[9] One possible consequence of devoting one's life to fulfilling a social role that no longer has meaning is poignantly described by Pauline Bart, "Mother Portnoy's Complaints," *Trans action,* vol. 8 (November–December 1970), pp. 69–80.

[10] Marijean Suelzle, "Women in Labor," *Trans action,* vol. 8 (November–December 1970), pp. 52–53. For statistics indicating the increase in women college graduates from 1900 to 1970 see *The American Almanac: The U.S. Book of Facts, Statistics, and Information for 1971* (New York: Grosset & Dunlap, Inc., 1971), p. 125.

[11] Janet Weitzner Salaff and Judith Merkle, "Women in Revolution: The Lessons of the Soviet Union and China," *Berkeley Journal of Sociology,* vol. 15 (1970), pp. 166–191. Nancy Milton, "Correspondence: Women and Revolution," *Socialist Revolution,* vol. 1 (November–December 1970), pp. 135–151, challenges Salaff and Merkle's interpretation of the role of women in contemporary China.

capitalism is likely to be a serious obstacle to social change, but even socialism—if it simply substitutes one economic system for another—will provide only partial liberation from debilitating sex roles.

While doing an admirable job of articulating the complexity of women's historical status, Mitchell seems to neglect the problem of male resistance to the restructuring of sex roles and the family. Nor does she consider in full the obstacles to feminist solidarity resulting from some of the peculiar features of sexual status. Yet both these matters, in addition to cultural and economic development, technology, and the pressures of the capitalist class and other institutional elites, have to be examined if one is to realistically assess the possibilities of eliminating sexism.

While the sources of male resistance to women's liberation are still obscure,[12] the problems of developing a feminist consciousness have been briefly explored. Alice Rossi and Aileen Kraditor mention several aspects of sex status that make analogies between women and other oppressed groups questionable in terms of whether collective action can be developed around sex role issues.[13] Unlike the poor and ethnic, racial, and religious groups, women are not segregated residentially or by class. The fact that they are likely to have their most intimate contact with men rather than each other is also a major obstacle to what might be called "sex consciousness."[14] It is hard to fight against those one loves. Rossi and Kraditor suggest that women are not only segregated by class among other statuses but are also socialized to live through others' achievements and to identify with their husbands' social class and status. The feminist movement has historically been dominated by middle-class women whose aims have generally not challenged middle-class values in regard to property, the family, and sexuality. Working-class women have been too caught up in economic insecurity to view their problems in sexual terms. Given these obstacles to feminist solidarity, it is not surprising that Mitchell refers to women's liberation as the "longest revolution."

[12] Kate Millet, *Sexual Politics* (New York: Doubleday & Company, Inc., 1970), pp. 23–58, attempts to examine the roots of patriarchy. Frederich Engels, *The Origins of Family, Private Property, and the State* (New York: International Publishers Co., Inc., 1942), also considers the origins of male domination, but the anthropological evidence he relies upon is no longer considered valid. See also H. R. Hays, *The Dangerous Sex: The Myth of Feminine Evil* (New York: Pocket Books, 1965).

[13] Alice Rossi, "Sex Equality: The Beginnings of Ideology", *The Humanist*, vol. 29 (September–October 1969), pp. 3–6, 16. Kraditor, *op. cit.*, pp. 3–24.

[14] Not only sex consciousness but collective consciousness in general is inhibited by the institution of the family which fosters atomization and competition between family units. In this sense the family, and even the "romantic love complex," functions as a safety valve for discontent experienced in other institutional spheres and isolates people from larger collectivities such as that of social class. While it would be perhaps impossible and probably undesirable to fight against romantic love, a socialist society might be able at least to encourage alternatives to the contemporary family.

Sexism and Society

Marlene Dixon

WHY WOMEN'S LIBERATION—2?

Rise of Women's Liberation

The old women's movement burned itself out in the frantic decade of the 1920s. After a hundred years of struggle, women won a battle, only to lose the campaign: the vote was obtained, but the new millennium did not arrive. Women got the vote and achieved a measure of legal emancipation, but the real social and cultural barriers to full equality for women remained untouched.

For over thirty years the movement remained buried in its own ashes. Women were born and grew to maturity virtually ignorant of their own history of rebellion, aware only of a caricature of blue stockings and suffragettes. Even as increasing numbers of women were being driven into the labor force by the brutal conditions of the 1930s and by the massive drain of men into the military in the 1940s, the old ideal remained: a woman's place was in the home and behind her man. As the war ended and men returned to resume their jobs in factories and offices, women were forced back to the kitchen and nursery with a vengeance. This story has been repeated after each war and the reason is clear: women form a flexible, cheap labor pool that is essential to a capitalist system. When labor is scarce, they are forced onto the labor market. When labor is plentiful, they are forced out. Women and blacks have provided a reserve army of unemployed workers, benefiting capitalists and the stable male white working class alike. Yet the system imposes untold suffering on the victims—blacks and women—through low wages and chronic unemployment.

With the end of the war, the average age at marriage declined; the average size of families went up; and the suburban migration began in earnest. The political conservatism of the fifties was echoed in a social conservatism that stressed a Victorian ideal of the woman's life: a full womb and selfless devotion to husband and children.

As the bleak decade played itself out, however, three important social developments emerged that were to make a rebirth of the women's struggle inevitable. First, women came to make up more than a third of the labor force, the number of working women being twice the prewar figure. Yet the marked increase in female employment did nothing to better the position of women, who were more occupationally disadvantaged in the 1960s than they had been twenty-five years earlier. Rather than moving equally into all

Reprinted from *Female Liberation*, edited by Roberta Salper, by permission of Alfred A. Knopf, Inc. Copyright © 1972 by Marlene Dixon. Marlene Dixon teaches sociology at McGill University, Montreal, and has written several articles on the status of women and the women's liberation movement.

sectors of the occupational structure, they were being forced into the low-paying service, clerical and semi-skilled categories. In 1940, women had held 45 percent of all professional and technical positions; in 1967, they held only 37 percent. The proportion of women in service jobs meanwhile rose from 50 to 55 percent.

Second, the intoxicating wine of marriage and suburban life was turning sour; a generation of women woke up to find their children grown and a life (roughly thirty more productive years) of housework and bridge parties stretching out before them like a wasteland. For many younger women, the empty drudgery they saw in the suburban life was a sobering contradiction to adolescent dreams of romantic love and the fulfilling role of woman as wife and mother.

Third, a growing civil rights movement was sweeping thousands of young men and women into a moral crusade—a crusade that harsh political experience was to transmute into the New Left. The American Dream was riven and tattered in Mississippi and finally napalmed in Vietnam. Young Americans were drawn not to Levittown, but to Berkeley, Haight-Ashbury, and the East Village. Traditional political ideologies and cultural myths, sexual mores and sex roles with them, began to disintegrate in an explosion of rebellion and protest.

The three major groups that make up the new women's movement—working women, middle-class married women, and students—bring very different kinds of interests and objectives to women's liberation. Working women are most concerned with the economic issues of guaranteed employment, fair wages, job discrimination, and child care. Their most immediate oppression is rooted in industrial capitalism and felt directly through the vicissitudes of an exploitative labor market.

Middle-class women, oppressed by the psychological mutilation and injustice of institutionalized segregation, discrimination, and imposed inferiority, are most sensitive to the dehumanizing consequences of severely limited lives. Usually well educated and capable, these women are rebelling against being forced to trivialize their lives, to live vicariously through husbands and children.

Students, as unmarried, middle-class girls, have been most sensitized to the sexual exploitation of women. They have experienced the frustration of one-way relationships in which the girl is forced into a "wife" and companion role with none of the supposed benefits of marriage. Young women have increasingly rebelled not only against passivity and dependency in their relationships, but also against the notion that they must function as sexual objects, being defined in purely sexual rather than human terms, and being forced to package and sell themselves as commodities on the sex market.

Each group represents an independent aspect of the total institutionalized oppression of women. Yet, in varying degrees all women suffer from economic exploitation, from psychological deprivation, and from exploitive sexuality. Within women's liberation there is a growing understanding that the common oppression of women provides the basis for uniting to form a powerful and radical movement.

Racism and Male Supremacy

Clearly, for the liberation of women to become a reality, it is necessary to destroy the ideology of male supremacy that asserts the biological and social inferiority of women in order to justify massive institutionalized oppression.

The ideology of male chauvinism can only be understood when it is perceived as a form of racism, based on stereotypes drawn from a deep belief in the biological inferiority of women. The very stereotypes that express the society's belief in the biological inferiority of women are images used to justify oppression. The nature of women is depicted as dependent, incapable of reasoned thought, childlike in its simplicity and warmth, martyred in the role of mother, and mystical in the role of sexual partner.

It has taken over fifty years to discredit the scientific and social "proof" that once gave legitimacy to the myths of black racial inferiority. Today most people can see that the theory of the genetic inferiority of blacks is absurd. Yet few are shocked by the fact that scientists are still busy "proving" the biological inferiority of women.

Yet one of the obstacles to organizing women remains women's belief in their own inferiority. This dilemma is not a fortuitous one, for the entire society is geared to socialize women to believe in and adopt as immutable necessity their traditional and inferior role. From earliest training to the grave, women are constrained and propagandized. Spend an evening at the movies or watching television and you will see a grotesque figure called woman presented in a hundred variations upon the themes of "children, church, kitchen" or "the chick sex-pot." Such contradictions as these show how pervasive and deep-rooted is the cultural contempt for women, how difficult it is to imagine a woman as a serious human being, or conversely, how empty and degrading is the image of woman that floods the culture.

Countless studies have shown that black acceptance of white stereotypes leads to mutilated identity, to alienation, to rage and self-hatred. Human beings cannot bear in their own hearts the contradictions of those who hold them in contempt. The ideology of male supremacy creates self-contempt and psychic mutilation in women; it creates trained incapacities that put women at a disadvantage in all social relationships.

It is customary to shame those who would draw the parallel between women and blacks by a great show of concern over the suffering of black people. Yet this response itself reveals a refined combination of white middle-class guilt and male chauvinism, for it overlooks several essential facts. For example, the most oppressed group within the feminine population is made up of black women, many of whom take a dim view of the black male intellectual's adoption of white male attitudes of sexual superiority. Neither are those who make this pious objection to the racial parallel addressing themselves very adequately to the millions of white working-class women living at the poverty level, who are not likely to be moved by this middle-class, guilt-ridden oneupmanship while having to deal with the boss, the factory, or the welfare worker day after day. They are already dangerously resentful of the gains made by blacks, and much of their "racist blacklash" stems from the fact that they have been forgotten in the push for social change. Emphasis on the real mechanisms of oppression—on the commonality of the process—is essential lest groups such as these, which should work in alliance, become divided against one another.

White middle-class males already struggling with the acknowledgment of their own racism do not relish an added burden of recognition: that to white guilt must soon be added "male." It is therefore understandable that they should refuse to see the harshness of the lives of most women—to face honestly the facts of massive institutionalized discrimination against women.

We must never forget that the root of the ideology of male superiority, female inferiority, and white racism is a system of white male supremacy. White male supremacy is part of the ideology of imperialism, first European, then American. The European powers stripped India, China, Africa, and the New World of their wealth in raw materials—in gold, slaves, in cheap labor. Such brutal forms of exploitation required justification, and that justification was found in the doctrines of white racial superiority and the supremacy of European and American "civilization" over the "heathen" civilizations of Africa, Asia, and Latin America. Even more, we must never forget that the doctrine of white supremacy included the *supremacy of white women* as well as of white men.

The rise of capitalism in the West was based upon the wealth looted from other civilizations at the point of a gun: imperialism was the root and branch of racism and genocide then as it is now. It is at the root of mass prostitution in Saigon, of the torture and murder of innocent Vietnamese and Indochinese women and children, of all the sufferings of war inflicted upon the innocent at home and in Indochina. White American women must understand their oppression in its true context, and that context *is* a brutal, antihuman system of total exploitation having its corporate headquarters in New York and its political headquarters in Washington, D.C. And white women must understand that they are part of the system, benefiting from the loot secured through genocide.

This is why we must clearly understand that male chauvinism and racism *are not the same thing*. They are alike in that they oppress people and justify systems of exploitation, but in no way does a white woman suffer the exploitation and brutalization of women who are marked by both stigmata: being female *and* nonwhite. It is only the racism of privileged white women, self-serving in their petty, personal interests, who can claim that they must serve their own interests first, that they suffer *as much* as black women or Indochinese women or any women who experience the cruelty of white racism or the ruthless genocide of American militarism.

The contradiction of racism distorts and contaminates every sector of American life, creeps into every white insurgent movement. Understanding their own oppression can and must help white women to confront and to repudiate their own racism, for otherwise there will be no freedom, there will be no liberation.

Marriage: Genesis of Women's Rebellion

The institution of marriage is the chief vehicle for the perpetuation of the oppression of women: it is through the role of wife that the subjugation of women is maintained. In a very real way the role of wife has been the genesis of women's rebellion throughout history.

Looking at marriage from a detached point of view, one may well ask why anyone gets married, much less women. One answer lies in the economics of women's position, for women are so occupationally limited that drudgery in the home is considered to be infinitely superior to drudgery in the factory. Secondly, women themselves have no independent social status. Indeed, there is no clearer index of the social worth of a woman in this society than the fact that she has none in her own right. A woman is first defined by the man to whom she is attached, but more particularly by the man she marries, and secondly by the children she bears and rears—hence the anxiety over sexual attractiveness, the frantic scramble for boyfriends and husbands. Having obtained and married a man, the race is then on to have children, in order that their attractiveness and accomplishments may add more social worth. In a woman, not having children is seen as an incapacity somewhat akin to impotence in a man.

Beneath all of the pressures of the sexual marketplace and the marital status game, however, there is a far more sinister organization of economic exploitation and psychological mutilation. The housewife role, usually defined in terms of the biological duty of a woman to reproduce and her "innate" suitability for a nurturant and companionship role, is actually crucial to industrial capitalism in an advanced state of technological development. In fact, the housewife (some 44 million women of all classes, ethnic groups, and races) provides, unpaid, absolutely essential services and labor. In turn, her assumption of all household duties makes it possible for the man to spend the majority of his time at his work place.

It is important to understand the social and economic exploitation of the married woman, since the real productivity of her labor is denied by the commonly held assumption that she is dependent on her husband, exchanging her keep for emotional and nurturant services. Household labor, including child care, constitutes a huge amount of socially necessary labor. Nevertheless, in a society based on commodity production, it is not usually considered even as "real work" since it is outside of trade and the marketplace. In a society in which money determines value, women are a group who work outside the money economy. Their work is not worth money, is therefore valueless, is therefore not even real work. And women themselves, who do this valueless work, can hardly be expected to be worth as much as men, who work for money.

Women are essential to the economy not only as free labor, but also as consumers. The American system of capitalism depends for its survival on the consumption of vast amounts of socially wasteful goods, and a prime target for the unloading of this waste is the housewife. She is the purchasing agent for the family, but beyond that she is eager to buy because her own identity depends on her accomplishments as a consumer and her ability to satisfy the wants of her husband and children. This is not, of course, to say that she has any power in the economy. Although she spends the wealth, she does not own or control it—it simply passes through her hands.

In addition to their role as housewives and consumers, increasing numbers of women are taking outside employment. These women leave the home to join an exploited labor force, only to return at night to assume the double burden of housework on top of wage work—that is, they are forced to work at two full-time jobs. No man is required or expected to take on such a burden. The result: two workers from one household in the labor force with no cutback in essential female functions—three for the price of two, quite a bargain. Regardless of her status in the larger society, within the context of the family, the woman's relationship to the man is one of proletariat to bourgeoisie. One consequence of this class division in the family is to weaken the capacity of oppressed men and women to struggle together against it.

For third-world people within the United States, the oppressive nature of marriage is reflected negatively—for example, motherhood out of wedlock is punished, either through discriminatory welfare legislation or through thinly disguised and genocidal programs of enforced sterilization. This society punishes unmarried women even more than it punishes married women. As a result, many third-world and poor white women want help with their families and need a husband in the home. The destruction of families among poor people, as a result of economic exploitation and social oppression, results in the deprivation of every facet of life for poor women and children. White middle-class women, bound up with the psychological oppression of marriage, have often been blind to the extent of suffering—and the extent of the needs—that the deliberate destruction of the families of the poor has created. Unemployment and pauperization through welfare programs creates very different problems than does the experience of boredom in the suburbs.

In all classes and groups, the institution of marriage nonetheless functions to a greater or lesser degree to oppress women; the unity of women of different classes hinges upon our understanding of that common oppression. The nineteenth-century women's movement refused to deal with marriage and sexuality and chose instead to fight for the vote and to elevate the feminine mystique to a political ideology. That decision retarded the movement for decades. But 1969 is not 1889. For one thing, there now exist alternatives to marriage. The cultural revolution—experimentation with life-styles, communal living, collective child rearing—have all come from the rebellion against dehumanized sexual relationships, against the notion of women as sexual commodities, against the hardship, alienation, and loneliness of American life.

Lessons must be learned from the failures of the earlier movement. The feminine mystique must not be mistaken for politics or legislative reform for winning human rights. Women are now at the bottom of their respective worlds and the basis exists for a common focus of struggle for women in American society. It remains for the movement to understand this, to avoid the mistakes of the past, to respond creatively to the possibilities of the present.

Economic Exploitation

Women's oppression, although rooted in the institution of marriage, does not stop at the kitchen or the bedroom door. Indeed, the economic exploitation of women in the work place is the most commonly recognized aspect of the oppression of women.

The rise of new agitation for the occupational equality of women also coincided with the reentry of the "lost generation"—the housewives of the 1950s—into the job market. Women from middle-class backgrounds, faced with an "empty nest" (children grown or in school) and a widowed or divorced rate of one-fourth to one-third of all marriages, returned to the work place in large numbers. But once there, they discovered that women, middle class or otherwise, are the last hired, the lowest paid, the least often promoted, and the first fired. Furthermore, women are more likely to suffer job discrimination on the basis of age, so the widowed and divorced suffer particularly, even though their economic need to work is often urgent. Age discrimination also means that the option of work after child rearing is limited. Even highly qualified older women find themselves forced into low-paid, unskilled, or semiskilled work—if they are lucky enough to find a job in the first place.

Most women who enter the labor force do not work for "pin money" or "self-fulfillment." Sixty-two percent of all women working in 1967 were doing so out of economic need (that is, were either alone or with husbands earning less than $5,000 a year). In 1968, 38 percent of American families had an income of less than $5,000 a year. Women from these families work because they must; they contribute 35 to 40 percent of the family's total income when working full time and 15 to 20 percent when working part time.

Despite their need, however, women have always represented the most exploited sector of the industrial labor force. Child and female labor were introduced during the early stages of industrial capitalism, at a time when most men were gainfully employed in crafts. As industrialization developed and craft jobs were eliminated, men entered the industrial labor force, driving women and children into the lowest categories of work and pay. Indeed, the position of women and children industrial workers was so pitiful and their wages were so small that the craft unions refused to organize them. Even when women organized themselves and engaged in militant strikes and labor agitation—from the shoemakers of Lynn, Massachusetts, to the International Ladies' Garment Workers and their great strike of 1909—male unionists continued to ignore their needs. As a result of this male supremacy in the unions, women remain essentially unorganized, despite the fact that they are becoming an ever larger part of the labor force.

The trend is clearly toward increasing numbers of women entering the work force: women represented 55 percent of the growth of the total labor force in 1962, and the number of working women rose from 16.9 million in

1957 to 24 million in 1962. There is every indication that the number of women in the labor force will continue to grow as rapidly in the future.

Job discrimination against women exists in all sectors of work, even in occupations that are predominantly made up of women. This discrimination is reinforced in the field of education, where women are being short-changed at a time when the job market demands higher educational levels. In 1962, for example, while women constituted 53 percent of the graduating high school class, only 42 percent of the entering college class were women. Only one in three people who received a B.A. and M.A. in that year was a woman, and only one in ten who received a Ph.D. was a woman. These figures represent a decline in educational achievement for women since the 1930s, when women received two out of five of the B.A. and M.A. degrees given, and one out of seven of the Ph.Ds. While there has been a dramatic increase in the number of people, including women, who go to college, women have not kept pace with men in terms of educational achievement. Furthermore, women have lost ground in professional employment. In 1960 only 22 percent of the faculty and other professional staff at colleges and universities were women —down from 28 percent in 1949, 27 percent in 1930, 26 percent in 1920. 1960 does beat the 20 percent of 1919: "you've come a long way, baby"— right back to where you started! In other professional categories, 10 percent of all scientists are women, 7 percent of all physicians, 3 percent of all lawyers, and 1 percent of all engineers.

Even when women do obtain an education, in many cases it does them little good. Women, whatever their educational levels, are concentrated in the lower-paying occupations. The figures tell a story that most women know and few men will admit: most women are forced to work at clerical jobs, for which they are paid, on the average, $1,600 less per year than men doing the same work. Working-class women in the service and operative (semiskilled) categories, making up 30 percent of working women, are paid $1,900 less per year on the average than are men. Of all working women, only 13 percent are professionals (including low-pay and low-status work such as teaching, nursing, and social work), and they earn $2,600 less per year than do professional men. Household workers, the lowest category of all, are predominantly women (over 2 million) and predominantly black and third world, earning for their labor barely over $1,000 per year.

Not only are women forced onto the lowest rungs of the occupational ladder, they are in the lowest income levels as well. The most constant and bitter injustice experienced by all women is the income differential. While women might passively accept low-status jobs, limited opportunities for advancement, and discrimination in the factory, office, and university, they choke finally on the daily fact that the male worker next to them earns more and usually does less. In 1965, the median wage or salary income of year-round, full-time women workers was only 60 percent that of men, a 4 percent loss since 1955. Twenty-nine percent of working women earned less than $3,000 a year as compared with 11 percent of the men; 43 percent of the women earned from $3,000 to $5,000 a year as compared with 19 percent of the men; and 9 percent of the women earned $7,000 or more as compared with 43 percent of the men.

Sexism and Society

What most people do not know is that in certain respects all women suffer more than do nonwhite men and that black and third-world women suffer most of all.

Women, regardless of race, are more disadvantaged than are men, including nonwhite men. White women earn $2,600 less than white men and $1,500 less than nonwhite men. The brunt of the inequality is carried by 2.5 million nonwhite women, 94 percent of whom are black. They earn $3,800 less than white men, $1,900 less than nonwhite men, and $1,200 less than white women.

There is no more bitter paradox in the racism of this country than that the white man, articulating the male supremacy of the white male middle class, should provide the rationale for the oppression of black women by black men. Black women constitute the largest minority in the United States, and they are the most disadvantaged group in the labor force. The further oppression of black women will not liberate black men, for black women were never the oppressors of their men—that is a myth of the liberal white man. The oppression of black men comes from institutionalized racism and economic exploitation, from the world of the white man.

Consider the following facts and figures. The percentage of black working women has always been proportionately greater than that of white women. In 1900, 41 percent of black women were employed, as compared to 17 percent for white women. In 1963, the proportion of black women employed was still a fourth greater than that of whites. In 1960, 44 percent of black married women with children under six years were in the labor force, in contrast to 29 percent for white women. While job competition requires ever higher levels of education, the bulk of illiterate women are black. On the whole, black women—who often have the greatest need for employment—are the most discriminated against in terms of opportunity. Forced by an oppressive and racist society to carry unbelievably heavy economic and social burdens, black women stand at the bottom of that society, doubly marked by the caste signs of color and sex.

Faced with discrimination on the job—after being forced into the lower levels of the occupational structure—millions of women are inescapably presented with the fundamental contradictions in their unequal treatment and their massive exploitation. The rapid growth of women's liberation as a movement is related in part to the exploitation of working women in all occupational categories.

Conclusion

Male supremacy, marriage, and the structure of wage labor—each of these aspects of women's oppression and exploitation has been crucial to the resurgence of the women's struggle. It must be abundantly clear that revolutionary social change must occur before there can be significant improvement in the social position of *all* women.

The heart of the movement, as in all freedom movements, rests in women's knowledge, whether articulated or still only an illness without a name, that they are not inferior—not chicks or bunnies or quail or cows or bitches or ass or meat. Women hear the litany of their own dehumanization each day. Yet all the same, women know that they are not animals or sexual objects or commodities. They know their lives are mutilated, because they see within themselves a promise of creativity and personal integration. Feeling the contradiction between the essentially creative and self-actualizing human being within her and the cruel and degrading less-than-human role she is compelled to play, a woman begins to experience the internal violence that liberates the human spirit, to experience the justice of her own rebellion. This is the rage that impels women into a total commitment to women's liberation, a ferocity that stems from a denial of mutilation. It is a cry for life, a cry for the liberation of the spirit.

Yet, we must never forget that we women are not unique in our oppression, in our exploitation. Understanding ourselves should help us understand all others like us and not divide us from them. We must also remember that in one way white American women are unique, for they suffer least of all: their experience cannot approach the abysmal suffering of the third-world women or of third-world men, subject to American racism and imperialism. How does one understand rape; forced prostitution; torture; and mutilation; twisted, crippled children; deformed babies; a homeland laid waste; memories of perpetual war; perpetual oppression? It is not a question of guilt; it is a question of revolutionary struggle.

Epilogue: 1969-1971

Nineteen sixty-nine was a year of explosive growth and measureless optimism for women's liberation. It was the year of sisterhood: "sisterhood is powerful!" "sisterhood is beautiful!" "sisterhood is unity!" The turning point for the women's struggle was 1969, the year in which the movement came up from underground by gaining recognition and legitimacy—recognition from the male-dominated white left and legitimacy as a protest "issue" in the larger society. The slogans of sisterhood reflected a joyful optimism, an overwhelming intuitive belief that *all* women could identify with each other, all women could struggle together—even lead—a vast movement of social transformation.

By 1971, the joyful optimism was increasingly being replaced by a sense of dismay and conflict in many women: "women's liberation is a nonstruggle movement"; "women's liberation is a racist movement"; "women's liberation is an apolitical movement"; "women's liberation is a class chauvinist movement"; "women's liberation is a liberal, middle-class movement." What did all of this mean? What had happened to the women's movement?

The United States of America had "happened" to women's liberation: all of the contradictions of a society torn by class and racial conflict, all of the contradictions of a society that is in fact based upon militarized state capitalism and institutionalized racism and class exploitation began to tear the women's movement apart. The apolitical simplicity of "sisterhood is unity" and "understand your own psychological oppression" was powerless to contend with or understand the internal, disruptive forces of the most exploitative, brutal, and complex oppressor nation in the history of Western imperialism—the United States of America.

The women's movement is no longer a struggling, tender shoot; it has become a mass movement; and women remain, often despite the movement, potentially a powerful, radical force. In the beginning, women were attacked from every quarter, most destructively from the left, for left politics became identified with male chauvinism. Originally, the attack from the left was corrupt, a ploy by radical men to keep women down. Now, however, the criticism does not come from the men, but from women within women's liberation. A movement that cannot learn from its past, that is too insecure and fearful to engage in self-criticism, that is too self-interested to be able to change its direction, too blind to see that all women are *not* sisters—that class exploitation and racism are fundamental to American society and exist *within* the women's movement—becomes a trap, not a means to liberation. In the brief critique that follows, I am correcting some of my own mistakes, for I too believed in sisterhood, I too believed that "common oppression provides the basis for uniting across class and race lines." In that belief I was wrong: this is what I have learned from the past year of the movement. There are many women and many groups within the women's struggle to which the following criticism does not apply, but there are still more who were, and still are, wrong.

Class Conflict

The mysticism of *sisterhood* disguised the reality that most women in women's liberation were white, young, and middle class, so that under all the radical rhetoric the movement's goals were reformist and its ideology was almost exclusively of middle-class female psychological oppression. The women's movement did not talk about *exploitation*, but about *oppression*—always in subjective terms. The women's movement did not talk about class struggle, nationalization of medicine, abolition of welfare, or the ultimate destruction of American imperialism. The needs of poor women, of working women, of black women were nowhere central to the demands or the rhetoric of women's liberation. The middle-class, reformist nature of the movement was not clearly and objectively revealed until the struggle over the equal rights amendment—an amendment that would have made *discrimination* unconstitutional but would not have included a single reference to exploitation, an amendment that would have benefited professional women at the expense of working-class women.

Fighting against *discrimination* is a middle-class, reformist goal—it says: let us *in* so that the privileges of our middle-class men can be extended to us middle-class women. Fighting against *exploitation* is revolutionary. To end exploitation, it is necessary to end "militarized state capitalism." To end class exploitation, it is necessary to abolish classes. To end racism, it is necessary to abolish white male supremacy, to abolish imperialism. White middle-class America, male and female, enjoys an affluence that is looted from half the world, that is stolen by means of poor white and black soldiers, that is turned into new cars and washing machines by workers, black and white, male and female. White middle-class America, *male and female*, enjoys incomes protected from inflation by means of the deliberate unemployment of workers, black and white, male and female, who suffer enforced pauperization so that the young girls of the middle class can go to the university and struggle for a women's center to give them a better education, the better to enjoy their class privileges, the better to explore the meaning of life and the adventures of a new, untrammeled sexuality. Genocide is committed against the people of Vietnam; war spreads to all the people of Indochina. So who cares? It's only a "penis war." It is of no concern to the young women of the middle class, who will never be soldiers, never be workers, never be on welfare, never suffer racism. The problem is *discrimination*. Women can only earn $10,000 a year teaching college while men earn $15,000 a year—that is the problem! "Sisterhood is unity! Don't criticize the movement! Don't make us feel guilty! Don't show us the blood on *our* hands— after all, we are oppressed too!"

Racism

The "black analogy" was originally used in women liberation to help women through their understanding of their own oppression, to understand the oppression of others. By 1971 the "black analogy" has become a tool of white racism. The cries "we are oppressed too" and even more terrible "we are equally oppressed" permitted white middle-class women to dismiss the black struggle, to dismiss their complicity in a racist system, to dismiss criticisms of the movement from black women as motivated by the influence "the male chauvinism of black men" has upon them—ultimately to complete the cycle of white middle-class racism by reducing black and third-world people within the United States to invisibility. White middle-class women, bloated with their own pious claims to oppression, blind within their own racism, refused to see that black women were trying to teach them something when they spoke at conferences, saying: "I am black and a woman, but am I first black or first a woman? First I am black." Or, "we fear the abortion program, it may be used against us." Or "we must destroy exploitation and racism *before* black women can be liberated—for what does it mean to us, black women, if you white women end discrimination? We are still black; we are still exploited; we are still destroyed and our children with us." All the white women could answer with was "black male chauvinism!" They remained completely blind to the fact that third-world people are a colony and a minority within the heart of the monster, that their survival depends upon a resolution to the contradiction of male chauvinism and male supremacy that *does not* divide black women and black men into antagonistic factions.

Female Chauvinism

The purest expression of self-serving middle-class ideology is reflected in the blind hatred of men that makes no distinction between the system of white male supremacy and male chauvinism. Only very privileged women can in the security of their class status and class earning power create a little "manless Utopia" for themselves. They need only withdraw from the psychological discomfort of male chauvinism to create a new and different life for themselves—they are not faced, as a class, with the necessity to struggle against another class; they are not driven by exploitation and repression to understand that male chauvinism is reactionary but that it can also be defeated, so that men and women can resolve the contradiction between them, emerge stronger, and unite in mutual opposition to their real enemies—the generals, the corporate bosses, the corrupt politicians.

Liberal Guilt

Liberal guilt is worthless. Appealing to women who are completely devoted to their own self-serving interests is equally useless. There is no mass movement in the United States that can avoid the contradictions of racism and class conflict, thus moralistic pleas are a waste of time. Nonetheless, women in the United States—and everywhere outside of the revolutionary world—are oppressed and exploited, suffer and die in silence. For the thousands and thousands of women who are poor, who are working class, who were born into the middle class but have turned away from it in disgust and revulsion, the women's movement, as a revolutionary struggle, remains their chief commitment and their only hope. Our challenge is to correct past mistakes, to learn what we must know to avoid future mistakes, to teach and to learn from each other. We must learn how to build, within the very heart of the monster, a revolutionary movement devoted to the liberation of all people in practice. Such a movement will not be self-serving, cannot be merely reformist. It must be political, must know history and economics, must understand that all revolutionary movements in the world today are interdependent. We can no longer be an island of affluence, blind to the lesson that what happens to women in Vietnam happens to us, that what happens to a black woman happens to us. The United States is not an empire that will stand for a thousand years, but is an oppressive monster that the peoples of the world will dismember and destroy before the world is all finished. We must choose which side we will be on—the path of revolution or the path of exploitation and genocide.

The women's movement is turning and twisting within its contradictions. Some women speed off into mysticism, claiming, but not explaining, how women by rejecting "male" politics and finding "female" politics effect world revolution—a world revolution in which the people's war in Vietnam plays no part, in which all previous world revolutions—Russian, Chinese, North Vietnamese, North Korean, Cuban—play no part. Still others seek escape in "sexual liberation," hoping to find, as does the youth movement, a personalized, individual salvation in a "life-style revolution" in which racism is dismissed as a problem of "black male chauvinism" and Vietnam is dismissed as a "penis war" of no concern to women. To be in the "vanguard," it is only necessary to love a woman sexually. Still others cling to the worn-out slogans of the early days, continuing with "consciousness raising" as weekly therapy and engaging in endless discussions of anti-elitism (an elite being anyone who does anything at all threatening to any woman in a small group) and "anti-elitist structure" in the organization of the women's center.

These tendencies reflect the other face of women's oppression, not anger or strength, but fearfulness, turning inward to avoid challenge, to avoid thinking, to avoid struggle, to avoid the large and frightening world of conflict and revolution, which cannot be contained within a small group or understood through the subjective oppression of a privileged woman. Women *are* mutilated, especially passive, nurturant middle-class women. They are made manipulative, dishonest, fearful, conservative, hypocritical, and self-serving. Celebrating women's weakness—elevating mutilation to a holy state of female grace—corrupts the movement into a reactionary and self-serving force.

Women are seen as absurd, and they blame the media. Women are criticized for being reactionary and racist. They howl "male defined," "male identified." Women are isolated from the liberation struggles of other people, and they scream that those movements are *male-dominated!* How many more excuses will be found until women have the strength to confront their mistakes and their failures? How many revolutions are we going to be called upon to make to assure rich and comforting interpersonal relationships and unhampered fucking for the people whose privilege is so great that they can afford to worry about their spirits instead of their bellies? How many more people are we going to help die in Indochina by howling that fighting against imperialism is "antiwoman" or a "penis war" or "dominated by men"? How long are we going to remain absurd because, in the eyes of the vast majority of peoples in the world, *we are absurd, self-seeking, blind,* and *ignorant!*

It is time, past time, to get our heads together, to listen to and learn from women who have made and are making revolutions, to study to fight, to fight to win, with strength and dignity and a proper respect for the suffering of others and a complete devotion to ending all oppression practiced against the majority of the peoples of the world, male and female, in the colonies of the monster and in the heart of the monster. Then, and only then, shall we know something of liberation.

Juliet Mitchell

WOMEN:
THE LONGEST REVOLUTION

Women in Socialist Theory

The problem of the subordination of women and the need for their liberation was recognized by all the great socialist thinkers in the 19th century. It is part of the classical heritage of the revolutionary movement. Yet today, in the West, the problem has become a subsidiary, if not an invisible element in the preoccupations of socialists. Perhaps no other major issue has been so forgotten. In England, the cultural heritage of Puritanism, always strong on the Left, contributed to a widespread diffusion of essentially conservative beliefs among many who would otherwise count themselves as "progressive." A *locus classicus* of these attitudes is Peter Townsend's remarkable statement:

> Traditionally Socialists have ignored the family or they have openly tried to weaken it—alleging nepotism and the restrictions placed upon individual fulfilment by family ties. Extreme attempts to create societies on a basis other than the family have failed dismally. It is significant that a Socialist usually addresses a colleague as "brother" and a Communist uses the term "comrade." The chief means of fulfilment in life is to be a member of, and reproduce a family. There is nothing to be gained by concealing this truth.

How has this counter-revolution come about? Why has the problem of woman's condition become an area of silence within contemporary socialism? August Bebel, whose book *Woman in the Past, Present and Future* was one of the standard texts of the German Social-Democratic Party in the early years of this century, wrote:

> Every Socialist recognizes the dependance of the workman on the capitalist, and cannot understand that others, and especially the capitalists themselves, should fail to recognize it also; but the same Socialist often does not recognize the dependance of women on men because the question touches his own dear self more or less nearly.

But this genre of explanation—psychologistic and moralistic—is clearly inadequate. Much deeper and more structural causes have clearly been at work. To consider these would require a major historical study, impossible here. But

Reprinted, with deletions, from Juliet Mitchell, "Women: The Longest Revolution," *New Left Review*, no. 40 (December 1966), pp. 11–37, by permission of *New Left Review*. Juliet Mitchell teaches English at the Universty of Reading, England. She is on the editorial board of the *New Left Review*, has been active in the British Women's Liberation Movement and is the author of *Woman's Estate*.

265

it can be said with some certainty that part of the explanation for the decline in socialist debate on the subject lies not only in the real historical processes, but in the original weaknesses in the traditional discussion of the subject in the classics. For while the great studies of the last century all stressed the importance of the problem, they did not *solve* it theoretically. The limitations of their approach have never been subsequently transcended.

Fourier was the most ardent and voluminous advocate of women's liberation and of sexual freedom among the early socialists. In a well-known passage he wrote:

> The change in a historical epoch can always be determined by the progress of women towards freedom, because in the relation of woman to man, of the weak to the strong, the victory of human nature over brutality is most evident. The degree of emancipation of women is the natural measure of general emancipation.

Marx quoted this formulation with approval in *The Holy Family*. But characteristically in his early writings he gave it a more universal and philosophical meaning. The emancipation of women would not only be as Fourier, with his greater preoccupation with sexual liberation saw it, an index of humanization in the civic sense of the victory of humaneness over brutality, but in the more fundamental sense of the progress of the human over the animal, the cultural over the natural:

> The relation of man to woman is the *most natural* relation of human being to human being. It indicates, therefore, how far man's *natural* behaviour has become human, and how far his *human* essence has become a *natural* essence for him, how far his *human nature* has become *nature* for him.

This theme is typical of the early Marx.

Fourier's ideas remained at the level of utopian moral injunction. Marx used and transformed them, integrating them into a philosophical critique of human history. But he retained the abstraction of Fourier's conception of the position of women as an index of general social advance. This in effect makes it merely a symbol—it accords the problem a universal importance at the cost of depriving it of its specific substance. Symbols are allusions to or derivations of something else. In Marx's early writings woman becomes an anthropological entity, an ontological category, of a highly abstract kind. Contrarily, in his later work, where he is concerned with describing the family, Marx differentiates it as a phenomenon according to time and place:

> . . . marriage, property, the family remain unattacked, in theory, because they are the practical basis on which the bourgeoisie has erected its domination, and because in their bourgeois form they are the conditions which make the bourgeois a bourgeois . . . This attitude of the bourgeois to the conditions of his existence acquires one of its universal forms in bourgeois morality. One cannot, in general, speak of the family "*as such.*" Historically, the bourgeois gives the family the character of the bourgeois family, in which boredom and money are the binding link, and which also includes the bourgeois dissolution of the family, which does not prevent the family

Sexism and Society

itself from always continuing to exist. Its dirty existence has its counterpart in the holy concept of it in official phraseology and universal hypocrisy. . . . (Among the proletariat) the concept of the family does not exist at all . . . In the 18th century the concept of the family was abolished by the philosophers, because the actual family was already in process of dissolution at the highest pinnacles of civilization. The internal family bond was dissolved, the separate components constituting the concept of the family were dissolved, for example, obedience, piety, fidelity in marriage, etc; but the real body of the family, the property relation, the exclusive attitude in relation to other families, forced cohabitation—relations produced by the existence of children, the structure of modern towns, the formation of capital, etc—all these were preserved, although with numerous violations because the existence of the family has been made necessary by its connection with the mode of production that exists independently of the will of bourgeois society.

Or, later still, in *Capital:*

It is, of course, just as absurd to hold the Teutonic-Christian form of the family to be absolute and final as it would be to apply that character to the ancient Roman, the ancient Greek, or the Eastern forms which, moreover, taken together form a series in historic development.

What is striking is that here the problem of women has been submerged in an anlysis of the family. The difficulties of this approach can be seen in the somewhat apocalyptic note of Marx's comments on the fate of the bourgeois family here and elsewhere (for example, in the *Communist Manifesto*). There was little historical warrant for the idea that it was in effective dissolution, and indeed could no longer be seen in the working-class. Marx thus moves from general philosophical formulations about women in the early writings to specific historical comments on the family in the later texts. There is a serious disjunction between the two. The common framework of both, of course, was his analysis of the economy, and of the evolution of property.

ENGELS

It was left to Engels to systematize these theses in *The Origin of the Family, Private Property and the State,* after Marx's death. Engels declared that the inequality of the sexes was one of the first antagonisms within the human species. The first class antagonism "coincides with the development of the antagonism between man and woman in the monogamous marriage, and the first class oppression with that of the female sex by the male." Basing much of his theory on Morgan's inaccurate anthropological investigations, Engels nevertheless had some valuable insights. Inheritance, which is the key to his economist account, was first matrilineal, but with the increase of wealth became patrilineal. This was woman's greatest single setback. The wife's fidelity becomes essential and monogamy is irrevocably established. The wife in the communistic, patriarchal family is a public servant, with monogamy she becomes a private one. Engels effectively reduces the problem of woman to her capacity to work. He therefore gave her physiological weakness as a primary cause of her oppression. He locates the moment of her exploitation at the point of the transition from communal to private property. If inability to work is the cause of her inferior status, ability to work will bring her liberation:

> ... the emancipation of women and their equality with men are impossible and must remain so as long as women are excluded from socially productive work and restricted to housework, which is private. The emancipation of women becomes possible only when women are enabled to take part in production on a large, social, scale, and when domestic duties require their attention only to a minor degree.

Or:

> The first premise for the emancipation of women is the reintroduction of the entire female sex into public industry . . . this . . . demands that the quality possessed by the individual family of being the economic unit of society be abolished.

Engels thus finds a solution schematically appropriate to his analysis of the origin of feminine oppression. The position of women, then, in the work of Marx and Engels remains dissociated from, or subsidiary to, a discussion of the family, which is in its turn subordinated as merely a precondition of private property. Their solutions retain this overly economist stress, or enter the realm of dislocated speculation.

Bebel, Engels' disciple, attempted to provide a programmatic account of woman's oppression as such, not simply as a by-product of the evolution of the family and of private property: "From the beginning of time oppression was the common lot of woman and the labourer. . . . *Woman was the first human being that tasted bondage,* woman was a slave *before the slave existed.*" He acknowledged, with Marx and Engels, the importance of physical inferiority in accounting for woman's subordination, but while stressing inheritance, added that a biological element—her maternal function—was one of the fundamental conditions that made her economically dependent on the man. But Bebel, too, was unable to do more than state that sexual equality was impossible without socialism. His vision of the future was a vague reverie, quite disconnected from his description of the past. The absence of a strategic concern forced him into voluntarist optimism divorced from reality. Lenin himself, although he made a number of specific suggestions, inherited a tradition of thought which simply pointed to the *a priori* equation of socialism with feminine liberation without showing concretely how it would transform woman's condition: "Unless women are brought to take an independent part not only in political life generally, but also in daily and universal public service, it is no use talking about full and stable democracy, let alone socialism."

The liberation of women remains a normative ideal, an adjunct to socialist theory, not structurally integrated into it.

THE SECOND SEX

The contrary is true of De Beauvoir's massive work *The Second Sex*—to this day the greatest single contribution on the subject. Here the focus is the status of women through the ages. But socialism as such emerges as a curiously contingent solution at the end of the work, in a muffled epilogue. De Beauvoir's main theoretical innovation was to fuse the "economic" and "reproductive" explanations of women's subordination by a psychological interpretation of both. Man asserts himself as subject and free being by opposing other consciousnesses. He is distinct from animals precisely in that he creates and invents (not in that he reproduces himself), but he tries to escape the burden of his freedom by giving himself a spurious "immortality" in his children. He dominates woman both to imprison another consciousness which reflects his own and to provide him with children that are securely his (his fear of illegitimacy). The notions obviously have a considerable force. But they are very atemporal: it is not easy to see why socialism should modify the basic "ontological" desire for a thing-like freedom which De Beauvoir sees as the motor behind the fixation with inheritance in the property system, or the enslavement of women which derived from it. In fact she has since criticized this aspect of her book for idealism:

> I should take a more materialist position today in the first volume. I should base the notion of woman as *other* and the Manichean argument it entails not on an idealistic and *a priori* struggle of consciences, but on the facts of supply and demand. This modification would not necessitate any changes in the subsequent development of my argument.

Concurrent, however, with the idealist psychological explanation, De Beauvoir uses an orthodox economist approach. This leads to a definite evolutionism in her treatment in Volume I, which becomes a retrospective narrative of the different forms of the feminine condition in different societies through time—mainly in terms of the property system and its effects on women. To this she adds various suprahistorical themes—myths of the eternal feminine, types of women through the ages, literary treatments of women—which do not modify the fundamental structure of her argument. The prospect for women's liberation at the end is quite divorced from any historical development.

Thus, the classical literature on the problem of woman's condition is predominantly economist in emphasis, stressing her simple subordination to the institutions of private property. Her biological status underpins both her weakness as a producer, in work relations, and her importance as a possession in reproductive relations. The fullest and most recent interpretation gives both factors a psychological cast. The framework of discussion is an evolutionist one which nevertheless fails noticeably to project a convincing image of the future, beyond asserting that socialism will involve the liberation of women as one of its constituent "moments."

What is the solution to this impasse? It must lie in differentiating woman's condition, much more radically than in the past, into its separate structures, which together form a complex—not a simple—unity. This will mean rejecting the idea that woman's condition can be deduced derivatively from the economy or equated symbolically with society. Rather, it must be seen as a *specific* structure, which is a unity of different elements. The variations of woman's condition throughout history will be the result of different combinations of these elements— much as Marx's analysis of the economy in *Precapitalist Economic Formations* is an account of the different combinations of the factors of production, not a linear narrative of economic development. Because the unity of woman's condition at any one time is the product of several structures, it is always "overdetermined." The key structures can be listed as follows: Production, Reproduction, Sex and Socialization of children. The concrete combination of these produces the "complex unity" of her position; but each separate structure may have reached a different "moment" at any given historical time. Each then must be examined separately in order to see what the present unity is and how it might be changed. The discussion that follows does not pretend to give a historical account of each sector. It is only concerned with some general reflections on the different roles of women and some of their interconnections.

Production

The biological differentiation of the sexes and the division of labour have, throughout history, seemed an interlocked necessity. Anatomically smaller and weaker, woman's physiology and her psycho-biological metabolism appear to render her a less useful member of a work-force. It is always stressed how, particularly in the early stages of social development, man's physical superiority gave him the means of conquest over nature which was denied to women. Once woman was accorded the menial tasks involved in maintenance whilst man undertook conquest and creation, she became an aspect of the things preserved: private property and children. All socialist writers on the subject mentioned earlier—Marx, Engels, Bebel, De Beauvoir —link the confirmation and continuation of woman's oppression after the establishment of her physical inferiority for hard manual work with the advent of private property. But woman's physical weakness has never prevented her from performing work as such (quite apart from bringing up children) —only specific types of work, in specific societies. In Primitive, Ancient, Oriental, Medieval and Capitalist societies, the *volume* of work performed by women has always been considerable (it has usually been much more than this). It is only its form that is in question. Domestic labour, even today, is enormous if quantified in terms of productive labour.[1] In any case women's physique has never permanently or even predominantly relegated them to

[1] Apologists who make out that housework, though time-consuming, is light and relatively enjoyable, are refusing to acknowledge the dull and degrading routine it entails. . . . Today it has been calculated in Sweden, that 2,340 million hours a year are spent by women in housework compared with 1,290 million hours in industry. The Chase Manhattan Bank estimated a woman's overall working hours as averaging 99.6 per week.

menial domestic chores. In many peasant societies, women have worked in the fields as much as, or more than men.

PHYSIQUE AND COERCION

The assumption behind most classical discussion is that the crucial factor starting the whole development of feminine subordination was women's lesser capacity for demanding physical work. But, in fact, this is a major oversimplification. Even within these terms, in history it has been woman's lesser capacity for violence as well as for work that has determined her subordination. In most societies woman has not only been less able than man to perform arduous kinds of work, she has also been less able to fight. Man not only has the strength to assert himself against nature, but also against his fellows. *Social coercion* has interplayed with the straightforward division of labour, based on biological capacity, to a much greater extent than generally admitted. Of course, it may not be actualized as direct aggression. In primitive societies women's physical unsuitability for the hunt is evident. In agricultural societies where women's inferiority is socially instituted they are given the arduous task of tilling and cultivation. For this coercion is necessary. In developed civilizations and more complex societies woman's physical deficiencies again become relevant. Women are no use either for war or in the construction of cities. But with early industrialization coercion once more becomes important. As Marx wrote:

> Insofar as machinery dispenses with muscular power, it becomes a means of employing labourers of slight muscular strength, and those whose bodily development is incomplete, but whose limbs are all the more supple. The labour of women and children was, therefore, the first thing sought for by capitalists who used machinery.

René Dumont points out that in many zones of tropical Africa today men are often idle, while women are forced to work all day. This exploitation has no "natural" source whatever. Women may perform their "heavy" duties in contemporary African peasant societies not for fear of physical reprisal by their men, but because these duties are "customary" and built into the role structures of the society. A further point is that coercion implies a different relationship from coercer to coerced than exploitation does. It is political rather than economic. In describing coercion, Marx said that the master treated the slave or serf as the "inorganic and natural condition of its own reproduction." That is to say, labour itself becomes like other natural things— cattle or soil: "The original conditions of production appear as natural prerequisites, *natural conditions of the existence of the producer*, just as his living body, however reproduced and developed by him, is not originally established by himself, but appears as his *prerequisite*." This is preeminently woman's condition. For far from woman's physical weakness removing her from productive work, her social weakness has in these cases evidently made her the major slave of it.

This truth, elementary though it may seem, has nevertheless been constantly ignored by writers on the subject, with the result that an illegitimate optimism creeps into their predictions of the future. For if it is just the bio-logical incapacity for the hardest physical work which has determined the subordination of women, then the prospect of an advanced machine tech-nology, abolishing the need for strenuous physical exertion would seem to promise, therefore, the liberation of women. For a moment industrialization itself thus seems to herald women's liberation. Engels, for instance, wrote:

> The first premise for the emancipation of women is the reintroduction of the entire female sex into public industry . . . And this has become pos-sible only as a result of modern large-scale industry, which not only per-mits of the participation of women in production in large numbers, but actually calls for it and, moreover, strives to convert private domestic work also into a public industry.

What Marx said of early industrialism is no less, but also *no more* true of an automated society:

> . . . it is obvious that the fact of the collective working group being com-posed of individuals of both sexes and all ages, must necessarily, *under suitable conditions,* become a source of human development; although in its spontaneously developed, brutal, capitalistic form, where the labourer exists for the process of production, and not the process of production for the labourer, that fact is a pestiferous source of corruption and slavery.

Industrial labour and automated technology both promise the preconditions for woman's liberation alongside man's—but no more than the preconditions. It is only too obvious that the advent of industrialization has not so far freed women in this sense, either in the West or in the East. In the West it is true that there was a great influx of women into jobs in the expanding industrial economy, but this soon levelled out, and there has been relatively little in-crease in recent decades. De Beauvoir hoped that automation would make a decisive, qualitative difference by abolishing altogether the physical differen-tial between the sexes. But any reliance on this in itself accords an indepen-dent role to technique which history does not justify. Under capitalism, automation could possibly lead to an ever-growing structural unemployment which would expel women—the latest and least integrated recruits to the labour force and ideologically the most expendable for a bourgeois society— from production after only a brief interlude in it. Technology is mediated by the total social structure and it is this which will determine woman's future in work relations.

Physical deficiency is not now, any more than in the past, a sufficient explanation of woman's relegation to inferior status. Coercion has been ameliorated to an ideology shared by both sexes. Commenting on the results of her questionnaire of working women, Viola Klein notes. "There is no trace of feminist egalitarianism—militant or otherwise—in any of the women's answers to our questionnaire; nor is it even implicitly assumed that women have a 'Right to Work.' " Denied, or refusing, a role in *production*, woman does not even create the *pre*conditions of her liberation.

Reproduction

Women's absence from the critical sector of production historically, of course, has been caused not just by their physical weakness in a context of coercion—but also by their role in reproduction. Maternity necessitates periodic withdrawals from work, but this is not a decisive phenomenon. It is rather women's role in reproduction which has become, in capitalist society at least, the spiritual "complement" of men's role in production. Bearing children, bringing them up, and maintaining the home—these form the core of woman's natural vocation, in this ideology. This belief has attained great force because of the seeming universality of the family as a human institution. There is little doubt that Marxist analyses have underplayed the fundamental problems posed here. The complete failure to give any operative content to the slogan of "abolition" of the family is striking evidence of this (as well as of the vacuity of the notion). The void thus created has been quickly occupied by traditional beliefs such as Townsend's quoted above.

The biological function of maternity is a universal, atemporal fact, and as such has seemed to escape the categories of Marxist historical analysis. From it follows—apparently—the stability and omnipresence of the family, if in very different forms. Once this is accepted, women's social subordination—however emphasized as an honourable, but different role (cf. the equal but "separate" ideologies of Southern racists)—can be seen to follow inevitably as an *insurmountable* bio-historical fact. The casual chain then goes: Maternity, Family, Absence from Production and Public Life, Sexual Inequality.

The lynch-pin in this line of argument is the idea of the family. The notion that "family" and "society" are virtually co-extensive terms, or that an advanced society not founded on the nuclear family is now inconceivable, is widespread. It can only be seriously discussed by asking just what the family is—or rather what women's role in the family is. Once this is done, the problem appears in quite a new light. For it is obvious that woman's role in the family—primitive, feudal or bourgeois—partakes of three quite different structures: reproduction, sexuality, and the socialization of children. These are historically, not intrinsically, related to each other in the present modern family. Biological parentage is not necessarily identical with social parentage (adoption). It is thus essential to discuss: not the family as an unanalysed entity, but the separate *structures* which today compose it, but which may tomorrow be decomposed into a new pattern.

Reproduction, it has been stressed, is a seemingly constant atemporal phenomenon—part of biology rather than history. In fact this is an illusion. What is true is that the "mode of reproduction" does not vary with the "mode of production"; it can remain effectively the same through a number of different modes of production. For it has been defined till now, by its uncontrollable, natural character. To this extent, it has been an unmodified biological fact. As long as reproduction remained a natural phenomenon, of course, women were effectively doomed to social exploitation. In any sense, they were not masters of a large part of their lives. They had no choice as to whether or how often they gave birth to children (apart from repeated abortion), their existence was essentially subject to biological processes outside their control.

CONTRACEPTION

Contraception which was invented as a rational technique only in the 19th century was thus an innovation of world-historic importance. It is only now just beginning to show what immense consequences it could have, in the form of the pill. For what it means is that at last the mode of reproduction could potentially be transformed. Once child-bearing becomes totally voluntary (how much so is it in the West, even today?) its significance is fundamentally different. It need no longer be the sole or ultimate vocation of woman; it becomes one option among others.

Marx sees history as the development of man's transformation of nature, and thereby of himself—of human nature—in different modes of production. Today there are the technical possibilities for the humanization of the most natural part of human culture. This is what a change in the mode of reproduction could mean.

We are far from this state of affairs as yet. In France and Italy the sale of any form of contraception remains illegal. The oral contraceptive is the privilege of a moneyed minority in a few Western countries. Even here the progress has been realized in a typically conservative and exploitative form. It is made only for women, who are thus "guinea-pigs" in a venture which involves both sexes.

The fact of overwhelming importance is that easily available contraception threatens to dissociate sexual from reproductive experience—which all contemporary bourgeois ideology tries to make inseparable, as the *raison d'être* of the family.

REPRODUCTION AND PRODUCTION

At present, reproduction in our society is often a kind of sad mimicry of production. Work in a capitalist society is an alienation of labour in the making of a social product which is confiscated by capital. But it can still sometimes be a real act of creation, purposive and responsible, even in conditions of the worst exploitation. Maternity is often a caricature of this. The biological product—the child—is treated as if it were a solid product. Parenthood becomes a kind of substitute for work, an activity in which the child is seen as an object created by the mother, in the same way as a commodity is created by a worker. Naturally, the child does not literally escape, but the mother's alienation can be much worse than that of the worker whose product is appropriated by the boss. No human being can create another human being. A person's biological origin is an abstraction. The child as an autonomous person inevitably threatens the activity which claims to create it continually as a *possession* of the parent. Possessions are felt as extensions of the self. The child as a possession is supremely this. Anything the child does is therefore a threat to the mother herself who has renounced her autonomy through this misconception of her reproductive role. There are few more precarious ventures on which to base a life.

Furthermore even if the woman has emotional control over her child, legally and economically both she and it are subject to the father. The social cult of maternity is matched by the real socio-economic powerlessness of the mother. The psychological and practical benefits men receive from this are obvious. The converse of women's quest for creation in the child is men's retreat from his work into the family:

> When we come home, we lay aside our mask and drop our tools, and are no longer lawyers, sailors, soldiers, statesmen, clergymen, but only men. We fall again into our most human relations, which, after all, are the whole of what belongs to us as we are in ourselves.

Unlike her non-productive status, her capacity for maternity *is* a definition of woman. But it is only a physiological definition. So long as it is allowed to remain a substitute for action and creativity, and the home an area of relaxation for men, women will remain confined to the species, to her universal and natural condition.

Sexuality

Sexuality has traditionally been the most tabooed dimension of women's situation. The meaning of sexual freedom and its connexion with women's freedom is a particularly difficult subject which few socialist writers have cared to broach. Fourier alone identified the two totally, in lyrical strophes describing a sexual paradise of permutations—the famous phalansteries. "Socialist morality" in the Soviet Union for a long time debarred serious discussion of the subject within the world communist movement. Marx himself —in this respect somewhat less liberal than Engels—early in his life expressed traditional views on the matter:

> . . . the sanctification of the sexual instinct through exclusivity, the checking of instinct by laws, the moral beauty which makes nature's commandment ideal in the form of an emotional bond—(this is) the spiritual essence of marriage.

Yet it is obvious that throughout history women have been appropriated as sexual objects, as much as progenitors or producers. Indeed, the sexual relation can be assimilated to the statute of possession much more easily and completely than the productive or reproductive relationship. Contemporary sexual vocabulary bears eloquent witness to this—it is a comprehensive lexicon of reification. Later Marx was well aware of this, of course: "Marriage . . . is incontestably a form of exclusive private property." But neither he nor his successors ever tried seriously to envisage the implications of this for socialism, or even for a structural analysis of women's condition. Communism, Marx stressed in the same passage, would not mean mere "communalization" of women as common property. Beyond this, he never ventured.

Some historical considerations are in order here. For if socialists have said nothing, the gap has been filled by liberal ideologues. A recent book, *Eros Denied* by Wayland Young, argues that Western civilization has been uniquely repressive sexually and in a plea for greater sexual freedom today compares it at some length with Oriental and Ancient societies. It is striking, however, that his book makes no reference whatever to women's status in these different societies, or to the different forms of marriage-contract prevalent in them. This makes the whole argument a purely formal exercise—an obverse of socialist discussions of women's position which ignores the problem of sexual freedom and its meanings. For while it is true that certain Oriental or Ancient (and indeed Primitive) cultures were much less puritan than Western societies, it is absurd to regard this as a kind of "transposable value" which can be abstracted from its social structure. In effect, in many of these societies sexual openness was accompanied by a form of polygamous exploitation which made it in practice an expression simply of masculine domination. Since art was the province of man, too, this freedom finds a natural and often powerful expression in art—which is often quoted as if it were evidence of the total quality of human relationships in the society. Nothing could be more misleading. What is necessary, rather than this naive, hortatory core of historical example, is some account of the co-variation between the degrees of sexual liberty and openness and the position and dignity of women in different societies. Some points are immediately obvious. The actual history is much more dialectical than any liberal account presents it. Unlimited juridical polygamy—whatever the sexualization of the culture which accompanies it—is clearly a total derogation of woman's autonomy, and constitutes an extreme form of oppression. Ancient China is a perfect illustration of this. Wittfogel describes the extraordinary despotism of the Chinese *paterfamilias*—"a liturgical (semiofficial) policeman of his kin group." In the West, however, the advent of monogamy was in no sense an *absolute* improvement. It certainly did not create a one-to-one equality—far from it. Engels commented accurately:

Monogamy does not by any means make its appearance in history as the reconciliation of man and woman, still less as the highest form of such a reconciliation. On the contrary, it appears as the subjugation of one sex by the other, as the proclamation of a conflict between the sexes entirely unknown hitherto in prehistoric times.

But in the Christian era, monogamy took on a very specific form in the West. It was allied with an unprecedented regime of general sexual repression. In its Pauline version, this had a markedly anti-feminine bias, inherited from Judaism. With time this became diluted—feudal society, despite its subsequent reputation for asceticism, practiced formal monogamy with considerable actual acceptance of polygamous behaviour, at least within the ruling class. But here again the extent of sexual freedom was only an index of masculine domination. In England, the truly major change occurred in the 16th century with the rise of militant puritanism and the increase of market relations in the economy. Lawrence Stone observes:

In practice, if not in theory, the early 16th century nobility was a polygamous society, and some contrived to live with a succession of women despite the official prohibition on divorce . . . But impressed by Calvinist criticisms of the double standard, in the late 16th century public opinion began to object to the open maintenance of a mistress.

Capitalism and the attendant demands of the newly emergent bourgeoisie accorded women a new status as wife and mother. Her legal rights improved; there was vigorous controversy over her social position; wife-beating was condemned. "In a woman the bourgeois man is looking for a counterpart, not an equal." At the social periphery woman did occasionally achieve an equality which was more than her feminine function in a market society. In the extreme sects women often had completely equal rights: Fox argued that the Redemption restored Prelapsarian equality and Quaker women thereby gained a real autonomy. But once most of the sects were institutionalized, the need for family discipline was re-emphasized and woman's obedience with it. As Keith Thomas says, the Puritans "had done something to raise women's status, but not really very much." The patriarchal system was re-tained and maintained by the economic mode of production. The transition to complete effective monogamy accompanied the transition to modern bourgeois society as we know it today. Like the market system itself, it represented a historic advance, at great historic cost. The formal, juridical equality of capitalist society and capitalist rationality now applied as much to the marital as to the labour contract. In both cases, nominal parity masks real exploitation and inequality. But in both cases the formal equality is itself a certain progress, which can help to make possible a further advance.

For the situation today is defined by a new contradiction. Once formal conjugal equality (monogamy) is established, sexual freedom as such—which under polygamous conditions was usually a form of exploitation—becomes, conversely, a possible force for liberation. It then means, simply, the free-dom for both sexes to transcend the limits of present sexual institutions.

Historically, then, there has been a dialectical movement, in which sexual expression was "sacrificed" in an epoch of more-or-less puritan repres-sion, which nevertheless produced a greater parity of sexual roles, which in turn creates the precondition for a genuine sexual liberation, in the dual sense of equality *and* freedom—whose unity defines socialism.

This movement can be verified within the history of the "sentiments." The cult of *love* only emerges in the 12th century in opposition to legal marital forms and with a heightened valorization of women (courtly love). It thereafter gradually became diffused, and assimilated to a *free* choice for *life*. What is striking here is that monogamy as an institution in the West antici-pated the idea of love by many centuries. The two have subsequently been officially harmonized, but the tension between them has never been abolished. There is a formal contradiction between the voluntary contractual character of "marriage" and the spontaneous uncontrollable character of "love"—the passion that is celebrated precisely for its involuntary force. The notion that it occurs only once in every life and can therefore be integrated into a volun-tary contract becomes decreasingly plausible in the light of everyday expe-rience—once sexual repression as a psycho-ideological system becomes at all relaxed.

Obviously, the main breach in the traditional value-pattern has so far been the increase in premarital sexual experience. This is now virtually legitimized in contemporary bourgeois society. But its implications are explo-sive for the ideological conception of marriage that dominates this society:

that of an exclusive and permanent bond. A recent American anthology *The Family and the Sexual Revolution* reveals this very clearly:

> As far as extra-marital relations are concerned, the anti-sexualists are still fighting a strong, if losing, battle. The very heart of the Judeo-Christian sex ethic is that men and women shall remain virginal until marriage and that they shall be completely faithful after marriage. In regard to premarital chastity, this ethic seems clearly on the way out, and in many segments of the populace is more and more becoming a dead letter.

The current wave of sexual liberalization, in the present context, could become conducive to the greater general freedom of women. Equally it could presage new forms of oppression. The puritan-bourgeois creation of woman as "counterpart" has produced the *precondition* for emancipation. But it gave statutory legal equality to the sexes at the cost of greatly intensified repression. Subsequently—like private property itself—it has become a brake on the further development of a free sexuality. Capitalist market relations have historically been a precondition of socialism; bourgeois marital relations (contrary to the denunciation of the *Communist Manifesto*) may equally be a precondition of women's liberation.

Socialization

Woman's biological destiny as mother becomes a cultural vocation in her role as socializer of children. In bringing up children, woman achieves her main social definition. Her suitability for socialization springs from her physiological condition: her ability to lactate and occasionally relative inability to undertake strenuous work loads. It should be said at the outset that suitability is not inevitability. Lévi-Strauss writes:

> In every human group, women give birth to children and take care of them, and men rather have as their speciality hunting and warlike activities. Even there, though, we have ambiguous cases: of course, men never give birth to babies, but in many societies . . . they are made to act as if they did.

Evans-Pritchard's description of the Nuer tribe depicts just such a situation. And another anthropologist, Margaret Mead, comments on the element of wish-fulfilment in the assumption of a *natural* correlation of feminity and nurturance:

> We have assumed that because it is convenient for a mother to wish to care for her child, this is a trait with which women have been more generously endowed by a careful teleological process of evolution. We have assumed that because men have hunted, an activity requiring enterprise, bravery, and initiative, they have been endowed with these useful aptitudes as part of their sex-temperament.

However, the cultural allocation of roles in bringing up children—and the limits of its variability—is not the essential problem for consideration. What is much more important is to analyze the nature of the socialization process itself and its requirements.

Parsons in his detailed analysis claims that it is essential for the child to have two "parents," one who plays an "expressive" role, and one who plays an "instrumental" role. The nuclear family revolves around the two axes of generational hierarchy and these two roles. In typically Parsonian idiom, he claims that:

> At least one fundamental feature of the external situation of social systems —here a feature of the physiological organism—is a crucial reference point for differentiation in the family. This lies in the division of organisms into lactating and non-lactating classes.

In all groups, he and his colleagues assert, even in those primitive tribes discussed by Pritchard and Mead, the male plays the instrumental role *in relation* to the wife-mother. At one stage the mother plays an instrumental and expressive role *vis-a-vis* her infant: this is pre-oedipally when she is the source of approval and disapproval as well as of love and care. However, after this, the father, or male substitute (in matrilineal societies the mother's brother) takes over. In a modern industrial society two types of role are clearly important: the adult familial roles in the family of procreation, and the adult occupational role. The function of the family as such reflects the function of the women within it; it is primarily expressive. The person playing the integrated-adaptive-expressive role cannot be off all the time on instrumental-occupational errands—hence there is a built-in inhibition of the woman's work outside the home. Parsons' analysis makes clear the exact role of the maternal socializer in contemporary American society. It fails to go on to state that other aspects and modes of socialization are conceivable. What is valuable in Parsons' work is simply his insistence on the central importance of socialization as a process which is constitutive of any society (no Marxist has so far provided a comparable analysis). His general conclusion is that:

> It seems to be without serious qualification the opinion of competent personality psychologists that, though personalities differ greatly in their degrees of rigidity, certain broad fundamental patterns of 'character' are laid down in childhood (so far as they are not genetically inherited) and are not radically changed by adult experience. The exact degree to which this is the case or the exact age levels at which plasticity becomes greatly diminished, are not at issue here. The important thing is the fact of childhood character formation and its relative stability after that.

INFANCY

This seems indisputable. One of the great revolutions of modern psychology has been the discovery of the decisive specific weight of infancy in the course of an individual life—a psychic time disproportionately greater than the chronological time. Freud began the revolution with his work on infantile sexuality; Klein radicalized it with her work on the first year of the infant's life. The result is that today we know far more than ever before how delicate and precarious a process the passage from birth to childhood is for everyone. The fate of the adult personality can be largely decided in the initial months of life. The preconditions for the latter stability and integration demand an extraordinary degree of care and intelligence on the part of the adult who is socializing the child, as well as a persistence through time of the same person.

These undoubted advances in the scientific understanding of childhood have been widely used as an argument to reassert women's quintessential maternal function, at a time when the traditional family has seemed increasingly eroded. Bowlby, studying evacuee children in the Second World War, declared: "essential for mental health is that the infant and young child should experience a warm, intimate and continuous relationship with his mother," setting a trend which has become cumulative since. The emphasis of familial ideology has shifted away from a cult of the biological ordeal of maternity (the pain which makes the child precious, etc.) to a celebration of mother-care as a social act. This can reach ludicrous extremes:

> For the mother, breast-feeding becomes a complement to the act of creation. It gives her a heightened sense of fulfilment and allows her to participate in a relationship as close to perfection as any that a woman can hope to achieve. . . . The simple fact of giving birth, however, does not of itself fulfil this need and longing. . . . Motherliness is a way of life. It enables a woman to express her total self with the tender feelings, the protective attitudes, the encompassing love of the motherly woman.

The tautologies, the mystifications (an *act* of creation, a *process* surely?), the sheer absurdities. . . . "as close to perfection as any woman can hope to achieve". . . point to the gap between reality and ideology.

FAMILIAL PATTERNS

This ideology corresponds in dislocated form to a real change in the pattern of the family. As the family has become smaller, each child has become more important; the actual *act* of reproduction occupies less and less time and the socializing and nurturance process increase commensurately in significance. Bourgeois society is obsessed by the physical, moral and sexual problems of childhood and adolescence. Ultimate responsibility for these is placed on the mother. Thus the mother's "maternal" role has retreated as her socializing role has increased. In the 1890's in England a mother spent 15 years in a state of pregnancy and lactation; in the 1960's she spends an average of four years. Compulsory schooling from the age of five, of course, reduces the maternal function very greatly after the initial vulnerable years.

The present situation is then one in which the qualitative importance of socialization during the early years of the child's life has acquired a much greater significance than in the past—while the quantitative amount of a mother's life spent either in gestation or child-rearing has greatly diminished. It follows that socialization cannot simply be elevated to the woman's new maternal vocation. Used as a mystique, it becomes an instrument of oppression. Moreover, there is no inherent reason why the biological and social mother should coincide. The process of socialization is, in the Kleinian sense, invariable—but the person of the socializer can vary.

Bruno Bettelheim, observing Kibbutz methods notes that the child who is reared by a trained nurse (though normally maternally breast-fed) does not suffer the back-wash of typical parental anxieties and thus may positively gain by the system. This possibility should not be fetishized in its turn (Jean Baby, speaking of the post-four-year-old child, goes so far as to say that "complete separation appears indispensable to guarantee the liberty of the child as well as of the mother"). But what it does reveal is the viability of plural forms of socialization—neither necessarily tied to the nuclear family, nor to the biological parent.

Conclusion

The lesson of these reflections is that the liberation of women can only be achieved if *all four* structures in which they are integrated are transformed. A modification of any one of them can be offset by a reinforcement of another, so that mere permutation of the form of exploitation is achieved. The history of the last 60 years provides ample evidence of this. In the early 20th century, militant feminism in England or the USA surpassed the labour movement in the violence of its assault on bourgeois society, in pursuit of suffrage. This political right was eventually won. Nonetheless, though a simple completion of the formal legal equality of bourgeois society, it left the socio-economic situation of women virtually unchanged. The wider legacy of the suffrage was nil: the suffragettes proved quite unable to move beyond their own initial demands, and many of their leading figures later became extreme reactionaries. The Russian Revolution produced a quite different experience. In the Soviet Union in the 1920's, advanced social legislation aimed at liberating women above all in the field of sexuality: divorce was made free and automatic for either partner, thus effectively liquidating marriage; illegitimacy was abolished, abortion was free, etc. The social and demographic effects of these laws in a backward, semi-literate society bent on rapid industrialization (needing, therefore, a high birth-rate) were—predictably—catastrophic. Stalinism soon produced a restoration of iron traditional norms. Inheritance was reinstated, divorce inaccessible, abortion illegal, etc.

> The State cannot exist without the family. Marriage is a positive value for the Socialist Soviet State only if the partners see in it a lifelong union. So-called free love is a bourgeois invention and has nothing in common with the principles of conduct of a Soviet citizen. Moreover, marriage receives its full value for the State only if there is progeny, and the consorts experience the highest happiness of parenthood,

wrote the official journal of the Commissariat of Justice in 1939. Women still retained the right and obligation to work, but because these gains had not been integrated into the earlier attempts to abolish the family and free sexuality no general liberation has occurred. In China, still another experience is being played out today. At a comparable stage of the revolution, all the emphasis is being placed on liberating women in *production*. This has produced an impressive social promotion of women. But it has been accompanied by a tremendous repression of sexuality and a rigorous puritanism (currently rampant in civic life). This corresponds not only to the need to mobilize women massively in economic life, but to a deep cultural reaction against the corruption and prostitution prevalent in Imperial and Kuo Ming Tang China (a phenomenon unlike anything in Czarist Russia). Because the exploitation of women was so great in the *ancien régime* women's participation at village level in the Chinese Revolution was uniquely high. As for reproduction, the Russian cult of maternity in the 1930's and 1940's has not been repeated for demographic reasons: indeed, China may be one of the first countries in the world to provide free State authorized contraception on a universal scale to the population. Again, however, given the low level of industrialization and fear produced by imperialist encirclement, no all-round advance could be expected.

It is only in the highly developed societies of the West that an authentic liberation of women can be envisaged today. But for this to occur, there must be a transformation of all the structures into which they are integrated, and an "*unité de rupture*." A revolutionary movement must base its analysis on the uneven development of each, and attack the weakest link in the combination. This may then become the point of departure for a general transformation. What is the situation of the different structures today?

Production   The long-term development of the forces of production must command any socialist perspective. The hopes which the advent of machine technology raised as early as the 19th century have already been discussed. They proved illusory. Today, automation promises the *technical* possibility of abolishing completely the physical differential between man and woman in production, but under capitalist relations of production, the *social* possibility of this abolition is permanently threatened, and can easily be turned into its opposite, the actual diminution of woman's role in production as the labour force contracts.

This concerns the future. For the present the main fact to register is that woman's role in production is virtually stationary, and has been so for a long time now. In England in 1911 30 per cent of the work-force were women; in the 1960's 34 per cent. The composition of these jobs has not changed decisively either. The jobs are very rarely "careers." When they are not in the lowest positions on the factory-floor they are normally white-collar auxiliary positions (such as secretaries)—supportive to masculine roles. They are often jobs with a high "expressive" content, such as "service" tasks. Parsons says bluntly: "Within the occupational organization they are analogous to the wife-mother role in the family." The educational system underpins this role-structure. 75 per cent of 18-year-old girls in England are receiving neither training nor education today. The pattern of "instrumental" father and "expressive" mother is not substantially changed when the woman is gainfully employed, as her job tends to be inferior to that of the man's, to which the family then adapts.

Thus, in all essentials, work as such—of the amount and type effectively available today—has not proved a salvation for women.

Reproduction Scientific advance in contraception could, as we have seen, make involuntary reproduction—which accounts for the vast majority of births in the world today, and for a major proportion even in the West— a phenomenon of the past. But oral contraception—which has so far been developed in a form which exactly repeats the sexual inequality of Western society—is only at its beginnings. It is inadequately distributed across classes and countries and awaits further technical improvements. Its main initial impact is, in the advanced countries, likely to be psychological—it will certainly free women's sexual experience from many of the anxieties and inhibitions which have always afflicted it. It will definitely divorce sexuality from procreation, as necessary complements.

The demographic pattern of reproduction in the West may or may not be widely affected by oral contraception. One of the most striking phenomena of very recent years in the United States has been the sudden increase in the birth-rate. In the last decade it has been higher than that of under-developed countries such as India, Pakistan and Burma. In fact, this reflects simply the lesser economic burden of a large family in conditions of economic boom in the richest country in the world. But it also reflects the magnification of familial ideology as a social force. This leads to the next structure.

Socialization The changes in the composition of the work-force, the size of the family, the structure of education, etc.—however limited from an ideal standpoint—have undoubtedly diminished the societal function and importance of the family. As an organization it is not a significant unit in the political power system, it plays little part in economic production and it is rarely the sole agency of integration into the larger society; thus at the macroscopic level it serves very little purpose.

The result has been a major displacement of emphasis on to the family's psycho-social function, for the infant and for the couple. Parsons writes:

> The trend of the evidence points to the beginning of the relative stabilization of a *new* type of family structure in a new relation to a general social structure, one in which the family is more specialized than before, but not in any general sense less important, because the society is dependent *more* exclusively on it for the performance of *certain* of its vital functions.

The vital nucleus of truth in the emphasis on socialization of the child has been discussed. It is essential that socialists should acknowledge it and integrate it entirely into any programme for the liberation of women. It is noticeable that recent "vanguard" work by French Marxists—Baby, Sullerot, Texier —accords the problem its real importance. However, there is no doubt that the need for permanent, intelligent care of children in the initial three or four years of their lives can (and has been) exploited ideologically to perpetuate the family as a total unit, when its other functions have been visibly declining. Indeed, the attempt to focus women's existence exclusively on bringing up children, is manifestly harmful to children. Socialization as an exceptionally delicate process requires a serene and mature socializer—a type which the frustrations of a *purely* familial role are not liable to produce. Exclusive maternity is often in this sense "counter-productive." The mother discharges her own frustrations and anxieties in a fixation on the child. An increased awareness of the critical importance of socialization, far from leading to a restitution of classical maternal roles, should lead to a reconsideration of them—of what makes a good socializing agent, who can genuinely provide security and stability for the child.

The same arguments apply *a fortiori,* to the psycho-social role of the family for the couple. The beliefs that the family provides an impregnable enclave of intimacy and security in an atomized and chaotic cosmos assumes the absurd—that the family can be isolated from the community, and that its internal relationships will not reproduce in their own terms the external relationships which dominate the society. The family as refuge in a bourgeois society inevitably becomes a reflection of it.

Sexuality It is difficult not to conclude that the major structure which at present is in rapid evolution is sexuality. Production, reproduction, and socialization are all more or less stationary in the West today, in the sense that they have not changed for three or more decades. There is moreover, no widespread *demand* for changes in them on the part of women themselves— the governing ideology has effectively prevented critical consciousness. By contrast, the dominant sexual ideology is proving less and less successful in regulating spontaneous behavior. Marriage in its classical form is increasingly threatened by the liberalization of relationships before and after it which affects all classes today. In this sense, it is evidently the weak link in the chain—the particular structure that is the site of the most contradictions. The progressive potential of these contradictions has already been emphasized. In a context of juridical equality ,the liberation of sexual experience from relations which are extraneous to it—whether procreation or property —could lead to true inter-sexual freedom. But it could also lead simply to new forms of neocapitalist ideology and practice. For one of the forces behind the current acceleration of sexual freedom has undoubtedly been the conversion of contemporary capitalism from a production-and-work ethos to a consumption-and-fun ethos. Riesman commented on this development early in the 1950's:

> . . . there is not only a growth of leisure, but work itself becomes both less interesting and less demanding for many . . . more than before, as job-mindedness declines, sex permeates the daytime as well as the playtime consciousness. It is viewed as a consumption good not only by the old leisure classes, but by the modern leisure masses.

The gist of Riesman's argument is that in a society bored by work, sex is the only activity, the only reminder of one's energies, the only competitive act; the last defense against *vis inertiae.* This same insight can be found, with greater theoretical depth, in Marcuse's notion of "repressive de-sublimation" —the freeing of sexuality for its own frustration in the service of a totally co-ordinated and drugged social machine. Bourgeois society at present can well afford a play area of premarital *non*-procreative sexuality. Even marriage can save itself by increasing divorce and remarriage rates, signifying the importance of the institution itself. These considerations make it clear that sexuality, while it presently may contain the greatest potential for liberation—can equally well be organized against any increase of its human possibilities. New forms of reification are emerging which may void sexual freedom of any meaning. This is a reminder that while one structure may be the *weak link* in a unity like that of woman's condition, there can never be a solution through it alone. The utopianism of Fourier or Reich was precisely to think that sexuality could inaugurate such a general solution. Lenin's remark to Clara Zetkin is a salutary if over-stated corrective:

> However wild and revolutionary (sexual freedom) may be, it is still really quite bourgeois. It is, mainly, a hobby of the intellectuals and of the sections nearest them. There is no place for it in the Party, in the class conscious, fighting, proletariat.

For a general solution can only be found in a strategy which affects *all* the structures of women's exploitation. This means a rejection of two beliefs prevalent on the left:

Reformism This now takes the form of limited ameliorative demands: equal pay for women, more nursery-schools, better retraining facilities, etc. In its contemporary version it is wholly divorced from any fundamental critique of women's condition or any vision of their real liberation (it was not always so). Insofar at it represents a tepid embellishment of the *status quo,* it has very little progressive content left.

Voluntarism This takes the form of maximalist demands—the abolition of the family, abrogation of all sexual restrictions, forceful separation of parents from children—which have no chance of winning any wide support at present, and which merely serve as a substitute for the job of theoretical analysis or practical persuasion. By pitching the whole subject in totally intransigent terms, voluntarism objectively helps to maintain it outside the framework of normal political discussion.

What, then, is the responsible revolutionary attitude? It must include both immediate and fundamental demands, in a single critique of the *whole* of women's situation, that does not fetishize any dimension of it. Modern industrial development, as has been seen, tends towards the separating out of the originally unified function of the family—procreation, socialization, sexuality, economic subsistence, etc—even if this "structural differentiation" (to use a term of Parsons') has been checked and disguised by the maintenance of a powerful family ideology. This differentiation provides the real historical basis for the ideal demands which should be posted: structural differentiation is precisely what "distinguishes an advanced from a primitive society (in which all social functions are fused *en bloc*)."[2]

In practical terms this means a coherent system of demands. The four elements of women's condition cannot merely be considered each in isolation; they form a structure of specific interrelations. The contemporary bourgeois family can be seen as a triptych of sexual, reproductive and socializatory functions (the woman's world) embraced by production (the man's world)—precisely a structure which in the final instance is determined by the economy. The exclusion of women from production—social human activity—and their confinement to a monolithic condensation of functions in a unity—the family—which is precisely unified in the *natural part* of each function, is the root cause of the contemporary *social* definition of women as *natural* beings. Hence the main thrust of any emancipation movement must still concentrate on the economic element—the entry of women fully into public industry. The error of the old socialists was to see the other elements as reducible to the economic; hence the call for the entry of women into production was accompanied by the purely abstract slogan of the abolition of the family. Economic demands are still primary, but must be accompanied by coherent policies for the other three elements, policies which at particular junctions may take over the primary role in immediate action.

Economically, the most elementary demand is not the right to work or receive equal pay for work—the two traditional reformist demands—but *the right to equal work itself*. At present, women perform unskilled, uncreative, service jobs that can be regarded as "extensions" of their expressive familial role. They are overwhelmingly waitresses, office-cleaners, hair-dressers, clerks, typists. In the working-class occupational mobility is thus sometimes easier for girls than boys—they can enter the white-collar sector at a lower-level. But only two in a hundred women are in administrative or managerial jobs, and less than five in a thousand are in the professions. Women are poorly unionized (25 per cent) and receive less money than men for the manual work they do perform: in 1961 the average industrial wage for women was less than half that for men, which, even setting off part-time work, represents a massive increment of exploitation for the employer.

EDUCATION

The whole pyramid of discrimination rests on a solid extra-economic foundation—education. The demand for equal work, in Britain, should above all take the form of a demand for an *equal educational system*, since this is at present the main single filter selecting women for inferior work-roles. At

[2] The capitalist mode of production separates the family from its earlier immediate association with the economy, and this marginality is unaffected directly by the transformation of the relations of production from private to public ownership in the transition to a socialist society. As the essence of woman's contemporary problem derives from this marginality, for this problem, *but for this problem only*, the distinction between industrial ind preindustrial societies is the significant one. Categories meaningful for one element of the social totality may well be irrelevant or even pernicious if extended to the whole of historical development. Similar arguments, but principally lack of space in a short article must excuse the total neglect of problems arising from class distinctions in the functions and status of women.

Sexism and Society

present, there is something like equal education for both sexes up to 15. Thereafter three times as many boys continue their education as girls. Only one in three "A"-level entrants, one in four university students is a girl. There is no evidence whatever of progress. The proportion of girl university students is the same as it was in the 1920's. Until these injustices are ended, there is no chance of equal work for women. It goes without saying that the content of the education system, which actually instils limitation of aspiration in girls needs to be changed as much as methods of selection. Education is probably the key area for immediate economic advance at present.

Only if it is founded on equality can production be truly differentiated from reproduction and the family. But this in turn requires a whole set of non-economic demands as a complement. Reproduction, sexuality, and socialization also need to be free from coercive forms of unification. Traditionally, the socialist movement has called for the "abolition of the bourgeois family." This slogan must be rejected as incorrect today. It is maximalist in the bad sense, posing a demand which is merely a negation without any coherent construction subsequent to it. Its weakness can be seen by comparing it to the call for the abolition of the private ownership of the means of production, whose solution—social ownership—is contained in the negation itself. Marx himself allied the two, and pointed out the equal futility of the two demands: ". . . this tendency to oppose general private property to private property is expressed in animal form; *marriage* . . . is contrasted with the community of women, in which women become communal and common property." The reasons for the historic weakness of the notion is that the family was never analysed structurally—in terms of its different functions. It was a hypostasized entity; the abstraction of its abolition corresponds to the abstraction of its conception. The strategic concern for socialists should be for the equality of the sexes, not the abolition of the family. The consequences of this demand are no less radical, but they are concrete and positive, and can be integrated into the real course of history. The family as it exists at present is, in fact, incompatible with the equality of the sexes. But this equality will not come from its administrative abolition, but from the historical differentiation of its functions. The revolutionary demand should be for the liberation of these functions from a monolithic fusion which oppresses each. Thus dissociation of reproduction from sexuality frees sexuality from alienation in unwanted reproduction (and fear of it), and reproduction from subjugation to chance and uncontrollable causality. It is thus an elementary demand to press for free State provision of oral contraception. The legalization of homosexuality—which is one of the forms of non-reproductive sexuality—should be supported for just the same reason, and regressive campaigns against it in Cuba or elsewhere should be unhesitatingly criticized. The straightforward abolition of illegitimacy as a legal notion as in Sweden and Russia has a similar implication; it would separate marriage civically from parenthood.

FROM NATURE TO CULTURE

The problem of socialization poses more difficult questions, as has been seen. But the need for intensive maternal care in the early years of a child's life does not mean that the present single sanctioned form of socialization—marriage and family—is inevitable. Far from it. The fundamental characteristic of the present system of marriage and family is in our society its *monolithism*: there is only one institutionalized form of inter-sexual or expression of them in our capitalist society is utterly simple and rigid. It is essentially a denial of life. For all human experience shows that intersexual and intergenerational relationships are infinitely various—indeed, much of our creative literature is a celebration of the fact—while the institutionalized expression of them in our capitalist society is utterly simple and rigid. It is the poverty and simplicity of the institutions in this area of life which are such an oppression. Any society will require some institutionalized and social recognition of personal relationships. But there is absolutely no reason why there should be only one legitimized form—and a multitude of unlegitimized experience. Socialism should properly mean not the abolition of the family, but the diversification of the socially acknowledged relationships which are today forcibly and rigidly compressed into it. This would mean a plural range of institutions—where the family is only one, and its abolition implies none. Couples living together or not living together, long-term unions with children, single parents bringing up children, children socialized by conventional rather than biological parents, extended kin groups, etc—all these could be encompassed in a range of institutions which matched the free invention and variety of men and women.

It would be illusory to try and specify these institutions. Circumstantial accounts of the future are idealist and worse, static. Socialism will be a process of change, of becoming. A fixed image of the future is in the worst sense ahistorical; the form that socialism takes will depend on the prior type of capitalism and the nature of its collapse. As Marx wrote:

What (is progress) if not the absolute elaboration of (man's) creative disposition, without any preconditions other than antecedent historical evolution which makes the totality of this evolution—i.e. the evolution of all human powers as such, unmeasured by any *previously established* yardstick—an end in itself? What is this, if not a situation where man does not reproduce himself in any determined form, but produces his totality? Where he does not seek to remain something formed by the past, but is the absolute movement of becoming?

The liberation of women under socialism will not be "rational" but a human achievement, in the long passage from Nature to Culture which is the definition of history and society.

chapter 7

The Knowledge Industry:
The Higher Learning in America

Educational institutions can liberate men from ignorance as well as provide a setting for indoctrination which serves the forces in a society that can best maintain their privileged positions if those not privileged are kept in relative ignorance.

Most teachers in elementary and secondary education recognize that their main task is not fostering intellectual liberation. Rather, in this country, as in virtually all others, the early educational experience is primarily concerned with socialization. The child is presumably taught rudimentary skills such as reading, writing, and simple mathematics which are indispensable for most occupations. Perhaps more importantly, he is imbued with a sense of discipline and is taught to identify positively with the cultural values and institutions of his society.[1] The school boards which play such a prominent role in determining the policy of primary and secondary schools are charac-

---

[1] Jules Henry, "American Schoolrooms: Learning the Nightmare," *Columbia University Forum,* vol. 6 (Spring, 1963), pp. 24–30; "Education for Stupidity," *The New York Review of Books,* vol. 10 (May 9, 1968), pp. 16–20.

teristically dominated by local businessmen, whose positions make a curriculum that upholds the values and concerns of a business civilization a certainty.[2]

This chapter deals exclusively with *higher* education in the United States. It suggests that even at advanced levels of learning, where the knowledge base presumably is founded upon free inquiry and a skeptical consciousness, the political economy of scholarship subverts the autonomy of the academy and channels intellectual energies into the service of private enterprise and the state.[3]

Although scholars readily admit that the nature of American elementary and secondary education has been heavily influenced by the needs of industry and government, they have been reluctanct to examine the political economy of *higher* education. There is a strong belief that the university is a place for free inquiry—and perhaps its last refuge. Thus, while acknowledging the efforts of business and political elites to affect the development of higher education, reputable analysts of the academy have maintained that such pressures were and are frequently resisted. After an exhaustive study undertaken during the McCarthy era, historians Richard Hofstadter and Walter Metzger conclude that though there are indeed threats to freedom in inquiry and academic freedom hangs like a "slender thread," the growth of understanding by teachers, administrators, and trustees, plus the influence of organizations such as the American Association of University Professors (AAUP), have permitted "a considerable measure of security for professors who have the hardihood to assert themselves."[4]

Their view, based upon an overly narrow reading of the historical record, is probably correct as far as it goes. Although the AAUP bowed before the onslaught of manipulated patriotism during World War I and made only feeble protests during the McCarthy era's campus witchhunts, the few *tenured* academic radicals can probably survive attempts by outside interests to remove them from universities.[5] The important question, and one

[2] Patricia Sexton, *The American School: A Sociological Analysis* (Englewood Cliffs, N.J.: Prentice-Hall, Inc., 1967), pp. 21–23, 29–30.

[3] There has been a great deal of debate on the proper relationship between educational institutions and the surrounding society. While some educators would prefer to restore colleges and universities to an "ivory tower" status, unconcerned with the relevance of knowledge to social needs, most would probably agree that some social service must be incorporated into the role of an educational institution. At the same time, few educators would wish scholarship to be totally or even primarily under the control of private industry or government. Institutional and faculty autonomy is perhaps considered the optimal solution when combined with a professional commitment to a rather vaguely defined "community service." My own view tends towards this position, but I feel that the "community" has been limited largely to the business class and its governmental allies. The poor and working classes rarely benefit from the activities that take place in universities and colleges.

[4] Richard Hofstadter and Walter Metzger, *The Development of Academic Freedom in the United States* (New York: Columbia University Press, 1955), p. 506.

[5] During periods of relative social tranquility the academic freedom of most faculty dissenters is often protected by university officials, particularly at the most prestigious institutions. When social turbulence develops, however, careers are more likely to be threatened for political reasons, even if a faculty member has tenure.

The Knowledge Industry

which David Horowitz faces in his article in this chapter, is whether the historical sources of university funding have not affected the structure and functions of the modern "multiversity" in a manner that has irrevocably bound the research and training orientations of these institutions to the material, political, and ideological needs of contemporary corporate capitalism. If Horowitz is correct in assessing the major significance of private "philanthropic" foundations in generating the capital for research and development during the formative period of the modern university, the occasional political firings of controversial professors represent only the top of an iceberg of academic subordination to outside interests.

While Horowitz goes into considerable detail on the role of private wealth in shaping the graduate training and research concerns of academics, we must also consider the even greater contribution made by the federal government to augment private philanthropy in the period after World War II.[6] Clark Kerr, former president of the University of California, reports that in 1960 higher education received approximately $1.5 billion from the federal government, one third of which went into university affiliated research centers and another third into project research on university campuses.[7] This expenditure represented a hundredfold increase in federal support for higher education since 1940. Moreover, these government funds accounted for an estimated 75 percent of the total university outlays for research.[8] The bulk of funds were given by the Department of Defense (32 percent) and the Department of Health, Education, and Welfare (39 percent).[9] The physical and biomedical sciences and engineering have received the greatest proportion of research funds, with the social sciences garnering only about 3 percent of the monies and the humanities being virtually excluded from governmental favor.[10]

Horowitz's article documents the concentration of private philanthropy at a handful of universities, whose near-monopoly in research and graduate training has shaped the orientation of American intellectual life. Similarly, federal research expenditures have been heavily concentrated among the same major institutions: MIT, Stanford, Harvard, Columbia, the University of Chicago, and Johns Hopkins University, as well as some of the major public universities such as the University of California.[11]

Kerr argues that dependence upon federal expenditures for university operations and research has not meant government control of higher education. It is true that the federal government does not monitor all the research that it funds. Nor does it generally prevent public disclosure of findings

[6] Clark Kerr, The Uses of the University (New York: Harper & Row, Publishers, 1966).
[7] Ibid., pp. 52–53. By 1970 the federal budget for higher education exceeded $4 billion.
[8] Ibid., p. 53.
[9] Ibid.
[10] Ibid., p. 54.
[11] James Ridgeway, The Closed Corporation: American Universities in Crisis (New York: Ballantine Books, Inc., 1969), pp. 212–213.

except in the large number of war-related research projects.[12] The effects of federal funding, like philanthropic fundings, are more subtle. Kerr says that control is minimized because "The federal government has customarily put scientifically trained persons in charge of science programs and they have operated fully within academic traditions."[13] Yet one wonders about the nature of these "academic traditions," which (as Horowitz shows) were heavily influenced prior to the rise of the "federal-grant university" by private wealth-holders as well as by the choice of "scientifically trained persons" to guide programs. Regardless of their scholarly reputations, radical academicians are hardly ever asked to serve on government research review boards.

If the budgetary power and political and ideological concerns of private wealth-holders and the government have played a decisive role in generating research priorities and structuring graduate training in the twentieth century, the fact that a few intellectuals such as C. Wright Mills managed to avoid the lure of academic stardom via servicing the needs of the political economy is a tribute to their personal courage or "hardihood," not to the character of institutions of higher learning.[14] As Horowitz suggests, the rewards for approved research and teaching are great and the punishment for nonconformity is quite predictable, even if dismissal is reserved for the most rebellious academics. An educational system that relies upon the rare martyr to generate critical scholarship and teaching is hardly a bastion of free inquiry.

The role of private foundations and federal grants in the development of higher education has been supplemented by the structure of policy control within individual institutions of higher learning. Despite the trend towards faculty self-governance in the routine operations of universities and colleges (for example, determining course content, grading procedures,

[12] Public disclosure of research does not guarantee that the fruits of scholarship will benefit all interested parties equally. For example, medical discoveries are useful primarily to private corporations that can afford to develop therapeutic technologies from the results of pure scientific inquiry and to diseased persons who can afford medical aid.

[13] Kerr, op. cit., p. 57.

[14] Contrary to popular belief the vast majority of academicians are not politically radical. See Paul Lazarfeld and Wagner Thielens, Jr., The Academic Mind: Social Scientists in a Time of Crisis (New York: The Free Press, 1958). See also Seymour Martin Lipset and Everett Ladd, Jr., ". . . And What Professors Think. . . ." Psychology Today, vol. 4 (November, 1970), pp. 49–51, 106. This fact permits a deeper understanding of the widespread belief among academicians that freedom of inquiry is not limited in the university. Almost all scholars' political beliefs are compatible with the approach to intellectual inquiry emphasized in graduate training. Thus, their freedom to pursue the research of their choice rarely will conflict with the need to support and service the existing political economy. Such support and service, as Horowitz shows, have been built into the theoretical frameworks and methodologies adhered to by academic disciplines. Radical scholars generally must challenge academic traditions in theory and methods to conduct research and thus can be charged with lacking professionalism. Their career limitations are not understood by most of their colleagues to be violations of academic freedom and political repression. This is, of course, a problem experienced by all innovators regardless of their political leanings, but is exacerbated in the case of politically unorthodox researchers.

personnel matters), *ultimate* authority still rests with boards of trustees who represent either the major benefactors of private institutions or the "public" in the case of state or municipal universities and colleges. The trustees can and increasingly have intervened in order to create new programs, eliminate threatening innovations, and fire recalcitrant faculty or administrators.

Not surprisingly, boards of trustees in both private and public institutions have always been dominated by representatives of the capitalist class. Thorstein Veblen's acidic commentary on the trustees of an earlier age as "captains of erudition," should not be taken as outdated polemic.[15] A recent study of five thousand college and university trustees reveals that 35 percent are executives of manufacturing, merchandising, or banking firms.[16] Other trustees are principally from the fields of law, medicine, and education. Among trustees of private universities, 49 percent are business executives compared to 36 percent for public universities. The percentages decrease as one moves to less prestigious institutions of higher learning such as private and public colleges and Catholic universities and colleges. This suggests that at the largest most innovative institutions which receive the great share of research funds and provide the highest-quality undergraduate and graduate training, policy making and the still considerable budgetary powers are more likely to be in the hands of businessmen.

A related finding of the study is that 49 percent of the trustees with business backgrounds and 31 percent of the other trustees believe that "running a college is basically like running a business"; moreover, 49 percent of the business trustees and 44 percent of the others "regard experience in high level business management as an important quality for a new president."[17] Among trustees at the private and public universities these overall figures are a few percentage points lower, perhaps reflecting a somewhat greater sophistication about the nature of the research and teaching process by trustees of prestigious institutions.

The social attitudes of the trustees leave little room for optimism among those who expect the governing body of an institution of higher learning to support free inquiry: 27 percent of the trustees do not believe that faculty members have the right to freely express their opinions; 40 percent believe that the university or college administration should control the contents of student newspapers; 60 percent advocate the screening of campus speakers; and 53 percent believe it reasonable to require faculty members to sign loyalty oaths.[18]

The social and political backgrounds of the trustees, notwithstanding their occupations and educational views, are likely to place them out of touch with new ideas and different subcultures. Most trustees are male Republicans, in their fifties; half earn more than $30,000 per year; 15 per-

[15] Thorstein Veblen, *The Higher Learning in America: A Memorandum on the Conduct of Universities by Business Men* (New York: Hill & Wang, Inc., 1957).

[16] Rodney Hartnett, "College and University Trustees: Their Backgrounds, Roles, and Educational Attitudes," in Jerome Skolnick and Elliott Currie, eds., *Crisis in American Institutions* (New York: John Wiley & Sons, Inc., 1970), pp. 267–273.

[17] *Ibid.*, p. 273.

[18] *Ibid.*, p. 270.

cent describe themselves as politically liberal, and less than 2 percent are black.[19]

Given the structure of power in American higher education, what general purposes do such institutions of advanced learning serve? Horowitz's article suggests that a major function of universities and colleges is to study the problems of the ruling class and avoid research and teaching that might be useful to those who wish to transform the political economy. James O'Connor's article in this chapter supplements Horowitz's analysis by listing briefly the other functions and "products" of the modern "knowledge industry."

Of the services that O'Connor mentions, the training of highly skilled professional and technical workers to serve industry and the state, and the development of new technology, products, and markets, are particularly sought by segments of the business class. According to Edward Denison, from 1929 to 1957 only 11 percent of the rate of national economic growth could be attributed to the growth of physical capital, compared to between 50 and 85 percent contributed by increases in the educational level of labor.[20] The change in the occupational structure of the United States in the twentieth century has meant a great decrease in the proportion of the labor force employed as farmers and unskilled laborers and a concomitant massive growth among professional, technical, and white-collar workers. The need to introduce labor-saving technology to cut costs, raise productivity, and increase the size of markets has led to Big Business support for the expansion of higher education, at public expense, in recent decades. Small businessmen, not dependent upon educated labor and capital-intensive technology, have frequently opposed government outlays for education. From their point of view, such expenditures have meant larger tax burdens, higher labor costs, and a weaker competitive position vis-à-vis the giant firms.

Big Business support for higher education has, of course, been selective. The hundreds of different academic degrees that can be obtained in American colleges and universities reflect the enormous occupational specialization resulting from the demands of new technology and its attendant social dislocations, not educational institutions' preoccupation with expanding knowledge for its own sake. The same thing can be said for the enormous increase in the number of college students in the United States during the past decades. This development has not been simply a consequence of the diffusion of the philosophy that a college education is the best way to promote an enlightened citizenry. Rather, it is primarily the result of industry's need for educated labor. Moreover, the lack of jobs available in the economy requires that an increasing proportion of young persons be channeled into activities not directly involved in the labor market. Among the residual functions of the university (and the armed forces) is the absorption of what would otherwise be a mass of unemployed and alienated young people.[21]

O'Connor's article mentions another function of the modern university

[19] Ibid., p. 267

[20] Edward Denison, The Sources of Economic Growth in the United States and the Alternatives before Us (New York: Committee for Economic Development, 1962).

[21] John and Margaret Rowntree, "Youth as a Class," International Socialist Journal, vol. 25 (February 1968), pp. 25–58.

which has increased in importance in recent years: the training of people to "solve," or rather meliorate, social problems and the related development of new techniques of intervention in domestic and foreign social crises. This function became more critical as the decay of cities, incidence of racial unrest, and resistance to American world economic, political, and military power magnified in the 1960s.[22] Nevertheless, the roots of this particular service to the political economy go back over a century to the Morrill Act of 1862, which set up colleges to aid farmers in agricultural development.

In the late nineteenth and early twentieth centuries the social and economic strains of industrialization created great turbulence in American cities and rural areas. In order to prevent the total breakdown of the political economy, ruling elites began to look toward the academic community for answers to the pressing problems resulting from capitalist development and contributing to the growth of radical movements which threatened to disrupt parliamentary capitalism. When academic reformers impressed by the example of Bismarck's "welfare state" began to support similar social welfare programs in America during the 1880s, corporate and government leaders showed little interest or sympathy. Only later, when the threat of social upheaval seemed real, did the partnership between the academy, corporations, and the state fully emerge.[23]

Possibly the first acceptance of the service ideology at a major American university occurred at the beginning of the new century. Liberal intellectuals at the University of Wisconsin developed what became known as the "Wisconsin idea," in which the university was seen as a provider of "nonpartisan" expertise to the world of government and industry.[24] Scholars such as Frederick Jackson Turner, Richard T. Ely, and University President Thomas C. Chamberlain desired to make Wisconsin a leading center of social sicence and social service which would help mediate between antagonistic social classes. Turner, the great American historian, expressed the nature of the social service ideal in the following manner during a commencement address at the University of Indiana in 1910:

> By training in science, law, politics, economics, and history the universities may supply from the ranks of democracy administrators, legislators, judges, and experts for commissioners who shall disinterestedly and intelligently mediate between contending interests. When the words "capitalistic classes" and "proletariat" can be used and understood in America, it is surely time to develop such men, with the ideal of service to the State, who may help break the force of these collisions. . . . It is hardly too much to say that the best hope of intelligent and principled progress in economic and social legislation lies in the increasing influence of American universities.[25]

[22] Ridgeway, op. cit., pp. 111–136.
[23] David Eakins, "The Development of Corporate Liberal Policy Research in the United States, 1885–1965," unpublished Ph.D. dissertation (Department of History, University of Wisconsin, 1966).
[24] Richard Hofstadter, Anti-intellectualism in American Life (New York: Alfred A. Knopf, 1962), pp. 199–203.
[25] Cited in ibid., pp. 200–201.

The notion of "service to the State" belied the spirit of nonpartisanship, of course, because the state itself was hardly neutral in the "collision" of "contending interests." Yet this fact was not even appreciated by many radicals,[26] and the preservation of the property system was certainly not considered a controversial issue by Turner and his colleagues.

The modest partnership between the academy and American business and political elites took on considerably more shape in the ensuing years. Academics played a considerable role in World War I. The development of psychological testing for draftees gave psychology respectability as a discipline. Loren Baritz examines this phenomenon and shows how the rise of psychology was further linked to its usefulness in labor-management relations.[27] Sociology gained in prestige largely because of its concern for the problems of the city and its contributions to industrial harmony.[28]

World War II consolidated the symbiotic relationship between government and the university, whose personnel played major roles in research and manpower training. Finally, the era of the Cold War and counterrevolution has witnessed the highest stage of service to the state. In the conduct of counterinsurgency such as the police training program in Saigon and the ill-fated Project Camelot,[29] social scientists actively collaborated with their physical science colleagues in serving American imperialism.

While the conscious service of capitalist institutions has been the most outstanding feature of the modern university, a neglected aspect of higher education has been its socialization of the young. Horowitz's discussion of the ideological roots underlying social research represents only the most blatant manifestation of this process. According to John McDermott, the very ideals of the academy—toleration, an emphasis on procedural as opposed to substantive rights, hierarchy, and cosmopolitanism—inadvertently create a cultural orientation that fails to equip many students for their future lives. This is particularly the case in the nonelite institutions, in which most students enrolled are destined to be low-level bureaucrats and clerks.[30]

On the basis of the evidence, it seems fair to characterize the contemporary university as a setting which inhibits the capacity for free inquiry. But, like all social institutions, the university cannot succeed totally in its institutional goals because of built-in contradictions. Because business and

[26] Gabriel Kolko, The Triumph of Conservatism: A Reinterpretation of American History, 1900–1916 (Chicago: Quadrangle Books, 1967); "The Decline of American Radicalism in the Twentieth Century," Studies on the Left, vol. 6 (September–October 1966), pp. 9–26. Also reprinted in Chapter 9 of this text.

[27] Loren Baritz, The Servants of Power: A History of the Use of Social Science in American Industry (New York: John Wiley & Sons, Inc., 1965), pp. 21–76.

[28] The Chicago school of sociology—Louis Wirth, Robert Park, W. I. Thomas, Frederick Thrasher, and their colleagues and students—became famous for its ethnographic accounts of "social disorganization" and social deviance in urban areas. For industrial harmony, see Baritz, op. cit., pp. 77–190.

[29] Martin Nicolaus, "The Professor, the Policeman and the Peasant," in Robert Perrucci and Marc Pilisuk, eds., The Triple Revolution: Social Problems in Depth (Boston: Little, Brown & Company, 1968), pp. 142–152. Irving Louis Horowitz, "The Life and Death of Project Camelot," in Ibid., pp. 153–169.

[30] John McDermott, "The Laying On of Culture," The Nation, vol. 208 (March 10, 1969), pp. 296–301. Also reprinted in Chapter 9 of this text.

government *need* well-trained, intelligent, and creative manpower, universities provide the resources that can contribute to the creation of a "nonfunctional" curriculum and the development of critical perspective by some of its students and professors. A library, a relatively unregulated work pace, and large numbers of young unattached persons mingling and exchanging ideas facilitate the development of dissenting life styles, ideas, and educational and vocational orientations. However, if dissension reaches a dangerous level, countermeasures may be expected. Dissent in American history has always been tolerated in small doses and in times of relative tranquility.

To consider some of the possibilities university decision-makers may entertain in more turbulent times, let us examine briefly some aspects of the Berkeley *Revised Academic Plan for 1969 to 1975*.[31]

In order to meet the changing needs of "society" the Plan envisages a reduction in the proportion of undergraduates in the student population of the notorious University of California campus.[32] Social science has not proven itself as indispensable as physical science to the political economy, while social science majors have been shown to be particularly volatile and disproportionately likely to become involved in campus disturbances. Perhaps this is why the Berkeley plan calls for a steep reduction in the number of social science majors, despite evidence of growing student demand for these majors.[33] Concomitantly, some biological and physical sciences have not experienced as great an increase in student demand in recent years; but, because of the great long-term need of government and industry for these scientists and, perhaps, because of the general political passivity of students majoring in biological and physical science, the Berkeley plan supports a much smaller reduction in the number of students majoring in these fields.[34]

The authors of the plan rationalize their rather cynical disregard of students and those neglected nonaffluent Americans whose well-being may be aided by social scientific knowledge if oriented toward their grievances by claiming that there would not be enough social science faculty to handle excessive numbers of students. Yet this teaching shortage would seem to create two options: either increase resources, including faculty, for social science instruction or cut student enrollment in this area. One suspects that the latter option was not chosen by accident.[35] The Berkeley plan illustrates the kind of restructuring of higher education one may expect in the name of academic freedom and university autonomy in a capitalist society where the needs of industry and its governmental partner ultimately determine the direction of intellectual endeavor.

[31] *Revised Academic Plan, 1969–1975: University of California Berkeley* (Sacramento, Calif.: The Regents of the University of California, 1969).
[32] *Ibid.*, p. 38.
[33] *Ibid.*, pp. 127–128. Interestingly, the major cuts seem to be in sociology, psychology, history and anthropology—disciplines which seem to produce a disproportionate number of student activists. Economics and political science, which are less associated with radicalism, do not suffer to the same extent.
[34] *Ibid.*, pp. 124–125, 127.
[35] A by-product of the reduction in undergraduate social science majors and the increase in graduate enrollments will be a limitation on the number of nontenured social science faculty, who have also been most prone to promote radical ideas and sympathize with student activism. See Lipset and Ladd, *op. cit.*

BILLION DOLLAR BRAINS:
HOW WEALTH PUTS KNOWLEDGE
IN ITS POCKET

I. Entrepreneurs of Higher Education

"Educate, and save ourselves and our families and our money from mobs."
—Henry Lee Higginson, Benefactor of Harvard, in a Fund-Raising Letter,
March 1886

Today's generation of students, who at this very moment are being suspended, beaten bloody and jailed for their efforts to end the subservience of intellect to power, loosen up entrance requirements, create new departments and colleges and attempt to make the university more relevant to their needs, might be interested in knowing how the system got set up in the first place. It did not, as it might seem, spring full-blown from the head of the absent-minded professor. The development of the modern American university was not left to the natural bent of those within its ivory towers; it was shaped by the ubiquitous charity of the foundations and the guiding mastery of wealth.

On an autumn day in 1875, a solemn ceremony in Nashville, Tennessee, marked the opening exercises of Vanderbilt University, whose benefactor, the semiliterate Cornelius Vanderbilt, figures in Gustavus Myers' *History of the Great American Fortunes* as "the foremost mercantile pirate and commercial blackmailer of his day." (His first millions were pilfered from the federal government, in very modern fashion, through the corruption of post office officials.) Commodore Vanderbilt's New York minister, the Reverend Charles F. Deems, had come down especially for the occasion, and during the concluding moments of the ceremony he rose to read the following telegram: "New York, October 4. To Dr. Charles F. Deems: Peace and goodwill to all men. C. Vanderbilt." Then Deems, a true servant of the pulpit and the purse, gazed up at a portrait of the benefactor hanging on the wall and intoned the Holy Scripture, Acts Ten, the Thirty-First Verse: "Cornelius, thy prayer is heard, and thine alms are had in remembrance in the sight of God."

Cornelius Vanderbilt was not the only wealthy patron of the times attempting to earn his passage through the eye of the needle by bestowing alms on collegiate supplicants. John D. Archbold, for example, chief bagman for Standard Oil, cast his benevolent grace on Syracuse University; Mrs. Russell Sage, whose husband began his career by stealing a railroad from the

Reprinted, with deletions, from David Horowitz, "Billion Dollar Brains: How Wealth Puts Knowledge in Its Pocket," *Ramparts*, May 1969, pp. 36–44. Copyright Ramparts Magazine Inc., 1969. By permission of the Editors. David Horowitz is an editor of *Ramparts* and the author of several books, including *The Free World Colossus* and *Empire and Revolution*.

city in which he was an official, blessed Rensselaer Polytechnic Institute with a new school of mechanical engineering; and there were hosts of others.

Prior to the Civil War, when the style of giving was still aristocratic and restrained, the largest single benefaction to a college had been Abbot Lawrence's $50,000 to Harvard. Colleges then were small, humble and well suited to their purpose as finishing schools and theological seminaries for the gentlemanly well-to-do. As the century matured, however, the rogues and robber barons of the new industrial age began to get into the act, demonstrating how paltry the conceptions of education had been in the preceding era. Rockefellers and Stanfords endowed whole institutions, not with tens of thousands, but tens of millions. The horizons of academe expanded. Greek and Latin, classical education, philosophy—these may have been fine for effete gentlemen but of what use were they in the *real* world? The real world, of course, was defined by the money which had suddenly become available for new and expanded institutions of learning.

From Stephen Van Rensselaer to Peter Cooper, from Charles Pratt (Standard Oil) to Andrew Carnegie, industrialists flocked to finance technological institutes which would honor and preserve their names (an important consideration for many who had amassed fortunes but no families) and promote the technical progress that would keep the money mills rolling. Nor was technology the only area of learning in which businessmen sought to open new paths. Joseph Wharton, a Philadelphia manufacturer of zinc, nickel and iron, was concerned that "college life offers great temptations and opportunities for the formation of superficial lightweight characters, having shallow accomplishments but lacking in grip and hold upon real things. . . ." To overcome the shallowness of the current college generation, Wharton proposed to the trustees of the University of Pennsylvania that they set up a "school of finance and economy." His plan was given a sympathetic hearing by the trustees. As one academic historian describes it: "The $100,000 Wharton offered to fulfill his proposal tempted the trustees into immediate acceptance"—and the Wharton School of Finance and Commerce was born.

Not only business schools and technical institutes but medical and other professional schools made their first appearance in this period. The college was giving way to the university. And the patrons of the new age were the captains of industry, the lords and masters of the times. The power of these men in education, as elsewhere, was a function not only of the size of their capital and their dispensations, which were gigantic, but of their aggressive dynamism as well. As givers, they became "entrepreneurs in the field of higher education."

The autobiography of G. Stanley Hall, president of Clark University, reveals that he was forced to break contracts at the orders of the founder, to reduce the scale of salaries because the founder wished to economize, and to add an undergraduate college to what he had planned as a graduate institution. This relationship was not wholly typical, in part because the president retained his independence of mind, even though he lacked the independent financial muscle to put his ideas into practice. Usually, college administrators were far more servile. Indeed, the attitude of the academic community as a whole towards its patrons bordered on sycophancy. The patrons of the university, being uncultivated themselves, often sought association with the men of learning. According to Walter Metzger, a recent historian of academic freedom, they received from academics "ornate courtesies of gratitude. They did not enter academe as intruders; they were welcomed into the realm and escorted to its high places by its very grateful inhabitants. Within the academic fraternity, to cultivate the goodwill of donors was a highly approved activity, betokening fine public spirit. To offend the bearer of gifts was an action sometimes defined as the deepest disloyalty and treachery. Cordiality was thus demanded of professors by the most compelling of motives—self-interest and the desire for social approval."

One of Major Higginson's primary concerns in conducting his philanthropic campaigns on behalf of Harvard had been that the end of aristocratic tutelage appeared to be imminent, that "Democracy has got hold of the world, and *will* rule." How fortunate, then, that with a little sprinkling of the wealth that was literally pouring into their pockets ("Think how easily it has come," Higginson remarked to one of his correspondents), the wealthy donors could sustain a filial relationship with the teachers of society's elite and the shapers of its knowledge: "Our chance is *now*—before the country is full and the struggle for bread becomes intense and bitter. . . . I would have the gentlemen of this country lead the new men, who are trying to become gentlemen. . . . Give one-fourth of your last year, and count it money potted down for quiet good."

And if any ingrates tried to raise an audible note of discord to mar the harmony of Knowledge and Industry, of the ideal and the practical, retribution was swift.

During the radical upsurge of the '80s and '90s, a series of exemplary firings of liberal scholars took place, usually as a result of the professors having linked some of their abstract ideas with the issues of the hour (populism, free silver vs. gold, the monopolistic trusts). As the liberal English economist J. A. Hobson pointed out at the time, "Advanced doctrine may be tolerated, if it is kept well in the background of pure theory; but, where it is embodied in concrete instances drawn from current experience, the pecuniary prospects of the college are instinctively felt to be endangered."

Of course, no college administration admitted that it was interfering with the spirit of free inquiry. Far from it. The professors were dismissed, the colleges said, not because of their views, but because of their lack of professionalism, their partisanship (justification of the status quo was of course considered in keeping with scholarly neutrality and objectivity). While the threat of dismissal was to retain a certain utility as an instrument for inducing "responsible" academic behavior, in the long run the actual costs of carrying it out were to prove excessively high. The protestations the administrators were already forced to make showed that, as a method of sanitizing higher education, the presumptive sack was too crude for scholars, and therefore inefficient.

Where it is available, however, the carrot is always more efficacious and gentlemanly than the stick. As education became more and more bound up with the success of the industrial system, therefore, the nexus of control

The Knowledge Industry

exercised over academics came increasingly to lie in the positive advantages which the established powers were able to bestow on a professionalism ready to serve the status quo and to withhold from "partisan" scholarship ranged against it. Advancement, prestige, research facilities, entrée into high society and later into government itself, were all reserved for responsible— and respectful—exemplars of the academic profession. Radicals were left to wither on the university vine.

Reinforcing this sophisticated approach was the appearance of a new institution on the educational scene, at once far more powerful than even Vanderbilts or Stanfords, and presenting a far less menacing front to the unsuspecting academic mind.

II. Enter the Big Foundations

"The very ambition of such corporations to reform educational abuses is itself a source of danger. Men are not constituted educational reformers by having a million dollars to spend."—Jacob Gould Schurman, President of Cornell, 1892–1920

"As one reviews the relationship between institutions of higher learning and the major foundations during the critical first two decades of this century," writes a former division chief of the Rockefeller Foundation, "One finds oneself wondering if it is too much to say that the foundations became in effect the American way of discharging many of the functions performed in other countries by the Ministry of Education." The division chief need not have been so modest.

Between them, the Rockefeller and Carnegie Foundations (there were several of each) had an annual revenue which, as a congressional report of 1915 pointed out, was "at least twice as great as the appropriations of the Federal Government for similar purposes, namely, educational and social service." But the lump sums only begin to tell the story.

In the first place, while the Carnegie and Rockefeller Foundations decided on an expenditure of funds during this period which amounted to a fifth of the *total* income of colleges and universities, "When one realizes . . . that essentially all the funds available to the foundations were free for the encouragement of innovation while almost all the regular income of the university was tied to ongoing commitments, it is easy to comprehend the overwhelming significance of the foundations' part." (Robert S. Morison, a former director of medical and natural sciences for the Rockefeller Foundation.)

In the second place, while the foundation millions really represent taxable surplus that ought to be in the hands of the community and dispensed by a real Ministry of Education, they actually come from the charitable trusts in the form of "gifts." And this very fact transforms their power and gives them a geometric possibility known as "matching." The Rockefeller Foundation offers to put up $10 million but stipulates that the beneficiary must raise two or three times that to receive its benefaction. This puts the Rockefeller

Foundation in the driver's seat, as far as conditions are concerned, and doubles or triples the power of its money. Thus, the massive endowment drives between 1902 and 1924 were inspired by the necessity of raising $140 million in order to receive $60 million from the Rockefeller's General Education Board. By 1931–32, it was estimated that the foundations had directly stimulated the giving of $660 million, or fully *two-thirds* of the total endowment of all American institutions of higher learning—colleges, universities and professional schools.

Furthermore, the potential for qualitative influence on the part of the foundations was enhanced by the fact that they were the largest single contributors to these endowment funds, and, more importantly, by the fact that as income sources they were *permanent* features of the educational scene, and hence their future goodwill had to be cultivated as well. This is probably the most subtle and significant new factor in the foundation approach to educational benefaction. For these are "perpetual trusts," and while a Cornelius Vanderbilt may die and leave his million to playboy heirs no longer interested in the training of tomorrow's elite, the Rockefeller and Carnegie Foundations which were here yesterday will be here in the future, managed by active leaders of the business world who understand the vital role that an educational establishment can play in the preservation and expansion of their wealth-producing system.

Andrew Carnegie did not originally set out to impose a general system of standards on American institutions of higher learning. Rather, he thought to make a grand gesture of generosity by using some of the millions he had stolen from the public through watered stock in his steel combines to ameliorate the condition of a dedicated and penurious segment of society: the college teacher. And so Carnegie announced that his Foundation would provide free pensions to all college teachers. It seemed like a very simple proposition.

But no sooner had the proposal been made than the president of the Carnegie Foundation, Henry S. Pritchett, advised the benefactor that higher education in America was in a state of utter confusion. Since, with the exception of a certification system associated with the University of Michigan, there were no general standards for defining a college or university, there was a plethora of conceptions of what a college should be. While among these institutions were diploma mills run solely for the profit of the proprietors—inevitable in a market system—there were also community financed and administered colleges, often set up by religious denominations and reflecting the needs of the communities themselves: chaos or freedom, depending on how you looked at it. President Pritchett looked at it and decided that "some criterion would have to be introduced [into the pension scheme] as to what constituted a college." After all, it wouldn't do to give a free pension to just any teacher. One must have standards. (Besides, there were economic constraints; in the end there wasn't even enough money to go around for teachers in the "bona fide" colleges certified by the Foundation.)

So the Carnegie Foundation announced that it was going to provide pensions for teachers in colleges; "colleges," according to the Foundation, were possessed of at least a $200,000 endowment (later this was escalated to

$500,000) or, in the case of State universities, an annual income of $100,000 —requirements which served to force the institutions into an even greater dependence on wealth. Colleges had strict entrance requirements, including so many hours of secondary education (these came to be known as "Carnegie units" and had a revolutionizing, and many would maintain damaging, effect on the secondary school curriculum). A college had at least eight distinct departments, each headed by a PhD (the beginning of the enthronement of that stultifying credential).

No institution that wanted to attract or retain quality teachers could afford to resist the Foundation's offer, and so these became the standards of the day. The process and its power was well exemplified in the Foundation's additional stipulation that institutions accepted into the program must give up their denominational affiliations. (In the broad university scene, this stipulation was subverted by the General Education Board which followed Carnegie's conditions in making its own grants, but chose to support the big denominational colleges while ignoring the small ones.) Among the colleges which gave up their religious character to receive Carnegie money were Wesleyan, Drury, Drake and Brown. Colleges which refused to comply with Carnegie and Rockefeller conditions were "left to die from financial starvation and other 'natural' causes."

The enormous implications of this sequence of events were remarked upon by the Walsh Commission, which in 1915 conducted the first government investigation of the foundations (and their relation to the industrial empires of the benefactors): "It would seem conclusive that if an institution will willingly abandon its religious affiliations through the influence of these foundations, it will even more easily conform to their will any other part of its organization or teaching." (Provided, of course, that the influence is ever so subtly exerted.)

What has to be remembered is that the reforms which the foundations had demonstrated such an impressive power in inducing were all in fields of college activity to which they were not directly appropriating a single dollar. Similarly, for the most part, they did not themselves invent the standards which they were able, via the power of their purse strings, to impose, but *selected* them from existing proposals. Ivy Lee, the Rockefeller public relations man who was one of the pioneers of the new benevolent image of corporate America, had described for the Walsh Commission the importance of appearances. "We know," Lee wrote, "that Henry VIII by his obsequious deference to the forms of law was able to get the English people to believe in him so completely that he was able to do almost anything with them." It was the *forms* of law, of democracy, that had to be observed to achieve maximum influence and power. Looked at *formally*, the foundations were imposing nothing. They did not invent the standards; the colleges were at every point free to accept or reject them. Their own role was not one of compulsion, but support. They were even advancing the cause of academic freedom by making the professors more secure. In the appearance of things, as opposed to their reality (which was quite the same as if the foundations had the force of law behind their prescriptions), lay the chief danger of foundation power. For its very subtlety was its strength. Where overt control would have been resisted, these no less effective forms of influences were tolerated. In the realm of the mind, the illusion of freedom may be more real than freedom itself.

If in the period of its origins the university was heavily dependent on foundation support, it was no less so in the period of its growth. As the university system expanded and non-foundation sources of income became available for endowment and building funds, administration and teachers' benefits, and other areas in which the foundations had played a pioneering role, the foundation directors began to shift their sights towards the new areas of innovation and growth. As the above-cited former division director of the Rockefeller Foundation put it, foundation funds were now "increasingly reserved for new and presumably venturesome undertakings which, once they had proved their worth, would be taken over by the universities' general funds." It was precisely the availability of foundation funds for the "growing edge" of knowledge, "for experimenting with new educational methods, developing research programs, and demonstrating the value of new knowledge," that made it possible for the foundations to maintain their guiding role in the shaping of higher learning in America. For with few exceptions, and until very recently, foundation funds were the only significant monies available for nonmilitary organized research and institutional innovation in the academic world.

The ability of the foundations to dominate the margins of growth in the university system was viewed with a critical and prophetic eye by Harold Laski, shortly after he had spent a few tumultuous semesters at Harvard. The passage of time has only made his perceptions more acute. "A university principal who wants his institution to expand," he wrote, "has no alternative except to see it expand in the directions of which one or other of the foundations happens to approve. There may be doubt, or even dissent among the teachers in the institution, but what possible chance has doubt or dissent against a possible gift of, say, a hundred thousand dollars? And how, conceivably, can the teacher whose work fits in with the scheme of the prospective endowment fail to appear more important in the eyes of the principal or his trustees than the teacher for whose subject, or whose views, the foundation has neither interest or liking? . . . What are his chances of promotion if he pursues a path of solitary inquiry in a world of colleges competing for the substantial crumbs which fall from the foundation's table? And, observe, there is not a single point here in which there is the slightest control from, or interference by, the foundation itself. It is merely the fact that a fund is within reach which permeates everything and alters everything. The college develops along the lines the foundation approves. The dependence is merely implicit, but it is in fact quite final . . . where the real control lies no one who has watched the operation in process can possibly doubt."

III.   What's Good for Harvard . . .

"There are two great clichés about the university. One pictures it as a radical institution, when in fact it is most conservative in its institutional

The Knowledge Industry

*conduct. The other pictures it as autonomous, a cloister, when the histor-
ical fact is that it has always responded, but seldom so quickly as today,
to the desires and demands of external groups."*—Clark Kerr, 1963

On paper, the contemporary American system of higher education looks
wonderfully diverse, a vast pluralistic sea of independent academic communities. There are more than 2000 institutions of higher education in
America, 800 publicly supported and 1400 private. Half the publicly supported
colleges are district or city schools and two-thirds of the private institutions
are denominational. If higher education were in practice anything like its
appearance on paper, then despite the historical evolution of the university,
its links to wealth and the ability of the foundations to dominate its innovational areas, the sheer quantity of institutions would cause the foundation
largesse to be spread so thin that its influence would evaporate.

The fact is, however, that the American system of higher education is a
highly centralized, pyramidal structure in which the clearly defined escalat-
ing heights intellectually dominate the levels below. Perhaps the most
tangible indication of the rigid hierarchy which characterizes the academic
community is the concentration of PhD programs in select prestige centers
at the apex of the pyramid. For the PhD is at once a validating credential and
the certificate of entry into the academic profession. It also represents an
arduous apprenticeship in the accepted principles and acceptable perspectives of academic scholarship; it defines the methodological and ideological
horizons which command academic respect and within which the "professional" operates.

Although there are over 2000 colleges and universities in America, 75
per cent of the PhD's are awarded in a mere 25 of them, institutions which
constitute a Vatican of the higher learning, the ultimate court of what can
and what cannot be legitimately pursued within the academic church. Most
of these select universities—Harvard, Yale, Princeton, the University of
Chicago, Columbia, Johns Hopkins, Stanford, MIT, Cornell—had emerged
as dominant institutions by the advent of World War I. Together with such
latecomers as the University of California, they form a relatively tight-knit
intellectual establishment. As David Riesman and Christopher Jencks observe
in their study, *The Academic Revolution*: "These universities have long been
remarkably similar in what they encourage and value. They turn out PhD's
who, despite conspicuous exceptions, mostly have quite similar ideas about
what their discipline covers, how it should be taught, and how its frontiers
should be advanced."

The similarity of ideas and perspectives among scholars who otherwise
lay strenuous claims to intellectual independence and ideological diversity
presents no real mystery to the outside observer—the apprenticeship and
training of academics within the centralized structure of the university system could be expected to produce no other result. The first stage in an academic career is the completion of a PhD, an effort which in the non-exact
sciences can take anywhere from five to ten years, and which is accomplished
under the watchful eyes and according to the principles and conceptions of
the already established masters of the guild. Having completed the PhD,

which represents his first serious work as a "scholar," the apprentice professor still has four to seven years of non-tenured status during which he is subject to review on an annual basis. This period of insecurity during which he is at the mercy of his tenured superiors (and in most institutions the university administrators as well) coincides with a time in his personal life when he has probably acquired a family and sunk some local roots. Hence the threat of being dispatched to the hinterlands should he fail to show—by publication of approved articles and further commitments of his intellectual energy and reputation—that he is still a responsible fellow and understands what is scholarly and professional according to accepted canons, is a real threat indeed. Especially when the action needed to dismiss him is the excessively simple and unobtrusive one of not renewing his contract at the end of the year. The Jesuits only asked for a human mind up to the age of seven years in order to control it forever; the American academic establishment has it to thirty-five. Is it any wonder that the product is generally so timid, conservative and conformist?

Responsibility for the monopolistic structure of the academic marketplace (a structure which neatly mirrors the economy on which it is founded) lies with the great foundations who at the outset of the university era made a calculated decision to create a "lead system" of colleges, which by virtue of their overwhelming prestige would set the standards for, and in effect dominate, the rest of the educational scene. Thus, while the foundations stimulated two-thirds of the total endowment funding of all institutions of higher learning in America during the first third of the century, "the major portion" of the funds they were responsible for were "concentrated in some 20 of these institutions." (Hollis, *Philanthropic Foundations and Higher Education*.)

Even more important than the concentration of endowment funds was the concentration of innovational and research funds, and funds for the creation of those facilities which provide the basis for a major center of learning. "The development of major university centers of research," an official account of the Rockefeller philanthropies explains, "became the most important part of the (Laura Spelman Rockefeller) Memorial's program. Chicago, Harvard, Columbia, Yale . . . and many others were assisted in developing rounded centers of social-science research. This frequently involved fluid research funds appropriated to the university to be used in its own discretion; aid to university presses; the provision of special sums for publication; grants to enable a number of the centers to experiment with different types of training . . . and various other devices for stimulating and encouraging the development of techniques and teaching in the social studies." In 1929, the chancellor of the University of Chicago, Robert Hutchins, summed up the achievements of this agency in the following terms: "The Laura Spelman Rockefeller Memorial in its brief but brilliant career (it was later merged with the Rockefeller Foundation) did more than any other agency to promote the social sciences in the United States."

The practice of concentrating funds in major university centers during this strategic period when the birth of institutions of research in the university complex took place has remained a permanent pattern of foundation financing. Thus the Ford Foundation distributed $105 million worth of grants in economics and business from 1951 through the first quarter of 1965, but 77.5 per cent of this went to only ten universities and five business-controlled research and policy organizations (Resources for the Future, the Brookings Institution, the Population Council, the National Bureau of Economic Research and the Committee for Economic Development). This has had an absolutely decisive effect in perpetuating the concentration of institution-alized knowledge which the direct endowment of individual wealth had instigated. In 1912, 51.6 per cent of the articles in the major academic journals of economics were written by economists from only ten universities. In 1962, although the individual universities had changed somewhat, 53.8 per cent of the articles were still being written at ten centers. Eight of these institu-tions were among those most favored by the Ford Foundation.

With few exceptions, of course, these major university research com-plexes coincide with the strongholds of the old wealth, the aristocratic centers of the American upper class (Harvard, Yale, Stanford, etc.). It is here that the channels to Wall Street and Washington are most open and inviting to the co-optable professor, and that social attitudes and traditions exert the most powerful and most subtle conservatizing pressures. (It is for just these reasons, moreover, that such schools can afford the flexibility that has earned them the undeserved reputation of being the most academically "free.")

One of the oldest of these centers outside the eastern Ivy League estab-lishment (where the connections are well known) is Stanford University, down the peninsula from San Francisco. While by no means unique, the Stanford Research Institute (SRI)-Stanford Industrial Park complex built around Stanford University provides, in fact, the most up-to-date example of the new levels of intimacy which Wealth and Intellect (and latterly the federal Defense establishment) have attained in the postwar period. (Only one Stan-ford trustee is not a corporate director: John W. Gardner, former president of the Carnegie Foundation, former secretary of Health, Education and Welfare, and presently head of the foundation/corporation-sponsored Urban Coalition.) William Hewlett and David Packard—two Stanford undergrad-uates who set up an electronics shop in their garage before World War II, got on the war production gravy train and eventually wound up with a billion-dollar military-industrial giant, the Hewlett-Packard Company—perhaps best exemplify the seamless web of vested interests which envelops this house of intellect.

Both Hewlett and Packard are trustees of Stanford and SRI, and both are directors of several large corporations in the Stanford Industrial Park. An impressive number of corporations in the park are in fact "spin-off" firms, resulting directly from research in Stanford's chemistry, electrical engineering and physics laboratories. Packard, who was recently named deputy secretary of Defense, is also a trustee of the National Merit Scholar-ship Corporation and the U.S. Churchill Foundation. Hewlett is a member of the President's Science Advisory Committee. Their positions of eminence in educational philanthropy and military-industrial moneymaking ("Profit is the monetary measurement of our contribution to society"—David Packard) are far from unique. Fellow SRI trustee and former Stanford University trustee Stephen D. Bechtel, of the Bechtel Corporation (builder of bigger and better military bases and longer oil pipelines), is also a trustee of the Ford Foundation. Another holder of dual trusteeships at Ford and Stanford is the Shell Oil Corporation, which has directors on the boards of both.

For the corporations involved in the Stanford-SRI-Industrial triangle, the relationship is pure gravy. Most of the industries involved are heavily research- and technology-oriented. The Bechtel Corporation, probably the biggest construction firm in the world, employs on a permanent basis (rather than under control) only 2000 people, most of them high-grade engineers. The electronics firms are similarly intellect-oriented; in the words of one journalistic account of the success-studded career of a Stanford professor who became a moving spirit in the SRI and finally a director of Hewlett-Packard and other "Stanford" corporations: "The industry's raw material is brainpower, and the university's students and professors are a prime source." Stanford not only supplies its corporations with the raw material, but provides refining facilities as well. Thus, under a new program Stanford engineering courses will be piped into the industrial enterprises via a four-channel TV network.

For the enterprising professor and student, the avenues to corporate success are manifold. William Rambo, associate dean of Stanford's engineering school, has said that he expects his students to become executives and company directors. All this opportunity for personal advancement (and aggrandizement) must inevitably have its effects on education. Perhaps as insightful a commentary as any was contained in James Ridgeway's impressions after visiting the SRI complex: "Professors once sneered at businessmen and the profit motive," he wrote, "but since they have been so successful in taking up the game themselves, the profit motive is now approvingly referred to as the 'reward structure.'"

IV. Rigging the Marketplace of Ideas

"Mr. Rockefeller could find no better insurance for his hundreds of millions than to invest one of them in subsidizing all agencies that make for social change and progress."—Frank P. Walsh, Chairman of the Commission on Industrial Relations, 1915

Dominating the avenues of prestige and supplying the main funds for social research within the universities, while providing the principal access to influence in the outside world, wealth has inevitably exerted the most profound, pervasive and distorting effects on the structure of knowledge and education in the United States. This has been achieved through lavish support and recognition for the kind of investigations and techniques that are ideologically and pragmatically useful to the system which it dominates, and by withholding support on any substantial scale from empirical research

The Knowledge Industry

projects and theoretical frameworks that would threaten to undermine the status quo. (Exceptional and isolated support for individual radicals may be useful, however, in establishing the openness of the system at minimum risk.)

Although it is an indubitable social fact that wealth provides the sea in which academic fish must swim, no self-respecting professor would admit to the full and unpleasant implications of that fact. Thus, Robert Dahl, former president of the American Political Science Association, and one of the most eminent beneficiaries of foundation support, while admitting that the foundations, "because of their enormous financial contributions to scholarly research, and the inevitable selection among competing proposals that these entail, exert a considerable effect on the scholarly community," maintains that "the relationship between foundation policy and current trends in academic research is too complex for facile generalities." (Of course there have been no systematic attempts by academics to investigate the cumulative impact of this relationship and discover even arduous generalities.) According to Dahl, "Perhaps the simplest accurate statement is that the relationship is to a very high degree reciprocal: the staffs of the foundations are highly sensitive to the views of distinguished scholars, on whom they rely heavily for advice." For a sophisticated analyst of political power this statement exhibits remarkable naivete. For it is precisely in determining which distinguished scholars (e.g., Professor Dahl or C. Wright Mills, S. M. Lipset or Herbert Marcuse) they choose to listen to that the foundations "determine" everything that follows.

The foundations themselves regard their funds as "risk capital" which can be employed "to demonstrate the validity of a new idea" (Morison). If the idea is successful, if the investment of funds covering facilities, research needs and salaries for collaborative effort establishes the idea in the intellectual mainstream, then full development can be financed from "normal" sources of capital (e.g., from the university budget, the corporations or the government).

A spectacular example of how the alliance between brains and money can become an unbeatable combination in the academic marketplace is afforded by the rise of the behavioralist persuasion and its offshoot pluralist ideology in the social sciences. Beginning as a localized academic phenomenon, with the benefit of the foundations' capital it ultimately achieved unchallenged national preeminence. The intellectual inspirer and organizer of the new "value-free," statistical-empirical outlook was Charles E. Merriam, and his department at the University of Chicago was the hothouse of its early development. Such stellar names in behavioralism as Harold Lasswell, V. O. Key Jr., David Truman, Herbert Simon and Gabriel Almond were either graduate students or, in the case of Lasswell, a faculty member, in Merriam's department before World War II.

A politically-oriented individual, as well as a political scientist (he ran for mayor of Chicago on a "Bull Moose" Republican ticket), Merriam began his organizing efforts in the academic world in the early '20s. As he himself summed up the crystallizing experience of his subsequent career, he had once gone to a high official of the University of Chicago and asked for a stenographer and other assistance in order to conduct an enquiry. The reply was that "the University could not possibly afford to aid all its professors in writing their books." The "answer" to this situation, wrote Merriam, "was the Social Science Research Building . . . and . . . the Public Administration Center"—both financed by the Laura Spelman Rockefeller Memorial, under the direction of Beardsley Ruml. (Ruml, who went from the Scott Company to the Carnegie Foundation to Rockefeller, was later to become dean of the Social Sciences Division at Chicago.)

The Rockefeller-Merriam team did not limit its horizons to local academic projects. The Social Science Research Council was founded in 1923, largely through Merriam's and Ruml's efforts, with Merriam as its chairman and Ruml as a member of its policy committee. Over the next ten years the Council, which was made up of representatives from the American Political Science Association, the American Sociological Society, the American Historical Association and four comparable groups in anthropology, economics, statistics and psychology, received $4.2 million in income. Of this, $3.9 million was from the Rockefellers, the rest from other private foundations. With these funds at its disposal, the Council became the "greatest single patron or clearing house of patronage for the social sciences," and throughout the Hungry Thirties this patronage was used extensively in behalf of the behavioral outlook.

The idea itself, of course, was ripe for the times. But as Dahl has noted: "If the foundations had been hostile to the behavioral approach, there can be no doubt that it would have had very rough sledding indeed." How many equally ripe ideas lacked the risk capital to demonstrate their validity?

After the war, the behavioral movement got into full stride, as Rockefeller, Carnegie and the mammoth new Ford Foundation (which briefly set up its own Behavioral Sciences Division) got directly into the act, financing an unprecedented proliferation of ambitious behavioral investigations and expensive but necessary survey research centers to amass and analyze the empirical data for behavioral studies. By then it was evident that the collaborative effort had paid off. In 1950, the behavioralist Peter Odegard was elected head of the American Political Science Association, and in subsequent years behavioralists held the presidency with increasing regularity; from 1965 to 1967, the behavioralists Truman, Almond and Dahl held the presidency, symbolizing the fact that theirs had finally become the established outlook in the field. (In a survey conducted among members of the Political Science Association in the early '60s to determine their opinion as to the best political scientists of the postwar period, only one of the top eight was not a behavioralist.)

In backing the behavioralists, the foundation trustees had not only backed men whose goodwill they enjoyed (the very mechanism of grant-giving assures this) but whose ideas had a definite utility from their interested point of view. The emphasis on observable behavior, and the acceptance of the given socio-economic framework as the basis of analysis, together with a scientific bias against the kind of theoretical probing which calls into question the basis of the status quo order itself, were naturally congenial to the men who put up the millions (as, no doubt, was the fact that behavioral infor-

310   The Knowledge Industry

mation which the scientists gathered about "masses" exceeded that gathered about "elites" by a factor of 100-1, according to behavioralist Karl Deutsch).

Moreover, the information gathered in survey research into the mass behavior of consumers, voters, trade unionists and organization members generally, as well as the techniques (e.g., of administration) developed out of the research, were obviously very useful from a manipulative point of view to the elites responsible for managing social systems and maximizing returns from the status quo. Behavioral studies soon were in high demand, from government to business directorates, from the military to the CIA. Indeed, the interest of the CIA provides one of the most bizarre and illuminating incidents in the history of behavioralism and its pluralist offspring.

One of the more important promoters of the behavioral mode within the American Political Science Association has been Evron Kirkpatrick, who has served as the executive director of the Association since 1954. Kirkpatrick's background for the job was interesting to say the least. At the end of World War II, he was assistant director of research and analysis in the OSS (intelligence). In 1946, he was assistant research director and projects control officer in Research and Intelligence for the State Department. In 1947, he became intelligence program advisor for State, and in 1948, chief of the external research staff, a position he held until 1952, when he assumed the additional post of chief of psychological intelligence. It was from this position that in 1954, Kirkpatrick was appointed executive director of the American Political Association. The political scientists seem not to have been at all curious about the background of their executive director until February 1967, when someone had the temerity to point out that Kirkpatrick was also president of a CIA-funded research organization called Operations and Policy Research Incorporated. (The treasurer of the American Political Science Association, Max Kampelman, turned out to be the vice president of Operations and Policy Research.)

When a group of political scientists at the University of Hawaii circulated a petition calling for the resignations of Kirkpatrick and Kampelman, it became clear that an investigation was in order. It was initiated by the president of the Association, Robert Dahl, and was conducted by four past Association presidents. These preeminent representatives of political science concluded that the Association "has received no funds directly [sic] from any intelligence agency of the government, nor has it carried on any activities for any intelligence agency of government." Moreover, "We wish to record our recognition of the dedication and services of these two men to the Association in the past and our full confidence in the value of their future services."

The notion that the only significant influences the CIA could exert through the executive director were the channeling of "tainted" funds or the use of the Association as a front or perhaps a spy network, represented a view of power that was astoundingly primitive.

The study of power, and the disbelief in its undemocratic and sinister concentration in American society, are of course the hallmarks of the pluralists, easily the most ideologically significant branch of the behavioralist school, and including such prestigious names as Peter Odegard, V. O. Key, S. M. Lipset, David Truman, Gabriel Almond and Dahl. These men have marshaled all the sophistication that the trade will bear to demonstrate that America is an effective democracy where no cohesive social group (and in particular no economic class) wields predominant political power in its own behalf. In a country in which six per cent of the population owns 50 per cent of the wealth, and where an upper class representing two per cent of the population holds majority positions in every significant institution of national power, the pluralists' panglossian views of American democracy are obviously worth their weight in gold.

Not so the views of the pluralists' main antagonist, C. Wright Mills, whose exposure of the "power elite" provided a whole generation with a basis for understanding the society around them, while bringing him ostracism and harassment from the academic establishment and a cold shoulder from the patrons of research. (Thus, while Dahl received $70,000 in grants from the Rockefeller Foundation in the wake of his pluralist study of New Haven, after writing *The Power Elite* Mills was abruptly cut off from foundations financing for his ambitious sociological projects.)

This points up what is perhaps the most far-reaching effect of the foundations' preeminent role in financing academic research, namely, the unbelievable dearth of organized information and systematic investigation of the men and corporate institutions that control the American economy, command the apex of the income pyramid, and dominate the strategic positions of power in the federal government. In the bibliography to *The Power Elite*, Mills lists eight studies of the American upper class which were useful to him. Not one of these was written by an academic.

The dearth has not gone unnoticed by the pluralists themselves. Observing that there is general recognition that business and politics have a more than passing relationship to one another, Robert Dahl in a recent essay draws attention to the fact that "during the past fifty years, only about a dozen articles have appeared on the subject of business in the pages of *The American Political Science Review*." Sociologists have not shown much greater interest, and at the American Sociological Association convention this year, they were justly excoriated by Martin Nicolaus: "Sociology is not now and never has been any kind of objective seeking out of social truth or reality . . . the eyes of sociologists, with few but honorable . . . exceptions, have been turned downwards, and their palms upwards."

How wide is the chasm of academic ignorance about the dominant institutions of the American political economy? Let one example stand for many:

Dillon, Read and Company is one of the most important investment banks in overseas areas, and a major financial underwriter of that number one political commodity, oil. Not surprisingly, therefore, as a recent study by Gabriel Kolko points out, Dillon, Read partners, including James V. Forrestal and Douglas Dillon, have occupied 18 key foreign policy posts in the postwar period, including those of secretary of the Navy and of Defense, chairman of the State Department's Policy Planning Staff, assistant secretary of State for Economic Affairs and secretary of the Treasury.

The interests which Dillon, Read partners promoted in Washington and the ongoing financial interests of the company were fatefully intertwined in

312   The Knowledge Industry

the fabric of American foreign policy. For example, Dillon, Read played a major financial role in prewar Germany during the rise of fascism and a major political role in postwar Germany—preventing the deconcentration of German industry and arresting the de-Nazification of the German power structure. Economically, Dillon, Read was deeply involved in the struggle over oil in the Middle East and central Europe in the early postwar period; politically, it was involved through James V. Forrestal—a central foreign policy figure at the time—in shaping the Truman Doctrine and other key Cold War strategies in the same areas.

Nor did Dillon, Read's influence end with the Truman Administration. Douglas Dillon and Paul Nitze played important roles in both the Eisenhower and Kennedy Administrations, in relation to major events in Europe, the Far East and southern Africa, where Dillon, Read is also a primary financial force.

In short, Dillon, Read is one of the most important institutions of power in America, a subject worthy, one would think, of a certain amount of attention from those who claim to be students of the structure and operation of American society and government. Yet as far as the 50,000 American political scientists, sociologists, economists and historians are concerned, Dillon, Read might as well not exist. There are 3,300,000 books in the library of the University of California. There is not one (academic or otherwise) on Dillon, Read and Company. The *Social Sciences and Humanities Index* is a cumulative guide to over 200 academic journals. In the last twenty-five years, it has not shown a single reference to Dillon, Read and Company. And Dillon, Read is not exceptional. Morgan Stanley, Brown Brothers, Harriman, First Boston Corporation and Lehman Brothers, investment houses of similar importance, go unmentioned. Then there are the law firms like Sullivan & Cromwell, with partners like the Dulles brothers and Arthur Dean and clients like Standard Oil, United Fruit and the internationally entrenched Schroder Banking Corporation. There is the Chase Manhattan Bank on whose board sits Douglas Dillon together with David Rockefeller and the heads of Standard Oil and AT&T. There is the incomparably important policy organization, the Council on Foreign Relations (see "Foundations," Part I, *Ramparts*, April 1969), which not a single academic has studied. Indeed, if one takes the two or three dozen law firms, banks and other financial and industrial institutions that make up what is euphemistically referred to as the New York establishment but is in fact the nerve center of the American ruling class, one will find that there has not been a single academic attempt to subject those institutions, their interest and power networks to systematic intellectual study.

Moreover, when one looks at the attempts that have recently been made to fill the gap, it is difficult to decide whether the advance is for better or for worse. Indeed, it is the positive effort to study business on an institutional basis (for only institutionally organized research can muster the resources necessary for such study) that demonstrates the full depths of corruption of the intellectual enterprise in the universities, a direct result of their continuing servile relationship to corporate wealth.

In 1964, a book appeared under the imprint of Wayne State University Press (Detroit) entitled *American Business Abroad: Ford on Six Continents.*

In a laudatory preface, Professor Allan Nevins of Columbia University writes: "As the most complete and scholarly account of the foreign activities of a great American industrial corporation yet written, this book claims the careful attention of all economists, historians, and business specialists." One of the coauthors of the book is project director of the History of American Business Operations Overseas project at the Columbia University Graduate School of Business. In their own preface, the authors explain how the book came to be written and how the research, which required substantial funds for travel all over the world, was financed: "Important in the initiation of the project was the role of Henry E. Edmunds, Director of Research and Information for the Ford Motor Company and the head of the Ford Archives. Mr. Edmunds encouraged us to lay the project before the Ford Fund (a "nonprofit" foundation) which subsidizes activity in the public interest(!). The fund made a generous grant to Columbia University, and we have worked as salaried employees of the University. We have been accountable only to Columbia University."

Nothing bespeaks the corruption of the university so eloquently as the blank innocence of this preface: the subsidization of the investigation by the subject to be investigated, the initiation of the project itself by the public relations officer of the party involved, and the ingenuous disclaimer that these facts would affect the scholarly objectivity of the report since its authors were accountable only to Columbia University. Columbia University indeed!

Although the business school of every university is of necessity the extreme center of its prostitution to corporate power, we have here the self-exposure of a relationship which is clearly general. Can anyone honestly believe that the foundations, which are based on the great American fortunes and administered by the present-day captains of American industry and finance, will systematically underwrite research which tends to undermine the pillars of the status quo, in particular the illusion that the corporate rich who benefit most from the system do not run it—at whatever cost to society —precisely to ensure their continued blessings? And where will the venture capital to establish the validity of radical ideas come from? Not, certainly, from the universities, whose funds are still controlled by corporate directors, who hold the university in trust and administer it for wealth and power.

James O'Connor

THE UNIVERSITY
AND THE POLITICAL ECONOMY

I

American colleges and universities have become key components of contemporary capitalism. They are an outstanding instance of the way in which
the economic system—the "base"—has become integrated with the political,
social, and cultural institutions—the "superstructure"—of the corporation
state. This integration is nowhere more evident than in the training functions
of the mass education system. The growth of capitalism in the present period
depends upon the availability of a large, highly skilled, technical-scientific
labor force. No one corporation can afford to train its own labor force for
there is no way to insure that its investment, once trained, will not seek
employment elsewhere. The costs of training therefore have to be socialized.
American colleges and universities, subsidized by government-collected taxes,
have taken on the social function of training skilled personnel and developing
knowledge for the needs of advanced capitalism. Far from merely "serving
corporate capitalism" by providing occasional research and consulting services, the universities have become a basic point of production.

II

In the United States today there are two important features of the capitalist mode of production: (1) *the acceleration of technological change*; and
(2) *the emergence of technical knowledge as a factor of production.*
1. With the overall rhythm of technological change accelerated, the life
span of fixed capital (plant and equipment) is shortened, labor skills rapidly
become redundant, and rationalization at the point of production is increased.
These tendencies have a number of causes: competition for markets between
industrial-finance groups; annual model and style changes of commodities;
built-in commodity obsolescence; political-military competition between the
U. S. and the Soviet Union; tax laws favoring accelerated depreciation of
plants and equipment; and the availability of cheap technical-scientific labor
power.
2. With the emergence of technical knowledge as a necessary factor of
production, economic growth increasingly depends more on the quality of
labor power and machinery and less on the absolute number of men and

Reprinted, with deletions, from James O'Connor, "The University and the Political Economy," *Leviathan*, vol. 1 (March 1969), pp. 14–15, by permission of
Leviathan.

machines in production.[1] Skilled, technical labor power replaces simple labor power, and the knowledge of the work force becomes a fundamentally important productive factor. This is widely recognized by corporate economists and administrators, the former in their literature on "investment in human capital," the latter in their reference to the university as part of the "knowledge industry."

The relationship between the acceleration of technological change and the emergence of technical knowledge as a factor of production is basically simple. The constant creation of new commodities, alterations of old commodities, redesign of equipment, reorganization of work processes, and research and development in new productive processes require a constantly expanding technical-scientific labor force. The existence of this labor force, trained by the universities under the guidance of the state and at the expense of the working class as a whole (via tax exploitation), in turn makes the creation of new commodities, redesign of equipment, etc., more profitable.

Because the state, not the individual corporation, takes financial responsibility for university-trained labor and university-developed technology, the element of risk for individual corporations is virtually eliminated. As a result, productivity and production can be raised to a level hitherto unimaginable.

III

Because science and technology are basically social in nature—they cannot be owned and controlled like a machine—private corporations and indeed individual countries have met with great difficulty in their attempts to monopolize these new productive forces. They cannot limit the diffusion of technical knowledge to even the capitalist world, much less to special interests within it. . . . The social character of scientific and technical knowledge means that ultimately no *private* form of business organization can completely contain and control it. For this knowledge to contribute to the benefit of the corporations, the intervention of the state is needed. In effect, a form of state capitalism must accompany the growth of the corporate conglomerate.

IV

There are four ways in which the state can and has intervened in the corporate economy. In each role the state uses the socialized product of the university: technical and administrative knowledge. First, industrial-financial

[1] In 1900, only 6.4 percent of the population were high school graduates; the figure today is 70 percent. School expenditures rose from $10.1 billion in 1950 to $22.4 billion in 1965. Projections put school expenditures at $30.4 billion in 1970 and $37.0 billion in 1975. . . . The Federal Government, due to the fiscal crisis of local and state governments, provides a rising share of public educational funds, rising from 1.8 percent in 1940 to 4.4 percent in 1960. . . .

interests use state power to socialize the costs of production—in particular, the costs of transforming raw labor power into technical-scientific labor power, the costs of retraining workers and the costs of research and development. Funds are acquired by the state through public taxation, transformed into college and university facilities, and used to purchase training personnel and to subsidize the industrial trainees.[2] Colleges and universities are thus not merely integral to the production process, but constitute another point of production, increasingly controlled, while not owned by the corporate bourgeoisie as a whole.

Second, these interests use state power not only to socialize costs, but also to subsidize demand. The development of science and technology has reached the stage at which all economic needs can potentially be easily satisfied. Commodity demand based on real economic needs rises only slowly, or not at all. Socially necessary labor steadily declines. Consequently, corporations are compelled to lay out larger and larger portions of profits on selling expenses, especially packaging, model changes, style changes, product differentiation, and forced commodity obsolescence, in order to maintain and expand the volume of demand by discouraging savings. In short, commodities contain both use values and waste; economic waste increasingly replaces use values, and socially unnecessary labor (that which produces waste) replaces socially necessary labor (that which produces use value). To acquire use values to meet economic needs, the working classes are compelled to consume waste—that is, pay for the expense of selling. The interpenetration of sales expenses and production costs, or waste and use values, is the basic method employed by business to maintain the level of demand.

As points of merchandising as well as points of production, colleges and universities help subsidize demand by accelerating the accumulation of waste. They are proving grounds for new marketing ideas, new products, new brands of "full employment" economics, etc. The activities of these "marketing departments" range from market research courses, home economics departments and seminars in Keynesian economics, to the art and industrial design schools which mobilize and apply creative talent to the latest problems of product design and packaging.

Third, the state has had to further embed itself in the corporate economy to help control the social risks resulting from its first two roles. The development of science and technology and the abundance of capital has led corporations to employ a capital-intensive technology despite the existing relative abundance of unskilled labor. From the standpoint of the corporations, it is more rational to combine technical-scientific labor power with capital-intensive technology than to combine simple labor power with labor-intensive technologies for the costs of training technical-scientific labor power are met by taxation falling on the population at large.

It is this system which has produced a large and growing stratum of unskilled, untrained workers, many of them black, who have never had

[2] At least 80 percent of the "progressive" Federal Personal Income Tax is appropriated at the basic 20 percent rate. The corporations shift the Corporation Income Tax to consumers in the form of higher prices. Excise, sales, and property taxes are all regressive relative to income. The tax burden as a whole thus falls almost altogether on the mass of wage and salary workers.

industrial work experience and never will. This "post-industrial" proletariat does not constitute a reserve army of the unemployed because it does not compete with the "technical-scientific" proletariat. Unemployed, under-employed, and employed in menial jobs in the private and state sectors of the economy, these workers, particularly the younger ones, have become increasingly politicized. In black organizations, poor peoples' associations, unions and welfare rights leagues, this group is politically in motion and constitutes a "social problem" of the first order for the corporation state.

The colleges and universities, in this case functionally inseparable from the state bureaucracy, are thus more and more preoccupied with questions of "social stability," "law and order," "social reform," and so on. The behavioral sciences, sociology, social psychology, economics, and other academic fields are oriented to "solving" pressing, "social problems" via the development of more refined instruments of social control and social discipline.

Finally, the state is employed at every step in the accumulation of capital abroad: in the acquisition of raw materials, the creation of investment opportunities, the creation of cheap labor havens, and the stabilization of international banking centers. The state guarantees foreign investments, stabilizes monetary systems under the reign of the dollar, provides the economic infrastructure for private investments and military groups, creates favorable tariff agreements, controls world commodity organizations, and generally exercises economic, political and military control over unstable areas (i.e., all underdeveloped areas).

The role of the colleges and universities in U.S. economic and political policy abroad corresponds to their role in the local political economy. They are points of imperialist rule. They develop and promote new weapons systems, new instruments of local, national, and international social control, new approaches to international marketing problems, and new economic theories which promote the hegemony of American business over world resources.

V

As a whole, therefore, the colleges and universities constitute four great overlapping departments of the U.S. ruling class—they are points of production, points of merchandizing, points of state bureaucratic social control, and points of imperialist rule. Most of the existing functions of colleges and universities fall into one or more of these categories.

To be sure, the smaller upper class liberal arts institutions still train governing elites—this has been their historical function. But the really important role of the university is to provide the kind of socialized technological-administrative skills outlined above. The colleges and universities therefore are not the "service stations" of the corporate system, but rather constitute a decisive and creative part of this system.

chapter 8

Societal and Human Development under Capitalism

The previous five chapters have been devoted largely to articulating the relationship between American capitalism and major social problems. While a drastically reformed capitalism may be able to minimize imperialism, poverty and economic insecurity, racism, and sexism, capitalism has distinctive features which place severe limitations upon societal and human development in societies oriented around this unique economic system.[1]

[1] Although conditions in so-called socialist countries such as the Soviet Union permit liberal apologists for capitalism to maintain that the problems of modern societies transcend the nature of economic systems, there is considerable evidence that many of the social and personal deformities experienced under capitalism are not universal or inherent in social organization. Specifically, much of the knowledge of postrevolutionary China becoming available to Americans suggest that it is possible to overcome uneven economic and social development, alienation, and class divisions to a great extent within the framework of genuine socialist institutions. See John Gurley, "Capitalist and Maoist Economic Development," in Edward Friedman and Mark Selden, eds., *America's Asia: Dissenting Essays on Asian-American Relations* (New York: Pantheon Books, Inc., 1971), pp. 324–356. See also Joshua Horn, *Away with All Pests: An English Surgeon in People's China, 1954–1969* (New York: Monthly Review Press, 1971). Jan Myrdal and Gun Kessle, *China: The Revolution Continued,* translated by Paul Britten (New York: Pantheon Books, Inc., 1971).

André Gorz's selection in this chapter is probably one of the most sophisticated critiques of capitalist societal and human development. He demonstrates how private enterprise creates false needs, interferes with the satisfaction of collective needs, distorts social and regional development; and how consumer ideology generates the privatization of needs, a function crucial in the maintenance of capitalist production. Gorz's discussion of the relationship between fundamental human needs and the historical transformation of the modes of their satisfaction is a penetrating exposure of the myth of progress. Although Gorz only discusses the particularities of the American case in order to illustrate a general thesis, the American reader should have little difficulty in relating abstract ideas to the realities of his or her everyday life.

Gorz's description of the normal operation of capitalism is an underestimation of the human costs in the United States of a political economy devoted to meeting the requirements of private enterprise rather than social welfare. American trade unionism's embrace of "business unionism" and the absence of even a conservatice labor or social democratic party have permitted capitalist ideology and practice to wreak havoc on cities and rural areas, to pollute the environment, and to foster rampant consumerism to a greater degree than in any other advanced capitalist society.

Another characteristic of all capitalist societies is alienated labor. That is, the worker in a capitalist economy does not own the means of production, has no control over the character and disposition of the fruits of his labor, and must exchange his labor power for money in order to survive, regardless of the possibilities for a free distribution of goods and services afforded by the productivity of the technology employed in the economy. C. Wright Mills' selection in this chapter is one of the finest analyses of the conditions of modern labor.[2] Although he focuses specifically on the problems and features of white-collar and bureaucratic work in the United States, he captures many of the universal aspects of alienated labor in capitalist societies.

In the remainder of this essay I would like to briefly supplement Gorz's and Mills' discussion of two problems which seem of major importance when one considers the quality of life today under American capitalism: the ecological crisis and the competitive ethos.

The recent outpouring of prose on the destruction of the physical environment has led to much anger and despair, but little theoretical insight into the sources of the problem. The existing literature typically attempts to locate the blame for impending ecological catastrophe on "all of us."

[2] See also Mills' crucial evaluation of the "human relations" approach to labor-management relations, "The Contribution of Sociology to Studies of Industrial Relations," *Berkeley Journal of Sociology*, vol. 15 (June 1970), pp. 11–32. Harvey Swados, "The Myth of the Happy Worker," in Robert Perrucci and Marc Pilisuk, eds., *The Triple Revolution: Social Problems in Depth* (Boston: Little, Brown & Company, 1968), pp. 234–240, dismisses any notion that blue-collar workers in mass-production industries no longer suffer from alienation. For a more recent statement, see Judson Gooding, "Blue Collar Blues on the Assembly Line," *Fortune*, vol. 82 (July 1970), pp. 69–71, 112–113, 116–117.

Societal and Human Development under Capitalism

Although all Americans contribute to the depletion of natural resources and various forms of environmental pollution through their particular patterns of consumption (for example, the use of automobiles), the problem does not lie essentially "with the people" but with a private enterprise economy predicated on wasteful production and consumption, rather than on social consciousness and an ecologically sound relationship to the physical environment.[3] American consumers are perhaps also culpable to the extent that they help perpetuate the destructive characteristics of the private economy and support governmental partnership with industry. But it should be recognized that the masses in their roles as consumers must operate within the same context of relative powerlessness as they do in their roles as voters and workers.

One of the major sources of environmental pollution is the concentration of business enterprise in metropolitan areas rather than their dispersal throughout the entire land area of the country. To relocate factories where preexisting transportation, communication, and educational infrastructures are absent would increase the cost of production. The drive to cut these costs is a necessary concomitant of the race for profits. But geographic concentration makes industrial waste and sewage more difficult to handle than would be the case if industry were dispersed.

The concentration of industry is also a consequence of the need for mass production, which can best be accomplished in economies of scale rather than small dispersed units. However, the need for continual mass production is in turn only rational because capitalism requires endless consumption. As Gayle Southworth points out:

> Profits will obviously be greater if people buy 2, 3, or 4 gadgets per year than if they buy only one. This is the reason cars and toys wear out so quickly. One of the reasons GMC, Ford and Chrysler oppose the development of steam powered cars (which are being shown to be almost pollution-free in a California experiment) is that they are almost indestructible. Not only are internal combustion engines extremely dirty, they are extremely susceptible to wear and tear.[4]

In addition to creating a massive problem of waste disposal, geographic concentration of industry is the prime cause of population density. People must live where they can work. As a consequence of the location of industry, approximately 75 percent of the American population lives on 1 percent of the land.[5] The resultant urban overcrowding is directly related to deteriorating city services, slum housing, and disease. The recent relocation of industry in suburbs has diminished this problem somewhat, but has substituted the increasing impoverishment of central cities because of the loss of the corporate and middle-class tax base. Ironically, the migration from

---

[3] Editors of *Ramparts, Eco-Catastrophe* (San Francisco: Canfield Press, 1970).
[4] Gayle Southworth, "Some Notes on the Political Economy of Pollution," *The Review of Radical Political Economics*, vol. 2 (Summer 1970), p. 76.
[5] *Ibid.*, p. 79.

metropolitan centers has been due, to no small degree, to the "urban blight" created by business concentration in the first place.

The endless consumption that is built into the capitalist system, as well as generating pollution, waste, and urban overcrowing, is also responsible for the absorption of huge amounts of precious natural resources. As the preeminent capitalist economic power, the United States consumes between 30 and 50 percent of the resources in the world.[6] Since the earth's supply of natural resources is finite, America's wasteful consumption is a severe threat to the economic development, and perhaps the survival, of the underdeveloped world.

The destruction of the environment through the normal operation of capitalist development is augmented by the long-established cooperative relationship between Big Business and the state, to which Gorz alludes. In America, the governmental support for limitless oil exploration, even at the cost of environmental destruction, and the total subsidy of the infrastructure required to sustain automobile use are the two most blatant examples of the use of state power to serve private enterprise.[7]

The "population explosion"—another environmental catastrophe given the rate of consumption of finite natural resources—while also superficially a problem caused by "all of us," is exacerbated by the logic of capitalist development.[8] While it would be foolish to suggest that population control is unnecessary, it is important to point out that the underutilization of resources in underdeveloped countries by native populations is related to the use and misuse of these same resources by giant capitalist enterprises because of their unending need for raw materials for production of useless, as well as useful, commodities.[9]

Finally, the fact that each American consumes approximately three hundred times the resources of a person from the underdeveloped world is another reflection of the endless generation of wasteful production and consumption that is the hallmark of capitalist development.[10]

It has been argued that many sources of ecological destruction are

[6] Hans Landsberg, *Natural Resources for U.S. Growth: Looking Ahead to the Year 2000* (Baltimore: The Johns Hopkins Press, 1964). Paul Ehrlich and Ann Ehrlich, *Population Environment Resources: Issues in Human Ecology* (San Francisco: W. H. Freeman and Company, 1970), p. 61.

[7] Harvey Molotch, "Oil in Santa Barbara and Power in America," *Sociological Inquiry,* vol. 40 (Winter 1970), pp. 131–144. Barry Weisberg, "(Ecology of Oil) Raping Alaska," in Editors of *Ramparts, op. cit.,* pp. 106–128. For the best analysis of the relations between the oil industry and the state, see Robert Engler, *The Politics of Oil: Private Power and Democratic Directions* (Chicago: University of Chicago Press, 1961). For government support of highways, see Southworth, *op. cit.,* p. 81.

[8] David Eakins, "Population and the Capitalism Bomb: A Review of Paul Erlich's *The Population Bomb,*" *Socialist Revolution,* vol. 1 (March–April 1970), pp. 145–152. See also Steve Weissman, "Why the Population Bomb Is a Rockefeller Baby," in Editors of *Ramparts, op. cit.,* pp. 26–41. Ronald Meek, ed., *Marx and Engels on the Population Bomb* (Berkeley, Calif.: Ramparts Press, 1971).

[9] Harry Magdoff, *The Age of Imperialism: The Economics of U.S. Foreign Policy* (New York: Monthly Review Press, 1969), pp. 27–66.

[10] Southworth, *op. cit.,* p. 74.

Societal and Human Development under Capitalism

rooted in the *functioning* of advanced *industrial* societies, whether they are capitalist or socialist. To the extent that economic growth and a "higher" standard of living are major goals of any nation, environmental resources will be depleted. Nevertheless, socialist societies, because of their commitment to economic and social planning, are more capable of dealing with ecological problems than are capitalist societies, which glorify the lack of planning by calling it "freedom." For example, while the major industrial nations are the principal contributors to world pollution (the United States accounting for 60 percent), the Soviet Union is a lesser offender than Japan, England, and West Germany even though her industrial output is greater than any of these capitalist countries and her population is about equal to that of all three combined.[11]

If capitalism increases man's destruction of nature, the competitiveness and resulting inequality that is a necessary by-product of capitalist economic and social life represents the institutionalization of man's destruction of his fellow man and himself. Mills' discussion of alienated labor in this chapter alludes to this characteristic of capitalism. Jules Henry's work on the American schoolroom provides a detailed examination of how children are socialized to fit the needs of capitalism.[12] The child learns to fear failure and to be wary of cooperation in his early years. Only in the family are competitive rules relaxed somewhat, because the psychic strains of endless insecurity and struggle against others would be unbearable without unconditional love and affection in at least one social setting.[13]

Several unique features of American history have contributed to the unprecedented legitimation of this competitive ethos in the United States. The absence of a significant feudal past permitted industrialization to occur without a legacy of elite paternalism and communitarian working-class traditions.[14] Moreover, the harsh wilderness, institutional vacuum, and extreme hardships of the early settlers and the Western pioneers increased the severity of human conflict in the formative years of the nation. Finally, the influence of Protestantism, with its emphasis on individualism, the sanctity of work, asceticism, and its doubts about salvation, possibly contributed to the emerging culture of industrial capitalism in America.[15]

While the absence of feudalism, the nakedness of American institutional structures, and Protestantism may have played a decisive role in creating a society based upon human competition, the extreme manifestations of this

[11] *Ibid.*, p. 86.
[12] Jules Henry, "American Schoolrooms: Learning the Nightmare," *Columbia University Forum*, vol. 6 (Spring 1963), pp. 24–30.
[13] Talcott Parsons and Robert Bales, *Family, Socialization and Interaction Process* (New York: The Free Press, 1955), pp. 35–186.
[14] Louis Hartz, *The Liberal Tradition in America* (New York: Harcourt Brace Jovanovich, Inc., 1955).
[15] Max Weber, *The Protestant Ethic and the Spirit of Capitalism*, translated by Talcott Parsons (New York: Charles Scribner's Sons, 1958). See Gabriel Kolko, "Max Weber on America: Theory and Evidence," in George Nadel, ed., *Studies in the Philosophy of History: Selected Essays From "History and Theory"* (New York: Harper & Row Publishers, 1965), pp. 180–197, for a review of the historical literature which tends to refute the Weber thesis as it applies to the American case.

feature of contemporary American society cannot simply be reduced to these factors. Social and cultural traditions may have aided the historical development of American capitalism and its ethos, but the ongoing requirements of capitalist economic and social relations have been the ultimate source of the almost pathological absence of cooperation that characterizes current American life. As Max Weber said in his conclusion to *The Protestant Ethic and the Spirit of Capitalism:*

> Since asceticism undertook to remodel the world and work out its ideals in the world, material goods have gained an increasingly and finally an inexorable power over the lives of men as at no previous period in history. . . . But victorious capitalism, since it rests on mechanical foundations, needs its [asceticism's] support no longer. . . . Where the fulfillment of the calling cannot directly be related to the highest spiritual and cultural values, or when, on the other hand, it need not be felt as simply economic compulsion, the individual generally abandons the attempt to justify it at all. In the field of its highest development, in the United States, the pursuit of wealth, stripped of its religious and ethical meaning, tends to become associated with purely mundane passions, which often actually give it the character of sport.
>
> No one knows who will live in this cage in the future, or whether at the end of this tremendous development entirely new prophets will arise, or there will be a great rebirth of new ideas and ideals, or, if neither, mechanized petrification, embellished with a sort of convulsive self-importance. For of the last stage of this cultural development, it might well be truly said: "Specialists without spirit; sensualists without heart; this nullity imagines that it has attained a level of civilization never before achieved."[16]

Weber's words—first published in a series of essays in 1904 and 1905—had great prophetic power. While suggesting that noneconomic motives contributed to the "capitalist spirit," he believed that they would be of less importance in understanding the maturing capitalist system. Today, the inner-directed entrepreneur of the eighteenth and nineteenth centuries is an anachronism. A decreasing proportion of Americans own productive property. Regardless of their incomes and life styles, most Americans work for others. To the extent that entrepreneurship is no longer a realistic goal, some of the ambitiousness and competitiveness of the past has been channeled toward attaining security in the bureaucratic order. This development, a function of the consolidation of monopolistic capitalism in the twentieth century, creates a different social character among Americans.[17] Competition in work is replaced by competition in consumption and for a safe position in the bureaucratic hierarchy. Restless ambition is followed by passive acquiescence to bureaucratic realities. In the creation of the "new" capitalist man the old passion for a calling may be increasingly absent, but an industrial culture based upon human antagonism still remains.

[16] Weber, *op. cit.*, pp. 181–182.
[17] Erich Fromm, *The Sane Society* (New York: Holt, Rinehart and Winston, Inc., 1955).

André Gorz

PRIVATE ENTERPRISE
AND THE PUBLIC INTEREST

1. The Superfluous before the Necessary

Does the man who eats red meat and white bread, moves with the help of a motor, and dresses in synthetic fibers, live better than the man who eats dark bread and white cheese, moves on a bicycle, and dresses in wool and cotton? The question is almost meaningless. It supposes that in a given society, the same individual has a choice between two different life styles. Practically speaking, this is not the case: only one way of life, more or less rigidly determined, is open to him, and this way of life is conditioned by the structure of production and by its techniques. The latter determine the environment by which needs are conditioned, the objects by which these needs can be satisfied, and the manner of consuming or using these objects.

But the basic question is this: what guarantees the adjustment of production to needs, both in general and for a specific product? Liberal economists have long maintained that this adjustment is guaranteed by the mechanism of the market. But this thesis has very few defenders today. Doubtless, if we do not look at the overall picture in optimum human and economic terms, but only at each product taken separately, then we can still maintain that a product totally devoid of use value would not find a buyer. Nevertheless, it is impossible to conclude that the most widely distributed products of mass consumption are really those which at a given stage of technological evolution allow for the best and most rational satisfaction (at the least cost and the least expense of time and trouble) of a given need.

In fact, under capitalism the pursuit of optimum human and economic goals and the pursuit of maximum profit from invested capital coincide only by accident. The pursuit of maximum profit is the first exigency of capital, and the increase of use value is no more than a by-product of this pursuit.

For example, let us take the case of the spread of disposable packaging for milk products. From the viewpoint of use value, the superiority of milk in a cardboard carton or yogurt in a plastic cup is nil (or negative). From the viewpoint of capitalist enterprise, on the other hand, this substitution is clearly advantageous. The glass bottle or glass jar represented immobilized capital which did not "circulate": empty bottles or jars were recovered and reused indefinitely, which entailed the cost of handling, collection, and

Reprinted, with deletions, from André Gorz, *Strategy for Labor*, translated by Martin Nicolaus and Victoria Ortiz (Boston: The Beacon Press, 1967), pp. 76–99. Reprinted by permission of the Beacon Press, copyright © 1964 by Editions du Seuil, English translation copyright © 1967 by Beacon Press. André Gorz is an editor of *Les Temps Modernes* in Paris, France. He has written several books, including *The Traitor* and *Le Socialisme Difficile*.

sterilization. The disposable containers, on the other hand, allow a substantial economy in handling, and permit the profitable sale not only of the dairy product but also of its container. To increase their profits, the big dairy firms thus forced the consumer to purchase a new product at a higher price although its use value remained the same (or diminished).

In other cases, the alternative between maximum profit and maximum use value is even more striking. The Philips trust, for example, perfected fluorescent lighting in 1938. The life of these fluorescent tubes was then 10,000 hours. Production of these tubes would have covered existing needs cheaply and in a relatively short period of time; amortization, on the other hand, would have taken a long time. The invested capital would be recovered slowly, and the labor time necessary to cover existing need would have declined. The company therefore invested additional capital in order to develop fluorescent tubes which burned for only 1,000 hours, in order thus to accelerate the recovery of capital and to realize—at the price of considerable *superfluous* expenditure—a much higher rate of accumulation and of profit.

The same holds true for synthetic fibers, whose durability, for stockings especially, has decreased, and for motor vehicles, which are *deliberately* built with parts which will wear out rapidly (and cost as much as longer-lasting parts would have).

Speaking generally, and regardless of the objective scientific and technical possibilities, technical development in terms of the criteria of maximum profit is often quite different from development in terms of criteria of maximum social and economic utility. Even when fundamental needs remain largely unsatisfied, monopoly capital objectively organizes scarcity, wastes natural resources and human labor, and orients production (and consumption) toward objects whose sale is most profitable, regardless of the need for such objects.

In general, monopoly capitalism tends toward a model of "affluence" which levels consumption "upward": the products offered tend to become standardized by the incorporation of a maximum of "added value" which does not perceptibly increase their use value. At the limit (a limit attained by an impressive range of products), the usefulness of an object becomes the *pretext* for selling superfluous things that are built into the product and multiply its price; the products are sold above all for their packaging and brand names (that is to say, advertising), while their use value becomes a secondary part of the bargain. The packaging and the brand name, moreover, are expressly designed to deceive the buyer as to the quantity, quality, and the nature of the product: tooth paste is endowed with erotic virtues, detergents with magic qualities, the automobile (in the U.S.) is extolled as a status symbol.

The apparent diversity of the products badly masks their true uniformity: the difference between brands is marginal. All American automobiles are identical with regard to the incorporation of a maximum of "packaging" and false luxury, to the point where an intense advertising campaign is necessary to "educate" the consumer, from school age on, to perceive the differences in detail and not to perceive the substantial similarities. This dictatorship of the monopolies over needs and individual tastes was broken in the

United States only from the outside, by the producers of European automobiles. "Upward" leveling, that is, leveling toward the incorporation of a maximum of superfluity, has been carried out in this instance to the detriment of the use value of the product, whose consumers were unable for years to reverse the tendency of an oligopoly to sell goods of a diminishing use value at a constantly increasing price.

The pursuit of maximum profit, to continue with this example of one of the pilot industries of the most developed country, was not even accompanied by scientific and technological fertility. The tendency to prefer the accessory to the essential, the improvement of the profit rate to the improvement of use value, has resulted in *absolute* wastage. None of the four major post-war technical innovations in automobile design: disc brakes, fuel injection, hydro-pneumatic suspension, rotating piston, originated in the American car industry—an industry which with every annual model change brings into conflict the two biggest manufacturing groups in the world. They compete mainly for maximum productivity, not for maximum use value. The notion that competition would be a factor in accelerating technical and scientific progress is thus, in large part, a myth. Competition does not contribute to technical progress unless such progress allows for the growth of profits. Technical progress, in other words, is essentially concentrated on productivity, and only incidentally on the pursuit of a human optimum in the manner of production and in the manner of consumption.

This is why, in all developed capitalist societies, gigantic waste coexists with largely unsatisfied fundamental needs (needs for housing, medical care, education, hygiene, etc.). This is also why the claim that capitalist profit (distributed or consumed) does not represent a great burden for the economy (about five per cent of the French national revenue) is a gross myth.

Certainly the confiscation of the surplus value consumed by the capitalists would not result in a perceptible improvement of the condition of the people or the workers. But nobody claims any longer that in order to transform society the principal attack must be leveled against the profits pocketed by individual capitalists, against the incomes of the great families and the major employers. What must be attacked is not the personal incomes created by capitalist profits; it is rather the orientation which the system and the logic of profit, that is to say of capitalist accumulation, impress on the economy and the society as a whole; it is the capitalist control over the apparatus of production and the resulting inversion of real priorities in the model of consumption. . . .

2. The Social Cost of Private Initiative

The effects of capitalist production on the environment and on society are a second source of waste and of distortion. In fact, what was said about the capitalist control over industry holds true *a fortiori* for the orientation of the economy in general. The most profitable production for each entrepreneur is not necessarily the most advantageous one for the consumers; the pursuit of maximum profit and the pursuit of optimum use value do not coincide when each product is considered separately. But if instead of considering the action of each entrepreneur (in fact of each oligopoly) separately, we consider the resulting total of all such actions and their repercussions on society, then we note an even sharper contradiction between this overall result and the social and economic optimum.

This contradiction results essentially from the limits which the criteria of profitability impose on capitalist initiative. According to the logic of this initiative, the most profitable activities are the most important ones, and activities whose product or result cannot be measured according to the criteria of profitability and return are neglected or abandoned to decay. These non-profitable activities, whose desirability cannot even be understood in capitalist terms, consist of all those investments which cannot result in production for the market under the given social and political circumstances, that is to say, which do not result in a commercial exchange comprising the profitable sale of goods and services. In fact this category includes all investments and services which answer to human needs that cannot be expressed in market terms as demands for salable commodities: the need for education, city planning, cultural and recreational facilities, works of art, research, public health, public transportation (and also economic planning, reforestation, elimination of water- and air-pollution, noise control, etc.)—in short, all economic activities which belong to the "public domain" and cannot arise or survive except as public services, regardless of the profitability.

The demand for the satisfaction of these needs, which cannot be expressed in market terms, necessarily takes on political and collective forms; and the satisfaction of these collective needs, precisely because it cannot be procured except by public services belonging to the collectivity, constitutes a permanent challenge to the laws and the spirit of the capitalist system. In other words, there is a whole sphere of fundamental, priority needs which constitute an objective challenge to capitalist logic. Only socialism can recognize the priority nature and assure the priority satisfaction of these needs. This does not mean that we must await the establishment of socialism or fight for socialism only by political campaigning. It means rather that the existence of this sphere of collective needs now offers the socialist forces the chance to demand and to achieve, in the name of these needs, the creation and the development of a sphere of services, a sphere which represents a popular victory and constitutes a permanent antagonism to the capitalist system and permanently restricts its functioning. We shall return to this point later.

The acuteness of this antagonism—and the sharpness of the contradiction between capitalist initiative and collective needs—necessarily grows. It grows principally as a result of the fact that collective needs and the cost of their satisfaction are not in principle included in the cost of capitalist decisions and initiatives. There is a disjunction between the direct cost of the productive investment for the private investor, and the indirect, social cost which this investment creates to cover the resulting collective needs, such as housing, roads, the supply of energy and water; in short, the infrastructure. There is also a disjunction between the computation of direct production costs by the private investor and the social cost which his investment will bring with it: for example, expenses for education, housing, transportation, various services; in short, the entrepreneur's criteria of profitability, which measure the desirability of the investment, and the criteria of human and collective desirability, are not identical. As a consequence, the collective needs engendered by capitalist investment are covered haphazardly or not at all; the satisfaction of these needs is neglected or subordinated to more profitable "priorities" because these needs were not foreseen and included in advance in the total cost of the project.

Thus, when a capitalist group decides to invest in a given project and a given locality, it need not bother to ask itself what degree of priority its project has in the scale of needs, what social costs it will entail, what social needs it will engender, what long term public investments it will make necessary later on, or what alternatives its private decision will render impossible. The decision of the capitalist group will be guided rather by the existing market demand, the available facilities and equipment, and the proximity of the market and the sources of raw materials.

The first result of this situation is that the decision of a private trust to invest does not in most cases have any but an accidental relationship to the real but non-marketable needs of the local, regional, or national unit: the model of development which monopoly capitalism imposes on insufficiently developed regions is as a general rule a colonial model. The balanced development of Brittany or Southern Italy, for example, if it were to answer real needs would in the first place demand investments to revive agricultural productivity, to assure local processing of raw materials, and to occupy the underemployed population in industries having local outlets. Priority thus would have to be given to educational and cultural services, to food and agricultural industries, to light industry, chemical and pharmaceutical manufacturing, to communication and transportation. If these priorities were chosen, the local communities could develop toward a diversification of their activities, toward a relative economic, cultural, and social autonomy, toward a fuller development of social relations and exchanges, and thus toward a fuller development of human relations and abilities.

Capitalist initiative functions only in terms of the existing *market* demand. If there is no such demand in the underdeveloped regions for the products capable of bringing about balanced development, then capitalist initiative will consist of setting up export industries in these regions. The resulting type of development, besides being very limited, will reverse the real priorities: the under-employed local manpower will be drained toward assembly workshops (although not to the extent of providing full employment), toward satellite factories which are sub-contractors of distant trusts, and toward the production or extraction of raw materials or of individual components which will be transformed or assembled elsewhere.

The local community, instead of being raised toward a new, richer internal equilibrium, will thus be practically destroyed by having a new element of imbalance grafted onto its already out-of-date structures: agriculture, instead of being made healthier and richer, will be ruined by the exodus of manpower and the land will be abandoned; the local industries, instead of being diversified in terms of local needs, will undergo specialization and impoverishment; local or regional autonomy, instead of being reinforced, will be diminished even more, since the centers of decision making for the local activities are in Paris or Milan and the new local industries are the first to suffer the shock of economic fluctuations: the quality of the local community's social relations, instead of being improved, will be impoverished; local manpower will get the dirtiest and the most monotonous jobs; the ancient towns will become dormitory cities with new cafés and juke boxes in place of cultural facilities; the former civilization will be destroyed and replaced by nothing; those of the new workers who do not travel one, two, or even three hours daily by bus to go to and from their work will be penned up in concrete cages or in shanty towns: in the mother country as well as in the colonies there is a process of "slummification." The colonies, at least, can free themselves of foreign colonialism; the underdeveloped regions in the mother country, however, are often irreversibly colonized and deprived of independent livelihood by monopoly capitalism, or even emptied of their population and turned into a wasteland.

The drift of industry toward the underdeveloped regions, in the conditions which have just been described, cannot really be compared to an industrialization of these areas. It tends rather to destroy all possibility of balance between the city and the countryside by the creation of new, giant agglomerations which empty the back country. The small peasants will not be able to rationalize their methods (that would require a policy of credit and equipment favoring cooperative or collective modes of farming); instead they will sell their holdings to the benefit of the agrarian capitalists. The former peasants will install themselves as shop keepers, café owners, or unskilled laborers in the new big city or in the capital. The drift of certain industries toward less developed regions is therefore not at all comparable to decentralization. On the contrary, it is only a marginal phenomenon of industry's tendency to concentrate geographically. Industry is attracted by industry, money by money. Both go by preference where markets and conditions of profitability already exist, not where these must first be created. Thus regional disparities tend to grow.

The principal cause of geographic concentration of industry has been the public prefinancing, during the past decades, of the social bases of industrial expansion in the highly dense zones: housing, transportation, trained manpower, infrastructure. Now, the savings realized by individual industries due to geographic concentration are an extra burden for the collectivity. After a certain point has been reached the operating costs of the large cities grow dizzily (long traveling time, air pollution, noise, lack of space, etc.). The overpopulation of the urban centers has as a counterpart the depopulation of non-developed areas below the threshold of economic and social viability, their economic and human impoverishment, and the obliteration of their potential; and the cost of the social reproduction of labor power is multiplied. . . .

This double process of congestion and decline has one and the same root: the concentration of economic power in a small number of monopolistic groups which drain off a large part of the economic surplus realized in production and distribution and which reinvest that surplus where conditions of immediate profitability are already present. Therefore the resources avail-

Societal and Human Development under Capitalism

able for a regional and social policy consonant with real needs are always insufficient, especially because monopoly competition engenders new consumer needs and new collective expenses which are incompatible with a government policy aimed at balanced development.

The costs of infrastructure (roads, transportation, city maintenance and planning, provision of energy and water) which monopoly expansion imposes on the collectivity as it spreads (namely in the congested zones), in practice make it impossible to provide such services in the areas where the need is greatest: the billions swallowed up by the great cities are in the last analysis diverted from economically and humanly more advantageous uses.

Furthermore, the cost of the infrastructure, which the orientation given by monopoly capitalism to consumption demands, represents an obstacle to the satisfaction of priority needs. The most striking example in this regard is that of the automobile industry. For the production of a means of evasion and escape, this industry has diverted productive resources, labor, and capital from priority tasks such as housing, education, public transportation, public health, city planning, and rural services. The priority given by monopoly capitalism to the automobile gets stronger and stronger: city planning must be subordinated to the requirements of the automobile, roads are built instead of houses (this is very clear in Italy, for example), and public transportation is sacrificed.

And finally the private automobile becomes a social necessity: urban space is organized in terms of private transportation; public transportation lags farther and farther behind the spread of the suburbs and the increasing distance required to travel to work; the pedestrian or the cyclist becomes a danger to others and himself; athletic and cultural facilities are removed from the city, beyond the reach of the non-motorized suburbanite and often even of the city dweller. The possession of an automobile becomes a basic necessity because the universe is organized in terms of private transportation. This process is halted only with difficulty in the advanced capitalist countries. To the extent that the indispensability of private automobiles has made life unbearable in the large, overpopulated cities where air, light, and space are lacking, motorized escape will continue to be an important—although decreasing—element in the reproduction of labor power, even when priority has returned to city planning, to collective services, and to public transportation.

3. Collective Needs

Monopoly expansion thus not only creates new needs by throwing onto the market mass consumption products symbolizing an alleged comfort which becomes a need because it is available; it creates needs by modifying the conditions under which labor power can be reproduced. In point of fact, the development of needs in capitalist society often results less from the improvement and the enrichment of human faculties than from an increase in the harshness of the material environment, from a deterioration in living conditions, from the necessity for more complex and more costly instruments to satisfy fundamental needs, to reproduce labor power.

The Marxist distinction between fundamental and historical needs thus becomes problematical and risks creating confusion in all cases where because of man's destruction or distortion of nature fundamental needs can no longer be satisfied—or even apprehended—except in a mediate manner. Between the natural origin of a need and its natural object, we note the interposition of instruments which not only are human products, but which are essentially social products. After the destruction of the natural environment and its replacement by a social environment, fundamental needs can only be satisfied in a social manner: they become immediately social needs; or, more exactly, fundamental needs mediated by society.

This is true, for example, of the need for air, which is immediately apprehended as the need for vacations, for public gardens, for city planning, for escape from the city; of the need for nightly rest, for physical and mental relaxation, which becomes the need for tasteful, comfortable housing protected against noise; of the need to eat, which in the large industrial cities becomes the need for food which can be consumed immediately after a day of work—that is, the need for cafeterias, restaurants, canned foods, and foods that require a minimum of preparation time; of the need for cleanliness, which in the absence of sunlight and natural beaches or rivers becomes the need for hygienic facilities, laundries, or washing machines, and so on.

In all these examples, the historical form which the fundamental need assumes cannot be confused with the historical need as such: the need in question is not a new and "rich" need which corresponds to an enrichment of man and a development of his faculties; it is merely an eternal biological need which now demands "rich" means of satisfaction because the natural environment has become impoverished, because there has been impoverishment of man's relation to nature, exhaustion or destruction of resources (air, water, light, space) which until now were taken as natural.

Now the nature of capitalist society is to constrain the individual to buy back individually, as a consumer, the means of satisfaction of which the society has socially deprived him. The capitalist trust appropriates or uses up air, light, space, water, and (by producing dirt and noise) cleanliness and silence gratuitously or at a preferential price; contractors, speculators, and merchants then resell all of these resources to the highest bidder. The destruction of natural resources has been social; the reproduction of these vitally necessary resources is social in its turn. But even though the satisfaction of the most elementary needs now must pass through the mediation of social production, service, and exchange, no social initiative assures or foresees the replacement of what has been destroyed, the social reparation of the spoliation which individuals have suffered. On the contrary, once its social repercussions and its inverted priorities have aggravated the conditions in which social individuals exist, private enterprise then exploits at a profit the greater needs of these same social individuals. It is they as individual consumers who will have to pay for the growth of the social cost of the reproduction of their labor power, a cost which often surpasses their means.

The workers understand the scandal inherent in this situation in a direct and confused manner. The capitalist trust, after having exploited them and mutilated them *in* their work, comes to exploit them and mutilate them *outside* of their work. It imposes on them, for example, the cost, the fatigue, and the long hours lost on public transportation; it imposes on them the search for and the price of housing, made scarce by the trust's manpower needs and made more expensive by the speculations which increasing scarcity produces.

The same thing holds for air, light, cleanliness, and hygiene, whose price becomes prohibitive. For example, great industrial concentration forces women to go to work for pay, because one paycheck in the family is not enough to buy the means necessary for the reproduction of labor power[1] in the big city. In the absence of public services, the mechanization of housework becomes a necessity: washing machines, refrigerators, ready-to-eat foods, semi-automatic stoves, and restaurants come to be a necessity. But the satisfaction of this need, even though it has its origin in the condition of social production and of social life, is left to private enterprise, which profits from it. Individuals have to pay for this satisfaction, so that a very important part of a working woman's wages which once were (wrongly) considered as "supplemental" income, serves only to cover the supplementary expenses women's work entails.

On the level of collective needs, and only on this level, the theory of impoverishment thus continues to be valid. The social cost of the reproduction of labor power (the simple reproduction, and as we shall show below, the wider reproduction) tends to rise as fast as or faster than individual purchasing power; the workers' social standard of living tends to stagnate, to worsen, even if their individual standard of living (expressed in terms of monetary purchasing power) rises. And it is extremely difficult, if not impossible, for urban workers to obtain a qualitative improvement in their living standard as a result of a raise in their direct wages within the framework of capitalist structures. It is this quasi-impossibility which gives demands in the name of collective needs a revolutionary significance.

The nature of collective needs, in effect, is that they often cannot be expressed in terms of monetary demands. They involve a set of collective resources, services, and facilities which escape the law of the market, capitalist initiative, and all criteria of profitability. These needs, inexpressible in economic terms, are at least virtually in permanent contradiction to capitalism and mark the limits of its effectiveness. These are the needs which capitalism tends to neglect or to suppress, insofar as capitalism knows only

[1] Labor power, according to Marx, is the quantity of productive energy expended by a worker during the process of work. In order to keep on working day after day, he must constantly reproduce his labor power; that is, he must eat, rest, sleep, keep healthy, etc. Similarly, the working class as a whole must be constantly reproduced: workers must raise children to replace them when they are old, and skills must be passed on from generation to generation. In the present volume, the phrase, "simple reproduction of labor power" generally refers to all the means necessary to reproduce and maintain labor power as of now; while "wider reproduction" refers to the totality of vocational training programs, educational institutions, public information media, and cultural facilities necessary to maintain and reproduce over time the sort of educated working force and administrative personnel required by a complex society whose technology and knowledge evolve at an ever-quickening pace. . . .

the *homo oeconomicus*—defined by the consumption of merchandise and its production—and not the human man, the consumer, producer, and user of goods which cannot be sold, bought, or reproduced. It is these needs which, although they are basically biological, all have a necessarily cultural and at least potentially creative dimension, due to the destruction by industry of a natural environment for which human praxis must substitute a new social environment and civilization.

Among these needs are:

1. Housing and city planning, not only in quantitative but in qualitative terms as well. An urban esthetic and an urban landscape, an environment which furthers the development of human faculties instead of debasing them, must be recreated. Now it is obvious that it is not profitable to provide 200 square feet of green area per inhabitant, to plan parks, roads, and squares. The application of the law of the market leads, on the contrary, to reserve the best living conditions for the privileged, who need them least, and to deny them to the workers who, because they do the most difficult and the lowest-paid work, need them profoundly.[2] The workings of this law also push the workers farther and farther from their place of work, and impose on them additional expense and fatigue.

2. Collective services, such as public transportation, laundries and cleaners, child day care centers and nursery schools. These are non-profitable in essence: for in terms of profit, it is necessarily more advantageous to sell individual vehicles, washing machines, and magical soap powders. And since these services are most needed by those who have the lowest incomes, their expansion on a commercial basis presents no interest at all for capital. Only public services can fill the need.

3. Collective cultural, athletic, and health facilities: schools, theatres, libraries, concert halls, swimming pools, stadiums, hospitals, in short, all the facilities necessary for the reestablishment of physical and intellectual balance for the development of human faculties. The non-profitability of these facilities is evident, as is their extreme scarcity (and usually great cost) in almost all of the capitalist countries.

4. Balanced regional development in terms of optimum economic and human criteria, which we have already contrasted to neo-colonialist "slummification."

5. Information, communication, active group leisure. Capitalism not only does not have any interest in these needs,[3] it tends even to suppress them. The commercial dictatorship of the monopolies cannot in fact function with-

[2] Under these circumstances the law of the market presents this additional absurdity: it makes the price of scarce resources like space, air, light, and silence rise dizzily, when by nature these resources *cannot be reproduced*. The seller of resources, however high a price he gets for them, has had no hand in their creation and is perfectly incapable of reproducing them. The sale and purchase of these resources is a pure and simple act of spoliation committed on the collectivity. Their socialization, that is to say their control and social allocation in terms of the simple criteria of need, is a fundamental demand.

[3] All information media show a deficit; only advertising, that is to say the sale of commercial "information" which they are paid to sell, allows some of them to balance their budgets.

out a mass of passive consumers, separated by place and style of living, incapable of getting together and communicating directly, incapable of defining together their specific needs (relative to their work and life situation), their preoccupations, their outlook on society and the world—in short, their common project. Mass pseudo-culture, while producing passive and stupefying entertainments, amusements, and pastimes, does not and cannot satisfy the needs arising out of dispersion, solitude, and boredom. This pseudo-culture is less a consequence than a cause of the passivity and the impotence of the individual in a mass society. It is a device invented by monopoly capital to facilitate its dictatorship over a mystified, docile, debased humanity, whose impulses of real violence must be redirected into imaginary channels.

4. Toward an Alternative Model

Collective needs are thus objectively in contradiction to the logic of capitalist development. This development is by nature incapable of giving them the degree of priority which they warrant.[4] This is why demands in the name of collective needs imply a radical challenge of the capitalist system, on the economic, political, and cultural levels.

From the economic point of view (as we have already said), the mechanism of capitalist accumulation automatically tends to give a high degree of priority to individual market needs, into which, because they are considered as the principal motive force of expansion, all collective needs are translated. The subordinate position of collective needs is even more evident in a highly developed capitalist economy such as the American or British, where a gigantic apparatus of commercial propaganda resorts to ever more perfected psychological tricks in order to excite and stimulate individual needs, while only isolated voices or bureaucratic apparatuses speak for collective needs. The attempt to counterbalance the dictatorship of monopoly capital over the means of information and individual education has always been ineffective because of the disproportion of forces: it is practically impossible for organs of information and education to fight against commercial propaganda so long, at least, as they address a dispersed and atomized public.

This practical impossibility is obviously due to the fact that collective needs can not be substantially defined except collectively. For it is impossible for any individual to obtain satisfaction of those needs which he feels (according to Marx's distinction) as a "social individual" rather than as an "accidental individual." Left to himself, he will always tend to demand individual goods rather than collective services or facilities—to demand, in other words, a "market economy" and a "society of consumption" rather than an economy and a society founded on service. This is for the simple

[4] Sweden is no exception to the rule, although the underdevelopment of collective facilities, compared with individual and private equipment, is less dramatic than elsewhere in certain respects. The official ideology of Sweden, indeed, implies that alienation of work must be accepted and that the worker must look for his freedom in private life and private consumption.

reason that he has some chance of someday obtaining a washing machine, a car, and the necessary wage increase; but as an "accidental individual" he has no chance of obtaining public laundry service, rapid and comfortable means of public transportation, parks and athletic facilities ten minutes from his home, or even suitable housing at a price he can afford.

The preference for the priorities and the values of the "society of consumption" for the ideology of mature capitalism is therefore not spontaneous; it arises out of the individuals' powerlessness to define and to prefer something else. Thus is created the spontaneous primacy of demands for greater consumption, demands in which the bourgeoisie joyfully thinks it recognizes the striving for a life in the bourgeois image: the working class is "becoming bourgeois," and even in its demands it seems to endorse the values of capitalist civilization. It seems to confirm that the acquisition and the enjoyment of private goods is the supreme goal of "man"; it seems to be caught in the trap of the merchants of pseudo-culture and of alleged affluence; it seems to demonstrate that needs and desires can be shaped by monopolistic production in terms of its own greatest profit.

The only thing that can be effective in destroying these myths is the outline of a social model of consumption—a way of life and a culture based on social service, on free communication and free time, on the satisfaction of cultural or creative needs, on the full development of human faculties. It is not enough to say that this model (which does not yet exist anywhere) must be socialist, that socialism means the subordination of the purpose and methods of production to human needs and development. It is necessary again to define the concrete substance of collective needs at their roots, and to give the certainty that satisfaction is not impossible. This can only be done in common by mass political and labor organization and action, by organizing and grouping individuals where their collective needs are experienced, by making them acquire a common consciousness of their common needs, at work and at home, and by defining with them the common goals of common actions, of mass demonstrations and of strikes.

Even this is no more than a beginning. The process set in motion by mass action shall not culminate in an electoral campaign on the theme of "The sky over the Ruhr must become blue again." If it is to be effective, this process must challenge the model and mechanism of capitalist accumulation in the name of a society based on public service; it must lead up to demanding that the investment function be socialized, that planning be democratized according to a scale of fundamental priorities which reflect needs and not the projection of past monopoly expansion. More concretely, and as a first step, there must be a struggle to make the capitalist trusts pay for the collective services and facilities which their activity renders necessary, services which are an integral part of the social cost of production and must be under the control and management of the workers.

The social model of the phase of transition toward socialism, and the superiority of socialism over capitalism, will emerge more concretely in the course of these struggles. And the partial victories won in this way, if they improve living conditions, will not thereby reinforce capitalism. On the contrary: the public expropriation of real estate, the socialization of housing construction, free medicine, the nationalization of the pharmaceutical industry, public cleaning and transportation services, an increase in collective facilities, regional development planning (elaborated and executed under the control of local assemblies and financed by public funds), and the *social control* of all these sectors which are necessarily outside of the criteria of profit—these things weaken and counteract the capitalist system from within. Their mere functioning as social services requires a constant struggle against the capitalist system itself, since they cannot be kept working without a form of social control over the whole process of capitalist accumulation and the latter's subordination to a democratically determined scale of priorities reflecting the scale of needs.

Expansion of the socialized sector, or the satisfactory operation of the already existing social services, can be obtained only by continually restricting the private sector, by increasingly limiting its "freedom" to produce and invest. The only way the socialized sector can survive is by limiting capital's sphere of autonomy and counteracting its logic, by restraining its field of action, and bringing its potential centers of accumulation under social control. The socialized sector must take control of the industries it depends upon (socialized medicine must control the pharmaceutical industry, social housing construction must control the building industry, for example), or else it will be nibbled away and exploited by the private sector, as has happened in France.

The defense of the socialized sector requires its expansion; and the functioning of the socialized sector demands that the private centers of capital accumulation (industrial and financial monopolies) be subordinated to it and placed under social control. This is why, far from stabilizing, "humanizing" or "socializing" capitalism, the socialized sector is a permanent contradiction in its midst. The bourgeoisie knows this well, often better than the working class movement. This contradiction can only sharpen with time, and at the same time sharpen the class conflicts, until one or the other sector succumbs to the final assault (which can, in the best of hypotheses, be peaceful) after successive partial setbacks. . . .

WORK

Historically, most views of work have ascribed to it an extrinsic meaning. R. H. Tawney refers to "the distinction made by the philosophers of classical antiquity between liberal and servile occupations, the medieval insistence that riches exist for man, not man for riches. Ruskin's famous outburst, "there is no wealth but life," the argument of the Socialist who urges that production should be organized for service, not for profit, are but different attempts to emphasize the instrumental character of economic activities by reference to an ideal which is held to express the true nature of man." But there are also those who ascribe to work an intrinsic worth. All philosophies of work may be divided into these two views, although in a curious way Carlyle managed to combine the two.

I. The various forms of Protestantism, which (along with classical economics) have been the most influential doctrines in modern times, see work activity as ulterior to religious sanctions; gratifications from work are not intrinsic to the activity and experience, but are religious rewards. By work one gains a religious status and assures oneself of being among the elect. If work is compulsive it is due to the painful guilt that arises when one does not work.

II. The Renaissance view of work, which sees it as intrinsically mean- ingful, is centered in the technical craftsmanship—the manual and mental operations—of the work process itself; it sees the reasons for work in the work itself and not in any ulterior realm or consequence. Not income, not way of salvation, not status, not power over other people, but the technical processes themselves are gratifying.

Neither of these views, however—the secularized gospel of work as compulsion, nor the humanist view of work as craftsmanship—now has great influence among modern populations. For most employees, work has a gen- erally unpleasant quality. If there is little Calvinist compulsion to work among propertyless factory workers and file clerks, there is also little Renaissance exuberance in the work of the insurance clerk, freight handler, or department-store saleslady. If the shoe salesman or the textile executive gives

Reprinted from C. Wright Mills, *White Collar: The American Middle Classes* (New York: Oxford University Press, 1951), pp. 218–238. From *White Collar: The American Middle Classes* by C. Wright Mills. Copyright 1951 by Oxford University Press, Inc. Reprinted by permission. The late C. Wright Mills taught sociology at Columbia University. Among the many books he wrote are *The New Men of Power*, *The Power Elite*, and *The Sociological Imagination*.

little thought to the religious meaning of his labor, certainly few telephone operators or receptionists or schoolteachers experience from their work any Ruskinesque inner calm. Such joy as creative work may carry is more and more limited to a small minority. For the white-collar masses, as for wage earners generally, work seems to serve neither God nor whatever they may experience as divine in themselves. In them there is no taut will-to-work, and few positive gratifications from their daily round.

The gospel of work has been central to the historic tradition of America, to its image of itself, and to the images the rest of the world has of America. The crisis and decline of that gospel are of wide and deep meaning. On every hand, we hear, in the words of Wade Shortleff for example, that "the aggressiveness and enthusiasm which marked other generations is withering, and in its stead we find the philosophy that attaining and holding a job is not a challenge but a necessary evil. When work becomes just work, activity undertaken only for reason of subsistence, the spirit which fired our nation to its present greatness has died to a spark. An ominous apathy cloaks the smoldering discontent and restlessness of the management men of tomorrow."

To understand the significance of this gospel and its decline, we must understand the very spirit of twentieth-century America. That the historical work ethic of the old middle-class entrepreneurs has not deeply gripped the people of the new society is one of the most crucial psychological implications of the structural decline of the old middle classes. The new middle class, despite the old middle-class origin of many of its members, has never been deeply involved in the older work ethic, and on this point has been from the beginning non-bourgeois in mentality.

At the same time, the second historically important model of meaningful work and gratification—craftsmanship—has never belonged to the new middle classes, either by tradition or by the nature of their work. Nevertheless, the model of craftsmanship lies, however vaguely, back of most serious studies of worker dissatisfaction today, of most positive statements of worker gratification, from Ruskin and Tolstoy to Bergson and Sorel. Therefore, it is worth considering in some detail, in order that we may then gauge in just what respects its realization is impossible for the modern white-collar worker.

The Ideal of Craftsmanship

Craftsmanship as a fully idealized model of work gratification involves six major features: There is no ulterior motive in work other than the product being made and the processes of its creation. The details of daily work are meaningful because they are not detached in the worker's mind from the product of the work. The worker is free to control his own working action. The craftsman is thus able to learn from his work; and to use and develop his capacities and skills in its prosecution. There is no split of work and play, or work and culture. The craftsman's way of livelihood determines and infuses his entire mode of living.

I. The hope in good work, William Morris remarked, is hope of product and hope of pleasure in the work itself; the supreme concern, the whole attention, is with the quality of the product and the skill of its making. There is an inner relation between the craftsman and the thing he makes, from the image he first forms of it through its completion, which goes beyond the mere legal relations of property and makes the craftsman's will-to-work spontaneous and even exuberant.

Other motives and results—money or reputation or salvation—are subordinate. It is not essential to the practice of the craft ethic that one necessarily improves one's status either in the religious community or in the community in general. Work gratification is such that a man may live in a kind of quiet passion "for his work alone."

II. In most statements of craftsmanship, there is a confusion between its technical and aesthetic conditions and the legal (property) organization of the worker and the product. What is actually necessary for work-as-craftsmanship, however, is that the tie between the product and the producer be psychologically possible; if the producer does not legally own the product he must own it psychologically in the sense that he knows what goes into it by the way of skill, sweat, and material and that his own skill and sweat are visible to him. Of course, if legal conditions are such that the tie between the work and the worker's material advantage is transparent, this is a further gratification, but it is subordinate to that workmanship which would continue of its own will even if not paid for.

The craftsman has an image of the completed product, and even though he does not make it all, he sees the place of his part in the whole, and thus understands the meaning of his exertion in terms of that whole. The satisfaction he has in the result infuses the means of achieving it, and in this way his work is not only meaningful to him but also partakes of the consummatory satisfaction he has in the product. If work, in some of its phases, has the taint of travail and vexation and mechanical drudgery, still the craftsman is carried over these junctures by keen anticipation. He may even gain positive satisfaction from encountering a resistance and conquering it, feeling his work and will as powerfully victorious over the recalcitrance of materials and the malice of things. Indeed, without this resistance he would gain less satisfaction in being finally victorious over that which at first obstinately resists his will.

George Mead has stated this kind of aesthetic experience as involving the power "to catch the enjoyment that belongs to the consummation, the outcome, of an undertaking and to give to the implements, the objects that are instrumental in the undertaking, and to the acts that compose it something of the joy and satisfaction that suffuse its successful accomplishment."

III. The workman is free to begin his work according to his own plan and, during the activity by which it is shaped, he is free to modify its form and the manner of its creation. In both these senses, Henri De Man observed, "plan and performance are one," and the craftsman is master of the activity and of himself in the process. This continual joining of plan and activity brings even more firmly together the consummation of work and its instrumental activities, infusing the latter with the joy of the former. It also means that his sphere of independent action is large and rational to him. He is responsible for its outcome and free to assume that responsibility. His problems and difficulties must be solved by him, in terms of the shape he wants the final outcome to assume.

IV. The craftsman's work is thus a means of developing his skill, as well as a means of developing himself as a man. It is not that self-development is an ulterior goal, but that such development is the cumulative result obtained by devotion to the practice of his skills. As he gives it the quality of his own mind and skill, he is also further developing his own nature; in this simple sense, he lives in and through his work, which confesses and reveals him to the world.

V. In the craftsman pattern there is no split of work and play, of work and culture. If play is supposed to be an activity, exercised for its own sake, having no aim other than gratifying the actor, then work is supposed to be an activity performed to create economic value or for some other ulterior result. Play is something you do to be happily occupied, but if work occupies you happily, it is also play, although it is also serious, just as play is to the child. "Really free work, the work of a composer, for example," Marx once wrote of Fourier's notions of work and play, "is damned serious work, intense strain." The simple self-expression of play and the creation of ulterior value of work are combined in work-as-craftsmanship. The craftsman or artist expresses himself at the same time and in the same act as he creates value. His work is a poem in action. He is at work and at play in the same act.

"Work" and "culture" are not, as Gentile has held, separate spheres, the first dealing with means, the second with ends in themselves; as Tilgher, Sorel, and others have indicated, either work or culture may be an end in itself, a means, or may contain segments of both ends and means. In the craft model of activity, "consumption" and "production" are blended in the same act; active craftsmanship, which is both play and work, is the medium of culture; and for the craftsman there is no split between the worlds of culture and work.

VI. The craftsman's work is the mainspring of the only life he knows; he does not flee from work into a separate sphere of leisure; he brings to his non-working hours the values and qualities developed and employed in his working time. His idle conversation is shop talk; his friends follow the same lines of work as he, and share a kinship of feeling and thought. The leisure William Morris called for was "leisure to think about our work, that faithful daily companion. . . ."

In order to give his work the freshness of creativity, the craftsman must at times open himself up to those influences that only affect us when our attentions are relaxed. Thus for the craftsman, apart from mere animal rest, leisure may occur in such intermittent periods as are necessary for individuality in his work. As he brings to his leisure the capacity and problems of his work, so he brings back into work those sensitivities he would not gain in periods of high, sustained tension necessary for solid work.

"The world of art," wrote Paul Bourget, speaking of America, "requires less self-consciousness—an impulse of life which forgets itself, the alternation of dreamy idleness with fervid execution." The same point is made by Henry James, in his essay on Balzac, who remarks that we have practically lost the faculty of attention, meaning ". . . that unstrenuous, brooding sort of attention required to produce or appreciate works of art." Even rest, which is not so directly connected with work itself as a condition of creativity, is animal rest, made secure and freed from anxiety by virtue of work done—in Tilgher's words, "a sense of peace and calm which flows from all well-regulated, disciplined work done with a quiet and contented mind."

In constructing this model of craftsmanship, we do not mean to imply that there ever was a community in which work carried all these meanings. Whether the medieval artisan approximated the model as closely as some writers seem to assume, we do not know; but we entertain serious doubts that this is so; we lack enough psychological knowledge of medieval populations properly to judge. At any rate, for our purposes it is enough to know that at different times and in different occupations, the work men do has carried one or more features of craftsmanship.

With such a model in mind, a glance at the occupational world of the modern worker is enough to make clear that practically none of these aspects are now relevant to modern work experience. The model of craftsmanship has become an anachronism. We use the model as an explicit ideal in terms of which we can summarize the working conditions and the personal meaning work has in modern work-worlds, and especially to white-collar people.

The Conditions of Modern Work

As practice, craftsmanship has largely been trivialized into "hobbies," part of leisure not of work; or if work—a marketable activity—it is the work of scattered mechanics in handicraft trades, and of professionals who manage to remain free. As ethic, craftsmanship is confined to minuscule groups of privileged professionals and intellectuals.

The entire shift from the rural world of the small entrepreneur to the urban society of the dependent employee has instituted the property conditions of alienation from product and process of work. Of course, dependent occupations vary in the extent of initiative they allow and invite, and many self-employed enterprisers are neither as independent nor as enterprising as commonly supposed. Nevertheless, in almost any job, the employee sells a degree of his independence; his working life is within the domain of others; the level of his skills that are used and the areas in which he may exercise independent decisions are subject to management by others. Probably at least ten or twelve million people worked during the 'thirties at tasks below the skill level of which they were easily capable; and, as school attendance increases and more jobs are routinized, the number of people who must work below their capacities will increase.

There is considerable truth in the statement that those who find free expression of self in their work are those who securely own the property with which they work, or those whose work-freedom does not entail the ownership of property. "Those who have no money work sloppily under the name of sabotage," writes Charles Péguy, "and those who have money work sloppily, a counter and different sloppiness, under the name of luxury. And thus culture no longer has any medium through which it might infiltrate. There no longer exists that marvelous unity true of all ancient societies, where he who produced and he who bought equally loved and knew culture."

The objective alienation of man from the product and the process of work is entailed by the legal framework of modern capitalism and the modern division of labor. The worker does not own the product or the tools of his production. In the labor contract he sells his time, energy, and skill into the power of others. To understand self-alienation we need not accept the metaphysical view that man's self is most crucially expressed in work-activity. In all work involving the personality market, as we have seen, one's personality and personal traits become part of the means of production. In this sense a person instrumentalizes and externalizes intimate features of his person and disposition. In certain white-collar areas, the rise of personality markets has carried self and social alienation to explicit extremes.

Thoreau, who spoke for the small entrepreneur, objected, in the middle of the nineteenth century, "to the division of labor since it divided the worker, not merely the work, reduced him from a man to an operative, and enriched the few at the expense of the many." "It destroyed," wrote F. O. Matthiessen, "the potential balance of his [Thoreau's] agrarian world, one of the main ideals of which was the union of labor and culture."

The detailed division of labor means, of course, that the individual does not carry through the whole process of work to its final product; but it also means that under many modern conditions the process itself is invisible to him. The product as the goal of his work is legally and psychologically detached from him, and this detachment cuts the nerve of meaning which work might otherwise gain from its technical processes. Even on the professional levels of white-collar work, not to speak of wage-work and the lower white-collar tasks, the chance to develop and use individual rationality is often destroyed by the centralization of decision and the formal rationality that bureaucracy entails. The expropriation which modern work organization has carried through thus goes far beyond the expropriation of ownership; rationality itself has been expropriated from work and any total view and understanding of its process. No longer free to plan his work, much less to modify the plan to which he is subordinated, the individual is to a great extent managed and manipulated in his work.

The world market, of which Marx spoke as the alien power over men, has in many areas been replaced by the bureaucratized enterprise. Not the market as such but centralized administrative decisions determine when men work and how fast. Yet the more and the harder men work, the more they build up that which dominates their work as an alien force, the commodity; so also, the more and the harder the white-collar man works, the more he builds up the enterprise outside himself, which is, as we have seen, duly made a fetish and thus indirectly justified. The enterprise is not the institutional shadow of great men, as perhaps it seemed under the old captain of industry; nor is it the instrument through which men realize themselves in work, as in small-scale production. The enterprise is an impersonal and alien Name, and the more that is placed in it, the less is placed in man.

As tool becomes machine, man is estranged from the intellectual potentialities and aspects of work; and each individual is routinized in the name of increased and cheaper per unit productivity. The whole unit and meaning of time is modified; man's "life-time," wrote Marx, is transformed into "working-time." In tying down individuals to particular tasks and jobs, the division of labor "lays the foundation of that all-engrossing system of specializing and sorting men, that development in a man of one single faculty at the expense of all other faculties, which caused A. Ferguson, the master of Adam Smith, to exclaim: 'We make a nation of Helots, and have no free citizens.' "

The introduction of office machinery and sales devices has been mechanizing the office and the salesroom, the two big locales of white-collar work. Since the 'twenties it has increased the division of white-collar labor, recomposed personnel, and lowered skill levels. Routine operations in minutely subdivided organizations have replaced the bustling interest of work in well-known groups. Even on managerial and professional levels, the growth of rational bureaucracies has made work more like factory production. The managerial demiurge is constantly furthering all these trends: mechanization, more minute division of labor, the use of less skilled and less expensive workers.

In its early stages, a new division of labor may specialize men in such a way as to increase their levels of skill; but later, especially when whole operations are split and mechanized, such division develops certain faculties at the expense of others and narrows all of them. And as it comes more fully under mechanization and centralized management, it levels men off again as automatons. Then there are a few specialists and a mass of automatons; both integrated by the authority which makes them interdependent and keeps each in his own routine. Thus, in the division of labor, the open development and free exercise of skills are managed and closed.

The alienating conditions of modern work now include the salaried employees as well as the wage-workers. There are few, if any, features of wage-work (except heavy toil—which is decreasingly a factor in wage-work) that do not also characterize at least some white-collar work. For here, too, the human traits of the individual, from his physique to his psychic disposition, become units in the functionally rational calculation of managers. None of the features of work as craftsmanship is prevalent in office and salesroom, and, in addition, some features of white-collar work, such as the personality market, go well beyond the alienating conditions of wage-work.

Yet, as Henri De Man has pointed out, we cannot assume that the employee makes comparisons between the ideal of work as craftsmanship and his own working experience. We cannot compare the idealized portrait of the craftsman with that of the auto worker and on that basis impute any psychological state to the auto worker. We cannot fruitfully compare the psychological condition of the old merchant's assistant with the modern saleslady, or the old-fashioned bookkeeper with the IBM machine attendant. For the historical destruction of craftsmanship and of the old office does not enter the consciousness of the modern wage-worker or white-collar employee; much less is their absence felt by him as a crisis, as it might have been if, in the course of the last generation, his father or mother had been in the craft condition—but, statistically speaking, they have not been. It is slow historical fact, long gone by in any dramatic consequence and not of psychological relevance to the present generation. Only the psychological imagination of the historian makes it possible to write of such comparisons as if they were of psychological import. The craft life would be immediately available as a fact of their consciousness only if in the lifetime of the modern employees they had experienced a shift from the one condition to the other, which they have not; or if they had grasped it as an ideal meaning of work, which they have not.

But if the work white-collar people do is not connected with its resultant product, and if there is no intrinsic connection between work and the rest of their life, then they must accept their work as meaningless in itself, perform it with more or less disgruntlement, and seek meanings elsewhere. Of their work, as of all of our lives, it can truly be said, in Henri Bergson's words, that: "The greater part of our time we live outside ourselves, hardly perceiving anything of ourselves but our own ghost, a colourless shadow. . . Hence we live for the external world rather than for ourselves; we speak rather than think; we are acted rather than act ourselves. To act freely is to recover possession of oneself. . ."

If white-collar people are not free to control their working actions they, in time, habitually submit to the orders of others and, in so far as they try to act freely, do so in other spheres. If they do not learn from their work or develop themselves in doing it, in time, they cease trying to do so, often having no interest in self-development even in other areas. If there is a split between their work and play, and their work and culture, they admit that split as a common-sense fact of existence. If their way of earning a living does not infuse their mode of living, they try to build their real life outside their work. Work becomes a sacrifice of time, necessary to building a life outside of it.

Frames of Acceptance

Underneath virtually all experience of work today, there is a fatalistic feeling that work per se is unpleasant. One type of work, or one particular job, is contrasted with another type, experienced or imagined, within the present world of work; judgments are rarely made about the world of work as presently organized as against some other way of organizing it; so also, satisfaction from work is felt in comparison with the satisfactions of other jobs.

We do not know what proportions of the U.S. white-collar strata are "satisfied" by their work and, more important, we do not know what being satisfied means to them. But it is possible to speculate fruitfully about such questions.

We do have the results of some questions, necessarily crude, regarding feelings about present jobs. As in almost every other area, when sponge questions are asked of a national cross-section, white-collar people, meaning here clerical and sales employees, are in the middle zones. They stand close to the national average (64 per cent asserting they find their work interesting and enjoyable "all the time"), while more of the professionals and executives claim interest and enjoyment (85 per cent), and fewer of the factory workers (41 per cent) do so.

Within the white-collar hierarchy, job satisfaction seems to follow the hierarchical levels; in one study, for example, 86 per cent of the professionals, 74 per cent of the managerial, 42 per cent of the commercial employees, stated general satisfaction. This is also true of wage-worker levels of skill: 56 per cent of the skilled, but 48 per cent of the semi-skilled, are satisfied.

Such figures tell us very little, since we do not know what the questions mean to the people who answer them, or whether they mean the same thing to different strata. However, work satisfaction is related to income and, if we had measures, we might find that it is also related to status as well as to power. What such questions probably measure are invidious judgments of the individual's standing with reference to other individuals. And the aspects of work, the terms of such comparisons, must be made clear.

Under modern conditions, the direct technical processes of work have been declining in meaning for the mass of employees, but other features of work—income, power, status—have come to the fore. Apart from the technical operations and the skills involved, work is a source of income; the amount, level, and security of pay, and what one's income history has been are part of work's meaning. Work is also a means of gaining status, at the place of work, and in the general community. Different types of work and different occupational levels carry differential status values. These again are part of the meaning of the job. And also work carries various sorts of power, over materials and tools and machines, but, more crucially now, over other people.

I. *Income* The economic motives for work are now its only firm rationale. Work now has no other legitimating symbols, although certainly other gratifications and discontents are associated with it. The division of labor and the routinization of many job areas are reducing work to a commodity, of which money has become the only common denominator. To the worker who cannot receive technical gratifications from his work, its market value is all there is to it. The only significant occupational movement in the United States, the trade unions, have the pure and simple ideology of alienated work: more and more money for less and less work. There are, of course, other demands, but they can be only "fixed up" to lessen the cry for more money. The sharp focus upon money is part and parcel of the lack of intrinsic meaning that work has come to have.

Underlying the modern approach to work there seems to be some vague feeling that "one should earn one's own living," a kind of Protestant undertow, attenuated into a secular convention. "When work goes," as H. A. Overstreet, a job psychologist writing of the slump, puts it, "we know that the tragedy is more than economic. It is psychological. It strikes at the center of our personality. It takes from us something that rightly belongs to every self-respecting human being." But income security—the fear of unemployment or under-employment—is more important. An undertow of anxiety about sickness, accident, or old age must support eagerness for work, and gratification may be based on the compulsion to relieve anxiety by working hard. Widespread unemployment, or fear of it, may even make an employee happily thankful for any job, contented to be at any kind of work when all around there are many workless, worried people. If satisfaction rests on relative status, there is here an invidious element that increases it. It is across this ground tone of convention and fear, built around work as a source of income, that other motives to work and other factors of satisfaction are available.

II. *Status* Income and income security lead to other things, among them, status. With the decline of technical gratification, the employee often tries to center such meaning as he finds in work on other features of the job. Satisfaction in work often rests upon status satisfactions from work associations. As a social role played in relation to other people, work may become a source of self-esteem, on the job, among co-workers, superiors, subordinates, and customers, if any; and off the job, among friends, family, and community at large. The fact of doing one kind of job rather than another and doing one's job with skill and dispatch may be a source of self-esteem. For the man or woman lonely in the city, the mere fact of meeting people at the place of work may be a positive thing. Even anonymous work contacts in large enterprises may be highly esteemed by those who feel too closely bound by family and neighborhood. There is a gratification from working downtown in the city, uptown in the smaller urban center; there is the glamour of being attached to certain firms.

It is the status conferred on the exercise of given skills and on given income levels that is often the prime source of gratification or humiliation. The psychological effect of a detailed division of labor depends upon whether or not the worker has been downgraded, and upon whether or not his associates have also been downgraded. Pride in skill is relative to the skills he has exercised in the past and to the skills others exercise, and thus to the evaluation of his skills by other people whose opinions count. In like manner, the amount of money he receives may be seen by the employee and by others as the best gauge of his worth.

This may be all the more true when relations are increasingly "objectified" and do not require intimate knowledge. For then there may be anxiety to keep secret the amount of money earned, and even to suggest to others that one earns more. "Who earns the most?" asks Erich Engelhard. "That is the important question, that is the gauge of all differentiations and the yardstick of the moneyed classes. We do not wish to show how we work, for in most cases others will soon have learned our tricks. This explains all the bragging. 'The work I have to do!' exclaims one employee when he has only three letters to write. . . This boastfulness can be explained by a drive which impels certain people to evaluate their occupations very low in comparison with their intellectual aspirations but very high compared with the occupations of others."

III. *Power* Power over the technical aspects of work has been stripped from the individual, first, by the development of the market, which determines how and when he works, and second, by the bureaucratization of the work sphere, which subjects work operations to discipline. By virtue of these two alien forces the individual has lost power over the technical operations of his own work life.

But the exercise of power over other people has been elaborated. In so far as modern organizations of work are large scale, they are heirarchies of power, into which various occupations are fitted. The fact that one takes orders as well as gives them does not necessarily decrease the positive gratification achieved through the exercise of power on the job.

Status and power, as features of work gratification, are often blended; self-esteem may be based on the social power exercised in the course of work; victory over the will of another may greatly expand one's self-estimation. But the very opposite may also be true: in an almost masochistic way, people may be gratified by subordination on the job. We have already seen how office women in lower positions of authority are liable to identify with men in higher authority, transferring from prior family connections or projecting to future family relations.

All four aspects of occupation—skill, power, income, and status—must be taken into account to understand the meaning of work and the sources of the gratification. Any one of them may become the foremost aspect of the job, and in various combinations each is usually in the consciousness of the employee. To achieve and to exercise the power and status that higher income entails may be the very definition of satisfaction in work, and this satisfaction may have nothing whatsoever to do with the craft experience as the inherent need and full devolopment of human activity.

The Morale of the Cheerful Robots

The institutions in which modern work is organized have come about by drift—many little schemes adding up to unexpected results—and by plan —efforts paying off as expected. The alienation of the individual from the product and the process of his work came about, in the first instance, as a result of the drift of modern capitalism. Then, Frederick Taylor, and other scientific managers, raised the division of labor to the level of planful management. By centralizing plans, as well as introducing further divisions of skill, they further routinized work; by consciously building upon the drift, in factory and in office, they have carried further certain of its efficient features.

Twenty years ago, H. Dubreuil, a foreign observer of U.S. industry, could write that Taylor's "insufficiency" shows up when he comes to approach "the inner forces contained in the worker's soul. . ." That is no longer true. The new (social) scientific management begins precisely where Taylor left off or was incomplete; students of "human relations in industry" have studied not lighting and clean toilets, but social cliques and good morale. For in so far as human factors are involved in efficient and untroubled production, the managerial demiurge must bring them under control. So, in factory and in office, the world to be managed increasingly includes the social setting, the human affairs, and the personality of man as a worker.

Management effort to create job enthusiasm reflects the unhappy unwillingness of employees to work spontaneously at their routinized tasks; it indicates recognition of the lack of spontaneous will to work for the ulterior ends available; it also indicates that it is more difficult to have happy employees when the chances to climb the skill and social hierarchies are slim. These are underlying reasons why the Protestant ethic, a work compulsion, is replaced by the conscious efforts of Personnel Departments to create morale. But the present-day concern with employee morale and work enthusiasm has other sources than the meaningless character of much modern work. It is also a response to several decisive shifts in American society, particularly in its higher business circles: the enormous scale and complexity of modern business, its obviously vast and concentrated power; the rise of successfully competing centers of loyalty—the unions—over the past dozen years, with their inevitable focus upon power relations on the job; the enlargement of the liberal administrative state at the hands of politically successful New and Fair Deals; and the hostile atmosphere surrounding business during the big slump.

These developments have caused a shift in the outlook of certain sections of the business world, which in *The New Man of Power* I have called the shift from practical to sophisticated conservatism. The need to develop new justifications, and the fact that increased power has not yet been publicly justified, give rise to a groping for more telling symbols of justification among the more sophisticated business spokesmen, who have felt themselves to be a small island in a politically hostile sea of propertyless employees. Studies of "human relations in industry" are an ideological part of this groping. The managers are interested in such studies because of the hope of lowering production costs, of easing tensions inside their plants, of finding new symbols to justify the concentrated power they exercise in modern society.

To secure and increase the will to work, a new ethic that endows work with more than an economic incentive is needed. During war, managers have appealed to nationalism; they have appealed in the name of the firm or branch of the office or factory, seeking to tap the animistic identifications of worker with work-place and tools in an effort to strengthen his identification with the company. They have repeatedly written that "job enthusiasm is good business," that "job enthusiasm is a hallmark of the American Way." But they have not yet found a really sound ideology.

What they are after is "something in the employee" outwardly manifested in a "mail must go through" attitude, "the 'we' attitude," "spontaneous discipline," "employees smiling and cheerful." They want, for example, to point out to banking employees "their importance to banking and banking's importance to the general economy." In conferences of management associations (1947) one hears: "There is one thing more that is wonderful about the human body. Make the chemical in the vial a little different and you have a person who is loyal. He likes you, and when mishaps come he takes a lot from you and the company, because you have been so good to him; you have changed the structure of his blood. You have to put into his work and environment the things that change the chemical that stimulates the action, so that he is loyal and productive. . . Somebody working under us won't know why, but . . . when they are asked where they work and why, they say 'I work with this company. I like it there and my boss is really one to work with.' "

The over-all formula of advice that the new ideology of "human relations in business" contains runs to this effect: to make the worker happy, efficient, and co-operative, you must make the managers intelligent, rational, knowledgeable. It is the perspective of a managerial elite, disguised in the pseudo-objective language of engineers. It is advice to the personnel manager to relax his authoritative manner and widen his manipulative grip over the employees by understanding them better and counting their informal solidarities against management and exploiting these solidarities for smoother and less troublesome managerial efficiency.

Current managerial attempts to create job enthusiasm, to paraphrase Marx's comment on Proudhon, are attempts to conquer work alienation within the bounds of work alienation. In the meantime, whatever satisfaction alienated men gain from work occurs within the framework of alienation; whatever satisfaction they gain from life occurs outside the boundaries of work; work and life are sharply split.

The Big Split

Only in the last half century has leisure been widely available to the weary masses of the big city. Before then, there was leisure only for those few who were socially trained to use and enjoy it; the rest of the populace was left on lower and bleaker levels of sensibility, taste, and feeling. Then as the sphere of leisure was won for more and more of the people, the techniques of mass production were applied to amusement as they had been to the sphere of work. The most ostensible feature of American social life today, and one of the most frenzied, is its mass leisure activities. The most important characteristic of all these activities is that they astonish, excite, and distract but they do not enlarge reason or feeling, or allow spontaneous dispositions to unfold creatively.

What is psychologically important in this shift to mass leisure is that the old middle-class work ethic—the gospel of work—has been replaced in the society of employees by a leisure ethic, and this replacement has involved a sharp, almost absolute split between work and leisure. Now work itself is judged in terms of leisure values. The sphere of leisure provides the standards by which work is judged; it lends to work such meanings as work has.

Alienation in work means that the most alert hours of one's life are sacrificed to the making of money with which to "live." Alienation means boredom and the frustration of potentially creative effort, of the productive sides of personality. It means that while men must seek all values that matter to them outside of work, they must be serious during work: they may not laugh or sing or even talk, they must follow the rules and not violate the fetish of "the enterprise." In short, they must be serious and steady about something that does not mean anything to them, and moreover during the best hours of their day, the best hours of their life. Leisure time thus comes to mean an unserious freedom from the authoritarian seriousness of the job.

The split of work from leisure and the greater importance of leisure in the striving consciousness of modern man run through the whole fabric of twentieth-century America, affect the meaningful experiences of work, and set popular goals and day-dreams. Over the last forty years, Leo Lowenthal has shown, as the "idols of work" have declined, the "idols of leisure" have arisen. Now the selection of heroes for popular biography appearing in mass magazines has shifted from business, professional, and political figures—successful in the sphere of production—to those successful in entertainment, leisure, and consumption. The movie star and the baseball player have replaced the industrial magnate and the political man. Today, the displayed characteristics of popular idols "can all be integrated around the concept of the consumer." And the faculties of reflection, imagination, dream, and desire, so far as they exist, do not now move in the sphere of concrete, practical work experience.

Work is split from the rest of life, especially from the spheres of conscious enjoyment; nevertheless, most men and many women must work. So work is an unsatisfactory means to ulterior ends lying somewhere in the sphere of leisure. The necessity to work and the alienation from it make up its grind, and the more grind there is, the more need to find relief in the jumpy or dreamy models available in modern leisure. Leisure contains all good things and all goals dreamed of and actively pursued. The dreariest part of life, R. H. Tawney remarks, is where and when you work, the gayest where and when you consume.

Each day men sell little pieces of themselves in order to try to buy them back each night and week end with the coin of "fun." With amusement, with love, with movies, with vicarious intimacy, they pull themselves into some sort of whole again, and now they are different men. Thus, the cycle of work and leisure gives rise to two quite different images of self: the everyday image, based upon work, and the holiday image, based upon leisure. The holiday image is often heavily tinged with aspired-to and dreamed-of features and is, of course, fed by mass-media personalities and happenings. "The rhythm of the week end, with its birth, its planned gaieties, and its announced end," Scott Fitzgerald wrote, "followed the rhythm of life and was a substitute for it." The week end, having nothing in common with the working week, lifts men and women out of the gray level tone of everyday work life, and forms a standard with which the working life is contrasted.

As the work sphere declines in meaning and gives no inner direction and rhythm to life, so have community and kinship circles declined as ways of "fixing man into society." In the old craft model, work sphere and family coincided; before the Industrial Revolution, the home and the workshop were one. Today, this is so only in certain smaller-bourgeois families, and there it is often seen by the young as repression. One result of the division of labor is to take the breadwinner out of the home, segregating work life and home life. This has often meant that work becomes the means for the maintenance of the home, and the home the means for refitting the worker to go back to work. But with the decline of the home as the center of psychological life and the lowering of the hours of work, the sphere of leisure and amusement takes over the home's functions.

No longer is the framework within which a man lives fixed by traditional institutions. Mass communications replace tradition as a framework of life. Being thus afloat, the metropolitan man finds a new anchorage in the spectator sports, the idols of the mass media, and other machineries of amusement.

So the leisure sphere—and the machinery of amusement in terms of which it is now organized—becomes the center of character-forming influences, of identification models: it is what one man has in common with another; it is a continuous interest. The machinery of amusement, Henry Durant remarks, focuses attention and desires upon "those aspects of our life which are divorced from work and on people who are significant, not in terms of what they have achieved, but in terms of having money and time to spend."

The amusement of hollow people rests on their own hollowness and does not fill it up; it does not calm or relax them, as old middle-class frolics and jollification may have done; it does not re-create their spontaneity in work, as in the craftsman model. Their leisure diverts them from the restless grind of their work by the absorbing grind of passive enjoyment of glamour and thrills. To modern man leisure is the way to spend money, work is the way to make it. When the two compete, leisure wins hands down.

part three

The Sources
of Stability
n American Society

chapter 9

The Maintenance of Capitalist Order: Legitimacy and Social Control

Throughout the first two parts of this text a rather formidable case has been made against American capitalism. Although the ideological spokesmen for laissez-faire capitalism have maintained that only an economy based upon private and unfettered enterprise can serve the cause of human liberty,[1] the empirical evidence strongly suggests either that this is not the case or that such "liberty" is historically related to class polarization, political elitism, imperialism, racism, sexism, poverty and economc insecurity, and profound societal disorganization and personal alienation. Moreover, the modern liberal contention that the state in capitalist society is able to

[1] Friederich von Hayek, *The Constitution of Liberty* (Chicago: University of Chicago: University of Chicago Press, 1960). Milton Friedman, *Capitalism and Freedom* (Chicago: University of Chicago Press, 1962). Irving Kristol, "When Virtue Loses All Her Loveliness," *The Public Interest*, No. 21 (Fall 1970), pp. 3–15.

meliorate the antisocial consequences of unfettered capitalist development has also been exposed as fanciful.[2]

The last decade has witnessed intense renewed opposition to the capitalist political economy. Whether the various movements for social change will succeed in bringing about a fundamentally new society remains an open question at this point. Certainly it is important to recognize that radical societal transformations are extremely rare. The longevity of unjust social structures is truly one of the most remarkable characteristics of recorded history.

The unique historical record of American economic and political stability has been a source of wonderment to a large number of social analysts of all political persuasions. Unfortunately, existing interpretations of this phenomenon capture a portion of the truth while ignoring large areas that can provide grist for the rival ideological camp's mill. Specifically, nonradicals are prone to ignore elite manipulation and coercion in the stabilization process.[3] At the same time, many radicals have overemphasized the role of elite coercion in limiting the development of popular movements in the past and present.[4] Actually, conflict, cooperation, repression, manipulation, and genuine consensus play significant roles in the stabilization of all social structures. It would be as great a mistake to believe that Hitler and Stalin ruled primarily by the use or threat of terror as to believe that the American labor movement's acceptance of and attachment to capitalism came about without the prior experience of employer and state violence serving to warn of the bleak prospects for successful overt class warfare.

While a significant ideological incorporation of nonelites has been characteristic of American history, a careful examination of America's past and present economic and political stability probably would reveal much greater elite manipulation and coercion in this process than most traditional

[2] One might well argue, as many classical liberals do, that state intervention has *exacerbated* social problems. Whether this is true—and in the area of foreign policy a good case can be made for this proposition—the capitalist class created the modern state and actively sought state aid to promote and preserve its interests. That economic elites under capitalism can somehow be prevented from acquiring political power is one of the most naïve beliefs advanced by the advocates of laissez-faire. Equally absurd is the notion that laissez-faire capitalism can function in its anarchic way without state regulation and police-power being required to maintain economic and political stability. See Karl Polanyi, *The Great Transformation: The Political and Economic Origins of Our Time* (Boston: The Beacon Press, 1957).

[3] Louis Hartz, *The Liberal Tradition in America* (New York: Harcourt Brace Jovanovich, Inc., 1955). Seymour Martin Lipset, *Political Man: The Social Bases of Politics* (New York: Doubleday & Company, Inc., 1960). Michael Rogin, *The Intellectuals and McCarthy: The Radical Specter* (Cambridge, Mass.: MIT Press, 1967), provides an excellent critique of the "consensus" and "pluralist" perspectives.

[4] Eugene Genovese, "The Legacy of Slavery and the Roots of Black Nationalism," *Studies on the Left,* vol. 6 (November–December 1966), pp. 3–26, criticizes Herbert Aptheker and others for overestimating the revolutionary inclinations of American slaves and underestimating the noncoercive factors which contributed to their relative docility. James Weinstein, *The Decline of Socialism in America, 1912–1925* (New York: Monthly Review Press, 1967), attributes the collapse of the Socialist party to internal factionalism after the Bolshevik Revolution as well as the post–World War I repression of radical dissent by the federal government.

academic scholarship has granted. Bruce C. Johnson's article in this chapter provides the kind of historical analysis of American political culture and its sociological roots essential to an understanding of the forces that made it difficult for radicalism to thrive and limited radical effects when social unrest was rampant. He argues that the identification of Federalist thought with a hated "aristocracy" and "monarchism" appears to have been truly indicative of mass opinion in the early nineteenth century, thus legitimizing laissez-faire. The defeat of federalism opened up significant opportunities for a more democratic political economy in the Jacksonian era, but the laws of capitalist development, combined with the political genius of the laissez-faire liberals, led to elite irresponsibility and ultimately to the growing rigidification of class lines without a corresponding class consciousness. The desire for economic freedom, defined as the opportunity to achieve pecuniary success rather than economic security or industrial democracy, sowed the seeds of the present American institutional and cultural crisis.[5] Along this path, however, a significant proportion of American nonelites willingly trod. When a working consensus broke down in the wake of the destruction of the homogeneous preindustrial community, Johnson as well as Evelyn Parks in her article on the police show how social control was maintained by force.[6]

My only major disagreement with Johnson's work is in his treatment of what he calls "new liberalism." His own discussion of the labor movement—coupled with evidence gleaned from Chapters 1, 2, 4, and 8 of this text—suggests that even the favored elements of labor have neither benefited greatly nor sought incorporation into the modern political economy without some ambivalence. While doing a masterful job of discussing elite cooptation and repression of oppositional forces in the period before the New Deal, Johnson largely ignores the contemporary relevance of these strategies.

Michael Mann's article in this chapter provides evidence that to the extent a conservative political culture has been adopted by the contemporary working class it is based primarily on elite manipulation rather than "true consciousness" resulting from working-class advances in economic and political life. His focus on the role of elementary and secondary education in political socialization, is not sufficiently developed, however, and it would be useful to consider at least two additional contributions the school system makes to social order: the reinforcement of passivity through social hierarchy in the classroom and the conservative functions of tracking, grading, and vocational counseling. It would seem reasonable to presume that authoritarian teacher-student relationships strengthen tendencies toward acquiescence

---

[5] William Appleman Williams, *The Contours of American History* (Cleveland: The World Publishing Company, 1961).

[6] As Johnson notes, the law, as a necessary component of police power, played a vital coercive role in limiting dissent, organized labor, and political radicalism. See Arnold Paul, *Conservative Crisis and the Role of Law: Attitudes of Bar and Bench, 1887–1895* (New York: Harper & Row Publishers, 1969). William Preston, Jr., *Aliens and Dissenters: Federal Suppression of Radicals, 1903–1933* (New York: Harper & Row Publishers, 1963). See also Mark Kennedy, "Beyond Incrimination: Some Neglected Facets of the Theory of Punishment," *Catalyst*, vol. 5 (Summer 1970), pp. 2–37, for a brilliant analysis of the political bases of the criminal sanction.

in other social situations and play a significant role in maintaining existing institutional arrangements. Similarly, tracking, grading, and counseling have functioned to make social immobility more likely and more acceptable to working-class youth as well as deflecting hostility away from the institutional arena by placing blame for failure on the individual student.[7]

John McDermott's article in this chapter supplements Mann by showing that the culture of nonelite colleges, in which many working-class and lower-middle-class youths receive training after high school, also serves to incapacitate most students politically.

Although Mann and McDermott are concerned primarily with the effects of educational institutions on the less advantaged classes, middle-class youth are no less influenced by their schooling. That they are more likely to derive certain benefits from the existing stratification system should not minimize the fact that their ideological acceptance of parliamentary capitalism helps stabilize the political economy.

In addition to the role of *formal* education in political socialization to create consensus, it is necessary to examine other institutional sources of cultural uniformity which, although imperfect in their effects, clearly influence large numbers of people to identify with the status quo. Stuart Ewen's and David Gross' articles in this chapter point to more subtle means of undermining a critical perspective toward American institutions and culture. Their analyses of the multiple functions advertising and mass culture serve in the stabilization of advanced capitalism are extremely valuable in documenting the power of the mass media in creating and reinforcing cultural uniformities, deflecting criticism away from social institutions and toward the individual, and offering solutions to social problems through individual consumption.

There are several possible objections to the view that the mass media function basically as instruments for ideological indoctrination. A principal one is that many controversial and "subversive" books, films, plays, and so on are presented to the public along with obvious establishment-oriented material. As Ralph Miliband points out, all media products do not have to be oriented to the status quo; success is achieved if the dissenting perspectives exposed to the public represent only a tiny proportion of cultural products.[8] Moreover, toleration for limited dissension is valuable in legitimizing the concept of "freedom of choice" under capitalism. The political economics of the culture industry make it virtually impossible for *Ramparts* to successfully compete with *Time* or for underground films to have as wide an audience as Hollywood productions.

What about the willingness of many established publishing houses and film studios to present extremely unorthodox books and films to the public? The best explanation for this seems to be, as Gross argues, that in a capitalist society, culture itself is primarily a commodity, even if it serves ideological

[7] Richard Rothstein, "Down the Up Staircase: Tracking in Schools," *This Magazine Is About Schools*, vol. 5 (Summer 1971), pp. 103–140.

[8] Ralph Miliband, *The State in Capitalist Society: An Analysis of the Western System of Power* (New York: Basic Books, Inc., 1969), pp. 219–238. See Robert Cirino, *Don't Blame the People: How the News Media Use Bias, Distortion and Censorship to Manipulate Public Opinion* (Los Angeles, Calif.: Diversity Press, 1971), for documentation of the overwhelming bias of the media in the United States.

ends. "Revolutionary" art is promoted even by conservative business interests, because it is in demand on the marketplace. In times of political conflict such as the present period, this demand may even become exceedingly large. Yet if American society continues to be torn by domestic revolt in the future as it has in recent years, the culture industry can reasonably be expected to restrain its economic appetite and begin to reduce or even eliminate its "subversive" offerings. If self-censorship does not occur, the federal government may well step in—as it has already threatened to do in the broadcasting and movie industries—to serve the *interests* of the business class in general, if not the immediate desires of certain firms.[9]

The enormous power of business advertisers over newspaper, magazine, radio, and television content makes the issue of governmental censorship in these significant media an academic question. Even if there were a public demand for muckraking journalism and controversial radio and television programming, the fact that advertising provides the bulk of total revenue for these media means that publishers, editors, and programmers have been more than sensitive to their advertisers' desires for uncontroversial articles and programs. In 1965 and 1966 over 70 percent of television revenues and 95 percent of radio revenues in the United States came from advertising. The printed media are only slightly less dependent upon this source of income. In the same period, over 70 percent of newspaper revenues were derived from advertising, compared to about 59 percent for magazines.[10]

A dramatic example of the effect of advertisers on mass culture is found in the October 26, 1960 issue of *Variety,* the entertainment trade publication. Quoted from an article entitled "Madison Avenue's Program Taboos" are a set of specifications for radio and television drama writers given by major national advertisers:

> In general, the moral code of the characters in our dramas will be more or less synonymous with the moral code of the bulk of the American middle class, as it is commonly understood. There will be no material that will give offense either directly or by inference to any organized minority group, lodge, or other organizations, institutions, residents, of any state or section of the country, or a commercial organization of any sort. This will be taken to include political organizations; fraternal organizations; college and school groups, industrial, business, and professional organizations; religious orders; civic clubs, memorial and patriotic societies, philanthropic

[9] The recent attempt by the Nixon administration to prevent the publication of *The Pentagon Papers*—classified documents pertaining to the origin and development of government policy in Vietnam—exemplifies this possibility. It should be noted that newspapers such as the *New York Times* are now "revealing" aspects of foreign policy that were largely available publicly in historical studies and memoirs of former government officials years earlier. The decision to *publicize* this material reflects a growing rift within the ruling class over the Indochina war, rather than a principled policy of printing "all the truth and nothing but the truth." As long as the *Times* (and other newspapers) basically supports government policy it is willing to engage in self-censorship and should be expected to continue to do so under similar circumstances. See James Aronson, *The Press and the Cold War* (Indianapolis: The Bobbs-Merrill Company, Inc., 1970).

[10] Brad Wiley, "The Entertainment Media as an Industry," *Leviathan,* vol. 1 (July–August 1969), pp. 10–12.

and reform societies (Anti-Tobacco League, for example); athletic organizations; women's group, etc. which are in good standing. . . . There will be no material for or against sharply drawn national or regional controversial issues. . . . Where it seems fitting, the characters should reflect recognition and acceptance of the world situation in their thoughts and actions, although in dealing with war, our writers should minimize the "horror" aspects. . . . Men in uniform shall not be cast as heavy villains or portrayed as engaging in any criminal activity. There will be no material on any of our programs which could in any way further the concept of business as cold, ruthless and lacking all sentiment or spiritual motivation.[11]

Any serious examination of the content of radio and television drama surely confirms the view that those who write the scripts for those productions have generally been attentive to the concerns of the advertising executives as manifested in the above guidelines.

In addition to the roles of the educational system and the media in developing or strengthening cultural orientations and beliefs compatible with the needs of the American political economy, several other factors have played crucial parts in undermining Western anticapitalist movements.[12]

In America, specifically, religion has been a bulwark against radical social change. The Catholic Church and Protestant fundamentalism have both served the needs of capitalism by their promotion of fanatical anticommunism. Marc Karson suggests that the Catholic Church played a vital role in fighting against radical ideas in the most important period in the development of the labor movement.[13] In the case of fundamentalism the picture is more complex. Many areas of present-day rightwing fundamentalism were strongholds of Southern populism in the late nineteenth century. Somehow the attacks on Eastern bankers and big businessmen for exploiting the poor were transformed into charges that these same people were atheistic Communists. A certain rationality and continuity can be seen in the evolution of populist thought to rightwing ideology. Unfortunately, only a few scholars such as G. William Domhoff have tried to take the political analysis of the extreme Right seriously.[14] Whatever the historic ties of Protestant fundamentalism with populism, its function in recent times has clearly been to undermine a class-based radical politics.

While this discussion and the articles by Johnson, Parks, Mann, Henry Ewen and Gross present important evidence for elite manipulation and coercion of nonelites in the service of capitalist order, this material should not be construed as testimony for a robotized view of the masses. As Mann suggests, along with an acceptance of many facets of capitalist ideology,

[11] Cited in D. W. Smythe and H. H. Wilson, "Cold-War-Mindedness and the Mass Media," in Neal Houghton, ed., *Struggle against History* (New York: Simon and Schuster, Inc., 1968), p. 70.

[12] Miliband, *op. cit.*, pp. 179–218, considers the role of national symbolism, literacy, suffrage, and business promotional groups in maintaining capitalist ideological hegemony.

[13] Marc Karson, *American Labor Unions and Politics* (Carbondale, Ill.: Southern Illinois University Press, 1958).

[14] G. William Domhoff, *The Higher Circles: The Governing Class in America* (New York: Random House, Inc., 1970), pp. 281–308.

the working-class experience of economic insecurity makes total ruling-class ideological hegemony very unlikely. Ethnic and racial minorities are hardly incorporated at all. Finally, among a small but growing sector of college youth and the "new working class" of professionals and para-professionals, the material rewards of capitalism no longer compensate for its cultural, social, and spiritual poverty.[15]

It is under the circumstances of an incomplete legitimacy, then, that capitalist economic and political elites must operate. As legitimacy for constituted authority tends to diminish, education and persuasion will be replaced by legal and extralegal repression. This tendency of democracy to transform itself into authoritarian rule has played a significant role in the failure of opposition movements seeking radical social change in the United States. Kolko's article concluding this chapter chronicles the historical incapacity of the American state to allow groups seeking to alter existing institutions the right to achieve power through electoral means. The repression of the Socialist party for its opposition to World War I and its growing electoral support together with the suppression of the Communist and Black Panther parties in more recent times should raise great doubt in the minds of those who believe that radical social change can be achieved "within the system."

Kolko's attack upon the Socialist and Communist party leaders for tacitly accepting the reality of the American elite's commitment to democratic procedures and the neutrality of the state is a penetrating critique of "parliamentary socialism."[16] He also criticizes the Socialist and Communist assumption that increasing federal power and organizing trade unions were steps towards socialism rather than means of strengthening capitalism. Thus, Kolko raises the tragic dilemma that reform, by ameliorating extreme suffering, may prevent the growth of a revolutionary movement.[17] In addition to his attack upon the Old Left and portions of the early reformist New Left (1960–1966),[18] Kolko is particularly vehement and provocative in his analysis of the anti-Communist Left that emerged in the United States and Western Europe during the Cold War. Although he exaggerates the ideological incorporation of nonelites and is unnecessarily pessimistic about potential mass support for radicalism, Kolko's work should sensitize the reader to the fact that the failure of American radicalism must be blamed, at least partially, on the theoretical and strategic blunders of the Left.

[15] Kenneth Keniston, Young Radicals: Notes on Committed Youth (New York: Harcourt Brace Jovanovich, Inc., 1968). Milton Mankoff and Richard Flacks, "The Changing Social Base of the American Student Movement," The Annals of the American Academy of Political and Social Science, vol. 395 (May 1971), pp. 54–67.
[16] See also Miliband, op. cit.
[17] For the opposite view, see André Gorz, Strategy for Labor: A Radical Proposal, translated by Martin Nicolaus and Victoria Ortiz, (Boston: The Beacon Press, 1967).
[18] From 1966–1971 radical activists increasingly rejected the electoral arena and, ultimately, reformism as means for the achievement of societal transformation. For an understanding and evaluation of the development of the New Left see Massimo Teodori, ed., The New Left: A Documentary History (Indianapolis: The Bobbs-Merrill Company, Inc., 1969). Mitchell Goodman, ed., The Movement toward a New America: The Beginnings of a Long Revolution (Philadelphia: Pilgrim Press/New York: Alfred A. Knopf, Inc., 1970). Harold Jacobs, ed., Weatherman (Berkeley, Calif.: Ramparts Press, 1970).

Bruce C. Johnson

THE DEMOCRATIC MIRAGE: NOTES TOWARD A THEORY OF AMERICAN POLITICS

I. The Problem and Existing Approaches

Most extant sociological theories of American politics are wrongheaded. I shall defend this hyperbole at some length below, though not in every nook and cranny of the field. My concern is the resolution of what is perhaps the major problem of American politics, the contradiction between its pervasive equalitarian rhetoric and the inequalitarian social structure within which it operates. More particularly, the problem is to see and to explain the massive blocks to equalitarian political action which are inherent in American politics. Louis Hartz' work on the liberal tradition in American politics represents a partial exception to my general indictment, and his theory is the starting point for my own.

Perhaps the major axis of recent American political sociology has been the debate between the pluralists and the power elitists. Pluralists typically deal with the equalitarian rhetoric/inequalitarian reality problem by minimizing the extent of the contradiction. Their work draws heavily on Tocqueville's *Democracy in America*. Yet this would appear to be an irrelevant model, for the democratic promise Tocqueville saw in the Jacksonian era never reached fruition. There has been almost no redistribution of income in an equalitarian direction during the last century in the United States, and rather less redistribution has taken place here than in most countries of Western Europe. Today, income disparities between strata in the United States are among the highest in the world. It is facts such as these that lead me to regard the application of Tocqueville's pre-industrial analysis of America to our contemporary situation as an exercise in myth-making rather than as relevant social analysis.

In rejecting contemporary pluralist formulations, one need not accept such evident alternatives as power elite theory. The latter school of thought is properly attentive to the fact of elite power in the United States, but it has by no means satisfactorily explained the stability of that power, the cultural dynamics behind its maintenance. The critical question, as stated, is the equalitarian rhetoric which dominates American political life. If it is not taken seriously, why does it persist? If it is taken seriously, why is it not a

Reprinted, with deletions and slight revision, from Bruce C. Johnson, "The Democratic Mirage: Notes toward a Theory of American Politics," *Berkeley Journal of Sociology*, vol. 13 (1968), pp. 104–143, by permission of the *Berkeley Journal of Sociology* and the author.

Bruce C. Johnson teaches sociology at the University of California at San Diego. He is a former editorial board member of the *Berkeley Journal of Sociology*.

source of political instability? The answer I would offer is that our political rhetoric is not substantively equalitarian, and that belief in it is spread unevenly (though systematically) through the American population. These two social facts are essential features of the contemporary structure of American politics, a structure which I term the "new liberalism."

The elaboration of these points into a theory will require a considerably closer look at the historical development of American politics than either pluralists or power elitists have regarded as necessary. I shall utilize a tripartite framework, one which is incidentally chronological. First, I shall analyze the establishment of the liberal unity, which was substantially complete by the time Andrew Jackson reached the Presidency. Next, I shall analyze the cracks in the liberal monolith induced by industrialization, as revealed by the political crisis America faced in the late nineteenth century. Finally, I shall analyze the negative resolution of that crisis in our time, the emergence of the new liberalism. While there is something of a dialectic in this argument, it is not one for which Marxist thought has prepared us. This is because the transcendence of liberalism was not achieved in this country. For America, liberalism is not a stage but the whole of her history.

Since neither the pluralists nor the power elitists have yet exhausted the possibilities for coherent theory inherent within their respective approaches to American politics, it may seem unjustified to move in a new direction. However, the inadequacies of these schools of thought are due less to the idiosyncrasies of work done so far than to the fundamental principles underlying each school. Pluralists are part of the American tradition of political analysis, while power elitists are part of the European one.[1] A brief defense of the usefulness of this broad dichotomy will serve to underscore the features of Hartz' work that make it new and important.

The intellectual traditions of America and Europe are quite distinct. The low level of contact between them is especially pronounced in the study of history and politics. American historians have expressed little concern over the philosophy of history; they have hardly participated in such great European debates as that over historicism and positivism. Their concerns have been more "substantial," as the prominence of Frederick Turner and Charles Beard testifies. Political science in America is similarly parochial, as its preoccupation with pluralism exhibits. American pluralism descends from Madison and Hamilton, not from Figgis, Cole, and Laski. American pluralists see groups as a means of disciplining individuals (e.g., civility, cross-pressures) to provide for societal cohesion and stability; European pluralists saw groups as a means of defending the liberty of individuals against a powerful state. The liberal state is *assumed* by American pluralists, though it is not by their European counterparts. American sociology is somewhat better off than history and political science, for it has not been allowed to forget its European heritage; however, even in this discipline, we hear much

[1] In light of the great influence of Tocqueville's work upon the pluralists, the separation between American and European political theory sketched below may seem overdrawn. Actually, the very fact of this influence confirms my analysis, since Tocqueville's work has functioned in the United States less as an intellectual tool than as a social myth.

of pluralism. Moreover, bodies of thought imported into American sociology from Europe do not often escape being fundamentally recast into a liberal pluralist framework.[2]

This dissimilarity between America and Europe in traditions of political analysis is ultimately due to basic differences in the political structures of the two areas. Samuel Huntington argues that American political institutions started out essentially similar to English institutions of the Tudor period, and that they have not evolved since that time (as English political insitutions obviously have). Louis Hartz would have it that American political institutions are liberal ones, but he agrees that they have not changed in the last three centuries. The extraordinary continuity in American politics has been philosophical as well as institutional. In Europe, social change and political change have been relatively congruent; thus, new economic interests produce new political ideologies. In American politics, however, new issues arise within the framework of a received and static doctrine. In consequence, the very meanings of key political concepts in America have changed over time. Such peculiarities of American politics as these have made its internal dynamics quite different from those of European politics.

Neither of these traditions of political analysis, American or European, is adequately equipped to explain American politics. Such native bodies of thought as the frontier thesis, American pluralism, or Perlman's theory of the labor movement are cultural mirrors, projections of national myths. As such, they are ultimately exercises in subjectivity rather than explanatory tools. To this argument, it may be objected that subjectivity is a component of all social theories, since they conceptualize only part of the evidence. While true, this fact does not ordinarily cripple the explanatory power of a theory, since alternate theories exist as a check. Where (as in Europe) a variety of political ideologies contend, it is easier to see the root assumptions and limitations of any one of them. In the United States, root assumptions are never challenged, and thus never examined. It is the theoretical consensus that makes American work cripplingly subjective.

We should not be too quick to see European theories as those alternate interpretations of American politics that could bring detachment and self-awareness to American theories. It is difficult for European political theories to grasp the American experience because they are geared to societies wherein political change is fairly congruent with other kinds of social change. Tocqueville, Weber, and Marx all understood America and Europe to be basically similar, so that America was understandable in the terms which they had elaborated for the European experience. Tocqueville and Weber both saw America as further along, "ahead" of European nations in a rather linear sense. To Marxists, America is behind Europe, as a case of "arrested development." Actually the United States is neither ahead of Europe nor behind it, but on a different path entirely.

[2] Theories of mass society are an example of this phenomenon; see Leon Bramson, *The Political Context of Sociology*, Princeton University Press, Princeton, N.J., 1961. One might also note that while early American sociologists were influenced by German thought, these influences were precisely that aspect of early American sociology that did not "take" in the long run.

Hartz' work reflects an alertness to this fundamental contrast between American and European politics. The heart of his method is the reiteration of that contrast at many levels. Hartz does not, however, fall into the "American uniqueness" trap. Sensitive to the particular American conditions, he is also detached from them. He reproves historians of both America and Europe for failing to overcome their separated perspectives. One can find fault with political scientists and political sociologists on the same grounds. The enormous growth of comparative studies which has occurred in these fields in the last fifteen years, has done little to improve this state of affairs. The comparative trend has thus far consisted largely of a surge of interest in underdeveloped countries. Since little sophisticated comparative work has yet focused on the United States, the task of conquering the intellectual provincialism that has characterized studies of American politics has just begun. Hartz' work is the most substantial effort in this direction which we possess at present.

Since the argument of this paper derives in fair measure from Hartz' theory, it is appropriate to briefly examine the theory's strengths and weaknesses. Hartz has published three books; all are preoccupied with American history, though their scope widens over time. *Economic Policy and Democratic Thought* (1948) deals with Pennsylvania during the century succeeding 1776; *The Liberal Tradition in America* (1955) deals with the whole of the American Republic; and *The Founding of New Societies* (1964) deals with five "fragment societies" (including the United States) which were born in an escape from Europe.[3] While wags may project a book on the world for 1975, I believe that Hartz has expanded his frame of reference as far as he wishes to. One indication that this is so is a certain turning back which *New Societies* exhibits; in it, Hartz goes to some effort to re-work problems ill-handled in *Liberal Tradition,* such as Puritanism and the racial question.

The Liberal Tradition in America is Hartz' best-known book, though in some respects undeservedly so. It spells out the impact which America's "fixed, dogmatic liberalism" has had on her political history. Centrally, the United States has lacked both a genuinely revolutionary tradition and a genuinely reactionary one, since all political factions have based their ideologies on property. Working from the status uncertainties and other attributes of this state of affairs, one can generate a rather interesting model of American class relations. The aspects of this model which most concern me at present are the unusual elite political and economic strategies it called forth, and their devastating impact on the mass of Americans. Even our

[3] In *New Societies*, Hartz wrote the overview and the chapters on the United States; others contributed other national histories. Of these, I would particularly recommend Richard Morse's essay on Latin America and Richard Rosecrance's essay on Austrialia. Hartz' fragmentation typology unifies the various chapters. The United States is characterized as a bourgeois fragment of Europe. Analogously, Australia is a proletarian fragment; Latin America is a feudal fragment; Canada is a bourgeois (English) and a feudal (French) fragment; South African is a bourgeois (Dutch) and a proletarian (English) fragment. This typology generally works very well, although the South African and Latin American cases are somewhat problematic, for neither developed entirely on an empty continent, as did the other three fragments.

equalitarian rhetoric was eventually adapted to the maintenance of elite power. Such ideological subtleties are Hartz' forte, but his framework can be adapted to "harder" analyses as well. . . .

Hartz' claim that a liberal unity has dominated and shaped American politics does not amount to a benign view of American history. In this respect, his work shares little with the consensual emphasis of authors such as Richard Hofstadter or Seymour Lipset. In fact, Hartz never uses the term "consensus" so far as I know. He remarks: "The argument over whether we should 'stress' solidarity or conflict in American politics misleads us by advancing a false set of alternatives." In Hartz' eyes, the liberal tradition has not eliminated conflict and tension from our history, but simply given it peculiar form.

Accepting or rejecting in toto such a grand theory as Hartz' is not my style. To me, his importance lies in the propositions specific to given eras and problems which are generated by the overall interpretation. In the rest of this paper I will explore the application of Hartz' ideas to the problem of the stability of American politics over the course of industrialization. If a goodly number of the sub-interpretations implicit in Hartz' work were demonstrated by comparative empirical research, his overall assertion of the importance of the liberal tradition would gain enormous significance.

II. An Alternate Perspective

In this paper, I am concerned both to discount the two prevailing schools of thought on American politics and to elaborate an alternative perspective. A certain forensic symmetry could be achieved were I to approach each issue under consideration with two negative arguments and a positive one. This is not possible, for no distinctive power elitist analysis exists for nineteenth century America. In fact, C. Wright Mills admits the rough validity of the pluralist analysis for the period up to 1886.[4] The conflict between the two schools is not fully joined until post-World War I America comes under scrutiny. Thus the negative concerns of this paper will be directed largely toward the pluralists for the nineteenth century, and will emerge in re both schools of thought only for the later period.

During the eight decades or so of industrialization in the United States (1840-1920), many popular movements arose to deal with its effects upon their followers' lives. Labor agitation is naturally the most important contributor here. In the United States, the agrarian sector of the economy was of significant size very late in industrialization, and farmers also contributed much to the popular agitation of this period. In analyzing the frustration of popular aspirations, I will draw evidence for specific points from labor and farmer movements, though to a certain extent my analysis applies to the third major protesting group of the era, the Negro populace, as well.

[4] Mills' discussion of the historical development of the American power elite is dismayingly superficial, especially given his oft-stated commitment to this kind of work.

Popular protest over the course of industrialization was less massive and less far-reaching (especially ideologically) in America than in Western Europe generally. There is surprisingly wide academic acceptance of the view that this difference was due to the high level of opportunity in nineteenth century America; this view extends, as noted, even to the power elitists. Actually, in all the forms in which the assertion of opportunity has been presented, it is unfounded. Before we can undertake a serious answer to the question of why farmer and worker mobilization for protest was halting and incomplete in industrializing America, we must dispose of the hardy historical myth of opportunity. It has taken four major forms over time.

The most venerable form of the opportunity myth is the frontier thesis. The essential idea is that the frontier acted as a safety valve to absorb urban discontent. The best known exponent of this theory was Frederick Turner, though it has been cited as a factor in American labor's conservatism by Marx, Trotsky, and Gunnar Myrdal as well. Recent historical studies have shown the safety valve idea to be unfounded, since it took considerable skill and cash to go west and to succeed there in the nineteenth century. Those members of the working class who did go west were in all likelihood not discontented laborers, but well-off skilled workmen. The unskilled who migrated from a given city were likely to remain part of the general urban labor market. Thus, if the safety valve had had any effect on the course of American labor history, it should have been to help radicalize the labor movement.

The second major form of the opportunity myth is the economic abundance thesis. The argument is that America's great natural resources and rapid economic expansion created a high standard of living, which in turn meant that subordinate classes in this country were relatively satisfied with their position. Note that this argument is distinct from the argument that social mobility has been high in the United States. The abundance thesis has been offered by Myrdal and Seymour Lipset: David Potter is perhaps its best known exponent. The first objection which may be made to it is that the material well-being of American workers and farmers over time has been exaggerated. Second, the hypothesis is conceptually inadequate. The argument that a high standard of living disposes a labor movement against radicalism is based on the notion that absolute rather than relative deprivation is the primary source of labor radicalism. This notion is not borne out by the facts, at least in the developed countries. In Sweden, for instance, a high standard of living coexists with a labor movement considerably more radical than the American one.

The most popular expression of the opportunity myth in America has been the stress on social mobility. This stress has presented itself in two specific hypotheses: occupational mobility and property mobility; these are the third and fourth forms of the opportunity myth. The occupational mobility argument has been made by Myrdal, Werner Sombart, and many others. It holds that in America many workers could rise in the economic and social structure, or at least that proportionately more could do so here than could in Europe. And if class relations were not fixed, there was no impetus to class action, or to collective action generally, for social rewards.

The belief that occupational mobility is, or has been, higher in the United States than in European countries has been discredited by recent research. Seymour Lipset and Reinhard Bendix' 1959 study, *Social Mobility in Industrial Society,* carefully reviewed available evidence and concluded that "the overall pattern of social mobility appears to be much the same in the industrial societies of various Western countries." One problem with their case was that data was not available for the period prior to 1900. In 1964, Thernstrom published a detailed study of social mobility in nineteenth-century Newburyport, Massachusetts. His conclusion was that occupational mobility was no easier for American laborers in the late nineteenth century than in the twentieth; if anything, it had been harder to come by in the past.

Thernstrom has made an ingenious attempt to save the opportunity myth by arguing salience for American workers of *property* mobility. He argues that the ability of workers to buy small homes and to accumulate savings, while remaining workers, was immensely meaningful to them. In a context of low expectations, this low-level social mobility seems to have been sufficient verification of the mobility ethic for the average worker. Actually Stephan Thernstrom's tables considerably overstate the level of property mobility of workers. In addition, Thernstrom's own findings lead one to believe that such property holding as did exist among workers was not a form of upward mobility at all. It seems to have been a pecuniary pattern of a defensive rather than an ambitious stripe. Savings were used to weather hard times rather than to get ahead. Immigrants (who were disproportionate savers) often sent money to the old country, to support relatives there or to bring them to the United States. The price of having funds available for this gesture was typically a bare subsistence existence and the early withdrawal of children from (mobility-aiding) school into jobs.

In sum, the general emphasis upon absence of mass grievances in industrializing America, on the existence of individual loopholes which gave workers and farmers little reason to protest, fails to convince. Actually, there was a considerable discrepancy in this period between the relatively high level of popular grievances and the minimal protest which they engendered. The liberal society concept offers an excellent framework for analysis of this discrepancy. We can get a purchase on the particular processes involved by examining a recurrent crisis phenomenon of American politics, the moralistic binge.

The phrase "moralistic binge" refers to the intolerant crusades supporting various absolutes in which Americans periodically engage. These absolutes include abolitionism, temperance, nativism, and anti-Communism. What is the genesis of such moralistic binges? Pluralists would have it that they emerge from the breakdown of independent group life among non-elites. The explanation has some plausibility, for moralistic binges have been more widespread in the nineteenth century than in the twentieth, and it has only been since the turn of the century that significant "group life" has emerged in the United States. However, participatory activity as a whole has probably declined in America in this century; there has been an enormous rise in social apathy. Political apathy will be discussed more fully below; what is relevant for the understanding of moralistic binges is the growth of cultural quiescence in our time. Puritanism supplied much of the fervor necessary for moralistic binges; the Great Awakening and the Great Revival (of the early eighteenth and early nineteenth centuries, respectively) were prototypical binges. The late nineteenth century growth of "mind cure" religions which made no demands on society was a reaction against Puritanism; in this century, this "other-directed" mode has spread beyond religion to other spheres of social life as well.

Reference to Puritanism helps us explain not only the incidence of moralistic binges, but also the functions they perform. Hartz has argued that being a "fragment society" poses enormous problems of self-definition. Based in migration to an empty continent, these societies had no part to offer them a national identity. The identity which did emerge was necessarily fragile, a fact which inspired rigid overreactions to developments which threatened the fragment. The Puritan colonies faced this problem, as did the liberal society which succeeded it. The fact that French Canada, another fragment society, has experienced similar moralistic binges shows that it is not any particularly Puritan intolerance that is involved here. The analogue of the fragment society's problem of self-definition for groups within society is the problem of status. Status is a far more important social issue in a fragment society than in a European one, for status positions are not clearly defined or differentiated from one another. In this situation, moralistic binges are an appropriate means for resolving status ambiguities; their relevance to this end is one reason they have recurred over time.

Joseph Gusfield argues correctly that status politics has proven no less rational than class politics in American history: "Far from being a pointless interruption of the American political system, [the politics of status goals] has exemplified one of its characteristic processes." However, within this context, Gusfield reaffirms the common distinction between class and status politics. Actually, status politics (at least in the form of moralistic binges) has not been an alternative to class politics in the United States, but a crisis version of that politics. Business elites have capitalized upon the petty bourgeois unease behind most moralistic binges to contain movements which challenged elite dominance. This was true of the free silver craze and the 1919 Red Scare, for instance. Even abolitionism served to divert attention from conditions in the factories owned by abolitionists. In sum, moralistic binges have not represented the breakdown of normal social action in this country so much as its exaggerated fulfillment. Moralistic binges do not threaten the American social order, as pluralists argue, but sustain it.

These remarks point out a critical defect in pluralist analysis. I do not refer to the common charge that pluralists fail to appreciate the extent to which political and economic power are concentrated in the United States. If pluralism could explain any political configuration, it could explain that one. There is more amiss with pluralism than an empirical implication: its very conception of power is inadequate. The idea of social pluralism, as applied to the United States, has usually featured two central propositions. First, social life consists of a series of distinct power centers whose interaction provides a rough mutual balancing. This idea comes from Madison, who believed that checks and balances upon fully mobilized social forces could stabilize a political situation. Realizing that this Madisonian premise is a fallacy, contemporary pluralists have added a second proposition designed to show that mobilization is actually incomplete. This is the notion that people's lives consist of a number of distinct spheres (so that, for instance, union membership does not influence a worker's life off the job). This proposition, however, is no less mechanistic than the first; in either its Madisonian or its contemporary form, pluralism fails to grasp the more subtle aspects of power and of the ways in which it becomes concentrated or dispersed, stabilized or relocated, in society. In America, these subtleties consist in fair measure of the ideological and cultural components of politics. Conceivably, a mechanistic conception of power could be of use in analyzing European politics, since there ideological differences mirror rather directly those wooden aspects of power upon which the pluralist conception focuses. In American politics, however, the ideological question is by no means so readily handled. Here, class conflict appears in such unlikely guises as the moralistic binge; no analysis which ignores this fact is ultimately of much use in analyzing American politics.

The United States is more properly regarded as a liberal society than as a pluralist society. By liberalism, I mean that Lockian philosophy which regards the state as a night watchman concerned only with the personal security of the citizens; the constricted liberal definition of politics gives primacy to economic action in society. It is less easy to define a liberal *society*. As the American orthodoxy, liberalism has many sides, some of which this paper seeks to illuminate. The prism is the orthodoxy itself—more amorphous at some points in the American experience than others, but never entirely absent. Benjamin Disraeli portrayed industrializing England as "two nations between whom there is no intercourse and no sympathy." In terms of standard of living and of income distribution, the same two nations existed in industrializing America; yet this economic cleavage acquired scant political expression. America remained "one nation," with a remarkable cultural and political uniformity.

The liberal tradition persisted during and after industrialization primarily because the mass of Americans were not able to build an alternative to it, though they sought to do so. The roots of this popular inability to sustain dissent or independent action lies in the weakness of *class community* in the United States. Working class neighborhoods existed in nineteenth century America, but few of them were real communities. The importance of class community as a foundation for sustained independent action has been affirmed by many studies.[5] Clerk Kerr and Abraham Siegel found that industries are most strike-prone when workers form an undifferentiated and socially isolated mass. In this situation, labor grievances quick become collective experiences, since they are shared by nearly everyone on a worker's social horizon. Homogeneity also enhances the communication and mobilization processes inherent in redressing grievances.[6] Nigel Young, in his discus-

---

[5] Class community/culture is a necessary but not sufficient condition for sustained radical action. Compare the relatively insular and ineffective working class culture in Great Britain to the politically relevant ones in Germany and Sweden.

sion of the British case, emphasizes more subtle aspects of class community, such as horizontal social controls and social supports and the emergence of defensive institutions.

There were, to be sure, situations where class community could be found in America throughout industrialization—in geographically isolated company towns for workers, and in the crop-lien system of the post-bellum South for farmers. Yet these are limiting cases, situations where class community could hardly be prevented from developing. They but reiterate the hostility to particularistic loyalties and communities inherent in the liberal tradition. What strikes one in general is the remarkable influence over popular life exerted by elites in America. Workers and farmers have been able to develop almost no autonomous institutions. American education has been considerably more uniform across class lines than has European education (see below). Religious institutions, when popular among workers, have been more elite-controlled in America than in Europe. Even the labor union, the institution one would expect to be most nearly autonomous, has not been safe from elite penetration. Labor spies have been much more widely used by American employers than by European ones.[7] Much of the rest of this paper will be concerned to elaborate how circumstances and elite design have combined to keep class community weak in America.

The themes of my argument are offered by Hartz' answer to the question at hand, his "law of Whig compensation." He writes that the Hamiltonian Federalists, after perforce failing at the European Whig strategy of *divide et impera,* learned

> the Alger mechanism of enchanting the American democrat and the "Americanistic" mechanism of terrifying him, which was the bounty they were destined to receive for the European strategies of which they were deprived. For the defeat of Hamilton, so long as the economy boomed, they were bound to get the victory of McKinley. One might call this the great law of Whig compensation inherent in American politics. The record of its functioning takes up a large part of American history.

---

[6] A number of observers have attributed importance to the distinctively high *geographic* mobility of American workers. Perlman believed that "moving on" typically entailed upward occupational mobility, a contention which Thernstrom's work refutes. The actual impact of geographic mobility upon radical action is mixed, for it tends to radicalize attitudes at the same time that it hampers stable interaction among workers. In some situations, American workers have made great use of geographic mobility, as when Wobblies gathered for free speech fights. In others, geographic mobility hurt their efforts, as when workers left the vicinity of a strike to look for jobs elsewhere. It seems best to regard geographic mobility not as an independent factor, but as an artifact of class community. The IWW created community among its mobile followers, but in other blue collar occupational groupings (where geographic mobility is not intrinsic to the job), such mobility is probably a good indicator of the weakness of class community.

[7] In the late 1920's, there was about one labor spy for every seventeen union members in the United States. In Britain, labor spies were used only very early in the nineteenth century (and, interestingly, by government rather than by employers). See Bernstein, *Lean Years,* pp. 84, 149; G. D. H. Cole and Raymond Postgate, *The British People, 1746–1946,* Methuen & Co., Ltd., London, 1961, Sections III and IV.

We can use Hartz' formulation to succinctly summarize elite strategy during industrialization: early use of Alger enchantment, followed by Americanist terror when that failed. Stress should be laid upon the terror rather than the enchantment, for the law of Whig compensation worked in American history without a boom. There were seven major economic depressions in this country between the Civil War and World War I. Speaking more sociologically, we can take "enchantment" as incorporation, and "terror" as legalist repression. Until around 1890, the American mass was composed largely of natives and old immigrants; ideological incorporation and the implication of American federalism kept class community (and thus insurgency) weak among them. The sudden influx after that time of the new immigrants, who possessed a full-blown class community, presented American elites with a radical new problem. Their response to this threat provides a case study in what might be called the repressive underside of American liberalism.

III. Early Industrialization: The Liberal Enchantment Obscures Grievances

At the outset of industrialization, in the Jacksonian era, the mass of Americans was thoroughly incorporated into the liberal structure. This is an important phenomenon; it has no parallel in Europe, where the masters and the servants (Tocqueville) could easily tell one another apart. Hartz regards ideology as the mainspring of this mass incorporation, a formulation I prefer to go beyond. A brief treatment of the substantive structural bases of the liberal unity will indicate the lines which a more extensive analysis could take. I will deal with the colonial educational system and the colonial economy.

A general system of elementary education was established considerably earlier in America than in England. Consequently, mass literacy was achieved here well over a century earlier than it was in England. This development laid the basis for the cultural uniformity that was to develop over time. While there were nations on the Continent (e.g. Denmark, Prussia) which established popular education almost as early as did America, the implications of this fact were quite different in the two situations. Bendix argues that there is an important element of national consensus in the establishment of the right to an elementary education. This is so, but the consensual element was much more important in America than in Europe, where popular education did little to undercut social hierarchy. In America, higher education became relatively widespread far earlier than it did in Europe; it remains to this day available to but the few in much of Europe. Also, colonial education went considerably farther than did its European counterpart toward creating a uniform national language and speech: dialect remains a significant clue to class background in Europe, though not in the United States. American education's search for broad uniformities bespeaks an important social fact, the atrophy of particularistic (especially class-based) communities and cultures.

The Maintenance of Capitalist Order

While one can find, at least in the Puritan colonies, systematic attempts to create a unitary culture, this is not the main reason it emerged. Hartz' fragment analysis carries us beyond conscious intentions here. It points, first, to America's nakedness of institutions. Before Europe modernized, education had already been established as the prerogative of the church; in America, no such prior claims existed to delay or modify the development of popular education. Second, the fragment analysis points to the relative uniformity of the colonists' European origins. This fact set America off from a nation like Canada, whose *dual* fragmentation became an important prop to stratification.

None of this is meant to deny that colonial America was significantly stratified. Not only did slaves and bound labor exist, but there was great status differentiation among free whites as well. However, very little internal economic conflict, of a type that would have threatened the emerging cultural unity, was generated in colonial America. The enormous labor shortage made the bargaining position of free (and even bound) labor very strong. Colonial real wages ranged from 30 per cent to 100 per cent higher than contemporary English ones. On a more general level, the sizable subsistence sector of the colonial economy was no source of economic strife; conflicts in the market sector of the economy were largely external, since it exported staples to England.

Once the Revolution was won, this bourgeois society was free to establish its own political structure. The one that emerged reflected the sense of unity sketched above. The men who drew up the Constitution deeply feared power and conflict, and envisaged a politics free of them. But this is no politics at all. These misconceptions would not have mattered a great deal, save for the fact that the Constitution was made very difficult to amend. In Europe, reform of the legal structure of politics continued to occur after more modern features (such as political parties) developed. The relatively immutable legal structure of American politics, by contrast, has become a massive anachronism. During industrialization, social conflicts unanticipated by the drafters of the Constitution emerged, and American politics could not adequately adapt. The most salient aspect of the Constitution vis a vis social conflict was . . . the *state by state* basis of national politics. . . . This feature was later to help negate that great positive aspect of the politics of the early Republic, widespread suffrage.

We are able, then, to indicate three structural bases for the ideological incorporation of the mass of Americans by the 1830's. The first two are popular education and economic circumstances. The third is the early achievement of manhood suffrage. Possession of the vote helped make it evident to the American worker and farmer that he was the social equal of any. Was not Andrew Jackson, a self-made man and a democrat, in the White House?

As industrialization began, America took abrupt leave of this liberal utopia. The Lynn, Massachusetts shoemakers complained in 1844 that their new economic relationship with manufacturers had created distinctions "anti-republican in character, which assimilate very nearly to those that exist between the aristocracy and the laboring classes of Europe." This complaint of an increase in social distance between classes had no small basis. Norman Ware has documented the degradation of the industrial worker which occurred in the early period of industrialization, the two decades preceding the Civil War. He concludes that workers were losing ground absolutely in the 1840's and relatively in the 1850's. By contrast, manufacturers were gaining enormous profits at this time; they did this by holding wages down while increasing worker productivity.

The basis for the rapid pace of American industrialization had been well-laid in the eighteenth and early nineteenth centuries. American economic growth was rapid from at least 1750 onward. Economic expansion was a major theme in the social life of the colonies and the early Republic; both the Revolution and the War of 1812 were fought in its name. The roots of this development are to be found partly in the ubiquity of the Protestant ethic, though the developing liberal tradition implied two more concrete facilitating conditions as well. First, popular education helped insure that the populace as a whole possessed the abilities and attitudes conducive to economic mobilization. Second, few legal reforms had to be undertaken in this early period; there were no feudal institutions that required adaptation or destruction for economic expansion to proceed.

Naturally, the liberal community could not substantively survive industrialization. The dramatic population growth and the emergence of serious economic conflict insured this. Yet liberalism *had* pointed America toward rapid industrialization. In fact, there was an ideological dynamic in America toward maintenance of liberal unity at a certain level. On this point, note the contrasting concerns of industrializing elites in America and Europe in their quest for legitimation. The European bourgeoisie had to legitimate entrepreneurial *activity*; in this respect they were oriented toward the aristocracy. Once entrepreneurial activity was accepted, legitimation of entrepreneurial *dominance* of the lower classes was readily obtained, by a straightforward application of feudal legacies of social hierarchy. The American bourgeoisie, by contrast, had much more trouble legitimating entrepreneurial dominance than entrepreneurial activity *per se*. In this respect, they were oriented toward the masses rather than the (non-existent) aristocracy. American industrializing elites could discover no element in the liberal tradition with which to ideologically extricate themselves from the lower classes. They could not cast off the lower classes, as in the Poor Law Reform in England, for this would be to abandon a paternalism that never was. Their only obvious ploy was to try and sustain the ideological incorporation of the masses, to maintain the impression of unity among equals.

Within this context, there occurred at the outset of industrialization a perceptible loosening of the community ties of early liberalism. The characteristics of the wide-ranging public debate which surrounded the emergence of the legal principle of limited liability in the United States make this clear. It is instructive to note the arguments which were popularly mounted during the 1830's and 1840's against the chartering of business corporations. One theme was the injustice of forcing small enterprises to compete with large ones, with "aristocracies." Another theme was community restraint on acquisitiveness, in the form of admonitions to honest toil and the moral use of wealth; it was argued that when liability was limited, responsibility to the community would atrophy. Another theme was the public interest; the slogan

The Maintenance of Capitalist Order

went: in a monarchy, corporations limit the power of the king, and in a democracy, they limit the power of the people.

These anti-corporate arguments reveal the wide-ranging impact of the
quite early acceptance of limited liability in the United States. Inequality of
opportunity was established. The ground was laid for the elite irresponsibility
which was to appear later. And the concept of a distinctive public interest
. . . was dissolved into a simple aggregate of private interests. These ideological redefinitions entailed a shift in the function of the state. To its task as the
defender of human rights and democracy was added the role of guarantor of
economic growth and power. These functions can conflict; at such times in
American history, the economy has typically come before the individual. In
sum, the continuity of liberalism following the onset of industrialization had
a manipulative, and even cynical, quality not previously present.

The pre-industrial incorporation of the mass of Americans into the
liberal framework gave business elites important ideological opportunities
during the first three decades of industrialization. Some of the most critical
episodes in the redefinition of fundamental social concepts occurred during
this period. Such redefinition is a political phenomenon unique to fragment
societies. More specifically, one of the major ideological concerns of business
elites early in industrialization is to limit the influence of equalitarian rhetoric.
The typical European strategy here was the assertion of counter-values of
hierarchy (e.g. deference). American elites, by contrast, engaged in a kind of
ideological imperialism, appropriating equalitarian rhetoric to their own ends.
The redefinition of the concept of equality itself was their signal victory in
this strategy.

During the first half century of American independence, much debate and
polemic took place over the meaning of equality. The concept's substantive
meaning (equality of condition; balanced distribution of status, income and
power) was a term in this debate, though its implications were so explosive
that few eminent men cared to endorse it. Even Thomas Jefferson never talked
of equality without countervailing reference to a "natural aristocracy." The
political salience of equality is shown by the fate of the Federalists. Their
open espousal of social hierarchy was a major cause of their political decline.
Post-Federalist elites absorbed this lesson and were more circumspect in their
attack on equality. By the Jacksonian era, they had gained their essential
victory. Equality had lost its substantive meaning and had been redefined as
"equality of opportunity." Daniel Webster was a critical figure in this emas-
culation of the levelling, democratic implications of the concept. The outcome
of this debate over equality shows the weakness of Lipset's argument that the
values of equality and achievement have continually conflicted over the
course of American history. Rather, by the 1830's, equality had been defined
as achievement in this country. Equality of opportunity is an inversion of substantive equality masquerading as its prerequisite; opportunity was not actually equal, and no promulgator of the new definition of equality intended it
to become so.

A similar analysis could be made of other American political concepts,
such as community, public, and liberty. All three lost their original meanings
during early industrialization. The upshot was that the mass of Americans

were denied even the skimpy conceptual resources with which they had entered industrialization. It became difficult for workers and farmers to define their opposition to elites, for the separateness of elite and mass was obscured rather than clarified by ideological developments. The pre-industrial incorporation of the American mass played a major role in their initial acquiescence before this ideological obfuscation. American farmers and workers entered industrialization with a greater faith in economic expansion than did their European counterparts. Ideologies of industriousness, efficiency, and social change were more widespread in this country at the outset of industrialization than they were in Europe.

In 1840, Orestes Brownson came forward with an all-encompassing critique of the philosophy of opportunity, of what would later emerge as the Horatio Alger ethic. His effort was ignored, because the philosophy of economic expansion had entrenched itself as the popular answer to American problems. Rather more was involved here than pious optimism. The belief in expansion fundamentally colored the social analysis which popular groups made. To accept the view that one's economic position depends upon prosperity and expansion (rather than, say, upon income redistribution) is very integrative vis a vis elites, whose economic position actually does depend upon economic expansion. The form which expansionism took among farmers was speculation, which was a major agrarian activity along the expanding frontier. The form which expansionism took among workers was the belief that a labor shortage was their *sine qua non*.[8]

The crash of 1873 dealt a severe blow to popular faith in economic expansion. At this time it became apparent to many that the redefinition of equality had concealed a fraud, that opportunity was not equal. Most workers ceased to believe that maintaining personal opportunity through a labor shortage was their major problem. Similarly, agrarian speculatory activity virtually ceased by the mid-1880's. The corollary of these abandoned bourgeois hopes was a sharp upswing in social protest. In the decade following 1876, there occurred an impressive wave of labor strikes. During the 1880's, agrarian protest moved beyond the inflationary concerns appropriate to speculation, a maturation which culminated in the radical Populist platform of 1892.

At the end of World War I, after a half-century of earnest protest, American farmers and workers had very little to show for their effort. The argument presented thus far prepares us to understand the extraordinary blocks to effectiveness which this insurgent activity faced. Popular political action was virtually impossible, either inside or outside the electoral framework. The mass of Americans could neither elect effective reformers nor build toward extra-legislative political action (e.g. a general strike). Let us examine these two in turn.

Electoral politics frustrates popular aspirations in the United States because its structure favors the formation of pre-electoral coalitions among economic adversaries. The distinction between pre-electoral and post-electoral political coalitions is important. Post-electoral coalitions are part of the very

[8] This belief was the primary rationalization for the race hatred which workers expressed so savagely in the New York "draft riots" of 1863. . . .

The Maintenance of Capitalist Order

stuff of democratic politics, the interplay of articulate interests. Pre-electoral coalitions typically stifle this interest articulation. When economic adversaries search for a program to mutually run on, the result is often not a self-interest program, but what Lipset calls the functional equivalent of one. Such a program provides its adherents with symbols to rally around (e.g. external scapegoats), but does not provide proposals actually relevant to the economic interests of the groups involved. The commitment is to abstract rather than concrete goals.

The propensity to irrelevancy characteristic of American politics is partly due to the ideological obfuscations analyzed above. But this state of affairs could not have sustained itself through industrialization had it rested on no more than an ideological impulse. The system has been further sustained by the legal structure of American politics. The federalist system erected by the Founding Fathers permits but two political parties in the long run. A two-party system favors pre-electoral coalitions, while a multi-party system favors post-electoral coalitions.

Lipset argues that a two-party system is better able to resist extremist inroads on political stability than is a multi-party system. This is only half-true. Two-parties polities readily produce right extremism, that is, intolerant movements which serve to maintain the existing distribution of social rewards. What two-party polities lack is left "extremism," that is, movements which serve to enlarge political and economic democracy. What renders Lipset's argument plausible is the fact that almost all nations with a two-party legal structure are fragment societies. In fragment societies, all political movements appear to be of the center; in particular, right movements do not have the clerical, etc. trappings of traditional European authoritarianism. Because of the overlap in these two ways of grouping nations, the party-system and fragment analyses perforce converge on this issue. In these societies, the right is favored and the left circumscribed by both the propensity to pre-electoral coalitions (party-system analysis) and by the propensity to moralistic binges (fragment analysis).

The critical feature of American federalism is the large size of the political units of national politics, viz. states. Given economic and social conflicts are much more likely to become politicized if they involve sectional antagonisms than if they do not. In other words, geographically concentrated groups have a better chance for political mobilization in America than do geographically dispersed groups. This is one major reason why there was an agrarian party but no labor party in late nineteenth century America. Both farmers and workers were faced with the same major party unresponsiveness at this time,[9] but the option of building a third party was available only to the geographically concentrated farmers.

American labor was very aware of the structural roadblocks presented

[9] Major parties were unresponsive to popular protest throughout the last half of the nineteenth century because they were controlled by industrializing elites. This indicates the non-pluralistic character of American politics; that is, its various features (two-party structure, moralistic binges) do not hamper all groups equally, as pluralist analysis would predict.

by electoral politics, and after 1896, its interest in this avenue of social action declined.[10] American farmers departed from politics more flamboyantly than did labor, but they were no less stymied by American liberalism. The Populists shifted from a radical economic program in 1892 to a non-radical quasi-economic program in 1896. Free silver was a textbook moralistic binge, which united rural America (farmers with their economic adversaries, small towners) in a quixotic crusade against urban America. The transformation, or deradicalization, of Populism between 1892 and 1896 can be laid directly to the weakness of class community among farmers. This can be demonstrated by a comparison of the two major wings of the Populist movement. Cotton-growing southern Populists were considerably more skeptical than were wheat-growing western Populists about free silver. The crop-lien system had created a viable class-community among cotton farmers, enabling them to better resist the ideological obfuscation which free silver offered.

Existing political channels were inadequate to cope with popular responses to the great disruptiveness of American industrialization. This inadequacy was so pronounced (and so beyond remedy) as to render the early achievement of manhood suffrage virtually hollow as a step toward democracy. Given these conclusions, one is led to ask why labor did not move beyond electoral politics to radical action, political or industrial.[11] The answer, as stressed above, is the absence of working class community. The point is worth reiterating here, for late in industrialization the American business elite was given an opportunity to refine and extend its strategies for destroying class community. This opportunity was created by the new immigration.

IV. Late Industrialization: The Liberal Terror Crushes Protest

During late industrialization, the combination of rapid industrialization and agrarian resistance gave an important impetus to immigration as the answer to the industrial labor supply problem. Immigrants began to arrive in noticeable numbers from Southern and Eastern Europe in the 1880's, and by 1896 these new immigrants were arriving in greater numbers than were "old" immigrants from Northern and Western Europe. The new immigrants were not a factor in the Knights of Labor or in the American Railway Union. However, by 1909, the new immigrants made up the majority of the industrial working class in the United States. The importance of this rapid change in the composition of the American working class is hard to overemphasize.

[10] The Socialist Party is only an apparent exception to this trend. The SP had an unimposing working class base; skilled workers were not interested, and unskilled workers were consistently mistreated by the SP. . . . The impressive vote totals gained by the SP during its first two decades did not bespeak organizational strength. They rather represented a personal tribute to Debs, as can be seen by the fact that the SP vote was consistently at least ten times larger than the SP membership.
[11] In isolated instances, it did so—viz. the IWW. This question of "what next" is less relevant for farmers, who were a declining class anyway. Still, one can point to two post-Populist agrarian organizations with radical features: the Southern Tenant Farmers Union and the National Farmers Organization.

The Maintenance of Capitalist Order

The new immigration caused a sharp break in the American working class tradition. The producers' philosophy represented by the Knights of Labor was forgotten almost overnight.[12] Its demise was aided by the limited organizational continuity between the two eras, as well as by such simple facts as the language problem. The old immigration brought proportionately more newcomers into American society than did the new immigration, but its effect on the native American working class was far less. Those elements of the old immigration which were least "American" (German, Scandinavian) tended to go into agricultural or petty bourgeois pursuits. The more "American" elements (British, Irish) were the ones which typically entered the American working class. Their influence there lay more in the reinforcement of selected existing tendencies than in the creation of whole new tendencies. Most notably, British and Irish immigrants contributed to AFL strength.

The new immigrants reacted vigorously to the industrial conditions they found in America. They were the backbone of many militant and cohesive strikes during the Progressive era. Strikes eased off during the war, but burst forth again in 1919, the most strike-bound year in American history. Many of the features of the American labor movement during this era, particularly its level of organization and hypercritical view of employers, are to be found in the mature labor movements of other nations. But in the American case, it is the break with the past, not the evolution from it, which bears emphasizing. The critical element which the new immigrants introduced to American labor was that of working class community. As David Brody writes of the 1919 steel strike,

> Strikes had the force of a communal action among immigrants. In Pueblo and elsewhere wives joined their men on the picket line. To violate the community will peculiarly disturbed the immigrant, for he identified himself, not primarily as an individual in the American manner, but as a member of a group. "Slavish" strikers in Monessen wanted to return to work, a company spy reported, but were "holding back for no other reason than that they would be called scabs and have a bad name among their fellow employees after the strike would be over."

This solidarity was based in ethnic culture and institutions. The strength of its hold on immigrants was increased by the fact that distinctions in the work place paralleled ethnic distinctions. There was little occupational differentiation among the new immigrants, who were almost entirely unskilled workers.

The turn of the century emergence of working class community in Amer-

---

[12] This older tradition has been much criticized, and often justly. But it is worth noting that Norman Ware, Chester Destler and other American labor historians have seen great missed potential in it. Their search has been for a "native radicalism." In Hartzian terms, these historians have argued for the existence in nineteenth century America of a democratic form of the liberal tradition which might have transcended the liberal consensus. I sympathize with these historians, and particularly with their attempt to escape the Commons-Marxist orthodoxy. However, I am not entirely convinced by their work as points made elsewhere in this paper should make clear. The dispute over native American radicalism cannot be settled unequivocally, but its existence reminds us to avoid retrospective determinism.

ica should not be regarded, despite its external roots, as an entirely unexpected shift in the course of American labor development. There are grounds for believing that fairly strong working class institutions of some type would have emerged during late industrialization in any case. This holds true even though European working class communities and cultures have usually had venerable roots. Tradition is not the only source of working class solidarity and militance, for traditions and ideologies must be embodied in institutions and structures to have continuing relevance. Atomization and fragmentation of the working class are characteristic features of the early industrializing period; thus the institutions of working class solidarity which emerge during late industrialization are new in an important sense even in Europe.[13] Similarly, the early absence of strong working class institutions in America cannot be the entire explanation for their later absence. On both sides of the Atlantic, a working class community could be expected to emerge during later industrialization as a situational response.

American business elites reacted with great coldness to the emergence of this first serious challenge to their power. Their short-run response was ruthless repression, and their long-run response was destruction of the class community in which the challenge was based. In both cases, their weapons were supplied by the liberal tradition.

Edward Shils has argued that a major difference between American and British society is the greater *civility* that is to be found in Britain. This is an apt general characterization of differences between the two countries in industrial relations. Both American and British labor historians have concluded that industrial conflict has been far more violent in the United States than in Britain. Shils argues that uncivil behavior is primarily a popular characteristic, an attribute of the populistic mass of Americans. Yet American businessmen have been less civil than American workers (or farmers) have been. Most of the violence surrounding American economic conflict has been instigated by elites. The suppression of the IWW is perhaps the outstanding episode of elite violence in the industrial sphere. Most worker violence in the United States has been a desperate response to elite violence. The major outbreak of violence in agrarian politics occurred in the 1890's. The community-based solidarity of the southern Populists kept them from being enchanted by that non-issue, free silver. It also led them to commit the ultimate heresy in Southern politics, crossing the color line. During the 1880's and early 1890's, the Populists made a determined attempt to build an *interracial* polit-

[13] It can be argued that rapid industrialization helps prevent creation (or re-creation) of working class community. In Britain, slow industrialization provided for a period of class abatement (c. 1849–1870). Young has stressed the importance of this period of quiescence in the growth of English working class institutions. . . . Bendix suggests a quite different argument of similar import. He remarks that the rise of the tertiary branch of economic production gives a pervasive influence to middle class standards of aspiration. From this one could infer that rapid industrialization, which continually alters the occupational structure in the direction of expansion of the tertiary sector, helps block the formation of a stable working class culture. . . . Comparing the American and British cases would tend to corroborate these arguments. However, we have in the Swedish case the coexistence of rapid industrialization and a flourishing working class culture.

The Maintenance of Capitalist Order

ical movement. Splitting the poor on racial lines had been a basic strategy of Southern business elites, and their response to the Populist challenge was unequivocal. During the 1892 campaign in Georgia, some fifteen Negroes and several whites were killed by the Democrats and an attempt was made on Tom Watson's life; this was but the most extreme aspect of a general repression. The Jim Crow tide of this era led directly to the wholesale disfranchisement of Negroes and poor whites in the South.

We should ask how this unsavory side of American business history was able to prosper in a polity not frankly authoritarian, one committed (in the schoolboy phrase) to "liberty and justice for all." Moralistic binges are part of the answer. Behind and beyond them has stood elite manipulation of the legal order to its own ends. Popular movements have faced legal restrictions in all advanced industrial nations, but in the United States these have been particularly extensively and intensively applied. Access to the legal order was for American elites both a weapon against popular movements and a smokescreen for other weapons. The level of repression thereby achieved surpassed even that imposed by Bismarck upon the German labor movement. American labor movements were penetrated and destroyed, not merely circumscribed and left to grow *sub rosa*, as in Europe. Legalism, as it may be called, was the distinctive American contribution to the panoply of anti-labor strategies found in developed countries. Its sources and functioning bear analyzing.

The distinctive legalism of American politics is well-known. It is reflected in such simple facts as the very high proportion of lawyers in public office in the United States relative to other countries. At the level of issues, legalism has been reflected in a continuing American disposition to see legal reform as an efficacious means of resolving social issues, as in Prohibition and Progressivism. The pre-eminent characteristic of legalism as a political stance is a fear of power. The whole political intent of legalistic reform movements is often to curb power. Moreover, the weak institutional devices they have proposed in order to effect the curbing display a fear of *wielding* power. At bottom, legalism seeks to end politics entirely.

Legalistic reform naturally failed to curb the power of the industrializing elites in America. In fact, it was transformed by elites into an efficient means of preserving their power. The American business world's appropriation of Progressive regulatory agencies to its own ends is by now well documented. In the area of labor disputes in particular, the most striking example of this is the use of the Sherman Act of 1890 to break strikes. The Sherman Act was intended to regulate business trusts, but for forty years it was characteristically used against labor rather than against business. If this seems remarkable, consider the fact that far more use of the anti-trust laws against labor occurred after 1914 (when the Clayton Act specifically exempted unions from anti-trust prosecution) than before 1914.

Throughout late industrialization, American courts not only directly used their powers to limit labor organization, but also gave legal sanction to virtually every form of employer hostility to labor. The sweeping scope of the law in the hands of American business is demonstrated by the infamous labor injunction. The injunction originated in English equity courts, as a device to prevent physical damage to property during pendency of a suit. It was a reasonable emergency legal device, though its potency led English courts to severely restrict its applicability. No such restraint characterized American courts when they adopted the injunction in the 1880's. They extended its scope to include intangible property as well as physical property. Consequently, in some cases American labor injunctions prohibited workers from engaging in any organizing activity whatsoever.

The single most important use of legalism against American labor occurred in the Pullman strike of 1894. This strike destroyed the American Railway Union, the first strong and effective mass labor organization to emerge in the United States.[14] One of the ARU's great strengths in the strike situation was the semi-skilled status of its members, which meant that strike-breakers could not easily be obtained. In the contemporaneous gas-workers' strike in Great Britain, this same striker indispensability insured the victory of the strike. However, such considerations did not deter American railroads in 1894; the injunction they obtained was the first use of the Sherman Act against labor. The contrast between the two trials which resulted from the Pullman strike shows nicely how legalism works culturally. Through legal action, the railroads sought to redefine the issue at hand from social grievances to law and order. They sought to make breaking the strike look like action in the public interest. The divergent outcomes of the two trials indicate the success of this strategy. The conspiracy case was argued in social terms; the ARU nearly won it before it was dismissed. The contempt case was argued in legal terms; the ARU lost it.[15]

Elites made less use of legalism in response to agrarian protest than in response to labor protest, largely because farmers confined themselves to electoral politics. In a way, however, the agrarian episodes of legalism are more important, for they reveal that even institutionalized protest can be rendered ineffective when American elites seek to defy it. In the nineteenth century, state courts had a notorious penchant for invalidation of any significant laws passed by Populist legislatures; the Canadian CCF, a comparable movement, received far more aid and comfort from provincial governments. The failure of the Non-Partisan League in North Dakota reveals that even popular control of all aspects of formal state power does not necessarily assure successful implementation of reforms. During World War I, NPL representatives enacted into law a program of state ownership of the wheat farmer's key economic institutions. The 1920–21 depression financially damaged the state-owned industries and the state bank, and private bankers seized the initiative. With the cooperation of other Midwestern financial interests, the solvency of the state of North Dakoa was successfully questioned.

[14] This shows how misleading it is to understand American labor history strictly in terms of particular organizations. The Knights of Labor, for instance, can be faulted for having poor leadership, a muddled financing system, and too benign a view of the employer. . . . However, the ARU shared none of these defects and was also beaten.

[15] Note, too, that the conspiracy case was a jury trial, while the contempt case was not.

American elites have been able to use the law in a manner virtually devoid of content or conceptual restraint. There are several reasons why, despite such distortions, the appeal to law is popularly successful. American patriotism, lacking most of the foci of language, custom and ancient tradition typical of European patriotisms, has always centered around our political institutions. The sacrosanctity which these institutions have gained through being the keystone of the "American way of life" has contributed to the relatively uncritical acceptance of whatever is done in their name. Moreover, state and nation are more closely linked in the United States than in other countries. For instance, the roles of head of state and head of government both inhere in the office of the Presidency, though they are typically separated in European nations. This makes it relatively easy to delegitimize dissent in America, for a challenge to the government can be cast as a challenge to the state. The concept of a loyal opposition (that is, loyal to the nation) is rather underdeveloped in the United States.

We have in legalism the means by which elite violence was carried out, but its ends are not entirely self-evident. Preservation of elite power was not the only end involved, for in many instances the intensity of the repression greatly overbalanced the reality of the threat which it met. The existence of elite violence was no indication of a "need" to go beyond normal channels for settling industrial disputes. The crux of the matter was the elite refusal to concede that *any* normal channels existed for settling industrial disputes. No good American worker has any grievances. Hartz, writing of the early twentieth century, remarks:

> While the material gap between the top and the bottom of American society was actually widened, the shattering even of the Hamilton distinctions of the earlier time meant that culturally it was more unified than ever. . . . An elite suspended between aristocratic frustration and bourgeois anxiety is bound to have some limitations, and one of these was that it did not always display the highest degree of responsibility. If it was "un-American" to be feudal, why should one bother with feudal paternalism? Power, as once again Ashley saw, came to be an end in itself for the new American giant, "his essential reward," which gave him the feeling, as with Pullman, that a "principle was involved" when labor unions struck.

American elites sought to repress industrial conflict out of existence because of a virtual inability to legitimate their power. Forced to use the democratic rhetoric they abhorred, elites had no adequate theories of status. The Alger ethic is a tangential justification for elite power: we're rich because we worked hard. But it still reflects the fundamental fact that American liberalism does not justify stratification, but denies that it exists. The problem of false consciousness is posed much more sharply in the U.S. than in Europe, and one result has been elite irresponsibility.

Legalistic repression was not a stable long-term solution to the elite dilemma, for it only presaged further disintegration of the social fabric. The more stable solution was the destruction of those particularistic communities which did not affirm the liberal consensus. The most significant effort in this direction was the Progressive era crusade to Americanize the new immigrants. Americanization demanded rather more of the new immigrants than the popular phrase "melting pot" implies. Assimilation was steadily pressed upon immigrants through public schools, settlement houses and political machines; it was also stimulated by periods of particularly virulent nativism. By defining community-based labor solidarity as foreign and unacceptable, Americanization performed a social control function for the new middle class of industrializing elites. By defining the WASP style of life as superior, Americanization performed a status function for the old middle class. The processes by which these two functions, social control and status, were carried out might be called hard and soft embourgeoisement, respectively. Hard embourgeoisement was primarily the work of the business community, and soft embourgeoisement the work of women and religious institutions.

Americanization directly blocked unionization efforts in some instances. Brody concludes that the Red Scare and the accompanying wave of nativism were major elements in the defeat of the 1919 steel strike. The long-term implications of Americanization were of a similar nature. Americanization resulted in a distinct weakening of the ethnic communities which the new immigrants had created in the United States. By the third generation, sanctions against aspirations to assimilation and mobility could no longer be enforced. When this occurred, ethnic communities had lost their regenerative powers. Working class community in Europe has been far sturdier than this.

This characterization of the new immigrants' communities as quickly and drastically undermined by Americanization may seem overdrawn. Many sociologists have concluded that substantial ethnic subcultures persist to this day in the United States. Yet Herbert Gans, a leading spokesman for this point of view, emphasizes that these surviving subcultures provide their members with little basis for economic or political action, and in fact hinder such action. Surviving ethnic subcultures may make life meaningful for their members, but they are no longer bases for building a better life. American nativism may have wished to accomplish more than this, but what it did accomplish was quite enough. When the new immigrants lost influence over their offspring, the radical labor movement which they had built atrophied.

It is entirely misleading to regard the assimilation of the new immigrants into the American way of life as a natural process or a forgone conclusion. The new immigrants did not have much choice in the matter, and comparative evidence leads one to conclude that they did not seek assimilation. Immigrants to other nations typically have retained far more of their European heritage than have American immigrants, and it is unlikely that selective migration accounts for this difference. Intolerance of ethnic diversity is a prominent characteristic of fragment societies, typically expressed in restrictive immigration policies, but also in high assimilation demands upon those who do immigrate. Far from being eager to assimilate, communities of new immigrants in America tended to split sharply on the issue. The more respectable sector of the community accepted it, while the working class sector opposed it. Even in the acceptance evinced by the former, we may perhaps be permitted to detect the rationalization of fate.

V. Today: The New Liberalism

Thus the industrializing period in the United States ended as it began, with an attempt to enforce the liberal consensus among the mass of Americans. But a strict return to the social relations characteristic of the Jacksonian era was not possible. Industrialization could not fail to have a permanent impact on American political life. The agrarian movement never recovered from its turn of the century defeats, for farmers were a declining social class. Labor and corporate business, however, were permanent fixtures in American society; and the conflict between them remained to be resolved. When the resolution came, it was negative: that is, to the advantage of business. By the time business power had been thus stabilized, the main outlines of the modern American political structure had been established. This structure is fundamentally liberal, so that there is continuity of a kind from the days of Madison and Tocqueville. Yet the realignment which began to emerge after 1896, and which was stabilized during the 1920's, is distinctive enough that it should be termed a *new* liberalism.

The new liberalism resembles pluralism, for it is based on the turn of the century emergence of group life in America. However, the new liberalism deviates from the pluralist model in one crucial respect. The various natural economic groupings did not simply become more cohesive and organized as such; rather they split internally and became organized around that split. The split was in each case between the wealthier and poorer elements of the grouping. This is the linchpin of the new liberalism: the *internal stratification* of natural economic groupings. Internal stratification has been the usual fate of the middle class during industrialization. Yet the disparity between the old and new middle classes has probably extended further in this country than in other industrially advanced nations. For instance, American big business has largely stripped the old middle class of even its cultural role; mass culture is more prominent in this country than in others. Moreover, internal stratification has emerged unexpectedly in this country in groups outside the middle class. Farmers, a group expected simply to decline in size and power as industrialization proceeds, have instead split into a highly productive elite of big farmers and an unproductive mass of small farmers. Labor, a group expected to rise in size and power as industrialization proceeds, has been internally stratified along skill lines.

Internal differentiation of this kind can be found among the agrarian and industrial masses of all developed nations, but nowhere is it so sharp as in the contemporary United States. In France, class community restrains the "better elements" among the mass from being co-opted. No similar restraints are operative in the United States. The processes by which an American labor elite and farmer elite came to abandon their poorer brethren and to make a separate peace with the corporate economy differed. The internal stratification of labor was a relatively circumstantial consequence of the ponderous workings of the liberal tradition. Among farmers, however, internal stratification was created by direct elite intervention. Let us examine the latter development first.

While late nineteenth century American farmers did vary in income and economic security, there were few developments in this era which made this differentiation socially or politically important. In particular, the Alger ethic of opportunity did not so contribute. The Alger ethic divided farmers into speculators and settlers, but this differentiation did not parallel and reinforce income differences; speculators were not markedly better off than settlers. The internal stratification of American farmers was essentially created by the agricultural education movement of the Progressive era. The agricultural education movement sought to persuade farmers to increase their productivity through extensive mechanization, soil improvement, and the like. The heavy capitalization involved would tie the farmer more closely to his old adversaries in the business community, bankers and merchants. Essentially, the agricultural education movement was a business-sponsored effort to economically and politically co-opt the farmer. Few farmers were amenable to change; business pressured them into giving agricultural education a full hearing with such devices as the threat to withhold credit. Those farmers already the best off were the most cooperative; thus the spread of the new farming techniques widened the existing economic differences among farmers. Today agrarian stratification is such that half the marketed farm products in the United States are produced by an eighth of the farmers.

The internal stratification of America labor had its beginnings in the late nineteenth century. Among workers, unlike farmers, ideological differences of the era reinforced existing status differences. Historical evidence indicates that after the 1873 disillusionment, very few workers had any faith in the Alger ethic of opportunity, though there was some interest in it among skilled workers. Actually it is questionable whether even skilled workers ever kept the Alger faith in its strict (that is, flamboyantly optimistic) form. The major ideological struggle within labor during the last quarter of the nineteenth century was over a more muted form of the liberal faith. Gomper's American Federation of Labor believed in economic expansion, not because it would make workers rich, but because it would reduce the competition for existing jobs. This was the reason why the AFL declined to risk aiding the mass organization of workers when such opportunities as the 1886 Haymarket affair and the 1894 Pullman strike presented themselves. The massive strikes of the era indicate that semi-skilled and unskilled workers had no interest in the job control strategy. They were moving away from this incorporative liberal analysis, and toward a more radical conception of labor's aims. Yet skilled workers had not entirely isolated themselves from the mass of workers below them at this time. Within the AFL, there was continuous left agitation up to the turn of the century. This agitation was strong enough to remove Gompers from the AFL presidency for one year.

The incipient skilled-unskilled split in American labor crystalized during the Progressive era. The final break was precipitated by the immigration question. The new immigrants were almost entirely unskilled workers, skilled positions being taken by native Americans and old immigrants. The usual differences between skilled and unskilled workers were exacerbated at this time by differences of language and culture. Skilled workers reacted coldly to the new immigrants' sudden appearance on the American scene. Spokesmen for craft unions invoked their labor shortage ideology to justify their opposition to immigration. These fears of job competition and wage depression were objectively unfounded, a fact that was known at the time. Moreover, explicitly nativist statements were often made by craft spokesmen. It was, then, both the liberal economic analysis and a generalized commitment to the American way of life (including liberal intolerance) that led skilled workers to distance themselves from unskilled workers at this time.

Most students of the American labor movement have regarded immigration as a critical factor in its history, but few have accurately interpreted its impact. It should be emphasized that it was not ethnic heterogeneity that splintered the American working class at this time, in the sense that ethnic cleavages in themselves hampered interaction and organization. Within the ranks of the unskilled, the various ethnic groups cooperated very well industrially and politically. This held true even when they literally could not understand one another. Nor was it true that American unions had trouble organizing the new immigrants. Established unions hardly tried to organize them, and had great success whenever they did try. The critical development was rather the failure of the (native) skilled workers to cooperate industrially with the new immigrants. Their actions made the skilled-unskilled gap a barrier which none could hurdle.

Over the years, Samuel Gompers and other spokesmen for American craft unions repeatedly stated that they would help organize the mass of American workers as soon as the skilled sector was securely organized. Their intentions may have been good, but their strategy was inappropriate to this larger end. The pace of American industrialization and the ferocity of American industrial conflict meant that the time for mass organization would never be so propitious as the AFL demanded that it be. American labor had to take risks; in this context, mass organization in the Progressive era would have been a sound gamble. The enormous expansion of the Knights of Labor into the ranks of the unskilled and semi-skilled during the 1880's had proven unstable, because its new members lacked a social basis for organizational tenacity. The new immigrants possessed, in ethnic community, just such a basis. In this light, the refusal of skilled workers to deal with the "un-American" new immigrants was disastrous for labor unity.

Having analyzed antecedents, let us describe the functioning of the new liberalism more explicitly. Contemporary interest groups typically have a narrow constituency, the upper fraction of a given economic grouping; their goals are narrow and concrete. Both of these features are new to American society. In the nineteenth century, interest group constituencies were larger and their goals were more general. The public interest was a more relevant conception in political life then than now. Being narrowly based, group goals today are often extreme. There is little impetus to mutual checking of demands. This is because the various interest groups are not fundamentally competing with one another. They all gain from the new liberalism; losses are absorbed by the unrepresented millions at the bottom of each natural economic grouping. It is not incidental that many are left out; the system is based on their exclusion.

The American elaboration of this process of internal stratification into a general principle of social life is the key to the stability of marked stratification in an ostensibly equalitarian society. The pluralistic representation of the upper sector of various groupings has enabled America to forget the bottom sectors involved. Are there reports of poor workers? Well, they have in the AFL-CIO a potential voice, should they choose to avail themselves of it. Are there reports of poor farmers? Well, they have in the American Farm Bureau Federation a potential voice, should they choose to avail themselves of it. It is conveniently assumed that the AFL-CIO and the AFBF speak for all workers and all farmers, or have the potential for doing so. Yet these organizations actually speak for a narrow upper stratum of workers and farmers. They are unlikely ever to jeopardize the gains of their narrow constituencies by reaching out to their poorer brethren.

These considerations introduce some new elements into the scholarly dispute over who rules America. A strict "power elite" analysis is difficult to sustain. While it can be easily demonstrated that most social decisions are made by a few persons, it is much harder to demonstrate that the interests of these elites converge or that they are autonomous *vis à vis* the rest of society. It is easier to attack the pluralists on their own ground, by denying that such decentralization of power as exists in America is a democratic phenomenon. The first element in such an argument is the fact of organizational oligarchy. If America's many private associations are internally undemocratic, how can they be essential to democracy? But this is not the entire point, for many private associations are as democratic as one could expect; they represent their constituencies well. These constituencies, however, are narrow and exclusive. The Tennessee Valley Authority, as interpreted by Philip Selznick, provides an excellent example of the undemocratic decentralization of power.

I suggest that the question of whether the contemporary structure of power in America significantly favors any one group or class is less significant than many assume. If different pluralist groups are unequal in power and influence, this is of little consequence, for they are not playing a zero-sum game. They all win; the mass loses. For example, the AFL-CIO and big business don't fight one another; they co-exist, and mutually benefit from the plight of unorganized labor and the petty bourgeoisie. In this context, the fact that business corporations have more power than does organized labor is not the central issue. The fact that there are many power groups in the United States does not mean that they constrain one another or that they are dependent on mass support. Each member of this broadly based oligarchy ignores the wider public.

The political consequences of the new liberalism have been extensive and negative. The scope of administrative politics has been enlarged at the expense of party politics. The defect of party politics, from the standpoint of new liberals, is that it involves the mass of Americans. This makes its outcome uncertain; new liberals have found that their political goals can be more readily achieved by direct interaction with government bureaucracies. The various interest groups have established extensive contact with the relevant administrative agencies—the broadcasting industry with the FCC, the lumber industry with the Forest Service, and so on. The extent of private infiltration of public regulatory agencies is shown by the fact that few private interests object to being so regulated.

Most Americans play little political role in the new liberalism. There has been a substantial increase in political apathy in the United States in the last three-quarters of a century. As Walter Burnham writes:

> The late 19-century voting universe was marked by a more complete and intensely party-oriented voting participation among the American electorate than ever before or since. . . . The 19-century American political system, for its day, was incomparably the most thoroughly democratized of any in the world.

The retreat from this achievement has been considerable. Burnham concludes that in present-day America, political apathy exists "on a scale quite unknown anywhere else in the Western world." His specific estimates for America are the following:

	Regular voters	Occasional voters	Non-voters
Late 19th-century	66%	10%	24%
1920's	33%	17%	50%
Present day	44%	16%	40%

In recent decades, while American voter turnout varied from 44% to 60%, voter turnout in Britain averaged around 80%. And in Sweden, voting participation has steadily increased over the last half-century, in stark contrast to the American trend.

The distinctively high political apathy in contemporary America requires an explanation which goes beyond the causes usually adduced for political apathy, such as differential access to information and cross-pressures. Such an explanation would have to deal with the additional fact that political apathy is more concentrated in lower status groups in America than it is in Western Europe. Political apathy is kept high in contemporary America because this helps stabilize the new liberalism. There are two mechanisms by which this end is accomplished. First, the formal barriers to electoral participation are higher in this country than in Western Europe generally. The need to meet residence requirements and to frequently re-register, and the fact that elections are held at a variety of times and invariably on a normal working day, all tend to keep people away from the polls. Second, the structure of the new liberalism helps insure that outsiders are a diverse group, sharing few substantive interests on which a political program might be built.

Some will seek to disclaim my melancholy perspective, even if they have followed me to this point, by referring to the 1930's. It will be argued that both the New Deal and the more radical activity of the depression decade represent a reinvigoration of American political life, a renewal of our democratic promise. The facts do not bear out this view. It is an error to regard the 1930's as one of the high points of protest and reform activity in American history. In the political sphere, Franklin Roosevelt's landslide election victories must be interpreted in light of the continuing political apathy. The highest voter turnout for FDR (1940) was lower than the turnout for any Presidential election between 1840 and 1908, inclusive. This is understandable if we note that the New Deal helped to establish the administrative politics which the new liberals favor. In the industrial sphere, depression developments were similarly muted.

When American mass unionization finally emerged in the 1930's, it had very limited aims. Even the Knights of Labor had possessed in "End wage slavery!" a cry more radical than anything the CIO later offered. The social philosophies of the new unionists such as Walter Reuther were little more radical than that of Gompers had been. Given the objective economic distress of the era, the moderation of American labor in the 1930's was remarkable. The Great Depression probably represented a sharper economic decline for the United States than for any other nation save Germany. Yet, compared to Germany and most other European nations, the United States of the 1930's was the very picture of social calm. Far less turmoil and challenge to the social order occurred in the United States than one would have expected. The roots of this anomaly lay in the earlier developments which I have analyzed.

The Wagner Act of 1935 and other reforms gave labor organizing its first effective legal protection, and helped to end the labor repression of old.[16] But, by the 1930's, labor was in little position to take advantage of this opportunity, for it had been internally stratified and socialized to an "American" way of thinking. Conflict between labor and capital was no longer openended. Labor was unable to translate the right to organize into substantive gains. An examination of shifts in distribution of personal income in the United States since 1929 is instructive on this point. The income share of the very rich has declined, but the essential gains have been made by the middle (and especially upper middle) class, not by the mass at the lower end of the scale.

The fear of democracy which has so long been a part of American liberalism has become in this century the dominant motif of American politics, and democracy has been curbed. In the European context, liberalism was a defense of freedom. In the American context, where it was the orthodoxy, liberalism has proven to be repressive. It is not my part to be a seer and to judge how stable the new liberalism, or the liberal tradition in general, will be. However, it should be noted that the new liberalism *has* resolved the class conflict in this country, albeit negatively. American class conflict has not moved toward a positive resolution, as in Sweden, nor has it remained unresolved, as in Britain. The mass of Americans have not had, and do not have, that strong class community needed to build toward sustained dissent. Such community could in principle yet emerge, but the splits among the American dispossessed run deep. If prognosis is demanded, I would offer the opinion that the American liberal tradition is more likely to be shattered from the right than from the left. Such a denouement would not be entirely unfitting.

[16] American unions had been given legal protection during World War I, but after the Armistice repression renewed in earnest.

Evelyn Parks

FROM CONSTABULARY TO POLICE SOCIETY: IMPLICATIONS FOR SOCIAL CONTROL

The history of social control in the United States is the history of transition from "constabulary" to "police society" in which the proliferation of criminal laws, enforcement officials, criminal courts and prisons was not essentially for the protection of the "general welfare" of society but was for the protection of the interests and lifestyles of but one segment of society—those holding positions of wealth, "respectability," and power. . . .

Transition from a Constabulary to a Police Society

The first official responsible for the enforcement of law and order in the New World was the constable. The law as written was oppressive—outlawing swearing, lying, sabbath breaking, and night walking—and gave to the constable almost totalitarian powers to enforce the laws. However, the constable did not use his power to discover and punish deviation from the established laws. Rather, he assisted complaining citizens if and when they sought his help. This reflected the conception of law during colonial times: the written law was regarded as an ideal, rather than as prescriptions actually to be enforced.

Initially, the constableship was a collective responsibility which all able-bodied men were expected to assume. It was not a specialized occupation or an income producing job, but a service to the community. The constableship was so thankless a task, however, that as early as 1653, fines were sometimes levied against anyone refusing to serve.

The constable served only during the day. At night, the towns formed a citizens' watch or nightwatch. Supposedly, each adult male took his turn, but as with the constable those who could hired substitutes. In contrast to our present police the concerns of the nightwatch were more closely related to the general welfare. They included looking out for fires, reporting the time, and describing the weather.

Thus, there was no one specialized agency responsible for social control. Not only was the power divided between the constable and the night watch, but initially, both were volunteer services rotated among the citizens. This lack of specialization of enforcement of law and order extended to a comparative lack of specialization in the punishment of offenders. Although prisons were constructed as early as 1637, they were almost never kept in

Extracted, with deletions, from Evelyn Parks, "From Constabulary to Police Society: Implications for Social Control," *Catalyst*, No. 5 (Summer 1970), pp. 76–97, by permission of *Catalyst* and the author. Evelyn Parks teaches sociology at Windham College, Putney, Vermont.

good enough condition to prevent jailbreaks. The financial costs of jails was considered prohibitive; corporal punishments, such as whippings, were preferred. Thus, there was no specialized penal system, staffed and available.

EARLY POLICE

The constabulary was not able to survive the growth of urban society and the concomitant economic specialization. Charles Reith writes that voluntary observance of the laws

> can be seen to have never survived in effective form the advent of community prosperity, as this brings into being, inevitably, differences in wealth and social status, and creates, on this basis, classes and parties and factions with or without wealth and power and privileges. In the presence of these divisions, community unanimity in voluntary law observance disappears and some other means of securing law observance and the maintenance of authority and order must be found.

By 1800 in the larger cities the constabulary had changed from a voluntary position to a quasi-professional one, being either appointed or elected and providing an income. Some people resisted this step, claiming that such police were threats to civil liberty, and that they performed duties each citizen should perform himself. However, in the 1840's and 1850's, the night watch was gradually incorporated into an increasingly professionalized police, establishing twenty-four hour responsibility and in other ways beginning to institute the type of law enforcement that we have today.

In the 1850's, cities began to employ detectives. The earliest detectives represented an attempt to apply the conception of the constableship to urban society. That is, the duties of the detective were to assist in recovering stolen property, not to prevent crime. However, this application of the constableship to the emerging urban society proved ineffective. For one thing, to recover stolen property effectively, familiarity with criminals was a necessary qualification and quite naturally ex-criminals were often hired. For another, detectives became corrupted through taking advantage of a system known as compromises. Under this system, it was legal for a thief to negotiate with the robbed owner and agree to return part of the stolen goods, if the thief could remain free. Detectives, however, would often supplement their salaries by accepting thieves' offers of a portion of the stolen goods in exchange for their immunity.[1]

Understandably, detectives were reluctant to devote their time to anything other than large-scale robbery. Murder, an amateur crime at this time, went uninvestigated. Detectives essentially served the private interests of big business at the expense of the general public.

By 1880, the detective force as such had acquired such adverse publicity

---

[1] . . . Today, "compromises" sometimes occur in civil rather than criminal court cases, or as "out of court" settlements, available only in white-collar criminality. . . .

The Maintenance of Capitalist Order

that in most places they were formally abolished. Their functions and services however were incorporated into the regular police. Compromises were no longer legally acceptable.

HISTORICAL SOURCES OF THE CHANGE
FROM CONSTABULARY TO POLICE

Central to the development of the professional police is the development of economic inequality. Seldon Bacon in his study of the development of the municipal police sees the increasing economic specialization and the resulting "class stratification" as the primary cause for the development of police. He argues that specialists could exploit the increasing dependence of the populace on their services. Cities responded by creating specialized offices of independent inspectors who attempted to prevent exploitation or cheating of the populace. For example, the necessity in New Amsterdam to rely on specialized suppliers of firewood led as early as 1658 to the employment of firewood inspectors. Regulation of butchers, bakers, and hack drivers showed the same consequences of the inability of the citizen to rely on his own resources in a period of increasing specialization.

By the time of the emergence of the professional police, the list of regulatory or inspectorial officials had grown quite long. Bacon describes the development of "the night police, the market police, street police, animal police, liquor police, the vagabond and stranger police, vehicle police, fire police, election police, Sunday police and so on." Gradually, many of these special police or inspectors were removed from the professional police to other municipal agencies. "Only slowly did regulation for the public good and the maintenance of order become themselves specializations and the full-time career police develop."

The other central element in the development of the professional police was rioting, which is closely related to economic inequality. Usually, riots are an attempt by the have-nots to seek a redress of grievances from those with power and wealth. The solid citizens, on the other hand, wanted to prevent riots, to stop the disturbances in the streets. An official history of the Buffalo Police states that in March of 1834 complaints of riot and disorder continued to pour in upon the Mayor. "Rowdies paraded the streets at night, unmolested, and taxpayers became alarmed regarding both life and property." Roger Lane writes of Boston, that "The problem of mob violence . . . soon compelled the municipality to take a more significant step, to create a new class of permanent professional officers with new standards of performance." David Bordua and Albert Reiss write:

The paramilitary form of early police bureaucracy was a response not only, or even primarily, to crime per se, but to the possibility of riotous disorder. Not crime and danger but the "criminal" and "dangerous classes" as part of the urban social structure led to the formation of uniformed and military organized police. Such organizations intervened between the propertied elites and the propertyless masses who were regarded as politically dangerous as a class.

From Constabulary to Police Society 393

Riots became so frequent that the traditional method of controlling them by use of military forces became less and less effective. Military forces were unable to arrive at the scene of trouble before rioting had already reached uncontrollable proportions. This illustrates how the military may be able temporarily to enforce laws but are ineffective for sustained law enforcement. The police, not the military, represent the continued presence of the central political authority.

Furthermore, in a riot situation, the direct use of social and economic superiors as the agents of suppression increases class violence.

If the power structure armed itself and fought a riot or a rebellious people, this created more trouble and tension than the original problem. But, if one can have an independent police which fights the mob, then antagonism is directed toward police, not the power structure. A paid professional police seems to separate "constitutional" authority from social and economic dominance.

These trends towards the establishment of a paramilitary police were given further impetus by the Civil War. It was the glory of the Army uniform that helped the public accept a uniformed police. Previously, the police themselves, as well as the public, had objected to uniforms as implying a police state with the men as agents of a king or ruler. A uniformed police was seen as contradictory to the ideals of the American Revolution, to a republic of free men. But after 1860 the police began to carry guns, although at first unofficially. Within twenty years, however, most cities were furnishing guns along with badges.

THE PROFESSIONAL POLICE AND THE NEW CONCEPT OF LAW

As the cities changed from a constabulary to a professional police, so was there a change in the conception of law. Whereas the constable had only investigated crimes in which a citizen had complained, the new professional police, were expected to *prevent* crime. A preventive conception of law requires that the police take the initiative and seek out those engaged in violating the law—those engaged in specific behaviors that are designated as illegal. Once an individual has been arrested for breaking a law, he is then identified, labelled and treated as a criminal. The whole person then becomes a criminal—not just an individual who has broken a law. Since now too, professional police were responsible for maintaining public order—seen as preventing crime—they came to respond to individuals who committed unlawful acts as criminal persons—as wholly illegitimate.

Processing people through this machinery stigmatizes people—i.e., publicly identifies the whole person in terms of only certain of his behavior patterns. At the same time, this often leads to acceptance by such persons of that identity. In this and other ways the transition to police society *created* the underworld. A professional police creates a professional underworld.

The "yellow press" which had emerged by the middle of the nineteenth century, focused on crime and violence. This helped confirm the new definition and stigmatization of the criminal person. Reporters obtained their stories by attending police courts. Police court reportage became so popular that even the conservative press eventually came to adopt it. And the police became guides to the newly discovered underworld.

The establishment of a professional police concerned with prevention increases the power of the state. Roger Lane writes:

> Before the 1830's the law in many matters was regarded as the expression of an ideal. The creation of a strong police raised the exciting possibility that the ideal might be realized, that morality could be enforced and the state made an instrument of social regeneration.

With the idea of prevention, then, law loses its status as only an ideal and becomes a real prescription actually to be enforced.

Those involved in the Reform Movements of the 1830's were quick to demand the services of the new police. Although, they had originally objected to hiring paid, daytime police, they soon began to welcome the police as part of the reform movement, seeing the police as "moral missionaries" eventually eliminating crime and vice. As Howard Becker writes, "The final outcome of a moral crusade is a police force."

During the first half of the 19th century, the professional police increasingly took over and expanded the duties of the constableship. This led to the police themselves becoming specialists in the maintenance of public order, which involved a transition to emphasizing the prevention of crime, and the role of law as ideal became an attempt to enforce laws as real prescriptions governing conduct. In this way the police, as an agency of the state, took over the function of social control from the members of the local community. The historical sources of the change were economic inequality and increasing riots. Thus, the police became an agency of those with wealth and power, for suppressing the attempts by the have-nots to re-distribute the wealth and power.

Thus, the professional police gave the upper classes an extremely useful and powerful mechanism for maintaining the unequal distribution of wealth and power: Law, which is proclaimed to be for the general welfare, is in fact an instrument in class warfare. . . .

It has been argued that the police and the legal system serve the interests of the powerful. This has been shown previously in that the powerful are able to get their own moral values passed as laws of the land—this is part of the definition of power. Also, however, they appear to be immune from the application or enforcement of the law. This can be substantiated by looking at the mechanics of enforcement. The police tend to divide the populace into two groups—the criminal and the non-criminal—and treat each accordingly. In police academies the recruits are told: "There are two kinds of people you arrest: those who pay the fine and those who don't."

William Westley asked the policemen in his study to describe the section of the general public that likes the police. Replies included:

> The law-abiding element likes the police. Well the people that are settled

down are polite to policemen, but the floater—people who move around—are entirely different. They think we are after them.

Westley concludes that "the better class of people," those from better residential neighborhoods and skilled workers, are treated with politeness and friendliness, because "that is the way to make them like you." In the policeman's relation to the middle class, "The commission of a crime by an individual is not enough to classify him a criminal."

> He sees these people [middle class] as within the law, that is, as being within the protection of the law, and as a group he has to observe the letter of the law in his treatment of them. Their power forces him to do so. No distinction is gained from the apprehension of such a person. Essentially, they do not fall into the category of potential criminals.

Whereas, for people in the slums, the patrolman feels that roughness is necessary, both to make them respect the policeman and to maintain order and conformity. Patrolmen are aware that it is slum dwellers' lack of power which enables him to use roughness and ignore "due process."

Skolnick writes that the police wish that "civil liberties people" would recognize the differences that police follow in applying search and seizure laws to respectable citizens and to criminals.

The immunity of those with power and wealth to having the law apply to them is so traditional that the police in one city were able to apply the normally withheld law enforcement to political officials as a measure of collective bargaining. The report of the activities of the Police Locust Club (police union), of Rochester, New York on the front page of the local newspaper is remarkable.

> The first move was to ticket cars owned by public officials for violations of the state Motor Vehicle Law.
> According to the club president, Ralph Boryszewski, other steps will include:
> Refusal to 'comply with requests from politicians for favors for themselves and their friends . . .'
> Cracking down on after-hours spots and gambling establishments 'which have been protected through the silent consent of public officials.'
> "These evils have existed as long as the police department has, and the public should know what's going on," Boryszewski said today, The slowdown is "really a speedup in enforcement of the law," he said. "The public won't be hurt, we're after the men who think they're above the law."

A Vermont urologist was charged with failure to file an income tax return for the years 1962, 1963, and 1964. However, he entered a plea of nolo on the 1964 charge only. "The judge said he accepted the lesser plea solely because it might jeopardize the doctor's standing in the medical profession."

Drug users who fail to fit the "dope fiend" image, that is, drug users who are from the "respectable" or upper classes, are not regarded as narcotic criminals and do not become part of the official reports. When the addict is a well-to-do professional man, such as a physician or lawyer, and is well spoken and well educated, then prosecutors, policemen, and judges alike seem to agree that "the harsh penalties of the law . . . were surely not intended for a person like this, and, by an unspoken agreement, arrangements are quietly made to exempt him from such penalties." The justification usually offered for not arresting addicted doctors and nurses is that they do not resort to crime to obtain drugs and are productive members of the community. "The only reason that users in the medical profession do not commit the crimes against property which other addicts do, is, of course, that drugs are available to them from medical sources."

The more laws a nation passes, the greater the possible size of the criminal population. In 1912, Roscoe Pound pointed out "of one hundred thousand persons arrested in Chicago in 1912, more than one-half were held for violations of legal precepts which did not exist twenty-five years before." Ten years ago, it was established that "the number of crimes for which one may be prosecuted has at least doubled since the turn of the century.

The increase has been in misdemeanors, not felonies. Sutherland and Gehlke, studying trends from 1900–1930 found little increase in laws dealing with murder or robbery. "The increase came in areas where there was no general agreement: public morals, business ethics, and standards of health and safety."

The prevention of felonies, and the protection of the community from acts of violence, is usually given as the *raison d'etre* of criminal law and the justification for a police system and penal sanctions. Yet, most police activity is concerned with misdemeanors, not felonies. Seldon Bacon writes.

> What are the crimes which hurt society so often and so intensely that the society must react to such disorder and must react in an effective way (i.e. with organization, equipment, and specialization)? The answer of the modern criminologist to this question is felonies. The case studies however, clearly indicate that society does not react in these ways to felonies nearly as much as to misdeameanors. Indeed, the adjustment to felonious activity is a secondary if not a tertiary sphere of action. Moreover, judicial studies of the present day point to the same findings, misdemeanor cases outnumber felony cases 100 to 1. Yet the criminologists without exception have labored almost exclusively in the sphere of felonies.

One writer noted that "in the three years from 1954 through 1956 arrests for drunkenness in Los Angeles constituted between 43 and 46 per cent of all arrest bookings." The importance of this is not in the prevalence of drunkenness as much as it is in the easy rationale afforded the police for maintaining order and conformity, for "keeping the peace." Now that marijuana smoking is apparently so widespread, laws preventing its use give police an excuse to arrest anyone they see as a threat to "order."

Becker writes, "In America, only about six out of every hundred major crimes known to police result in jail sentences." In addition, only about twenty per cent of original reports find their way into criminal statistics. It appears then, that the police have considerable discretion in deciding which violators to punish, or in deciding when an individual has committed a violation.

From Constabulary to Police Society   397

The greater the number of punitive laws, and the stiffer the penalties, the easier it is to attempt enforcement of any *one* law. Police threaten prostitutes with arrest, using the threat to get a lead on narcotic arrests; if the prostitute informs, then there is no arrest or reduced charges. Liquor laws can be used to regulate or control "homosexual" bars. Burglary informants as well as narcotic informants are usually addicts. Skolnick writes, "In general, burglary detectives permit informants to commit narcotic offenses, while narcotic detectives allow informants to steal."

As early as 1906, Professor Ernst Freund commented upon the range of criminal legislation. "Living under free institutions we submit to public regulation and control in ways that appear inconceivable to the spirit of oriental despotism."

As the laws increase in range and number, the population is criminalized, especially the population from low-economic background, minority racial groups, or non-conformists in other ways. John I. Kitsuse writes about those labeled as deviant.

> For in modern society, the socially significant differentation of deviants from the non-deviant population is increasingly contingent upon circumstances of situation, place, social and personal biography, and the bureaucratically organized activities of agencies of control.

The vast number of our laws provides the means for selective enforcement, and selective enforcement means the immunity of the rich and powerful. The greater the number of laws, the easier it is to control those without power and wealth. The content of the laws is not crucial for purposes of social control. What is crucial is the power to establish the "language of punishment" (or conversely, "the language of legitimacy"), the power to institute both the enforcers of law—the police—and the violators of law—the criminals.

The Maintenance of Capitalist Order

Michael Mann

THE SOCIAL COHESION
OF LIBERAL DEMOCRACY

It is now some years since Dahrendorf and others made their attacks on consensus theory and their pleas for a "mixed theory" of social cohesion. But, despite all the complexities of individual sociologists' arguments, there is still agreement between almost all theorists that *some* minimal degree of value consensus exists in liberal democratic societies, permitting them to handle conflict and remain stable. What is especially surprising is that this belief is at its strongest among latter-day conflict theorists, who admit that value consensus exists but deny its "validity" by their use of "false consciousness." In this paper I will attempt empirical testing of the theories of both "consensus" and "false consciousness" sociologists.

The theoretical orthodoxy of those I loosely term "consensus theorists" is to be found in this quotation from an editorial introduction to an American symposium on political socialization:

> Political socialization refers to the learning process by which the political norms and behaviors acceptable to an ongoing political system are transmitted from generation to generation . . . A well-functioning citizen is one who accepts (internalizes) society's political norms . . . Without a body politic so in harmony with the ongoing political values, a political system would have trouble functioning smoothly . . ." (Sigel, 1965:1; for a similar statement see Rose, 1965:29).

Using such an approach, several well-known studies have argued that the stability and "success" of democratic societies depend on the sharing of general political and prepolitical values. In these studies, Great Britain and the United States are taken as examples of successful liberal democracies and often contrasted explicitly or implicitly with "less successful" democracies (e.g. Almond and Verba, 1963; Lipset, 1964; Easton and Dennis, 1967). Thus, Dahl (1967:329–330), reviewing previous studies, concludes that "Americans ordinarily agree on a great many questions that in some countries have polarized the citizenry into antagonistic camps. One consequence of this massive convergence of attitudes is that political contests do not usually involve serious threats to the way of life of significant strata in the community," while Rose has stated ". . . enduring consensus is one of the most distinctive features of politics in England" (1969:3; see also his 1965 work).

Reprinted from Michael Mann, "The Social Cohesion of Liberal Democracy," *American Sociological Review*, vol. 35 (June 1970), pp. 423–439, by permission of American Sociological Association. Michael Mann teaches sociology at the University of Essex, England. He is the author of two forthcoming books, *Industry and Community* and *Consciousness and Action among the Western Working Class*.

We now might ask "what is this consensus about?" And here different writers would produce different answers. Firstly, there are those who stress the commitment of social members to *ultimate values*, of which examples might be generalized beliefs in equality and achievement (Lipset, 1964). Others, however, stress commitment to social *norms*, of which well-known examples are an adherence to the "rules of the democratic game" and opposition to those who introduce strong conflictual elements (such as class ideology) into politics (Dahl, 1967; McKenzie and Silver, 1968). Finally, there are writers who stress commitment to *beliefs* about how society is actually organized, of which there are two main varieties. The first stresses the harmonistic structure of society and political elites (against, say, a belief in class conflict), while the second stresses the essential benevolence of other individuals within the society, for example, the trustworthiness of others (see respectively Easton and Dennis, 1967, and Almond and Verba, 1963). According to these writers, widespread commitment to any or all of these values, norms and beliefs confers legitimacy and stability on present social structure. The "false consciousness" writers agree that this widespread commitment exists, but deny that it thus confers legitimacy on society. Before turning to their arguments, however, let us examine the conceptual problems arising from the asserted link between consensus and social cohesion. There are in fact four main objections to the statement that shared values integrate and legitimate social structures.

1. Most general values, norms and social beliefs usually mentioned as integrating societies are extremely vague, and can be used to legitimate any social structure, existing or not. As Parsons (1951:293) notes, conservatives and revolutionaries alike appeal to common values of "social justice," "democracy," and "peace." Even the most monolithic of societies is vulnerable to radical appeals to its core values. For example, medieval rebels were often clerics appealing to common Christian values, as did John Ball in the 1381 Peasants' Revolt in England:

> When Adam delved and Eve span,
> Who was then a gentleman?

But at the same time respectable, established clerics unwittingly primed their congregations by emphasizing these "leveling" aspects of Christianity in their sermons (Owst, 1961: Chaps. 5 and 6). Most "consensus theorists" accept the force of this argument. Dahl, for example, though concluding that the stability of American democracy rests on consensus about fundamentals, admits that these are often vague and of doubtful influence on actual behaviour (see also Rose, 1965:30).

2. Even if a value is stated precisely, it may lead to conflict, not cohesion. For while some values unite men, others necessarily divide them. An extreme example of this fact is the consensus among the Dobu people on the values of suspiciousness and treachery (quoted by van der Berghe, 1963). The more consensus there is about such values, the greater the ensuing conflict. Clearly it is only some values which lead to integration, and we had better stick to safe statements like "the more widely interpersonal trust is valued, the

greater the social integration" (cf. Almond and Verba, 1963). In short, we have to specify the content of a value if we are to predict its consequences.

3. The standards embodied in values are absolute ones, and it is difficult for such absolutes to co-exist without conflict. For example, the modern Western values of "achievement" and "equality"—emphasized by Lipset—each limit the scope of the other. Turner (1953–54) has noted that such value-conflict is ubiquitous in societies, which develop ways of "insulating" values from each other. Cohesion is therefore affected by the relative success of society's insulation processes as well as by the nature of the values themselves.

4. The final objection is related to the third: where insulation processes operate, cohesion results precisely because there is no common commitment to core values. For example, in a society which values achievement, a lower class is more likely to acquiesce in its inequality if it places less stress on achievement aspirations than on other values. Moreover, the cohesion of any functionally differentiated society must partly depend on the learning of role-specific values. In a business firm, for example, though all managers may need some degree of commitment to common organizational goals, they also need differential commitment to role values—the engineer to product quality, the accountant to cost, the personnel manager to industrial peace—for the survival and efficiency of the firm. Thus either role- or class-specific values may contribute more to social cohesion than general core values.

As I have indicated, these problems have been perceived by consensus theorists. Their modifications of a naive, traditional view of consensus (such as Kingsley Davis, 1948, posited) have been paralleled by recent modifications to "conflict theory" which in the modern context means Marxist theory.

Just as no consensus theorist would posit the existence of complete harmony, no Marxist would claim that complete disharmony characterized society. He would admit, firstly, that some form of social cooperation is necessary in the pursuit of scarcity, and, secondly, that subordinate classes within society always appear to "accept" their position at least to some extent (Giddens, 1968:269). Yet the precise meaning of this word "accept" has greatly troubled Marxists. We must distinguish two types of acceptance: *pragmatic* acceptance, where the individual complies because he perceives no realistic alternative, and *normative* acceptance, where the individual internalizes the moral expectations of the ruling class and views his own inferior position as legitimate. Though pragmatic acceptance is easy to accommodate to Marxism, normative acceptance is not, and the unfortunate popularity of the latter concept has contributed to the inadequacies of much modern Marxist theory.

Writers like Marcuse (1964) and Hacker (1957) have agreed with the consensus theorists that value consensus does exist, and that normative acceptance characterizes the working class in present-day liberal democracies. Such a position can be only reconciled with a Marxist approach by utilizing the concept of "false consciousness" and asserting that normative acceptance is "false" in the sense that it leads workers to ignore their true interests. Yet false consciousness is a dangerous concept, for if we define interests totally independently of the orientations of those concerned, "religious mania alone speaks here" (Geiger, quoted by Dahrendorf, 1959:175). Nevertheless, the

The Social Cohesion of Liberal Democracy   401

concept of false consciousness is tenable if we can demonstrate two or three things: that an indoctrination process has occurred, palpably changing working-class values, or that the indoctrination process is incomplete, leaving indoctrinated values in conflict with "deviant" ones in the mind of the worker; and thirdly, in *both* cases we still have to be able to rank the rival sets of values in order of their "authenticity" to the worker if we are to decide which is more "true." This is a formidable task, barely begun by Marxists. On the first point they are in conflict with the many research findings which show that it is comparatively difficult for the mass media and other indoctrination agencies to change existing values (to which they might justifiably reply that as ruling-class values are in essence traditional, they do not have to be taught afresh). The second point they have obscured by general denunciations of total indoctrination. The third problem of "authenticity" has always been faced by Marxists, but has been too often solved by assertion rather than by evidence.

We are now in a position to derive testable propositions from each of the broad theoretical positions described above. The crucial questions are empirical: *to what extent do the various classes in society internalize norms, values and beliefs which legitimate the social order?* And, *do such norms, values and beliefs constitute true or false consciousness,* as defined above? Present sociological writings offer no coherent answer to these questions. One distinguished group of writers has argued that a "minimum" legitimating consensus does exist in certain liberal democracies, thereby contributing to the stability of their regimes (e.g. Almond and Verba, 1963; Dahl, 1967; Easton and Dennis, 1967). But other empirical investigations of the extent of political value consensus in one of those liberal democracies, the United States, provide opposite conclusions and, moreover, provide hints that the individual's own internal belief system may not be consistent (Agger et al., 1961; McClosky, 1964, Prothro and Grigg, 1960, Converse, 1964). An impasse has been reached. As Easton has remarked (1965:197): ". . . the actual specification of the degree of consensus . . . is an empirical rather than a theoretical matter and is one that has never been fully faced up to, much less resolved through testing whole systems." Such is the intention of the main part of this paper.

The Data

The data consist of a variety of findings from other writers' empirical investigations into value-commitment in Britain and the United States. The values, norms, and beliefs analyzed here are all ones supporting, or destructive of, the present social structure of those countries. Most concentrate on issues regarding the legitimacy of the social stratification system. Following Parkin (1967), I have labeled supporting values *dominant*, and destructive values *deviant*. Dominant values are generally promulgated by ruling groups to legitimate their rule; deviant values, by groups contesting that legitimacy.

Nearly all the results used here consist of responses to agree-disagree questions. They are presented in Tables 1 to 4. The first column of these tables contains the investigator's name and reference, together with references to other studies which produce similar findings. The second column gives brief details of the sample used, and the third column give the gist of the question asked. The fourth column gives details of subsamples where available. This paper gives only the subsamples corresponding to the broad occupational stratification hierarchy in liberal democracies, with the groups presented in descending order.[1] The term "class" will be loosely used in the text to describe the main groups, though the authors of the studies themselves use a variety of terms. The fifth column shows the percentage agreement among the sample to the question. The final column presents a classification system designed to show briefly which, if any, theory the finding tends to support. If 75% or more of respondents agree with a dominant value, the final column contains "Dominant Consensus." If 75% agree with a deviant value, this is labeled "Deviant Consensus." Obviously, 75% is an arbitrary cutoff point between consensus and dissensus, but its general level seems not unreasonable. Where a clear majority of a sample endorses a value, this may still be a significant finding, and thus any agreement of between 60% and 75% has been labeled either "Dominant" or "Deviant Dissensus," according to the direction of the majority. Where there is almost complete, i.e., between 40% and 60%, disagreement, this has been labeled simply "Dissensus." One further classification has been made: where class differences emerge, in that upper classes endorse dominant values significantly more, and deviant values significantly less, than lower classes, this is labeled "Dissensus between Classes."[2]

One important reservation must be made before we turn to the actual results: this type of secondary analysis of published material suffers from important methodological disadvantages. One major problem is that the questions actually used in different studies are rarely identical, and—as all sociologists well know—very slight changes of cue in a question can produce markedly differing results. This difficulty will not be shirked—for example, the effect on respondents of the single word "class" will be discussed—but as we are looking for consistency between findings from different surveys, question bias will usually be randomized. The same should also apply to the difficulties of comparing responses of samples of differing compositions at different points of time and place. However, it must be emphasized that conclusions drawn from such secondary analysis can be only tentative until confirmed by primary research.

[1] There is no analysis in this paper of racial aspects of stratification, though these are obviously extremely important in the United States, and increasingly so in Britain.

[2] The reverse trend does not in fact occur. Note that no tests of *statistical* significance are used here—the populations sampled by the studies are too diverse and ill-reported for this. "Significant" differences indicates merely "clear" differences in this paper.

Results

In this section we analyze respondents' views on the legitimacy of social structure, and particularly class structure, in Britain and the United States. As the principal function of a social stratification system is to regulate the distribution of scarce resources, we will start by observing how much people, particularly working-class people, want those scarce resources.

Sociological studies of "achievement motivation" are our first pieces of evidence. Several have shown that almost all persons, of whatever class, will agree with statements like "It is important to get ahead" (Scanzoni, 1967:456; Mizruchi, 1964:95; Veness, 1962:153), and some useful pointers to what respondents mean by this are now emerging. Most important, working-class people are more likely than middle-class people to think of success as achieved solely in the occupational sphere, and are more likely to conceive of it as materialistic, economic success (Mizruchi, 1964:77–90). The crucial question then is "Can their economic aspirations be met, given the constraints of the stratified occupational system?" There is evidence that the answer to this is "No." In a comparative analysis of British and American schoolboys, Stephenson demonstrated that the lower the social class of the boy, the more his occupational aspirations outran his occupational expectations. Thus, later on it is the working class pupils ". . . who lower most their aspirations when it comes to considering plans or expectations" in the occupational sphere (Stephenson 1959:49; for supporting evidence see Caro and Pihlblad, 1965). This process seems to continue in the world of work itself. It has been a frequent research finding in industrial sociology that, in identical jobs, older workers are more satisfied than younger ones. The most probable explanation of this is Kornhauser's, applied to his own findings: ". . . men in the routine types of work come over the years to accept and make the most of their situation" (1967:77). From a very early age the lower class person begins to realize that he is at the bottom of a stratification hierarchy (Bettelheim and Sylvester, 1950; Himmelweit et al., 1952). Probably starting with universalistic achievement values, he gradually redefines his aspirations in a more and more role-specific way, so that his lot can become acceptable.

The nature of this "acceptance" is, of course, crucial as I argued earlier. Does this redefinition of goals lead to normative or to pragmatic acceptance? One test of this is the extent to which lower classes regard as legitimate the opportunity structure which has disadvantaged them. In this respect, dominant values are clear: success comes to those whose energies and abilities deserve it, failures have only themselves to blame. Is this argument accepted by lower class persons? Table 1 provides an answer.

We can see that, by and large, the samples hold dominant beliefs about the opportunity structure. Though these results show clearly the biasing effects of leading questions, almost all respondents endorse the key cues of "ability" and "hard work" while much smaller numbers endorse "luck," "pull" and "too hard for a man." Yet there are slight indications here that these beliefs might not be of great significance for the respondents. Thus the Blauner and the Mercer and Weir studies show that respondents are more likely to be cynical about the opportunity structure that confronts them in

Table 1. The Legitimacy of the Opportunity Structure

Author	Sample	Statement	Subsample	% Agreement	Classification
Mizruchi (1964:82) (cf. Berelson et al., 1954:58; Lenski, 1963:165)	U.S. small town adults	Ability determines who gets ahead	a) Social Classes I-III b) Social Classes IV, V	97 92	Dominant Consensus
Veness (1962:144)	a) English boys and girls aged 13-17, representative national sample	Hard work (and not luck or influence) is how to get on	a) Grammar School b) Technical School c) Modern School	88 93 88	Dominant Consensus
	b) Boys only	Status achieved by effort in children's essays	a) Grammar School b) Technical School c) Modern School	79 63 30	Dissensus between classes
Kornhauser (1965:210)	U.S. male workers	Luck and "pull" determines who gets ahead	a) White collar b) Nonfactory workers c) All factory workers (including d and e) d) Small town factory workers e) Routine production workers	13 26 36 32 50	Dissensus between classes Dominant consensus in middle class
Blauner (1964:206)	U.S. factory workers national sample	"cynical" factors determine promotion in own organization	·	39	Dominant Dissensus
Mercer & Weir (1969:122)	English male clerical and technical workers, large town	Ditto	·	28	Dominant Dissensus
McKenzie & Silver (1968:140)	English urban working class. Labour and Conservative voters only	Too hard for a man with ambition to get ahead	·	51	Dissensus

Table 2. Harmonistic and Conflictual Images of Society

Author	Sample	Statement	Subsample	% Agreement	Classification
Form & Rytina (1969:23)	U.S. adults, medium town (the "analytic sample")	Holding pluralist models of society rather than class or power elite models	a) Rich b) Middle c) Poor	65 59 57	Borderline Dissensus Class differences not significant
Lewis (1964–65:176)	U.S. white males, medium town	Rating U.S. citizenship more important than class membership	•	"Almost" 90	Dominent Consensus
Manis & Meltzer (1954:33–35)	U.S. male textile workers, medium town with history of labour disputes	a) Social classes are inevitable and desirable b) Social classes are either enemies or in conflict, or partners or in paternalistic relationship	• • •	56 33 46	Dissensus Dissensus
Leggett (1964:230)	U.S. male manual workers, metropolis	The rich get the profits	a) Employed b) Unemployed	62 76	Deviant Dissensus
McClosky (1964:370)	U.S. national ("general electorate") sample	a) The laws are rich man's laws b) Poor man doesn't have a chance in the law courts	• •	33 43	Dominant Dissensus Dissensus
Kornhauser (1965:220) cf. Haer, 1956–57:140; Lipsitz, 1964:957	U.S. male workers	Big business has too much power	a) White collar workers b) All factory workers	54 79	Dissensus between classes Deviant consensus within lower class

Author	Sample	Statement	Subsample	% Agreement	Classification
Nordlinger (1967:178)	English male urban manual workers[1]	Class conflict is important in England	• •	55	Dissensus
McKenzie & Silver (1968b:135) [cf. Cannon, 1967:168]	English urban workers. Labour and Conservative voters only	Upper class has always tried to exploit working class	• •	51	Dissensus
Goldthorpe et al. (1968b:26)	English affluent workers, medium town	The laws favour the rich	a) White collar b) Manual workers	59 72	Virtual deviant Dissensus
Mercer & Weir (1969:121)	English male clerical and technical workers, large town	Management and workers are a team, and not on opposite sides	• •	54	Dissensus
Goldthorpe et al. (1968a:73, 85)	As above	a) Ditto b) Work study engineers are antiworker	a) White collar b) Manual workers Manual workers only	76 67 55	Dominant Dissensus Dissensus
Goldthorpe et al. (1968b:26) [cf. Cannon, 1967:168; McKenzie & Silver, 1968:127]	As above	a) Big business has too much power b) Trade unions have too much power	a) White collar b) Manual workers a) White collar b) Manual workers	63 60 72 43	Deviant Dissensus Dissensus between classes

[1] As only one third of manual workers vote Conservative, the Conservative bias of this sample has been removed by weighting double the % of Labour voters

their actual working lives. This kind of interpretation is strengthened by the Veness (1962) findings. These are based on schoolchildren's essays describing imaginary "successes" in future life. Very large class differences emerge in the essays. In the essays of the grammar and technical school boys (destined for the most part for occupational success), success and status are seen as coming from steady achievements in the occupational sphere. In those of the secondary modern boys (the future manual workers), however, the idea of cumulative status is usually absent, and, instead, success comes from either a quiet, happy life or sudden fame in sport and entertainment. From this, it seems probable that, though lower class children may endorse general platitudes about the importance of ambition, these have little actual relevance for their own life-projects. Turner (1964), in his study of American high-school seniors, also comes to this conclusion, stressing that we can only assess the importance of values in society by considering their *relevance* to peoples' lives.

For further tests of our theories we can turn to respondents' images of the entire social structure to see whether *they* hold to theories of harmony or conflict. Table 2 presents the relevant findings.

This mass of conflicting results permits no easy generalizations. It is true that significant class differences in the direction predicted by Marxist theory emerge in several parts of this table. But not even the statement "Big business has too much power" evokes deviant consensus among the working class of both countries. In only two other cases is there even a clear majority for a deviant value among the working class: for "The rich get all the profits" and (probably) for "The laws favour the rich."[3] And when we examine these most favoured statements we see none mentions "class" and all are couched in what might be termed simplistic "common man" language. By contrast in Table 2, all the more abstract and sophisticated models of society evoke less support, whether they be basically dominant or deviant in content. We may note, for example, in the studies of Form and Rytina (1969) and of Manis and Meltzer (1954) that dissensus results from presenting alternative abstract theories of society to working class respondents. Moreover, the single word "class" produces dissensus among them whenever it occurs, except significantly when in the Lewis study it is decisively rejected in favour of nationality. This, then, is another problem to be faced later: why is the working class able and willing to produce deviant simplistic views of society but not deviant abstract ones?

Another type of study which enables us to perceive men's images of ongoing social structure is analyzing "political efficacy," that is a man's estimate of his own ability to affect the political government. A belief in high efficacy is certainly consonant with what we have termed dominant values, though a belief in low efficacy is not necessarily deviant to the extent of supporting the redistribution of political power. The relevant research findings are set out in Table 3.

---

[3] Taking note of McClosky's statement that more of the lower occupational groups in his sample have significantly deviant beliefs than higher groups (1964: 371). He does not, however, present these differences statistically.

Table 3. Images of Political Efficacy

Author	Sample	Statement	Subsample	% Agreement	Classification
Thompson & Horton (1960: 191–4) [cf. for white collar, Haer, 1956–7: 140]	U.S. adults, small town	Neither exercising nor believing in possibility of exercising political control ("politically alienated")	a) Managers and Officials b) Professionals c) White collar d) Labour	33 38 47 68	Dissensus between classes
McClosky (1964:371)	U.S. national "general electorate" sample	a) Nothing I do has any effect on politics b) No use being interested in politics	. .	62 21	Deviant Dissensus Dominant Consensus
Nordlinger (1967:97) [cf. McKenzie & Silver, 1968:124]	English male urban manual workers	People like me have no ability to influence government	.	43	Dissensus
Agger et al. (1961:479) [for b cf. Berelson et al. 1954:58; Kornhauser et al., 1956:190]	U.S. adults in metropolitan area	a) People are very frequently manipulated by politicians b) Politicians usually represent the general interest	.	60 58	Deviant Dissensus Dissensus
Nordlinger (1967:105, 109)	As above	Selfish minority groups control government Which groups? a) big business, rich, upper classes b) trade unions	. . .	63 65} 17}	Deviant Dissensus N.B. Total= c 110% Deviant Dissensus

409

Table 4. Norms Relating to Class Action and Equality

Author	Sample	Statement	Subsample	% Agreement	Classification
Kornhauser (1965:213–220)	U.S. male workers	a) Workers should have more control of industry	a) White collar	37	Dissensus between classes
		b) Always side with union against company	b) All factory workers	60	Deviant dissensus
Leggett (1964:230)	U.S. male manual workers, metropolis	All factory workers		60	
		a) Supporting working-class action in rent protest	a) Employed	31	Dissensus
		b) Wanting wealth equally divided	b) Unemployed	46	
Nordlinger (1967:178)	English male urban manual workers	a) In favour of reducing class differentials	a) Employed	9	Dominant Consensus
			b) Unemployed	16	Deviant Consensus
			· ·	79	
Benney et al. (1956:140–141) (for b cf. Goldthorpe et al. 1968a:109)	English adults, medium town	a) Large inequalities are wrong	· ·	48[1]	Dissensus
		b) Workers should have more control in industry		47	Dissensus
Nordlinger (1967:181)	As above	b) Working class should stick together to get ahead	· ·	41	Dissensus
Sykes (1965:303)	Scottish males, nationalized steelworks	Preferring to bargain with employer collectively	a) Clerks	4	Consensus within, dissensus between classes
			b) Workers	100	
McClosky (1964:369)	U.S. national "general electorate" sample	a) Government should give work to unemployed	· ·	47	Dissensus
		b) Government should give everyone good standard of living	· ·	55	Dissensus
Lenksi 1963:152 (cf. Kornhauser, 1965:218)	U.S. adults, metropolis	Government should do more for housing, unemployment, education, etc.	a) Middle Class	40	Dissensus
			b) Working Class	57	
Key (1965:124)	U.S. national sample	Ditto	a) Nonmanual	28	Dominant
			b) Manual	31	Dissensus

[1] This figure was arrived at by averaging the percentages among Labour and Conservative voters, who are equally represented in the country as a whole but not in Benney's sample.

410

All but one of the questions produce dissensus among respondents. Again, however, significant class differences appear, with at least half the working-class respondents choosing the mildly deviant alternative. Clearly then we must consider the possibility, argued by Thompson and Horton (1960), that there is considerable political alienation among the working class. And at the very least, the numerous inconsistencies in political beliefs emerging in the McClosky study indicate that a person's attitudes to political authority may have little significance for him. Again, we have to consider not only a person's stated attitude but also its importance for him.

From the confused images of society revealed in Tables 2 and 3, we might predict that confusion would also be evident in working-class norms regarding political action, and this is indeed revealed in Table 4.

Here, the two statements supporting class action (Leggett a and Nordlinger b) produce dissensus. The statement "Workers should have more control in industry" produces no consistent majority. Very few of one working-class sample want wealth equally divided, only about half of another mixed-class sample think that large inequalities are wrong, but in a third, working class, sample there is consensus in favour of reducing class differentials (one possible explanation of the last finding is that "class" is such an unpopular term that almost everyone is in favour of reducing it). Clearly, if most social groups had consistent and meaningful normative systems, the results would be less affected by the exact wording of questions, the composition of samples, etc.

A further trend emerges from Table 4 which we also noticed in Table 1: that deviant values are more likely to be endorsed if they are presented as relevant to respondents' everyday lives. Thus 60% of Kornhauser's (1965) samples say that in disputes they always side with the union and only 5% with the company, while all of Sykes' (1965) manual workers, in marked contrast to his clerks, support collective rather than individual bargaining. Note also that in Table 2, 55% of Goldthorpe et al's (1968a) manual sample saw work study engineers as opposed to worker interests, though 67% had in general seen worker-management relations in harmonistic terms. Again there seems to be a disjunction between general abstract values and concrete experience.

Such a disjunction is the main theme of Free and Cantril's (1967) study of American political attitudes, and their evidence can advance our argument considerably. They asked respondents two series of questions to test their liberalism/conservatism, the first on specific issues of government intervention in favour of redistribution (which they term the "operational" spectrum), the second on general issues of individualist versus interventionist philosophies (the "ideological" spectrum). Typical examples are, in the first spectrum, "Do you approve of Medicare?" and in the second "We should rely more on individual initiative . . . and not so much on governmental welfare programs." Table 5 presents their main results.

As the authors comment, the results are positively schizophrenic, with a large proportion of the electorate operationally liberal but ideologically conservative. Significantly, white manual workers are among the most schizoid groups (though Negroes are consistently liberal). Similar findings have also

Table 5. Ideological and Operational Spectrums in American Political Attitudes (Source: Free and Cantril, 1967:32)

	Ideological Spectrum		Operational Spectrum	
Completely Liberal[1]	4%	⎫	44%	⎫
		⎬ 16%		⎬ 65%
Predominantly Liberal	12	⎭	21	⎭
Middle of the Road	34		21	
Predominantly Conservative	20	⎫	7	⎫
		⎬ 50%		⎬ 14%
Completely Conservative	30	⎭	7	⎭
	100%		100%	

[1] The scoring system is quite complicated and the reader is referred to Free and Cantril, pp. 220–221.

been reported by Selznick and Steinberg (1969:220). Such findings have obvious bearing on the problem of false consciousness discussed earlier in this paper: it is interesting that writers as obviously non-Marxist as Free and Cantril (1967) should conclude their study by remarking that present American ideology is out of touch with American realities (i.e. false) and should therefore be reformulated.

Finally, we can examine the suggestion that political and social stability is in part a function of consensus on pre-political values. Many writers have argued this, asserting in particular that liberal democracy "works" because its members trust each other. The most satisfactory evidence for this comes from Almond and Verba's (1963) influential study, but even their findings seem rather suspect on closer examination. It is indisputable that their results show a greater degree of consensus on values such as interpersonal trust among British and American respondents than among respondents in the "less successful" democracies of Italy, Mexico, and West Germany. However, there are equally significant differences in value-commitment according to the only (and indirect) measure of social class used, the formal education of the respondent. The least educated groups are consistently the least politically confident and trusting. Moreover, when Almond and Verba produce their results on the extent of commitment to the norm of interpersonal trust, they tend to obscure one very significant finding, which is difficult to fit into their general theoretical position. It is that the *degree* of value commitment, even in Britain and the United States, is still minimal. In Table 4 (on page 267) Almond and Verba demonstrate that more respondents in Britain and the States than in the other countries agree with five similar statements whose tenor is that "people can be trusted." But additionally, on two of the five items in the U.S. and on three of them in Britain, only a minority of respondents show themselves as "trustful." Also, in Table 5 (on page 269), a majority of those with only primary education in these countries agree with the deviant statement "No one is going to care much what happens to you, when you get right down to it," which statement Almond and Verba think "reflects the most extreme feeling of distrust and alienation" (p. 268). Unfortunately, the authors do not present the results of the other questions according to educational level, but it would not be unreasonable to assume that the majority of lower class respondents would emerge as distrustful on the less extreme questions. Clearly, Almond and Verba's analysis of the stability of liberal democracy is at best partial, neglecting as it does the lack of value consensus between classes.

From all these findings four trends, which are in need of explanation, clearly emerge:

1. value consensus does not exist to any significant extent;
2. there is a greater degree of consensus among the middle class than among the working class;
3. the working class is more likely to support deviant values if those values relate either to concrete everyday life or to vague populist concepts than if they relate to an abstract political philosophy;
4. working class individuals also exhibit less internal *consistency* in their values than middle-class people.

We can now return to our general theories with these trends in mind.

Discussion

If there is not value consensus, what remains of value consensus theory? Obviously the more extreme and generally stated versions of the theory are untenable, but many others have been rather more cautious, asserting merely that some "minimum" level of consensus about certain "critical" value is necessary to social cohesion. As this level is never precisely specified, we cannot very easily come to grips with the argument. Let us approach the problem by asking *why* some measure of consensus is considered necessary for social cohesion. The answer lies in one of sociology's most sacred tenets: that values are by definition beliefs governing action. As action itself must be considered nonrandom, and as men do actually cooperate with one another, then it would seem to follow that there is some degree of congruence between their values. This seems plausible, for if men cooperate they must come to some form of agreement, explicit or implicit, to share power. There is, of course, no such social contract which does not rest on shared normative understandings (Durkheim, 1964:206–19).

But when we consider whole complex societies, it is not clear that all social members can be considered as parties to the social contract. The ordinary participant's social relations are usually confined to a fairly narrow segment of society, and his relations with society as a whole are mostly indirect, through a series of overlapping primary and secondary groups. We may characterize his meaningful life as being largely on an every-day level. Thus his normative connections with the vast majority of fellow citizens may be extremely tenuous, and his commitment to general dominant and deviant values may be irrelevant to his compliance with the expectations of others. As long as he conforms to the very specific role behavior expected of him, the political authorities may not trouble themselves with his system of beliefs. If this is so, we might develop the following hypothesis: *only those actu-*

ally sharing in societal power need develop consistent societal values. There are two available tests of this hypothesis and both support it. Firstly, Mc-Closky (1964) has shown that there is a far greater internal consistency in the political values of political activists in the United States than in the population at large.[4] Clearly it is the former who daily face the problems of power-sharing. Secondly, there are the various class differences demonstrated earlier in this paper, and obviously, the middle class is closer to centers of power than is the working class. Etzioni (1964) has argued persuasively that the normative orientations of lower participants in "utilitarian" organizations like the industrial firm are largely irrelevant to the quality of their role-performance. Might this be also true of the lower classes in liberal democracy? Their compliance might be more convincingly explained by their pragmatic acceptance of specific roles than by any positive normative commitment to society. There is even evidence that lower class parents and children are in a similar relationship: Rosen (1967) shows that the working-class parent disciplines his children by "eliciting specific behavioral conformities" from them, whereas the middle-class parent attempts more to persuade his children to internalize norms and to generalize them to a variety of situations. The attachment of the lower classes to the distant state may be expected to be far less normative and more pragmatic than their attachment to the primary familial group.

While rejecting more extreme versions of harmonistic theories, we must also do the same with Marxist ones. There is little truth in the claims of some Marxists that the working class is systematically and successfully indoctrinated with the values of the ruling class. Though there is a fair amount of consensus among the rulers, this does not extend very far down the stratification hiearchy. Among the working-class there is almost complete dissensus on most of the general dominant-deviant political issues we have investigated. We have seen that two types of deviant values are widely endorsed by working class people; firstly, values which are expressed in concrete terms corresponding to everyday reality, and, secondly, vague simplistic divisions of the social world into "rich" and "poor." Everyday social conflict is experienced, and to some extent is referred to what Ossowski has described as the eternal struggle between "rich" and "poor," "rulers" and "ruled," "idle drones" and "worker bees" (Ossowski, 1963:19–30). But the one is concrete and the other is vague; there is no real political philosophy uniting the two in the working-class consciousness. Instead, at the political level are rather confused values with surprisingly conservative biases. How these political values come to be is of crucial theoretical importance, for it is their presence which keeps the working-class from noncompliance in the political order. It is not value-consensus which keeps the working-class compliant, but rather a *lack* of consensus in the crucial area where concrete experiences and vague populism might be translated into radical politics. Whether a harmonistic or a conflictual theory can best account for their compliance now turns on whether this lack of consensus is "free" or "manipulated," on how it is

[4] See also Converse's (1964) excellent argument on this point: he maintains that it is a tiny minority consisting of highly educated, political activists which has an internally consistent, considered, and stable set of political beliefs.

produced. Though we need more studies of the operation of socialization processes, at least one of them, the school system, has been extensively studied.

Studies of the school systems of Britain and the United States have generally concluded that the school is a transmitter of political conservatism, particularly to the working-class. Hess and Torney (1967) find that the school is the most important political socialization agency for the young child, and that its efforts are directed toward the cultivation of nationalism and a benevolent image of established political authority. Greenstein stresses benevolence, too, noting that the child's view of the world is deliberately "sugarcoated" by adults: "Books such as *Our Friend the Farmer* and *How the Policeman Helps Us* are couched in language which closely resembles some of the preadolescent descriptions of the political leaders reported in this survey" (1965:46). Both Zeigler (1967) and Litt (1963) stress how teachers strive to keep the conflictual elements of politics out of the classroom unless, paradoxically, they are dealing with upper class children. As Litt puts it, politics is presented as a ". . . formal mechanistic set of government institutions with the emphasis on its harmonious legitimate nature rather than as a vehicle for group struggle and change." (1963:73). Abrams (1963) comes to a similar conclusion from his review of textbooks used in British schools: he notes that they often try to avoid mentioning nonbenevolent occurrences such as economic slumps or industrial conflict, and where they cannot avoid them, the events are presented as "just happening" with no real attempt at explanation. Other studies have shown that schools also attempt to inculcate individualism and competitiveness in pupils; e.g., the child is taught that any form of achievement is gained at the expense of others (e.g. Henry, 1965; Friedenberg, 1963). It is of especial interest that the dominant values thus taught in schools are precisely the ones we have already noted as being present in adult working-class consciousness. Individualism we saw expressed strongly in Table 1, while a strong preference for ties of nationality over class, was also evident in Table 2. Furthermore, Litt and Zeigler's observations about teaching on the American political system enable us to trace back the origin of another supposed American core-value, belief in the legitimacy of the Constitution (see Dahl, 1967, for an assertion of the importance of this value to American democracy).[5]

We must be careful to specify the limits of this indoctrination. It is rarely direct, though the daily oath to the U.S. flag, or the granting of holidays to children in Britain if they will cheer visiting royalty, clearly come into this category. More usually, dominant-deviant issues are not presented at all to children. The essential point is that "the realities of the political process" (to use Litt's phrase) and the populist deviant tradition of the lower class are ignored in the classroom. Presumably the working class child learns the latter from his family and peers;[6] certainly he experiences something of the former when he enters the world of work, so his manipulated socialization is only

[5] Respondents' attitudes on this issue have not been analyzed here, as there is no comparable British issue.
[6] Though the evidence here is conflicting. Hess and Torney (1967) state that the families they investigated also transmit nationalism and political benevolence, but Carter (1962) finds that British working class families transmit a cynical populism.

partial. We may aptly describe these socialization processes as the mobilization of bias (the phrase of Bachrach and Baratz, 1962). As the child gets older, he becomes increasingly cynical in his political and social attitudes (Hess and Easton, 1960; Hess, 1963; Greenstein, 1965), but he has difficulty in putting them into abstract terms. What has been ignored in childhood is unlikely to be grasped in adulthood, given working class difficulties with abstract concepts (cf. Bernstein, 1961; findings replicated by Hess and Shipman, 1965). Hence we can see agencies of political radicalism, like the trade unions and the British Labour Party, struggling against their opponents' ability to mobilize the national and feudal symbols to which the population has been taught to respond loyally in schools and in much of the mass media (McKenzie and Silver, 1968:245). Thus the most common form of manipulative socialization by the liberal democratic state does not seek to change values, but rather to perpetuate values that do not aid the working class to interpret the reality it actually experiences. These values merely deny he existence of group and class conflict within the nation-state society and therefore, are demonstrably false.

Thus there are strong suggestions that the necessary mixed model of social cohesion in liberal democracy should be based more on Marxist conflict theory than sociologists have usually thought. A significant measure of consensus and normative harmony may be necessary among ruling groups, but it is the absence of consensus among lower classes which keeps them compliant. And if we wish to explain this lack of consensus, we must rely to some extent on the Marxist theories of *pragmatic role acceptance* and *manipulative socialization*. Of course, the existence of contrary harmonistic processes is feasible. Alongside coercive processes there may exist elements of voluntary deference, nationalism, and other components of normative integration in liberal democracy. It is often difficult to distinguish the two. Yet sociologists can no longer assert that these elements produce value consensus between social members and value consistency within them. Thus whatever "legitimacy" liberal democracy possess is not conferred upon it by value consensus, for this does not exist.

However, these results do not contradict all such affirmations of the legitimacy of social structure. Though I have demonstrated the existence of present-day false consciousness, this is insufficient as a total explanation of pragmatic role acceptance. For the reason why most working-class people do "accept" (in whatever sense) their lot and do not have consistent deviant ideologies, we must look back to the historical incorporation of working-class political and industrial movements in the 19th and 20th centuries within existing structures. Dahl's historical analysis would lead to the same conclusion as that of Marcuse, that the institutionalization of class conflict has resulted in a closing of the "political universe." But, of course, whereas Marcuse stresses that this process was itself dominated by the manipulative practices of the ruling class,[7] Dahl has stressed its elements of genuine and voluntary compromise. Clearly, the historical as well as the present-day theory must be a

[7] For a rather more detailed and better argued statement of this, see R. Miliband, 1961.

"mixed" one. Yet one obstacle to the development of a more precise mixed theory in the past has been the failure of most sociologists to take the Marxist tradition in social theory seriously. In particular, they have dismissed the crucial concept of "false consciousness" as being non-scientific. Yet in this paper we have seen fulfilled two of the preconditions for an empirically-grounded theory of false consciousness. Firstly, we saw quite clearly a conflict between dominant and deviant values taking place within the individual. Secondly, we found some evidence of the alternative precondition, the actual indoctrination of dominant values. Thus the third precondition, the ranking of conflicting values by an analysis of "who gains and who loses" can be investigated, and some relevant suggestions have been made here. The central argument of this paper is that the debate between harmonistic theories and Marxist theories must be an empirical one. The way is open to further empirical investigations.

REFERENCES

Abrams, P. (1963), "Notes on the Uses of Ignorance." Twentieth Century (Autumn): 67–77.

Agger, R. E., M. N. Goldstein, and S. A. Pearl (1961), "Political cynicism: Measurement and meaning." Journal of Politics 23:477–506.

Almond, G., and S. Verba (1963), The Civic Culture. N. J.: Princeton University Press.

Bachrach, P., and M. S. Baratz (1962), "Two faces of power." American Political Science Review, 56:947–952.

Benney, M., A. P. Gray and R. H. Pear (1956), How People Vote: A Study of Electoral Behaviour in Greenwich. London: Routledge and Kegan Paul.

Berelson, B. R., P. F. Lazarsfeld, and W. N. McPhee (1954), Voting. University of Chicago Press.

Bernstein, B. (1961), "Social class and linguistic development: A theory of social learning." Pp. 288–314 in A. H. Halsey et al. (eds.), Education, Economy and Society. Glencoe: The Free Press.

Bettelheim, B., and E. Sylvester (1950), "Notes on the impact of parental occupations." American Journal of Orthopsychiatry, 20:785–795.

Blauner, R. (1964), Alienation and Freedom. Chicago University Press.

Cannon, I. C. (1967), "Ideology and occupational community: A study of compositors." Sociology, 1:165–185.

Caro, F. G., and C. T. Pihlblad (1965), "Aspirations and expectations." Sociology and Social Research, 49:465–475.

Carter, M. P. (1962), Home, School and Work. Oxford: Pergamon Press.

Converse, P. E. (1964), "The Nature of belief systems in mass publics." Pp. 206–261 in D. E. Apter (ed.), Ideology and Discontent. Glencoe: The Free Press.

Dahl, R. A. (1967), Pluralist Democracy in the United States: Conflict and Consent. Chicago: Rand McNally.

Dahrendorf, R. (1959), Class and Class Conflict in an Industrial Society. London: Routledge and Kegan Paul.

Davis, K. (1948), Human Society. New York: Macmillan.

Durkheim, E. (1964), The Division of Labor in Society. New York: The Free Press.

Easton, D. (1965), A Systems Analysis of Political Life. New York: John Wiley.

Easton, D., and J. Dennis (1967), "The child's acquisition of regime norms: Political Efficacy." *American Political Science Review*, 61:25–38.

Easton, D., and R. D. Hess (1962), "The child's political world." *Midwest Journal of Political Science*, 6:229–246.

Etzioni, A. (1964), *A Comparative Analysis of Complex Organization.* New York: The Free Press.

Form, W. H., and J. Rytina (1969), "Ideological beliefs on the distribution of power in the United States." *American Sociological Review*, 34:19–31.

Free, L. A., and H. Cantril (1967), *The Political Beliefs of Americans.* New Brunswick: Rutgers University Press.

Friedenberg, E. (1963), *Coming of Age in America.* New York: Random House.

Giddens, A. (1968), " 'Power' in the recent writings of Talcott Parsons." *Sociology* 2 (September):257–272.

Goldthorpe, J. H., D. Lockwood, F. Bechhofer, and S. Platt (1968a), *The Affluent Worker: Industrial Attitudes and Behaviour.* Cambridge University Press.

——— (1968b), *The Affluent Worker: Political Attitudes and Behaviour.* Cambridge University Press.

Greenstein, F. I. (1965), *Children and Politics.* New Haven: Yale University Press.

Hacker, A. (1957), "Liberal democracy and social control." *American Political Science Review*, 51:1009–1026.

Haer, J. L. (1956–57), "Social stratification in relation to attitude toward sources of power in a community." *Social Forces*, 35:137–142.

Henry, J. (1965), "Attitude organization in elementary school classrooms." Pp. 215–233 in G. D. Spindler (ed.), *Education and Culture.* New York: Holt, Rinehart and Winston.

Hess, R. D. (1963), "The socialization of attitudes toward political authority: Some cross national comparisons." *International Social Science Journal*, 15:542–559.

Hess, R. D., and D. Easton (1960), "The child's image of the president." *Public Opinion Quarterly*, 24:632–644.

Hess, R. D., and V. C. Shipman (1965), "Early experience and the socialization of cognitive modes in children." *Child Development*, 36:869–886.

Hess, R. D., and J. V. Torney (1967), *The Development of Political Attitudes in Children.* Chicago: Aldine.

Himmelweit, H., A. H. Halsey, and A. N. Oppenheim (1952), "The views of adolescents on some aspects of the Social class structure." *British Journal of Sociology*, 3:148–172.

Key, V. O. Jr. (1965), *Public Opinion and American Democracy.* New York: Knopf.

Kornhauser, A. W., A. L. Sheppard, and A. J. Mayer (1956), *When Labor Votes.* New York: University Books.

Kornhauser, W. (1965), *The Mental Health of the Industrial Worker.* New York: John Wiley.

Leggett, J. C. (1964), "Economic insecurity and working-class consciousness." *American Sociological Review*, 29:226–234.

Lenski, G. (1963), *The Religious Factor.* New York: Anchor Books.

Lewis, L. S. (1964–65), "Class consciousness and the salience of class." *Sociology and Social Research*, 49:173–182.

Lipset, S. M. (1964), *First New Nation.* London: Heinemann.

Lipsitz, L. (1964), "Work life and political attitudes: A study of manual workers." *American Political Science Review*, 58:951–962.

Litt, E. (1963), "Civic education, community norms and political indoctrination." *American Sociological Review*, 28:69–75.

Manis, J. G., and B. N. Meltzer (1954), "Attitudes of textile workers to class structure." *American Journal of Sociology* 60:30–35.

Marcuse, H. (1964), *One-Dimensional Man.* London: Routledge and Kegan Paul.

McClosky, H. (1964), "Consensus and ideology in American politics." *American Political Science Review,* 58:361–382.

McKenzie, R., and A. Silver (1968), *Angels in Marble: Working-class Conservatives in Urban England.* London: Heinemann.

Mercer, D. E., and D. T. Weir (1969), "Orientations to work among white collar workers." Pp. 112–145 in Social Science Research Council (eds.), Social Stratification and Industrial Relations. Cambridge: Social Science Research Council. Revised version of paper forthcoming in John H. Goldthorpe and Michael Mann (eds.), Social Stratification and Industrial Relations. Cambridge University Press.

Miliband, R. (1961), *Parliamentary Socialism.* London: Allen and Unwin.

Mizruchi, E. H. (1964), *Success and Opportunity.* New York: The Free Press.

Nordlinger, E. A. (1967), *The Working Class Tories.* London: MacGibbon and Kee.

Ossowski, S. (1963), *Class Structure in the Social Consciousness.* London: Routledge and Kegan Paul.

Owst, G. R. (1961), *Literature and Pulpit and Medieval England.* Oxford: Blackwell.

Parkin, F. (1967), "Working class conservatives: A theory of political deviance." *British Journal of Sociology,* 18:278–290.

Parsons, T. (1951), *The Social System.* London: Routledge and Kegan Paul.

Prothro, J. W., and C. W. Grigg (1960), "Fundamental principles of democracy: Bases of Agreement and Disagreement." *Journal of Politics,* 22:276–294.

Rose, R. (1965), *Politics in England.* London: Faber.

————— (1969), *Studies in British Politics.* London: Macmillan, 2nd Edition.

Rosen, B. C. (1967), "Family structure and value transmission." Pp. 86–96 in R. J. Havighurst et al. (eds.), *Society and Education.* Boston: Allyn and Bacon.

Scanzoni, J. (1967), "Socialization, n achievement and achievement values." *American Sociological Review,* 32:449–456.

Selznick, G. J., and S. Steinberg (1969), "Social class, ideology, and voting preference." Pp. 216–226 in C. S. Heller (ed.), *Structured Social Inequality.* New York: Macmillan.

Sigel, R. (1965), "Assumptions about the learning of political values." *Annals of the American Academy of Political and Social Science,* 361:1–9.

Stephenson, R. M. (1958), "Stratification, education and occupational orientation." *British Journal of Sociology,* 5:42–52.

Sykes, A. J. M. (1965), "Some differences in the attitudes of clerical and of manual workers." *Sociological Review,* 13:297–310.

Thompson, W. E., and J. E. Horton (1960), "Political alienation as a force in political action," *Social Forces,* 38:190–195.

Turner, R. (1953–54), "Value conflict in social disorganization." *Sociology and Social Research,* 38:301–308.

————— (1964), *The Social Context of Ambition.* San Francisco: Chandler.

Van den Berghe, P. L. (1963), "Dialectic and functionalism: Toward a theoretical synthesis." *American Sociological Review,* 28:695–705.

Veness, T. (1962), *School Leavers: Their Aspirations and Expectations.* London: Methuen.

Zeigler, H. (1967), *The Political Life of American Teachers.* Englewood Cliffs, N.J.: Prentice-Hall.

John McDermott

CAMPUS MISSIONARIES:
THE LAYING ON OF CULTURE

I

About a year ago I accepted an invitation to speak "against the war," at, let's call it, the University of Dexter. It is located in the city of that name, one of the major manufacturing towns of the Midwestern industrial belt. Since Dexter is somewhat off the main circuit for anti-war speech-making, I read up on the university and the town, and what I found made me look forward to my visit.

The university tended to draw most of its students from the town itself. They came heavily from working-class families and were often the first in their families to attend college. Frequently English was not the only language spoken at home. More significant was the fact that the city itself had at one time considerable fame for working-class militancy. One of the great early strikes of the depression was fought in Dexter, and the issue was not settled in the workers' favor until they had fought the National Guard to a draw in pitched street battles. Before that the city had been a center of Socialist Party activity, and still earlier, a stronghold of IWW sentiment. Thus I looked forward to my visit as an opportunity to talk to the kind of students seldom reached by Movement speakers.

It wasn't. Attendance at the well-publicized meeting was spotty; those who came tended to be about evenly divided between faculty and graduate students, almost all of whom were from outside the state. And there were no students at the party to which I was taken later in the evening, though they had helped plan the meeting, for student segregation is the campus rule at Dexter, no less within the Movement than outside it. Perhaps it was that or perhaps my disappointment at the absence of "normal" students at the evening's meeting; anyhow, I deliberately forced the party to become a meeting. It had taken no great powers of observation to note that the anti-war movement at Dexter, and, by extension, its Left, was largely a preserve of the faculty and some fellow-traveling graduate students, and I was interested to discover why that was so. In particular, I wanted to explore the role these teachers had adopted to their "normal" students and to examine with them the contradiction between that professional role and their wider political

Reprinted, with deletions, from John McDermott, "Campus Missionaries: The Laying On of Culture," *The Nation*, no. 208 (March 10, 1969), pp. 296–301, by permission of *The Nation*. John McDermott teaches at the State University of New York at Old Westbury and is the author of numerous articles on the Vietnam war. He is a founder of the New University Conference and former editor of *Viet-Report*.

aspirations. I have taught in several universities, I've suffered the same contradiction and was unable to overcome it.

The most prominent feature of the discussion which followed, and of all the subsequent ones I've started on the same subject in similar situations, was that the faculty, to a man, still aspired to teach in elite schools. Dexter, after all, is what is popularly known as a "cow" college. A state school, it gets those students who, for lack of skill or money or interest, don't go to the main state university and couldn't "make" the liberal arts colleges in the area, even if they wanted to. Its students are very much vocationally oriented and still tied to their families. Most of them live at home.

Dexter is frequently under nuisance attack by some right-wing faction or other. It pays rather badly and is not in an attractive metropolitan area. Its library is inferior, it provides little research money, and the teaching loads are heavy. The administration is fusty and conservative, as is much of the faculty.

My faculty friends, obviously talented men and women, had not reconciled themselves to this exile. They depreciated the region, the town, the university and, especially, the students, even the graduate students. Loyalty and affection they reserved for the graduate schools from which they had come, and they reflected this feeling in their teaching and counseling by relating only to that one student in a hundred who might go on to one of those prestigious graduate schools. Those were the students who shared with them the culture of books and civility—and scorn for Dexter; who might by their success at a "good" graduate school justify the faculty's exile in Dexter.

Of course they didn't put it that way, and neither did I when I taught in similar places. They saw themselves as embattled missionaries to the culturally Philistine. They worked hard and creatively with the students who merited hope. As for the others, these men and women, in spite of their expressed scorn, nourished a vision, hesitantly expressed, of a society in which no student would be oppressed by cultural bondage to ignorance, vocationalism, anti-intellectualism and provincialism. In fact, that attitude and hope gave rise to and was expressed in their left-wing politics.

The guests at the party were woefully ignorant of the background of their "normal" students. They were vaguely aware that most of them came from working-class families, though what that might mean aside from greater resistance to formal education they had no idea. They had no knowledge either of Dexter's militant labor traditions. This was sad, for it penalized the faculty in a number of ways. To cite an apparently trivial instance, most of the faculty present were concerned over attacks made on the university by the right wingers in town. Respect for free speech and expression had an important place in their scale of values, and they tried to convey it to their classes, using all the familiar academic examples, from HUAC witch hunting and Joe McCarthy, to Stuart Mill, Milton and Sophocles.

Yet that they might relate the principle of free expression to the problems of Wobbly agitators in the 1910s or of CIO organizers in the 1930s (or of white-collar workers in the 1970s)—in short, relate it to the actual cultural history (or future) of their own students—never occurred to them. Instead, they were put off when the students responded to the alien and seemingly irrelevant world of HUAC and Milton and academic freedom with either passive unconcern or active hostility.

I believe this example successfully characterizes how the great majority of faculty behave in schools like Dexter, including, especially, the left wing of the faculty. Socialized like all their fellows into a rigid professional role by their university, graduate school and early professional experiences, they have neither the information nor the inclination to break out of that role and relate openly and positively to the majority of their students who cannot accept the culture of the university world as their own.

University professors as a group seem exceptionally uncritical of the limited value—and values—of a university education and the acculturation it represents. In their view, a student who is really open to his classroom and other cultural experiences at the university will, as a rule, turn out to be more sophisticated, more interested in good literature, more sensitive morally than one who is less open or who has not had the benefit of college. The student will also be free of the more provincial ties of home, home town, region and class. In short, most academics take it as an article of faith that a student benefits by exchanging his own culture for that of the university. It is by far the most common campus prejudice.

And it would be harmless enough if it were limited in its sanction to those students who allow their university education to "take," who do well at university work and will go on to graduate school and then to a place within the university world or, perhaps, into some other related profession. University attitudes and values are appropriate to that world. But what about the others, the cultural rednecks, the "normal" boy and girl at a place like Dexter? Do they really profit from acquiring the attitudes, values, life style, and so forth of the peculiar culture whose institutional base is the university? One way of attacking this question is to ask to what extent those values, attitudes and life style may be usefully transferred to other institutional settings —to little towns and big cities, to industrial or agricultural life, to life in a corporation or in government.

That was about as far as we went at that party a year ago. We agreed that we were part of a university system which was actively engaged at its Dexters in destroying whatever indigenous culture might remain among the American working class. We recognized that, consciously or not, we had assumed an invidious clerical relationship to our student laity. Like medieval priests or missionaries to the heathen, we dispensed a culture to all our students, despite the fact that a scant few could participate in it. For the others, the language of that culture, like Latin to the colloquial, was grasped largely in rote phrases, its symbols and doctrines recognized but only dimly understood. To the extent that this majority of students acquired the external trappings of the university, they seemed both culturally pacified and made culturally passive. Pacified because they were acculturated away from their own historical values and traditions; passive because they could at best be spectators of a culture whose home remained an alien institution.

The Maintenance of Capitalist Order

II

In the year that has passed since my visit to Dexter my views of the relationship of general culture to political culture have very much developed under the influence of Edward Thompson's *The Making of the English Working Class.* I find particularly persuasive and suggestive Thompson's demonstration of how certain aspects of the general culture of the English working class, over a period of time and under the stress of events, came to support a specifically political culture—that is, to enlarge its capacity to define its social interests and to struggle successfully in their behalf. I shall cite several instances of this, for I want later to use them to illuminate the problem at Dexter from a new and, I think, hopeful standpoint.

Thompson shows that the movement into the factories in England of the late 18 and early 19th centuries was made up of two distinct streams. One was the movement of poor, dispossessed rural persons to the city and the factory in search of opportunity; the other of highly skilled, often literate craftsmen being pushed down the social and economic ladder by the new forces of industrialism and technology. The former, abruptly torn from their rural poverty, had some reason to view the change as an improvement. The cultural shock of the transition, the traditional passivity to authority, the stimulus of urban life, and the novelty of cash wages might easily have disguised for a time the exploitative nature of their place in the new factory system. The urban craftsmen, however, having a sense of their own skill and worth, with still lively guild traditions, and a strong sense of declining status and economic position, were most unlikely to think of the factory experience as a road to opportunity. They knew it for the oppression it really was. It was the meeting of these two groups that proved so creative for the future of the working-class movement. The skilled printers, weavers and mechanics recognized that their lot was cast with the unskilled rural migrants, and they became a creative element among the larger mass. Their literacy, their talent for organization, their family and folk memories that working people had once lived secure in their homes, livelihoods and craftsmanship, were transferred over the years to the mass of working people. But they were transferred with a radical difference. By contributing them to the cause of the entire working class, what might otherwise have been merely a narrow defense of guild interests was instead universalized into a struggle for the rights of all Englishmen, a struggle for the rights of man.

Thompson also shows how important for the new working-class movement was the experience so many workers had in the Dissenting Churches. Men and women who, over the years, had learned to contend with the problems of maintaining a minister's salary, keeping up the church and parsonage, administering an active religious and social program, and organizing regional church activities were able to apply these skills to nascent working-class organizations. Of particular importance was their long experience of persecution at the hands of the Church of England. Both ministers and congregations had learned how to preserve their churches and beliefs in the face of official hostility and repression. Thus when Pitt, Burke and their successors attempted to destroy the new workingmen's organizations, these were able to go underground, preserving their organizations, maintaining their programs and extending their networks throughout the country.

Still another general cultural factor cited by Thompson as a primary support for the growing working-class movement was the belief among the English lower classes that they were "freeborn Englishmen." The phrase had no precise meaning, but it was habitually called into play to criticize or resist any arbitrary act against the populace and its organizations, any claim to special place by the upper classes, any innovation in government control over the speech, writing, travels or associations of the common people. It was a useful and eminently flexible weapon in the hands of the working-class movement against the power of the capitalists and the wiles of Edmund Burke.

What makes Thompson's work of more than antiquarian interest is the suggestive analogy it offers to situations such as that at Dexter. There is a double movement into such universities today, somewhat as there was a double movement into the factories of England two centuries ago. On the one hand, a flood of lower-class young people is moving into these universities, seeking entree into the old independent professional middle class which university attendance supposedly affords. It is necessary to add "supposedly," for passage through a non-elite university no longer qualifies one for that kind of life. The jobs for which the Dexters and the junior colleges prepare students are elementary and secondary teaching, the lower levels of social work, white-collar hire, petty management—that is, employments which were once semi-professional, but which now are being rapidly industrialized by bureaucracy, managerial science and the IBM machine. Thus the lower-class boys or girls who go to Dexter only appear to escape from the world of industry; they are really taking the first vocational step into a new kind of industrial life.

The second movement into such institutions as Dexter is of a gifted minority of educated persons, who identify with the values, accomplishments and prestige of elite professions, but are forced by the economics of academic employment to take positions they consider beneath their skills, their sense of worth and accomplishment, their lively memories of the recent past.

But here the analogy with Thompson's English working class begins to break down, for these latter specifically and pointedly refuse to make common cause with the lower-class students with whom they share daily existence. This gifted Left minority does not help the students to develop an effective and vital popular political culture. On the contrary, it often occupies the vanguard of a university culture which, as I suggested above and now wish to argue more fully, pacifies lower-class students.

III

The most obvious political characterization of university culture is that it lives by, and presents to its students, the values and attitudes appropriate to its own upper-middle-class life style—a style that is part of the older, now declining, professional middle classes. As indicated above, a university education did once promise membership in the professional classes. This meant

The Maintenance of Capitalist Order

that university graduates could ordinarily expect a life of considerable social and economic independence, some measure of personal influence in local business and political communities, significant autonomy and initiative in carrying out their daily work, and thus the possibility of enjoying the pride that follows from personal accomplishment and craftsmanship.

Could it be clearer that no such life awaits the graduates of the nation's Dexters? Today a degree from a second- or third-line institution is a passport to a life style of high consumption and of reasonable job security. But it will probably be an industrial life style, characterized by social and economic dependence on a large institution, by little or no political or social influence, and by participation in rationalized work processes wherein one must try merely "to get by and not step on anybody's toes." Consider, therefore, how the professionally oriented values of the university's culture might function in such an industrial environment. High on the scale of university values, now and in the past, stands the virtue of tolerance—not only personal tolerance in the face of new or differing ideas, attitudes and values but the belief that tolerance itself is of greater personal and social value than the substance of almost any set of creeds. Such a value was useful in the professional worlds of the past, for it would normally help diminish conflict in a middle class made up of highly autonomous individuals. And in elite circles even today it diminishes the weight assigned to ideological differences and helps to harmonize the social and political relations of our pluralistic, semi-autonomous industrial, educational, government and other managers. It carries the advantage, too, that it opens managers to the merits of technological and organizational novelty in a political economy strongly oriented to such innovations.

But how does this belief function for the young men and women of Dexter, who will normally occupy the lower and middle levels of great institutional bureaucracies, and who may have reason to resist those very same innovations: speed-up, compulsory overtime, more and more alienating work processes, forced transfer to another city or region, institutional propaganda, Muzak and the other normal tyrannies of personnel managers? Is it a value that helps them to initiate or continue those collective struggles which are necessary to defend or enhance their interests; or does it rob them of the moral and ideological assurance which must support the beliefs of people who challenge the social legitimacy and retributive power of authority?

A second political aspect of university culture is its almost uniform hostility to the institutions of local and community life. Many churches, fraternities, veterans' associations, councils and boards upon which local and community life in America is built are havens of the narrowest sorts of provincialism, racism, intellectual baiting, babbittry and jingoism. For these reasons, and for reasons having to do with the demands of the national economy for college-trained persons, the tendency of university experience is to propel the young away from local and community life and toward national life and its institutions. A result of the university's liberalism, cosmopolitanism and technologism, this tendency is supported by the national culture, by the students themselves, and by their parents.

But it should be combated by those, like my friends at Dexter, who are interested in building mass resistance to the prevailing currents of American life. A young person from Dexter, unless extraordinarily gifted or fortunate, has almost no means of gaining influence in national politics. And to the extent that university culture directs great masses of lower- and lower-middle-class young people into the institutions of national rather than local and community life, it assists in disenfranchising them from political influence. Of course, the conventional representatives of university culture argue that the decline of local politics and local institutions is inevitable, given the institutional needs of 20th-century industry and government, the gradual nationalization of American life, and the march of technology—i.e., liberalism, cosmopolitanism and technologism. But we should begin to question whether this inevitability amounts to more than advantageous prejudice. For the kind of society which these university spokesmen describe as inevitable appears to be coincidentally one in which the Ph.D. takes its place with property and birth as a means to political influence and social status.

Similarly, the ignorance, racism and the like which characterize so much of local life should not put us off. Given the preoccupation of the Left, over the past epoch, with national rather than local concerns and institutions, it is not surprising that local America has become a playpen of unchallenged right-wing attitudes, persons and organizations. Of course, one could not expect, even under the best conditions, that the life style of local America will rival the faculty club in gentility, civility, humanist learning and other caricatures of university life. But that is not its test, any more than the theological elegance of the Dissenting Churches was the test of their usefulness to a struggling movement of ordinary Englishmen. Those who are today concerned about a different kind of economic barbarism and a similar kind of world-wide crusade should draw the appropriate lessons.

A third political aspect of university culture is its latent hostility to two of the more valuable and humane realities in current popular culture. One cannot move around this country without being impressed by its egalitarianism, that is the depth and vitality of the ordinary American's feeling that he is as good as the next fellow. And the other reality so important in our popular culture is the well-nigh universal belief among our people that they possess an extraordinary range and variety of substantive rights. Like the belief in "the freeborn Englishmen," the belief in substantive rights is often vague and contradictory. Nevertheless, the history of popular political movements is the history of ordinary people acting in behalf of what they believe to be their substantive rights.

It would be too much to say that the university's culture is uniformly hostile to these popular realities, for the situation is ambiguous. However, it is not difficult to identify important hostile tendencies. Thus in contrast to the normal American acceptance of the principle of equality, the professoriat strongly values formalized differences of age, academic rank, scholarly reputation and, it may even be, accomplishment. The effect of this sort of deference is somewhat difficult to gauge and it may be tendentious on my part to believe that it influences student attitudes on legitimacy, authority and equality. Perhaps the issue is instead that university men and women, by failing to provide a living example of egalitarian relationships, merely fail to

The Maintenance of Capitalist Order

make common cause with the American people in their resistance to the hierarchic tendencies implicit in the social and economic system.

A more secure case can be made against the disposition in the university world to identify right not with substantive but with procedural matters. Peter Gay expressed this position in the Summer 1968 issue of *Partisan Review*: ". . . democracy is essentially procedural and what matters is not so much (important though it may be) what a given policy is as how it is arrived at. . . ." Persons as fortunately placed as Professor Gay, whose substantive rights are well established in easily available procedures, have an understandable tendency to overlook the fact that, for example, tenure, sabbaticals, choice of hours, and freedom of expression on the job—are virtually unknown outside the academic world. Obviously there are other, important and thorny issues here as well. Without going into them at any length, note that the test of Professor Gay's remark is its fidelity to historical fact. From that point of view, it tends to obscure the fact that the great libertarian and democratic turning point in postwar American political history, a turning point with great promise still, came not from the narrow defense of procedural rights by academic and other liberals against Joe McCarthy in the 1950s but from the assertion of substantive rights in the 1960s by mass movements of students, blacks, professors and ordinary Americans.

The students at Dexter, and a great part of their countrymen, rightly view the liberal and academic preference for procedural right as a defense of privileges which they themselves are denied. Many view the principle of academic freedom, for example, as they view some of the laws of property. It is a tricky device which enables professors to do things, like criticize the dean or the country, for which ordinary people can be fired; just as the law of property is a tricky device which enables installment houses and loan companies to do things for which ordinary people can be sent to jail. The goal is not to do away with academic freedom, or any other hard-won libertarian procedure. A better approach would be to shape a university culture which would help to extend Professor Gay's tenure, sabbaticals, and freedom of expression on the job to everyone, on campus and off.

The existence of hostile tendencies toward egalitarianism and the primacy of substantive right is very much related to still a fourth political aspect of university culture. Even though the university is the home and source of much of the libertarian ideology within our culture, it is often the source of authoritarian ideology as well. I have two cases in mind. The first has to do with the extensive commitment to technologism found among many faculty members. A considerable body of university opinion believes with Zbigniew Brzezinski that the promises of modern technology demand for their social realization a society characterized by "equal opportunity for all but . . . special opportunity for the singularly talented few." The evasiveness of the formula should not be allowed to obscure the authoritarian social and political processes which are envisioned and justified by it—processes today best exemplified in the area of national security, where the equal voting opportunities of all are nullified by the special bureaucratic opportunities open to a singularly talented few. The second of the university's authoritarian ideologies I call clericism. To borrow from Brzezinski's formula, it is the claim to "equal cultural rights for all, but special cultural authority for a singularly scholarly few." I refer to the still widespread (but declining) academic belief that, whatever else culture may include, it also includes the Western Heritage, the Western Tradition, the Literary Tradition, the traditions of reason and civility, etc., and that these are most fully embodied in the profession of academe and the written treasures of which academe is priestly custodian and inspired interpreter.

This principle underlies faculty sovereignty over curricular matters, justifies any and every required course, oppresses first-year graduate students, and received its most prosaic formulation in the observation by Columbia's vice dean of the graduate facilities that ". . . whether students vote 'yes' or 'no' on an issue is like telling me they like strawberries." Clericism and technologism have their good points; no one wishes seriously to derogate either the social or the moral value of good scholarship or competent technology. But as principles under which to organize cultural or political life they are distinctly hostile to the interests of great numbers of non-elite students, the social classes from which they are drawn, and especially the social classes they will constitute when they leave the university. For clericism and technologism, like the doctrines of apostolic succession and of property which they tend to replace, transpose major areas of social concern from the purview of all to the treasure house of the few. Culture, no less than politics, is a critical factor in the nature of social organization; in the distribution of power, reward and status; in the infliction of powerlessness, oppression and despair. This is becoming increasingly understood with regard to politics, where ten years of war, urban decay and increasing social chaos seem to have been the fruit of the same decade's obeisance to technology's claims. But I am not persuaded that clericist depredations on culture are similarly recognized.

As I think was made clear at the start of this essay, the faculty at Dexter did not feel called upon to know the specific cultural history and experiences of the students they taught. Neither they nor anyone in the academic profession consider it their task to use their own superior symbolic gifts and wider historical culture of their students, to clarify its ambiguities, to criticize it, purging it of its moral (not geographical) provincialism, and thus to assist the students to develop a culture which is at once personally ennobling and politically self-conscious. On the contrary, at Dexter and elsewhere the faculty assume that it is their duty to replace the students' actual culture with an alien culture. Missionaries from these graduate schools, like clergy from colonial empires everywhere and in every time, feel confident that what they bring is good for the natives and will improve them in the long run. In culture, as elsewhere, this is manifestly not so.

Consider the matter of historical traditions. No acculturation worth the name should be permitted to block the transmission of Dexter's militant working-class traditions. Even granting, as is probably the case, that only a small minority of the Dexter students are children of depression workers or the earlier Wobblies, to assist, even if only negatively, in destroying these traditions is to minimize for most of the students the opportunity to discover

The Maintenance of Capitalist Order

the reasons for their attitudes on a score of moral and social questions, the reality of their social lives, and the possibility of rebuilding a more humane culture in Dexter for their own advantage. White intelligentsia recognize this danger when they peer across cultural lines at blacks or Vietnamese; why are they so blinded by the class lines of their own society? It should come as no surprise, therefore, that the anti-intellectualism of the students is often as deep and as bitter as the hatred exhibited by other colonial peoples toward foreigners and their works.

A university culture which related positively and creatively to the traditions and history of the working classes, blue collar and white collar, would find allies not only among the hippies and the leftists of Smith and Williams but from the squares of Dexter as well.

What is particularly disturbing about cultural pacification in the university is that it is not entirely an accidental phenomenon. At least since Herbert Croly's *Promise of American Life* (1909), America's dominant historians have been strongly nationalist, more interested in discovering and celebrating the American essence or character, the national mainstream, consensus or moral epic, or the peculiar quality of our national integration, than in emphasizing its divisions, especially those based on class. It has often crossed my mind that when liberal historians two decades hence write the chronicle of the Southern freedom movement of the early 1960s or of the anti-Vietnamese War movement of today, they will find imaginative and persuasive reasons to show that the first was really part of the New Frontier and the second of the Great Society. It was thus that their predecessors have managed to reduce the richness and variety of popular revolt in the 1930s to the bureaucratic dimensions of a Washington-based "New Deal."

Fortunately, some of the younger historians, such as Staughton Lynd and Jesse Lemisch, have begun to undermine the epic poetry of the Crolyites by reviving interest in the history of popular insurgency in America. Thus they have created the possibility that at least at some universities young people will be reacquainted with the real diversity and conflict of their past. More than that, and without exaggerating its importance or extent, this new scholarship provides a point of departure for a fundamentally different university culture than the one I have been describing.

IV

Faced with the vast social diversity of America and in opposition to the variety and strength of its Populist traditions, the thrust of university culture is to pacify its working-class "natives" and thus, I believe, to help preclude any fundamental change in national politics and priorities. Because of the surge of rebellion on campus since last spring, it is likely that this is understood better now among faculty than it was at the time I visited Dexter. But many university men and women, comparing the university's cultural values to those of industry, the mass media and the military, or to the restless hostility of lower- and working-class America, remain partisans and priests of academe, convinced that for all its faults it is, at least minimally, a humane alternative to its rivals. . . .

Stuart Ewen

ADVERTISING:
SELLING THE SYSTEM

Mass reproduction is aided especially by the reproduction of masses. . . .
the masses are brought face to face with themselves.—Walter Benjamin

Proletarianization, meaning that process by which human life is implicated in the universe of bourgeois production, has always been a cultural
"offering." Karl Marx initiated his argument for a critique of culture from the
conceptual touchstone of proletarianization; as the mode of culture itself,
the process of proletarianization stood at the heart of his understanding of
modern history. Marx argued further, in pursuit of his radical understanding,
that a critique of culture was inextricably bound up in the revolutionary
perception of civil society. Concomitant with any "stage of development of
[the] material powers of production," Marx wrote in his "Preface to a
Critique of Political Economy," specific and corresponding social formations
and relations of production would arise. Thus it would appear that to focus
historical attention on the study of *social production*—that is, on the specific
means and consequences of the process of proletarianization (the trans-
valuation of "use-value" into "exchange value")—could hardly qualify as a
methodological innovation, since Marx long ago both located and formulated
its primacy. Yet few contemporary studies of emerging industrial culture
deal seriously with the problem of perception as a social formation; a notable
exception is E. P. Thompson's brilliant social history of the clock, *"Time,
Work-discipline, and Industrial Capitalism,"*[1] which views the emergence of
industrial capitalism as a world-historic shock that beyond being a significant
change in the "material powers of production," required its participants to
assume a critically altered perception of time—of reality. Thompson concludes his essay with the instructive though implicit admonition that "there is
no such thing as economic growth which is not, at the same time, growth or
change of a culture; the growth of social consciousness."

The emergence of bourgeois social production meant the creation of a
social life style over and above a work style prescribed by the conditions of
the job. While the history of nineteenth-century social production and

Reprinted, with deletions and revisions, from Stuart Ewen, "Advertising as Social
Production," *Radical America*, vol. 3 (May–June 1969), pp. 42–56, reprinted by per-
mission of *Radical America* and the author. Stuart Ewen is a graduate student in
history at the State University of New York at Albany and has received his mas-
ter's degree from the University of Rochester. He is a former associate editor of
Radical America and field secretary for the Student Non-Violent Coordinating
Committee (SNCC). He has coedited *Social Textures of Western Civilization: The
Lower Depths* and written numerous articles for the underground press.

[1] E. P. Thompson, "Time, Work-discipline, and Industrial Capitalism." *Past &
Present*, No. 38 (December, 1967).

proletarianization seems largely informed by the boundaries of work, it should be viewed more radically as informed by that *social style*. Corresponding to a definite, and in our terms primitive, arrangement of the material forces of production, the social style seems precluded by the work style only when one fails to view the nature of work as exigent to a specific level of social production. To view proletarianization in early industrial America solely as the creation of "workers" in the most colloquial sense (i.e., people to work in factories) ignores the social mode of the system. In short, the most significant aspect of capital was that it historically defined the limitations of all social bonds within its expanding arena of influence. In the early period of accumulation, its social definition is perhaps most clearly located in the factory relations between capitalist and worker, yet to isolate the work style as the sole mode of proletarianization in the nineteenth century is as deceptive as the work of bourgeois "culture critics"; work which takes issue with the character of consumption culture, branding its anomalous, while accepting the "positive" integrity of our social institutions and the tenets of our political economy. Both the conceptual isolation of the work style and the writings of bourgeois culture critics extricate particular aspects of social capitalism from their *totality*.

Contemporary proletarianization extends far beyond the creation of workers to man the productive machinery of industry. Although the proletarianization of nineteenth century capitalism was—as it continued to be—a process of habituation to a *social style*, its limits were narrower and its focus less specific than the proletarianization of contemporary capitalism. The nature of the productive machinery and its capacity to produce (and have its products consumed) meant a very privatized and work oriented proletarianization—a privatized level of social production. "Worker" indicated "wheelhorse." The number of hours spent on the job; the introduction of a "clock-time" oriented work day; the imposition of a routinized moderation and thrift that was bent on making an essentially non-industrial work force "socially responsible"; and the ideological *embourgeoisment* of religious and other cultural institutions were the often self-conscious attempts on the part of an industrial bourgeoisie to educate people to production. These aspects of industrial life must be seen as attempts not to create fourteen hour-per-day workers, but proletarian men and women.

The development of a more highly technologized capitalism promised to disengage vast numbers of "wheelhorse" proletarians from their previous social role. In the process of producing vast quantities—"mass" numbers—of goods for consumption, it necessarily altered the character, although not the substance of their proletarianization. *Character* and *substance* have often been confused and fused in the description of the "beneficial" *choices, freedoms, leisures,* and *affluence* that have been "attained" by the modern industrial worker. Such "gains" are generally regarded as having elevated the contemporary "mass" above its previous proletarian status.

Yet the maintenance of the notion "mass" should give pause to such sanguinity. *Choice, freedom, leisure,* and *affluence* can not be viewed as transhistoric absolutes in the context of corporate capitalism, but rather as the *historic* demarcations of the elements of *proletariat*—those aspects of *social style* which commit the proletariat to, rather than extricate it from, serving the continual fiscal needs of bourgeois society. An appraisal of the quality and direction of *choice* reveals its link of commitment to the counter-human consumer market. Apparent disengagement from proletarian life represents its opposite: a further involvement in that life. *That which appears to be is not.*

Consumption, likewise, is not what it appears to be. Though generally considered (and ideologically defined) as increasingly expanding *time off from production,* leisure time consumption is rather a modern social-economic formation that, like factory discipline, commits our *TIME,* our LIVES, to the maintenance of the ascendant bourgeois class. Sebastian de Grazia pointed out the fatal contradictions of our leisure and the substance of (alienated and deferred) pleasure when he cryptically noted that "consumption gobbles time up alive."[2]

During the 1920's the creation of an advanced advertising bureaucracy was an attempt to put culture to more efficient work for capitalism. While in the minds of both capital and labor, early industrial proletarianization was closely associated with the productive plant and its disciplines, the intensified use of cultural apparati (media) in the proletarianizing process tended to obfuscate that association. While the ad industry was bureaucratically linked to the industrial machinery, its products were capitalistic *art forms* which publicly ignored any bourgeois complicity except insofar as their message implored people to consume. The advertising industry's ability to perform such an obfuscation was deliberate and historical; historical in that advanced technological art forms were increasingly conducive to camouflaging their source. Walter Benjamin has noted that as technologically reproduced art is designed for prolific exhibition, the notion of authenticity—the sense of there being *an original*—is lost.[3] The essential element in each work of mechanically reproduced art is its immediacy, its every showing, rather than its ability to be located absolutely "in time and space." The consumer, confronted with a commercial advertisement, views but an off print, not the economic-cultural apparatus from which it is generated and his own life in relation to that apparatus. As such, he has only his own critical abilities with which to draw connections between "art" and its source. As the social style of technological corporatism, and art forms themselves, represent a continual assault on that ability to critique—attempting, as Herbert Marcuse would have it, to absorb all opposition—that critical ability itself may be domesticated; the "connection" between art and source reduced to a pacified epigram of modern life.

It was this sense of immediacy, the apparent lack of source, which gave advertising its particular value as an efficient productive tool. Advertising was a way of projecting the necessitated values and activities of the system which broke from the traditional context of proletarianization, and correlated these values and activities to an ideological notion of pleasure. The "per-

[2] Sebastian de Grazia, *Of Time, Work and Leisure* (1962), p. 211.
[3] Walter Benjamin, "The Work of Art in the Age of Mechanical Reproduction," (1936), in *Illuminations* (1968). This essay originally appeared in the *Zeitschrift fur Sozialforschung,* V. 1 (1936).

formance principle" (to borrow from Marcuse's *Eros and Civilization*) which capitalism demanded, was appealingly cloaked in the garb of the "play/pleasure principle" which capitalism denied.

It is with these concepts in mind that the following is presented.

I

In 1910, Henry Ford instituted the "line production system" for "maximum production economy" in his Highland Park (Mich.) plant.[4] The innovation, though in many ways unsophisticated, and hardly educated as to its own implications, was the beginning of a momentous transformation in America's capacity to produce. In quantitative terms, the change was staggering. On the 1910 line, the time required to assemble a chassis was twelve hours and twenty-eight minutes. "By spring of 1914, the Highland Park plant was turning out over 1000 vehicles a day, and the average labor time for assembling a chassis had dropped to one hour and thirty-three minutes."[5]

Mass production was a way of making production more economical. Through his use of the assembly line, Ford was able to utilize "expensive, single-purpose" machinery, along with quickly trained, "single-purpose" workmen to make a single-model, inexpensive automobile at a rate which, with increasing sophistication, continued to dwarf not only the production levels of pre-massified industry, but the output of less refined mass production systems.[6]

By the 1920's, interest in and employment of the industrial potential of mass production extended far beyond the automobile industry. In recognition of such industrial developments, the United States Special Census of 1921 and 1923 offered a study of productive capacity[7] which was one of the first general discussions of its kind.[8] Consumer goods manufacturers increasingly recognized that mass production and mass distribution were "necessary" steps toward survival in a competitive market. Edward Filene, of the Boston department store family, and a businessman founder of the consumer union movement, recognized and articulated the competitive compulsion of mass production; competition, said Filene, ". . . will compel us to Fordize American business and industry."[9]

And yet, what Filene and others meant by "Fordizing" American industry transcended the myopic vision of Henry Ford. While Ford stubbornly

[4] Alfred Dupont Chandler, *Giant Enterprise* (1964), p. 29. Chandler is citing the "Federal Trade Commission Report on the Motor Vehicle Industry."

[5] Chandler, p. 26.

[6] ". . . during a period of eighteen years commencing in 1908, Ford Motor Company manufactured and offered for sale only one basic model of passenger automobile . . . This was the (black) Model T." See Chandler, pp. 27, 37.

[7] Harold Loeb, *National Survey of Potential Product Capacity* (1935), p. 3.

[8] This may be seen as a response to a combination of things. Aside from the fact of proliferating mass production methods, the 1921 depression/"buyers' strike" served as an impetus to this study.

[9] Edward A. Filene, *The Way Out* (1925), p. 93.

held to the notion that ". . . the work and the work *alone* controls us,"[10] others in the automobile industry,[11] and (for our purposes) more importantly, ideologues of mass industry outside of the auto industry, viewed the strategy of production in broad social terms. Before mass production, industries had produced for a limited consumer market. With a burgeoning capacity to produce, industry promised to become distended in comparison to traditional non-proletarian markets and conventional buying habits. While traditional markets had been viewed as a distinct and dependable receptacle for consumer goods, "scientific" production promised to make the conventional notion of "consumer" anachronistic.[12]

The mechanism of mass production could not function unless markets became more dynamic, growing horizontally (nationally), vertically (into social classes not previously among the consumers), and ideologically. "Ideological" growth refers to the needs of a mass industrial capitalism to produce, change, or habituate men into responding to the demands of the productive machinery. The corollary to a freely growing system of goods production was a "systematic, nationwide plan to endow the masses with more buying power," a freely growing system of consumer production.[13] The modern mass producer could not depend upon an elite market to respond to his productive capacity. From a dependence upon local markets or localized markets scattered nationally,[14] the manufacturer was forced to "count on the whole United States if he [was] going to manufacture a large enough quantity of goods to reduce the cost to the point where he [could] compete with other manufacturers of the same goods,"[15] and subsequently distribute his mass produced ware more efficiently and profitably. He was required to create an ideological bridge across traditional social gaps; section, taste, need, and class, which could congeal prejudices in his favor.

Considering the quantitative possibilities of mass production, the question of "national markets" became one of qualitatively changing the nature of the American buying public. In response to the exigencies of the productive system of the twentieth century excessiveness replaced thrift as a social

[10] Chandler, p. 143.
[11] Noteably Alfred P. Sloan of General Motors. Sloan saw productive strategy in broad social terms. His biography, *My Life With General Motors*, gives an account of these early developments.
[12] Loeb, p. xv. In regard to "the capacity of the nation to produce goods and services. If full advantage were taken of existing resources, man power, and knowledge . . . every new invention, every improved method, every advance in management technique, will increase the final quantitative estimate." Such a question would be answered by "a running inventory of our approach to perfection rather than a research into existing capacity as determined by production." The survey considered such a potential too open-ended to effect meaningful speculation.
[13] Edward A. Filene, "The Consumer's Dollar," *John Day Pamphlets* 41 (1934), p. 13.
[14] *Printers' Ink* (hereafter, *P.I.*) vol. 124, no. 12, p. 180. As the trade journal for the ad industry dating back into the 19th century, *Printers' Ink* is an invaluable source for any research in this field.
[15] Ernest Elmo Calkins, *Business, the Civilizer* (1928), p. 10.

The Maintenance of Capitalist Order

value. It became imperative to invest the laborer with a financial power and a psychic desire to consume.

By the end of the depression of 1921, "productive machinery was so effective that even more so than before much greater markets were absolutely necessary than those provided by the existing public buying power."[16] As the question of expanding old and creating new markets became a function in the massification of industry, foresighted businessmen began to see themselves as social producers. It was a necessity for them to organize their businesses not merely around the production of goods, but around the creation of a buying public, men and markets correlative to such goods production. "The changes that we shall be obliged to make in production," noted Filene, "will lead to pretty thorough overhauling of our machinery and methods of distribution, and, in the end, both the quantity and quality of consumption will be dictated by them."[17] As the "twentieth-century industrialist realized to a greater extent than did his predecessors, that he must understand the living world contained by his factory,"[18] so too did he realize that he must understand, and manipulate, as part of his productive apparatus, the total world occupied by his workers. The necessity to "influence human conduct," the knowledge that goods production meant social production, gave some businessmen's rhetoric a revealing idiom; they spoke of "human conduct" or the "consumer's dollar" as industrial discoveries, or as more valuable to manufacturing "than the uses of electricity or steel."[19] Within an ideal of a "scientifically" managed industry raw materials and consumers were both viewed as malleable. They both would have to be shaped by the demands of the production line, pecuniary interests, and the increasingly managerial tools of capital.

As capitalism became increasingly characterized by mass production and the subsequent need for mass distribution, traditional expedients for the real or attempted manipulation of labor were transformed. While the nineteenth-century industrialist coerced labor, both on and off the job, to be the "wheelhorse" of industry, modernizing capitalism sought to change "wheelhorse" to "worker," and "worker" to "consumer," on and off the job.[20]

To the worker on the job within modernizing industries, the movement toward mass production had severely changed the character of his labor. The modern manufacturing plant culminated a trend of industrialism which made him a decreasingly "significant" unit of production. "The man who had been the more or less creative maker of the whole of an article became the tender of a machine that made only one small part of the article."[21] The time required to teach the worker the "adept performance" of his "operation on assembly work" was a matter of a few hours.[22] This development had significant repercussions both in terms of the way in which a laborer viewed

---

[16] "The Consumer's Dollar," p. 29.
[17] The Way Out, p. 50.
[18] Loren Baritz, The Servants of Power (1960), p. 15.
[19] Whiting Williams, Mainsprings of Men (1923), p. 297.
[20] Whiting Williams, What's on the Worker's Mind (1920), p. 317.
[21] The Way Out, p. 62–3.
[22] Mainsprings of Men, p. 51.

his proletarian status, and in terms of the manufacturer's need to mass distribute the mountainous fruits of mass production. The two phenomena merged in the redefinition of that proletarian status. While mass production defined labor's work in terms of monotony, and rationalized his product to a fragment, some businessmen spoke of "economic freedom" or "industrial democracy"[23] as the blessing promised the worker by modern production methods. Yet the "freedom" and "democracy" offered by mass industry stopped short of a freedom to define the uses, or to rearrange the relationships, of production. "The industrial democracy I am discussing," Filene assured those who might fear its anti-capitalist implications, "has nothing to do with the Cubist politics of class revolution."[24] What was meant, rather, was that modern industrial production required that workers be free to "cultivate themselves" among the uncontestable fruits of the new industrial cornucopia.

The endowment of the masses with "industrial democracy" was seen as a complex and involving process. Their traditional role in capitalism had afforded them neither the cash nor the conviction to be so "democratized." It was imperative that the worker, "desire(s) a larger share in the mental and spiritual satisfactions of the property of his daily job much more than *a larger share in the management of the enterprise which furnishes that job.*"[25]

Not only was this alleged democracy designed to define the modern worker as a smoothly running unit of industrial production, but it also tended to define protest and proletarian unrest in terms of the desire to consume, making it also profitable. By protesting for the right to be better consumers, the aspirations of labor would be profitably coordinated with the aspirations of capital. Such convictions implicitly attempted to divest protest of its anti-capitalist content. Modern labor protest should have no basis in class antagonism.[26]

By the twenties, the ideological vanguard of the business community saw the need to endow the masses with what economic historian Norman Ware has called the money, commodity, and psychic wages (satisfactions), correlative and responsive to the route of industrial capitalism.[27] A major part of this endowment was the movement toward objective conditions which would

[23] *The Way Out*, p. 127.

[24] *Ibid.*, p. 137.

[25] *Mainsprings of Men*, p. 127.

[26] By the 1920's, wide-spread elements of the union movement had accepted such an ideology. Among others, William English Walling of the Labor Progressives, dissolved the class struggle in one fell swoop. Almost paraphrasing the ideologues of scientifically planned capitalism, he felt that "to bring labor to the maximum productivity, the American labor movement believes, requires new organization and policies in the administration of industry." Walling, *American Labor and American Democracy* (1926), p. 233.

Walling spoke of *labor* and *consumer* as interrelated aspects of the total life of the American worker. His concern for consumer rights reflected the ideology of progressive capital no less than did the writings of Edward Filene, who although he had one foot in the 'consumer category,' placed his other on the side of financial power rather than in the monotony of factory life.

[27] Norman Ware, *Labor in Modern Industrial Society* (1935), p. 88.

The Maintenance of Capitalist Order

make mass consumption feasible: higher wages and shorter hours. Giving official credence to such visions, Herbert Hoover noted that "High wages [are the] very essence of great production."[28] In 1923, Julius Barnes, president of the U.S. Chamber of Commerce, spoke of the need to *prevent* the overconcentration of wealth, which threatened the development of a "broad purchasing market necessary to absorb our production."[29] Certainly the movement to higher wages preceded the twenties but it is mainly in the literature of the twenties (and later) that this is linked to a general strategy to consumerize the worker. As early as 1914, Henry Ford had instituted the five dollar work day wage, but his innovation coexisted with a nineteenth-century Protestant value system which the worker was expected to maintain.[30] This system significantly clashed with the "economic freedom" that, out of necessity, attempted to subvert the moderation earlier valued for the masses.

The question of shorter hours was also tantamount to offering labor the "chance" to expand the consumer market. And yet, "chance," as "industrial democracy," and as "economic freedom" were subterfuges, in so much as these alleged freedoms and choices meant a transformed version of capitalism's incessant need to mold a work force in its own image. "As modern industry [was] geared to mass production, time out for mass consumption becomes as much a necessity as time in for production."[31] The shortening of hours was seen as a qualitative as well as quantitative change in the worker's life, without significantly altering his relation to power over the uses and means of production. In addition to increasing the amount of leisure, it was hoped that shorter hours would productively determine, "to some extent, the use of leisure and consumption."[32] Shorter hours and higher wages were seen as a first step in a broader offensive against notions of thrift and an attempt to habituate a national population to the exigencies of mass producion. A capitalism that had previously required the worker to "live, move, and [have] his being *there on the job*"[33] was now, among some industries, trying to undo such notions and realities of "the job." Now priorities demanded that the worker spend his wages and leisure time on the consumer market. Realizing that earlier conditions had not been "favorable to such a worker's finding in, say the sector of his home the sought-for satisfactions of forward movement and distinction," Whiting Williams, personnel director for a steel company, and an ideologue of "scientific" management, felt that labor had developed a "suspicion" of such "sought-for satisfactions." Once again linking the rhetoric of freedom to the necessities of capitalism, Filene noted that

[28] Walling, p. 212.
[29] *Ibid.*
[30] In an attempt to assure that his workers carried on a 'moderate' life off the job, Ford developed a *Sociological Department*, staffed by thirty investigators who were "empowered to go into the workers' homes to make sure that no one was drinking too much, that everyone's sex life was without blemish, that leisure time was profitably spent, that no boarders were taken in, that houses were clean and neat." Baritz, p. 33.
[31] Ware, p. 101.
[32] *Ibid.*, p. 94.
[33] *What's on the Worker's Mind*, p. 299.

modern workmen have learned their habits of consumption and their habits of spending (thrift) in the school of fatigue, in a time when high prices and relatively low wages have made it necessary to spend all the energies of the body and mind in providing food, clothing and shelter. We have no right to be overcritical of the way they spend a new freedom or a new prosperity until they have had as long a training in the school of freedom.[34]

Within the vision of consumption as a "school of freedom," the entry onto the consumer market was described as a "civilizing" experience. "Civilization" was the expanded cultural world which flowed from capitalism's broad capacity to commodify material resources. The experience of civilization was the cultural world this capacity produced.

And yet the "school of freedom" posed various problems. The democratic terminology within which the profitable vision of consumption was posed did not reveal the social and economic realities that threatened that vision. In terms of economic development, the financial growth of industrial corporations averaged 286% between 1922 and 1929. Despite some wage hikes, and relatively shorter hours in such industries,[35] the average manufacturing wage earner showed a wage increase of only 14% during this same period.[36] The discrepancy between purchasing power and the rate of industrial growth was dealt with in part by the significant growth of installment selling[37] that followed the 1921 "buyer's strike."

Despite the initiation of a corporate credit system which offered consumers supplementary money, the growth of the productive system forced many industrial ideologues to realize the continuous need to psychically habituate men to consumption beyond the level of familiar structural change.

II

The man with the proper imagination is able to conceive of any commodity in such a way that it becomes an object of emotion to him and to those to whom he imparts his picture, and hence creates desire rather than a mere feeling of ought.[38]

Modern advertising must be seen as a direct response to the needs of mass industrial capitalism. Second in procession after the manager of the production line, noted Whiting Williams, "came the leader who possessed

[34] *The Way Out*, p. 202.

[35] Ware, p. 95. According to Ware's studies, union manufacturing labor averaged 40–48 hours per week. Non-union labor in similar industries averaged 50 hours per week; while labor in more traditional areas, mills, shops, were working 48–60 hours per week.

[36] *Ibid.*, pp. 16–17.

[37] Robert S. Lynd, "The People as Consumers," in *Recent Social Trends*: Report of the President's Research Committee on Social Trends (1933), vol. I, p. 862. Such credit buying was initiated primarily in the automobile industry, with the General Motors Acceptance Corporation (GMAC).

[38] Walter Dill Scott, *Influencing Men in Business* (originally published 1911)—(1928 revised edition enlarged by Delton T. Howard.)—p. 133.

the ability to develop and direct men's desires and demands in a way to furnish the organized mass sales required for the mass production made possible by the massed dollars."[39] Advertising, as a part of mass distribution within modernizing industries, became a major sector for business investment. Within the automobile industry, initiated by the broad and highly diversified G.M oligopoly, distribution came to account for about one-half of that investment. Among producers of smaller consumer goods, the percentage of capital devoted to product proliferation was often greater.[40]

In the 1920's, advertising played an increasingly significant role in industry's attempt to develop a continually responsive consumer market. Although committed national corporations saw advertising as an invaluable integrant of critical economic planning,[41] its acceptance was hardly universal. A mass advertising industry developing in concert with the mass needs of industrial corporations was continually selling itself to industry. Between 1918 and 1923, a greater percentage of articles in the advertising trade journal, *Printers' Ink,* were devoted to ways of convincing "ancient" corporations that advertising was a given of modern industrialism, than were devoted to advertising and merchandising techniques. During the 1920's, however, advertising grew to the dimensions of a major industry. In 1918, total gross advertising revenues in General and Farm magazines was $58.5 million. By 1920 the gross had reached $129.5 million; and by 1929, $196.3 million. Such figures do not include newspaper revenues, or more significantly, direct-to-buyer advertising which still comprised a major, though declining, sector of the industry.

In an address to the American Association of Advertising Agencies (27 October 1926), Calvin Coolidge noted that the industry now required "for its maintenance, investments of great capital, the occupation of large areas of floor space, the employment of an enormous number of people."[42] As the production line had insured the efficient creation of vast quantities of consumer goods, ad men spoke of their product as "business insurance"[43] for profitable and efficient distribution of these goods. While line management tended to the process of goods production, social management—advertisers— hoped to make the cultural milieu of capitalism as efficient as line management had made production. Their task was couched in terms of a secular religion for which the advertisers sought adherents. Calvin Coolidge, applauding their secular clericism, noted that "advertising ministers to the spiritual side of trade."[44]

The reality of modern production dictated the creation of vast national markets. Although many corporations boasted of having attained national

[39] *What's on the Worker's Mind*, p. 317.
[40] "In some lines, such as whiskey and milk, distribution cost is from four to ten times the cost of production." Chandler, p. 157.
[41] Harry Tipper, et al., *Advertising: Its Principles and Practice* (1921), pp. 16–18. See also, Alvin Hunsicker "Stabilizing Profits Through Advertising," *P.I.*, vol. 124, no. 13, p. 81.
[42] Frank Spencer Presbrey, *The History and Development of Advertising* (1929), p. 620.
[43] Calkins, p. 236.
[44] Presbrey, p. 625.

markets without the aid of advertising, *Printers' Ink*, the trade journal, argued that these "phantom national markets" were actually inefficient, unpredictable, and scattered aglommerations of heterogeneous local markets.[45] Advertising offered itself as a means of efficiently creating consumers and as a way of homogeneously "controlling the consumption of a product."[46] The significance of the notion of efficiency in the creation of consumers lies in the fact that the modern advertising industry, like the modern manufacturing plant, was an agent of mass social production. As Ford's assembly line utilized "expensive single-purpose machinery" to produce automobiles inexpensively and at a rate that dwarfed traditional methods, the costly machinery of advertising that Coolidge had described set out to produce consumers, likewise inexpensively and at a rate that dwarfed traditional methods. To create that body efficiently the advertising industry had to develop universal notions of *what makes people respond*, going beyond the "horse sense" psychology that had characterized the earlier industry.[47] Such general conceptions of human instinct offered to provide ways of reaching a mass audience via a universal appeal. Considering the task of having to build a mass ad industry to attend to the needs of mass production, the ad men welcomed the work of psychologists in the articulation of these general conceptions.[48]

The ideological vanguard of the business community found the social psychology of such men as Floyd Henry Allport useful in terms of developing a universal appeal to consumers.[49] Such theories seem to give an ideological cohesion to much of what one sees in the advertising of the twenties. The notion of man as the object of continual and harsh social scrutiny that underscored the argument of much of the ad texts of the decade (Part III), found at least close companionship within the psychological professions. Explicating his notion on the way in which man develops a sense of himself from infancy, Allport asserted that "our consciousness of ourselves is largely a reflection of the consciousness which others have of us. My idea of myself is rather my own idea of my neighbor's view of me."[50]

Whether or not the general conception of "self" as propounded by Floyd Henry Allport had a direct bearing on the *Weltanschauung* held by advertising in the 1920's is not clear. It was generally conceded however, that a "knowledge of people—human nature—"[51] was as necessary a constituent of social production as the line manager's knowledge of his raw materials was to goods production. While agreeing that "human nature is more difficult to control than material nature,"[52] ad men nonetheless discovered in such general notions of human selfconception useful tools for advertising, given their desire to predictably control men in order to create new habits and desires for consumer products.

[45] *P.I.*, vol. 124, no. 12, p. 180.
[46] *Ibid.*, vol. 124, no. 5, p. 152.
[47] Baritz, p. 27.
[48] *Ibid.*, p. 26.
[49] *Mainsprings of Men.*
[50] Floyd Henry Allport, *Social Psychology* (1924), p. 325.
[51] Calkins, p. 123.
[52] Scott, p. 3.

Beyond the search for a general conception of human nature, ad men spoke in specific terms of "human instincts" which if properly understood could induce people "to buy a given product if it was scientifically presented. If advertising copy appealed to the right instincts, the urge to buy would surely be excited."[53] The utilitarian value or traditional notion of mechanical quality was not sufficient to move products at the necessary rate and volume required by mass production.

Such traditional appeals would not change the disposition of potential markets to consumption. Instead, it would offer each product isolatedly, not in terms of the social-economic consumerization (i.e., proletarianization) of men, but through an appeal to traditional notions of quality. The advertisers were concerned with effecting a self-conscious change in the psychic economy, which could not come about if they spent all their time talking about a product, and none talking about the "reader." The appeal to instincts was a way of "scientifically" controlling mass goods distribution. Advertising literature, following the advent of mass production methods, increasingly spoke in terms of appeals to instinct. Anticipating later implementation, by 1911, Walter Dill Scott, psychologist/author of *Influencing Men in Business,* noted that "goods offered as means of gaining social prestige make their appeals to one of the most profound of the human instincts."[54] Yet the instinct for "social prestige" as well as others of a broad "constellation"[55] of instincts were channeled into the terms of the productive system. The use value of "prestige," of "beauty," of "acquisition," of "self-adornment," or of "play" was placed in the service of advertising's basic purpose—to provide effective mass distribution of products. Carl A. Naether, an ideologue of advertising for women, demonstrated how the link might be effected between "instinct" and mass sales.

> An attractive girl admiring a string of costly pearls just presented to her would in no few cases make the one seeing her in an advertisement exclaim: "I wish that *I, too,* might have a set of these pearls and so enhance *my* personal appearance." Such and similar longings are merely expressions of real or fancied need for what is advertised.[56]

The creation of "fancied need" was crucial to the modern advertiser. The transcendence of traditional consumer markets and buying habits required people to buy not to satisfy their own fundamental needs, but rather, to satisfy the real, historic needs of capitalist productive machinery. Advertising was a way of making people put time and energy into what Calvin Coolidge referred to as their "education"[57] to production. The investment of time and energy in deliberation over an advertisement, as described

---

[53] Baritz, p. 26.
[54] Scott, p. 132.
[55] Baritz, p. 26.
[56] Carl A. Naether, *Advertising to Women* (1928), p. 97.
[57] "When we stop to consider the part which advertising plays in the modern life of production and trade, we see that basically it is that of education . . . it makes new thoughts, new desires and new actions." Presbrey, p. 620.

by Scott,[58] enacted in requisite microcosm the commitment of one's total time and energy to consumption. Advertising demanded but a momentary participation in the logic of consumption. Yet hopefully that moment would be expanded into a life style by its educational value. A given ad asked not only that an individual buy its product, but that he experience a self-conscious perspective that he had previously been socially and psychically denied. By that perspective, one was able to ameliorate social and personal frustrations through his access to the marketplace.

In light of such notions as Allport's "social self," and other self-objectifying visions of popularity and success,[59] a new cultural logic was projected by advertising beyond the strictly pecuniary one of creating the desire to consume. The social perception was one in which people ameliorated the negative condition of social objectification through consumption, material objectification. The negative condition was portrayed as social failure derived from continual public scrutiny. The positive goal emanated from one's *modern* decision to armor himself against such scrutiny with the accumulated "benefits" of industrial production. Social responsibility and social self-preservation were being correlated to an allegedly existential decision that one made to present a mass produced public face. Man, traditionally seen as exemplary of God's perfect product, was now hardly viable in comparison with the man-made products of industrial expertise. The elevation of man's works in the cosmos which had effected the half-way covenent among New England Puritans was now being secularized into the realm of mass social production. It was felt that capitalism through an appeal to instincts—ultimately feelings of social insecurity—could habituate men to consumptive life.[60] Such social production of consumers represented a shift in the social and political priorities of the cosmos, which has most probably characterized much of the "life" of American industrial capitalism. The functional goal of national advertising was the creation of desires and habits. In tune with the need for mass distribution that accompanied the development of mass production capabilities, advertising was trying to produce in readers personal needs which would dependently fluctuate with the expanding marketplace.

Exposing an affirmative vision of capitalist production, Calvin Coolidge reassured the members of the ad industry in 1926 that "rightfully applied, it [advertising] is the method by which the desire is created for better things."[61] The nature of this desire and not, incidentally, the nature of capitalism required an unquestioning attitude towards the uses of production. The use of psychological methods, therefore, attempted to turn the consumer's critical

[58] Scott, p. 43.
[59] "Physical or sex attraction . . . other things being equal, qualities which make one pleasing to look at or to caress render their possessor popular to many and loved by not a few." Allport, p. 365.
[60] Not incidental to this direct appeal to the consumer's self image, advertisers argued that "heavy expenditures for consumer advertising by a manufacturer . . . (might) induce merchants to favor him with orders." Harold Maynard, et al., *Principles of Marketing* (1927), p. 439.
[61] Presbrey, p. 622.

functions away from the product and toward himself. The determining factor for buying was self-critical and ideally ignored the intrinsic worth of the product. The Lynds, in their study of *Middletown,* noted that unlike ads of a generation before, modern advertising was

> concentrating increasingly upon a type of copy aiming to make the reader emotionally uneasy, to bludgeon him with the fact that decent people don't live the way he does. . . . This copy points an accusing finger at the stenographer as she reads her motion picture magazine and makes her acutely conscious of her unpolished finger nails . . . and sends the housewife peering anxiously into the mirror to see if her wrinkles look like those that made Mrs. X in the advertisement "old at thirty-five" because she did not have a Leisure Hour electric washer.[62]

Advertising hoped to elicit the "instinctual" anxieties of social intercourse. Cutex Hand Preparations translated well-prepared hands as armor for success. Hoping to prepare the psyche for such an argument, they declared in crescendo

> You will be amazed to find how many times in one day people glance at your nails. At each glance a judgment is made. . . . Indeed some people make a practice of basing their estimate of a new acquaintance largely upon this one detail.

Even those whose physical appearances were marketably "safe," who appeared to be "the picture of health," were warned of their natural contingencies. Listerine was offered as an agent to militate against "The Hidden Wells of Poison" that lurk and conspire against the "program[s] of pleasure" of even the most beautiful women.

The Lynds saw advertising "and other channels of increased cultural diffusion from without [as] rapidly changing habits of thought as to what things are essential to living and multiplying optional occasions for spending money."[63] The critical analysis offered by the Lynds found unwitting support in predominant advertising theory. It was recognized that in order to get people to consume and, more importantly, to keep them consuming, it was more efficient to endow man with a critical selfconsciousness in tune with the "solutions" of the market place, than to fragmentarily argue for products on their own merit. Writing in *Printers' Ink,* Frederick P. Anderson spoke of the industry's conscious attempt to direct man's critical faculties against himself or his environment, "to make him self-conscious about matter of course things such as enlarged nose pores, bad breath. . . ."[64]

In mass advertising, the consciousness of a selling point was precisely the theorized "self-consciousness" of the modern consumer which had occa-

---

[62] Robert and Helen Lynd, *Middletown* (1929), p. 82.
[63] *Ibid.,* pp. 81–2.
[64] *P.I.,* vol. 136, no. 8, p. 130.

Advertising: Selling the System

sioned the Lynds' remarks.[65] This consumer self-consciousness was clearly identifiable with the continuous need for product proliferation that increasingly informed mass industry. Linking the theories of "self-consciousness" to the exigencies of capitalism, one writer in *Printers' Ink* commented that "advertising helps to keep the masses dissatisfied with their mode of life, discontented with *ugly things* around them. Satisfied customers are not as profitable as discontented ones."[66]

III

In his sympathetic book on the *History and Development of Advertising,* Frank Presbrey articulated the conception of a predictable, buying, national population in proud and patriotic terms. "To National Advertising," noted Presbrey, "has recently been attributed most of the growth of a national homogeneity in our people, a uniformity of ideas which, despite the mixture of races, is found to be greater here than in European countries whose population is made up almost wholly of people of one race and would seem to be easier to nationalize in all respects."[67] Presbrey's conception of "national homogeneity" was a translucent reference to what Calvin Coolidge saw as "the enormous capacity for consumption of all kinds of commodities which characterizes our country."[68]

The idea that advertising was producing a homogeneous national character was described within the trade as a "civilizing influence comparable in its cultural effects to those of other great epoch-making developments in history."[69] Yet not all of the conceptions of advertising were expressed in such epic and trans-historical terminology. Sensitive to the political and economic context of such notions as "civilizing," "national homogeneity," and "capacity for consumption," William Allen White bridged the gap between "civilization" and civil society, noting that modern advertising was particularly a formation of advanced capitalist production. Aiming his critique at internal and external "revolutionist" threats to capitalism, White turned contemporary conceptions of revolution on their head. Reasserting the efficacy of the American Revolutionary tradition, he argued that advertising men were the true "revolutionists." Juxtaposing the consumer market to revolution of a socialistic variety, White presented a satirical political

[65] In "The People as Consumers," Robert Lynd further characterized the advertising of products of mass technology in terms of the questions of 'uniformity' and the nature of the modern capitalist market place.

"Technological uniformity and complexity . . . tends to remove further the complex of characteristics blanketed by a brand name from the sorts of empirical comparisons that were more often possible a generation ago. . . . There is a ceaseless quest for what advertising men call 'million dollar ideas' . . . to disguise commodities still further by identifying them with cryptic characteristics." *Recent Social Trends* (I), pp. 876–7.

[66] *P.I.*, vol. 150, no. 6, p. 163.
[67] Presbrey, p. 613.
[68] *Ibid.*, p. 622.
[69] *Ibid.*, p. 608.

strategy to halt the "golden quest" for consumer goods. "I would cut out the advertising and fill the editorial and news pages with material supplied by communists and reds. That would stop buying—distribution of things. It would bring an impasse in civilization, which would immediately begin to decay."[70] Identifying ad men with the integrity and survival of the American heritage, White numbered advertising among our sacred cultural institutions.

Through advertising then, consumption took on a clearly cultural tone. Within governmental and business rhetoric, consumption assumed an ideological veil of nationalism and democratic lingo. The mass "American type," which defied unity on the bases of common ethnicity, language, class, or literature, was ostensibly born out of common desires—mass responses to the demands of capitalist production. Mass industry required a corresponding mass man, cryptically named him "Civilized American," and implicated his national heritage in the marketplace. By defining himself and his desires in terms of the good of capitalist production, the worker would implicitly accept the foundations of modern industrial life. By transforming the notion of "class" into "mass," business hoped to create a massified "individual" who could locate his needs and frustrations in terms of the consumption of goods rather than the quality and content of his life (work).

Advertisements aimed at transforming pockets of resistance contained the double purpose of sales and "civilization." Resistance to the universal type appeals to modern advertising was often dealt with in racial or national terms. In an article dealing with immigrant readers of the domestic foreign language press, a writer in *Printers' Ink* noted that these *less American* elements of the population had not yet been sophisticated to the methods of modern advertising. While other Americans were portrayed as responding to appeals to universal instinct, the author noted that "Swedes and Germans . . . study the most minute detail of anything they consider buying."[71] It was felt that a particular form of advertising had to be developed to temporarily accommodate immigrant and other defined resistance to nationalization. While it was suggested that for immediate sales ads could be written offering extensive proof of a product's intrinsic worth, other forms of advertising assumed the task of the "democratization" which Edward Filene had exalted. "Antidote advertising" and other, less theoretical tactics were designed to repudiate antique beliefs which had no place in *the social style* of modern industrial life. Often, such ads were geared to make people ashamed of their origins and, consequently, the habits and practices that betrayed them as alien. The Sherwin Cody School of English advertised that a less than perfect mastery of the language was *just* cause for social ostracism. "If someone you met for the first time made . . . mistakes in English . . . what would you think of him? Would he inspire your respect? Would you be inclined to make a friend of him? Would you care to introduce him to others as a close friend of yours?"[72] Rather than arguing that a knowledge of the language would be helpful in conversation and effective communica-

[70] *Ibid.*, p. 610.
[71] *P.I.*, vol. 140, no. 5, p. 108.
[72] See Presbrey, 'Illustrated Appendix.'

tion, the ad argued that being distinguishable from the fabricated national norm, a part of advertising's mythologized homogeneity, was a justification for social failure.

In an attempt to massify men's consumption in step with the requirements of the productive machinery, advertising increasingly offered mass-produced solutions to "instinctive" strivings, as well as to the ills of mass society itself. If it was industrial capitalism around which crowded cities were being built, and which had spawned much of the danger to health, the frustration, the loneliness and the insecurity of modern industrial life, the advertising of the period denied complicity. Rather, the logic of contemporaneous advertising read: one can free himself from the ills of modern life by embroiling himself in the maintenance of that life. A 1924 ad for Pompeian facial products argued that

> unless you are one woman in a thousand, you must use powder and rouge. Modern living has robbed women of much of their natural color . . . taken away the conditions that once gave natural roses in the cheeks.[73]

Within such literature, the term "modern living" was an ahistorical epithet, devoid of the notion "Modern Industrial Society," and rent with visions of the benefits of civilization which had emerged, one would think, quite apart from the social conditions and relations to which these "benefits" therapeutically addressed themselves. On the printed page, modern living was defined as "heated houses, easy transportation, and the conveniences of the household." To the reader it may have meant something considerably different: light-starved housing, industrial pollution, lack of nutrition, boredom. In either sense, modern life offered the same sallow skin and called for a solution through consumption. Within such advertisements, business called for a transformation of the critique of bourgeois society to an implicit commitment to that society.

The reality of modern goods production and distribution called for a dependable mass of consumers. The advertising which attempted to create that mass often did so by playing upon the fears and frustrations evoked by mass society. Within a massifying culture, the ads offered mass-produced visions of individualism by which people could extricate themselves from the mass. While on the level of ideological consciousness, people were being offered commoditized individuality, on the level of the marketplace their acceptance of that individuality meant an entrenchment within the dependable mass of consumers that advertising was attempting to build. The rationale was simple. If a person was unhappy within mass industrial society, advertising was attempting to put that unhappiness to work in the name of that society.

In terms of the self-conscious use of language by advertisers, the idea was to "hitch" concepts and feelings which were familiar to readers and link them to a new and profitable context,[74] the marketplace. In an attempt to boost mass sales of soap, the Cleanliness Institute, a cryptic front group for the soap and glycerine producers' association, pushed soap as a "Kit for

[73] The *Ladies Home Journal*, May 1924, p. 161.
[74] *P.I.*, vol. 133, no. 2, p. 196.

Climbers" (social, no doubt). The illustration was a multitudinous mountain of men, each climbing over one another to reach the summit. At the top of this indistinguishable mass stood one figure, his arms outstretched toward the sun, whose rays spelled out the words "Heart's Desire." The ad cautioned that "in any path of life, that long way to the top is hard enough—so make the going easier with soap and water." In an attempt to build a responsive mass market, the Cleanliness Institute appealed to what they must have known was a major dissatisfaction with the reality of mass life. Their solution was a sort of mass pseudo-demassification.

A good deal of drug and toilet goods advertising made more specific references to the quality of industrial life. Appealing to dissatisfaction and insecurities around the job, certain advertisements not only offered their products as a kind of job insurance, but intimated that through the use of their products one might become a business success, the capitalist notion of individual "self-" fulfillment.

Listerine, whose ads had taken the word "halitosis" out of the inner reaches of the dictionary and placed it on "stage, screen and in the home," offered this anecdote:

> He was conscious that something stood between him and greater business success—between him and greater popularity. Some subtle something he couldn't lay his hands on . . . Finally, one day, it dawned on him . . . the truth that his friends had been too delicate to mention.

When a critical understanding of modern production might have helped many to understand what actually stood "between them and greater business success," this ad attempted to focus man's critique against himself—how his body has kept him from happiness. Within the world view of a society which was increasingly divorcing men from any notion of craft, or from any definable sort of product, it was also logical that "you couldn't blame a man for firing an employee with halitosis to hire one without it." The contingency of a man's job was offered a non-violent, apolitical solution. It offered man as the victim of himself, the fruits of mass production as his savior. Ads constantly hammered away at everything that was his own; his bodily functions, his self-esteem, and offered something of theirs as a socially more effective substitute.

In addition to the attempt on the part of advertising to habituate men to buying as a solution to the particular realities of a growing industrial society, ad men presented products as means to what they viewed as instinctual ends. Speaking often to women,[75] ads offered daintiness, beauty, romance, grace, security, and husbands through the use of certain products. Traditional advertising had conceived of these "ideals" as integrants of a Protestant notion of thrift and moderation. The dainty woman, a pillar of sense and temperance within the home, had been characterized as physically divorced

---

[75] Carl Albert Naether noted that "Women buy 80–90% of all things in general use in daily life." The breakdown of this generalization specified: 90% of the dry goods, 87% of the raw and market foods, 67% of the automobiles, 48% of the drugs, etc. Naether, p. 4, (citing figures from Hollingsworth, *Advertising and Selling*).

from the marketplace not to mention her self. Increasingly, within the texts of ads in the twenties, these desires are fulfilled on the marketplace. Thrift no longer cohabitates with daintiness, but threatens to prevent it. Positioning goals such as marriage, romance, social grace, etc., ads begin telling women that through the consumption of their products, those goals could be reached. Within the rhetoric of these ads, the accumulation of various products, each for a separate objectified portion of the body, was equated with the means to success. Correlative to Allport's vision of "social self," advertising offered the next best thing to people who were unhappy or could be convinced that they were unhappy about their lives, a *commodity self*; an appropriate popular, successful conglomeration of mass-produced breath, hair, teeth, skin, and feet. Each portion of the body was to be viewed critically, as a *potential* bauble in a successful assemblage. Woodbury's soap was offered as a perfect treatment for the "newly important face of Smart Today"; another product promised to keep teeth white. "A flashing smile is worth more than a good sized bank account. It wins friends." After she has used Caro Cocoanut Oil Shampoo, a dashing gentleman informs the lady, "I'm crazy about your hair. *It's* the most beautiful of any here tonight." Within the vision offered by such ads, not only was social grace and success attainable, but also defined through the use of specific products. You don't make friends, your commoditized smile "wins" them; your embellished hair, and not you, is beautiful. "Smart today" required one to compete on a social marketplace, though it would be gone tomorrow, yielding its momentary, though cataclysmic, importance to a newly profitable "smart today." As the ads intimated that anything natural about the consumer was worthless or deplorable and tried to make him schizophrenically self-conscious of that notion, they offered weapons by which even people with bad breath, enlarged nose pores, corned feet and other such maladies could eclipse themselves and "succeed."

As notions of failure were to be perceived within a style of self-denigrating paranoia, notions of success were likewise portrayed in purely self-involved terms. Though the victorious heroines of cosmetic advertisements always got their man, they did so out of a commodity defined *self-fetishization* which made that man and themselves almost irrelevant to the quality of their victory. Their romantic triumphs were ultimately commercially defined versions of the auto-erotic ones of Alban Berg's prostitute, *Lulu*, who declares that "When I looked at myself in the mirror I wished I were a man—a man married to me."

During the twenties, civil society was increasingly characterized by mass industrial production. In an attempt to implicate men and women within the efficient process of production, advertising built a vision of culture which bound old notions of "civilization" to the new realities of civil society. In what was viewed as their instinctual search for traditional ideals, people were offered a vision of *civilized man* which was transvaluated in terms of the pecuniary exigencies of society. Within a society that defined real life in terms of the monotonous insecurities of mass production, advertising attempted to create an alternative organization of life, which would serve to channel man's desires for self, for social success, for leisure, away from himself and his works, and toward a commoditized acceptance of "civilization."

The Maintenance of Capitalist Order

David Gross

CAPITALISM AND CULTURE

Today culture is generally thought of in terms of entertainment. It is acknowledged as escape from everyday routine, and consequently it is associated with leisure, relaxation, and comfort of the mind. The humdrum life of the workaday world, and the world of "culture" are seen as opposites, each belonging to a fundamentally different sphere of activity. When one attends a "cultural event" he literally enters a qualitatively different realm, in time as well as space. Familiar reality temporarily recedes into the background and culture is experienced as absolute separateness from ordinary life. This is why the acquisition of culture has lately become such a popular pastime; it promises a sublimity that routine existence cannot possibly supply. If one's job is miserable, then culture can soothe him after hours; if one experiences life as boorish and oppressive, there is the stereo set and the recent crop of "best-sellers" to make him forget (and of course become cultured at the same time). Culture is always the medication waiting to be applied to disaffection. The more intolerable contemporary life becomes, the greater will be the demand for culture.

So firmly implanted is the idea that culture is the opposite of everyday life that the argument of this essay may at first glance appear absurd. What I want to pursue in the following pages is the dual notion (1) that culture, far from being an escape from oppressive conditions as is generally believed, is actually the foremost instrument of oppression; and similarly (2) that culture no longer stands aside or remains epiphenomenal to the struggle for a better society, but is, in fact, at the very center of that struggle. In the Twentieth Century, Thomas Mann has said, "everything becomes politics." This statement might more accurately be re-phrased by saying that in the Twentieth Century everything, including politics, eventually becomes "culture." If this is so, then no radical critique of society can dispense with a cultural critique —or perhaps even be conceived of apart from one. At present, the insufficiency of contemporary life is made palatable by the culture that accompanies it; but if the falsity of this culture were exposed, then the true nature of social reality would be revealed for what it is: simple oppression. The job of cultural criticism is to remove the masks that now disguise the otherwise bare facts of social domination.

One of the weaknesses of the American Left in contrast to the European is that it has never developed a genuinely radical theory of culture. With few exceptions, the traditional Left accepted the bifurcation of (elite) culture and ordinary life as natural and inevitable. As a result it never achieved any

Reprinted, with deletions, from David Gross, "Toward a Radical Theory of Culture," *Radical America*, vol. 2 (November–December 1968), pp. 1–14, by permission of *Radical America*. David Gross teaches history at the University of Colorado.

insights into the crucial role that culture plays in legitimizing and solidifying capitalist society; nor did it see the liberating possibilities that new concepts of culture could offer for the fight against an increasingly totalitarian and regimented way of life.

Two recent works help to correct this oversight: Theodor W. Adorno's *Prisms* and Herbert Marcuse's *Negations: Essays in Critical Theory*. Both contain important essays that go a long way toward defining the reactionary nature of modern culture (and also its revolutionary potential). In what follows I rely to a great extent on these two books in an attempt to sketch what might be termed a radical theory of culture.

Culture in the Bourgeois Epoch

The bourgeois epoch of culture should be considered apart from its present-day successor for reasons which will be developed later. For the moment, the bourgeois culture age refers to the period of Western history— roughly from 1820 to 1920—when the traditional bourgeoisie was at its height. During this time culture, like everything else, fell under the prevailing influence of the middle class. A number of consequences followed from this.

For one thing, culture was compartmentalized. It was understood to be a quality of mind, a certain sophistication of thought, which was quite far removed from the realm of necessity. Culture meant appreciation of eternal values and an easy familiarity with the elevating thoughts of former ages. As such, it was identical with Matthew Arnold's phrase "sweetness and light," but had nothing to do with the material or "lower" aspects of human existence. Thus a cleavage emerged in the domain of middle-class values which was never overcome. Between useful and functional activity on the one hand, and thought or art on the other, an absolute barrier was erected. There came to be no effective communication between the two—and none desired. The result of this division was not only the relegation of culture to a world of pure essences above and beyond "the real" world, but also an irreparable split between thought and action, mental and spiritual work. This schizophrenia of the psyche has remained characteristic of bourgeois consciousness to the present time.

The bifurcation between the "realm of necessity" and the "realm of culture" led to something unexpected: material practice was "exonerated from responsibility for the true, the good, and the beautiful," since these were already realized in the exclusive sphere of culture. In other words, culture became an independent realm of value separated from the struggle for existence; it was not expected to react back upon the factual world, but rather to stay apart from it. Similarly, an individual became "cultured" by realizing culture "from within" and "without any transformation of the state of fact." In the world of abstract culture, he could experience everything that is denied to him in ordinary existence, including the feeling of permanence in change, purity amidst impurity, freedom amidst unfreedom. Culture, by opposing the beauty of the soul to bodily misery and external bondage, "entered increasingly into the service of suppression . . . once bourgeois rule began to be stabilized." (Herbert Marcuse) . . .

That was the first consequence of culture in the bourgeois epoch. By leaving the material world to itself, it allowed the natural laws of society (the laws of the market economy) to work themselves out unchecked. For the middle class as a whole the arrangement was ideal because it permitted the bourgeois to live a humane and cultured life at home and a ruthless one at work without seeing any contradiction in his behavior.

But a second consequence followed which was equally important. This was the realization that culture was not only a respite from labor; if utilized in the right way it was also much more—a helpful accoutrement for social and economic advancement. The possession of culture was drawn upon for its hidden use value, that is for the magical qualities it seemed to confer over and above one's working productivity. Becoming "cultured" was one means of ascending the social scale, and the ability to speak of cultural matters was a mark of status, a symbol that one had arrived. Even though culture itself (as a collection of eternal, super-mundane values) remained apart from the material world, in practice the veneer of culture was increasingly "used" for purposes exterior to it. At first distinctions were made between pure culture one one hand and its practical use on the other; but eventually even these became blurred or non-existent as large segments of the middle class began to look to culture for what it could offer in real, tangible terms. Thus the bourgeoisie began to talk about the "benefits" of culture rather than about its spiritual truth; they gradually came to think of it as a means to an end and no longer as an end in itself.

This development, however, was not simple or clear-cut: it had at least two discernible aspects or phases to it. In the beginning, the utility value of culture was viewed in terms of the status-knowledge it bestowed upon its aspirants. At this stage culture in the abstract was still thought of as a spiritual dimension, but this did not prevent the middle class from converting it into something more practical. . . . This meant, in effect, that culture was transformed into knowledge, its most immediate exchange value, and increasingly came to be thought of as the spiritual equivalent of money.

It was in opposition to this development that the term "cultural philistinism" was coined. The cultural philistine was simply the bourgeois who equated culture with knowledge, and knowledge with power. To him, culture was "a social commodity which could be circulated and cashed in on as social coinage for the purpose of acquiring social status. Cultural objects were transformed into values when the cultural philistine seized upon them as currency by which he bought a higher position in society—higher, that is, than in his own opinion he deserved either by nature or birth." (Hannah Arendt).

Whereas real culture aims at inner, personal qualities, the educated bourgeois of the early Nineteenth Century sought just the opposite: objectified knowledge. By confusing learning with culture he attempted to acquire an extensive familiarity with cultural values as objectively given. As a result, the idea of culture was cut off from its subjective moorings; it became, in a word, crystallized thought or what Hegel called "objectified Spirit." No longer was it essential that one really be cultivated. All that were necessary were the signs and symbols of culture which one could display quickly and facilely for rapid advancement.

This development already foreshadowed the second phase of the bourgeois concept of culture. In the late Nineteenth and early Twentieth Century its meaning changed once again. This time culture came to be identified not with a quality of mind, and not even with knowledge per se, but rather with the possession of certain kinds of cultural objects, which by their very nature conferred a prestigious cultural status on their owners. This new notion of culture grew concomitantly with the rise of industrial production and the absolute ascendancy of the bourgeoisie in the social and economic spheres. The difference between culture as useful learning and culture as material display may simply be the difference between an early and a late phase of bourgeois thought. The first reflects the spirit of the middle class jockeying for position, and the second reflects their self-satisfaction as a firmly established leisure class.

Another way to put it is as follows: In an age of economic scarcity and limited production an aspiring class is forced, almost by necessity, to define culture as knowledge, for it alone is accessible in virtually unlimited quantities. However, in a period of greater wealth, culture can be thought of in other ways—in terms of material goods, for example. This change actually occurred in the second half of the Nineteenth Century. Culture came to be thought of as commodity acquisition. Instead of being defined as knowledge, which has a ready exchange value, it was objectified and materialized into exquisite and hard-to-come-by objets d'art. Culture, then, became something that accrued to things, and therefore to the owners of things. The new cultural style manifested itself most visibly in hoarding.

One of the few who saw this development as it happened was Thorsten Veblen. In his *Theory of the Leisure Class*, he pointed out that the individual bourgeois, though still interested in improving his position in the social hierarchy, had discovered new ways of doing it. He simply spent his money as uselessly as possible, proving thereby that he was wealthy enough to do so. For him, culture meant ostentation and conspicuous display. Consequently, it was viewed in terms of material objects that could be purchased, or rather as the honorific prestige that went along with the purchase. As such, it was an aesthetic way of advertising prowess—a refined but unmistakable means of flaunting one's power, loot, and profit. . . .

By the beginning of the Twentieth Century, and more particularly after the First World War, the late-bourgeois notion of culture began to be democratized. Culture began to be synonymous with "cultural goods," and the "fanticism of utensils" . . . now became standard throughout all of society. Only at this point—when the idea of culture as a commodity became widespread—did critics begin to speak with horror of "mass culture." They forgot that the materialization of spiritual values into manipulatable objects was fully developed in upper-bourgeoisie circles well before it became popular among the "masses."

Culture in the Age of Mechanical Reproduction

In the contemporary period the legacy of bourgeois culture remains, but at the same time it has been transformed into something nearly unrecognizable. The main reason for this change . . . is the new phenomenon of technical mass production. Once this had been introduced on a large scale, the old spiritual and elitist notion of culture began to fade. In its place came a new concept of culture—one that was in harmony with a more advanced stage of capitalist production.

This is made clear by comparing the culture of Veblen's time with that of the present day. It is true that in 1900 culture was already materialistic since it was thought of as so many commodities which bestowed cultural importance on their possessors. Nevertheless, this view demanded that the cultural goods be rare and relatively limited, or else they would lose their status signification. The last thing this kind of culture wanted was to become "common." It fought against the rise of a cultural industry, and insisted that culture remain exclusive if it was to continue to be culture at all. The enemy was not so much the traditionally uncultured population as it was the market managers and the psycho-technicians who would bring the world of culture to everyone—and at enormous profits to boot. . . .

In this the conservative elements of the old middle class lost out to the new progressive wing. The more aggressive bourgeois of the Twentieth Century had essentially different ideas—not about the nature of culture, but about its use—and were eager to put these ideas into effect. Though in agreement with their predecessors that culture appertained more to objects than to indeterminable spiritual values, they struck out on untried paths by turning culture over to the consumer. It was through their initiative that a whole new market was opened up: the cultural market. Because of these entrepreneurs the notion of culture as sacrosanct was destroyed. Instead, culture was described as everyone's possession; there was no man or woman who could not be cultured or have the appurtenances of culture (in the form of reproductions and cheap imitations) in the home. In the Twentieth Century, then, a totally novel field of enterprise was discovered and exploited; but this was possible only after the notion of culture was entirely removed from the realm of scarcity and turned over in toto to the realm of production. (It was also necessary, in the short run at least, for profit to be more important than culture. The old established bourgeoisie were often willing to forego absolute profit in order to "enjoy" culture, and this is one reason why they did not exploit the new markets.)

The shock effects of this development were cataclysmic as far as the meaning of culture was concerned. Now it no longer meant, as it did earlier, the retreat from the processes of production and consumption. On the contrary, culture increasingly came to be identified with the very processes themselves. The gap between the spiritual and material dimensions of life began to close for the first time; but this was not because a modus vivendi had been reached between them, but rather because the spiritual elements of culture tended to disappear altogether. Formerly the middle class made distinctions between culture and everyday life, between the ideal and the real worlds; but in the Twentieth Century culture gradually began to be associated with ordinary consumption. . . . As a result, its transcendental and spiritual qualities vanished as it became increasingly bound up with the commercial market.

A related consequence is also worth mentioning. As culture moved into the fields of mass production it became indistinguishable from mass entertainment. This, too was something new. By being trivialized into an amusement or a leisure-time diversion, culture began to be closely identified with the entertainment industry—even to the extent of catering to "mass opinion, the mass recreational product, and the generalized emotional response." (Richard Hoggart). Hannah Arendt has commented on this by noting that culture has ceased being the "social commodity" it had been in the last century. At that time it was used, abused, or desecrated for a variety of selfish reasons, but it was not consumed like all other commodities. Today it is otherwise, for the needs of advanced capitalism demand that traditional culture become consumer culture—that is to say, entertainment. Cultural goods must literally be "used up," devoured, and destroyed so they can make way for new ones which are now merchandised at an ever-quickening pace.

If culture is becoming synonymous with mass entertainment, it is also becoming the linear continuation of production, and hence an integral part of the rationality of the system. Yet it is usually experienced as something quite different: the liberation from production or the "flight from an unbearable reality." (Leo Lowenthal). This is perhaps the most striking example that one can find of contemporary false consciousness. The idea that culture is an escape from the workaday world is illusory, because in truth it is a preparation for more consumption and for a re-invigorated working day in order to keep the economy going. The cleavage between culture and the routine of daily life (which really existed in the past) is now only apparent. It survives in the minds of people who think that in the enjoyment of culture they are separating themselves from the tedium of the customary. In reality they are immersing themselves more deeply in it, for consumer culture is an indispensable adjunct to modern capitalism—even when it seems to be a respite from it. At the present time, culture of this kind binds one more closely to the economy and legitimizes the status quo by beautifying and even advertising in it. In the words of Situationists, culture becomes the "ideal commodity, the one which sells all the others."

This state of affairs is properly referred to as "mass culture." (This is an apt description, but only to the extent that it means the wholesale distribution of false values and the prostitution of real cultural objects into marketable "things"; if the phrase is used contemptuously, as it often is, to describe the vertical filtering of values from an elite to the larger whole, then it becomes a meaningless term of snobbery and reproach.) The most pronounced feature of contemporary "mass culture"—the one thing which most clearly distinguishes it from bourgeois culture—is that between the cultural object and the individual there is a new mediation that never existed before: namely technology. This intervening factor has had a profound effect on the shape of modern culture. Not only has it been responsible for the mass production of

The Maintenance of Capitalist Order

cheap imitations, of rewritten and digested copies, of condensed and fabricated versions of great art and literature, but it has also greatly affected, and in some cases determined, what will be called culture, what it will look like, and what its message will be. Technology is not simply a means of cultural reproduction; it actually has a decisive role to play in deciding the form and content of the cultural product. Now for the first time what is produced becomes destined for reproduction. The value of a work of art no longer lies in its autonomy, but now lies in its ability to be manufactured and sold on a mass scale. The result is that the authenticity of a cultural artifact, its immediacy and historicity, are seriously damaged. As Walter Benjamin put it, "The technique of reproduction detaches the reproduced object from the domain of tradition. It substitutes a plurality of copies for a unique existence. . . . (This) lead(s) to a profound shattering of tradition which is the reverse side of the contemporary crisis and the renewal of humanity."

What has been described so far is the devolution of high culture into mass culture. This means, among other things, (1) that high culture has lost its transcendent spirituality; (2) that it has been metamorphosed into a fetishized object; (3) that it has become subject to the laws of the market, thereby losing its autochthonous value; and (4) that it has become tangled in the web of technology in ways which harm its very essence.

. . . There is also another type of culture which has not been mentioned: folk culture. It still persists in certain localities, but its future is threatened by the growing penetration of mass culture into every area of life. Like imperialism, mass culture is compelled to expand its markets; hence its own dynamic forces it to usurp the old forms of folk culture and integrate them into a homogenized popular culture. The "traits" of folk art and music continue to survive even within popular culture, but they become contrived rather than spontaneous, strained rather than natural. Today genuine folk culture exists only where the mass media have not yet reached.

All of this has to do with the deteriorating effect that the bourgeoisie, and later the phenomenon of mechanical reproduction, have had on the quality of culture, but it says nothing about the effect that contemporary culture has had upon society. What role does culture play in the present age? Is it a critic of society or an accomplice? Is it antagonistic or integrative? Does it stand apart or is it in the center of contemporary social life?

These questions open up a whole new area of discussion which for lack of space cannot be gone into in great detail. Sufficient documentation exists to indicate that popular or mass culture serves the interests of social domination. It tends to legitimize and sanctify the status quo, and induce the individual to adjust to the "givenness" of society as it is presently constituted. For example, when culture is defined in terms of amusement or enjoyment it helps solidify the powers-that-be since it makes no unreasonable demands on them. It asks for nothing that cannot be satisfied, and in some cases it asks for only that which can be satisfied. This only tends to reinforce one-dimensionality because it narrows consciousness to a safe social level. Similarly, a culture that maintains a steady level of banality and compels passive acquiescence to it because "that's all there is" lays the groundwork for social and political manipulation. People come to expect little from life; they become conditioned to the mediocre even while they secretly crave for things to be different. In this state of mind they become grateful for every novelty presented to them under the guise of cultural innovation. The art of improvising and distributing these novelties, however, lies with the existing power structure, which uses them for purposes of social stabilization and "undreamed-of psychological control." (Theodor Adorno). By instilling automatized reactions and a mood of general receptiveness, mass culture weakens the tendencies of individual resistance to social domination. The result is that people forget how to act by waiting to be acted upon. Closely related to this is still another point. Popular culture tends to define "reality" as the immediate given, the concrete. This implies that what exists does so necessarily, and that what is natural must for that reason be real. In an age of mass culture, men are prevented from seeing other dimensions to life—and consequently they come to believe that there must not be any. Culture, which should be a means of heightening awareness, now works for the opposite principle: the contraction of awareness. The result: culture continues and intensifies the hypertrophy of human consciousness, whereas it should point the way toward total renewal. As Irving Howe has noted, people "accept mass culture and daily experience precisely to the degree that the two blend. By now neither can be maintained without the other, which is why there prevails in this country such a blurred notion of what human experience is and such an inadequate notion of what it should be." In other words contemporary culture, by being incorporated into daily life and work, serves to meliorate the status quo, and teaches men to accommodate themselves to it.

In intriguing and not always visible ways, culture in the age of mechanical reproduction has a constraining effect upon modern consciousness. At the same time it also performs a valuable social function (for the rulers) by contributing (perhaps even unwillingly) to the solidification of the "given" in society. . . .

The Maintenance of Capitalist Order

Gabriel Kolko

THE DECLINE OF AMERICAN
RADICALISM IN THE TWENTIETH CENTURY

I

Existing theories on the failure of American socialism in the 20th century provide ample opportunity for American society to indulge in self-congratulation, and this perhaps explains why no one has defined a truly satisfactory view of the problem. The absorption of third party platforms by major parties, the economic prosperity of a society that met the economic grievances that led to the formation of socialist parties in other nations, the consensual, Lockean basis of an American liberalism which was broad enough to accept the demands of the left, the religious and radical conservatism of the American workers, social mobility, or limited trade union job consciousness—all these generally accepted interpretations have permitted a narrower view than is justified of the nature of the historical context in which American radicalism failed. If each has some merit, their collective thesis by-passes a somewhat less attractive possibility that American socialism failed partly because of its own internal life and ideology, but primarily because in crucial respects American society and politics in the 20th century have also failed in a world wracked by war and repression. Indeed, given the cataclysmic nature of a great part of the century, tepid views of the demise of socialism avoid the tenor of the period by ignoring the relationship of the failure of organized American socialism to the failure not just of American politics and diplomacy, but also to the intellectual and political collapse of the left everywhere in the Western world. It is worth considering some of the internal and external causes of the decline of American radicalism.

The intellectual and political heritage of Marxism did not prepare the left in America and Europe for the complexities of the 20th century, if only because, exegetical citations notwithstanding, Marxism and all its later varieties and schools prior to World War I accepted a paralyzing and debilitating optimism which was inherited from the intellectual tradition of the idea of Progress. Defeat as a possibility of long-term, even permanent duration was never entertained, and a social theory that cannot consider this option is not merely intellectually unsatisfactory but misleading as a basis of political analysis and action. Ignoring the intellectual issue of possessing an accurate account of past events, mechanistic optimism led socialists to slight the negative consequences of action or inaction in relation to desired goals,

Reprinted, with deletions, from Gabriel Kolko, "The Decline of American Radicalism in the Twentieth Century," Studies on the Left, vol. 6 (September–October 1966), pp. 9–26, by permission of Studies on the Left.

and to try to fit every major event of political and economic development into a pattern of inevitable progression that justified optimism. Such determinism led to quietism, even celebration and opportunism, as socialists everywhere welcomed the events that led to their undoing. Never was it considered that societies have options to succeed and to fail in the attainment of desired goals, and that the precarious relationship of means to ends warranted continuous concern. Social democracy and bolshevism alike, sharing the premises of historical liberalism, avoided considering the possibility of tragic history, a viewpoint that might be based on secular premises but which placed, as the price of success, a greater burden on superior thought and appropriate social action at critical junctures in history. The need for decisive action in unpredictable situations had no meaningful place in either socialist or, after 1918, bolshevik political strategy, since the normal evolution of things did not warrant it, and for this reason the paralysis of the left in the face of reaction before World War I or between the two World Wars is quite explicable.

The relevance of Marxism to the 20th century depends less on its function as an inspiration of radical faith and commitment than its value as an intellectual system capable of being applied in an elucidating manner to social reality. After the demise of Austrian socialism and Rosa Luxemburg it may be argued that, on the level of social and economic analysis, Marxists produced remarkably little of value, and hence Marxism's function as an ideology and exaltation of social change was hopelessly limited for the tasks at hand. And since the Western left in general was theoretically impoverished, it should come as no surprise that the American left was not much below the intellectual par of the international movement. There is nothing "exceptionalist" about the fact that not one important or original socialist theoretician emerged in the entire history of American socialism—a best it produced charismatic figures or men of rare degrees of integrity admired for their constancy and dedication. Although American socialism on an organizational level was infinitely weaker than European socialism, what is important is that Western European social democracy and bolshevism could never translate mass political movements into political success—in the form of a substantially new social order—and for many of the same reasons that prevented the emergence of a serious American left.

What were the intellectual causes of the impotence of socialism and its failure to develop a dynamic social theory appropriate to the complicated economic and political realities of this century?

Marx undoubtedly wished his intellectual system to serve as the beginning of a theoretical reservoir that his successors were to continuously apply and amplify, but the fact is that it was not. What may have been a stimulus for social change eventually constricted it as the left failed to keep abreast of the evolution of modern capitalism and society. This widening gap between theory and reality often led to the application of 19th century premises to 20th century conditions, and Marxism became the deadening burden on the left—the opium of optimism and certitude Marx assimilated in the prior century disarmed the revolutionists of the 20th century save, as in the case of Lenin, where the will to power led to the abandonment of ideology. The socialists certainly did not fail because of Marxism, but because their reliance on a stultified view of it was used to justify action for which no better rationale was found. Marxism was primarily effect rather than cause, but it failed to correct opportunism and optimism.

Marx and Engels early took their stand against the assumption of the utopian socialists that industrial technology was malleable and capable of decentralized controls and direction by men for their own social purposes. To Marx and the Marxists the inevitable centralization and monopolization of industry under capitalism was not only a prerequisite to a new social order but its best guarantee. Marxists, from the American Socialist Party to the Mensheviks, dismissed tampering with this inexorable trend as a hopeless undertaking. After the economic imperatives of the system had spun itself into a giant tangled superstructure, capitalism would presumably choke under its own weight and contradictions.

Such an interpretation of the evolution of capitalism logically led to a consideration of the fragility of the economy in the larger social context rather than an inquiry into the extent to which big business might have weaknesses not necessarily involving constant and variable capital, surplus value, or rates of profitability, but rather weaknesses reflecting innovation, decentralization of the market, or the international economy. American socialists, with the possible exception of William E. Walling, hardly discussed the prospects for the economy in a way that hinted that the character and function of the political order might be deeply influenced by the needs of the economy, changing the features of both politics and economics in some decisive fashion requiring a political theory of change superior to Engels' last expression of Marxism. This shortcoming was just as true in Europe among the dominant schools of socialism as it was in America.

It is not unfair to suggest that the parliamentarian and legalist theory of social change which the American and European socialists accepted in theory and practice before the First World War, and that the bolsheviks of Western Europe accepted in practice from the mid-1920's onward, was also a logical outcome of Marxist theory. It would be very easy indeed to catalog Marx and Engels' comments concerning the need for revolutionary action, but both in their response to anarchism and the spectacular electoral triumph of German Social Democracy Marx and Engels eventually opted for left *politics* as the crucial means of social change in the West, and hence implicitly for a liberal political theory that assumed that the political structure, in the last analysis and despite corruption, was a classless tool available to the workers.

The belief in the efficacy of the ballot box and the ultimate neutrality of the state laid the basis for the subsequent parliamentary mechanism, naivete and failure of Western European socialism. A logical conclusion of this premise was a serious misconception of the functions of the state in the economy and society. American socialists could therefore see state intervention in the economy as a kind of surrogate socialism, perhaps reflecting the interests of small business against big industry, as Walling interpreted it, but an important step toward true socialism. And with their faith in parliamentarianism European socialism was led down the less uncomfortable path of the "politics of responsibility," and an accommodation to a fragile and reluctantly liberal order that failed after 1914 to stem the demise of that system before the challenges of war and reaction. Responsibility to an irresponsible society did in fact lead to the attainment of certain minimal goals in Western Europe—to a kind of welfare state—but the socialist movement failed to reverse the deeply regressive aspects of Western capitalism that periodically expressed itself in crises that threatened to wipe out, and frequently did so, welfarism and much else besides, including the socialists. The view of socialists in America and Europe alike by 1914 was that for all their limitations the existing political forms could be utilized for a clean fight for a clean victory, a victory that would not be borne in terror, struggle and counter-terror. For the new world the socialists wished to create before 1914, the outlines of which Marx, Engels and their successors only vaguely specified, the inherited structural forms were still viable. Both the American and European socialists accepted this assumption.

The vehicle for exploiting this structure was the working class, which in its dynamism, strikes and organizations created in the face of repression and conflict, seemed to be engaged in a continuous process which was, certainly in its American context, best characterized by the term "struggle." The socialists interpreted this struggle as having a revolutionary meaning involving decisive social change rather than limited ends, a confusion that historical experience has yet to prove justified. It seemed inconceivable that this epic of heroism and sacrifice might be directed toward something less than heroic and ennobling goals. The American socialist movement, and certain revisionist schools in Europe as well, also saw the need for winning over men of good will from the middle-classes, classes that had economic problems also driving them to socialism, but in the last analysis the concept of the working class was the core of the theory of change.

Looking at the emergence of new efforts to regulate the economy prior to the First World War, socialists everywhere failed to understand the political-economic process they were living through, a process that was pragmatic, haphazard and hardly comprehended by even its most sophisticated advocates. Nothing in socialist theory, much less *laissez faire* and marginal economic theory, prepared socialists for the possibility that a class-oriented integration of the state and the economy in many key areas would rationalize and strengthen capitalism. This process could only reinforce modern capitalism in a way that not only made Marxian economics obsolescent, but which made democratic social change, and the political instrumentalities supposedly available for that purpose, more remote. In this process of development, socialists, almost without exception in the United States and generally in Europe, misinterpreted capitalism's desire to strengthen itself with seemingly neutral techniques of sophisticated economic planning, techniques which nothing in the socialist intellectual heritage helped them to understand and which by their endorsing helped lead to the almost willing demise of the left. Like orthodox advocates of *laissez faire*, many socialists believed that state intervention in the economy was a step toward socialism.

In all this the response of American socialism was not exceptional. The question is not merely why socialists failed to build a party in the United States, as important and as uniquely American as these causes may be, but why socialists also failed on the decisive intellectual issues where they were well organized. To the extent that the complexities of 20th century capitalism and politics outstripped American socialism, it may be suggested that it failed for the same reasons that the European socialists failed.

II

Yet the distinctive American causes for the failure of socialism and radicalism in the 20th century also deserve reconsideration. These causes were both external to the organized socialist groups, rooted in the unique character of the larger social order, and internal, reflecting the special qualities of parties and their followers.

The political and intellectual history of the Socialist Party, much less the Communist Party, is far better described and understood by historians than that of perhaps either major party over a similar period, and this fascination with causes that have failed rather than those that have succeeded affords me the luxury of generalizing on the thorough research of others. The genesis of American socialism until 1900 was colorful, like an intellectual hothouse, but not more so than that of the British Labor Party, which was at least as exotic. Socialism as a cause touched every interesting intellectual current—Christians who saw in polite socialism a way to bring a piece of heaven to earth, funny-money advocates seeking deeper solutions than free silver, cooperative colonization groups, led by Eugene Victor Debs, that could appeal to John D. Rockefeller as a "Christian gentleman" to bring the frontier opportunities back to America, discontented intellectuals seeking to end the alienation of industrial society, followers of Edward Bellamy's Nationalist movement, and, of course, the Marxist-oriented elements that were to effectively dominate the party after 1901 when the Socialist Party was formed out of an amalgam of various groups.

The internal world of the Socialist Party until 1912 was not unlike that of German Social Democracy, from which it absorbed many of the doctrinal positions of both Eduard Bernstein's revisionist school and his seemingly left critics. The Party was not merely partially German on ideological issues —borrowing from the Bernstein-Kautsky debate was a convenience, not a cause—but also in the classic bureaucratic sense described by Robert Michels in *Political Parties*. From this viewpoint the Socialist Party was a party of functionaries, officials and an elite quite impatient with rank-and-file democracy and dissent. The Party, like most pre-World War I European Social Democratic parties, was bolshevik in structure though fairly democratic in organizational theory. Later in 1919 the men who controlled the Party before the war were to expel the vast bulk of the members for their support of bolshevik theory as well, just as they had expelled the embarrassingly non-parliamentarian Industrial Workers of the World faction at the 1912 convention. The Party had never actively sought to enlist the vast slum and industrial working class, and in purging the I. W. W., it broke with its already minimal pre-war mass working class contacts. It was, to cite Trotsky's unkind but apt remark, a party of dentists, and always remained so at the leadership levels.

The middle-class character of the majority of Socialist leaders reflected their belief that the middle-class and skilled workers were the most promising for membership, and this unconsciously required a crucial conformity to dominant prejudices, assumptions that guaranteed that the political strength of the Socialists could never exceed the 900,000 votes of the 1912 election unless the Party radically altered its tactics—which it never did. In the area of trade unionism the Party always maintained its primary contacts with the A. F. of L., which at this time was the most conservative major union in the world.

The position of the Socialist Party on civil rights and racism was hardly designed to win support from the Negro community either. Before the war the Socialist Party tolerated within its ranks social segregation, the exclusion of Negroes from Southern white locals and theories of racial superiority. The Party passed only one resolution on Negro rights—a weak one—between 1901–12. Anti-Oriental prejudice was common as well, and on this question, as well as the larger issue of immigration restriction, the Party followed the conservative, even reactionary leadership of the A. F. of L. It made little effort before the war to enroll immigrants or to publish sufficient non-English materials, and what little was produced in this field was generally from local and individual initiative.

The expulsion of the I. W. W. in 1912 soon cost the Party an important minority of its 125,000 members, but new circumstances were nevertheless to result in a victory for its left wing. The Party lost most of its intellectuals to the pro-war cause, but its intransigent position against the war—until 1917 there was nothing unique about its neutralism—attracted vast electoral support. In the 1917 municipal elections it increased its percentage of total votes received from three to eight times by campaigning on an anti-war platform, its vote being considerably greater in areas with large Yankee populations. Indeed, by 1919 the Party's membership was almost restored to its 1912 peak, but the complexion of that membership had radically altered. Thirteen percent of the Party belonged to foreign language sections in 1912, 53 percent in 1919. The Socialist Party had moved to the left for the first time, had become a party of immigrants, and was making significant electoral gains.

Although internecine disputes have wracked the Socialist Party since 1919 and would have destroyed it in any case, it is worth noting that at the very moment American Socialism appeared on the verge of significant organizational and political success, it was attacked by the combined resources of the Federal and various state governments. Elected candidates were denied their seats in Congress and various state assemblies, immigrant leaders were deported under the Espionage and Sedition Acts, numerous leaders of the Party were jailed, newspapers were denied mailing privileges and otherwise harassed, and in many localities the club, lock and prison ended Party activity. If the Government used war and patriotism as justification, it should be recalled that leading progressives, with rare exceptions, also supported the Red Scare and repressive laws for reasons always implicit in pre-war progressive ideologies. Progressives wished to integrate the labor and immigrant community into an ordered, homogeneous society, and they feared socialism might be the consequence of their failure to do so. Roosevelt had never equivocated on the use of force against dissident labor, and consistently endorsed major infractions of the civil liberties of unions and their leaders. Progressivism to men such as Roosevelt was designed, among other things, to head off the threat of socialism by reforming capitalism. The United States Steel Corporation, accepted by Roosevelt as a model of enlightened business, could introduce both welfare measures and Pinkertons when needed. In brief, if labor could not be voluntarily integrated into the social order by good works, it was to be tailored to size by chopping off its unmanageable left by any means appropriate to the task, including suppression. Only when one takes this equation into account can we comprehend the near unanimity of pre-war reformers in favor of Wilson's Red Scare and the Espionage and Sedition Acts.

In a sense the failure of American radicalism was due, at least between 1917 and 1920, to the failure of American politics to operate according to the conventionally accepted but rarely practiced ideal theories of democratic political processes. American Socialism was unable to appreciate the limitations this breakdown might have for their own concept of change, a view that remained static until it was too late. To the extent the true character and the efficacy of a political structure is revealed only under the test of pressure and crisis, it can be suggested that Socialists shared a generally-held sublime innocence concerning the resilience of American democracy during crisis. For Socialists this naivete was decisive, since their stake in the validity of existing mechanisms of change was vital—for others, the fixity of the political machine merely reinforced their interests in the status quo.

Looking at American society and politics before the First World War the Socialists could see a class structure as an objective fact, and sufficient tumult and noise within it to impute to it a seemingly dynamic aspect. Such dynamics could be measured, and if amplified held out hope of vindicating the socialist theory of change. Classes, strata and competing interests were recognized by Marx, though he neither created them nor was he the first to discover their existence. Since politics was based ultimately on conflict, the class context of such conflict might lead to decisive social change. Yet one other possibility existed which socialists refused to consider, but which Thorstein Veblen had proposed before the war. American society could also be understood as a class structure without *decisive* class conflict, a society that had conflict limited to smaller issues that were not crucial to the existing order, and on which the price of satisfying opposition was relatively modest from the viewpoint of the continuation of the social system. In brief, a static class structure serving class ends might be frozen into American society even if the interests and values served were those of a ruling class. A sufficiently monolithic consensus might voluntarily exist on the fundamental questions indispensable to the continuation of the existing political and economic elites, and their primary interest would be respected in the last analysis. The functionally dominant conception of interests, the prime values of the society, did not have to be essentially classless, as Louis Hartz and recent theorists of consensus have argued, but merely accepted by those segments of society without an objective stake in the constituted order. This, I believe, was the point that Veblen was making, not in order to rationalize the dominance of business in American life but to explain the extent of its obvious spiritual and material pervasiveness.

The best argument for such an interpretation is the fact that at no time in American history in this century has the labor movement or the dispossessed translated their struggles for specific demands into a larger demand for fundamental change. The mythology of American society as one that welcomes opportunity and equality for all—as if a vaguely defined rhetoric is more realistic than a frank appreciation of the functionally inegalitarian and class nature of America—extends not only to labor, but even to civil rights activists who seek entry of the Negro into a society that is inherently stratified and class-oriented in decisive ways having nothing to do with race. And if everyone does not share this consensus consciously, and indeed even if the majority neither agrees nor disagrees but is apathetic on such matters, the least that can be said is that no one has been able to redirect such apathy toward a meaningful alternative. Indeed, even the apathetic usually permit the consensual ideology of American life to be defined for them during times of crisis and pressure, and they accept erstwhile national goals which are in fact class goals and interests. The apathy itself proves less than the fact that conscious deviations from manipulated consensual values have been roughly disparaged in this century as "Hunism," "pacifism," "bolshevism," or what have you, suggesting that although voluntary most of the time, the power of legal authority has also reinforced and defined consensus to save society from dangers the possibility of functional democracy posed to the existing order.

The failure of the Socialist Party, therefore, also reflected the consensual and voluntarily accepted total domination of American political ideology, an ideology that was conveniently described as classless, and in recent years as the end rather than the total triumph of ideology, in order to reaffirm the ideal view of the neutral, free and untrammelled nature of the political mechanism. American radicals accepted this mythology and tried to play the game according to rules that were quite irrelevant to social and political reality, a reality that was obscured until the exercise of nominal political rights threatened to become unmanageable and Red Scares, the manipulation of electoral laws and the like were required to reinforce a consensus that was equivalent to class domination. And since the force of challenges to this control was rarely very great, and the American left was usually incapacitated by its own internal weaknesses, the true character of politics as a means for confirming and legitimizing the existing order was rarely revealed. For the American left to regard this historical experience frankly would also have required a willingness to reorient their descriptive social theory and their concept of change. To consider the union movement as wedded to reform capitalism would have called for a less reverent, flexible view of labor. To regard the electoral structure as free only when it was not exercised would have demanded new tactics, tactics which also might have been inappropriate in light of the seemingly pervasive support for the social order by those with the smallest stake in it. That the society might have been, quite voluntarily and even happily, functionally totalitarian in its monolithic character would have required the rejection of the political optimism of the 19th century, an optimism that not merely rationalized unimportant gestures that constituted a make-believe world of democratic rhetoric concealing controlled politics, but also offered the left some hope of eventual success. That success was perhaps unobtainable in a game so completely loaded required a realism that bordered on a willingness to accept a tragic view that possibly involved writing off America as an arena for social progress in the 20th century.

And rather than consider these unpleasant alternatives the American left after 1919 continued in its ritual acts of self-destruction.

One of the more common interpretations of the failure of the American left—defined to include both the Socialist and Communist Parties after 1919— ascribes its demise to the success of American capitalism. This view might make sense applied to a period of full employment, but for a decade after 1929 both the left and the larger social structure in which it operated had failed, and well before the New Deal reforms allegedly stole its thunder and presumably impinged on its basic demands, the Socialist Party was quite dead. It existed, of course, but never as a serious factor in shaping American politics or labor unionism toward some socially meaningful new departure. What it called "life" was a factional precociousness that sharpened the pole-mical talents of its brighter young followers, talents many were later to employ to their own advantage as key spokesmen for anti-communism after the Second World War.

The leaders of the Socialist Party during the 1920's fell into quieter, bureaucratic ways, managing their existing institutions, building their private careers and maintaining a doctrinal purity which was by this time well to the left of that prevalent in the pre-war party. The Communists, despite their anti-parliamentarian rhetoric, ran their first Presidential candidate in 1924, and differed only slightly from the Socialist Party in their functional political premises. The Communist Party too was primarily a party of recent immi-grants, and during the 1920's its amoebic internal life kept it preoccupied with Trotskyists and Lovestonites. Though it created its own organizational forms for the purpose, it duplicated the union and other activities of the Socialists. In brief, just as Social Democracy was bolshevized into bureau-cratic channels before the war, Bolshevism was being social democratized toward parliamentarian and unionist directions after 1924 in a way hardly designed to create a new order where others had failed.

The divisions in the Socialist Party after 1933 do not warrant much consideration. Factors having to do with age, politics or psychology kept the Party in factional turbulence to the extent that from 22,000 members in 1934 it dropped to 7,000 in 1938 and 2,000 in 1941, and has not exceeded the last figure since that time. During the 1930's the majority of the Socialist Party's members were foreign-born or first generation, and this pattern of immigrant domination was even more widespread in the Communist Party. In this con-text both parties became a kind of fraternal center—the majority of the literature of the Socialist Party was not in English—for lonely migrants who might raise funds at banquets for the Scottsboro boys but were essentially adjusting as best they could to a strange, new life. What was ultimately more important to such leftists was the conviviality of the banquet hall and comrades who spoke the mother tongue. These activities might also finance the work of the more earnest younger men who were wholly committed to politics as they defined it and, especially in the case of the Communists after 1935, might be caught in the euphoria and passion of organizing the C.I.O., going to Spain or participating in student movements. Even when the Communists lost their capacity to attract the young and the earnest they could still, even in the worst days of McCarthyism, retain their banquet hall followers whose social roots were grounded in the activities of the I.W.O. or other organizations—aging and bewildered people who were transformed in the social imagery into conspirators posing a serious danger to society.

The intellectual problems of the Socialists and Communists in America were very much like those of their associates in Europe. Throughout the 1930's the European left was fighting a losing, rear-guard battle and drifting along with the capitalists toward a world conflagration. The left was characterized by futile efforts to respond to the initiatives of reaction. The Western European left, the Communist Parties included, was incapable of breaking out of the mold of a parliamentarianism no longer resilient enough to provide the decisive leadership necessary for social change capable of stopping the tide of the Right. "Socialism" from this time onward became merely another, more technically sophisticated way of managing an effete European capitalism, and after the Popular Front period, and especially during 1944–47, the Communists frequently shared in this game by courting respectability via cabinet posts in France, Belgium and Italy, an effort that frequently made the practical domestic function of the Communist Party in Western Europe indistinguishable from that of the Social Democrats and liberal centrist parties.

It may perhaps be suggested that in fact the institutional and economic heritage of Western capitalism limited the European left, and hence doomed it to failure. If so, the left in both Europe and America never seriously acknowledged the dilemma, but persisted in giving obeisance to socialist doctrines that molded their political action to a concept of change. The dominant political leaders of these movements rarely contemplated that the left was participating in the strengthening of capitalism. This lack of reflection characterized the American left even more than the European, for here there was no intellectual core capable of grasping these dilemmas.

III

The sins of the Bolshevik left after the Second World War are well documented, so much so that the history of the American Communist Party in all its dimensions has become a major, well financed and thoroughly debilitating concern which has been both a cause and reflection of the demise of the American left. In its worst aspect it suggested that the Communist Party was an important experience in post-World War I American history, just as paranoid McCarthyites had suggested. At best it was a dialogue with Mc-Carthyism on terms and issues defined by that movement, critical only insofar as it applied higher canons of evidence. This concern engaged an articulate sector of the non-Communist Party left that implicitly regarded a discourse on an unimportant and impotent party as a more serious undertaking than a confrontation of basic social and political questions. Indeed, the issue of the Communist Party gave the left an excuse to postpone and ultimately avoid dealing with the much more significant and difficult issues facing it in an age of nuclear terror.

It was not unexpected that the non-communist left might focus so closely on the Communist Party, since anti-communism had become a categorical imperative of American life, and a way for the left to integrate itself with the larger assumptions of their society and perhaps make itself more plausible. Succumbing to the mood of the times, even while proclaiming a higher if not clearly defined morality, the American left gradually took over even more of the crucial assumptions of conventional politics, aligning itself with the more liberal wings of the Cold War in the hope, quite as chimerical, that it would succeed with the liberals in a way it had not been able to do with the workers. Turning an astringent eye on the faults of the bolsheviks, the post-war left could not recognize its own, much less see that their moral defects were very much in the same category as those it attributed to the bolsheviks. Both had lost critical perspective toward their favorite side, neither had anything new to say in regard to the American scene and its mechanics of change. The Eastern European situation was described by the socialists in the blackest detail, but little was said, for example, about the actions of French socialist ministers who in Indo-China, Madagascar and Algeria committed horrors on behalf of an old order that paled those of bolsheviks groping their way against resistance toward new societies. The moral distinctions that were evoked on behalf of anti-communism were obscured when it was necessary to give critical support to the West.

Such policies were a logical concomitant of social democratic biases, but not entirely conscious. With the exception of those who gave up social-ism for sociology and a technical precociousness which produced formal structural theories with less historical relevance than even hobbled socialist theses, American socialism of the non-Communist variety was characterized by a pervasive dilettantism. Crucial political judgments were made on the basis of the most casual information, and a precise focus on the institutional operation of society, politics and foreign relations was just as lacking as before the war. Socialism as an intellectual system became, for the most part, impressionist and literary, which added a sensitivity to subtle problems in only a few areas. Alienation and mass culture—the former had been a familiar complaint of radicals for decades—were deemed worthy of closer inquiry than economics or diplomacy. The post-war left preferred taking its insights from political novelists who, for all their perception, saw the world through a looking glass that obscured important distinctions that could be defined only by viewing society directly. A mediocre novelist such as George Orwell was far more influential than considerably more intelligent social scientists, and his success was based on the political favor with which his views were held.

Once socialists regarded totalitarianism, much less bolshevism, as a cause of the world crisis, rather than as the effect of the collapse of liberalism and Western politics, it was possible for socialists to enlist, with reservations that did not change their basic commitment, in the cause of the "Free World." The results were catastrophic. American radicals soon found themselves cutting the edge of their criticism and explicitly acknowledging the community of interests and assumptions with American politics and society that had always been implicit. In this position they were at a premium, their talents and books overpraised as they titillated a jaded and casual upper middle-class, professional audience. A few might sincerely maintain a semblance of critical integrity by dissecting marginal aspects of American life and politics, aspects that if altered would leave the larger society intact, but by 1952 no important neutralist or third-camp foreign policy position could be found among articulate radicals. And what was never willingly tolerated, above all, was a hard, dispassionate, uncommitted look at the competing worlds, their attainments as well as their shortcomings, much less a searching view of the foundations of American society and its purposes and historic role in the post-1945 crisis. Stronger claimants to intellectual and literary importance who failed to accept these premises were isolated or ignored by upper bohemia and the intellectual set connected with universities and the "cultural media." Only the subterranean world of the beats and isolated renegades claimed Kenneth Patchen; Europeans published Karl Korsch, who built a major reputation in France without ever being acknowledged in the country he resided in the last 25 years of his life; the anti-communist left read but also reviled C. Wright Mills. The post-war generation recognized the need for new ideas, and the call for the application of intelligence became a static posture, but little more. Intelligence was rarely applied to specific American issues in a way that increased knowledge, and studies of communism failed to alter this deficiency.

In the name of humanism, socialists in the United States gradually but firmly aligned themselves with the American cause in the deepest political and cultural sense—Castro, the Vietminh and the victims of the post-war world crisis became first as guilty as their potential executioners, as culpable morally, and then deserted in a manner that increasingly absolved the executioners. The impact of the Western resistance against revolutionary movements, especially in Eastern Europe and China, was rarely considered in evaluating the social systems that emerged. Again victims were condemned for their responses to the crimes of their executioners, as if the Cubans, Vietnamese and Chinese had chosen with deliberate malice to violate a humanist tradition they too evoked and claimed to act upon. The power of the old orders to shape the form of the new systems, and what was transitional or permanent, defensive or deliberate in the synthesis was never considered. Economic development as a justification of their action was dismissed as narrow economism, as if economic development were worth nothing. The losses involved in such a process were carefully examined, but never weighed and balanced against the gains, particularly in those areas that had precious little intellectual freedom or political democracy to lose. Growth rates and their distribution struck many as meaningless, and for *litterateurs* as uninteresting. That the difference between bolshevik totalitarianism with bread, and capitalist totalitarianism without bread, is the elimination of hunger, filth and death was gainsaid. That a dynamic society that ends starvation is freer in a crucial sense, and saves far more life than it may willingly or unwillingly destroy, is a point that was never confronted, even when politically meaningful options to the status quo or controlled planned economies did not exist.

To have considered these questions would have meant a rupture between the non-communist American left and the social order to which it had accommodated itself. To re-examine the political context of socialism closely might have meant a new and sympathetic alignment with forces throughout the world that have rejected the hegemony of American leadership, and it would have meant a return to isolation and discomfort. By the end of the 1950's the left which emerged from the Socialist Party tradition of the 1930's was incapable of making this adjustment. For 50 years the American left, because of ideological roots and optimistic belief in the efficacy of transforming the existing order, had been grounded in the acceptable myths and premises of the existing order. In the context of the world conflict, to refuse to align itself with the United States would have been equivalent to breaking the illusion of being political men with a political future. To assume otherwise would have been to take the unenviable and pessimistic position that radicalism, given the social and political realities of America, had moved beyond politics not because it had no political ideas but because it finally acknowledged it had no political means. The left would have been beyond politics not because politics is unimportant, but because the control and exercise of power is nominally democratic but in reality voluntarily totalitarian. To refuse to support the American cause would have shattered the last illusions concerning the nation's ability to tolerate dissent which does not choose to mark out areas of agreement on fundamental assumptions.

Instead radicals sought to remain politically "relevant" at the expense of their ability to protest against injustice emphatically and negatively. They found it necessary to argue for the existence of a viable political structure in the hope description would eventually assume the nature of self-fulfilling prophecy, even if their description of the political process sounded strangely similar to those of the academic schoolmen who confused liberal rhetoric with reality. At no time did they attempt to articulate a sense of history which generalized on the consistency in United States' policies at home and abroad, for this could only lead to seeing the politics of liberal rhetoric as a trap, and the pessimistic consequences of such a realization were not considered to be worth the loss of the assumption, if not illusion, that radicals were still free agents of potential power in a situation that was plastic and retained cause for hope.

The failure of the left by the end of the 1950's did not eliminate the need for a left, nor did their forced optimism alter the graver realities which underlay American domestic affairs and foreign policy. That a "new left" should have emerged was both predictable and logical, and that it should have all-too-many of the characteristics of the older left should not be surprising. Its factionalism is debilitating, and its view of the Negro and poor is not unlike that of the old leftists or Wobblies who cultivated illusions concerning mass industry or migrant workers. There is no serious awareness that modest gains for the Negro and poor may make far-reaching successes, the prerequisite of permanent social change, impossible. A society that is poisoned produces poisoned responses and men, and those who do not succumb to these pressures may find themselves a very small minority of the white and black community—a rare minority of principled radicals with a commitment that is not likely to gain followers in the milieu of aborted movements of progress.

The new left has had the political courage to challenge the politics of the status quo, though it too frequently hopes that the existing political mechanism may somehow be applied to serve its own radical ends. But it has not asked sharp or relevant questions concerning the intellectual premises of the old left, and has merely rejected its chronic anti-communism and myopia concerning the liberals in the Democratic Party. To succeed intellectually where the old left failed, the new left will have to find fundamentally new and far-reaching premises, premises that are not obsequious in the presence of the ghosts of the 18th and 19th centuries. And to succeed politically it must find dynamic possibilities and forces of movement in a social order in crisis, forces it must frankly acknowledge may not exist as permanent or decisive factors for social change. Having rejected the conservative, futile politics of the old left, the new left has yet to define a solid alternative, much less begin to create it. . . .

epilogue

The Political Economy of Cultural and Social Revolution

Whenever one seeks to incorporate the "lessons of history" in speculations about the future of any society, the first rule should be to throw up one's hands in despair. The record of historical prophecy by professional social analysts has generally proved no more encouraging than that of politicians and millenarianists. The leading economists of the 1920s believed with Herbert Hoover that the American economy was destined for unlimited and uninterrupted expansion. To forecast the Great Depression would have endangered the reputation of any economist. Similarly, in our time, sociologists and political scientists were unable to predict the emergence of the militant extraparliamentary movements for fundamental social change in the 1960s, despite massive research on racial and ethnic minorities and students in the years preceding the protest marches, sit-ins, riots, and the early signs of urban guerrilla warfare in the United States.

From these two examples it might be argued that we should never overestimate the stability of any society, however tranquil things may appear at a given moment. Yet it is also true that societies with profound institutional

471

contradictions have avoided economic and political collapse for centuries.[1] In fact, the entire history of human civilizations testifies to the durability of political economies beset by chronic social pathology. Thus, those who view the recent social unrest in America as necessarily leading to a fundamentally new institutional and cultural structure are perhaps as likely to be in error as those who continue to foresee stability. As Seymour Martin Lipset suggests in a complacent but insightful article: "History, fortunately or not, operates cyclically as well as secularly. Cultural styles, political trends, intellectual orientations have a tendency to be self-exhausting. As they move to extremes they produce counter-reactions."[2]

Lipset argues that many of the "symptoms" heralding radical social change such as intense antimilitarism, generational revolt, alienation, and cultural revolt have occurred frequently in twentieth-century America without leading to a collapse of the system. At a theoretical level he criticizes "structural trend analysis," which perceives frequently recurring social phenomena (for example, student unrest) as the unique and inevitable results of long-term changes in the institutional characteristics of societies, phenomena which signal the birth of a new epoch. However, Lipset is speaking with the knowledge that American parliamentary capitalism has survived the onslaught of militant social movements from the Left and Right. Without this knowledge, how would he have written about the ascension of an American communism, socialism, or fascism? Would he describe the French, Russian, and Chinese revolutions as the result of the unparalleled genius of tiny bands of revolutionaries who exploited routine social problems in ways that brought about the transformation of entire social systems? If so, Lipset would seemingly embrace a variant of the "Great Man" theory of history, in which social change is dependent upon historical accidents which permit a few individuals to prevent restoration of the natural equilibrium of social life in otherwise unexceptional periods of social stress.

While social revolution has always involved the concatenation of fortuitous circumstances and the organizational genius of relatively small numbers of known or unknown political activists able to channel mass disaffection toward political ends, I would still maintain that certain features are "necessary" in all societies entering a revolutionary period. Some of these features are what Lipset would call structural trends, or long-standing structural features of a society; others are structurally based symptoms of the disintegration of ruling political and economic elites. Whether the existence of these preconditions of revolutionary change actually result in social revolution may also depend upon the relative capabilities of revolutionary and counterrevolutionary "leaders" and groups, the intervention of outside force, and a good deal of luck. These factors, however, should rightfully be considered "sufficient" conditions for social revolution.

[1] Barrington Moore, Jr., *Social Origins of Dictatorship and Democracy: Lord and Peasant in the Making of the Modern World* (Boston, The Beacon Press, 1966), pp. 314–410.
[2] Seymour Martin Lipset, "The Banality of Revolt," *Saturday Review*, vol. 53 (July 18, 1970), p. 34.

REVOLUTIONARY CHANGE IN OTHER SOCIETIES

Before I examine the particularities of the American case in the 1970s in regard to origins of the present crisis and the prospects for revolutionary change from the Left (or Right), it will be helpful to consider some factors which have been preconditions for the radical transformation of the economic, political, legal, and cultural institutions of societies that have undergone revolutionary change in the modern era.[3]

The most significant symptom exhibited by societies entering revolutionary periods is the delegitimation of existing political and economic elites. This process permits oppositional groups to freely organize and agitate and frustrates the attempts of elites to isolate and discredit them. Since ruling elites encompass a small minority of the population in any society, they must rely primarily upon their ability to solve social problems and/or to maintain ideological hegemony in order to preserve legitimacy. Ideological hegemony is maintained by a popular acceptance of an elite-sponsored set of cultural values and beliefs that legitimizes or obscures the fact that the political economy is serving the interests of one class or stratum rather than of society as a whole. Elite ideology also defines role behavior in other crucial social settings (for example, the family, educational institutions) which function to solidify existing power relationships.

Under what conditions does delegitimation occur? An examination of the great revolutions of the modern era suggests several sources of delegitimation. First and foremost, prerevolutionary periods are characterized by severe social problems which challenge the capabilities and, more importantly, the loyalties of elites. Barrington Moore, Jr., perhaps the foremost contemporary authority on comparative revolution, believes that in such periods there

. . . has been the appearance of very sharp conflicts of interest within the dominant classes themselves. In all major revolutions so far, the symptom has been apparently insoluble financial problems. Behind the symptom has been acute disagreement—insoluble contradictions might for once do as a meaningful empirical term here—over how to resolve stresses posed by the rise of new social relationships and, more specifically, over which social groups are to bear the costs of these new arrangements. This split

[3] I am assuming that the American ruling class, like all previous ruling classes, will not permit the overthrow of the economic, legal, and political foundations of its power even if this were to be accomplished through legal (that is, parliamentary) means. My article in Chapter 2 and Kolko's in Chapter 9 of this text cast grave doubt upon the thesis that parliamentary capitalism can be transformed into genuine socialism (as opposed to European-style social democracy) by a *primary* emphasis on "working within the system." A partial test of this thesis may be forthcoming in Chile where the elected Marxist president is seeking the parliamentary road to socialism. See Paul Sweezy and Harry Magdoff, "Peaceful Transition to Socialism?" and Oskar Lange, "On the Policy of Transition," *Monthly Review*, vol. 22 (January, 1971), pp. 1–18, 38–44, respectively. See also Eric Hobsbawm, "Chile: Year One," *The New York Review of Books*, vol. 17 (September 23, 1971), pp. 23–32.

in the dominant classes has quite different causes in successive historical epochs and in different countries. Hence there is little to be gained to reduce it to a single pattern of events.[4]

Whereas Moore seems correct in avoiding a *single* generalization about the sources of splits in the dominant classes in prerevolutionary periods, his most exhaustive study of comparative paths to modernization finds that acute conflicts between and within elites and among elites and nonelites have been produced by problems of foreign domination; humiliation in war; collection of state revenues; and the relative claims on state power and resources of landlords, peasants, urban dwellers, and the emerging commercial class.[5] Political elites generally have failed to solve these problems because they had neither the material nor political resources to do so and/or were compromised by their strong ties to social strata or classes whose short-run self-interests brought economic catastrophe to the mass of the population.[6]

While insoluble contradictions may have manifested themselves in crises of a cyclical nature, Moore's comparative work indicates clearly, contra Lipset, that the traditional structural arrangements, cultural orientations, and short-run interests of elites made them ill equipped to handle the problems likely to emerge after the introduction of new economic, political, and social relations by indigenous forces or forcefully from abroad.

Although the existence of an insoluble contradiction is essential in the process of delegitimizing elites, other factors must also be present to transform a loss of confidence in the old order into a willingness to aid, actively or passively, in its overthrow. As stated earlier, hopelessly corrupt brutal political systems which generated or at least tolerated widespread misery have frequently operated for generations, even centuries, without serious opposition. For discontent to be expressed in revolutionary actions rather than in fatalistic withdrawal from political activity, people have to believe in an alternative to the existing system. In this connection, the "desertion of the intellectuals" in revolutionary periods, appears to be an important factor not only in destroying the ideological hegemony of the existing elites but in projecting, however vaguely, an appealing vision of a new society.[7]

Despite the common belief that intellectuals are alienated from authority throughout history they have performed valuable services in supplying elites with justifications for or obfuscations of existing social and political arrange-

[4] Barrington Moore, Jr., "Revolution in America?" *The New York Review of Books*, vol. 12 (January 30, 1969), p. 6.

[5] Moore, *op. cit.*, 1966.

[6] It is, of course, always possible to second guess the elites of regimes that have succumbed to social revolution and point out how easily they might have avoided disaster if they had only known what the modern researcher does. Nevertheless, irrationality has always played a role in human history and the *theoretical* possibility of resolving social contradictions without revolution should not blind social analysts to the fact that elites, like all humans, are sometimes unable or unwilling to do what is both urgent and possible.

[7] Crane Brinton, *The Anatomy of Revolution* (New York: Vintage Books, 1960), pp. 41–52. Moore, *op. cit.*, 1969, p. 6.

ments. Moreover, their formulations have been disseminated to the masses in ways calculated to integrate the latter into the society. While some dissenting intellectuals are found in every society, revolutionary eras are characterized by a widespread discrediting of old ideas and intellectual leaders by dissenting groups which exert significant influence over at least the most potentially active sector of the population: youth. In modern times, classical and contemporary liberalism as well as Marxism have captured the imagination of the intellectual stratum and then penetrated in crude form into the consciousness of large numbers of common people. Thus, these ideologies have become key ingredients in social reform and even revolution.

At this juncture it should be noted that the failure of the political system to solve fundamental economic problems and the desertion of the intellectuals can also be preconditions for social reforms that fall short of revolution.[8] Moore, echoing Leon Trotsky's firsthand analysis of the Russian Revolution, believes that the one factor that distinguishes mass movements which result in reform from those which culminate in revolution is the "loss of unified control over the instruments of violence: the army and the police." He is convinced that "without control or neutralization of the government's armed forces, revolutionary movements do not have the shimmer of a ghost of a chance."[9] A disciplined well-organized armed force can induce submission in a society that has lost all faith in its political elites.

Thus far the discussion of preconditions for social revolution has concentrated upon the disintegration of elite unity and efficacy and the erosion of elite legitimacy and control over the means of coercion. Having maintained that the masses must be able to believe in the desirability and possibility of an alternative to their present situation, we must now examine the importance of the masses *feeling* that they can overthrow the old order *themselves* with or without organized revolutionary leadership. Mass perceptions of the possibility of success in revolution is a crucial factor in determining the extent of insurrectionary behavior. Such behavior is often triggered by the immediate, short-term inability of certain groups to endure a sudden deterioration of consumptive standards within the context of general economic hardship. Food shortages, increasing prices, and excessive taxation have often been the proximate causes of both peasant and urban rioting.[10] But if mass action is to spread and create the possibility of revolution, not mere rebellion, those who are not among the most oppressed must be drawn into the struggle.

People who are alienated from the political system and afraid to risk their material and physical security must have some confidence that their

---

[8] Moore, *op. cit.,* 1969, p. 6.

[9] *Ibid.*, p. 6. See also Leon Trotsky, *The Russian Revolution: The Overthrow of Tzarism and the Triumph of the Soviets*, selected and ed. by F. W. Dupee (New York: Doubleday & Company, Inc., 1959), pp. 97–147.

[10] Moore, *op. cit.*, 1969, p. 8. See also James Davies, "The J-Curve of Rising and Declining Satisfactions as a Cause of Some Great Revolutions and a Contained Rebellion," in Hugh Davis Graham and Ted Robert Gurr, eds., *The History of Violence in America: Historical and Comparative Perspectives* (New York: Bantam Books, 1969), pp. 690–730.

minimal needs for survival can be met under chaotic conditions. With the exception of the invariably small number of ideologically committed revolutionaries and the hopelessly deprived groups who feel they have little to lose even in death, most persons worry whether their commitment to insurrection will jeopardize whatever small comforts are theirs. Striking workers and crowds have little capacity to provide food, clothing, and shelter on more than a temporary basis. And, unless the police and armed force are neutralized or won over, such groups cannot provide protection against violent military repression. If the movement does not quickly spread, most persons will probably begin within a matter of days or a few weeks at the most to reestablish ties with their normal sources of minimal material security.[11] Strikers and pillaging masses will soon return to familiar work routines. This process is most likely to occur in urban settings where populations are highly vulnerable because of their lack of material self-sufficiency. Peasant insurrections usually must be put down by armed force, since the insurrectionists control food supplies and are not nearly as dependent upon external sources of sustenance as urban dwellers.[12]

A widespread belief that the ruling elites have lost self-confidence, are divided amongst themselves, and are incapable of restoring order facilitates the spread of insurrectionary behavior. In addition, the resort to violent repression by elites—especially when misdirected—is both a cause and a consequence of delegitimation and spurs the process on. The relationship between repression and radicalization may be more complicated, however, than it has seemed to liberal elites and militant advocates of "confrontation politics." There is evidence that repression succeeds in radicalizing people only when they feel that those being repressed are engaged in legitimate activity, whether it is legal or not.[13] However, if a repressive policy is carried out in a sufficiently thorough, brutal, and fear-inspiring manner—as in contemporary Greece—it still may inhibit insurrectionary behavior despite an increase in mass disaffection.

Given that control or neutralization of the armed forces is necessary for a revolution to succeed, another factor that makes potential rebels hopeful is a belief that the army is not willing to defend the old regime or that there is at least disunity among the soldiers. This condition is most likely to exist when the army is demoralized by defeat, especially in an unpopular war, or when its ranks are filled by members of groups who feel alienated from the political system.

Finally, a key ingredient in motivating many people to join the revolutionaries is the belief that these forces are committed to achieving total victory in their struggle against the ruling elites. Highly visible elements of the population such as soldiers are particularly influenced by this consideration. As Trotsky writes of the all-important behavior of the Tzar's army during the February 1917 revolution:

---

[11] Moore, *op. cit.*, 1969, pp. 8–9.

[12] *Ibid.* See also Martin Oppenheimer, *The Urban Guerrilla* (Chicago: Quadrangle Books, 1969).

[13] Edward Gude, "Batista and Betancourt: Alternative Responses to Violence," in Graham and Gurr, *op. cit.*, pp. 731–747.

... the more the soldiers in their mass are convinced that the rebels are really rebelling—that this is not a demonstration after which they will have to go back to the barracks and report, that this is a struggle to the death, that the people may win if they join them, and that this winning will not only guarantee impunity, but alleviate the lot of all—the more they realize this—the more willing they are to turn aside their bayonets, or go over with them to the people. In other words, the revolutionists can create a break in the soldiers' mood only if they themselves are actually ready to seize the victory at any price whatever, even the price of blood.[14]

The growth of widespread insurrection does not seem to depend heavily upon the prior agitation or organizational work of professional revolutionaries. However, the spread of insurrection, even when it encompasses a majority or strategic minority of the population, is no guarantee that social revolution will succeed. At this point, the resolute behavior of organized political groups, such as the Bolshevik party in October 1917 appears necessary to sustain the revolution. The difference between the partial or abortive revolutions of February 1917 in Russia and May 1968 in France and the successful conclusion of the French, Russian and Chinese revolutions, has rested clearly upon the capacities of organized political groups.[15] Once mass insurrectionary activity has taken hold and the army has ceased to play a role in maintaining the status quo, the fate of the society has been decided to a great extent by the resourcefulness and flexibility of revolutionary and counterrevolutionary leadership. This does not mean that it is theoretically impossible for ordinary members of society to sustain a revolution without organized leadership; it only suggests that modern history does not include instances of this occurrence.

In turning now to the prospects of an American social revolution, the reader should be warned again that the future is in no way bound by the "laws" of the past. The patterns characteristic of societies that have undergone revolutionary change may not be applicable to the contemporary American case.

THE AMERICAN CASE CONSIDERED

The current crisis in American society is, in part, no crisis at all; that is, many characteristics of the contemporary period which make social analysts question the viability of parliamentary capitalism in the United States do not represent unique mass responses to extraordinary historical developments. As preceding chapters in this text have shown, racism, sexism, imperialism, poverty and economic insecurity are not recent phenomena which have suddenly darkened the American landscape. Similarly, American

[14] Trotsky, op. cit., p. 117.
[15] Ibid. It is illuminating to compare the role of the Chinese Communist party during the civil war period, described by William Hinton, Fanshen: A Documentary of Revolution in a Chinese Village (New York: Monthly Review Press, 1967), with its French counterpart in May 1968 as analyzed by Daniel Singer, Prelude to Revolution: France in May 1968 (New York: Hill & Wang, Inc., 1970).

education has rarely been concerned with extending the frontiers of knowledge and liberating human potential except as a by-product of serving the needs of the political economy. Finally, the capitalist dominance of the political system and the subordination of public power to private interest have been so characteristic of our national experience that the disclosures of professional muckrakers such as the late Drew Pearson have become relegated to the back pages of newspapers rather than creating the front page headlines they often merit.

Just as the social problems of our age have deep roots in American history, violent protest has also been a timeless mode of redressing grievances. From Shay's Rebellion in the early days of the republic to the IWW of late industrialization, extraparliamentary movements for radical social change have arisen during periods of mass discontent. Past disruptions of normalcy did not lead to the revolutionary overthrow of parliamentary capitalism. Rather they led to violent repression of extreme dissidents and some reform to alleviate the intense frustrations of their "constituency" without a fundamental change in the political economy. Both the carrot and the stick have played significant roles in the maintenance of social order throughout American history.[16]

What would constitute a crisis for the political economy would not be the presence of enormous social problems, mass discontent, nor violent upheaval, but the inability of contemporary ruling elites to successfully employ the sophisticated conservative policies of their ancestors to a situation which, despite superficial similarities, differs in several respects from the past.

The recent wave of militant protest and rebellion and the increasing delegitimation of the political system seem to be a response to contemporary societal features ultimately traceable to the failure of American political institutions and culture to resolve the unique cultural and economic problems that emerged from both the changes and continuities in the advanced capitalist mode of production and distribution. To concretize this rather abstract analysis, it will be necessary to examine the development of the American political economy and culture in the late nineteenth and twentieth centuries.

Economic and Cultural Contradictions of Advanced Capitalism   The post–Civil War era was one of rapid economic growth in the United States. It was also, however, a period in which the dynamics of capitalist accumulation caused severe cyclical fluctuations in the economy. The increasing productivity of labor—a consequence of massive investment in labor-saving technology—created an unprecedented volume of output. Yet, simultaneously, the replacement of human labor by machinery coupled with the income inequality inherent in the capitalist mode of distribution contributed to ineffective "demand" and frequent depressions.[17] The severe depressions of the 1870s and 1890s were particularly troubling because hungry workers gained an anticapitalist education from the knowledge that poverty was no longer a

---

[16] James Weinstein, *The Corporate Ideal in the Liberal State; 1900–1918* (Boston: The Beacon Press, 1968). William Preson, Jr., *Aliens and Dissenters: Federal Suppression of Radicals, 1903–1933* (New York: Harper & Row, Publishers, 1963).

[17] Charles Hession and Hyman Sardy, *Ascent to Affluence: A History of American Economic Development* (Boston: Allyn and Bacon, Inc., 1969), pp. 399–503.

function of natural scarcity, but an anticipated outcome of the needs of private enterprise for *profitable* production.

Gareth Stedman Jones' article in Chapter 3 indicates the enormous concern that the possibility of chronic depressions generated among political and economic elites. Basically, it was felt that if the increasing surplus generated by newly mechanized agricultural and industrial work could not be consumed domestically, and other outlets were unavailable, production would inevitably be reduced and unemployment would increase; this situation would lead to a further reduction in purchasing power, consumer demand, production, and a collapse of the economy. The agrarian and urban unrest fomented by populists and militant workers during the seventies and nineties provided the impetus for the policy of "Open Door imperialism" which has continued to be both a cause and a consequence of American foreign activity to this day. American elites believed that the only alternative to economic expansion abroad was a wholesale redistribution of national wealth. This choice would have required a dismantling of the system of parliamentary capitalism that the elites truly believed in and benefited from.[18]

Whether political and economic elites could have followed other policies without risking the destruction of a cherished political economy should not simply be evaluated by economists, who characteristically ignore precisely the cultural and political impediments to "rational" behavior which account for the fascination and tragedy of human history.[19]

The imperialist "solution" to the problem of failing to absorb surplus production at home represented a limited response to the dilemma facing the maturing American capitalist system as the nineteenth century receded and the "Fordization" of industry promised even greater gains in labor productivity than before. American capitalism was moving from a period of "accumulation," in which the expansion of manufactured goods production required an increase in the proportion of the *industrial* labor force, to the era of "disaccumulation," which is characterized by the increase in manufactured goods production and a proportional *decrease* in the size of the labor force engaged in this sector of the economy.[20] This development, although not

---

[18] William Appleman Williams, *The Roots of the Modern American Empire: The Growth and Shaping of Consciousness in a Marketplace Society* (New York: Vintage Books, 1970), suggests that there was considerable nonelite support for imperial expansion, especially among farmers. The crucial question, however, is whether such support was crucial in the development of foreign policy or whether imperialism was likely to occur even if nonelites were indifferent or opposed to it. See Gabriel Kolko, *The Roots of American Foreign Policy: An Analysis of Power and Purpose* (Boston: The Beacon Press, 1969), pp. 11–13.

[19] This essay is primarily concerned with the *historical* roots of the contemporary American condition and is therefore not oriented toward an analysis of the validity of elite belief systems. Whether imperialism was necessary for preserving capitalism and class privilege is not as significant as whether elites believed so and continue to.

[20] Martin Sklar, "On the Proletarian Revolution and the End of Political-Economic Society," *Radical America*, vol. 3 (May–June 1969), pp. 8–18. The disaccumulation process began in the agricultural sector in the late nineteenth century as output became inversely related to the proportion of agricultural workers in the labor force.

unique to *capitalism,* had different consequences than it would in an equally productive socialist society not oriented toward consumerism.

The most threatening aspect of disaccumulation in a capitalist context was the clear implication that people would be *technically* able to satisfy their needs for food, clothing, and shelter without devoting as much time to commodity production as during earlier stages of industrial development. Under these circumstances a widespread dramatic growth in leisure time for all Americans might have occurred. Such possibilities endangered the structure of capitalist economic institutions and social class relationships. Capitalism could not endure without masses of people willing to work long hours to earn money to spend satisfying endless "needs" through individual consumption. To eliminate the exchange-value of goods and simply distribute them freely on the basis of professed need or desire would mean the demise of a class-based economic and social structure. In order to meet the crisis of disaccumulation, capitalists would either have to "create" new needs through mass persuasion or coercive means (for example, planned obsolescence) or satisfy old needs in new ways if people were to be induced to continue working arduously and thereby foster profitable investment outlets. The alternative strategy would be to restrict the output of essential goods and services to restore an artificial but profitable scarcity. This approach would probably have socially explosive consequences under circumstances of potential abundance.

Faced with the perils of capitalist prosperity, President Warren Harding in 1921 sponsored the Conference on Unemployment under the initiative of Secretary of Commerce Herbert Hoover. The conference led to the formation of several standing committees whose task was to conduct research on the American economy. In 1929 one of these bodies, the Committee on Recent Economic Changes, issued its final two-volume report, which exhaustively documented what was soon to be confirmed in the lives of millions of Americans: the illusion of permanent prosperity and progress under the capitalist mode of production. According to the report, per capita labor productivity had increased by 60 percent between the end of the last century and 1929. This phenomenon had resulted in a labor shift away from manufacturing and agriculture with a concomitant rise in unemployment unprecedented in prosperous times.[21]

The analysis of the Committee on Recent Economic Changes together with that of the Committee on Recent Social Trends (which had begun its work under President Herbert Hoover in 1929) contributed to changes in the thinking of business leaders associated with giant financial and industrial corporations. In retrospect, perhaps the most significant aspect of new business thinking was the recognition that the mass psychology appropriate to the period of capitalist accumulation—deferred gratification, thrift, asceticism, and inner-directedness—was dysfunctional in the era of mass production. The rapid growth of advertising and consumer financing through installment debt were not only designed to increase short-run domestic aggregate demand but also to change the very life style of Americans to one com-

[21] *Ibid.,* pp. 14–16.

patible with the giant corporations' insatiable quest for profitable investment.[22] The old mass psychology was to be replaced by one emphasizing hedonism, consumption, and hypersensitivity to community tastes. But, because the traditional link between employment and income was to be maintained even in an era of unlimited productive capabilities, the work-oriented discipline was not to be tampered with. Leisure was considered as a reward for hard work and material success, not as something that could be granted as a consequence of the new technology under different social, political, and economic relations.

Although imperialism, advertising, and installment buying could help alleviate the problem of overproduction, political and economic elites recognized that other dramatic changes in the political economy would have to supplement these strategies for maintaining the prosperity on which the social order and their own class privilege depended. Thus, groups of liberal industrialists, bankers, and statesmen who were committed to enlightened self-interest began during the 1920s to carry on the work of the prewar National Civic Federation in rationalizing and reforming the unstable capitalist economy.[23] Martin Sklar summarizes the general policies with which these groups responded to the problems resulting from disaccumulation:

> Without at this point going into the details of the response, suffice to say that in the private sector, trade associations, agricultural cartel arrangements (cooperatives), and corporate consolidation, and in the public sector, government intervention with credit and subsidies to agriculture and transportation, export financing and promotion, public works, and money and credit management, all tracing back to the Wilson period, were continued and elaborated further in the Harding, Coolidge, and Hoover Administrations. As Secretary of Commerce and President, Hoover along with prominent men from large industrial, commercial, and financial corporations . . . warmly supported and worked for the adoption of measures along these lines. They viewed it as a government responsibility to ameliorate unemployment with public works, to facilitate and protect imperialist corporate enterprise abroad, and to stabilize the investment cycle by appropriate subsidy, price-support, and credit measures designed to encourage the advance of productivity and hence profitable investment opportunities, while *restricting the volume of products* thrown onto the domestic market. They spoke glowingly of the era of "abundance," but warned and took action against *too much of it,* which in their view would disastrously derange the private market economy and throw the whole system of employment-for-income and private discretionary investment into hopeless disarray. Their approach amounted to government-fostered production *restriction,* secular inflation, and aggressive imperialist expansion, to sustain the flow of profitable investment and the capitalist domination of the labor force within the framework of the corporate-industrial system.[24]

[22] *Ibid.,* p. 17.
[23] Weinstein, *op. cit.*
[24] Sklar, *op. cit.,* p. 18.

The proposals of business elites met considerable opposition from other members of the business community who were associated with smaller firms not likely to benefit from government intervention in the economy nor from the legitimation of the demands of even the conservative trade unionism exemplified by the American Federation of Labor (AFL).[25] The significance of the historic split in the twentieth century between the moderate or corporate liberal Big Business (oligopolist) elites associated first with the National Civic Federation and later with such organizations as the Committee for Economic Development and the Council on Foreign Relations, and the conservative business establishment, composed largely of the heads of smaller corporations, operating in a competitive market, and oriented to the programs of the National Association of Manufacturers and chambers of commerce, will be discussed in greater depth at a later point. It should be noted, however, that the program of the moderates was not incorporated into the political economy until the reforms of the New Deal and the post-World War II permanent war economy demonstrated the necessity and utility of state stabilization of the economy through the regulation of aggregate demand. Even today, as I shall argue, corporate conservatives strongly oppose many of the programs sponsored by corporate liberals.

This rather extensive discussion of the development of the American political economy and the rationale of its proponents suggests that the fundamental problem of handling "abundance" has been deferred, not solved with the rise of modern corporate liberalism and the so-called Welfare-Warfare State. In fact, it is in the nature of a capitalist economy that such problems can never be solved. Each level of prosperity must be the basis not of a major reduction of labor or a wholesale distribution of the fruits of technology (regardless of demand backed up by purchasing power), but of a vigorous attempt to create new wants, through salesmanship or planned obsolescence. Those who believe economic and political elites are "imprisoned" by the needs of technology are mistaken. The priorities of maintaining capitalism largely determine both the introduction of new technologies and their ultimate use.

I have argued that the impact of the capitalist disaccumulation process on the American economy resulted in expanding the role of the federal government to include the promotion and regulation of economic activity and the corporate sponsorship of a new culture better suited to the needs of capitalism in the era of mass production. It is now necessary to indicate how political, economic, and cultural changes due to the "resolution" of the disaccumulation crisis affected the consciousness of segments of the American population. To begin with, the difficulties arising from the erosion of the traditional capitalist virtues of hard work and deferred gratification created a profound malaise among many persons in the growing educated middle class. Those whose education and material well-being allowed them to experience the limitations of a cultural and economic structure exalting

[25] G. William Domhoff, *The Higher Circles: The Governing Class in America* (New York: Random House, Inc., 1970), pp. 111–250.

consumerism and able to deliver endless quantities of superfluous commodities, but incapable of developing a meaningful alternative to the continual pursuit of wealth, began to explore new life styles and identify with new values.

The first manifestation of the alienation of the educated middle class was Progressivism. A major thrust of middle-class Progressivism was an attack on political corruption and the neglect of the poor.[26] But the traditional noblesse oblige of the more secure social classes was supplemented by the "permissive" educational philosophy of John Dewey, the attack on Victorian morality implicit in the new Freudian psychology, and the "revolution" in the arts. These trends indicated a deepening alienation from hierarchical social relationships and asceticism—the pillars of traditional capitalist society. By the 1920s a "counterculture," similar in many respects to the democratic and hedonistic youth culture of the current period, emerged in response to the impact of disaccumulation and the post-World War I disillusionment with politics on the young educated middle classes.[27]

Sociologists such as Lipset acknowledge that the cultural revolt of the 1920s bears a striking resemblance to that of the 1960s and early seventies only to suggest that parallels are indicative of the "banality of revolt." These critics fail to understand that, rather than representing discrete and unrelated rebellious periods in American history, the alienation of the educated younger generation of the pre-Depression era was a response—albeit limited—to the same structural and cultural crisis that has shaped the youth culture of today.[28]

Among the factors that retarded the growth and significance of the emerging counterculture in the United States after the 1920s was the onset of the Great Depression. A culture preoccupied with the quality of human relations and the heightening of self-awareness and personal development is possible when a social group has solved the more pressing problem of material security. Although there was considerable unemployment in the twenties, the life of the educated middle class was characterized by great affluence and seemingly limitless opportunity. The Depression destroyed the illusions of those who expected a millennium of prosperity. In this process the "cultural" radicalism of the post–World War I years was subordinated to economic and political radicalism in the 1930s. The radicalization of the young intelligentsia of the 1930s was aided by the infusion of socialist ideology by upwardly mobile children of working class immigrants.

The history of the flirtation with socialism and communism that marked a moment in the lives of many of the educated young during the Depression years has yet to be written with the detachment of those not identified with

[26] This aspect of Progressivism was only a component of the political philosophies and policies of the leading Progressive politicians, Theodore Roosevelt and Woodrow Wilson. See Weinstein, op. cit., and Gabriel Kolko, The Triumph of Conservatism: A Reinterpretation of American History, 1900–1916 (New York: The Free Press, 1963).

[27] Sklar, op. cit., pp. 18–36.

[28] Richard Flacks, "Young Intelligentsia in Revolt," Trans action, vol. 7 (June 1970), pp. 47–55.

the protagonists in the events and struggles of that time. Generally, much of the political radicalism of the educated middle-class Socialists and Communists seems to have been rhetorical. By the 1930s, the Socialist party was impotent and without a mass base in the working class.[29] More significantly, a Stalinized Communist party—whose considerable efforts in the great organizing drives that established the CIO were undermined by its tragic allegiance to the theoretical perspectives and political needs of a nonrevolutionary Soviet Union—placed severe limitations on radical political developments during the Depression.[30]

Those young people who did not become permanently disillusioned with leftwing or even liberal politics and ideology as a consequence of the embittered and futile internecine battles of the Left were generally attracted to the Roosevelt New Deal. Many of them found their desire for public service satisfied by their employment in the professions or in the growing governmental bureaucracy created to deal with the massive social problems threatening to destroy capitalist society in the wake of the Depression.[31] The New Deal invective against the "economic royalists" and the bitter feelings Roosevelt inspired among small businessmen and the less pragmatic Big Business elites could easily have given the impression that the political system was at last working in behalf of the common man against the wishes and interests of the capitalist class.

If the failure of the Socialist and Communist Left permitted the incorporation of alienated young adults into the political and ideological universe of corporate liberalism during the 1930s, World War II, renewed prosperity, and the total eclipse of political radicalism under the impact of Stalinism and McCarthyism reduced dissent to a bare minimum between 1940 and 1960.

Though an economic and political critique of American society was rarely expressed publicly in these two decades, the heritage of cultural Progressivism—with its emphasis on democratic participation, education, and personal freedom—still influenced the private lives of the now middle-aged liberals of the 1950s. They may have perceived the outside world as relatively benign, but it was clearly not utopian. These well-to-do highly educated liberals inculcated their children with the values of intellectual skepticism, moral commitment, and free expression—even though they themselves had made an unintended accommodation to American institutions.[32] Moreover, though strong political dissent was virtually absent from the American scene, the writings of several popular social critics represented a severe indictment of a culture infused with the values of the market-

[29] James Weinstein, The Decline of Socialism in America, 1912–1925 (New York: Monthly Review Press, 1967). David Shannon, The Socialist Party of America: A History (New York: Crowell-Collier and Macmillan, Inc., 1955).

[30] An annotated bibliography on the activities of the American Communist party can be found in Brian Peterson, "Working Class Communism: A Review of the Literature," Radical America, vol. 5 (January–February 1971), pp. 38–44.

[31] Flacks, op. cit.

[32] Kenneth Keniston, Young Radicals: Notes on Committed Youth (New York: Harcourt Brace Jovanovich, Inc., 1968).

place.[33] If a welcome affluence and the lack of alternative models prevented many of the older generation from breaking politically with American society, their offspring, not scarred by the material insecurity of the Depression or the bitter political struggles and disappointments of the past, could give voice again to the previously muted critique of a business civilization.

The Hungarian and Cuban revolutions provided the spark that invalidated the view of monolithic communism necessary for the continuance of the Cold War psychology. The civil rights movement gave young American students an opportunity to become passionately involved in a domestic struggle for social change. And perhaps most important, the student movement in the early 1960s grew out of a profound dissatisfaction with a society that appeared to promise the possibility of a higher stage of human development, but offered instead a future of affluence without purpose, alienated labor, and a recapitulation of the experience of the older generation.

When the New Left first surfaced in the United States in the early 1960s its adherents were a tiny minority distinguished by their unusual social backgrounds. Research carried out by Richard Flacks and Kenneth Keniston, among others, indicated that the early New Leftists were largely the children of the young educated middle class of the late 1920s and 1930s.[34] They absorbed the rudiments of a cultural and institutional critique of American capitalism from their liberal parents, but also recognized how a concern for material security and a fear born of political disillusion and repression forced the older generation to compromise with a social order it could not truly legitimize. Many of the young activists who went south to organize poor blacks or worked in Northern ghettoes recognized that they would have to cut their ties with the affluent society, materialism, authoritarianism, and the puritanism of the past in order to develop personally and change the culture and institutions of their society.

Because the New Left originated in the alienated experience of *atypical* American youth, the earliest explanations for its appearance stressed the importance of unorthodox family socialization. But recent evidence that aspects or by-products of this new culture have been diffused to more typical American university students—the children of the so-called silent majority— suggests that the revolt on the campuses reflects a more generalized re-

[33] David Reisman, et al., *The Lonely Crowd: A Study of the Changing American Character* (New Haven, Conn.: Yale University Press, 1950). Erich Fromm, *The Sane Society* (New York: Holt, Rinehart and Winston, Inc., 1955). Paul Goodman, *Growing up Absurd: Problems of Youth in the Organized System* (New York: Random House, Inc., 1960). William H. Whyte, *The Organization Man* (New York: Simon and Schuster, Inc., 1956). Arthur Miller, *Death of a Salesman: Certain Private Conversations in Two Acts and a Requiem* (New York: The Viking Press, Inc., 1949). C. Wright Mills, *White Collar: The American Middle Classes* (New York: Oxford University Press, 1951). A singular exception to the political acquiescence of the non-Communist Left of the 1950s was Mills' *The Power Elite* (New York: Oxford University Press, 1956).

[34] Richard Flacks, "The Liberated Generation: An Exploration of the Roots of Student Protest," *Journal of Social Issues*, vol. 23 (July, 1967), pp. 52–75. Keniston, *op. cit.*

sponse to a growing cultural and political crisis resulting from the disaccumulation process.[35]

Because their families sensitized them to the failings of American society and provided them with the material standards to recognize the limits of affluence, the early student activists were naturally most likely to be a critical vanguard against the social order. Yet to understand the movement's growth beyond this vanguard and its significance in comparison to the youth revolt of the 1920s, we must examine the changing status and experience of the unprecedented numbers of affluent young people who flooded the campuses in the mid-1960s in response to the needs of industrial and government bureaucracies.

In the twentieth century, under the impact of disaccumulation, American capitalists have been forced to create new markets and products, cut production costs by introducing new technology in order to compete successfully in the international marketplace, and solve the numerous material and social problems that have accompanied urbanized advanced capitalism. The expansion of the professional and technical labor force, from 4.6 percent of the total number of employees in 1910 to 14.4 percent in 1970, has been the most dramatic indicator of the changing needs of the political economy.[36] In addition to the expansion of the professional and technical labor force, however, there has been a concomitant increase in the proportion of other sectors of the white-collar stratum, namely, those engaged in clerical and sales work. This category rose from 10.4 percent of the labor force in 1910 to 23.6 percent in 1970.[37] The importance that educated labor plays in the modern capitalist economy can perhaps be understood best by noting that between 1929 and 1957 educational upgrading of the American labor force accounted for between 50 and 85 percent of the rate of economic growth compared to an estimated 11 percent attributed to the growth of physical capital.[38]

The general upgrading of the skill levels of the labor force and the other needs of modern capitalism has required an unprecedented expansion of the "knowledge industry," a complex of secondary and higher educational institutions and auxiliary centers for training and research. Whereas in 1920 only 16.8 percent of the seventeen-year-olds in the population received high school diplomas, 79.5 percent of this age group were graduated in

[35] Milton Mankoff and Richard Flacks, "The Changing Social Base of the American Student Movement," *The Annals of the American Academy of Political and Social Science*, vol. 395 (May 1971), pp. 54–67.

[36] Data on the composition of the labor force from 1870 to 1960 is taken from Benjamin Solomon and Robert Burns, "Unionization of White Collar Employees," in Richard Lester, ed., *Labor: Readings on Major Issues* (New York: Random House, Inc., 1965), p. 132. The proportion of professional, technical, and kindred employees in the labor force for 1970 is computed from *The American Almanac: The U.S. Book of Facts, Statistics, and Information for 1971.* (New York: Grosset & Dunlap, Inc., 1971), p. 225.

[37] *American Almanac, op. cit.*, p. 225.

[38] Edward Denison, *The Sources of Economic Growth in the United States and the Alternatives before Us* (New York: Committee for Economic Development, 1962).

1970.[39] In higher education, 129 of every 1000 students who had entered the fifth grade in 1926 were enrolled in college in 1935; 454 of every 1000 student who had entered the fifth grade in 1961 were enrolled in the freshman class of a university or college in 1969.[40]

The massive increase in enrollment has led to an expansion of educational opportunity to larger proportions of the general population, an intensification of competition at each level of schooling, and a relative loss of security and status for degree holders. The bureaucratization of education at even the highest levels has reflected the increasing "proletarianization" of the young intelligentsia—who must seek careers not as free professionals, but as salaried specialists in industrial and government bureaucracies. While many of the young intelligentsia of the 1920s and 1930s were alienated from American culture and social institutions, they were nevertheless able to anticipate distinctive opportunities for free creative work in which they would have considerable control over the decisions affecting their lives. Their counterparts in the late 1960s and the 1970s, cannot realistically envision any measure of intellectual satisfaction nor opportunities for meaningful decision-making under the more rationalized occupational structure of the present period.

During the early post–World War II period the memory of the Great Depression and the Cold War hysteria lessened the impact of the proletarianization of the young intelligentsia, and the vast majority of students were willing to be trained to fill the needs of the corporate political economy. But, as the belief in continuous prosperity spread and higher education became more available, a greater number of students became dissatisfied with consumer culture, the bureaucratization of education, and an anticipated worklife. A deep but still unarticulated malaise began to characterize campus life.[41]

The political and economic elites' dreams of a technically creative but socially and politically submissive intelligentsia were undermined by the very conditions of modern education and labor. Despite the competition, impersonality, and irrelevance of most higher education, students were able to gain from the few dissenting intellectuals who survived the campus purges of the McCarthy years or their own peers a sense that the present held little of value and the future would be the present writ large. Moreover, the growth of new knowledge, even technical knowledge, increasingly separated each new cohort of students from the beliefs and preoccupations of the older generation. By the midsixties the generalized dissatisfaction of the affluent young had begun to crystallize into a fairly coherent counterculture based largely upon a rejection of authoritarianism and puritanism, on the one hand, and a commitment to personally fulfilling and socially meaningful work, on the other.

The growing significance of educated labor in the economy of advanced capitalism as well as the accompanying emphasis upon supplying human services along with commodities has placed the young intelligentsia of

[39] *American Almanac, op. cit.,* p. 125.
[40] *Ibid.,* p. 126.
[41] Kenneth Keniston, *The Uncommitted: Alienated Youth in American Society* (New York: Harcourt Brace Jovanovich, Inc., 1965).

the contemporary period in a strategic position in the political economy. As professionals and subprofessionals in the burgeoning health, education and welfare bureaucracies (public and private) and as journalists, editors, and filmmakers in the media, recent college graduates have been increasingly sensitized to the inherent failings of parliamentary capitalism in meeting human needs, their own inability to effect personal and social change without rejecting traditional occupational roles and institutional arrangements, and their potential power to mobilize citizens to struggle for better human services and lives richer materially and qualitatively. The very affluence of this new generation of intelligentsia has permitted it to feel secure and alienated enough to challenge the organization of human services in a capitalist society. The development and impact of free clinics and educational institutions, welfare rights organizations, and the underground press and film corps testify to the possibilities of opposition to capitalist institutions emerging from the cultural alienation of the educated middle class. The building of counterinstitutions and organization of workers within existing human service bureaucracies and culture industries will continue to characterize the thrust of educated middle-class radicalism for some time. While the counterculture has been generally limited to human service workers trained in the social sciences and humanities, the recent concern over ecological destruction may spur the expression of alienation among young scientists (for example, engineers, chemists) working in the manufactured goods sector of the economy and beginning to appreciate the contradiction between the potentially liberating role of science and technology and its perversion in the service of capitalism (for example, planned obsolescence).

Thus far the economic and cultural changes generated by twentieth-century capitalist disaccumulation have been discussed solely in terms of their influence on the lives of the educated upper-middle class. Yet these unprecedented developments have had equally profound consequences for the working class.

In addition to creating a sizable professional and technical class the disaccumulation process has brought about the decline of farm workers, the small rural and urban businessman and the so-called free professional class (for example, fee-practicing doctors, real estate agents). Whereas nearly 40 percent of the labor force was engaged in agricultural work, principally as self-employed farmers, at the turn of the century, only about 4.6 percent of the labor force was working on farms by 1969.[42] Moreover, the proportion of self-employed businessmen and free professionals in the nonagricultural sector of the economy declined from approximately 25 percent in 1900 to less than 11 percent in 1969.[43] The decline of the farmer and small capital-

[42] The shift from agricultural to industrial and "service" work between 1870 and 1930 is documented by Victor Fuchs, *The Service Economy* (New York: Columbia University Press, 1968), p. 24. Data on the decline in the agricultural sector of the labor force in the contemporary period can be found in *Manpower Report of the President* (Washington, D.C.: Government Printing Office, 1970), p. 228.

[43] *Manpower Report,* op. cit., p. 228. It is estimated that about 10 percent of the professional and sales group is self-employed, which would add about 2 percent to the 9.1 percent listed as "self-employed."

ist in the face of rising labor productivity in the era of the giant financial and industrial corporation has reduced the vast majority of the labor force to the level of salaried employees or wage earners working increasingly in private or public bureaucracies. The blue-collar working class (of craftsmen, operatives, and laborers) has accounted for 35 to 40 percent of the employed civilian population for several decades.[44] If one adds the almost 12 percent of employees in agricultural labor and the nonprivate household service work, as of 1970, it is clear that the manual working class still represents about half of the labor force.[45]

The transformation of the labor force has gradually undermined the "rugged individualist" philosophy of the old middle class by eroding the economic power of that class. At the same time the growing proletarianization and bureaucratization of the work process has discredited the model of Horatio Alger—whatever its vitality may have been for the worker in the past.[46] While considerable upward mobility does exist, it generally results from the overall growth of the economy, the transformation of the occupational structure, and, less significantly, from small intergenerational movements within families rather than from the movement of large proportions of workers' children into the professional ranks.[47] The son of a worker will probably earn much more in real wages than his father during the course of his work life, but his *relative* position in the social class structure will probably remain the same. Moreover, his relationship to authority in the work place will probably also remain the same, even if he moves up to a white-collar, subprofessional, or even professional, status.

The decline of the old middle classes and the increasing bureaucratization and proletarianization of the labor force have contributed to the widespread decline of traditional capitalist culture crystallized in the Protestant ethic and the Alger myth. Traditional culture, which rationalized economic inequality in a period of relative scarcity, no longer serves the needs of a capitalist economy in an era of mass production. As noted previously, modern business and political elites, realizing the disjunction between culture and economic structure, sought to affect a cultural "revolution" without signifi-

[44] Everett Kassalow, "White Collar Unionism in the United States," in Adolf Sturmthal, ed., *White Collar Trade Unions: Contemporary Developments in Industrialized Societies* (Urbana, Ill.: University of Illinois Press, 1966), p. 307, covers 1940 to 1960. For more recent data see *The American Almanac, op. cit.*, p. 225.

[45] *The American Almanac, op. cit.*, p. 225. The solid middle class of salaried and free professionals, technical, and kindred employees and managers, officials, and proprietors makes up approximately 25 percent of the labor force. The lower-middle, or white-collar, class of sales and clerical workers accounts for the remaining 25 percent.

[46] Moses Rischin, ed., *The American Gospel of Success: Individualism and Beyond* (Chicago: Quadrangle Books, 1968). Stephen Thernstrom, *Poverty and Progress: Social Mobility in a Nineteenth Century City* (Cambridge, Mass.: Harvard University Press, 1964).

[47] There are no figures available which indicate the proportion of workers' male children who become members of the propertied economic elite (i.e. big businessmen). Only about 10 per cent become self-employed or salaried professionals. See Peter Blau and Otis Dudley Duncan, *The American Occupational Structure* (New York: John Wiley & Sons, Inc., 1967), pp. 432–435.

cant changes in the logic of the capitalist productive and distributive apparatus. The upper-middle classes and their university educated offspring have
embraced certain portions of the new culture. Although the limitations of consumer culture have contributed heavily to the upper-middle class youth revolt
and the malaise of their parents, massive consumption was economically
possible for this group. At the same time, however, the spread of mass communications, particularly television, has diffused aspects of the culture of affluence to groups whose "rising expectations" were not backed up by the
purchasing power to effectively "demand" the commodities flowing from
capitalist production.

Under the capitalism of an earlier day poverty was a sign of individual
moral failure. The poor were thought to be either lazy or sinful. In the more
remote past religious teachings gave the economically deprived a sense of
inner worth, at least in the eyes of God. Due to the secularization of American
capitalism and their greater awareness of the basically unstable character of
its operation, the poor are less inclined to accept the contempt of the more
advantaged or the consolations of religion. The system today justifies its
existence largely on material grounds and those who have been left out of
the "affluent society" are likely to be increasingly enraged by their exclusion.

Delegitimation of American Institutions The preceding analysis has
suggested that the process of capitalist disaccumulation in the United States
has led to disjunctions between culture and economic structure and posed a
serious challenge to the American political economy. The historic governmental and corporate response to disaccumulation—consumerism, aggressive economic expansion abroad, militarism, limited government regulation
of the economy, and minimal and inadequate social welfare legislation—
succeeded until the mid-1960s in maintaining widespread legitimacy for the
political system. In the past few years, however, the growing militancy of
black and other minorities—together with working class economic stagnation
and the apparent inconsistencies in foreign policy manifested by the détente
with the Soviet Union and China and the continuing of the Indochinese war—
has led, because of the increased visibility of the state in the modern era, to
considerable delegitimation of political elites from both major political parties,
the political system, and other major social institutions.

Because of the legacy and continued operation of personal prejudice
and discrimination, most black and nonwhite Americans are generally unable
to take advantage of the opportunities open to educated white labor and are
particularly victimized by the institutional racism caused by the structural
transformation of the American economy. The nonwhite population is concentrated in the unskilled, semiskilled, and service occupations, which have
been either slightly declining or growing at a slower rate than other sectors.[48] This concentration, along with discrimination, has kept unemployment

[48] *Social and Economic Conditions of Negroes in the United States, Bureau of
Labor Statistics Bulletin*, no. 332 (Washington, D.C.: Government Printing Office,
October 1967), pp. 41–42. Changes within the occupational structure between
1958 and 1969, can be found in *Manpower Report*, op. cit., p. 226.

levels extremely high among nonwhites, particularly teenagers.[49] In addition, the urbanization of nonwhites that resulted from agricultural mechanization and wartime labor shortages has generated a growing and concentrated déclassé population of culturally distinct and profoundly alienated persons. Extreme poverty among blacks in particular has placed pressures on the underdeveloped urban public services, which cannot meet their needs under the existing political economy of welfare. Moreover, the federal government's commitment of great resources in foreign affairs has led many nonwhites to conclude that the government's limited and inadequate response to the "urban crisis" is based upon an unwillingness, not an inability, to combat racism and poverty.

Given these structural sources of the increasing alienation among the urban nonwhite poor, it would appear that they are the foremost victims of disaccumulation. Their labor power is in less demand than ever before by advanced capitalism, and they cannot be given adequate incomes because such a policy would undermine the relationship between employment and compensation basic to the capitalist mode of distribution.

The increasing militancy in the ghettos and the rejection of the capitalist political economy particularly among the young have been a function of the rising educational levels of achievement without comparable material improvement, the persistence of racial and ethnic discrimination, the awareness that the "laws of the market" invariably operate against the interests of the poor, and the diffusion of consumer ideology and secularization. Moreover, the models of revolutionary nationalism in Africa and Latin America in the 1960s have helped create an anticolonial ideology increasingly accepted by the militant political groups which seem to be gaining influence in the ghettos.

If nonwhites are being threatened by new and old forms of racism and the long-term economic growth of the American economy, the blue- and white-collar working class has seen its economic position imperiled in recent years by rising inflation and taxation in conjunction with deteriorating work conditions and the threat of automation. The increasing concentration of industry, the growing military budget, and the added expenditures needed to finance the Indochinese war have been the principal factors in the failure of nonagricultural workers in private industry to increase their average spendable real weekly earnings since 1965 after approximately three decades of generally rising real wages.[50] In addition, the long-term internationalization of American capitalism may further erode the wage structure and working conditions of Americans employed in the private sector of the economy. Whereas prior to World War I American capitalism engaged in only limited world commerce its industrial and financial hegemony in the past few decades has made economic and political leaders extremely sensitive to the imperatives of international competition. The relatively high wages

[49] *Social and Economic Conditions of the Negro, op. cit.*, pp. 30, 32.

[50] *Economic Report of the President* (Washington, D.C.: Government Printing Office, 1970), p. 214. Real wages or earnings consider variations in the cost of living over time and are therefore better indicators of changes in the standard of living than indices based on current prices.

American workers earned in the past because of an historic labor shortage, the enormous productivity of American industry, and its isolation from world economic competition, may be threatened by the recovery of Japanese and European capitalism from the ravages of World War II. With industrial concentration, state aid, low wages, and the introduction of the latest technologies, advanced foreign capitalist corporations are vigorously competing with their American counterparts. Already foreign-made steel, automobiles, electrical appliances, textiles, and certain machines are successfully "invading" America's domestic and foreign markets because of the growing productivity and lower labor costs of capitalist enterprise abroad.[51]

This challenge, only in its initial stages, is apparently being met in ways that will undoubtedly undermine the living standards and/or working conditions of the American worker in the private sector. On the one hand, the giant corporations which were willing and able in the past to concede to demands for higher wages are beginning to resist them more tenaciously because higher labor costs will inevitably lead to higher prices and a decreasing share of world export sales and profits. The internationally oriented business community will also continue to build factories abroad and to introduce new technology to reduce labor costs and increase productivity.[52] By reducing prices, these developments will enable American firms to compete more favorably with foreign competition. Even when the introduction of new technology does not threaten employment, it results in "speedup," a process of extracting more and more productivity per man/hour without an accompanying increase in the workers' pay.[53]

Increased pressure on working-class living standards is also supplied by the rising costs of public services and welfare programs needed to meet the demands of population growth, urbanization, and the failure of the private economy to generate full employment. Moreover, the regressive tax structure places most of the burden on low-income families directly through sales taxes and indirectly through property taxes, which result in higher rents. At the same time, the tax structure reduces the proportion of revenues accruing from corporate taxation.[54] The tax burden is increasingly felt to be

[51] Ernest Mandel, "Where Is America Going?" *New Left Review*, no. 54 (March–April 1969), pp. 11–14.

[52] Fred Block, "Expanding Capitalism: The British and American Cases," *Berkeley Journal of Sociology*, vol. 15 (1970), pp. 138–165. Stanley Weir, "The U.S. Labor Revolt," in Maurice Zeitlin, ed., *American Society, Inc.: Studies in the Social Structure and Political Economy of the United States* (Chicago: Markham, 1970), pp. 485–495. President Nixon's recent economic plan suggests the state will be playing a crucial role in trying to maintain the world economic hegemony of American capitalism during the coming years. A major component of the Nixon strategy is a wage stabilization policy. This has already led to the abrogation of existing contracts between management and labor and may include an expansion of antistrike legislation.

[53] In the automobile industry, for example, it has been reported that many young workers have to take pep pills to maintain the increased work pace while older ones can no longer continue on their jobs. Weir, *op. cit.*, pp. 491–492.

[54] Gabriel Kolko, *Wealth and Power in America: An Analysis of Social Class and Income Distribution* (New York: Frederick A. Praeger, Inc., 1962), pp. 30–45. See also James O'Connor, "The Fiscal Crisis of the State," *Socialist Revolution*, vol. 1 (March–April 1970): 65–73.

unjust because of its inequity and also, perhaps, because some of the programs revenues finance—particularly space, military, and welfare projects—have lost legitimacy.[55]

The failure of the Democratic party, the so-called party of the common man, to intervene in behalf of the working class, and the mistaken belief that large and undeserved monies are being channeled to the nonwhite poor have combined with deteriorating economic conditions to loosen the ties between the working class and that party. The current sympathy for George Wallace among some workers is rooted only partially in racist sentiment and represents a growing hostility toward both the Democratic party and the AFL-CIO leadership which has identified with that party and failed to protect the unionized sectors of the working class from management's economic assault on living standards, job conditions, and job continuance.[56] The 1968 Wallace campaign was not merely racist, but had elements of populism perhaps even more appealing to large numbers of economically hard-pressed Americans who felt themselves increasingly at the mercy of big government, business, and labor. The absence of a viable labor or leftwing political party has sent a significant proportion of the working class into the Wallace camp.[57]

The final source of political delegitimation since the 1960s has been the conduct of American militarized imperialism under conditions which have made public support increasingly doubtful. As long as American foreign policy was directed toward preserving American security and protecting European societies from fascism or alleged Soviet designs it was fairly easy to arouse public support for virtually any form of foreign intervention. Americans who knew little of capitalism's needs for constant expansion, could readily identify with the "plight" of peoples with whom they shared a common cultural heritage. But as the threat to European parliamentary capitalism receded and American statesmen and economic elites turned their attention toward the so-called Third World, they have not been able to conduct costly policies, particularly if they involve protracted commitments, without considerable popular opposition.

Both geography and racism have combined to diminish the sense of threat to American domestic life and the empathy for the alleged loss of freedom of nonwhite peoples if communism triumphed in Asia, Africa, and

[55] *Gallup Opinion Index,* no. 46 (April 1969), p. 20. *Gallup Opinion Index,* no. 50 (August 1969), pp. 11, 50. *Gallup Opinion Index,* no. 25 (July 1967), p. 17.

[56] Weir, *op. cit.* See also Seymour Faber and James Rinehart, "Structural Sources of Working Class Political Unrest," unpublished paper presented at the annual meeting of the Society for the Study of Social Problems, Washington, D.C., 1970.

[57] It should be noted that the vast majority of workers did not vote for Wallace in the 1964 Presidential primaries or in the 1968 Presidential election. Moreover, a great deal of Wallace support, particularly in 1964, came from voters outside the working class. See Michael Rogin, "Wallace and the Middle Class: The White Backlash in Wisconsin," *Public Opinion Quarterly,* vol. 30 (Spring 1966), pp. 98–108. In March 1970 the Gallup poll included an item asking people to "vote for either Nixon, Humphrey, or Wallace." Sixteen percent of the manual workers preferred Wallace, as compared to 9 percent of the professionals and businessmen and 8 percent of the white-collar workers. *Gallup Opinion Index,* no. 57 (March 1970), p. 6.

other parts of the underdeveloped world. The spectacle of the world's mightiest country destroying tiny Korea, Cuba, and Vietnam also made it somewhat difficult to enlist great public support for military activity in defense of *our* "national security." Attempts to link the anticolonial and antiimperialist revolutions in the underdeveloped world with the conspiratorial machinations of "international Communism" became equally problematic when the Soviet Union both opposed revolutionary activity and successfully courted American presidents with a policy of "peaceful coexistence." The military strength of the Soviet Union, particularly its nuclear capabilities, played a decisive role in the relaxation of the Cold War. American elites recognized that they had to tone down the more strident antiSoviet invective and refrain from "liberating" Eastern Europe if nuclear war were to be averted. The developing American-Soviet rapprochement, however, made it increasingly hard to justify protracted war in distant Asia to fight for the very freedom we let expire in Hungary and Czechoslovakia.

Despite the contradictions in American foreign policy since 1950 it was not until the Vietnam war that masses of Americans seriously began to question not only the wisdom but the morality of military intervention abroad. This process could only occur because of the tenacity of the Vietnamese resistance to American military power. If the war had ended quickly with an American victory, it is doubtful that widespread delegitimation of the political system would have occurred. Except for the small proportion of students and intellectuals who knew enough about Vietnamese history to oppose American policy on moral grounds as early as the late 1950s and early 1960s, most citizens were content to question only whether it was necessary to spill American blood in altruistic defense of Asians. The length and savagery of the war have provided the time for a majority of Americans to wish to terminate our efforts there even if it meant suffering a defeat. The revelation of systematic war crimes, the duplicity of the American and South Vietnamese governments, and the tenacity of the North Vietnamese and National Liberation Front have raised disturbing parallels between the United States foreign policy and that of the old-fashioned imperialists. Given the intense popular disillusionment with this longest war in American history, it seems likely that at least in the foreseeable future government leaders will be unable to prevent revolutionary upheavals without incurring major domestic opposition. If the United States is forced to tolerate the erosion of its empire, she may eventually have to face the internal contradictions of disaccumulation her pursuit of empire was designed to forestall.

The most profound effect of the Vietnam war has been the delegitimizing of the political system. The war has also had a "multiplier effect" as other vital social institutions have become discredited as a consequence of their complicity in the war effort. Thus, the armed forces—always defensive because of their adherence to authoritarian social relations in a society presumably founded on social equality—have suffered an additional loss of prestige in Vietnam because of their inability to "win" and because of the perpetration of genocidal acts. As noted earlier, public opinion polls have clearly indicated a sharp decline in support for defense expenditures in recent years; and the amount of politically motivated rebellion within the army has reached serious proportions. There is even some question as to the reliability of the armed forces as an instrument of war and domestic social control. President Nixon's decision to shift from a ground to an air war in Indochina and his desire to phase out the draft reflect the delegitimation of the armed forces, particularly among the young. If the armed forces lose their effectiveness and a "volunteer" army proves unworkable, this major source of established power may be neutralized.[58]

The war has also served to discredit the legal system for those whose antiwar activity has resulted in contact with the police and the courts. Increasingly visible police violence against *middle class* dissenters has turned large numbers of affluent students and liberals against the most salient enforcers of law. The indictments, trials, and convictions of respected antiwar activists and the unwillingness of the Supreme Court to even consider the constitutionality of the war has created a widespread disrespect for the law among the young intelligentsia and the liberal community.[59] Of course, the poor, especially those who are nonwhite, have long appreciated the fact that the law in its "impartiality" is more likely to harass, arrest, and punish them for acts that wealthier people engage in with impunity.

Finally, the exposure of the ties between higher education and the military apparatus—germ warfare perfected at the University of Pennsylvania, secret police trained in Saigon under the auspices of Michigan State; CIA-sponsored research projects and institutes at Ivy League universities—has undermined the image of "institutional neutrality" so necessary for disseminating the "value-free" social theory that invariably seems to legitimate the political economy of parliamentary capitalism. It is doubtful that the current movements for free universities, black studies, and women's studies, could have been launched without exposure of the one-sided "service" orientation of the university.

The attack on university commitments to service American imperialism and capitalism and the scholarship that buttresses such service has forced university administrations to give more critical and antiestablishment perspectives a stronger voice or to further undermine respect for the academy by suppressing these views. As the university has become a center for a radical counterculture under the long-term impact of disaccumulation and the recent delegitimation of the political, legal, and educational systems, federal and private resources have been channeled away from its portals. Although the contraction of financial support may well reverse the trend towards permissiveness and unorthodoxy on the campus, it will invariably increase the frustration of high school students and undergraduates unable

[58] History seems to suggest that a civilian army is much more likely to desert the government during a period of social breakdown. Thus, those who seek social revolution in the United States should oppose the development of a volunteer force despite its likely popularity among draft-age youth. Moreover, given the fact that a volunteer army would have to rely upon material incentives to recruit manpower, the poor would probably serve in the armed forces in even greater proportion than under the inequitable draft of today.

[59] Undoubtedly, the enforcement of drug laws has also played a major role in undermining the legitimacy of the law, the judiciary, and the police among young middle class drug users.

to continue their studies, and graduates told of teacher overproduction despite crowded classrooms and the pervasive ignorance in the land. A massive and politically directed alienation of intellectuals may well ensue if their developing critical awareness of the realities of the American political economy is coupled with an abrupt loss of status and material well-being. The increasing unionization of university faculty may be the first symptom of this process.

Prospects for Reform, Revolution, or Counterrevolution The previous section has examined the historical sources of the fairly substantial delegitimation of the American political system and other social institutions that has taken place in the late 1960s and early 70s. Whether the problems of creating a culture and socioeconomic structure for a stable advanced capitalism without empire will prove insurmountable will depend largely upon the ability of the American ruling elite to recognize the gravity of the present situation and to act with enlightened self-interest.

The absence of a socialist or communist ideological tradition and institutional base in the working classes has made it possible, up to now, for minimal reform to accomplish what major reform has barely succeeded in doing in Europe. Given this lack of a serious challenge to the hegemony of bourgeois ideology, delegitimation of the political system in the United States has only been remotely possible in the aftermath of severe historic crises such as the Great Depression, widespread racial violence, a prolonged lost and immoral war. In France and Italy, by contrast, the ascendance of anti-capitalist ideology in the factories, bureaucracies, and universities has made the institutions of parliamentary capitalism tremble under much less trying circumstances. If the American ruling elites cannot "solve" (that is, significantly meliorate) the most pressing economic, social and cultural challenges in the next two decades, a social and ideological base for social revolution may develop.

Rather than imprudently attempt to predict the future development of American society, I will consider some of the factors which strengthen or weaken the chances for fundamental social reforms, the presence of which would contribute to the stability of parliamentary capitalism.

At the outset needed reform would have to be inaugurated and implemented largely by the state apparatus, mainly the government, with cooperation from the judiciary and the administrative bureaucracies. The concentration of the corporate economy has undoubtedly created unprecedented possibilities for coordinated change in the productive and distributive policies of the most powerful economic units. Nevertheless, the imperatives of capitalist enterprise are unlikely to permit massive investment in socially beneficial but economically unprofitable projects, remuneration based upon need rather than "marginal utility," and production for use rather than profit. To expect otherwise would be to assume that capitalists will commit "class suicide"—something quite unprecedented in the history of all ruling classes.

As for some widespread "cultural revolution" or changes in "the hearts and minds" of ordinary Americans, their lack of power over largely impersonal institutional forces can permit much personal change within the context of institutional stability. Many contemporary bureaucrats smoke marijuana, sleep on water beds, and sympathize with the poor without it affecting *in any way* the demands of institutional life.[60] This state of affairs is precisely what has *accounted* for the alienation of the young intelligentsia. Individual conversion alone cannot provide the solution under the normal conditions of social stability. In revolutionary moments, however, personal orientations may have decisive import.

What are the possibilities of government mobilizing men and resources to address the potentially explosive short-run and long-run problems of American society? Undoubtedly, some members of the political elite and ruling class have the wisdom and flexibility under duress to work for a fundamental reform of American capitalism, which would truly incorporate the black and other nonwhite "colonies" into the system, improve the social and economic status of the working class, and redistribute wealth to provide enough profitable investment at home to peacefully adjust to the end of empire. In addition, the American ruling class and political elite have a greater ability through the use of advanced scientific knowledge and communications technology to sensitize themselves to the nature of potentially explosive societal problems and evaluate policy alternatives in the light of cost-benefit analysis. Had Herbert Hoover been surrounded by contemporary economists, the Great Depression might well have been averted. Moreover, under capitalism, unlike feudalism, the renunciation of privilege ordinarily involves a quantitative rather than a qualitative loss of power. Because of its immense wealth and the abundant resources of the continental United States, the American capitalist class can probably afford to accept even major reforms without giving up all its privileges. Finally, although most Americans believe that the political economy of the United States is the most advanced in the world, Western Europe and the Scandinavian countries present everpresent proof that introduction of greater governmental economic controls and welfare legislation will not necessarily imperil the capitalist system. Thus, radical reforms can be accepted more gracefully in America than if these foreign models were not available. Their existence should eliminate or at least reduce the prospect of an irrational defense of institutional arrangements not essential for the maintenance of class privilege.

Despite the advantages of America's contemporary ruling class in coping with massive social problems generated by the disjunction between the economic structure and the sociocultural structure, several features of the political economy may impede the possibility of swift and far-reaching reform. As suggested above, the very nature of capitalism makes the ruling class unable to gain a comprehensive understanding of the general needs of the system. However concentrated the economic structure may have become, it is still basically decentralized. This decentralization impedes class consciousness for all but a few leading representatives of the capitalist

[60] Charles Reich is currently the most popular exponent of revolution through changing "consciousness." For a critical review of his rather banal book, *The Greening of America* (New York: Random House, Inc., 1970), see Andrew Kopkind, "The Greening of America: Beyond the Valley of the Heads," *Ramparts*, vol. 9 (March 1971), pp. 51–52.

class. Most capitalists cannot see beyond their immediate economic interests or those of their industry. This short sightedness prevents a coordinated effort, particularly one that sacrifices short-run interests for class interests. Moreover, the structurally based ideological unity and diversity *within* the ruling class (and their political manifestations) and the combination of political centralization and decentralization characteristic of the American polity may present a formidable roadblock to the peaceful reformation of capitalist institutions.

As suggested earlier the term "ruling class" is a misnomer. Actually, the capitalist class, while sharing the ideological premises of bourgeois political economy and operating its businesses in order to maximize profitable investment and growth, has been seriously divided throughout the twentieth century on the crucial matter of social reform. The structural basis for this historic split in the ruling class has been the coexistence of monopolistic or oligopolistic industry and the competitive small business sector of capitalist enterprise.[61] The economic and political representatives of giant industry— the Committee for Economic Development, Council on Foreign Relations, Business Advisory Council and the dominant moderate wings of both the Republican and Democratic parties—have generally favored the needs of large corporations and banks as opposed to those of smaller businessmen. These bodies have worked for increases in defense spending *and* welfare outlays; have been influential in the creation of multiversities and the legitimation of labor unions; and have rejected isolationism in favor of imperialist expansion via investment, "free" trade, and foreign "aid." Moreover, they reject puritanism and deferred gratification, the values crystallized in the Protestant ethic, and endorse consumer ideology. Finally, the moderate Big Business sector supports civil liberties and dislikes racist ideology. This dominant outlook represents the seemingly contradictory needs of enterprises caught in the web of disaccumulation. Overseas expansion, a growing consumer class, and an expansion of human education, toleration, and freedom are promoted as long as they will ultimately stabilize advanced capitalism.

On the other side, through the National Association of Manufacturers, chambers of commerce, and right wings of the Republican and Democratic parties, the leaders of the small, or national, business community oppose Big Business and government, the welfare state, *and* some props of modern imperialism (especially foreign aid and free trade). In addition, the conservative small business sector of the capitalist class is opposed to cosmopolitanism, permissive and progressive education, federal aid to schools, civil liberties, and racial integration. These outlooks are characteristic of those who operate in the competitive small business world, who do not trade or invest abroad, who do not require educated labor or advanced technology, and who have traditionally embraced the asceticism and "work and save" ethic of early capitalism.

[61] According to the U.S. Senate Small Business Committee, an enterprise employing less than 250 persons, having $500,000 or less in assets and no more than $1,000,000 in business volume is considered small. John Bunzel, *The American Small Businessman* (New York: Alfred A. Knopf, 1962), p. 30.

If either of these contending "class-conscious" groups within the ruling capitalist class could totally dominate the American political structure the corporate moderates would bring prosperity for a larger number, more racial and economic justice, better education, a higher culture, and a greater likelihood of excessive government power, militarism and war. The business conservatives, on the other hand, would follow the path of poverty, racism, ignorance, provincialism, old-fashioned virtue, limited government, and possibly more peaceful coexistence with other nations. The incomplete victory of the political perspectives associated with giant corporate enterprise has meant the coexistence of prosperity and poverty, civility and intolerance, education and ignorance, institutional and personal racism, the visibility of big government and the veto power of local elites, the Playboy philosophy and Horatio Alger, and highly impersonal and personal forms of genocide.

It is perhaps an exaggeration to emphasize the divisions within the politically articulate and active ruling class when their shared values are much more significant than their differences and each tolerates the most socially dysfunctional features of the other's program while vigorously fighting that which is most progressive or benign. Thus, the small business conservatives, while not generally involved in economic activity which requires imperialism, can vociferously support the activities *inaugurated by the "moderates"* in the name of anticommunism. And while opposing the "big government" of welfare spending, these small business groups have great respect for the work of the FBI, the House Unamerican Activities Committee, and other state agencies which tend to restrict civil liberties by their beliefs and practices. For their part, the corporate moderates are often more concerned about small business attacks on corporate-governmental collusion and the "protectionist" sentiment of the small business-conservative coalition than about these groups' disdain for liberal education, civil liberties, and their strict adherence to traditional puritan morality.

Despite considerable mutuality, the split within the ruling-class leadership and rank and file can be expected to widen as the urgency of social reform becomes apparent. The economic problems which would abound in a demilitarized postimperial America could possibly be meliorated if the domestic market were totally reorganized for peace and profitable investment. This policy of isolationism would not be met by formidable opposition for reducing imperialism and militarism *per se* since it is primarily the giant international corporate and financial interests whose representatives traditionally make foreign policy and benefit from overseas economic activity and military spending. While anticommunist crusaders and military men might resist, neither has much legitimacy at this time and the general public would probably be inclined to support a policy of isolationism after the experience in Indochina.

Opposition to a policy of genuine economic and military isolationism would most likely be generated by the need to modernize the economy. This modernization would have to overcome the small business–conservative resistance to massive doses of welfare legislation financed by radically progressive taxation calculated to produce genuine income transfers and stimulate domestic aggregate demand. Such a reconstruction program would probably fail because of the still considerable power of conservative forces in national, state, and local legislatures and because of the resistance and hostility of most small and large businessmen to this kind of radical reform and the changes it would occasion in their daily business decisions. Even among the corporate liberal sector of the ruling class, only a small proportion have what Marx would call class consciousness. As mentioned, the centripetal and anarchic forces inherent in capitalist production would make it difficult for most of the capitalists to see clearly the requirements for maintaining the total system. If they could be brought to such an understanding by their leaders under the conditions of social turmoil, they might still be economically incapable of the self-sacrifice necessary to sustain the social order. Under such circumstances, the leadership which had commanded respect in more tranquil times might be delegitimized by its ruling-class constituency.

The ruling-class resistance to solving the problems of American militarism and imperialism and to reorienting the economy to peace and autarky (economic self-sufficiency) would probably become more tenacious when it came to eliminating racism and the economic plight of the working classes. The ideological split between big and small business is most critical in this realm because economic rationality is fused with radically different ideological tendencies. Small businessmen not only cannot afford to pay higher wages, employ unnecessary labor, and invest in socially useful but unprofitable enterprises but also are inclined to believe the poor (especially when nonwhite) are lazy and/or incompetent and responsible for their own suffering. The small businessmen have not accepted the modern economic proofs that poverty can be produced by prosperity, and they believe firmly in the prerogatives of businessmen to make all economic decisions regardless of the social consequencies. Decision-making without controls is the freedom this sector of the ruling class fervently defends. On the other side, the corporate liberal leaders' constituents would generally be able to make economic and ideological adjustments required for racial and working-class pacification. But many of them would still resist the abandonment of "capitalist rationality" in employment and investment policy-making.

The sabotage of federal civil rights and welfare reforms (with corporate liberal sponsorship) by legislative conservatives and small businessmen indicates the critical weakness of a federalist ("states' rights") political structure and decentralized economy in handling a crisis that requires self-sacrifice at the local level. The increased visibility of the federal government makes it vulnerable to concerted attack, while the reality of significant *undemocratic* political and economic decentralization prevents the effective redress of grievances. If the riots and strikes of May 1968 had occurred in the United States instead of France, the President, unlike DeGaulle, could never have promised *and* delivered the reforms needed to defuse what had become a revolutionary situation. The dictatorial power of the French leader and the great control of the state over the economy and educational institutions made the government not only the focus of mass discontent but also more capable of weathering the storm.

In the domestic racial and economic problems facing the American political system, the public has also exercised veto power at times. The erosion of real wages and the resultant tax revolt as well as racist sentiment in the population make concessions to the white and nonwhite poor extremely hazardous for even the most liberal political elites. The surprising vitality of some laissez-faire notions in this era of monopoly capitalism and big labor testify to the usefulness of "rugged individualism" as an ideological smoke-screen behind which economically self-serving behavior flourishes. Popular opposition to the racial and welfare programs of enlightened corporate liberals tends to further polarize an already divided nation.

The foregoing analysis suggests that the American political system may well be characterized by a precondition for revolution: an increasingly bitter split in the ruling class over how to resolve severe social and economic problems. This split, both a product and further cause of delegitimation, is widened under modern technological conditions. As Daniel Bell observes:

> The United States is, for the first time, a national society. It has long been a "nation" in the sense of achieving a national identity and a national symbolism. But it is only in the last thirty years, because of the revolution in communications and transportation, that the United States has become a national *society* in the fundamental sense that changes taking place in one section of the society have an immediate and repercussive effect in all the others. One can see this most clearly in the "contagion effects" of the race situation. The pictures on national television of police dogs snarling at Negro marchers in Selma, Alabama, brought so widespread a reaction that in forty-eight hours 10,000 people joined Martin Luther King in a new march.[62]

The polarization and radicalization of people have clearly been catalyzed by the television coverage of urban and campus riots, the "police riot" at the 1968 Democratic Convention, the assassination of Martin Luther King, Jr., the horrors of the Vietnam war, and the killings at Kent State University. In the coming decade or two, the dramatization of social problems and conflict and the uncertain future of the armed forces and the intellectual stratum may create the possibility of social revolution—if the ruling class is incapable of restoring political legitimacy by unifying itself behind a program of thor-oughgoing economic, political, and social reform.

It has been argued, however, that there is no certainty that an upheaval would be to the advantage of the working class, intelligentsia, poor, and mi-nority groups, that is, a Left revolution. Public opinion polls show that a majority of Americans seem to be highly conservative and stability-seeking even when stability might entail the loss of civil liberties.[63] Most speculation about the

[62] Daniel Bell, "Unstable America: Transitory & Permanent Factors in a National Crisis," *Encounter*, vol. 34 (June 1970), p. 20.

[63] When asked if "Everything considered, would you say that, in general, you approve or disapprove of wiretapping?", 45 percent of those polled by Gallup approved. *Gallup Opinion Index*, no. 51 (September 1969), p. 14. In an earlier poll, a majority (54 percent) felt that the *best* way to handle looters during race riots would be to have the police shoot them on sight. *Gallup Opinion Index*, no. 37 (July 1968), p. 17.

effects of student and black protest in the contemporary period suggests that the extraparliamentary activity on the Left, particularly acts of civil disobedience and sabotage involving violence, will drive the "silent majority" into the hands of American fascists. The activity of "hard hats" and the popularity of George Wallace, along with the activities of Vice President Agnew and the Department of Justice under Attorney General Mitchell, are viewed as omens of a political drift to the extreme Right. What are the possibilities of such an outcome in the event of a failure of reform?

I am inclined to doubt that an extreme Right movement would have much chance of gaining popular support and/or control of the government. For example, the success of fascism in Germany was not a result merely of economic depression and social unrest. The Nazi party was able to attract the intellectuals and the young as well as to appeal to the traditional military and religious values felt strongly by anxious farmers, small businessmen, and white-collar workers.[64] Nazism never had much support in the blue-collar working class, which was suspicious of its "socialist" claims and remained loyal to the Social Democrats or voted Communist. In the United States today, the young student and professional stratum is moving to the Left. There is no military caste or tradition comparable to that of Imperial and Weimar Germany. The farm population and small business class are declining numerically and in economic and political power. The nonprofessional white-collar stratum is made up increasingly of women, who are apparently more liberal than men.

But what of the blue-collar working class? Although declining slightly in proportion to the rest of the labor force since 1950, blue-collar workers still represented 36.2 percent of the total number of employees over age sixteen and 47.7 percent of male employees in 1969.[65] Earlier it was noted that conditions of economic hardship and status loss have moved many of these workers to sympathize with the Wallace movement. What direction are they likely to move in if their ties to the Democratic party and their trade union leadership are further eroded? Might not an American fascism rely upon a social base of workers who, unlike the German working class, lack a socialist perspective and long for social stability in a period of bewildering social turbulence?

My views on this question are consistent with those expressed by political scientist Richard Rubenstein:

> It is erroneous to assume that what any group "really" wants is either stability *or* change; most groups want both simultaneously. By measuring reactions and testing group responses at a time when existing political

[64] William Sheridan Allen, *The Nazi Seizure of Power: The Experience of a Single German Town, 1930–1935* (Chicago: Quadrangle Books, 1967). David Schoenbaum, *Hitler's Social Revolution: Class and Status in Nazi Germany, 1933–1939* (New York: Doubleday & Company, Inc., 1966).

[65] *Manpower Report, op. cit.*, p. 226. If one includes nonprivate household service workers and farm laborers in the blue-collar working class, the proportion of manual workers in 1969 was 48.2 percent and 56.3 percent if only males in the labor force are included.

configurations are beginning to break up . . . one will almost always find a vast majority of those polled leaning towards stability. There are several reasons for this: the inevitability of change is not yet accepted; initial reactions to conduct which seems unusual and "disorderly" are usually negative. . . . Thus, at the beginning of what we might call the revolutionary process, the Right always seems extremely strong. As the process continues, however, initial reactions to social disorder are qualified. The society becomes conditioned to accepting a higher degree of political militancy and social turbulence (compare the front-page newspaper coverage of the 1964 disturbance at Berkeley with the minimal reporting of the much more serious People's Park disturbance of 1969). The irreversibility of change is increasingly accepted and the question is not *whether* there will be change or order but what *kind* of change will prevail.[66]

Social scientists who treat public opinion data seriously, especially in times of rapid social change, are terribly simplistic in their assumptions about the nature of "political opinion." Most people have very complex opinions, which are often not logically related. Coherent ideologies are rarely found among workers.[67] For example, while the blue-collar working class tends to be more hostile than the middle class to dissenters, manual workers are, and always have been, more disaffected with the war in Vietnam.[68] Moreover, in an extensive study of American opinion conducted in 1964, Free and Cantril found most Americans to be philosophically conservative but operationally liberal.[69] For example, people support rugged individualism in theory while they favor the expansion of welfare state legislation. When asked to describe in their own words, what they wanted out of life, the great majority of those interviewed mentioned improving their economic position to achieve a decent standard of living, health and happiness for themselves and their families, educational opportunities for their children, and peace.

The above portrait of "public opinion" seems at odds with prevailing stereotypes because opinion polls generally report questions without determining how salient either the question or the answer may be to the respondent. In addition, responses to one set of items—attitudes towards the

[66] Rubenstein, *op. cit.*, pp. 183–184. See also Harvey Molotch, "The Radicalization of Everyone?," in Peter Orleans and William Russel Ellis Jr., eds., *Change, Race, and Urban Society* (Berkeley, Calif.: Sage Publications, 1971), pp. 517–560.

[67] Michael Mann, "The Social Cohesion of Liberal Democracy," *American Sociological Review*, vol. 35 (June 1970), pp. 423–439. Also reprinted in Chapter 9 of this text.

[68] Richard Hamilton, "A Research Note on the Mass Support for 'Tough' Military Initiatives," *American Sociological Review*, vol. 33 (June 1968), pp. 439–445. See also *Gallup Opinion Index*, no. 57 (March 1970), pp. 10–11. The findings reported in this poll are consistent with every other sampling of public opinion since the beginning of the Vietnam war.

[69] Lloyd Free and Hadley Cantril, *The Political Beliefs of Americans: A Study of Public Opinion* (New Brunswick, N.J.: Rutgers University Press, 1967).

Vietnam war, for example—are rarely correlated with other attitudes—such as those pertaining to dissenters or the welfare state.

Perhaps the greatest shortcoming of political analysis through examination of public opinion data is that responses to questions are verbal, and, more significantly, are given in a situation in which social order and atomization reign. Although a respondent may be sincere when he claims he is relatively pleased with his job, external events and the pressure of his co-workers may lead him to participate in a militant strike the next day.[70] Surely, it was difficult to predict on the basis of General DeGaulle's rising popularity as measured by public opinion polls shortly before May 1968, that France would soon narrowly avert social revolution.

Finally, even if public opinion polls do accurately reflect public opinion, such "voting" for public policies would be significant only if political activity were confined to the election booth. Once politics moves "to the streets" the sentiments of a sixty-year-old housewife are hardly as important in determining the outcome of extraparliamentary social conflict as the behavior of a twenty-five-year-old male communications worker, truck driver, factory worker, or policeman. That is why even when young people make up only a small minority of the population, their attitudes are taken so seriously by governments. In America the views of youth are not yet crystallized. The leftward drift of college students has not yet been matched by a corresponding movement among working class youth. Yet, the diffusion of the university-based youth culture and political alienation to high schools, factories, and the armed forces, coupled with the growing educational achievement levels and relative affluence of young workers, suggests that many of the concerns of those on the campuses may soon be shared by their working-class cohorts.[71]

A more serious obstacle to a future social revolution than an American fascism is the weakening of social bonds among Americans, which has been furthered by geographical mobility as well as popular culture and the less socially conscious aspects of the youth culture. The seeming disintegration of the family has, thus far, not led to satisfactory communal ties, but frequently has fostered an atomized insecurity and a rationale for sexual exploitation. The conservatism and corruption of most existing trade unions have prevented people of all social classes and ages from seeking economic, political, and social solidarity and experimentation in democratic forms of decision-making through these institutions. The remnants of the old individualistic liberal tradition which Louis Hartz stresses so much in analyzing the absence of an American Left,[72] still seems to be plaguing those who seek to organize for revolutionary activity. Americans of all ages seem predominantly hostile to collective economic and political action. Only the Depression of the thirties appears to have created collective consciousness and, even then, only

[70] Faber and Rinehart, op. cit., pp. 2–3.

[71] Judson Gooding, "Blue-Collar Blues on the Assembly Line," Fortune, vol. 82 (July 1970), pp. 69–71, 112–113, 116–117.

[72] Louis Hartz, The Liberal Tradition in America (New York: Harcourt Brace Jovanovich, Inc., 1955).

briefly.[73] At that time corporate liberalism, not socialism, captured the allegiance of the people because of the decline of the Left in the 1920s.[74]

Nevertheless, despite the power of the ruling elites to coerce and coopt, the past decade has witnessed the steady growth of ideas based upon a vision of social cooperation and the militant revolt of masses of people working collectively at times if not always. Whether these stirrings of revolt are the first concrete manifestations of social revolution or the death throes of social strata whose aspirations were incompatible with advanced capitalism cannot be determined at this time by the "laws" of societal evolution. Although Americans have been caught in a web of national mythology, perhaps to a greater extent than other peoples, the "American Dream" has turned into a nightmare in recent years. This has caused great suffering, but also permitted the possibility of choosing a new path. The failure, thus far, to build viable organized vehicles for revolutionary struggle and to develop ideology, program, strategy, and tactics appropriate and appealing in the American context, should not result in a cynical dismissal of the likelihood of a revolutionary transformation in the coming generation. Nevertheless, the enormity of the stakes compels one to hope that the barbarism that has so rudely awakened us from dreaming will not seize the day while we attempt to clear the sleep from our eyes.

[73] Studs Terkel, *Hard Times: An Oral History of the Great Depression* (New York: Avon Books, 1971).
[74] Weinstein, *op. cit.*

BIBLIOGRAPHY

The following bibliography contains some of the major works with which a serious student of societal development in general and American society in particular should be familiar. This bibliography is hardly exhaustive, but provides a starting point for more specialized inquiry. Limitations of space have forced the exclusion of many fine examples of scholarship. The first section, on general societal development, includes some of the most significant attempts to understand how social systems evolve. And, because existing knowledge makes it impossible to accurately predict the direction of American and world history, in the light of so many unanticipated events in the twentieth century, a list of a few periodicals that provide valuable continuous coverage and analysis of contemporary world affairs follows. After these general, overall references, the reader will find chapter-by-chapter listings and, finally, material relevant to the Epilogue.

General Societal Development

Baran, Paul. *The Political Economy of Growth*, 2nd ed. (New York: Monthly Review Press, 1968).

Bloch, Marc. *Feudal Society,* translated by L. A. Manyon (Chicago: University of Chicago Press, 1963).

Dobb, Maurice. *Studies in the Development of Capitalism,* rev. ed. (New York: International Publishers Co., Inc., 1964).

Huizinga, Johan. *The Waning of the Middle Ages: A Study of the Forms of Life, Thought, and Art in France and the Netherlands in the XIV and XV Centuries* (New York: Doubleday & Company, Inc., 1954).

Mandel, Ernest. *Marxist Economic Theory,* translated by Brian Pearce (New York: Monthly Review Press, 1969), 2 vols.

Marx, Karl. *Pre-Capitalist Economic Formations,* ed. with an introduction by E. J. Hobsbawm (New York: International Publishers Co., Inc., 1965).

Marx, Karl. *Capital: A Critique of Political Economy,* edited by Frederick Engels (New York: International Publishers Co., Inc., 1967), 3 vols.

Marx, Karl. *The Grundrisse,* ed. and translated by David McLellan (New York: Harper & Row, Publishers, 1971).

Mayer, Arno. *Dynamics of Counterrevolution in Europe, 1870–1956: An Analytic Framework* (New York: Harper & Row, Publishers, 1971).

Moore, Barrington, Jr. *Social Origins of Dictatorship and Democracy: Lord and Peasant in the Making of the Modern World* (Boston: The Beacon Press, 1966).

Polanyi, Karl. *The Great Transformation: The Political and Economic Origins of Our Time* (Boston: The Beacon Press, 1957).

Sweezy, Paul. *The Theory of Capitalist Development* (New York: Monthly Review Press, 1968).

Thompson, Edward P. *The Making of the English Working Class* (New York: Vintage Books, 1963).

SUGGESTED PERIODICALS

Monthly Review. An American monthly independent Marxist journal which provides useful analysis of the American economy as well as of world politics.

New Left Review. A British neo-Marxist bimonthly journal of radical scholarship and political analysis.

The New York Review of Books. A non-Marxist left-liberal biweekly journal which specializes in analytic reviews of significant contemporary scholarship.

Socialist Revolution. An American neo-Marxist bimonthly journal similar to *New Left Review.*

The American Political Economy

THE STRUCTURE AND DYNAMICS OF AMERICAN CAPITALISM

Baltzell, E. Digby. *Philadelphia Gentlemen: The Making of a National Upper Class* (New York: The Free Press, 1958).

Baran, Paul. *The Political Economy of Growth,* 2nd ed. (New York: Monthly Review Press, 1968), pp. 1–133.

Foner, Philip. *The History of the Labor Movement in the United States* (New York: International Publishers Co., Inc., 1947, 1955, 1964, 1965), 4 vols.

Hacker, Louis. *The Triumph of American Capitalism: The Development of Forces in American History to the End of the Nineteenth Century* (New York: Simon and Schuster, Inc., 1940).

Kolko, Gabriel. *Wealth and Power in America: An Analysis of Social Class and Income Distribution* (New York: Frederick A. Praeger, Inc., 1962).

Perlo, Victor. *The Empire of High Finance* (New York: International Publishers Co., Inc., 1957).

Pessen, Edward. "The Egalitarian Myth and the American Social Reality: Wealth, Mobility, and Equality in the 'Era of the Common Man,'" *The American Historical Review,* vol. 76 (October 1971), pp. 989–1034.

Tanzer, Michael. *The Sick Society: An Economic Examination* (New York: Holt, Rinehart and Winston, Inc., 1971), parts I, III, IV.

THE AMERICAN STATE: THE PRIVATE USE OF PUBLIC POWER

Conkin, Paul. *FDR and the Origins of the Welfare State* (New York: Crowell-Collier and Macmillan, Inc., 1967).

Domhoff, G. William. *The Higher Circles: The Governing Class in America* (New York: Random House, Inc., 1970).

Domhoff, G. William. *Who Rules America?* (Englewood Cliffs, N.J.: Prentice-Hall, Inc., 1967).

Engler, Robert. *The Politics of Oil: Private Power and Democratic Directions* (Chicago: University of Chicago Press, 1961).

Kolko, Gabriel. *The Triumph of Conservatism: A Re-interpretation of American History, 1900–1916* (Chicago: Quadrangle Books, 1967).

Lynd, Staughton. *Anti-Federalism in Dutchess County: A Study of Democracy and Class Conflict in the Revolutionary Era* (Chicago: Loyola University Press, 1962).

Lynd, Staughton. *Class Conflict, Slavery and the United States Constitution* (Indianapolis: The Bobbs-Merrill Company, Inc., 1968).

Miliband, Ralph. *The State in Capitalist Society: An Analysis of the Western Systems of Power* (New York: Basic Books, Inc., 1969).

Moore, Barrington, Jr. *Social Origins of Dictatorship and Democracy: Lord and Peasant in the Making of the Modern World* (Boston: The Beacon Press, 1966), "The American Civil War: The Last Capitalist Revolution," pp. 111–155.

Pearson, Drew, and Jack Anderson. *The Case against Congress: A Compelling Indictment of Corruption on Capitol Hill* (New York: Simon and Schuster, Inc., 1968).

Preston, William, Jr. *Aliens and Dissenters: Federal Suppression of Radicals, 1903–1933* (New York: Harper & Row, Publishers, 1963).

Weinstein, James. *The Corporate Ideal in the Liberal State, 1900–1918* (Boston: The Beacon Press, 1968).

Williams, William Appleman. *The Contours of American History* (Cleveland: The World Publishing Company, 1961).

The Political Economy of American Social Problems

AMERICAN IMPERIALISM AND MILITARISM

Ambrose, Stephen. *Rise to Globalism: American Foreign Policy, 1938–1970* (Baltimore: Penguin Books, 1971).

Baran, Paul. *The Political Economy of Growth,* 2nd ed. (New York: Monthly Review Press, 1968), pp. 134–300.

Horowitz, David. *The Free World Colossus: A Critique of American Foreign Policy in the Cold War* (New York: Hill & Wang, Inc., 1965).

Kolko, Gabriel. *The Politics of War: The World and United States Foreign Policy, 1943–1945* (New York: Vintage Books, 1970).

Kolko, Gabriel. *The Roots of American Foreign Policy: An Analysis of Power and Purpose* (Boston: The Beacon Press, 1969).

La Feber, Walter. *The New Empire: An Interpretation of American Expansion, 1860–1898* (Ithaca: Cornell University Press, 1963).

Magdoff, Harry. *The Age of Imperialism* (New York: Monthly Review Press, 1969).

Perlo, Victor. *Militarism and Industry: Arms Profiteering in the Missile Age* (New York: International Publishers Co., Inc., 1963).

Tanzer, Michael. *The Political Economy of International Oil and the Underdeveloped Countries* (Boston: The Beacon Press, 1969).

Williams, William Appleman. *The Tragedy of American Diplomacy* (Cleveland: The World Publishing Company, 1959).

POVERTY, ECONOMIC INSECURITY, AND THE WELFARE STATE

Caplovitz, David. *The Poor Pay More: Consumer Practices of Low Income Families* (New York: The Free Press, 1963).

Caudill, Harry. *Night Comes to the Cumberlands: A Biography of a Depressed Area* (Boston: Little, Brown & Company, 1961).

Elman, Richard. *The Poorhouse State: The American Way of Life on Public Assistance* (New York: Dell Publishing Co., Inc., 1966).

Harrington, Michael. *The Other America: Poverty in the United States* (New York: Crowell-Collier and Macmillan Inc., 1962).

Kolko, Gabriel. *Wealth and Power in America: An Analysis of Social Class and Income Distribution* (New York: Frederick A. Praeger, Inc., 1962).

Miller, S. M., and Pamela Roby, *The Future of Inequality* (New York: Basic Books, Inc., 1970).

Piven, Frances Fox, and Richard Cloward. *Regulating the Poor: The Functions of Public Welfare* (New York: Pantheon Books, Inc., 1971).

Terkel, Studs. *Hard Times: An Oral History of the Great Depression* (New York: Avon Books, 1971).

Thernstrom, Stephan. *Poverty and Progress: Social Mobility in a Nineteenth Century City* (Cambridge, Mass.: Harvard University Press, 1964).

Ware, Norman. *The Industrial Worker: The Reaction of American Industrial Society to the Advance of the Industrial Revolution, 1840–1860* (Chicago: Quadrangle Books, 1964).

RACISM: DOMESTIC COLONIALISM AND NEOCOLONIALISM

Allen, Robert. *Black Awakening in Capitalist America: An Analytic History* (New York: Doubleday & Company, Inc., 1969).

Brown, Dee. *Bury My Heart at Wounded Knee* (New York: Holt, Rinehart and Winston, Inc., 1970).

Fredrickson, George. *The Black Image in the White Mind: The Debate on Afro-American Character and Destiny, 1817–1914* (New York: Harper & Row, Publishers, 1971).

Genovese, Eugene. *The Political Economy of Slavery: Studies in the Economy and Society of the Slave South* (New York: Vintage Books, 1965).

Jacobs, Paul, and Saul Landau (with Eve Pell), eds. *To Serve the Devil: A Documentary Analysis of America's Racial History and Why It Has Been Kept Hidden* (New York: Vintage Books, 1971), 2 vols.

Jordon, Winthrop. *White over Black: American Attitudes towards the Negro, 1550–1812* (Baltimore: Penguin Books, Inc., 1969).

McWilliams, Carey. *North from Mexico: The Spanish-Speaking People of the United States* (Philadelphia: J. B. Lippincott Company, 1949).

Prewitt, Kenneth, and Louis Knowles. *Institutional Racism in America* (Englewood Cliffs, N.J.: Prentice-Hall, Inc., 1970).

Willhelm, Sidney. *Who Needs the Negro?* (New York: Schenkman, 1970).

SEXISM AND SOCIETY

Kraditor, Aileen. *Up from the Pedestal: Selected Writings in the History of American Feminism* (Chicago: Quadrangle Books, 1968).

Morgan, Robin, ed. *Sisterhood Is Powerful: An Anthology of Writings from the Women's Liberation Movement* (New York: Random House, Inc., 1970).

Sullerot, Evelyne. *Woman, Society and Change,* translated by Margaret Scotford Archer (New York: McGraw-Hill, Inc., 1971).

THE KNOWLEDGE INDUSTRY: THE HIGHER LEARNING IN AMERICA

Baritz, Loren. *Servants of Power: A History of the Use of Social Science in American Industry* (New York: John Wiley & Sons, Inc., 1965).

Chomsky, Noam. *American Power and the New Mandarins: Historical and Political Essays* (New York: Random House, Inc., 1969).

Caplow, Theodore, and Reece McGee. *The Academic Marketplace* (New York: Basic Books, Inc., 1958).

Ridgeway, James. *The Closed Corporation: American Universities in Crisis* (New York: Ballantine Books, Inc., 1969).

Wallerstein, Immanuel, and Paul Starr, eds. *The University Crisis Reader* (New York: Vintage Books, 1971), 2 vols.

SOCIETAL AND HUMAN DEVELOPMENT UNDER CAPITALISM

Chinoy, Ely. *The American Automobile Worker and the American Dream* (New York: Doubleday & Company, Inc., 1955).
Editors of *Ramparts, Eco-Catastrophe* (San Francisco: Canfield Press, 1971).
Goffman, Erving. *The Presentation of Self in Every-Day Life* (New York: Doubleday & Company, Inc., Anchor Books, 1959).
Henry, Jules. *Culture against Man* (New York: Random House, Inc., 1963).
Marcuse, Herbert. *Eros and Civilization: A Philosophical Inquiry into Freud* (Boston: The Beacon Press, 1966).
Mills, C. Wright. *White Collar: The American Middle Classes* (New York: Oxford University Press, 1951).

The Sources of Stability in American Society

THE MAINTENANCE OF CAPITALIST ORDER: LEGITIMACY AND SOCIAL CONTROL

Aronson, James. *The Press and the Cold War* (Indianapolis: The Bobbs-Merrill Company, Inc., 1970).
Barnouw, Erik. *A History of Broadcasting in the United States* (New York: Oxford University Press, 1966, 1968, 1970), 3 vols.
Cirino, Robert. *Don't Blame the People: How the News Media Use Bias, Distortion and Censorship To Manipulate Public Opinion* (Los Angeles, Calif.: Diversity Press, 1970).
Friedenberg, Edgar. *Coming of Age in America* (New York: Vintage Books, 1965).
Goodman, Paul. *Compulsory Mis-Education* (New York: Vintage Books, 1965).
Hartz, Louis. *The Liberal Tradition in America* (New York: Harcourt Brace Jovanovich, Inc., 1955).
Lasch, Christopher. *The Agony of the American Left* (New York: Alfred A. Knopf, 1969).
Miliband, Ralph. *The State in Capitalist Society: An Analysis of Western Systems of Power* (New York: Basic Books, Inc., 1969), pp. 179–238.
Paul, Arnold. *Conservative Crisis and the Rule of Law: Attitudes of Bar and Bench, 1887–1895* (New York: Harper & Row, Publishers, 1963).
Preston, William, Jr. *Aliens and Dissenters: Federal Suppression of Radicals, 1903–1933* (New York: Harper & Row, Publishers, 1963).
Rogin, Michael. *The Intellectuals and McCarthy: The Radical Specter* (Cambridge, Mass.: M.I.T. Press, 1967).
Rosenberg, Bernard, and David Manning White, eds. *Mass Culture: The Popular Arts in America* (New York: The Free Press, 1957).
Schiller, Herbert. *Mass Communications and American Empire* (New York: August M. Kelley, Publishers, 1969).
Zeigler, Harmon, *The Political Life of American Teachers* (Englewood Cliffs, N.J.: Prentice-Hall, Inc., 1967).

The Political Economy of Cultural and Social Revolution

REVOLUTIONARY CHANGE IN OTHER SOCIETIES

General

Eckstein, Harry. "On the Etiology of Internal Wars," *History and Theory,* vol. 4 (1965), pp. 133–163.

Moore, Barrington, Jr. *Social Origins of Dictatorship and Democracy: Lord and Peasant in the Making of the Modern World* (Boston: The Beacon Press, 1966).

Stone, Lawrence. "Theories of Revolution," *World Politics,* vol. 18 (January 1966), pp. 159–176.

Soviet Union

Deutscher, Isaac. *The Unfinished Revolution: Russia, 1917–1967* (New York: Oxford University Press, 1967).

Trotsky, Leon. *The Russian Revolution: The Overthrow of Tzarism and the Triumph of the Soviets,* selected and ed. by F. W. Dupee (New York: Doubleday & Company, Inc., 1959).

Cuba

Huberman, Leo, and Paul Sweezy. *Cuba: Anatomy of a Revolution* (New York: Monthly Review Press, 1968).

Karol, K. S. *Guerrillas in Power: The Course of the Cuban Revolution,* translated by Arnold Pomerans (New York: Hill & Wang, Inc., 1970).

Yglesias, Jose. *In the Fist of the Revolution: Life in a Cuban Country Town* (New York: Vintage Books, 1969).

China

Belden, Jack. *China Shakes the World* (New York: Monthly Review Press, 1971).

Hinton, William. *Fanshen: A Documentary of Revolution in a Chinese Village* (New York: Monthly Review Press, 1967).

Horn, Joshua. *Away with All Pests: An English Surgeon in People's China, 1954–1969* (New York: Monthly Review Press, 1971).

Karol, K. S. *China: The Other Communism,* translated by Tom Baistow (New York: Hill & Wang, Inc., 1967).

Myrdal, Jan, and Gun Kessle. *China: The Revolution Continued* (New York: Pantheon Books, Inc., 1971).

Nee, Victor. *The Cultural Revolution at Peking University* (New York: Monthly Review Press, 1969).

THE AMERICAN CASE CONSIDERED

Allen, Robert. *Black Awakening in Capitalist America: An Analytic History* (New York: Doubleday & Company, Inc., 1969).

Binzen, Peter. *Whitetown, U.S.A.* (New York: Random House, 1970).

Flacks, Richard. *Youth and Social Change* (Chicago: Markham, 1971).

Gans, Herbert. *The Levittowners: Ways of Life and Politics in a New Suburban Community* (New York: Pantheon Books, 1967).

Gitlin, Todd, and Nanci Hollander. *Uptown: Poor Whites in Chicago* (New York: Harper & Row, Publishers, 1970).

Hodges, Donald Clark. "Cynicism in the Labor Movement," in Maurice Zeitlin, ed. *American Society, Inc.: Studies of the Social Structure and Political Economy of the United States* (Chicago: Markham, 1970), pp. 439–446.

Jacobs, Harold, ed. *Weatherman* (Berkeley, Calif.: Ramparts Press, 1970).

Mandel, Ernest. "Where Is America Going?" in Zeitlin, *op. cit.*, pp. 508–524. *American Society, Inc.: Studies of the Social Structure and Political Economy of the United States* (Chicago: Markham, 1970), pp. 508–524.

Mankoff, Milton, and Richard Flacks. "The Changing Social Base of the American Student Movement," *The Annals of the American Academy of Political and Social Science*, no. 395 (May, 1971), pp. 54–67.

Moore, Barrington, Jr. "Revolution in America?" *The New York Review of Books*, vol. 12 (January 30, 1969), pp. 6–12.

Oppenheimer, Martin. *The Urban Guerrilla* (Chicago: Quadrangle Books, 1969).

Peck, Sidney. *The Rank-and-File Leader* (New Haven, Conn.: College and University Press, 1963).

Rubenstein, Richard. *Rebels in Eden: Mass Political Violence in the United States* (Boston: Little, Brown & Company, 1970).

Singer, Daniel. *Prelude to Revolution: France in May 1968* (New York: Hill & Wang, Inc., 1970).

Tanzer, Michael. *The Sick Society: An Economic Examination* (New York: Holt, Rinehart and Winston, Inc., 1971), pp. 165–233.

Teodori, Massimo, ed. *The New Left: A Documentary History* (Indianapolis: The Bobbs-Merrill Company, Inc., 1969).

Weir, Stanley. "U.S.A.: The Labor Revolt," in Zeitlin, *op. cit.*, pp. 466–501.

Wilensky, Harold. "Class, Class Consciousness and American Workers," in *ibid.*, pp. 423–437.

Young, Alfred, ed. *Dissent: Explorations in American Radicalism* (DeKalb, Ill.: Northern Illinois University Press, 1968).

Index

A

Academic freedom, 427
Academic Revolution, The (Riesman and Jencks), 305
Achievement motivation, 404–408
Adorno, Theodor W., 450, 456
Advertising, 359–360, 430–448
  notion of failure used by, 447–448
  as producer of national homogeneity, 444–445
  psychology of, 440–444
  resistance to, 445
Affluent Society, The (Galbraith), 56–57
AFL, 16, 60, 62, 63, 64, 65, 66, 70, 72, 379, 386, 387, 388, 462, 482, 493
Afro Americans (*see* Blacks)
Agency for International Development (A.I.D.), 114, 166–167
Alaska, 141
Allen, Horace, 143
Allport, Floyd Henry, 440, 442, 448
Almond, Gabriel, 309, 311, 400, 401, 402, 412–413

Amalgamated Clothing Workers, 66–69 *passim*
American Business Abroad: Ford on Six Continents, 313–314
American Capitalism: The Concept of Countervailing Power (Galbraith), 46
American Civil War, 136–139, 148, 207, 209–212
American foreign policy, 88–89, 119–151, 170–174, 493–495
  as anticommunist crusade, 125
  political economy of, 123
  private organizations for the study of, 124
  world exports and, 153–164
  world power retained by, 169–174
American history, differing interpretations of, 132–133
American imperialism, 119–151
  bourgeois, 139–143
  and the Cold War, 134
  formally anti-imperialist ideology of, 134

Cultural philistinism, 451–452
Culture, in age of mechanical reproduction, 453–456
  bourgeois epoch of, 450–452
  and Capitalism, 449–456
  daily life and, 449–451
  folk, 455
  mass produced, 453–455
  and oppression, 449–451
  popular, 454–456
  and societal development, 449, 451–452

D

Dahl, Robert, 74, 76, 82, 83, 309, 310, 311, 312, 399, 400, 416
Dahrendorf, R., 203–204, 399
Dark Ghetto (Clark), 217
Democracy, liberal, 399–419
Democracy in America (Tocqueville), 362
Democratic party, 493, 498
Depression, Great, 122, 483–484, 487, 496, 497, 504–505
Detectives (see Police)
Dillion, Douglas, 312, 313
Dillon, Read and Company, 312–313
Division of labor, 343–344, 348, 352
Dixon, Marlene, 247, 249, 251–264
Dizard, Jan, 215, 231–245
Domhoff, G. William, 85, 86, 88, 89, 126, 360
Dulles, John Foster, 162, 172

E

Earley, James, 53
Ecological crisis, 320–322, 327
Economic Policy and Democratic Thought (Hartz), 365
Economics, Keynesian, 22–24
  laissez faire, 22–23
  Marxian, 22–24
Economy, international, 152–174
Education, 286–287
  bureaucratization of, 487
  elementary and secondary, 357, 486–487

Education (cont.)
  higher, 289–318, 372, 486–487
    behavioralists in, 309–311
    big business support for, 294, 296
    boards of trustees in institutions of, 293–294
    consumerism and, 317
    and corporate capitalism's needs, 291, 292, 315–318
    cultural pacification in institutions of, 420–429
    dissension in, 297, 485–486
    entrepreneurs of, 298–301
    federal support for research in, 291–292
    foreign policy and, 318
    hierarchy of, 305
    and the military, 495
    political aspects of institutions of, 425–428
    political economy of, 290
    and private foundations, 292, 298–314
    and production costs, 316–317
    and social service ideal, 295–296, 317–318
    and socialization of the young, 296
  political conservatism transmitted through, 415–416
Elitism, 75–76, 82–85, 89, 473, 474
  See also Power elitists
Engels, Friedrich, 267–268, 270, 272, 275, 276, 459
England, 126, 129, 150
Eros and Civilization (Marcuse), 432
Eros Denied (Young), 275–276
Ewen, Stuart, 358, 361, 430–448

F

False consciousness, concept of, 401–402
Family, 283–284, 287, 288
  nuclear, 279, 281
Family and the Sexual Revolution, The, 278
Fanon, Frantz, 222, 223
Farmers, decline of, 488–489

Marxism, 4, 5, 6, 82, 457, 458–459, 475
Marxist theory, 401, 402, 408, 414, 416, 417
Mass consumption, 434–448, 479–480
Mass production, 233–439, 448, 453, 480
Mead, Margaret, 278, 279
Means, C. C., 50
Media, mass, 358, 402
Merriam, Charles, 309–310
Metzger, Walter, 290, 300
Mexican Americans, 207, 208, 224
Mexico, 141
Michels, Robert, 461
Middletown (Lynd), 75, 443–444
Miliband, Ralph, 21, 46–58, 74, 83, 90–91, 92, 358
Military establishment, 112–113
Military-industrial complex, 126–129, 151
Mills, C. Wright, 17, 59, 75–76, 82, 83, 88, 132, 243, 292, 312, 320, 323, 336–352, 366, 468
Minority groups in U.S., 207–208, 215, 219
   See also American Indian; Blacks in U.S.; Mexican Americans
Mitchell, Juliet, 249–250, 265–288
Mobility, occupational, 368
   social, 367–368
Monogamy, 276, 277
Monroe Doctrine, 131, 137, 142, 143, 145, 148
Moore, Barrington, 6, 209–210, 473–474, 475
Moralistic binge in U.S., 368–370, 378, 381
Mueller, Willard, 19
Myrdal, G., 198, 205, 367

N

NAACP, 233
Nadler, Marcus, 25, 30
Naether, Carl A., 441
National Alliance of Businessmen, 237, 240
National Association of Manufacturers, 143, 482, 498
National Civic Federation (NCF), 16, 60, 61, 87, 481, 482

National Labor Union, 15
National Recovery Administration (NRA), 64–65, 68–69, 71
National Security Council, 124
Nationalism, cultural, 222–224
Nazism, 122–123, 502
Negations: Essays in Critical Theory (Marcuse), 450
Negroes (*see* Blacks in U.S.)
Nevins, Allan, 314
New Deal, 35, 70–72, 175, 389–390, 429, 482, 484
New Industrial State, The (Galbraith), 16, 21, 46–58
New Left, 3, 485
New Men of Power, The (Mills), 349
Nicholson, J. L., 196
Nixon, Richard, 495

O

Occupational mobility, 368
O'Connor, James, 81, 94–115, 294–295, 315–318
Oglesby, Carl, 120–121
Open Door Policy, 126, 145–150 *passim*, 161
Opportunity, myth of, 367–368, 464
Origin of the Family, Private Property and the State, The (Engels), 267–268
Ossowski, S., 414
Overstreet, H. A., 346–347

P

Packard, David, 307–308
Parks, Evelyn, 357, 361, 391–398
Parsons, T., 400
Paternalism, employer, 13–14
Peguy, Charles, 343
Perlo, Victor, 18, 20–21, 25–45, 128–129
Philippines, 131, 132, 144
Plumb, J. H., 210
Pluralism, 3, 74–76, 82–93, 362, 363–364, 366, 368, 369–370, 385, 388
Point Four program, 162
Police, 391–393

Scott, Walter Dill, 441, 442
Second Sex, The (de Beauvoir), 269
Seward, William, 140–142, 144
Sexism, 181, 246–250
  black women as victims of, 253
Sexuality, 275–278, 284–285
Sheehan, Robert, 49, 50, 52, 53
Sherman Act (1890), 381, 382
Siegel, Abraham, 370
Sigel, R., 399
Silent majority, 485, 502
Sklar, Martin, 481
Slavery, 137, 207, 208–212, 218, 223
Smith, Adam, 21, 22
Social control in the U.S., 391–398
Social Democracy, German, 459, 461
  Swedish, 90, 91
Social mobility, 367–368
Social Mobility in Industrial Society,
    (Lipset and Bendix), 368
Social production, 430–431
Social Science Research Council, 310
Socialism, 328, 336, 361
  American, 457–470, 483–484
  liberation of women under, 288
Socialist Party, 16, 361
Socialist theory, women in, 265–270
Socialization, political, 399, 415–417
  process of, 278–281, 283–288 *passim*
Sombart, Werner, 367
South America, 141–142, 145, 147, 163,
    164, 171, 174
Southworth, Gayle, 321
Soviet Union, 119–120, 122, 494
  women in, 281–282
Spain, 143
Spanish-American War, 131, 132, 143–
    145
Stalin, Joseph, 122–123
Standard Oil of New Jersey, 28
Stanford Research Institute (SRI), 307
State aid to industries, 95–101
State budget, combined with corporate
    capital, 101–115
  functions of, 94–115
  highway expenditures in, 96–98
State in Capitalist Society, The (Mili-
    band), 90
Status politics, 369
Stephenson, R. M., 404

Stock ownership, 18, 24–25
  concentration of, 27–30
  and influence in corporate affairs, 32–
      34, 49–55, 73
  institutional, 30–32
Stone, Lawrence, 276
Strachey, John, 204
Strong, Josiah, 142
Studebaker-Packard, 41
Student activists, 486
Suburbs, 98–101
Sweezy, Paul, 20, 22, 37, 42, 53, 109
Swope, Gerard, 63–64, 68, 70

T

Taylor, Frederick, 348–349
Technology, production and, 315–316
Theory of the Leisure Class (Veblen),
    452
Thernstrom, Stephan, 368
Third World, 89, 120, 131, 153, 157, 164,
    170–173, 174, 256, 259, 260, 262, 493
  American loans to, 165–167
  and capitalism, 112
  exports of, 158–164
  U.S. economic power over, 161–174
  U.S. opposition to reforms in economy
      of, 170–174
Thompson, Edward, 6, 423–424, 430
Thomson, Dorothy, 203
*Time, Work-discipline, and Industrial
    Capitalism* (Thompson), 430
Titmuss, R., 200–201
Tocqueville, Alexis de, 11–12, 21, 362,
    364, 372
Townsend, Peter, 265
Trade unions (*see* Labor unions)
Transportation budget, 96–98
Turner, Frederick, 143, 295, 363, 367

U

Unemployment, among blacks in U.S.,
    232
  in Britain, **193**
  in socialist countries, 182
  in U.S., 181, 182–183, 214
  in Western Europe, 182